Lawyers

A CRITICAL READER

Edited by

RICHARD L. ABEL

The New Press · New York

Published in the United States by The New Press, New York
Distributed by W.W. Norton & Company, Inc., New York

The New Press was established in 1990 as a not-for-profit alternative to the large, commercial
publishing houses currently dominating the book publishing industry. The New Press operates in
the public interest rather than for private gain, and is committed to publishing, in innovative ways,
works of educational, cultural, and community value that might not normally be commercially viable.

Book design by
[sic]

Printed in Canada

9 8 7 6 5 4 3 2

CONTENTS

CHAPTER 12. BEYOND MARKET CONTROL: PROFESSIONAL ASSOCIATIONS AND THE PUBLIC INTEREST

CHAPTER 13. SELF-REGULATION: PROMULGATING AND ENFORCING ETHICAL RULES

CHAPTER 14. CULTURAL IMAGES OF LAWYERS

CHAPTER 15. IS THERE "UNMET LEGAL NEED"?

CHAPTER 16. HOW DO PEOPLE GET LAWYERS AND LAWYERS GET BUSINESS?

CHAPTER 17. WHEN DO AND SHOULD LAWYERS RENDER PRO BONO LEGAL SERVICES?

CHAPTER 18. REPRESENTING THE POOR

CHAPTER 19. LAWYERS AND SOCIAL CHANGE: INSTITUTIONS

CHAPTER 20. LAWYERS AND SOCIAL CHANGE: STRATEGIES

INTRODUCTION

AT least since Tocqueville, a century and a half ago, numerous commentators have marvelled at—and worried about—the influence of lawyers in American life. Lawyers dominated the Constitutional Convention and have continued to be greatly overrepresented in federal and state executives and legislatures. There are more lawyers per capita in the United States than in any other country (although who counts as a lawyer complicates comparison). The large law firm is a distinctively American innovation, which now dominates transnational practice (if with increasing competition). Lawsuits and legal investigations dominate American political and social life: sensational murder trials (O.J. Simpson), terrorist acts (the Oklahoma City and World Trade Center bombings), racial hostility (the beating of Rodney King, Bernard Goetz's shooting in the New York subway), political scandals (Watergate, Iran-Contra, Whitewater), famous Supreme Court decisions (*Brown v. Board of Education, Roe v. Wade*), and popular culture (*L.A. Law, Law and Order, N.Y.P.D. Blue*).

Despite such prominence, there is widespread ignorance about lawyers and, worse, considerable misinformation. I hope this Reader will help to remedy that. It is intended for anyone interested in learning more about these central actors in our political, social, economic, and cultural life. Such insights may be especially relevant to anyone thinking of becoming a lawyer. Finally, the Reader is intended for use in courses on the legal system and legal profession in both college and law school.

I begin with the most difficult question all lawyers confront: in speaking for others do they become morally implicated in the *ends* of their clients? Next I introduce the profession through overviews of its evolution, demography, and social structure. With that map, I turn to the two end points on the spectrum of private practice. Despite the low prestige of solo and small-firm practice, nearly two-thirds of private practitioners work in firms with fewer than six lawyers. Because these are the lawyers with whom most individual clients interact, it is essential to understand the nature of the lawyer–client relationship and how lawyers transform their clients' objectives. Although fewer than 15 percent of private practitioners work in firms with more than fifty lawyers and fewer than 10 percent in firms with more than one hundred, it is the megafirms that grab headlines and enjoy the pinnacle of wealth, prestige, and influence. Consequently, I examine their emergence and possible futures, as well as the way they shape responses to ethical dilemmas.

Socialization and recruitment to occupational roles profoundly shape all professions. Almost everyone finds law school an overwhelming experience—but how does it actually change students? Until the middle of this century, the legal profession deliberately restricted entry by women and racial minorities and marginalized the few who overcame those obstacles. To what extent does the profession and each of its components now reflect the gender and racial composition of the population? What could be done to improve its representativeness, in light of the sexual division of child-rearing responsibility and the backlash against racial affirmative action?

A wide variety of theories have been advanced to help us understand professions: Weberian theories of social closure and collective mobility, neoclassical economic theories of rent-seeking behavior and information asymmetries, Marxian theories of proletarianization and exploitation, and Durkheimian theories of community and altruism. I explore these competing frameworks in two ways, through a historical account of the transformation of American legal education and by contrasting the common law tradition (to which American lawyers belong) with the civil law professions of Europe and its former colonies.

Professions offer their members not only material rewards but also social honor. How successful is this facet of the "professional project?" Do bar associations advance the public interest by seeking to reform the legal system? How effective is self-regulation, and will it withstand challenges from government agencies, judges, and civil liability? How does popular culture portray lawyers?

Until recently, virtually all legal services were distributed through the market. Once we acknowledge that they are not just another commodity, like ice cream, where can we find principles to guide their allocation? Are there empirical data that should inform this decision? Twenty years ago, professions prohibited almost all promotional activity. Now that the Supreme Court has extended some First Amendment protection to commercial speech, what kinds of advertising and solicitation must be allowed? Do lawyers' claims to be professionals create an obligation of

altruism? Do lawyers render free legal services? Should they be required to do so? How much, what kind, and through what mechanisms? What are the experiences of those who represent the poor and disadvantaged—the satisfactions and frustrations of legal services lawyers and public defenders?

Lawyers do not just operate within the legal system; they also have the potential to transform it. Some do so by changing the rules through litigation and legislation. Others focus on subtly subverting power relationships between citizens and the state, clients and lawyers. How effective are those efforts?

The excerpts that follow are accompanied by questions intended to provoke individual reflection and collective discussion, as well as annotated bibliographies to guide further reading and research. Those wanting a more systematic overview may wish to consult my book *American Lawyers* (1989) or the four volumes comparing legal professions across nearly 20 countries, which I edited with Philip S. C. Lewis, *Lawyers in Society* (1988–89, 1995). I am grateful to the authors and publishers for permission to reprint these excerpts, all of which have been edited extensively. I also want to thank the hundreds of students who have reacted to earlier versions of these readings.

Chapter One

THE FUNDAMENTAL DILEMMA
OF LAWYERING:
THE ETHICS OF THE HIRED GUN

"How can you represent such a client?" That question—the hardest to answer—underlies all lawyer jokes and the profession's constant obsession with its reputation. In common law jurisdictions the glib reply long was: the adversary system.* This came under serious scrutiny in the 1970s.† David Luban's essay offers a devastating criticism of that rationale.

THE ADVERSARY SYSTEM EXCUSE[1]
David Luban

GEORGE Sharswood, whose 1854 *Legal Ethics* is the great-grandparent of the current ABA Code of Professional Responsibility, wrote: "The lawyer, who refuses his professional assistance because in his judgment the case is unjust and indefensible, usurps the functions of both judge and jury." Murray Schwartz calls this the "Principle of Nonaccountability":

> When acting as an advocate for a client...a lawyer is neither legally, professionally, nor morally accountable for the means used or the ends achieved.

Add to this the "Principle of Professionalism":

> When acting as an advocate, a lawyer must, within the established constraints upon professional behavior, maximize the likelihood that the client will prevail.

---

* E.g., Charles Curtis, "The Ethics of Advocacy," 4 *Stanford Law Review* 3 (1952); Charles Horsky, *The Washington Lawyer* (1952); Max Kampelman, "The Washington Lawyer: Some Musings," 38 *George Washington Law Review* 589 (1970); Monroe Freedman, *Lawyers' Ethics in an Adversary System* (1975); Murray Schwartz, "The Professionalism and Accountability of Lawyers," 66 *California Law Review* 669 (1978).

† E.g., Richard Wasserstrom, "Lawyers as Professionals: Some Moral Issues," 5 *Human Rights* 1 (1975); Marvin Frankel, "The Search for Truth: An Umpireal View," 123 *University of Pennsylvania Law Review* 1031 (1975); William Simon, "The Ideology of Advocacy: Procedural Justice and Professional Ethics," 1978 *Wisconsin Law Review* 29.

and you get what is usually taken to be the professional morality of lawyers. I shall argue (1) that a lawyer's nonaccountability does depend on the adversary system; (2) that the adversary system is not a sufficient basis for it; and (3) thus, that while the Principle of Professionalism may be true, the Principle of Nonaccountability is not.

INSTITUTIONAL EXCUSES

On February 7, 1973, Richard Helms, the former director of the Central Intelligence Agency, lied to a Senate committee about American involvement in the overthrow of the Allende government in Chile. Santiago proved to be Helms's Waterloo; he was caught out in his perjury and prosecuted. Helms claimed that requirements of national security led him to lie to Congress. We can only speculate, however, on how the court would have viewed this excuse for, in fact, the case never came to trial; Helms's lawyer, the redoubtable Edward Bennett Williams, found an ingenious way to back the government down. He argued that national security information was relevant to Helms's defense and must be turned over to Helms, thereby confronting the government with the unpleasant choice of dropping the action or making public classified and presumably vital information. The government chose the first option and allowed Helms to plead guilty to a misdemeanor charge.

I don't know if anyone ever asked Williams to justify his actions; had anyone attempted to do so, they would presumably have been told that Williams was simply doing his job as a criminal defense attorney. The parallel with Helms's own excuse is clear—he was doing his job, Williams

---

1. In David Luban (ed.), *The Good Lawyer*. Totowa, NJ: Rowman & Allanheld, 1984. Reprinted with permission.

was doing his—but it is hard to miss the irony. Helms tried to conceal national security information; therefore he lied. Williams, acting on Helms's behalf, threatened to reveal national security information as part of a tactic that has come to be called "graymailing." One man's ends are another man's means. Neither lying nor graymailing (to say nothing of destabilizing elected regimes) is morally pretty, but a job is a job, and that was the job that was. So, at any rate, runs the excuse.

What could justify the conduct of such lawyers? A famous answer is the following statement of Lord Henry Brougham:

> An advocate, in the discharge of his duty, knows but one person in all the world, and that person is his client. To save that client by all means and expedients, and at all hazards and costs to other persons, and, amongst them, to himself, is his first and only duty; and in performing this duty he must not regard the alarm, the torments, the destruction which he may bring upon others. Separating the duty of a patriot from that of an advocate, he must go on reckless of consequences, though it should be his unhappy fate to involve his country in confusion.

My main question is this: does the adversary system really justify Brougham's position? I hope that the example of Helms and his lawyers has convinced you that a more general issue is lurking here, the issue of what I shall call institutional excuses. We can state the main question in full generality in this way: can a person appeal to a social institution in which he or she occupies a role in order to excuse conduct that would be morally culpable were anyone else to do it? Plausibly, examples exist in which the answer is yes: we do not call it murder when a soldier kills a sleeping enemy, although it is surely immoral for you or me to do it. There are also cases where the answer is no, as in the job "concentration camp commandant" or "professional strikebreaker." Here, we feel, the immorality of the job is so great that it accuses, not excuses, the person who holds it.

This suggests that an important feature of a successful institutional excuse is that the institution is itself justified. I think that is partly right, but I do not think it is the whole story: I shall argue that the kind of justification that can be offered of the institution is germane to the success of the excuses it provides.

THE ADVERSARY SYSTEM AND THE TWO PRINCIPLES

On the face of it, Brougham's exhortation is as terse a characterization as one could hope to find of amorality; it is reminiscent of Nietzsche's description of the old Teutonic code: "To practice loyalty and, for the sake of loyalty, to risk honor and blood even for evil and dangerous things."

The way it is currently phrased, in the ABA's Code of Professional Responsibility, is this:

> The duty of a lawyer, both to his client and to the legal system, is to represent his client zealously within the bounds of the law.... In our government of laws and not of men, each member of our society is entitled...to seek any lawful objective through legally permissible means; and to present for adjudication any lawful claim, issue, or defense.

It sounds nicer than Zarathustra or Brougham, but in fact there is no difference. Nor does the phrase "within the bounds of the law" mitigate this. For the law is inherently double-edged: any rule imposed to limit zealous advocacy (or any other form of conduct, for that matter) may be used by an adversary as an offensive weapon. In the words of former Judge Marvin E. Frankel, "the object always is to beat every plowshare into a sword." "Zeal" means zeal at the margin of the legal, and thus well past the margin of whatever moral and political insight constitutes the "spirit" of the law in question.

It is at this point that the adversary system looms large, for it provides the institutional excuse for the duty of zealous advocacy. What, then, is the adversary system? We may distinguish narrow and wide senses. In the narrow sense, it is a method of adjudication characterized by three things: an impartial tribunal of defined jurisdiction, formal procedural rules, and most importantly for the present discussion, assignment to the parties of the responsibility to present their own cases and challenge their opponents'. The attorneys are their clients' agents in the latter task. The duty of a lawyer in an adversary proceeding is therefore one-sided partisan zeal in advocating his or her client's position. This, in turn, carries with it familiar collateral duties, the most important of which are disinterestedness and confidentiality. Each of these is best viewed as a prophylactic designed to enhance the quality of partisan advocacy: forbidding lawyers who have conflicts of interest from advocating a client's cause is meant to forestall the possibility of diluted zeal, and forbidding lawyers from divulging clients' confidences and secrets is meant to encourage clients to give their lawyers information necessary for effective advocacy. These duties of zeal, disinterestedness, and confidentiality—which I have elsewhere called the Three Pillars of Advocacy—form the core of an attorney's professional obligations.

The structure of the adversary system, then—its fission of adjudication into a clash of one-sided representations—explains why Schwartz's Principle of Professionalism holds. But it explains the Principle of Moral Nonaccountability as well. If advocates restrain their zeal because of moral compunctions, they are not fulfilling their assigned role in the adversary proceeding. But, if lawyers must hold themselves morally accountable for what they do in the course of the representation, they will be morally obliged to restrain their zeal whenever they find that "the means used or the ends achieved" in the advocacy are morally wrong. Therefore, or so the syllogism goes, the structure of adversary adjudication must relieve them of moral accountability, and that is how the adversary system entails Schwartz's Principle of Nonaccountability—how, that is, the adversary system is supposed to provide an institutional excuse for moral ruthlessness.

All this holds (if hold it does) only within the context of adjudication. Lawyers, however, commonly act as though Schwartz's two principles characterized their relationship with clients even when the representations do not involve the courtroom. Thus, there is a wide sense of the adversary system in which it is defined by the structure of the lawyer-client relationship rather than the structure of adjudication. When lawyers assume Schwartz's two principles in negotiations and counseling as well as courtroom advocacy, and attribute this to the adversary system, they are speaking of it in the wide sense.

☙

CRIMINAL VERSUS NONCRIMINAL CONTEXTS

Monroe Freedman argues that zealous adversary advocacy of those accused of crimes is the greatest safeguard of individual liberty against the encroachment of the state. The good criminal defense lawyer puts the state to its proof in the most stringent and uncompromising way possible. Better, we say, that a hundred criminals go free than that one person be wrongly convicted. I think this is right as far as it goes, but as general defense of the adversary system it is beside the point for two related reasons. The first is that it pertains only to criminal defense and thus is irrelevant to the enormous number of civil cases tried each year. Most people I have spoken with about lawyers' ethics assume that the paradigm of the morally dubious representation is the defense of the guilty criminal, the defense that gets a murderer back out on the street. This, I suspect, is a reflection of a perception of the justice system as primarily concerned with protecting the lives and property of Decent People (meaning us) from You Know Who (meaning you know who). It is You Know Who that needs watching, not the real estate speculator, the slumlord, the redliner, the discriminatory employer, the finance company, the welfare officials who won't give recipients their due, or the police.

It is this public preoccupation with crime and criminals, I think, that leads writers to focus their justifications of Broughamesque advocacy on criminal defense. They are reacting to an assault from the Right, an assault that sees the rights of the accused as a liberal invention leading to anarchy. Now, emphasizing the role of lawyers in safeguarding individual liberty may indeed be the best defense against the Law and Order attack on lawyers. Criminal defense is, so to speak, the "worst-case scenario," and it might be assumed that any defense of advocacy that works there works everywhere else as well.

In fact, and this is my second point, criminal defense is a very special case in which the zealous advocate serves atypical social goals. The point is one of political theory. The goal of zealous advocacy in criminal defense is to curtail the power of the state over its citizens. We want to handicap the state in its power even legitimately to punish us. And so the adversary system is justified, not because it is a good way of achieving justice, but because it is a good way of hobbling the government and we have political reasons for wanting this. The argument, in other words, does not claim that the adversary system is the best way of obtaining justice. It claims just the opposite: that it is the best way of impeding justice in the name of more fundamental political ends, namely, keeping the government's hands off people.

It seems, then, that focusing on the adversary system in the criminal context obscures the issue of how it works as a system of justice, and for this reason I shall talk only about arguments attempting to vindicate it as a system of justice. There are two sorts of arguments: those claiming that the adversary system is the best way of accomplishing various goals (consequentialist arguments), and those claiming that it is intrinsically good (nonconsequentialist arguments).

CONSEQUENTIALIST JUSTIFICATIONS OF THE ADVERSARY SYSTEM

Truth

The question of whether the adversary system is, all in all, the best way of uncovering the facts of a case at bar sounds like an empirical question. I happen to think that it is—an empirical question, moreover, that has scarcely been investigated, and that is most likely impossible to answer. This last is because one does not, after a trial is over, find the parties coming forth to make a clean breast of it and enlighten the world as to what really happened.

The kind of empirical research that can be done, then, is laboratory simulations: social psychology experiments intended to model the adversary proceeding. Obviously, there are inherent limitations on how closely such experiments can correspond to actual trials, no matter how skillfully they are done. In fact, the only experiments of the sort I know of are those of Thibaut, Walker, and their associates, and these are far from perfect modelings of the adversary and "inquisitorial"—meaning French- and German-style—systems that they are comparing. Even so, the results are instructive: they show that in some

situations the adversary system works better, while in others the inquisitorial system does, and furthermore, that the participants cannot tell which situation they are in. This would hardly surprise us: it would be much more astounding to discover a greater difference in veracity between the Anglo-American and Continental systems, for surely such a difference would after so many centuries have become a commonplace in our folklore.

Given all this, it is unsurprising to discover that the arguments purporting to show the advantages of the adversary system as a fact finder have mostly been nonempirical, a mix of a priori theories of inquiry and armchair psychology.

Here is one, based on the idea, very similar to Sir Karl Popper's theory of scientific rationality, that the way to get at the truth is a wholehearted dialectic of assertion and refutation. If each side attempts to prove its case, with the other trying as energetically as possible to assault the steps of the proof, it is more likely that all of the aspects of the situation will be presented to the fact finder than if it attempts to investigate for itself with the help of the lawyers. This theory is open to a number of objections. First of all, the analogy to Popperian scientific methodology is not a good one. Perhaps science proceeds by advancing conjectures and then trying to refute them, but it does not proceed by advancing conjectures that the scientist knows to be false and then using procedural rules to exclude probative evidence.

The two adversary attorneys, moreover, are each under an obligation to present the facts in the manner most consistent with their client's position—to prevent the introduction of unfavorable evidence, to undermine the credibility of opposing witnesses, to set unfavorable facts in a context in which their importance is minimized, to attempt to provoke inferences in their client's favor. The assumption is that two such accounts will cancel out, leaving the truth of the matter. But there is no earthly reason to think this is so; they may simply pile up the confusion.

Legal Rights

It is sometimes said, however, that the point of the adversary system is not that it is the best way of getting at the truth, but rather the best way of defending individuals' legal rights. Put this way, however, it is clear that the argument trades on a confusion. My legal rights are everything I am in fact legally entitled to, not everything the law can be made to give. For, obviously, a good lawyer may be able to get me things to which I am not entitled.

To this it might be replied that looking at it this way leaves the opponent's lawyer out of the picture. Of course, the reply continues, no one is claiming that a zealous adversary advocate is attempting to defend legal rights: he or she is attempting to win. The claim is only that the clash of two such adversaries will in fact defend legal rights most effectively.

But what reason do we have to believe this, other than a question-begging analogy to eighteenth-century economic theories of the Invisible Hand, theories that are themselves myth rather than fact? Every skill an advocate is taught is bent to winning cases no matter where the legal right lies. If the opponent manages to counter a lawyer's move with a better one, this has precisely nothing to do with legal rights. In the Middle Ages lawsuits were frequently tried by combat between hired champions. Each was charged with defending the legal right of his employer, but surely the fact that one swordsman successfully filleted the other did not mean that a right was established. Now, of course, judicial combat did not involve argument about rights. But neither does graymailing, "dollaring to death," driving up an opponent's costs by getting his or her law firm disqualified, preemptorily challenging a juror because he or she seems too smart, or even masking an invalid argument with what Titus Castricius called "the orator's privilege to make statements that are untrue, daring, crafty, deceptive and sophistical, provided they have some semblance of truth and can, by any artifice, be made to insinuate themselves into the minds of the persons who are to be influenced."

At this point an objection can be raised to my argument. The argument depends on a distinction I have drawn between what a person is, in fact, legally entitled to and what the law can be made to give. But this is a suspect distinction because it is based on the notion that there are legal entitlements other than what the law, in fact,

gives. American Realism, the dominant jurisprudential theory of this century, was primarily responsible for throwing cold water on the notion of entitlements-in-themselves floating around in some sort of noumenal never-never land. The law is nothing other than what the courts say it is.

The objection fails, however, for it cuts the ground out from under itself. If legal rights are strictly identical with what the courts decide they are, then it is simply false that the adversary system is the best defender of legal rights. Any system whatsoever would defend legal rights equally well, as long as courts decided cases on the basis of that system.

There is, however, a legitimate insight concealed in the Realist objection. Whether or not legal rights are anything beyond what the courts say they are, it is the courts that are charged with adjudicating them. And—the point continues—if lawyers were given discretion to back off from zealous advocacy, they would have to prejudge the case themselves by deciding what the legal rights actually are in order to exercise this discretion. Lawyers would be usurping the judicial function. I think that the insight contains an important argument for the adversary system that we have not yet considered.

Ethical Division of Labor

This argument is no longer that the excesses of zealous advocacy are excused by appealing to the promotion of truth or the defense of legal rights. Rather, it is that they are excused by what Thomas Nagel calls "ethical division of labor." The idea is that behavior that looks wrong from the point of view of ordinary morality is justified by the fact that other social roles exist whose purpose is to counteract the excesses resulting from role-behavior. Zealous adversary advocacy is justified by the fact that the other side is also furnished with a zealous advocate; the impartial arbiter provides a further check.

Will this do the trick? The answer, I am afraid, is no. Suppose that a lawyer is about to embark on a course of action that is unjustified from the point of view of ordinary morality, such as attempting to win an unfair, lopsided judgment for a client from a hapless and innocent party. A zealous adversary advocate will do whatever he or she can to avoid the opposing counsel's attempt to foil his or her designs. But such an advocate surely cannot claim that the existence of the opposing counsel morally justifies these actions. Certainly the fact that a man has a bodyguard in no way excuses you for trying to kill him, particularly if you bend all your ingenuity to avoiding the bodyguard.

The problem is this: the checks-and-balances notion is desirable because if other parts of the system exist to rectify one's excesses, one will be able to devote undivided attention to the job at hand and do it better. It is analogous to wearing protective clothing in a sport such as fencing: knowing that one's opponent is protected, one is justified in going all out in the match. But in the adversary system the situation is different, since the attorney is actively trying to get around the checks and balances: here the analogy is to a fencer who uses a special foil that can cut through the opponent's protective clothing. To put the point another way, the adversary advocate attempts to evade the system of checks and balances, not rely on it to save his or her opponents.

The structure of bureaucratic institutions such as the legal system lends itself to divided responsibility. Those who write the rules, those who give the orders, and those who carry them out each have some basis for claiming that they are not at fault for any wrong that results. But this is unacceptable. As Hannah Arendt observed,

> In a fully developed bureaucracy there is nobody left with whom one can argue…. Bureaucracy is the form of government in which everybody is deprived of…the power to act; for the rule of Nobody is not no-rule, and where all are equally powerless we have a tyranny without a tyrant.

A final division-of-labor argument exists different from those we have just been considering. This is the general line of argument of the ABA-AALS Joint Conference Report. It is based on a point emphasized by the Realists, namely, that lawyers spend very little of their time or attention on actual litigation. Mostly they are involved in other activities: document-drafting, deal-making, negotiation, giving advice, and so forth. The Joint Conference Report seizes on this fact to argue for a separation of lawyerly functions, with a corresponding separation of norms of professional behavior in accord with the nature of those functions. The report restricts no-holds-barred zeal to the role of advocate, a role that, to repeat, lawyers do not occupy very much of the time. As to the morally troubling cases, the lawyer is permitted or even required to advise the client against "a course of conduct technically permissible under existing law, though inconsistent with its underlying spirit and purpose." This the lawyer does by reminding the client of the "long-run costs" of such conduct. I suppose some clients engaged in morally shady projects may be dissuaded by being told how they are harming society, but surely these are just the people least likely to listen. The Joint Conference Report's ominous rumbling about long-run costs is mere Panglossian piety, which harmonizes society's loss with the client's, when, in fact, society's loss is often the client's gain. The argument also omits the key point that, after lawyers have offered their "quiet counsel," they will still have to press forward with the representation if the client won't be dissuaded. Perhaps the lawyer can say that he or she gave morality the old college try, and his or her heart is pure. Our worry, however, was not about impure hearts, but about dirty hands. And those haven't become any cleaner.

The Joint Conference Report's theory that most lawyerly functions are nonadversarial is, I might add, bad sociology. Lawyers, I have suggested, commonly act as though all their functions were governed by the Principles of Professionalism and Nonaccountability. It follows, then, that lawyers commonly act as though all their functions were adversarial. This is true even of the counseling and drafting functions, the report's prime examples of nonadversarial legal activities.

NONCONSEQUENTIALIST JUSTIFICATIONS OF THE ADVERSARY SYSTEM

It may be thought, however, that assessing the adversary system in consequentialist terms of how it will get some job done misses the point. Some social institutions, such as participatory democracy, are justifiable despite the fact that—maybe even because—they are inefficient. The moral standing of such institutions has a noninstrumental basis.

Adversary Advocacy as Intrinsically Good

When we seek out the services of a professional, we have the sense of entrusting a large chunk of our life to this person, and the fact that he or she takes on so intimate a burden and handles it in a trustworthy and skillful manner when the stakes are high seems commendable in itself. Such arguments are frequently made: they are based on the idea that providing service is intrinsically good. No finer statement of this exists, in my opinion, than Mellinkoff's. He sees the paradigm client as the "man-in-trouble."

> Cruelty, oppression, deception, unhappiness, worry, strain, incomprehension, frustration, bewilderment—a sorcerer's bag of misery. These become the expected. Then the saddest of all human cries: "Who will help me?" Try God, and politics, and medicine, and a soft shoulder, sooner or later a lawyer. Too many do. The lawyer, as lawyer, is no sweet kind loving moralizer. He assumes he is needed, and that no one comes to see him to pass the time of day. He is a prober, an analyzer, a scrapper, a man with a strange devotion to his client. Beautifully strange, or so it seems to the man-in-trouble; ugly strange to the untroubled onlooker.

Charles Fried thinks of the lawyer as a "special-purpose friend" whose activity—enhancing the client's autonomy and individuality—is an intrinsic moral good. This is true even when the lawyer's "friendship" consists in assisting the profiteering slumlord to evict an indigent tenant or enabling the wealthy debtor to run the statute of limitations to avoid an honest debt to an old (and less well-off) friend.

Both arguments are attempts to show that a lawyer serving a client is engaged in an intrinsic moral good. Mellinkoff's, however, really shows something much weaker, that a lawyer serving a man-in-trouble is (even more cautiously: can be) engaged in an intrinsic moral good. If the client is a graymailing company or Fried's friend-in-need, we are confronted with no man-in-trouble, and the intuitions to which Mellinkoff's argument appeals disappear. Indeed, if these were the typical clients, the real men-in-trouble—the victims of these predators—might be better off taking their chances in the war of all against all than seeking to have their "autonomy" vindicated legally. The trouble with Mellinkoff's argument is that he makes clients look more pitiable than they are.

Fried, on the other hand, is willing to bite the bullet and argue that it is morally good to represent the man-in-no-trouble-in-particular, the man-who-troubles-others. Your friendly neighborhood anticompetitive multiglomerate is nobly served by a special-purpose friend who helps extract that pound of flesh. Fried constructs a "concentric-circles morality" in which, beginning with an absolute right to self-love based on our own moral standing, we work outward toward those closest to us, then to those whose connections are more remote. Fried's idea is that the abstract connection between a remote person (even a person-in-trouble) and the agent exercises too slight a claim on the agent to override this inclination toward concrete others. This justifies lavishing special care on our friends, even at the expense of "abstract others," and since lavishing care is morally praiseworthy, once we swallow the notion that a lawyer is a special-purpose friend, we are home free with the intrinsic moral worth of the lawyer-client relation.

Several of Fried's critics focus on the fact that the friendship analogy is question-begging: Fried builds enough lawyerly qualities into his concept of friendship that the rest of the argument virtually writes itself. It does seem to me, however, that the analogy captures, albeit in a distorted form, some of the legitimate notion of professionals as devoted by the nature of their calling to the service of their clients. Fried's analogy contains a grain of truth.

This does not, however, vindicate the adversary system. For the friendship analogy undercuts rather than establishes the Principle of Nonaccountability. We are not—except for Nietzsche's Teutons and G. Gordon Liddy—willing to do grossly immoral things to help our friends, nor should we be. Lord Brougham's apology may be many things, but it is not a credo of human friendship in any of its forms. Fried realizes the danger, for he confesses that

> not only would I not lie or steal for...my friends, I probably also would not pursue socially noxious schemes, foreclose the mortgages of widows or orphans, or assist in the avoidance of just punishment. So we must be careful lest the whole argument unravel on us at this point.

The method for saving the argument, however, is disappointing. Fried distinguishes between personal wrongs committed by a lawyer, such as abusing a witness, and institutional wrongs occasioned by the lawyer, such as foreclosing on widows. The latter are precisely those done by the lawyer in his or her proper role of advancing the client's legal autonomy and—preestablished harmony?—they are precisely the ones that are morally OK. That is because the lawyer isn't really doing them, the system is.

This last distinction has not been very popular since World War II, and Fried takes pains to restrict it to "generally just and decent" systems, not Nazi Germany. With this qualification, he can more comfortably assert: "We should absolve the lawyer of personal moral responsibility for the result he accomplishes because the wrong is wholly institutional."

This last sentence, however, is nothing but the assertion that institutional excuses work for lawyers, and this should tip us off that Fried's argument will be useless for our purposes. For consider: our whole line of argument has been an attempt to justify the adversary system by showing that the traditional lawyer-client relation is an intrinsic moral good. Now it seems that this can be established by Fried's argument only if we are permitted to cancel the moral debit column by means of an institutional excuse; but that can work only if the institution is justified, and we are back where we started.

The Social Fabric Argument

The remaining arguments are distinct but closely related. They are two variants of the following idea, which may be called the "social fabric argument":

> Regardless of whether the adversary system is efficacious, it is an integral part of our culture, and that fact by itself justifies it.

The first variation is based on democratic theory: it claims that the adversary system is justified because it enjoys the consent of the governed. The second variation is based on conservative theory: it claims that the adversary system is justified because it is a deeply rooted part of our tradition.

According to the social fabric argument, the moral reason for staying with our institutions is precisely that they are ours. We live under them, adapt our lives and practices to them, assess our neighbors' behavior in their light, employ them as a standard against which to measure other ways of life. Traditional institutions bind us—morally and legitimately bind us—because we assimilate ourselves to our tradition (variation 2). In the language of political theory, we consent to them (variation 1). They express who we are and what we stand for.

This way of looking at the adversary system is quite different from the claim that it promotes the discovery of truth, or the protection of legal rights, or the rectification of wrongs. Those arguments are consequentialist in character: they are attempts to justify the adversary system on the basis of what it does. The social fabric argument justifies it on the basis of what we do, or who we are. Let us look at the variants.

The *consent argument* claims that the adversary system is part of the social contract. The adversary system is justified because it enjoys the consent of the governed, the highest moral compliment that can be paid to it in a democracy. An immediate problem with the argument, however, is that we obviously do not *explicitly* consent to the adversary system. Nobody asked us, and I don't suppose anyone intends to. If the argument is to work, the consent must be *tacit* consent, and then we are entitled to wonder how we can tell that it has been given. One test is simply that, over an extended period of time, we have incorporated the institution into our shared practices. Michael Walzer makes this suggestion: "Over a long period of time, shared experiences and cooperative activity of many different kinds shape a common life. 'Contract' is a metaphor for a process of association and mutuality." There is a problem with this account, however: just because people do not have the energy, inclination, or courage to replace their institutions we should not conclude that they want them or approve of them. But unless they want them or approve of them, people's endurance of institutions does not make the institutions morally good. The verb "consent" can mean either "put up with" or "actively approve." Only the latter has the moral force required to show that the institution is a positive moral good, but only the former is revealed by the mere existence of "our common life."

Thus, the most we get from tacit consent arguments, such as Walzer's appeal to our "common life," is a demonstration that we are not obliged to dismantle the adversary system. To get anything stronger, we must appeal to a different concept in democratic theory from consent: we must show that people *want* the adversary system. In Rousseau's language, we must show that having an adversary system is our "general will."

Does the adversary system pass such a test? The answer, I think, is clearly no. Few of our institutions are trusted less than adversary adjudication, precisely because it seems to license lawyers to trample the truth, legal rights, and common morality. The argument fails.

Seeing that it fails and why, can motivate the second variation, which we may call the *tradition argument*. Consent theorists assume that we have no political obligations except those we consent to, but as Hume noted, "would these reasoners look abroad into the world, they would meet with nothing that, in the least, corresponds to their ideas, or can warrant so refined and philosophical a system." On the contrary, as Hume argued, people commonly consent to institutions because they take themselves to be obligated to them, rather than the other way around. We feel that traditional institutions lay claim to us, even when they themselves originated through violence or usurpation.

A Burkean argument for the adversary system would appeal to its place in our traditions and claim that we are under a moral obligation to spurn "speculations of a contingent improvement" that would tear this tradition apart. There is much to be said for Burkean argument, if for no other reason than its rejection of a shallow and philistine conception of progress. But it does not apply to the adversary system.

In the first place, it ignores the fact that there is no constant tradition: common law constantly modifies the adversary system. Indeed, the adversary advocate is a recent invention within that changing tradition. In Great Britain, criminal defense lawyers were not permitted to address the courts until 1836; in America, criminal defendants were not guaranteed counsel until 1963.

Civil litigants are still not guaranteed counsel, even in quasi-criminal matters such as a state's attempt to take a child from its parent. It is hard to see the adversary system as "a clause in the great primaeval contract."

In the second place, the adversary system is an ancillary institution compared with those with which Burke was concerned. In William Simon's words,

> It's one thing to talk about the dangers of utopian change when you're talking about ripping the whole society apart to restructure it from top to bottom. But there are plenty of ways of abolishing adversary ethics which, from a larger point of view, are really just marginal social reforms which, whether good or bad, hardly suggest the likelihood of Burkean dangers.

THE ADVERSARY SYSTEM EXCUSE

So far the course of argument has been purely negative, a persecution and assassination of the adversary system. By this time you are entitled to ask what I propose putting in its place. The answer is: nothing, for I think the adversary system *is* justified.

I do not, let me quickly say, have an argumentative novelty to produce. It would be strange indeed for a social institution to be justified on the basis of virtues other than the tried and true ones, virtues that no one had noticed in it before. My justification is rather a version of the tradition argument, but purged of its ideological overtones: I shall call it the "pragmatic justification" or "pragmatic argument" to suggest its affinity with the relaxed, problem-oriented, and historicist notion of justification associated with American pragmatism. The justification is this:

First, the adversary system, despite its imperfections, irrationalities, loopholes, and perversities, seems to do as good a job as any at finding truth and protecting legal rights. Second, some adjudicatory system is necessary. Third, it's the way we have always done things.

CONCLUSION AND PERORATION

My argument countenances adversarial ruthlessness as a blanket policy only in criminal and quasi-criminal defense, and thus only in these situations is the adversary system available as an institutional excuse. What does all this mean in noncriminal contexts, where this institutional excuse based on political theory is unavailable? The answer, very simply, is this. The adversary system possesses only the slightest moral force, and thus, appealing to it can excuse only the slightest moral wrongs. Anything else that is morally wrong for a nonlawyer to do on behalf of another person is morally wrong for a lawyer to do as well. The lawyer's role carries no moral privileges and immunities. Am I not saying that a lawyer may be professionally obligated to do A and morally obligated not to do A? That is indeed what I am saying. When moral obligation conflicts with professional obligation, the lawyer must become a civil disobedient. Not that this is likely to happen. Lawyers get paid for their services, not for their consciences. But so does everyone else. As we do not expect the world to strike a truce in the war of all against all, we should not expect lawyers to. Shen Te, the Good Woman of Setzuan, says:

> I'd like to be good, it's true, but there's the rent to pay. And that's not all: I sell myself for a living. Even so I can't make ends meet, there's too much competition.

That, of course, is the way the world is, and criticizing an ideology won't change the world. The point of the exercise, I suppose, is merely to get our moral ideas straight: one less ideology is, after all, one less excuse.

DISCUSSION QUESTIONS

1. Think about the range of principal-agent relationships and the extent to which agents are implicated in the *ends* pursued by their principals or even the *identity* of their principals. Mercenary soldiers and political consultants might occupy one extreme and physicians the other. Where would you place the following: advertising or public relations agencies, government officials (including police, soldiers)? Is it acceptable for them to change sides (as lawyers are permitted to do—even required by the British "cab rank" rule)? Before Dick Morris went to work for Bill Clinton, he wrote a speech for a Republican candidate ridiculing the president for wanting to "make our military a joke." A woman who founded Mothers Against Drunk Driving after her daughter was killed now lobbies for breweries and restaurants resisting stricter laws against drunk driving.

Some professional models refuse to pose for advertisements of certain products—tobacco, alcohol, hair straighteners, or skin lighteners. Some pharmacies are refusing to sell tobacco. How would you distinguish their moral situation from that of lawyers?

Does the lay public agree that lawyers are not morally responsible for the ends they seek or the clients they represent? Consider the lawyers who represented those accused of communism during the 1950s red scare. Republican Wayne Allard defeated Democrat Tom Strickland in the 1996 election for Colorado's senator partly by publicizing the fact that Strickland's law firm represented polluters, ski-resort developers, and truckers while the candidate claimed to be an environmentalist.

2. Consider the roles lawyers play. If criminal defense lies at one extreme of moral nonaccountability, can (must) a lawyer perform that role regardless of the identity or character of the accused and crime charged? Did a Canadian defense lawyer commit professional misconduct by concealing six videotapes showing his client, Paul Bernado, sexually abusing two teenage girls he later murdered?[2] What lawyer roles lie at the opposite extreme of the spectrum? Are there situations in which a lawyer is entitled (required) to decline representation? In which you would do so? Does it depend on *which* lawyers are declining representation (public/private, free/feed, solo/large firm)? The composition of the profession? Whether the adversary has equal representation? Santa Monica City Attorney Robert M. Myers was fired for refusing to draft a law criminalizing homelessness; can his position be justified?

What about the following situations:

A. Assisting a Southern school district to resist integration for decades after the *Brown* decision.

B. Writing an unenforceable contract, such as an invalid agreement not to sue.

C. Stalling while the statute of limitations runs; or using court delay to drive down a settlement.

---

2. *New York Times* A4 (2.24.97)

D. Using a legal argument you find morally offensive, e.g., prior sexual conduct by a rape victim to show consent, or homosexuality to challenge child custody.

E. Lobbying for a law you oppose or against one you favor, e.g., delaying FDA regulation of tobacco.

F. Acting in a facilitative capacity for an organization you oppose, e.g., the acquisition of property by a neo-fascist group, or South Africa's attempt to evade the international boycott. Should a black ACLU lawyer represent the KKK in its attempt to keep its membership secret? Should an American Jew (Abraham Sofaer) represent Libyan leader Muammar el-Qaddafi? (The *New York Times* thought not.)

3. If you believe that lawyers ought to adhere to their own moral principles in their representational roles (at least more than they do now), what are the obstacles? How would we have to restructure the legal profession, the legal system or society to increase such autonomy? Should a prosecutor's office excuse employees from handling death penalty cases? "Three strikes" cases? Should a law firm excuse women and minorities from defending employment discrimination? What would be the consequences of such changes for the distribution of legal services? Which kinds of clients presently benefit from the Principle of Nonaccountability?

Is it appropriate for law students to boycott an on-campus law firm interview because of the firm's clients—as Harvard students did when Sidley & Austin defended Colorado's initiative banning local antidiscrimination ordinances protecting homosexuals? What about picketing the firm's office? About 20 percent of the 175 lawyers at Shook, Hardy & Bacon, the largest law firm in Kansas City, work on tobacco defense; would that be relevant to you in accepting a job offer from them? When and for what reasons do lawyers reject clients now? Is it appropriate for a client to withdraw business from a firm because of its other clients?

SUGGESTED READING

David Luban has elaborated his views in *Lawyers and Justice: An Ethical Study* (Princeton, 1988) and engaged in a debate with William Simon about the adversary excuse for criminal defense in 91 *Michigan Law Review* 1703-72 (1993); see also William Simon, *The Practice of Justice: A Theory of Lawyers'*

Ethics (1997). The numerous accounts of the O.J. Simpson trial raise these issues, e.g., Lawrence Schiller and James Willworth, *American Tragedy* (Random House, 1996). Contrast the strained apologetics of Harvard Law School professor and former Solicitor General Charles Fried, "The Lawyer as Friend: The Moral Foundations of the Lawyer-Client Relation," 85 *Yale Law Journal* 1060 (1976) with the tirade by black feminist activist Florynce Kennedy, "The Whorehouse Theory of Law," in Robert Lefcourt (ed.), *Law Against the People* (1971). Stephen Pepper argues that different considerations must govern transactional lawyering: "Counseling at the Limits of the Law: An Exercise in the Jurisprudence and Ethics of Lawyering," 104 *Yale Law Journal* 1545 (1995). Drawing on historical research concerning the emergence of corporate lawyers at the end of the nineteenth and beginning of the twentieth centuries, Robert Gordon claims that they do and should urge their moral views on clients: "Legal Thought and Legal Practice in the Age of American Enterprise, 1870-1920," in Gerald L. Geison (ed.), *Professions and Professional Ideologies in America* (University of North Carolina, 1983); "The Independence of Lawyers," 68 *Boston University Law Review* 1 (1988); "Corporate Law Practice as a Public Calling," 49 *Maryland Law Review* 255 (1990). Ronald Gilson contends that economic pressures have made it increasingly difficult for them to do so, "The Devolution of the Legal Profession: A Demand Side Perspective," 49 *Maryland Law Review* 869 (1990). Rob Atkinson offers an ethical riposte: "A Dissenter's Commentary on the Professionalism Crusade," 74 *Texas Law Review* 259 (1995); "How the Butler Was Made to Do It: The Perverted Professionalism of *The Remains of the Day*." 105 *Yale Law Journal* 177 (1995). David Wilkins has addressed the dilemma of representing hateful clients: "Race, Ethics, and the First Amendment: Should a Black Lawyer Represent the Ku Klux Klan?" 63 *George Washington Law Review* 746 (1995). I offer my own thoughts about professionalism in "The Contradictions of Legal Professionalism," in School of Justice Studies, Arizona State University, eds., *New Directions in The Study of Justice, Law and Social Control* (Plenum, 1989), "Taking Professionalism Seriously," 1989 (1) *Annual Survey of American Law* 41 (1989).

Chapter Two

AN OVERVIEW OF
THE AMERICAN LEGAL PROFESSION

Like all social institutions, legal professions experience long eras of relative stability punctuated by short bursts of rapid change. The history of American lawyers can be crudely periodized as follows: an English heritage (including a divided profession, some of whose barristers trained at the London Bar); the flight of many lawyers allied to the Tory cause following the Revolution; the successful Jacksonian attack on privilege, which eliminated almost all entry barriers for white men; the effort to "professionalize," begun in the 1880s by the American Bar Association and largely complete by the 1930s; the displacement of apprenticeship by university legal education; the demographic effects of the two World Wars and the economic impact of the Great Depression; and the end of a long period of stasis in the 1970s, with the rapid growth of law school enrollments, including increasing numbers of women and racial minorities, and the expansion of law firms. The next selection summarizes these events and locates them within a sociological theory.

THE TRANSFORMATION OF THE AMERICAN LEGAL PROFESSION[1]
Richard L. Abel

IN recent decades, the American legal profession has undergone changes whose speed and magnitude are without historical precedent. The number of lawyers more than doubled between 1950 and 1980 and seems likely to do so again by the end of the century. As a result, the profession is becoming dramatically younger. Once almost exclusively a white male enclave, the profession now admits significant numbers of women and members of ethnic minorities, although African American and Latino entrants remain greatly underrepresented. In addition, the dominance of

private practice and of solo and small-firm practitioners within that category—which long has been more pronounced in the United States than in any other country—is declining with the growth of public and private employment and the expansion in law firm size. Although we will not be able to assess the full ramifications of these changes until the cohorts that entered the profession before the mid-1960s have retired, the new patterns are sufficiently clear and striking to demand provisional reflections.

All occupations in capitalist societies seek to control their markets. Professions are distinguished from other service providers by their strategic choices and relative success. American lawyers constructed the contemporary legal profession between the 1870s and 1950s. They developed local, state, and national bar associations; promulgated ethical codes; and established disciplinary procedures. These associations were instrumental in controlling the production of qualified producers of legal services by redefining and tightening professional entrance requirements. Around the turn of the century, formal legal education rapidly displaced apprenticeship. Law schools lengthened the period of study from one or two years to three, and their examinations weeded out many students. Part-time evening schools unaccredited by the American Bar Association gradually disappeared as state bars refused to accept their degrees. Law school tuition rose. Law schools and state bars began to require an undergraduate degree. Bar examinations became universal, written, and difficult, and the examiners required prospective legal practitioners to possess American citizenship, state residence, and good character. Partly as a result of these entry barriers, the population/lawyer ratio was higher in 1970 than it had been in 1890.

Professional associations also sought to con-

1. 20 *Law & Society Review* 7 (1986). Reprinted with permission.

trol production *by* producers of legal services. They waged campaigns against the unauthorized practice of law by other occupations, entering agreements dividing the market with realtors and bankers. They prohibited lawyer advertising and solicitation, sporadically enforcing these bans in highly publicized campaigns against low-status "ambulance chasers." They attacked and successfully curtailed prepaid legal services plans, which threatened to take business from nonmember lawyers. They promulgated minimum fee schedules, punishing those who engaged in price competition. Some state bars erected high protective walls against out-of-state lawyers. Bar associations maintained that legal services to the poor should be provided only through the charitable efforts of philanthropies and volunteer lawyers; when Britain established a state-supported legal aid scheme in 1949, American lawyers recoiled in horror at the threat to professional independence posed by this specter of creeping socialism.

The legal profession that emerged in the first half of the twentieth century was distinctive in both composition and structure. Despite the strong nativist sentiments of professional elites and xenophobic bar associations, the relatively lenient entry standards that prevailed until the late 1930s and the availability of part-time legal education allowed large numbers of second-generation immigrants, whose parents were skilled workers or small entrepreneurs, to become lawyers. But the profession explicitly discriminated against both blacks, who were excluded from the American Bar Association and many law schools, and women, who were denied entry to some law schools until the 1950s and 1960s. In consequence, blacks remained about 1 percent of the legal profession and women less than 5 percent as late as 1970. Because the number of entrants declined from 1928 to 1947, under the influence of the Great Depression and even more of World War Two, the profession grew progressively older and, presumably, more conservative. The postwar profession also was dominated by private practitioners (almost 90 percent) and, among them, by solo practitioners (more than 60 percent).

When we assess recent changes against this background, we find that each element has been seriously eroded. First, the entry barriers painfully constructed over half a century have failed to withstand assault by the growing number aspiring to become lawyers. This should not be surprising. Supply control in a capitalist economy can never be more than temporary; its very success engenders more vigorous attacks. Restrictions on the production of lawyers during the boom years of the 1950s and 1960s created an imbalance between the supply of legal services and the demand, leading to a rapid increase in starting salaries. Beginning associates in large firms, who earned $7,000 in the mid-1960s, commanded twelve times as much thirty years later. But money has not been the only incentive; the civil rights, women's, consumer, and environmental movements all made law an integral part of their social activism. Furthermore, the first two movements irretrievably delegitimated the ascriptive barriers of race and gender, more than doubling the numbers who could aspire to be lawyers.

The growth of public tertiary education also greatly expanded the population qualified to enter law school, while credential inflation made a professional degree more essential to continued membership in the middle class. At the same time, better-educated students found it easier to graduate from law school and pass the bar examination. The United States Supreme Court struck down exclusions of noncitizens, out-of-state residents, and those who deviated from the political or sexual mainstream. Although the American Bar Association continued to exercise its accreditation powers, the number of approved law schools rose more than 25 percent in fifteen years, and student enrollments in those schools more than doubled. Thus, although the profession still exerts some control over entry, the rate of production of lawyers has risen greatly. That rate appears to have stabilized, albeit at a level more than three times what it was in the mid-1960s.

Declining control over the production *of* producers has been accompanied by an erosion of control over production *by* producers. It seems plausible that the former is at least partly responsible for the latter. The greater number of lawyers, especially in recent cohorts, must compete with each other more aggressively. Furthermore, there is evidence that younger lawyers are more critical than their elders of restrictive practices, which tend to favor the more established practitioner. But the attack on professional privilege also has been waged by a strange alliance between the liberal consumer movement and the laissez-faire economists who criticize any state regulation. In response to these diverse stimuli, the Supreme Court has invalidated minimum fee schedules and most restrictions on advertising (although not solicitation), and the United States Justice Department forced the American Bar Association to stop favoring open-panel over closed-panel group legal service plans by threatening an antitrust prosecution. Legal clinics have pioneered the mass production of routine legal services for middle-class individuals through advertising and price cutting. The professional market also is threatened by lay competitors, who publish handbooks, produce forms, offer advice, and represent clients before administrative tribunals—indeed, do everything except appear in court.

Faced with an excess supply of law graduates and heightened competition from both within and outside the profession, lawyers displayed greater interest in demand creation as a strategy of market control. Advertising, legal clinics, and prepaid plans are examples. But the greatest transformation occurred in the profession's attitude toward state support for legal services to the poor. In the 1950s, lawyers were united in opposing any government role. When President Kennedy launched the OEO Legal Services Program in 1965, it secured the support of the ABA governing body, but state and local bar associations and many rank-and-file lawyers remained skeptical or openly hostile. Yet when President Reagan repeatedly sought to abolish the Legal Services Corporation, he was greeted with protests from every bar association in the country, whether national, state or local, specialist or generalist, liberal or conservative. Furthermore, the profession pushed steadily (although with limited success) for the diversion of funds from staffed offices employing full-time salaried lawyers to "judicare" programs reimbursing private attorneys for representing poor clients. The fear that state intervention would curtail professional autonomy seems to have evaporated in the face of potential benefits.

Many of the forces explaining the profession's growth also account for changes in its composition. Women are more than 40 percent and racial minorities more than 10 percent of entrants. An important question is how they will be distributed across professional strata. We have known for several decades that lawyers are sharply stratified in prestige and wealth along such variables as clients served, subject-matter specialization, employment versus independent practice, firm size, and location within the public or private sectors. The growth of the profession and the erosion of restrictive practices continue to intensify this stratification. Solo and small-firm practitioners are most deeply affected by competition from new entrants, who engage in advertising and price cutting, while the upper echelon of the profession enjoys ever-greater wealth, power, and status. There is a substantial danger that disproportionate numbers of minority lawyers will be relegated to the bottom of this hierarchy by discrimination, law school grades that reflect inadequate prior education and continuing economic disadvantage, and commitment to work for social justice.

The future of women lawyers is likely to be more complicated. On one hand, women often chose career paths different from those of men, partly influenced by patriarchal family relations, partly in anticipation of discrimination at work. They tended to prefer salaried employment, especially in the public sector (such as legal aid and public defender offices and government), to private practice and, within the latter category, solo practice to small firms. On the other hand, women do at least as well as men in law school, and many have joined large firms, although they appear to attain partnership more slowly and less frequently. The increase in female entry seems to have narrowed the class backgrounds of lawyers (perhaps because upper-class women are better able to overcome sex discrimination), whereas the entry of minorities may have had the opposite effect. To the extent that stratification within the professional hierarchy comes to be paralleled by race and gender differences, it will be harder to legitimate.

The growth of the legal profession also poses another kind of challenge. Declining bar admissions from 1928 to 1946, stasis until the early

1960s, and recent dramatic growth charged a small cohort of elderly white men with the governance of associations that deeply affect the lives of a very large younger cohort with significant female and minority membership. Since the younger generation of lawyers will not ascend to positions of power for another decade or two, given the strongly gerontocratic character of professional governance, the divergence of interests, styles, and demography between rulers and ruled is likely to generate considerable tension.

Greater numbers, together with other changes, also have influenced the structures within which lawyers practice. The solo practitioner—that paradigm of the independent professional—no longer dominates the profession. Although a larger fraction of lawyers still practice by themselves in the United States than in any other common-law country, the category is likely to shrink (at least proportionally) as a result of competition from legal clinics, prepaid plans, and laypersons, which achieve economies of scale by investing heavily in advertising, and word processing, and employing cheap labor. (Yet solo practice continues to offer the only alternative for new entrants who cannot find jobs.) At the other extreme within the private-practice spectrum, large firms have been growing in size and numbers, augmenting their capital investments, and enlarging their subordinate labor force. Once again, we can expect these trends to persist as firms seek prestige (of which size is an important symbol), compete for clients (corporate conglomerates and multinationals as well as wealthy individuals) by adding specialties and opening branch offices, and strive to enhance profitability (significantly correlated with the ratio of associates to partners).

The decline of solo practice and the growth of larger firms both contribute to the increasing number of employed lawyers. Firms not only employ more associates but also keep them in that status for longer periods, sometimes indefinitely. The number of lawyers employed by business and government has also increased. More than nine out of every ten law school graduates now begin their careers as employees, and many are content to remain in that status; women, for example, may want to limit their working hours in order to raise a family, and both female and

minority lawyers may fear that client prejudices will deny them business if they open their own practices. If these trends are extrapolated, a profession that was 85 percent self-employed in 1948 and about 60 percent self-employed in 1980 soon may be more than half employees.

Finally, the changes in size, composition, structure, and function have serious implications for one of the characteristics most central to the concept of the profession—self-governance. First, the growing number and diversity of lawyers have made it difficult for any association to speak on their behalf. The result has been less a struggle for power within traditional organizations (the ABA and state and local bar associations) than the proliferation of rival organizations based on gender, ethnicity, age, politics, or functional specialization. These centrifugal tendencies threaten to rip apart that bulwark of professional control, the integrated bar, which combines compulsory membership with state power. In its place we may find a plurality of voluntary (and thus weaker) trade associations, free to pursue their self-interests, arrayed against a state regulatory agency over which lawyers exert greatly reduced control.

Second, there is growing doubt, both within and outside the profession, about lawyers' capacity and commitment to regulate themselves and, perhaps in response, continuing encroachment on professional autonomy by external regulators. The ABA's 1981 revision of legal ethics, a mere decade after the last major overhaul, revealed considerable normative dissensus among lawyers, perhaps reflecting their growing heterogeneity. State disciplinary processes are periodically wracked by scandals about systematic underenforcement. Some bar associations have transferred disciplinary responsibility to an independent state agency to avoid charges of self-dealing. Changes in the composition and structure of the profession also make effective discipline problematic. On one hand, the large firm is a powerful bureaucratic organization, jealously guarding control over its members and remaining relatively impervious to external influence. Similarly, neither ethical rules nor disciplinary mechanisms speak meaningfully to lawyers employed by business or government. On the other hand, if disciplinary investigations and sanctions continue to focus disproportionately on lower-status practitioners, these processes may be accused of racial as well as class bias.

> External forces are eager to fill the vacuum presently left by ineffective or illegitimate professional self-regulation. Clients can take action, either individually, as when (with increasing frequency) they sue for malpractice, or collectively, as when a labor union oversees the competence of lawyers serving its members through a group plan. In addition, government can act on behalf of consumers, as when the U.S. Supreme Court, the Justice Department, or the Federal Trade Commission challenges restrictive practices. Although American government is not the paymaster of private lawyers, as government is under legal aid schemes in other countries, this may yet occur, and it would greatly enlarge the amount of state intervention within the market for legal services. Thus, the changes of the last decade have impaired the profession's capacity to take unified action and witnessed the growth of both consumers and the state as competing loci of regulation.

Professions are historically specific institutions for organizing the production and distribution of services. Only a few occupations have succeeded in attaining the status of a profession during the last hundred years. Because they have granted their members high prestige, considerable wealth, and insulation from capitalist relations of production, many other occupations have emulated them, if with only mixed success. For the same reasons, lawyers have sought to retain their professional privileges, deploying both the force of tradition and the sentiments of nostalgia in a vain effort to resist change. But the experience of the last two decades strongly suggests that we are witnessing the decline of the professional configuration, if not yet its demise.

Today the production *of* producers is occurring at levels lawyers did not choose and through mechanisms over which they exercise little influence. Attempts to reassert control—by creating specializations that require further training, for instance—are partial measures at best and have the unfortunate effect of promoting intraprofessional rivalry and fragmentation. Lawyers also have lost considerable control over production *by* producers; as a result, they find it more difficult to defend the restrictive practices that survive and suffer more intense competition, which accelerates the spread of capitalist relations of production within legal practice. To the extent that lawyers respond to this erosion of market control by adopting a strategy of demand creation, they run the risk of intensifying rather than moderating competition, becoming more dependent on the state rather than regaining autonomy, and organizing hitherto atomistic consumers into collectivities that can challenge professional dominance.

Lawyers today look less and less like a homogeneous category of independent professionals. Employees are a growing minority and soon will be a majority. Stratification into two hemispheres divided by backgrounds, clients, functions, structures, rewards, and associations is irreversible and growing. At the base of this hierarchy, the solo practitioner, long the embodiment of professional autonomy, is facing an ever more hostile economic environment, lost prestige, and declining numbers. At the apex of the hierarchy, the large firm is growing in size and prominence while simultaneously becoming more bureaucratic and less independent. As professional heterogeneity increases, stratification may come to be associated with racial and gender differences. If so, it will be seen as a form of illegitimate discrimination rather than an indispensable aspect of a benign meritocracy. Divisions of race, gender, age, class, structure of practice, and politics make it increasingly difficult for a single association to represent all lawyers. For similar reasons, professional self-regulation is being undermined from within while it is being challenged from without. Is it useful to continue viewing lawyers as members of a profession when they no longer control their market, when they are divided by demographic characteristics, rewards, structures, functions, and voluntary associations, and when they are losing the privileges of self-regulation?

With this historical synopsis as a foundation, we turn to a statistical snapshot of the contemporary profession.

THE FUTURES OF AMERICAN LAWYERS: A DEMOGRAPHIC PROFILE OF A CHANGING PROFESSION IN A CHANGING SOCIETY[1]
Robert L. Nelson

IN the last two decades there has been a veritable explosion in both the number of lawyers and the size of the legal services industry. Between 1977 and 1989, revenues devoted to legal services increased by some 480 percent, to a total of $75 billion. Thus legal services grew almost twice as fast as the gross national product (which expanded by some 260 percent), and substantially faster than health services (which grew by some 370 percent to a total of $250 billion). Receipts from business legal services grew at an annual rate of 15 percent between 1967 and 1982, while receipts from individual clients grew at a vigorous but lower rate of 11.7 percent. Between 1980 and 1988 the number of law firms with more than 100 lawyers grew by 196 percent, the number with 51–100 lawyers by 91 percent, and the number with 21–50 lawyers by 68 percent. In contrast the number of law firms overall increased by 11 percent. In 1972 the top 50 firms received an estimated 5.1 percent of receipts for all law firms; by 1987 their share had increased to 7.8 percent, a 50 percent increment.

THE NUMBER AND DISTRIBUTION OF LAWYERS ACROSS PRACTICE SETTINGS

The growth in the number of lawyers is in part a product of population growth and the rise of professionalism generally. Table 1 reports the pattern of change in the number of lawyers, doctors, government employees, and the total population from 1900 to 1990 by ten-year intervals. The population of the United States has more than tripled over the period, but lawyers, doctors, and

government employees have exceeded the general rate of population growth. The increase in new lawyers may result in part from the increased number of college graduates produced by the "baby boom." The proportion of the population aged 20–29 years, which makes up the vast majority of law school applicants, increased from 15.7 percent in 1950 to 18 percent in 1980. From 1970 to 1980 the total number in this age group increased 50 percent, less than half the rate of increase in the number of lawyers. Although the number of doctors exceeded the number of lawyers in the period before 1930, the two groups have similar patterns of sustained growth through 1970 and a takeoff in the period 1970–80.

TABLE 1

Decennial Change (%) in Number of Lawyers, Doctors, Government Employees, and Total Population

YEAR	LAWYERS	DOCTORS	CIVIL SERVANTS	POPU-LATION
1910	6.5	16.0	–	21.0
1920	7.0	-0.7	–	14.9
1930	30.9	7.9	–	16.1
1940	13.4	6.7	–	7.2
1950	1.1	14.9	43.1	14.4
1960	15.8	17.0	37.6	19.0
1970	28.6	20.5	47.9	13.3
1980	112.0	61.0	22.6	11.5
1990	24.4	17.8	10.0	10.3

However, the number of lawyers grew twice as quickly as doctors in the 1970s, and 50 percent higher in the 1980s.

Government employment also has increased during this period. Since 1940 the number of civilian government employees has quadrupled. Most government employment is at the state and local level. It grew from 3.3 million in 1940 to more than 14 million in 1990. Federal employment increased from 1.1 million in 1940 to 3.1 million in 1990. The expansion of government should create work for lawyers, both inside government and for lawyers representing clients

---

1. 44 *Case Western Reserve Law Review* 345 (1994). Reprinted with permission.

before government. But the percent increase in government employment in the two decades, 1970–80 and 1980–90, is much lower than the percent increase in lawyers.

The growth of government legal staffs may be particularly relevant. The total number of government lawyers more than doubled from 19,614 in 1948 to 44,167 in 1970. By 1980 it reached 70,512, a 60 percent rise. From 1980 to 1988, government lawyers increased by 19 percent to some 84,182. Thus the rate of increase is lower than for the profession as a whole.

American lawyers are still overwhelmingly engaged in private law practice, in contrast to many continental legal systems where larger proportions are in the judiciary and private employment. Table 2 displays the distribution of lawyers across practice settings nationally from 1948 to 1988. Almost nine out of ten lawyers in 1948 were private practitioners, and two-thirds of these were solo practitioners. The proportion in private practice has declined by about 20 percent, to a little more than seven out of ten lawyers nationally. The presence of solo practitioners in the profession has declined much more substantially, from 61 percent in 1948 to 46 percent in 1960 to 33 percent nationally in 1980 and 1988.

It is the organizational practice settings of law firms, private industry, nonprofit institutions, and government, therefore, that have come to occupy an increasing proportion of legal positions. About 10 percent of the profession works in private business or nonprofit organizations. These sectors outgrew the profession's overall rate of increase until the 1970–80 period but did not keep pace in the 1980s, resulting in a slight decline in their proportion among lawyers. Lawyers working for the government follow a very similar pattern. Due to problems of double-counting lawyers who worked part-time for government, the statistics for government lawyers are probably inflated for the years 1948 to 1970, but government lawyers probably grew as a proportion of the profession throughout the 1948 to 1980 period, and only in the 1980s have their numbers decreased as a percentage of the total profession.

Table 3 shows that the most dramatic organizational change in the profession in the last decade has been the growth of large law firms. Among private practitioners, solos and small firms still make up a large majority of the profession—some 63 percent of private practitioners were in firms of one to five lawyers in 1988—but

TABLE 2

National Distribution of Lawyers (%)
by Practice Setting

SETTING	1948	1951	1954	1957	1960	1963	1966	1970	1980	1988
PRIV. PRACTICE	89.2	86.8	85.5	80.1	76.2	74.7	73.5	72.7	68.3	71.9
SOLO	61.2	59.0	57.5	51.9	46.3	42.1	39.1	36.6	33.2	33.2
PARTNERS	23.6	23.2	23.3	23.3	24.1	26.1	27.1	28.5	26.3	27.0
ASSOCIATES	4.4	4.6	4.7	4.9	5.8	6.5	7.2	7.6	8.8	11.7
PRIV. EMPLOY.	3.2	5.7	6.9	8.3	9.2	10.2	10.6	11.3	10.9	9.8
EDUCATION	—	0.6	0.6	0.6	0.7	0.8	0.9	1.1	1.2	1.0
GOVERNMENT	8.3	9.8	9.6	10.3	10.2	10.9	10.8	11.1	10.8	9.0
LOCAL	4.7	3.9	3.9	3.3	3.3	2.9	2.6	2.4	5.6	5.3
STATE	—	1.8	1.6	1.7	1.7	2.4	2.6	2.9	3.7	5.3
FEDERAL	—	4.1	4.1	5.3	5.2	5.6	5.6	5.8	1.5	3.7
JUDICIAL	4.2	3.6	3.6	3.3	3.2	3.3	3.4	3.2	3.6	2.7

TABLE 3

National Distribution of Private Practitioners by Firm Size (%)

Year	SOLO	2	3	4	5	6–10	11–20	21–50	51+
1980	48.6	8.8	6.1	4.4	3.1	9.0	6.5	6.1	7.3
1988	46.2	6.7	4.6	3.4	2.6	7.8	7.1	7.0	14.6

Firm Size

very large firms now make up a much greater share of the private bar than ten years ago. Only a little more than 13 percent of private lawyers in 1980 were in firms of more than twenty attorneys, and only 7 percent were in firms of more than fifty lawyers. By 1988, 22 percent of private practitioners worked in firms of more than twenty lawyers. The percentage of lawyers in firms of fifty or more had doubled, so that about one in seven private attorneys worked in firms of fifty or more. Almost one in ten lawyers practiced in firms of 100 or more.

INCOME AND EMPLOYMENT RATES

The data on income by firm size demonstrate clearly the economic benefits of gaining a large-firm position. The relative earnings of lawyers in different practice settings has become substantially more dispersed in recent years. Table 4 presents income data from a variety of sources. In the early 1960s, partners in firms of any size made about 2.5 times the incomes of sole proprietors or beginning associates in Wall Street firms or beginning corporate counsel. By 1975, partners were averaging three times what solo practitioners made and twice what Wall Street associates made. By 1980, the earnings ratio was 3.25 between partners and solos and only 1.5 between partners and Wall Street associates. The relative earnings of partners and sole practitioners stayed about the same through 1986, but by this time partners as a group averaged earnings that were only 1.38 times more than what Wall Street associates make. The decline in the partner/Wall Street associate ratio was due in part to compositional effects. That is, we are comparing partners in small firms with associates in the very biggest firms. Indeed the average profits per partner in the top 100 law firms in 1986 were $305,000, which was 4.7 times more than the starting salary for Wall Street associates. Those beginning Wall Street associates, in turn, were making 2.3 times more than solo practitioners as a group, twice as

TABLE 4

Lawyer Income by Practice Setting ($)

YEAR	SOLO	PARTNER	STARTING ELITE NY ASSOCIATE	STARTING ASSOCIATE (MEDIAN)	STARTING CORP. COUNSEL (MEAN)
1960	7,257	17,090	—	—	—
1963	8,763	20,660	7,000	—	—
1968	11,216	27,820	15,000	—	9,338
1974	14,675	41,092	22,000	14,500	14,223
1980	18,119	58,917	38,000	23,000	20,911
1985	24,990	85,640	54,000	32,500	29,004
1990	35,730	123,756	85,000	48,000	39,500

much as the median salary for all starting associates, almost three times the starting salaries of small-firm associates, and twice the mean starting salary of corporate counsel. And, as the table shows, average profits per partner at these top firms rose very rapidly to $424,000 in 1990, until they receded somewhat to $400,000 in 1991.

The escalation of the salaries of Wall Street associates can in part be traced to supply and demand considerations. The large corporate law firms that require graduates from elite law schools have grown much faster than the graduating classes from preferred law schools. If we rely on the categories of "elite" and "prestige" schools employed by Heinz and Laumann, we can readily demonstrate the problem faced by rapidly expanding corporate law firms. Table 5 reports that elite law school enrollments made up 10 percent of total ABA approved enrollments in the period from 1941 to 1960, and prestige schools contributed between 14 percent and 17 percent during the period. Between 1970 to 1990, the percentage of elite and prestige students among the total began to decline. The most recent percentages are 4.3 percent elite and 9.8 percent prestige. In absolute numbers there has been almost no change in the number of elite law school students from 1970 to present. The law schools in the prestige category grew by some 1,400 students, a 12 percent increase from 1970 to 1990. During the period 1980 to 1988 alone, the number of lawyers in law firms with more than 50 attorneys more than doubled, from some 27,018 to some 75,912.

The dispersion of lawyers' salaries should give pause to college students and others contemplating legal careers. Potential law students may not comprehend such complexities. The NALP [National Association for Law Placement] 1991 survey reported that the median starting salary for private practitioners was $51,000, and that the interquartile range (between the 25th and 75th percentile) was $35,000 to $65,000. The NALP estimate may be high. NALP probably receives a larger proportion of salary data from higher-status schools and higher-paying employers than from other schools and employers. Yet the NALP data present encouragement to potential law school applicants. Mean earnings for males aged 25–30 with four years of college in 1987 were $31,596; for women, they were $23,307. The prospects for economically rewarding work in the legal profession appear to remain high, even if there is more uncertainty today than in the 1980s.

Starting salaries for public interest positions (which do not include public defenders) were $25,500 (median) in 1991. For government jobs (including public defenders), the median starting pay was $30,000. Thus public interest jobs begin at one-half the median for positions in private practice, and some $18,000 below the median starting salary for positions in business or private industry.

WOMEN AND MINORITIES

Perhaps the most dramatic demographic change in the legal profession in the last two decades has been the increasing numbers of women. Table 6 gives the percentage of women in the population of law students from 1940 to 1990. As late as 1971 women represented less than 10 percent of law

TABLE 5

Enrollment in Elite and Prestige Law Schools

SCHOOL	1941	1950	1960	1970	1980	1990
Elite						
NUMBER	2232	4347	4692	5744	5561	5828
PERCENT	10.1	8.2	10.7	6.7	4.3	4.4
Prestige						
NUMBER	3048	7041	7215	11,582	13,578	13,019
PERCENT	13.8	13.3	16.5	13.5	10.5	9.8
TOTAL	22,033	53,025	43,695	86,028	128,983	132,433

TABLE 6

Women as Percentage of ABA-Approved Law School Enrollments

YEAR	1940	1944	1950	1961	1965	1970	1975	1980	1985	1990
PERCENTAGE	4.3	21.8	3.1	3.6	4.2	8.5	22.9	34.2	40.1	42.5

TABLE 7

Lawyer Employment 1988 by Sex and Age (%)

	ALL LAWYERS		UNDER 40		40+	
EMPLOYMENT	M	F	M	F	M	F
PRIVATE PRACTICE	73.0	66.4	78.2	67.7	69.3	62.8
FEDERAL JUDICIARY	0.3	0.5	0.2	0.4	0.4	0.6
FEDERAL GOVERNMENT	2.9	4.8	3.2	4.8	2.6	4.8
OTHER JUDICIARY	2.4	1.6	0.7	1.1	3.6	3.0
OTHER GOVERNMENT	4.2	8.1	5.2	8.4	3.4	7.1
PRIVATE INDUSTRY	9.2	9.4	8.6	9.8	9.6	8.3
PRIVATE ASSOCIATION	0.5	1.1	0.5	1.2	0.4	1.1
LEGAL AID/PUBLIC DEFENDER	0.8	2.3	1.2	2.5	0.5	1.7
EDUCATION	1.0	1.5	0.6	1.1	1.2	2.4
INACTIVE	5.9	4.3	1.5	2.9	9.0	8.0

TABLE 8

Distribution of Private Practitioners by Firm Size, Sex, and Age (%)

	ALL LAWYERS		UNDER 40		40+	
	M	F	M	F	M	F
SOLO	45.9	47.8	38.1	42.8	52.0	61.7
2 LAWYERS	7.1	4.2	5.7	3.4	8.2	6.8
3 LAWYERS	4.9	2.6	4.5	2.4	5.3	3.2
4 LAWYERS	3.6	2.3	3.6	2.3	3.6	2.4
5 LAWYERS	2.7	1.9	2.8	2.0	2.7	1.6
6–10 LAWYERS	8.1	6.4	9.1	6.9	7.3	5.0
11–20 LAWYERS	7.1	6.8	8.8	7.8	5.8	4.2
21–50 LAWYERS	6.9	7.8	9.0	8.8	5.2	4.7
51–100 LAWYERS	4.9	6.2	6.4	7.2	3.6	3.4
100+ LAWYERS	8.8	14.0	12.0	16.4	6.2	7.8

students. This proportion grew rapidly throughout the 1970s until some 34 percent of legal enrollments were women. The presence of women continued to increase until 1989, when it reached some 42.7 percent, and remained roughly unchanged in 1990.

Women tend to be distributed differently from men among types of legal employment. As table 7 demonstrates, even when we control for age, women are less likely to work in private practice and more likely to work in government and legal aid or public defender positions than are men. The 1991 NALP data also reveal this pattern. One-third of the women, but one-quarter of the men, in the class of 1991 took positions in government, judicial clerkships, or with public interest groups. Women also are distributed somewhat distinctively among private law firms of different size (see table 8). Women tend to be overrepresented among the smallest and the biggest firms. A higher percentage of women are solo practitioners compared to men, a difference that is especially striking for lawyers older than forty. As of 1983, women in large law firms had much higher rates of turnover than their male colleagues. Recent surveys indicate more progress. A *National Law Journal* survey of the 250 largest law firms in 1989 found that 9.2 percent of partners were women, compared to 2.8 percent in 1981. My own estimates from the California bar survey suggest that a significant proportion of women are making partner but at a lower rate than men. Among lawyers in private practice who have ten or more years of experience and thus sufficient seniority to be partners, I calculated that 33 percent of women were partners, compared to 42 percent of men.

Minorities also have entered the legal profession in unprecedented numbers in the last two decades, yet they present a very different pattern from women. Table 9 lays out the historical statistics on law school enrollment. Minority enrollment has climbed relatively steadily throughout the period, from 4.3 percent in 1969 to 13.1 percent in 1990. This contrasts with the far more explosive growth of women. And if we examine the composition of minority law students, we can see that a substantial proportion of the increase is due to the two minority groups who have the highest median family earnings among minorities: Asians and other Hispanic Americans. In the last five years African Americans increased their presence in law schools from 4.8 percent to 5.1 percent. Mexican Americans gained 0.2 percent and Puerto Ricans gained 0.1 percent from 1986 to 1990. Other Hispanic Americans moved from 1.5 percent to 1.9 percent of the enrollment. Asian Americans grew from 1.9 percent to 3.3 percent in the same period. This last group alone represents 42 percent of the total growth in minorities in law schools over the last five years.

Minorities pursue different careers than white lawyers do, either out of choice or to avoid discrimination. According to the NALP survey of the class of 1991, only 44 percent of blacks took jobs in law firms, compared to 62 percent of whites and Asians. Four of ten black graduates took jobs in government or judicial clerkships, compared to 25 percent of all graduates. Hispanics, African Americans, and Native Americans were all more likely to take public interest jobs (4.2 percent, 5.5 percent, and 7.2 percent, respectively) than were whites or Asians, of whom 1.6 percent took public interest positions. According to the California bar survey, a majority of these minority lawyers are either sole practitioners or government attorneys. The most notable difference between black attorneys and white attorneys is in law firms. In the California survey, 9 percent of blacks but 28 percent of whites were law firm partners. Among the 250 largest firms, only 2.2 percent of associates and 0.9 percent of partners were black. In a sample of elite law firms in New York, Chicago, Los Angeles, and Washington, D.C., Elizabeth Chambliss found that in 1990, 6.5 percent of associates were minorities, and 1.7 percent of partners were minorities. Thus, while there has been some increase in the proportion of minorities in the upper precincts of the profession, it has come very slowly, and blacks in particular have not gained substantially. Although black partners have increased their presence in the biggest firms since 1981, the percentage of black associates declined slightly between 1981 and 1989.

Women and minorities have become a substantial presence in the legal profession but are far more likely to work in less remunerative, if not lower-status, positions. The NALP survey reported that among 1991 graduates, the median starting salaries for males increase with age. Men aged 20–25 had a median starting salary of $38,000, and older males received more than the national median of $40,000. Women graduates received starting salaries that were below the national median, and women older than 40 received the lowest median salary of these groups. For the California bar, white males consistently receive higher incomes from practice than do white women or minorities, even after accounting for years in practice. If we treat $100,000 as the threshold of high earnings, there are relatively few differences in the least senior group of attorneys. But in the group with five to nine years of experience, some 26 percent of white males are high earners compared to 16 percent of white females and 19 percent of minorities. The group in practice 10 to 19 years shows more inequality. A majority of white males (53 percent) attract a high income, while only about one-third of white women and minorities (35 percent and 31 percent, respectively) do so.

TABLE 9

Racial Minorities in ABA-Approved Law Schools

YEAR	AFRICAN AMERICAN	MEXICAN AMERICAN	PUERTO RICAN	OTHER HISPANIC	ASIAN AMERICAN	AMERICAN INDIAN	TOTAL %
1969–70	2,128	412	61	75	—	72	4.3
1971–72	3,744	883	94	179	480	140	5.9
1972–73	4,423	1,072	143	231	681	173	6.6
1973–74	4,817	1,259	180	261	850	222	7.2
1974–75	4,995	1,362	272	392	1,063	265	7.5
1975–76	5,127	1,443	333	406	1,099	295	7.4
1976–77	5,503	1,588	335	538	1,324	301	8.1
1977–78	5,305	1,564	350	617	1,382	363	8.2
1978–79	5,350	1,649	423	716	1,424	390	8.1
1979–80	5,257	1,670	441	706	1,547	392	8.4
1980–81	5,506	1,690	442	882	1,641	414	8.7
1981–82	5,789	1,756	396	1,037	1,755	402	8.4
1982–83	5,852	1,739	418	1,249	1,947	406	9.1
1983–84	5,967	1,744	450	1,302	1,962	441	9.3
1984–85	5,955	1,661	407	1,439	2,026	429	9.9
1985–86	6,052	1,635	412	1,632	2,153	462	10.4
1986–87	5,894	1,568	422	1,875	2,303	488	10.1
1987–88	6,028	1,641	459	1,971	2,656	492	10.8
1988–89	6,321	1,657	478	2,207	3,133	499	11.3
1989–90	6,791	1,663	483	2,850	3,767	527	12.1
1990–91	7,432	1,950	506	2,582	4,306	554	13.1

The last two readings offered overviews of the entire profession. The next presents the most detailed profile available of lawyers in one large city—Chicago. It acutely exposes their social organization, especially the fault lines that divide them into distinct, often distant, sometimes opposed fragments.

CHICAGO LAWYERS:
THE SOCIAL STRUCTURE OF
THE BAR[1]

John P. Heinz and Edward O. Laumann

DISTRIBUTION OF LAWYERS' EFFORT
AMONG THE FIELDS OF LAW

TABLE I indicates the total number of practitioners who spent at least 5 percent of their professional time in each of the fields and an estimate of the percentage of total legal effort expended by Chicago's metropolitan bar in each of the fields. We have divided the fields into two broad categories, corporate versus personal and small business. These categories are further subdivided into clusters of fields that disproportionately share practitioners, as we demonstrate below when we discuss the interdependencies among fields. While there is nothing especially problematic about the numbers of practitioners, our estimates of legal effort are considerably more conjectural. We thus offer these results as a first approximation only.

We estimate that somewhat more than half (53 percent) of the total effort of Chicago's bar is devoted to the corporate client sector, and a smaller but still substantial proportion (40 percent) is expended on the personal client sector. More than half of the lawyers in Chicago spend some of their time in one or more of the fields in the "general corporate" cluster, and 627 of the 699 practicing lawyers devote at least some fraction of their effort to either the "general corporate" or the "personal business" cluster. On the other hand, these two substantial segments of the profession are largely separate. Only 56 of our respondents devoted as much as 25 percent of their time to a personal business field and at least

25 percent to a general corporate field—these overlapping lawyers are fewer than 17 percent of the total number of respondents who practice in those fields at least 25 percent of their time. The relatively small degree of overlap in the practice of these two groups of fields is, perhaps, surprising when we consider that the substance of legal work for personally owned businesses may not be far different from work for small corporations.

Only one field of law commands the exclusive attention of as many as half of its practitioners—criminal prosecution. Of the others, only patents even comes close to this criterion of specialization of effort, with 40 percent of its practitioners doing that work exclusively. Corporate tax comes in a very distant third, with 22 percent of its practitioners reporting full-time activity. All the other fields tend to cluster fairly tightly around the average of 5 to 6 percent full-time practitioners. The median number of fields of practice to which our respondents devoted as much as 5 percent of their time was 2.7.

SOCIAL DIFFERENTIATION WITHIN
THE PROFESSION

Figure 1 depicts the relationships among the fields of law, representing them as points in two-dimensional space and accounting for their positions on a number of variables. Fields with similar profiles lie in close proximity (i.e., share a region of Euclidean space); those with greater differences on the variables lie at greater distances from one another. The nine variables used in this analysis are:

1. Business clients (mean percentage of income received from clients that are businesses rather than persons)

2. Stability of practice (mean percentage of clients represented for three years or more)

3. Lawyer referrals (mean percentage of clients obtained through referrals from other lawyers)

4. Freedom in choice of cases (percentage of practitioners indicating wide latitude in selecting clients)

5. Negotiating and advising (percentage of practitioners indicating their work often involves negotiating and advising rather than the use of highly technical procedures)

1 Evanston, Illinois: Northwestern University Press, 1994 (rev. ed.). Reprinted with permission.

TABLE I

Number of Practitioners and Estimated Percentage of Total Effort Expended
in Various Fields of Law by Chicago Lawyers

FIELDS OF LAW	CLUSTER SIZE	NUMBER OF PRACTITIONERS IN FIELD	ESTIMATED PERCENTAGE OF TOTAL LEGAL EFFORT
A. CORPORATE CLIENT SECTOR		541	53
1. *Large corporate*	242		
Antitrust (defense)		47	2
Business litigation		56	3
Business real estate		80	4
Business tax		51	3
Labor (management)		39	2
Securities		53	2
CLUSTER TOTAL			16
2. *Regulatory*	110		
Labor (unions)		18	1
Patents		45	4
Public utilities and administrative		52	4
CLUSTER TOTAL			9
3. *General corporate*	396		
Antitrust (plaintiffs)		24	1
Banking		60	3
Commercial (including consumer)		102	3
General corporate		262	11
Personal injury (defendant)		73	6
CLUSTER TOTAL			24
4. *Political*	46		
Criminal (prosecution)		20	2
Municipal		30	2
CLUSTER TOTAL			4

TABLE I *(continued)*

B. PERSONAL/SMALL BUSINESS CLIENT SECTOR		421	40
1. *Personal business*	287		
General litigation		53	2
Personal real estate		153	5
Personal tax		57	3
Probate		195	8
CLUSTER TOTAL			18
2. *Personal plight*	296		
Civil rights		41	2
Criminal (defense)		91	5
Divorce		153	6
Family		84	3
Personal injury (plaintiffs)		120	6
CLUSTER TOTAL			22
C. GENERAL, UNSPECIFIED LEGAL WORK	248	248	8
TOTAL		699	101

6. Government employment (percentage of practitioners employed by federal, state, or local government)

7. Local law school (percentage of practitioners who attended any of four local law schools in Chicago: De Paul, Kent, Loyola, John Marshall)

8. High-status Protestants (percentage of practitioners who state a preference for Congregational, Presbyterian, Episcopal, or United Church of Christ)

9. Jewish origin (percentage of practitioners who report either Jewish religion or ethnicity)

The relationships among the fields form a structure that may be interpreted as roughly U-shaped. The fields that serve corporations lie to the right; fields that serve persons lie to the left. Fields that serve either a mixture of the two or special sorts of corporations such as governments or labor unions fall toward the middle. Only one of the nine variables used in the multidimensional scalogram analysis explicitly measures the type of client. The vertical dimension of the structure appears to be related to the distinction between litigation and office practice. The fields

with higher rates of court appearances tend to be higher in the space. Other general patterns in the structure are perhaps less striking, but they are surely discernible. The median size of the law firm or other practice organization increases as one moves from the upper left counterclockwise around the U. Client volume and the percentage of practitioners who attended a local law school both move in the opposite direction, increasing as one proceeds clockwise around the U. The percentage of stable clients generally increases as one moves toward the bottom of the figure.

The most prestigious fields of law are at the upper right of the U and the least prestigious are at the upper left. Prestige, in fact, decreases in a very orderly clockwise fashion; the correlation between our measure of the prestige order of the fields and their order on the U is .9. A small cluster of high-status fields representing the largest corporations lie at the upper right of the U. Generally, the work for larger business corporations appears to be concentrated higher on the right side of the U, and the size of the businesses represented then decreases as one moves down. Moving clockwise, we encounter a group of fields dealing with financial transactions, particularly those regulated by government. Farther clockwise, a more diffuse cluster contains the remainder of the corporate sector. The field of probate law—which, of all the personal client fields, most deals with the transmission of wealth and thus with the wealthier personal clients—is a part of this general cluster but is on its upper left periphery, nearest to the other personal client fields.

The remaining fields in our personal business group are included in the next cluster of points in the figure, still moving clockwise.

Finally, we find four of the five fields of the personal plight group in the upper left quadrant of the U. The fifth, civil rights, is a special case. Because half of its practitioners are full-time government employees, we could in fact define civil rights work as a governmental function and place the field in the political group of the corporate sector, which is about where it appears in the figure.

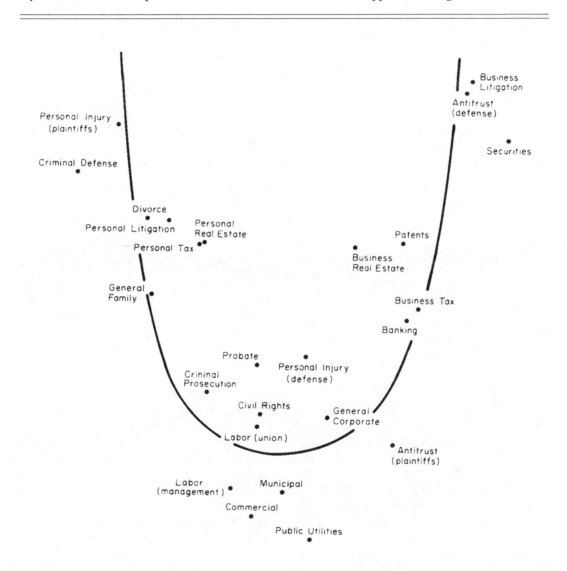

FIGURE I

Much of the differentiation within the legal profession is secondary to one fundamental distinction—the distinction between lawyers who represent large organizations (corporations, labor unions, or government) and those who represent individuals. The two kinds of law practice are the two hemispheres of the profession. Most lawyers reside exclusively in one hemisphere or the other and seldom, if ever, cross the equator.

Lawyers who serve major corporations and other large organizations differ systematically from those who work for individuals and small businesses, whether we look at the social origins of the lawyers, the prestige of the law schools they attended, their career histories and mobility, their social or political values, their networks of friends and professional associates, or several other social variables. Our thesis that the profession is divided into two quite distinct, largely separate hemispheres rests on the proposition that the principal independent variable is not a continuum, like wealth, but a dichotomy, the difference between corporate and personal clients.

In addition to the difference in social power associated with these two types of clients, the nature of the interaction between lawyer and client may also differ systematically with client type. Most individuals, even the wealthiest persons, will not devote any substantial portion of their time and energy to direct supervision of their lawyer's work. Persons who are not wealthy will usually be too busy earning a living to use their time for this purpose, and wealthy individuals will usually have better things to do. Organizations, however, will give an employee the responsibility for looking after the organization's legal affairs. Thus, lawyers are likely to have greater freedom of action, greater control over how they practice law, if their clients are individuals rather than corporations or other large organizations.

The professional's freedom from client control is often cited as one of the most fundamental of the characteristics that distinguish the professions from other occupations. But our argument suggests, quite ironically, that the lawyers who serve the more powerful, corporate clients are likely to be less "professional" in this respect than are those who serve the less powerful clients, individuals.

Size, Separation, and Specialization of the Two Hemispheres

Though the two principal parts of the Chicago bar are not exactly equal in size, the total amounts of effort devoted to each and the total numbers of lawyers practicing in them are roughly comparable. The corporate sector is somewhat larger, but not so much so as to overwhelm the personal client practice or to render it insignificant. More than three-quarters of the practicing lawyers devoted at least some of their time to fields in the corporate client sector, while more than three-fifths of them devoted time to personal client fields. There is, then, substantial overlap in these categories—that is, a number of lawyers practiced in both hemispheres—but a solid majority of the practicing lawyers worked exclusively in one hemisphere or the other. Only about two-fifths of them reported devoting any time to work in both hemispheres. And if we look not merely at whether they spent any time at all in fields in both sectors but take the devotion of at least 25 percent of their time to a field as a measure of greater commitment to that area of practice, we find that only 101 of our respondents (i.e., only about one-seventh of the 699 practicing lawyers) devoted that much time to fields in both of the hemispheres.

The division of labor along client lines may mean that lawyers become devoted to such a narrow range of interests that they have little stake in or dependence on lawyers who serve other sorts of clients. Client specialization thus may have consequences for the integration and coherence of the profession. If specialization has not only disaggregated lawyers' interests but created conflicts among them, we would expect these conflicts to emerge in disputes over "territory," over the monopolization or control of types of work or clients.

Fifty years ago, for example, the organized bar might readily reach a consensus that lawyers were the proper persons to search real estate titles and to handle the closings of home sales. Performance of these functions by anyone else would have been said to constitute "the unauthorized practice of law." Today, the bar is sharply divided on this issue. There is now a substantial interest group within the profession consisting of lawyers who regularly represent real estate brokers and title companies. It is, of course, these clients who would engage in that "unauthorized practice." Rather than retain lawyers to perform these routine tasks, the title companies would prefer to use their own, less-well-paid employees to do these jobs, keeping for themselves any profit that is to be made on the services. The paradigm of the general practitioner—the nineteenth-century lawyer or perhaps the present-day small-town lawyer—would represent home buyers or sellers one day and the local real estate agent the next. But specialization within the profession has now created, in addition to the group of lawyers who represent the brokers, a second distinct faction: neighborhood lawyers who almost never represent large real estate brokers or title companies but have many middle-class clients who buy and sell their homes and small businesses. For this second interest group, real estate closings are bread and butter. The two groups have reason to conflict. And they do.

The conflicts need not be motivated exclusively (or even primarily) by self-interest or client interest. Like other persons, lawyers have private causes. They may act as "moral entrepreneurs," and this may bring them into conflict with other lawyers who have opposing moral principles. But their principles may also be influenced by their areas of practice. The corporate lawyers who dominate the Association of the Bar of the City of New York advocate "no-fault" systems of automobile accident compensation. They never touch a personal injury case. And they are vigorously opposed by the personal injury plaintiffs' lawyers, whose voice is the American Trial Lawyers Association.

Social Differentiation of Lawyers and Clients

There are, of course, subdivisions within the two hemispheres of the profession. The most important of these is the distinction between litigation and office practice. In Figure 2, the "corporate hemisphere" is at the right and the "personal hemisphere" is at the left, the circle being further subdivided into quadrants that engage in, respectively, corporate litigation, office practice for corporate clients, office practice for personal clients, and litigation for persons.

In our data, however, we do not find that the structure is so neatly circular. The two sorts of litigation fields—those representing corporate clients and those representing persons—are sepa-

FIGURE 2

rated by a considerable social distance. A closer rendering of the arrangement of the fields in social space, therefore, more nearly resembles a U than an O. At the bottom of the U—that is, in the office practice fields—the difference between the hemispheres in wealth of clients, the nature of their legal work, and the character of the relationships among lawyers and clients is probably less pronounced than it is in the litigation fields at the top of the U. The great bulk of the office practice done for persons is no doubt work done for relatively wealthy individuals on such matters as estate planning, personal income tax avoidance, and real estate sales. There is also a considerable volume of commercial law work (debtor–creditor, contracts, Uniform Commercial Code matters) done for businesses owned or controlled by individuals. This work is probably much more like the office practice of law for corporate clients than is corporate litigation like personal litigation. Corporate litigators often represent the largest corporations, but personal client litigation is more likely to involve the low- to moderate-income end of the personal client spectrum. Thus, defendants in criminal cases, evictions and repossessions, and plaintiffs in personal injury and civil rights claims are likely to have below-average incomes. Parties to divorce cases that consume much litigation time almost surely have above-average incomes, but they need not be wealthy. It is therefore likely that social distinctions will be greater between lawyers engaged in litigation for the two, broad sorts of clients than between practitioners in the two types of office practice.

DISCUSSION QUESTIONS

1. How did the contemporary profile of the profession differ from your preconceptions? Where did your expectations come from? What are the divisions within the profession; what caused them; how are they likely to change in the future; how could they be changed; what are their consequences for lawyers and society?

2. What are the principal trends of recent decades? What explains them? How would you extrapolate them into the future? Do you expect them to continue, intensify or decline, reverse? What is their significance for lawyers and society? Do any of these trends disturb you? If so, how could they be changed? Does it surprise you that law school applications and enrollments stagnated and actually declined in the early 1990s?

3. In thinking about these questions, you may find it useful to compare lawyers with other professions or occupations, consider other time periods, or look at professions (including lawyers) in other countries.

SUGGESTED READING

Statistical data on lawyers may be found in the U.S. Census, the Annual Review of Legal Education, and the American Bar Foundation's *Lawyer Statistical Report* [the latest of which are Barbara A. Curran and Clara N. Carson, *Supplement to the Lawyer Statistical Report: The U.S. Legal Profession in 1988* (1991); *The Lawyers' Statistical Report: The U.S. Legal Profession in the*

1990s (1994)]. States also survey their professions, e.g., Illinois State Bar Association, "Economics of Legal Services in Illinois: a 1975 special bar survey," 64 *Illinois Bar Journal* 73 (Oct. 1975); "The Economics of Law Practice in Michigan," 53 *Michigan State Bar Journal* (May 1974); W. L. Blaine, *Where to Practice Law in California: Statistics on Lawyers' Work* (1976). Earlier overviews and analyses include J. C. York and R. D. Hale, "Too Many Lawyers? The Legal Services Industry: Its Structure and Outlook," 26 *Journal of Legal Education* 1 (1973); Barbara Curran, "The Legal Profession in the 1980s: A Profession in Transition," 20 *Law & Society Review* 19 (1986); Richard H. Sander and E. Douglass Williams, "Why Are There So Many Lawyers? Perspectives on a Turbulent Market," 14 *Law & Social Inquiry* 431 (1989).

Believing the profession a useful scapegoat, politicians as various as Jimmy Carter and Dan Quayle complained there are too many lawyers. Now academics have tried to give the argument respectability: Stephen P. Magee, William A. Brock, and Leslie Young, "The Invisible Foot and the Waste of Nations: Lawyers as Negative Externalities," in *Black Hole Tariffs and Endogenous Policy Theory* (1989). The case has been demolished: Frank B. Cross, "The First Thing We Do, Let's Kill All the Economists: An Empirical Evaluation of the Effect of Lawyers on the United States Economy and Political System," 70 *Texas Law Review* 645 (1992); 17(4) *Law & Social Inquiry* (1993) (symposium).

Much writing within the profession advances what Robert Gordon calls the "declension theory": paeans to the good old days, jeremiads about the future. See the following by a Yale Law School dean, Harvard Law professor, and prominent practitioner: Anthony T. Kronman, *The Lost Lawyer: Failing Ideals of the Legal Profession* (1993); Mary Ann Glendon, *A Nation Under Lawyers: How the Crisis in the Legal Profession Is Transforming American Society* (1994); Sol M. Linowitz, *The Betrayed Profession: Lawyering at the End of the Twentieth Century* (1994). For more optimistic futurology, see Ronald W. Staudt, "Does Grandmother Come With It? Teaching and Practicing Law in the 21st Century," 44 *Case Western Reserve Law Review* 499 (1994).

Chapter Three

SOLO AND SMALL-FIRM PRACTICE

Although solo practitioners declined from three out of five lawyers in 1948 to one out of three in 1988, even at the later date nearly half of all lawyers still practiced in firms of five or fewer. Perhaps reflecting their lower status, small-firm lawyers rarely appear in newspapers or fictional depictions in novels, television, or film (except as courageous criminal defense lawyers). The following excerpt from a recent empirical study based on lengthy interviews with more than 100 randomly selected small-firm and franchise lawyers in the outer boroughs and suburbs of New York City corrects that deficiency.

THE BUSINESS OF PRACTICING LAW: THE WORK LIVES OF SOLO AND SMALL-FIRM ATTORNEYS[1]
Carroll Seron

PROFESSIONALISM VERSUS COMMERCIALISM
The Decision to Become a Lawyer

FOR most practitioners, the call of the mobility escalator emerges as the defining ingredient in the decision to go to law school. As David Friedman, an entrepreneur in Queens, put it, echoing others, Jewish boys become either doctors or lawyers, "unless they are really retarded—then they become accountants." Another theme was a concern to "be of service" and to "help." Amy Moskowitz, an associate in a small firm in suburban Queens, said: I'm a very...hands-on, person-to-person kind of person. And I felt that I either wanted an area like law, where I could make a difference, or I wanted to pursue psychology." Others claimed they had just *always* wanted to be a lawyer; they had read a biography of Louis Nizer, Melvin Belli, or Clarence Darrow, had gone to watch trials, remembered Perry Mason. This diffuse sense of passion about law was somewhat more commonly expressed by women.

---

1 Philadelphia: Temple University Press, 1996. Reprinted with permission.

Getting Started

There were two fairly typical career trajectories. One group began by working for the government. An equally notable group began as associates or employees of solo or small-firm practitioners; they often switched jobs any number of times and then moved on to set up their own practices. Less typical was the small group of those who began their careers in major Wall Street law firms.

Attorneys described three fairly distinct though not mutually exclusive strategies of coping with the initiation rites of professionalization. Some cultivated an informal network of attorneys and court officials on whom they could call to ask questions, copy legal forms, or clarify court procedures. Some learned by watching other lawyers and then trying out what they saw. Ever clever, Maisie Streep "made the point of casually running into [attorneys] before [trial] and just sat down for an hour, talking about their cases." A minority of attorneys learned through mentors. Mark Valesquez of the Bronx and Daniel Friedman of Queens are the protegés of powerful, local political bosses who served them as mentors. These attorneys reported that "getting started" took five years.

Expectations

Workplace Expectations. The entrepreneurial lawyers began their careers with a crystal-clear sense of what they wanted—and eventually got. Many reported having worked as investigators for insurance companies, where they realized that this was one area where a "poor boy" could make a living. Art Strauss and Sam Roth made it abundantly clear that they knew they would be successful because they were excellent salespeople.

The desire for autonomy runs throughout the work lives of these attorneys. Martin Minkowicz, who shares space and a secretary with his father in a predominately working-class Long Island community, said, "I wanted my *own* practice." Others knew that they did *not* want to work in a large firm. Daniel Levine "didn't want to be a cog in a wheel," and Renaud White thought "corporate law seemed awfully dull!"

A small group of women reported that they modified their expectations about work because of children or other family obligations. Mary Anne Gallister, with solid legal credentials, acknowledged that "a lot of things changed… when I got pregnant. Once I knew that I was going to have a child…a big-firm practice went out the window."

Financial Expectations. Cash flow, an uncertain client base, a vulnerability to the ups and downs of the market, and the very nature of legal work explain why most of these attorneys do not feel financially secure. For many women married to successful baby boomer men, much of their sense of financial security comes from a spouse's handsome earnings or from a sense that they can control the scope of their work because they have support. For single attorneys whose earnings may be neither very predictable nor grand, security comes from knowing that they do not have to support anyone else. The married baby boomer men are the most tentative on the subject of security.

GETTING CLIENTS

Social Networks and Community Ties

Richard Leavitt enjoyed the benefits of his father's earlier labors to build a legal practice in a remote community of Westchester County. When he joined his dad, he did what any aspiring lawyer must do to meet people:

> You join what I call the animal clubs. You join the Elks…. In my case, it was the Jaycees and the B'nai B'rith and the local Democratic Party and the local political party. [I've been] past state council for the Jaycees, an officer in the Elks; I headed up the town's United Way.

Most of these attorneys overwhelmingly agree that, with time, the single most important source of new clients is referrals from former clients. Most pointed out that referrals from professional colleagues—other lawyers, real estate agents, accountants or bankers—though neither as typi-

cal nor as important a source as client referrals, are another important source of business. Alan Gentile thanks colleagues and clients by doing "Christmas cards plus oranges." He also gets referrals from about 15 realtors and mails them "a bushel of tangelo oranges…. I *might*, if there's a promotion and I find out about it, I might send them one of those cheese-and-salami things from Hickory Farms or Wisconsin Cheeseman; that was *never* necessary three or four years ago [before the recession]." Not surprisingly, the task of cultivating and socializing with clients tends to fall to partners rather than associates, though some male associates did discuss client-getting as an aspect of their job, whereas female counterparts did not.

Victor Cutolo said that friends and family are a big but "unfortunate" source of business because…

> …they're a pain; they feel they can call you any time and it's very hard to be candid. For example, if somebody is being a jerk about taking a settlement, you…have got to tell them…. Your friends don't like to hear that….

It can also be difficult to bill friends who "always call you up for advice. It is always cheap!" One group of men, however, have turned family and friends into a positive client-getting resource. These men reported that work has come through local sports activities, high school friends who now own businesses, or special interest clubs. Martin Minkowicz reported: "I have a lot of my childhood friends who are accountants; a couple are bankers. They deal in businesses that are always looking for lawyers and they mention my name." Donald Irons relies on his well-known connections on Staten Island and his chance to be a coach at "St. Francis High School [which is] like being associated with Staten Island itself…." None of the women, however, belonged to any extracurricular local clubs at the time of the interview. This nexus in the client-getting networks of private lawyers suggests a gendered nuance that complements a gendered economy of social capital or a differential access to "extra" time.

The Traditionalists

Building from this shared, if porous, social network, some attorneys reject all other techniques and carefully construct a traditional professional model for client-getting. In a profession with high turnover, these are the survivors; in an area of practice that tends to involve work with one-shot cases, many of these attorneys represent long-standing clients; in a region with some highly precarious economic niches, these firms are situated in upscale Manhattan or growing suburban hubs marked by a postindustrial economy.

Experiments with Client-Getting

The typical experimenter is a practitioner who begins with a core of referrals and builds a client base through professional networks and local activities, coupled with various forays into advertising or solicitation. Whether these attorneys place ads in local or citywide newspapers, develop brochures, or advertise on television, their efforts tend to be reluctant and haphazard. Typically, these attorneys have a modest listing in the Yellow Pages. Some join prepaid plans but rarely get any business that way. All try advertising at some point in their careers but tend to approach the decision with a professional's eye to form rather than a businessperson's eye to the bottom line. Most agreed that community-based Yellow Pages are the preferred place to advertise. The clients who come in through the Yellow Pages may be less desirable prospects, but the ads do tend to pay for themselves.

Offering prepaid plans through direct mail advertising is neither very effective nor profitable. The promoters of prepaid plans, such as Hyatt Legal Services, market a networking device between consumers and lawyers. On the consumer side, they sell plans through direct mail to potential clients; in turn, they develop groups by state of participating attorneys who are paid a very small retainer and agree to take cases from these plan members at a "reduced" or, in some instances, a flat fee. Most who had joined such a plan reported that they never heard anything from it and, indeed, usually could not remember its name. Eric Smith of Manhattan was one of the very few attorneys to report getting any work

from prepaid legal plans, but his efforts are limited to a closed, union-side legal plan.

> I represent a League Players Association. The way I got that was that we represent unions in the AFL-CIO. When that union joined the AFL-CIO, there was a meeting at the Sheraton Center, and I was invited to come to that meeting through a contact that I had through a labor firm that represented them.... As a result of that I was able to acquire them as a client.

As to newspaper advertising, Joseph Fitzsimmons, a solo practitioner and former lawyer at Jacoby and Meyers, said, "I don't have the money for it! I'm not saying it's a bad way to obtain clients, but unless you have $25,000 a year minimum for an advertising budget, you're just throwing your money away." His assertion reflects an entrepreneur's logic that advertising must be deep, wide, and long-range to be effective. Further, newspaper advertising begins to raise the issue of the "line": some of these practitioners regard it as "unprofessional." When they do advertise, it tends to be in local papers or in special event papers. These attorneys try newspaper advertising without a clear or long-term game plan in mind; in each instance, they drop the advertising when it does not pay for itself.

Non-advertising newspaper coverage, however, may be a source of business. Eliot Klein, a Manhattan lawyer, had some cases with...

> ...substantial verdicts, over a million, two million dollars, and the local paper where I live had written them up.... It was a very nice spread, and I called them and I complimented them on what they had written and that it was very nice. Then they asked me if, well, would I make a donation?...So I gave them a few dollars or something.

Nora Charles-Cox tries to get her name known in the community through her efforts on "public service type of things." For instance, she said, "I recently spoke at the YWCA. I was asked to speak on a panel, and that was covered really heavily by the press.... I've had several shows that I've been involved in that have run on cable and several things on the radio...." A recurring attitude among the experimenters is that although they do participate in many of these new opportunities, they tend to be somewhat passive, somewhat reluctant.

The vast majority of experimenters feel that television advertising crosses the social divide between professional and unprofessional solicitation. Victor Cutolo asked, "Can you really take anything seriously that you see on TV?" Some pointed out that they do not advertise on television because of what their colleagues will think or because of potential damage to their reputation.

Most of these attorneys would agree with Mendel Rosenbaum's observation:

> A majority [of cases] are routine in the sense that they involve things I've done before, I'd say probably—I don't know—80 percent....

Further, they corroborate an observation of Nora Charles-Cox that their professional practices do not entail very much legal research. Rather, it is the "people side" of the law that complicates their work and makes each case different.

A Family Affair: The Collegial Organization of Small-Firm Practice

For partners in small, traditional law firms, friendship—if not the family—is the concept that captures the essential dynamic of their organization. The majority of these partnerships are between men of approximately the same age, many of whom met at other firms or in school, or shared office space and decided to start a firm together. Typically, partners explain, their agreement is verbal. By contrast, an associate in a small firm is an employee—somewhat marginal, isolated, or cut off from the partners. A partnership "track"—the essential building block of the corporate law firm—does not exist in most small-firm practices. Although associates *may* become partners, there are no cues, no time frames, no ground rules, no clear expectations. Associates also reported that they are not quite sure how or if they are formally evaluated. The question of evaluation returns to an image of family, of fitting in, of being the right kind of person.

The process of hiring associates reveals the embeddedness of small firms in a local community. Most typically, partners reported, they look for attorneys with some work experience; they try to avoid hiring a recent law school graduate unless the individual worked for them while in school. They also prefer someone from the immediate area; the rationale is that they have watched the person function in court or in the local district attorney's office; they "know" his or her reputation.

Although small firms are generally computerized, there is a wide variation in the degree of automation. All legal forms and documents are now stored in word processors or computers and are available on-line. The more sophisticated firms have systematized forms and documents and coded them by area of practice: wills, opinion letters, trust agreements, supply agreements, and so on. Over a quarter of these attorneys reported that their firm has some type of computerized calendaring and billing system in place. Yet with few exceptions, these lawyers do not use on-line legal research tools, network their computers between support and professional staff or between home and office, or foresee the need for more sophisticated capability such as desktop publishing. Typically, these attorneys reported that they very rarely start from scratch but work from boilerplate material that a secretary generates and they modify to fit the particulars at hand. Yet most of these associates and partners tend to take pride in claiming that they are "illiterate" about computers or that their "hands never touch the keyboard"; they prefer to communicate with a secretary or paralegal or typist through dictation equipment. The organizational division of labor between professional and support functions is also encrusted with a deep layer of social distinctions. More typically than not, attorneys referred to support staff as "our girls." The conceptual work of lawyering, the mental or technical work itself, is not especially esoteric, difficult, or complex in most of these legal matters—a point these attorneys acknowledge. Therefore, the recurring reference to secretarial-manual staff as "girls" and the resistance to doing work at a terminal become important buttresses for the claim that a professional's work is distinguished by the authority to determine what needs to be done.

Being Your Own Boss: The Organization of Solo Practice

Some attorneys, opting for even more independence than collegiality allows, work on their own. Seymour Kaplowitz of Manhattan summed it up for most: "The advantages are easy enough. You're your own boss. You make your own hours; you take the time that you need to devote to the projects that you want. You're not harassed in the sense that someone is looking over your shoulder, and you don't have to report to anyone." Some attorneys who have been in partnerships alluded to the downside of such a "marriage": "One out of two go belly up after a few years." The relative isolation, the "frenetic" nature of solo practice, and, in some instances, the disrespect from peers are keenly felt, to be sure, but these factors do not outweigh the advantages.

For many in full-time solo practice, however, the major disadvantage is that the work includes running a small business, a demand that many assumed they were sidestepping when they opted for *professional* careers. Compared to those in small firms, attorneys in solo practice are more likely to perform support tasks themselves. In fact, all the part-time women do their own support work.

"THE MANAGING-MARKETING END"

The most nationally visible entrepreneurial firms have been Jacoby and Meyers and Hyatt Legal Services, but 13 of the attorneys I interviewed have equally innovative approaches to the business of law. In interviews with partners at both Hyatt Legal Services and Jacoby and Meyers, the first thing I was told was that "old-fashioned" legal practice is not efficient, that it is very feasible to separate administration from service delivery and to establish standard operating procedures for attorneys in the field because most legal matters that individuals face are so straightforward. These firms limited in-house service delivery to specific matters, such as wills, divorces, or real estate closings in New York. At Jacoby and Meyers, bankruptcy, criminal, and personal injury cases were assigned to specialists who,

depending on demand, were either in the direct employ of the firm or working on an "of-counsel" (retainer) basis.

Both Hyatt Legal Services and Jacoby and Meyers began with the premise that extensive advertising through television and the Yellow Pages would make it possible to centralize the strategies of client-getting by gearing the message to a wide market share, to an entire media market. They claimed that they could handle a volume business because the legal services they offered were relatively simple. Hence, partners at headquarters developed training manuals and standard practices designed to instruct attorney-employees how to handle a case in the field. Centralized management also dealt with the acquisition of equipment, real estate decisions, consumer complaints, and—for Hyatt—the marketing and selling of prepaid plans. A primary task of managing was to train new associates. Both firms had decentralized attorney recruitment from headquarters to regional offices to increase efficiency. Lawyers at Jacoby and Meyers talked about case tracking and reports to headquarters in a manner quite different from the approach of their more traditionally oriented colleagues. A managing attorney had to learn to keep an eye on statistics and case flow, to think of cases in terms of dollars and cents, and to incorporate support staff into the organizational design of the local office.

Marketing Legal Services

Art Strauss used Jacoby and Meyers as a point of departure to explain the marketing strategy for his large workers' compensation firm, with headquarters in an outer Long Island manufacturing hub and six satellite offices.

> [W]hen I [attended] law school, I never sat in my regular class…. I knew everybody when I graduated…just as a friendly "hi," and that is what I started my practice on. So classmates right out of law school were a good source. And family and friends, that is your first source.
>   Then you do announcements through the bar…. And as the clients come in, they tell their friends, relatives…. You start to build up your client-to-client network…. And each time that somebody would come in [you would ask] who referred you? So you send a nice letter, thank you for sending so-and-so….

Then, you start [tracking] where you [are] getting the most success…. So if I was getting a lot of
firemen, then I'd be pushing other firemen.

When he became the partner in charge of business development…

…the first thing I did with our marketing campaign
was to create a logo….Jacoby and Meyers work[ed]
because it is two names. All right? People can
remember two; they can't remember three, and for-
get four!…I also took out an 800 number [with a
jingle telephone number]….once we got the firm
identified, the next step would be to develop that
marketing campaign.

The campaign was wide and systematic, beginning with the publication of a brochure that "paid
for itself" within a month. One of his partners
sent it to a union official of a uniformed service
after he had met him at a reception; they were
called to be interviewed to represent union members and got the job—because the brochure got to
the right desk. He and his partners give presentations to doctors and sell a loose-leaf book about
workers' compensation. Additionally, the firm
sends flyers and advertises on the radio and a cable
television station. His "mix" also includes half-
page ads in six countywide Yellow Pages, "a must!"
They have done well with advertising in the TV
guide section of *Newsday*; other newspaper ads
have not, however, shown a return. Two independent public relations people assist him because "I
don't know how to do a video; or I don't know…
how to make a news article look interesting."

The efforts of Sam Roth and Alan Fine rival
those of Art Strauss. Beginning with a specialized and delimited area of practice in personal
injury and an "educational" message, Roth's marketing includes full-page ads in the Queens and
Nassau Yellow Pages because, he claimed, people
who look up a name there are "knowledgeable,
interested, consumer[s]. They have a real problem and they want real help…. The calls are generally excellent." He explained that radio does
not work because…

…the basic consumer listens to the radio in the car
on the way to work. And I think it is difficult for
him to take a pencil and paper….I am not selling
perfume or cars; I'm selling a service. I want somebody who is lying in a hospital bed, with his leg up
in the air, and he's a captive audience to my television set.

He regularly attends conferences of the Trial
Lawyers Marketing Association and "has scripts
in the drawer" for the next step: a television campaign directed to the entire New York metropolitan media market in conjunction with plans to
open offices in specific locations.

Alan Fine, like his colleagues on Long Island,
has a highly specialized and limited practice,
focusing on immigration. About 15 years ago he
was asked to write a weekly column on current
immigration issues for the largest Korean newspaper in the United States. Realizing that it
looked like "legalization might be coming in," he
accepted the invitation and has been writing the
column ever since. Following the *Bates* decision[2]
he began to advertise in the Korean and other
ethnic newspapers, such as *India Abroad*. In addition, he participates in a cable television show
"twice a month for about twelve minutes every
other Sunday, which I do with another lawyer
and we split the costs" and that "everybody
watches." Every Monday night he does a half-
hour radio program, speaking for fifteen minutes
and then taking calls on the air. His television
and radio style is "like a type of documentary."
He also produces "a lot of brochures," which he
hands out when he does lectures: "A lot of them
are from governmental material that I just regur-
gitated…."

Daniel Friedman invests about 10 percent of
his gross earnings in print advertising in the *New
York Post* and the *New York Daily News*—which
at the time of the interview he called "excellent
sources of business"—and in the Yellow Pages.
He maintains a battery of telephone numbers
that he varies with the ads so that his staff can
link the inquiry to the advertising source.
Reflecting that he did not get any calls from ads
in Jewish newspapers, he asked, "Do you know
any Jewish person who doesn't know half a dozen
attorneys?"

Mark Stevens explained that his firm has done
some television advertising, but its efforts are
essentially limited to various kinds of legal plans,
including closed, union plans for professional
and service employees as well as prepaid for-
profit plans marketed by other companies. For

---

2 See Chapter 16.

this firm, getting business is a matter of "encouraging more [union] locals to come in," which is the exclusive responsibility of partner Warren Seidman. Stevens, Seidman, and a third partner take a long-term view toward investing in legal plans as a way to build a solidly middle-class client base of midlevel professionals such as teachers and public service employees, who, over the course of a lifetime, will, in all probability, have a variety of fairly predictable legal needs. At the time of the interview, Stevens estimated that about two-thirds of the firm's client base came from plans.

> Here, we're trying to establish more of a liaison that is going to last for a period of time. So we take our clients, making sure that the real estate work is right and the house closes and everything is done the way it is supposed to, or that [if] the matrimonial client…comes into some money, I have the financial adviser that I can forward to her. And I have the insurance people…. You know, we're not going to make a fortune out of the $65-an-hour client. But, if the $65-an-hour client talks to two of her friends who come in and say, "You did a great job for Zoe, can you help me?" I am going to get two clients at $200 an hour.

Plans, then, can be both the base for a stable business and a "loss leader" means of bringing in other, higher-paying clients. Keeping a close eye on the bottom line, Stevens reported that his firm's "cafeteria" plans (those whose members may pay a small fee per month for additional benefits), offered through unions, started out "with four or five thousand members; now we have twenty thousand…[and] that's a significant increase over a real short period of time."

Getting one's name in the news is another strategy. In addition to his storefront operation in a Hispanic neighborhood of the Bronx, Mark Valesquez explained that he does "some famous cases. Right now, I'm on trial in the Central Park jogger case." Although Denise Dewey began by saying "I don't advertise" and "it is just not my way of doing business," a different picture began to unfold as she indicated that there had been some articles about her cases in the *Post* and the *Daily News*. She said she would "seek" interviews: "I called up on a rape case I had last year…and Channel 5 did a thing on the news." "I know the reporter who reports the New York county cases

for the *Post*…. I'll knock on his door and say hi sometimes. He came and watched a couple of summations…." One of her former clients who is in public relations…

> …was interested in doing something as a result of her trial; she wants to write a book or whatever…though right now [we're] in the process of working up a video. I am going to do that and explain rights of crime victims and things like that. They will then distribute it to various community centers.

Managing Legal Services

Many of these entrepreneurs have gone beyond the somewhat rigid, factory-like model developed by Jacoby and Meyers. At four personal injury firms, one attorney is the "owner," and lawyer-employees are "independent contractors." Art Strauss and his partners have taken specialization a step further thanks to the computer. At any given time, 40 operators are answering questions on about 7,500 open cases. The firm represents clients in approximately 1,000 hearings a month. With the aid of a computerized docketing system, the operators handle inquiries from clients and prepare the cases. Attorneys take over only at the point of the hearing. Every case is entered and given a docket number, and "every phone call that comes in is documented." "Each client is in the computer, and the information is there." So when a client calls, one of the 40 operators can answer the question, and they "don't have to leave their desk all day long." Additionally, the computer system automates much of the work related to preparation for a hearing and, he claimed, eliminates the need for *all* lawyer–client contact until the actual eve of the hearing. "Hearing letters go out just by pressing a button."

Whatever the marketing and managing strategies devised by these entrepreneurs, they carefully track the return on their advertising investments and know where their clients come from. Whenever a client comes in, the first question asked is how he or she heard about the firm. Typically, this information is recorded on a standard form that is inserted in a client's file. Alan Fine takes case tracking a step further.

> I track it by sending each client when the case is finished…a questionnaire…. [The cover letter] says you don't have to put your name down—it's anony-

mous, but we code the envelope so we know who it is....if there's something positive or negative about any of my people, they get a copy of it.

SERVING CLIENTS AND CONSUMERS

Entrepreneurial legal practice is service oriented, but as in other postindustrial organizations a concern with service emphasizes efficiency and cost rather than process and quality. At Jacoby and Meyers I was told that the firm looked for attorneys who are "entrepreneurial," who are willing to work long hours, hustle, and take risks. As a managing attorney at a local Jacoby and Meyers office put it, in weighing the relative importance of entrepreneurial and legal skills, the former is "more important" because the latter can "always be bought." Or, asked what clients want from an attorney, Michael Fitzgerald, an associate at a storefront firm on Long Island, said that for "most clients, it's a toss-up [between] whether it's fast and cheap or cheap and fast!" Denise Dewey explained that working with clients is "all communication and salesmanship."

Being More Than a Technician

Overwhelmingly, the men and women who part company with the entrepreneurs agree that qualities such as the "personal touch," "communication," and a willingness to cultivate a "bedside manner" are their most important professional skills in working with clients. Carol Shapiro, who has been practicing law for about 15 years, commented, "I haven't yet had a client who, you know, was looking for Clarence Darrow.... I think they obviously want an adequate and competent representation. But they *also* need people who are good listeners." Maisie Streep supported herself by selling cookware during law school and while she studied for the bar; in fact, she developed a very successful franchise. Asked to describe the balance between legal and social skill, she said:

> It's definitely business and social acumen as opposed to legal knowledge [that makes a difference with clients]. It's not legal knowledge! It's people.... [It] really goes back to cookware.... The reason I was good at the cookware is that I was very good at keeping the employees motivated and, you know, figuring out which people to hire and who not to hire.

What Does a Client Want?

Most of the attorneys claimed that *each* client expects to be treated as special, when in fact each client is actually one of many, often with problems that the attorney has heard before. Marshall Meyer, a Manhattan lawyer, had a particularly telling insight about the demands of client expectations.

> You might be saying something for the thousandth time, and the client might be hearing it for the first time. Making certain that you try to put yourself in the position of the client and making certain that, if you were in that position, you would understand what the lawyer is saying to you is absolutely essential for establishing an effective rapport.

Whatever the specifics of the pressure, when attorneys describe what clients want in a lawyer, it is some variation on a demand for *their time*. Most of these practitioners imply that an entrepreneurial concern to be fast and cheap must be balanced by the demands to be responsive and caring.

The most concrete manifestation of time pressures translates into demands to return telephone calls. The work lives of these men and women are dominated by the telephone, and it plays the major role in organizing (or disorganizing) the days (and nights) of personal-plight lawyers. When asked to describe a typical day, Harold Christopher turned to his diary and summarized it this way.

> I came in and I had a telephone call with...a client. I don't know how specific you want me to be, but...[I had] another telephone call, a prospective client. A third telephone call about a client, a fourth telephone call—a trust fund, to be more specific. The next [call] was a corporate client, talking to the attorney on the other side. Next, a telephone call with someone involved with prepaid legal, an individual who had a problem with a noncovered matter.... Back to that same corporation [and a call. Then] another client, [a] telephone call with the president of the association [and at least four calls back to the client]. Then a call from another prepaid legal services plan [member] who had a problem with a car lease and wanted to have me speak with her about it; in fact, she's coming in today. Then I drafted a modification of a lease for a private client. The next [thing] I did was I talked with another client about his estate plan. The next [call] was another business client who has problems. Then I talked with the tenant [and some more telephone calls ensued].

When I interviewed Brian Dolan at a local court in lower Manhattan, he described what his morning had already been. "I took the subway to Foley Square and…came into this building and checked the calendar in the main courtroom downstairs." Then he "found the man who answers the calendar for me and a lot of other attorneys" before getting a cup of coffee. Next he went to the housing court to make sure that the court was open and that his client [a tenant] was there; he also found the attorney for the other side and told them both that he would return later. From there "I went to the eleventh floor where I had another two matters; that's the commercial part…. Then I came back down to the eighth floor to check the case with the tenant," after which he found me to explain that he was running behind schedule—and he was off again. When he could not find the judge he had been looking for, "I called up my office recording machine; I had eleven messages! And I wrote down all of those and returned a few of those calls from up there." Finally, before returning to find me in the hallway, he settled the case in housing court and two commercial cases. Once we finished our interview, he said, he would report the settlements to the judge's clerk, go back to his office, check messages and return more telephone calls; then he would do some paperwork in the evening after dinner. I was left with the overwhelming impression that the men and women who go to court on a regular basis find it difficult if not impossible to structure their time in a predictable manner.

DISCUSSION QUESTIONS

1. In some national legal professions divided between courtroom lawyers and business advisers, the former (British barristers, French *avoués*) were *required* to practice alone. What is the justification? In all legal professions, solo practice historically antedated other arrangements. Why was this so? Why has solo and small-firm practice persisted? Why has its proportion of practitioners declined? Do you expect further decline?

2. What attracted small-firm lawyers to the legal profession? To that locus of practice? How does this differ from the motivation to enter other kinds of law practice? Are there gender differences? How are motivations likely to affect lawyer behavior? What do you find attractive and unattractive about small firm practice? About solo practice?

3. How do recruitment, socialization, and promotion in small-firm practice differ from those processes in other legal roles?

4. How do these lawyers get and keep clients? How does this differ from large firms? Is the behavior of small-firm lawyers economically rational? What explains the strategies they use? Do you approve? Would you suggest others? How are these practices gendered? What are the consequences of such gendering?

Which lawyers use what kinds of advertising? What explains those decisions?

What are the advantages and disadvantages of prepaid plans for both lawyers and clients? How do lawyers become involved in such plans?

5 What knowledge and skills do these lawyers deploy? Do these satisfy the criteria for professionals? Were they acquired in law school? Tested by the bar examination? Could nonlawyers perform these tasks? Should they be allowed to do so?

6. Were you surprised by Seron's description of the social organization of the firm? Troubled? How does it differ from that of large firms?

7. How do you understand the division of labor within the firm: between lawyers and nonlawyers, between people and computers? How is this gendered? How does it differ in solo practice?

8. How do the "franchises" differ from other small firms? Do you expect them to displace independent practice? Why? Would you favor that development? What do you find attractive and unattractive about them from the perspective of lawyers? Clients?

9. What is the relationship between who the clients are, the kind of services they seek, how

lawyers obtain clients, and the quality of work they perform? Which clients do these marketing efforts reach? Which do they miss? How do large- and small-firm lawyers differ in their relationships with adversaries, court and agency personnel, other lawyers?

10. What do small-firm lawyers think clients want? Are they correct about this? Does the incentive structure give clients what they want? If "autonomy" is the hallmark of a profession, do small-firm lawyers enjoy it?

SUGGESTED READING

The classic study of solo and small-firm practice in Chicago in the 1950s is Jerome Carlin, *Lawyers on Their Own* (1962; reprinted 1994). His second book, *Lawyers' Ethics: A Survey of the New York City Bar* (1966) also focuses on that stratum. Douglas Rosenthal, *Lawyer and Client: Who's In Charge* (1974) looks at personal injury plaintiffs' lawyers in New York; and Hubert O'Gorman, *Lawyers and Matrimonial Cases: A Study of Informal Pressures in Private Professional Practice* (1963) examines family lawyers there. For a contemporaneous study of a medium-sized midwestern city, see Joel Handler, *The Lawyer and His Community* (1967); for an earlier study in a similar milieu, see Emily P. Dodge, "Evolution of a City Law Office," 1955 *Wisconsin Law Review* 180, 1956: 35. For historical accounts, see Harry M. Caudill, *Slender Is the Thread: Tales from a Country Law Office* (1987); C. Robert Haywood, *Dodge City and Its Attorneys, 1876–86* (1988). On competition between small-firm lawyers and other occupations, see Quintin Johnstone and Don

Hopson Jr., *Lawyers and Their Work: An Analysis of the Legal Profession in the United States and England* (1967); "Note: Unauthorized Practice of Law and Pro Se Divorce: An Empirical Analysis," 86 *Yale Law Journal* 104 (1976).

Small-town lawyers in Nebraska today are described in Donald J. Landon, "Clients, Colleagues, and Community: The Shaping of Zealous Advocacy in Country Law Practice," 1985 *American Bar Foundation Research Journal* 81; "LaSalle Street and Main Street: The Role of Context in Structuring Law Practice," 22 *Law & Society Review* 213 (1988); *Country Lawyers: The Impact of Context on Professional Practice* (1990); see also the comparative review essay by Jon Johnsen, "Rural Justice: Country Lawyers and Legal Services in the United States and Britain," 17 *Law & Social Inquiry* 415 (1992). On lawyers employed by legal clinics of the Jacoby & Meyers or Hyatt Legal Services variety, see Jerry Van Hoy, "Selling and Processing Law: Legal Work at Franchise Law Firms," 29 *Law & Society Review* 703 (1995); for earlier studies, see T. J. Muris and F. S. McChesney, "Advertising and the Price and Quality of Legal Services: The Case of Legal Clinics," 1979 *American Bar Foundation Research Journal* 179; Carrie Menkel-Meadow, *The American Bar Association Legal Clinic Experiment: An Evaluation of the 59th Street Legal Clinic* (1979). Seron presents some additional data and interpretation in "Managing Entrepreneurial Lawyers: A Variation on Traditional Practice," in Robert Nelson, David M. Trubek, and Rayman L. Solomon (eds.), *Lawyers' Ideals/Lawyers' Practices* (1992), "New Strategies of Getting Clients: Urban and Suburban Lawyers' Views," 27 *Law & Society Review* 399 (1993).

Chapter Four

LAWYER-CLIENT INTERACTION

Although sociologists of medicine have devoted considerable energy to studying, and criticizing, the ways in which medical professionals deal with patients,* sociologists of law only recently began to ask similar questions about lawyers and clients. Some attributed this omission to the difficulty of gaining access to lawyers' offices, allegedly because an observer would jeopardize the client's privilege to prevent the lawyer from breaching confidentiality.† But the physician–patient privilege is just as important and medical confidences usually more intimate. Furthermore, many laypeople are more afraid, and ignorant, of lawyers than of doctors. The following account shows the profound ways in which lawyer–client interaction shapes the experience of law.

LAW AND STRATEGY IN THE DIVORCE LAWYER'S OFFICE[1]

Austin Sarat and William L. F. Felstiner

WE observed cases over a period of 33 months in two sites, one in Massachusetts and one in California. This effort consisted in following one side of 40 divorce cases, ideally from the first lawyer–client interview until the divorce was final. Our major objectives were to describe the ways in which lawyers present the legal system and legal process to their clients, to identify the roles that lawyers adopt in divorce cases, to describe the actual content of legal work, to analyze the language and communication patterns through which lawyers carry out these

---

* E.g., Howard Waitzkin, *The Politics of Medical Encounters: How Patients and Doctors Deal with Social Problems (1991).*

† Compare Brenda Danet, Kenneth Hoffman, and Nicole Kermish, "Obstacles to the Study of Lawyer–Client Interaction: The Biography of a Failure," 14 *Law & Society Review* 905 (1980), with Maureen Cain, "The General Practice Lawyer and Client," 7 *International Journal of the Sociology of Law* 331 (1979).

1 20 *Law & Society Review* 93 (1986). Reprinted with permission.

functions, and to examine the ways that lawyer–client interaction affects the development and transformation of divorce disputes.

In this conference the lawyer presents the legal process of divorce largely in response to questions or remarks by the client. Throughout the conference the client persists in focusing on the restraining order until finally she asks:

Client: How often does a case like this come along—a restraining order of this nature?

Lawyer: Very common.

Client: It's a very common thing. So how many other people are getting the same kind of treatment I am? With what, I presume, is very sloppily handled orders that are passed out.

Lawyer: Yeah, you know, I talked, I did talk to someone in the know—I won't go any further than that—who said that this one could have been signed purely by accident. I mean, that the judge could have if he looked at it now—said, I would not sign that, knowing what it was, and it could have been signed by accident, and I said, well, then how does that happen? And he said, well, you've got all this stuff going; you come back to your office, and there's a stack of documents that need signatures. He says, you can do one of two things: you can postpone signing them until you have time, but then it may be the end of the day; the clerk's office is closing, and people who really need this stuff aren't going to get the orders, because there's someone else that needs your attention, so you go through them, and one of the main things you look for is the law firm or lawyer who is proposing them. And you tend to rely on them.

The lawyer thus states that a legal order of immense consequence to this woman may have been handled in a way that in several respects is inconsistent with the formalist image of a rational system: it may have been signed by accident. Moreover, the lawyer claims that he has received this information from "someone in the know," someone he refuses to identify. By this refusal, he implies that the information was given improperly, in breach of confidence. Furthermore, the lawyer's description of how judges handle court orders suggests a high level of inattention and routinization. Judges sign orders without reading them to satisfy "people who really need this stuff." While the judge is said to ignore the substance of the order, he does pay attention to the lawyer or law firm who requests it. The legal process is thereby portrayed as responding more to reputation than to substantive merit. Thus, the client is introduced to a system that is hurried, routinized, personalistic, and accident-prone.

Throughout this conference, the theme of the importance of insider status and access within the local legal system is reinforced by references to the lawyer's personal situation. The conference begins with a description of his close ties to the district attorney:

Observer: You're what? You're on a jury?

Lawyer: Well, no, I'm sitting there waiting to get questioned. It's a criminal case, and I think the chances of my being selected are rather remote, because I just came back from lunch with the district attorney. And then the next question will be: How often does this happen? And I'll say, with some degree of regularity. And they'll say, with whom? Who else do you guys eat with when you meet? And I'll say, nobody.

Shortly afterward, he reminds the client that he serves on occasion as judge *pro tem* in divorce cases:

Lawyer: Let's see. We've appeared in court and then I went to be a judge. Now I'm meeting with you, and…

The client responds by inquiring about a case that she had observed earlier:

Client: How did you decide the case of the overextended New Vista attorney?

Lawyer: Oh, he…No, New Verde attorney, New Beach. The other attorney, the overextended—

Client: I love the Perry Mason titles.

Lawyer: He was…Oh, let's see. There were four matters. He stipulated to the child custody. I gave the wife all the attorney's fees she asked for and made a notation that the request was less than I knew it cost to prosecute the action. I held him in contempt for not paying the doctors, and…ah…

Client: You didn't put him in jail, I presume.

Lawyer: No, I didn't put him in jail. I would have if they had asked me to. And the fourth one was the

child support. In chambers, they had asked for $275, and I gave them $300. So…And he wanted to pay what? $25 a month, or some thing.

Client: Hard-nosed judge. Whew.

The lawyer later claims that he knows one of the judges involved in this client's case well enough to tell him off in private ("I'll tell you, when this is over, I'm going to take it to John Hancock and I don't think he'll ever do it again") and that he supported the other's campaign for office. These references suggest that a lawyer's capacity to protect his client's interests depends in part on his special access to the system's functionaries, who will react to who he is rather than what he represents. We found this emphasis on insider status, reputation, and local connections repeatedly in the cases that we observed. The lawyer in this case and the other lawyers we studied generally presented themselves as well-connected insiders, valuable because they are known and respected rather than because they are expert legal technicians.

The kind of familiarity with the way the system works that insiders possess is all the more important in divorce cases because the divorce process is extremely difficult to explain even to discerning outsiders.

Client: Tell me just the mechanics of this, Peter. What exactly is an interlocutory?

Lawyer: You should know. It's your right to know. But whether or not I'm going to be able to explain this to you is questionable…. It's a very…It's sort of simple in practice, but it's very confusing to explain. I've got an awful lot of really smart people who've—who I haven't represented—who've asked me after the divorce is over, now what the hell was the interlocutory judgment?

The communications that we have been discussing are, for the most part, explicit. The message is in the message. But there is also a way in which the language that the lawyer employs to describe the legal process communicates something about that process itself. Although this lawyer is articulate and knowledgeable, his reactions to many of the client's questions are nevertheless circuitous and confusing. Interviews with clients, as well as our observations, suggest that this failing is common. Instead of direct description, lawyers frequently use analogies that seem to obscure more than they reveal. This practice, of course, may be seen as a simple problem of communication. Yet it also suggests that law and legal process are themselves so dense and erratic that they pose a formidable barrier even to well-educated and intelligent laypeople.

Another example of this impenetrability is seen when the lawyer is once again pressed to explain why the restraining order was imposed:

> *Lawyer*: Ever since I've been practicing law in Pacificola, I've had [Mike Cohen]—I like him; I respect him; he's a hard worker; and I think he's very, very honest; I supported him in his campaigns, so on and so forth—but I have had difficulty understanding how Mike Cohen thinks. It is [difficult]—and I have an analogy that I thought of today. While my jury panel was on a break, I went in to watch him, and there was a district attorney that he was questioning. They were going to sentence some guy—it was a probation revocation—they were going to sentence him to county jail. The district attorney had earlier argued that he ought to be sent to the state prison. The judge turns to the district attorney and says, well, now, when I send him to county jail, I want to do this, this, this, this, this, but this is my problem; I don't know if I can do this, do this, do this. And the district attorney started to help him solve his problem, then said, wait a minute; I don't know what I'm doing. I don't want him to go to county jail; this guy belongs in state prison.... You just said you were going to think about sending him to county jail, and now you want me to tell you how to do it; I think you're wrong, and I'm not going to tell you how to do it wrong. Now those weren't his exact words, but then Cohen had some more chin music and then continued it for another day, so that he could think it over. And he had an excuse. He said, well, I need some more evidence on this, and I need some.... And I talked to the district attorney afterwards, and I said, it was so clear to me what was going on. It was as though you, as one side, say, judge, the way I see this case it's a matter of five plus five plus five divided by three equals five. Now, you have made a tentative ruling where you say, five plus five plus five equals fourteen. Now, you want me to tell you how you come up with a right answer after you've made the first false conclusion. And I can't do it. And that's what happened. He just...

At its clearest point this answer suggests that the restraining order, like the county jail sentence, rested on a "first false conclusion." What that conclusion is the lawyer never does say. But in the course of constructing the parallel narrative about the sentencing hearing, he suggests that

the mind of the judge is unfathomable, that the judge did not know the limits of his own powers, that the district attorney, at least for a moment, did not know his own interests, and that in the end time had been wasted pursuing a course of action based upon a mistaken premise. Judges, in particular, do not fare well when divorce lawyers describe the legal process to their clients.

Moving from the restraining order to the question of how a settlement could be reached, the client asks why her lawyer did not acknowledge to the other side what he had shared with her: namely, that a court battle might end in defeat. In response, the lawyer might simply have said that it is poor strategy in a negotiation to tell the other side that you recognize that you may lose. Instead he says:

> *Lawyer*: Okay. I'll do it in my usual convoluted way, using lots of analogies and examples. When you write to…when a lawyer writes to an insurance company, representing a person who's been injured in an automobile accident, usually the first demand is somewhat higher than what we actually expect to get out of the case. I always explain that to clients. I explain it very, very carefully. I don't like to write letters of any substance without my client getting a copy of it, and inevitably, I will send a copy of it to my client with another letter explaining, "This is for settlement purposes. Please do not think that your case, which I evaluate at $10,000, is really worth $35,000." And then months later when I finally get the offer to settle for $10,000, I will convey it to my client, and they'll say, well, I've been thinking about this, and I think that you're right; it really was worth $35,000. I then am in a terrible position of having to talk my own client down from a number that I created in the first place and that I tried to support and convince them—of course, they wanted to be convinced, so it was easy—that's the difference between a letter that you send to your adversary and a letter that you, or than what you communicate to your client…. You have hired me to represent your interests. I do that in two fashions. One, I tell you the way I truly see the picture, and then I try to advance your cause as aggressively as I can. Sometimes—almost always—those are inconsistent. I mean, the actions, the words, and so forth are inconsistent.

Like the example of the county jail sentence the lawyer used earlier, this example is also drawn from an area of law unrelated to divorce. The lawyer's point is the hypocrisy of orthodox settlement negotiations. Even if warned, he claims, clients are likely to confuse demands and values.

That is their error. In the legal process words and goals, expressed objectives and real objectives, are usually "inconsistent."

Not only is the legal process inconsistent, but it cannot be counted on to protect fundamental rights or deal in a principled way with the important matters that come before it. Thus, the lawyer validates the client's expressed belief that her rights are neither absolute nor secure in the legal process. As they discuss what they ought to demand in trying to negotiate a settlement, the client says:

> *Client*: Sure. I mean, that's as much as can be expected, I believe. Am I right in that?
>
> *Lawyer*: I think so, too.

The relationship of law to values like fairness and justice is discussed more explicitly. At that point the client muses about her goals and hopes about the legal process of divorce.

> *Client*: Well, I mean, I'm a liberal. Right? A liberal dream is that you will find social justice, and so here was this statement that it was possible to fight injustice, and you were going to protect me from horrible things like judicial abuse. So that's, uh, it was really nice.

To the client, "justice" demands that the error of the restraining order be righted. For the lawyer, that kind of justice simply gets in the way of what for him is the real business of divorce: to reach a property settlement, not to right wrongs or vindicate justice. There is, if you will, a particular kind of justice that the law provides, but it is not broad enough to include the kind that the client seeks. For her, justice requires some compensation, or at least an acknowledgment that she has "been treated unjustly." When she finally gets the lawyer to speak in terms of justice, he admits that it cannot be secured through the legal process.

> *Client*: But as you say, if you want justice in this society, you look somewhere other than the court. I believe that's what you were saying to Bob.
>
> *Lawyer*: Yeah, that's what I said. Ultimate justice, that is.

Legal justice is thus juxtaposed to ultimate justice. The person seeking such a final accounting is clearly out of place in a system that focuses much more narrowly. Thus the failure of law to

provide justice is, for her, a failure to validate her position. The language of justice also serves to bolster her image of herself as an innocent, rather gracious, victim of an evil husband and his untrustworthy lawyer.

While many clients think of the legal process as an arena for a full adversarial contest, most divorce disputes are not resolved in this manner. Although not all lawyers are equally dedicated to reaching negotiated agreements, most of those we observed advised their clients to try to settle the full range of issues in the case.

The conference we are examining revolves around two major issues: (1) whether to ignore or contest the restraining order; and (2) what position to take concerning disposition of the family residence. Substantively, the order is not as important as the house itself, which received much less attention and generated much less controversy. Both issues, however, force the lawyer and client to decide whether they will retain control of the case by engaging in negotiations or cede control to the court for hearing and decision. The lawyer definitely favors negotiations.

> *Lawyer*: Okay. What I would like your permission to do then is to meet with Foster, see if I can come up with or negotiate a settlement with him that, before he leaves…I leave his office or he leaves my office, he says, we've got something here that I can recommend to my client, and I can say, I've got something here that I can recommend to my client. My feeling is, Jane, that if we reach that point, both lawyers are prepared to make a recommendation on settlement to their respective clients, if either of the clients, either you or Norb, find something terribly disagreeable with the proposal that we have, then the lawyers have come to between themselves, then the case just either can't be settled or it's not ripe for settlement. But we would have given it the best shot. But I wouldn't…as you know, I'm very concerned about wasting a lot of time and energy trying to settle a case where two previous attempts have been dismally unsuccessful.

The major ingredient of this settlement system is the primacy of the lawyers. They produce the deals, while the clients are limited to initial instructions and after-the-fact ratification. Furthermore, if the professionals are content with the agreement they have devised, dissatisfied clients not only have nothing to contribute but also had perhaps better seek psychotherapy:

Lawyer: And if we have to come down a little bit off the 10 percent to something that is obviously a real good loan—9 percent—a percentage point on a one-year, eighteen-month, $25,000 loan does not make that much difference to you. And that's worth settling the case, and I'll say, Jane, if we're going to court over what turns out to be one percentage point, go talk to Irene some more. So that's the kind of a package that I see putting together.

The client in this case is reluctant to begin settlement negotiations until some attention is paid to the restraining order. While she acknowledges that she wants a reasonable property settlement, she reminds her lawyer that that is not her exclusive concern:

Client: Yes, there's no question in my mind that that [a property settlement] is my first goal. However, that doesn't mean it's my only goal. It's just my first one. And I have done a lot of thinking about this and so it's all this kind of running around in my head at this point. I've been looking very carefully at the parts of me that want to fight and the parts of me that don't want to fight. And I'm not sure that any of that ought to get messed up in the property settlement.

The lawyer responds by acknowledging that he considers the restraining order to be legally wrong and that he believes it could be litigated. Thus he confirms his client's position and inclination on legal grounds. Yet he dissents from her position and opposes her inclination to fight on other grounds. First, he states that the restraining order, although legally wrong, is "not necessarily…completely wrong" because it might prevent violence between spouses. In this way lawyers present themselves as both an ally and an adviser embracing the wisdom of a long-term perspective.

Second, the lawyer is worried that an effort to fight the restraining order would interfere with the resolution of the case, that is, of the outstanding property issues. Thus when the client asks whether the issue of the restraining order has been raised with her husband's lawyer, her lawyer says:

Lawyer: Well, I've talked to him. My feelings are still the same. They're very strong feelings that what has been done is illegal, that I want to take it to the Supreme Court. I told Foster off. I basically told him the contents of the letter. I said that I think that Judge Cohen is dead wrong, and I would very much like to litigate the thing. On the other hand, I have

to be mindful of what Irene said, which is absolutely correct. Does that move us toward or away from the ultimate goal, which is the resolution of the case and what you told me when we started off now in very certain terms.

Time and again in our study we observed lawyers attempting to focus their clients' attention on the issues the lawyers thought to be major while the clients often concentrated on matters that the lawyers considered secondary. While the disposition of the house in this case will have long-term consequences for the client, the restraining order, as unjust as the lawyer understands it to be, is in his view a temporary nuisance. His sense of justice and of the long-term best interests of his client lead him to try to transform this dispute from a battle over the legality and morality of the restraining order to a negotiation over the more narrow and tangible issue of the ultimate disposition of the house and other assets, which he believes can and should be settled.

In attempting this transformation, the lawyer allies himself with the therapist:

Lawyer: I agree with Irene that that [fighting the restraining order] is not the best way…. It's probably the worst way. This [negotiating] hopefully is the best way.

This reliance on the therapist is noteworthy because it is often assumed that a therapeutic orientation is antithetical to the adversarial inclination of law and the legal profession.

The client's own ambivalence toward settlement continues throughout the conference. In discussing a letter that her lawyer had prepared to send to the other lawyer outlining their position on the restraining order, she says:

Client: So it was an important letter, and I didn't realize how much I wanted to continue fighting until I read the first portion of this letter…. It kind of let me feel that finally…I'd found a knight in shining armor.

To which the lawyer responds:

Lawyer: Ouch.

The transference reflected in her reference to a "knight in shining armor," a female client's substitution of her male lawyer for her failed husband, may not be unusual in divorce cases, but nowhere in our sample is it as explicit as it is here.

A minute later this client substitutes a different metaphor when she asks:

Client: Are you familiar with Chief Joseph?

Lawyer: No.

Client: He was a Nez Perce Indian, and he fought the troops of the U.S. government for years and finally he saw that his whole tribe would be killed off and the land devastated so he put down his weapons. And I think the full quote is something like: "From the time the moon sets, I will fight no more forever." I went away that day, that Monday, feeling that this fight had to end, and that's still what I feel.

Lawyer: Now, orient me as to…

Client: That went on Monday evening, the day of the hearing, to Norb.

Lawyer: Okay. After…It was after Irene and you and I spoke, but it was before the last conversation you and I had and it preceded…

Client: Your letter, your draft.

Lawyer: My draft, and it also preceded Norb's proposal.

Client: Yes.

Lawyer: So Norb's proposal is in response to this, presumptively.

Client: That's right.

Lawyer: Okay.

Client: I think that's accurate. One of the thoughts I had that afternoon was that—probably it came a lot from what Irene had to say—that I've been arguing with this man for a good many years of my life. You know, first in the living room, then involving family and friends, then involving therapists, and now involving attorneys. How many forums am I going to spend arguing with this person? And I really want the war to end. So that's my basic conflict. I feel I've been treated unjustly. I feel there's a very good case here, but I don't want to fight any more. And that's what this really is about—a continuing war. So a part of me is still very much with Chief Joseph—I don't want to fight any more. There are other and better things to do with this life.

However, as they move further into the discussion of whether to fight or settle, the client begins to interpret settlement as a capitulation and to reiterate her own ambivalence about how to proceed.

Client: And I think I feel some level of fear about

this process of negotiation and how much more I'm going to have to give up. I don't feel tremen— you know, there's a part of me that does not feel very satisfied with having capitulated repeatedly, and now we're simply doing it with a property settlement.

Lawyer: That's, yeah, that's a…

Client: I mean, I don't want to fight and I do want to fight, right? That's exactly what it comes down to.

Lawyer: Yes, you're ambiguous.

Client: Oh, boy, am I ever. And I have to live with it.

She may have to live with her ambivalence, but her lawyer needs a resolution of this issue. The lawyer seeks this resolution by allying himself with the "don't fight" side of the struggle. Her advocate, her "knight," has thus become the enemy of adversariness. Through him the legal system becomes the champion of settlement. Ironically, the client's ambivalence serves to validate the lawyer's earlier suggestion that he might be wasting his time and her money trying to settle this case because she might refuse at the last minute to agree to a deal.

The conference reaches closure on the fight/settle issue when the lawyer again asks whether he has her authority to negotiate on the terms they had discussed and repeats his earlier warning that this is their last chance for a settlement:

Lawyer: Well, then I will make a…my best effort— we are now coming full circle to where we were this morning, which is fine, which is where we should be. I will make my best effort to effect a settlement with Foster along the lines that you and I have discussed and the specific terms of which I can say to you, Jane, I recommend that you sign this. The decision, of course, is yours. If you don't want to sign it, we're going to go ahead with the litigation on the restraining order and probably a trial. Things can change. We can effect a settlement before the restraining order, which is highly unlikely, or between the time the restraining order issue is resolved and the actual time of trial, maybe there will be another settlement. I'm not going to suggest or advise, after this attempt, that either one of us put any substantial energy in another try at settlement. I just think it's a waste of time and money.

The lawyer's reference to "coming full circle" reflects both the centrality of the dispositional question and the amount of time spent talking about issues the lawyer considers to be peripheral. Having invested that time, the lawyer secures what he wanted, both an authorization to negotiate and an agreement on the goals that he will pursue. The client, on the other hand, has aired her ambivalence and resolved to try to end this dispute without a legal contest.

Lawyers thus legitimate some parts of human experience and deny the relevance of others, but they do not explicitly state what is required of the client. Rather, the approved form of the legal self is built up from a set of oppositions and priorities among these oppositions.

The negotiation of the legal self in this case begins by focusing on the relative importance of emotions engaged by the legal process and the symbolic aspects of the divorce as opposed to its financial and material dimensions. Throughout this conference the lawyer warns his client not to confuse the realms of emotion and finance and instructs her that she can expect the legal process to work well only if emotional material is excluded from her deliberations.

The client is, in the first instance, eager to let her lawyer know that she feels both anger and mistrust toward many participants in the legal process. This combination of feelings is clearly expressed as she talks about the restraining order and the manner in which it was issued:

Client: So I was a total ass. I moved out of the house and left myself vulnerable to that, which I was certainly not informed of by any attorney in the process of mediation. And I was setting myself up for that.

Lawyer: In my view, it would have been a rather extraordinary attorney that could have advised you of that, because, in my view, that's not the law. So I'm hard-pressed to see how a lawyer could have said, don't move out of the house or you may prejudice your situation by moving out of the house.

Client: But obviously, some attorney did, right? We have the case of Paul Foster, who interprets the law in that fashion. Well, I'm angry about all that. However….

The client continues to express her anger throughout the conference, especially when the conversation turns directly to her husband's lawyer.

Client: The other option I see could have been that Norb would have gotten different legal advice from the beginning. So the thing, I suppose, that I'm con-

cerned about, I'm concerned about Foster. I'm concerned about the kind of person he is. I distrust him as thoroughly as I do Norb, and I think you have been very measured in your statements about him. I think he's a son of a bitch, and there's nothing I've seen that he's done that changed my mind about that. And I think that he has a client that can be manipulated.

The client's mistrust is not reserved exclusively for the opposition. She is, to an extent, wary of her own lawyer as well:

Client: But when I think of myself—you know, this is a very vulnerable time in my life, and one of the things that has happened is a major trust relationship has ended. And then suddenly in the space of what—six weeks or something—I'm supposed to entrust somebody else, not only with the intimate details of my life, but with the responsibility for representing me. And that's not easy for me under any circumstances. I really like to speak for myself.

Given her concerns about her husband and the lawyers involved in the case, it is not surprising that the issue of trust is paramount when the client considers how to try to reach a negotiated agreement:

Client: One of the things I'm feeling is a tremendous discontent that some form of negotiation is going to now begin without any act from Norb that establishes trust.

…

Client: Ahh. It doesn't seem that I have a lot of options. I simply will have to accept that, and I guess I will have to live with that pain…. I think it's dreadfully unfair. But it doesn't seem that I can get any satisfaction, so I'll have to…

Lawyer: That's not entirely true. You can litigate. Strongly we can litigate.

Client: Well, I think the only question then is whether or not an overture then is even possible before litigation. I'm not sure. I mean, yes, I have these things separated in my mind, but how can I trust this human being to do anything? I don't know if I can. I feel that pretty strongly.

Lawyer: I don't blame you. I don't blame you at all.

Because she feels betrayed by her husband, the client wants "some gesture from him" as a means of establishing the basis for negotiations. Moreover, she feels that she is already two points down vis-a-vis her husband. First, he has the house and has denied her any access to it, although her departure was an act of generosity done for the good of the marital community. Second, she "knows" that he is going to get the house and that she will at best get half its market value. She repeatedly asks the lawyer about gestures or concessions to even this score:

> *Client*: So I wrote this as a draft to send to Norb…And obviously I'm still waffling…. I mean, I don't know exactly how to give up this hearing. Part of me says, it's real clear and I ought to. But I want some gesture from him.
>
> …
>
> *Client*: Okay. That's not going to be a problem for me, alright? I don't think that one percentage point is going to be a problem for me. This is the problem for me. I feel that, even to get to this point, I have given up a substantial amount. One thing that I've given up is the home in Pacificola. I don't give a fuck how much cash Norb gives me, I'm not going to be able to re-create that scene, and that's just a fact of real estate in Pacificola. I want the negotiation to begin there. I want some attention to be paid to what I have already conceded to even get to this point.
>
> …
>
> *Client*: I just think that's a very, very big concession, and I think if I'm to take another kind of settlement, then that is the first thing that ought to be seen. Now, that's a very good faith negotiation thing for me to do, say, okay, Norb has this tremendous emotional investment in the house; I'm willing to let go of mine.
>
> …

How does the lawyer respond to the client's emotional agenda, to her efforts to define those parts of herself that are legally relevant? With respect to the problem of trust and the need for a gesture, the lawyer once says, "Ouch," once, "I don't blame you," and once he changes the subject. He does tell the client that her husband is unlikely to reestablish trust by giving up the restraining order. In addition, there is a brief exploration of whether she could buy the husband's share of the house, an alternative doomed by earlier recognition that it would involve an expensive and probably fruitless court battle. There is a joke about taking $25,000 to forget the restraining order. Otherwise nothing is said.

Why? Lawyer and client could have discussed the kind of gestures short of unconditional sur-

render that might have satisfied her and been tolerable to her husband. The lawyer could have explored the possibility that the husband might agree to his client's occasional, scheduled visits to the property or to $5,000 more than a 50/50 split in recognition of giving up the house. Perhaps he feared that further exploration might complicate his efforts to have his client focus on reaching an acceptable division of property. There can be little doubt that this objective governed his thinking.

> *Lawyer*: Okay, Now, that disagreement—or, it wasn't even a disagreement—that—where we weren't on the same wavelength—was really a matter of style than of end result. Right?
>
> *Client*: You mean, what part?
>
> *Lawyer*: Where you said was that you wanted me to start these negotiations by making it clear that major concession was being made at the outset and it was being made by you.
>
> *Client*: Yes.
>
> *Lawyer*: Okay, I understand that now. Let's come back to the end of it…. What am I shooting for? Okay, I agree. That's the way it ought to be begun, and that point ought to—during my conversations, I ought to keep coming back to that, if I have to use it. Just make that strongly. But what am I shooting for? What's the end result? Is it what I was talking about initially?
>
> *Client*: Sure. I mean, that's as much as can be expected, I believe. Am I right in that?

The lawyer proposes to turn the client's demand for concessions into an opening statement and implies that an equal division of assets is the only possible legal settlement. The client, on the other hand, appears to believe that it is dangerous to trade values with someone that you do not trust for both the chance that they will take advantage of you in making the deal and the probability that they will fail to do what they promise are increased. The lawyer is, and can afford to be, disinterested in trust. Protection of his client does not lie in fostering goodwill and mutual respect between the spouses but rather in the terms of the bargain and in its enforcement powers. His duty is to see that the settlement agreement is fair to his client, whatever the motives or morals of the other side may be, and that the structure of the agreement guarantees that his client gets what she bargained for or its substitute, or at least the best approximation available.

By playing down the question of trust the lawyer is telling the client that the emotional self must be separated from the legal self. Gestures and symbolic acknowledgment of wrongs suffered belong to some realm other than law. He is, in addition, defending himself against a kind of emotional transference. Much of the emotion talk in this conference involves the lawyer himself, directly or indirectly. In the discussion of trust the client makes the lawyer into a kind of husband substitute ("a major trust relationship has ended. And then…I'm supposed to entrust somebody else…"). The client described him as her "knight in shining armor," an image of protection and romance; she acknowledges having sexual fantasies about him and she speaks of her expectation that he would protect her from "judicial abuse."

By downplaying emotions and signaling the limited relevance of gestures, the lawyer defends himself against both the transference and the test. He must find a way to be on his client's side (e.g., repeatedly acknowledging the legal error of the restraining order) and, at the same time, to keep some distance from her (e.g., responding "Ouch" to the image of the knight).

To maintain this balance the lawyer acknowledges the difficulty of separating emotional and property issues, but continually reminds the client of its necessity if they are going to reach what he calls a "satisfactory disposition" of the case:

> *Lawyer*: I mean, people have a very, very hard time of separating whatever it is—so I think for shorthand, we call it the emotional aspect of the case—from the financial aspect of the case. But if there is going to be a settlement, that's kind of what has to happen, or the emotional aspect of the case gets resolved and then the financial thing becomes a matter of dollars and cents and the client decides, I'm tired and I don't want to fight over the last $500 or the last $100.

The need to exclude emotional issues is thus linked to a warning that emotions can jeopardize satisfactory settlements. The notion of satisfactory disposition, however, is itself problematic. The lawyer's definition of "satisfactory" tends to exclude the part of the client's personality that is angry or frustrated. Satisfactory dispositions are financial. The question of who is satisfied is left unasked. For the client, no definition of the case that ignores her emotions seems right; to the lawyer, this is the only definition that seems acceptable. Moreover, the responsibility for finding ways to keep emotions under control is assigned to the client. The lawyer offers no help in this task even as he acknowledges its relevance for this client and for the practice of divorce law. If no settlement is reached it will, at least as far as their side is concerned, be because of a failure on the part of the client.

Throughout this conference the lawyer stresses the need for two parallel separations: the separation of the emotional issues from the legal and the separation of the client and her husband.

> *Client*: I mean, I don't want to fight and I do want to fight, right? That's exactly what it comes down to.
>
> *Lawyer*: Yea, you're ambiguous.
>
> *Client*: Oh, boy, am I ever. And I have to live with it.
>
> *Lawyer*: That's right. I'd say the ambiguity goes even deeper than the issue of fighting and not fighting. It's how…The ambiguity is what Irene talked about and that is it's the real hard one—it's terminating the entire relationship. You do and you don't, and the termination…I mean, you're angry; you're pissed off. You've said that. And are you ready to call a halt to the anger, and I'm not so sure that that's humanly possible. Can your rational mind say, okay, Jane, there has been enough anger expended on this; it is time to get on with your life. If you are able to do that, great. But I don't know.

As the lawyer sees it, the client will only be able to make an adequate arrangement with her husband when she can contemplate their relationship unemotionally. As the client sees it, the second separation seems impossible if the first is carried out. She cannot become free of her husband if she thinks about legal problems in material terms only—if she fails to take her feelings into account she will continue to be affected by them. Thus, the program the lawyer presents to the client appropriates her marriage to the realm of property and defines her connection to her husband exclusively in those terms. She, on the other hand, sees property issues embedded in a broader context. The client speaks about the separation of the emotional and financial issues as being difficult to effect because it is unnatural. The market does not exhaust her realm of values, and she has difficulty assigning governing priority to it. Yet this is what the lawyer indicates the law requires.

DISCUSSION QUESTIONS

1. What does the client want from the lawyer? What is the client's image of the ideal lawyer? Where do clients get these ideas? How do clients present themselves to lawyers? How do clients control lawyers? How much did these clients participate in shaping legal strategies? Should they have participated more? If so, how could we increase the client's role? Judith Kaye, Chief Judge of the New York Court of Appeals, recently promulgated new rules to prevent matrimonial lawyers from exploiting their financial, legal, and emotional power over clients.[2]

2. What does the lawyer want from the client? What is the lawyer's image of the ideal client? How do lawyers present themselves to clients? How do lawyers control clients?

3. Do lawyers and clients differ in their conceptions of how the legal system does and should work? Their beliefs about the legitimacy of the legal system? Their attitudes towards the adversary, opposing counsel, the judge? How do they misunderstand or ignore each other?

4. How do the objectives and incentives of lawyers and clients differ? How do they change over time? What does each believe can be compromised or is non-negotiable? Politicians, the media, and others blame lawyers for Americans' alleged litigiousness. Does this reading support such a criticism? How do clients and lawyers choose between negotiation, mediation, and litigation? Sociologists of law seek to understand how disputes are transformed over time.[3] How did the lawyer–client interaction described in this reading transform the dispute?

5. How does the lawyer–client relationship differ across subject matters: family, criminal, personal injury, property? How does it differ between individual and corporate clients? Among individuals by the gender, race, and class of both lawyers and clients? How does it differ from other client–professional relationships, e.g., with physicians, clergy, psychotherapists, teachers, architects?

SUGGESTED READING

The authors have published other parts of their study in articles and a book: "Law and Social Relations: Vocabularies of Motive in the Lawyer–Client Interaction," 22 *Law & Society Review* 737 (1988); "Lawyers and Legal Consciousness: Law Talk in the Divorce Lawyer's Office," 98 *Yale Law Journal* 1663 (1989); "Enactments of Power: Negotiating Reality and Responsibility in Lawyer–Client Interaction," 77 *Cornell Law Review* 1447 (1992); *Divorce Lawyers and Their Clients: Power and Meaning in the Legal Process* (1995). For an early observational account of how lawyers transform their client's goals, see Maureen Cain, "The General Practice Lawyer and the Client: Toward a Radical Conception," 7 *International Journal of Sociology of Law* 331 (1979).

There are accounts of the interaction between divorce lawyers and clients in other jurisdictions: New England—Craig A. McEwan, Lynn Mather, and Richard J. Maiman, "Lawyers, Mediation, and the Management of Divorce Practice," 28 *Law & Society Review* 149 (1994); Wisconsin— Howard Erlanger, Elizabeth Chambliss, and Marygold Melli, "Participation and Flexibility in Informal Processes: Cautions from the Divorce Context," 21 *Law & Society Review* 593 (1987); Marygold Melli, Howard Erlanger, and Elizabeth Chambliss, "The Process of Negotiation: An Exploratory Investigation in the Context of No-Fault Divorce," 40 *Rutgers Law Review* 1133 (1988); Karen Winner, Divorced from Justice (1996) England—Richard Ingleby, "The Solicitor as Intermediary," in Robert Dingwall and John Eekelaar (eds.), *Divorce Mediation and the Legal Process* (1988); Richard Ingleby, *Solicitors and Divorce* (1992); and the Netherlands—John Griffiths, "What Do Dutch Lawyers Actually Do in Divorce Cases?" 20 *Law & Society Review* 135 (1986).

---

2 *New York Times* A15 (5.5.93), A1 (8.17.93), B12 (11.8.93).

3 E.g., William L. F. Felstiner, Richard L. Abel, and Austin Sarat, "The Emergence and Transformation of Disputes: Naming, Blaming, Claiming…," 15 *Law & Society Review* 631 (1980–81); Lynn Mather and Barbara Yngvesson, "Language, Audience, and the Transformation of Disputes," Id. 775.

And there are studies of interaction in other subject areas: contract—Stewart Macaulay, "Lawyers and Consumer Protection Laws," 14 *Law & Society Review* 115 (1979); Mark C. Suchman and Mia L. Cahill, "The Hired Gun as Facilitator: Lawyers and the Suppression of Business Disputes in Silicon Valley," 21 *Law & Social Inquiry* 679 (1996); personal injury—H. Laurence Ross, *Settled Out of Court* (1970); Douglas E. Rosenthal, *Lawyer and Client: Who's in Charge?* (1974); Hazel Genn, *Hard Bargaining: Out of Court Settlement in Personal Injury Actions* (1987); and criminal defense—Carl Hosticka, "We Don't Care What Happened, We Only Care About What Is Going to Happen," 26 *Social Problems* 599 (1979); Kenneth Mann, *Defending White-Collar Crime: A Portrait of Attorneys at Work* (1985); Roy B. Flemming, "Client Games: Defense Attorney Perspectives on Their Relations with Criminal Clients," 1986 *American Bar Foundation Research Journal* 253, "If You Pay the Piper Do You Call the Tune? Public Defenders in America's Criminal Courts," 14 *Law & Social Inquiry* 393 (1989); Michael McConville, Jacqueline Hodgson, and Lee Bridges, *Standing Accused: The Organization and Practice of Criminal Defence Lawyers in Britain* (1994). The large plea-bargaining literature is also relevant.

Chapter Five

LARGE FIRMS

Although large firms contain a relatively small proportion of American lawyers (just 9 percent in firms over 99 in 1988, 14 percent in firms over 49), they enjoy disproportionate influence and visibility both within the profession and outside and, of course, wealth and social standing. Furthermore, they continue to proliferate and grow in all major economic centers. The first reading describes their emergence and present form and then offers an original explanation for their evolution and predictions about their future.

WHY THE BIG GET BIGGER: THE PROMOTION-TO-PARTNER TOURNAMENT AND THE GROWTH OF LARGE LAW FIRMS[1]

Marc Galanter and Thomas M. Palay

THE large law firm and its distinctive style of practice emerged around the turn of the century. These lawyers are highly specialized and ordinarily divided into departments (for example, corporate, banking, real estate, litigation). Work for clients includes planning, counseling, negotiation, and representation in a wide range of settings. Since relations with clients are enduring, big-firm lawyers tend to take up problems early and to monitor the effects of their work.

These firms are hierarchical. The working groups that serve clients consist of senior and junior lawyers. The latter are hired on the basis of their qualifications directly from prestigious law schools. The work of these junior lawyers is supervised and reviewed by seniors. Training is imparted to young lawyers in the course of a prolonged (four- to ten-year) apprenticeship, normally ended either by promotion to partnership or by departure from the firm.

Like the hospital as a way to practice medicine, the big firm provides the standard format for the practice of law. And yet, the growth and prosperity of big firms is accompanied by a palpable anxiety. The observation that lamentations about commercialization and the loss of professional virtue have recurred regularly for a century suggests caution about taking these misgivings at face value. But we submit that something is different this time around. The present "crisis" is the real thing. In the past 20 years or so the big firms have undergone a set of striking changes aptly described as transformation.

In the mid-1950s only 38 law firms in the United States had more than 50 lawyers—and more than half of these were in New York City. By 1985, over 500 firms had more than 50 lawyers, and firms with more than 100 grew from less than a dozen in 1960 to 251 in 1986. In 1968 the largest firm in the United States had 169 lawyers, and the twentieth largest had 106 lawyers. In 1988, the largest firm had 962 lawyers, and 149 firms had more lawyers than the largest firm of 1968.

In addition to size, the most visible and striking changes in the big law firm have occurred in recruitment. Starting in the 1970s, lateral movement became more frequent and widened out from individual lawyers, to whole departments and groups within firms and, finally, to whole firms. A casual search of the legal press from 1985 to 1989 produced a list of 71 mergers, involving 83 firms with more than 50 lawyers. As firms become larger, the task of maintaining an adequate flow of business becomes more precarious and firms more prone to splitting up or failing. Firms are more vulnerable to defections by valued clients or by the lawyers to whom those clients are attached. Size multiplies the possibility of conflicts of interests, and the resulting tension between partners who tend old clients and those who propose new ones can often lead to a breakaway.

Contemporaneous with the growth of big law firms, in-house corporate law departments grew

---

1. 76 *Virginia Law Review* 747 (1990). Reprinted with permission.

in size, budget, functions, authority, and aggressiveness. In their relationship with outside law firms, today's enlarged corporate legal departments impose budgetary restraints, exert more control over cases, demand periodic reports, and engage in comparison shopping among firms.

At the same that business clients retracted much routine work into their corporate law departments, they experienced a great surge of litigation and other risk-prone, high-stakes transactions. Suddenly, the corporate work of large outside firms shifted from its historic emphasis on office practice back toward the litigation from which the large firm had turned away in its infancy. The new aggressiveness of in-house counsel, the breakdown of retainer relationships, and the shift to discrete transactions have made conditions more competitive. Firms rationalize their operations and engage professional managers and consultants; firm leaders worry about billable hours, profit centers, and marketing strategies. "Eat what you kill" compensation formulas emphasize rewards for productivity and business-getting over "equal shares" or seniority. Some firms take on marketing directors.

In the last ten years the time required for promotion to partner has lengthened, firms have become more highly leveraged—that is, the ratio of associates to partners has risen—and the chances of becoming a partner are perceived to have decreased. At the same time, firms have increased the use of personnel who are either not promoted to partner or are never eligible for promotion. A cadre of permanent salaried personnel (paralegals, second-tier associates, and permanent associates/senior attorneys) now surrounds the core, which in some instances contains non-lawyers. As firms have grown, they simply have outpaced earlier methods of monitoring and coordinating personnel, recruiting associates, and generating revenues. To survive, firms have adapted by slowing growth, generating new sources of income, remolding existing governance structures, or accepting decreased (or at least different) profit distributions.

To understand why firms have restructured requires inquiry into why they have grown so fast and why staffing and revenue constraints have begun to impose restrictions on growth. We argue that the big firm, comprised of partners and associates who are incipient partners, contains an inherent dynamic of growth. This is a by-product of the governance structure developed to permit the efficient sharing of human capital. If the environment permits, the firm will grow exponentially. That growth, however, changes the character of the firm. Informality recedes, collegiality gives way, notions of public service and independence are marginalized, and the imperative of growth collides with notions of dignified passivity in obtaining business. Eventually the firm faces the necessity of reorganizing to support ever larger increments or to suppress growth. Either reorganization is likely to jeopardize collegiality, independence, and public service.

To build a model of why law firms grow, we used Martindale-Hubbell to create growth histories for the 50 largest law firms in 1986 (Group I) and 50 smaller but still large firms in 1988 (Group II). The results indicate that the total number of attorneys has grown substantially since each firm's inception and that much of this growth has occurred since 1970.

Many observers subscribe to a "shock theory," which posits constant, though different, absolute amounts of growth and implies that *rates* of growth were decreasing both prior to 1970 and again after the "external shock" around that date. Closer inspection, however, reveals a more complex growth history. The slope, rather than remaining constant, appears to increase even before 1970. Similarly, post-1970 levels of growth also appear to increase over time. In fact, from 1922 onward, most big law firms grew by a constant (or possibly increasing) *percentage* each year.

We propose an alternative explanation: The constant increases imply an *exponential* growth pattern in which a firm's early growth will appear—in absolute numbers—quite unremarkable. An exponential function is not a bad approximation of the actual data, especially in the earlier years; but a kinked linear function fits better after 1970. Combining the external "shock" component of the kinked linear function model with the exponential growth theory results in a hybrid in which firms grow at exponential rates before and after 1970, but the constant percentage of growth differs in each period.

For those who conceive of law-firm growth curves as kinked lines, a theory is needed principally to explain the reason for the steeper angle of ascent after 1970. A theory that seeks to account for kinked exponential law firm growth must explain not only the "kink" but the underlying nonlinear growth pattern as well.

An attorney, like any other producer, combines labor with the capital she has accumulated over time. Most of a lawyer's capital consists of human assets: a pre–law school endowment of intelligence, skills, and general education; legal education and experience-dependent skills; professional reputation; and relationships with clients. We assume that at least some attorneys will have surplus human capital as a result of the constraints on their personal supply of labor, which is ultimately fixed by the working hours in the day. Capital is nonrival if its employment by one user does not prevent other users from simultaneously receiving the identical benefit from the same asset; a standard example is a highway up to the point of congestion. Sharing client relationships and reputation with, or transferring experience-dependent skills to, another attorney does not diminish the benefit the "owner" or other lawyers can derive from those assets. Most attorneys possess a mix of shareable and unshareable assets. For instance, while trial attorneys cannot lend their courtroom presence, they can share the knowledge of how to pick a jury or take a deposition. Net borrowers of human capital typically obtain access to it by selling their labor to those who have a surplus.

Imagine a sole practitioner, P, who has shareable surplus human capital. She would like to lend or rent these assets to A, an attorney with little human capital of his own but a full complement of labor. P might contract with A to produce an output, using his labor and her capital, which one of them then would sell to a client. If P markets the product, as is typically the case, she would pay A the marginal product of his labor and capital, retaining the remainder—minus overhead and other support costs—as compensation for her capital. We refer to the institutional arrangement for conducting these activities as a governance mechanism. We can imagine two extreme possibilities. P could depend entirely on markets, remaining a sole practitioner, renting her capital to A, and agreeing to purchase his output for a price or forward it to the client, who would compensate A. Or P could organize the sharing of her capital as a firm, hiring A and selling the additional output to her client.

In a world without transaction costs, there is no a priori reason a law firm must result from contracting among attorneys. We interact, however, in an economy replete with transaction costs. Long-term agreements render the parties vulnerable to the opportunistic conduct of their trading opposites. P has three potential concerns. A might "grab" assets P lends to him, departing with a client in tow. A may "leave" prematurely (or threaten to do so), taking firm-specific skills and information for which P has paid but not amortized fully. And A might "shirk," thereby depriving P of her expected returns.

The existence of a large number of substitute sources of supply and demand will render problems of this sort negligible. But where assets are either transaction-specific or unique, substitutes will not readily exist. Once P undertakes to train A, the associate will become moderately unique. To fire and replace A entails a willingness on P's part to sacrifice, and then replicate, her investments in him. P also makes transaction-specific investments in client relationships. When P "lends" this asset to A and permits him to do some of the client's work, she places these past investments at substantial risk. A might produce inferior work, breach the client's confidence, or cause P to lose a case. Alternatively, A might gain the client's trust and then demand more money from P by threatening or attempting to leave with the client in tow. P's investments in her reputation are similarly unique.

A also has concerns about potential opportunistic conduct. He needs assurance that P will fairly compensate him for his labor and for any human capital he brings to or develops on P's behalf. A may also seek assurance that if he meets implicit conditions, P actually will promote him. Both parties must be able to obtain inexpensive and reliable indicators of A's effort or output, or at a minimum, both parties must have identical information about A's productivity. But monitoring output in the provision of legal services to clients is difficult and costly. Ultimately, the assessment of A's output comes down to a subjective evaluation of performance. In addition, neither P nor A can easily separate one individual's contribution from that of others. This problem is especially acute where, as generally happens, P is both co-contributor and supervisor and therefore has an incentive to understate A's contribution. A will hesitate to produce a maximum effort for fear that P will not reward him adequately. The realization that many of the human-capital investments he has made are specific to P's business compounds A's concerns. Thus P has significant bargaining advantages in establishing the value of and the return on these assets.

Both sides, therefore, make increased expenditures *ex ante* to protect themselves against the possibility that the other party will attempt to exploit its *ex post* bargaining advantage. These expenditures take the form of governance mechanisms that are bilateral and unique to the parties. The firm in general (and the law firm in particular) is one such specialized governance structure.

To this point we simply have adapted the transaction-cost, asset-specificity argument to the problem of sharing human capital to explain the *existence* of law firms. We argue here that the rapid growth we currently observe relates directly to the specific governance structure used by law firms. An attorney with lots of surplus human capital to share confronts two competing incentives: to hire as much labor as possible to use her capital, and to monitor carefully any attorney she hires. We argue that the mechanism chosen in most firms to monitor performance *has led inevitably* to a pattern of exponential growth.

First, to assure the partners that they will receive the proper return on investments in client relationships, reputation, or skills they impart to associates, firms defer payment of some percentage of the associate's salary, denying it to those who act opportunistically. Partners still must find some method of motivating associates not to shirk. The big law firm typically ties the payment of its deferred bonus to the outcome of what we call the "promotion-to-partnership tournament." The rules are simple. For a fixed period of time (six to ten years), the firm pays salaries to associ-

ates who neither grab nor leave. At each successive stage in the hierarchy part of the associate's salary increase includes a deferred bonus for nonopportunistic behavior. In addition, the firm implicitly tells its associates that it constantly evaluates them for a "super-bonus," paid in the form of promotion to partner. After the fixed period of time has expired, the firm ranks the players in a particular class and declares the top x percent the winners. Though it has been the typical practice, there is no intrinsic reason that the firms must fire the losers.

Associates now have an incentive to produce the maximum combination of legal work and human capital. By declaring up front that, on average, it will promote a fixed percentage of associates, the firm obligates itself to distribute a fixed amount of compensation to the winners. The associate easily can verify that the firm pays out the agreed-to prizes by observing how the present and preceding classes fare and whether the firm continues to recruit new classes of associates.

The promotion-to-partner tournament, originally instituted as a mutual monitoring device, contains an internal dynamic that explains why law firms must grow. Growth occurs because, at the end of the tournament, the firm must replace not only the losing associates who depart but also all those who win and are promoted. By replacing promoted attorneys the firm grows by the number of promotions.

Our argument goes further and asserts that a by-product of the promotion-to-partner tournament is that the firm very likely will grow by more than the number of newly promoted partners. The firm's growth rate will depend upon the ratio of associates to partners in the base year, the percentage of associates promoted, and the number of associates that it must hire the next year to replace the newly promoted partners and to meet the next period's associate-to-partner ratio. If the promotion percentage remains constant over time, then the firm will grow at an exponential rate if the associate-to-partner ratio remains constant. If the associate-to-partner ratio rises, the percentage growth rate will increase.

Thus our claim that firms will tend to grow (at least) exponentially depends upon our argument that each firm's promotion percentage remains reasonably constant and the ratio of associates to partners either remains constant or increases. Empirically, there is evidence supporting both propositions. We observe no obvious upward or downward trend in the associate promotion rate for 90 percent of Group I firms and 86 percent of Group II firms. Similarly, associate-to-partner ratios showed no downward trend for 76 percent of Group I and 78 percent of Group II firms.

The number of associates per partner that a firm can hire depends upon two factors: the monitoring resources of the firm and the amount of human capital each partner in the firm possesses. For most large firms, choosing the promotion percentage effectively chooses the firm's future level of capital per partner. The associate-to-partner ratio tends to remain constant or to increase because firms generally establish promotion percentages designed to cultivate new partners with at least as much human capital as the average of the existing partners. They do so for two reasons. One is the concern that less-endowed partners would attempt to "tax" the more "wealthy" existing partners. Second, the firm bases a significant percentage of a partner's income on the average productivity of the firm; a firm that promotes associates with less capital than the average partner will lower the firm's future average productivity.

Once a firm establishes the promotion percentage it will be costly to change. The integrity of the firm's compensation package depends upon the associates' ability to observe the promotion percentage. A firm that (implicitly) advertises one promotion percentage, but then unpredictably lowers it at the end of the tournament, will have difficulty recruiting in the future. So long as the number of promotions exceeds departures from the partnership, each promotion to partner will lead to net increases in both the number of partners and the number of associates at the firm. Because the promotion percentage is constant and the associate-to-partner ratio is constant or increasing, the firm's percentage growth rate will be constant (exponential) or increasing (faster than exponential). We emphasize this point because a firm that grows exponentially will eventually exhibit large jumps in membership quite apart from any external shocks.

The continued existence of small law firms is not inconsistent with our argument. First, there are the incipient big firms. Second, some firms have made a conscious decision to remain small. Firms that neither expand their monitoring resources through promotion (or lateral hires) nor screen and filter associates will find that their existing monitoring resources place absolute limits on the size they can achieve. Small boutique law firms often follow promotion patterns of this nature. Generally, associates remain associates throughout their tenure with the firm. Similarly, a firm that promotes associates only as partners leave will remain small. Third, the vast majority of firms probably remain small simply because they do not have surplus, shareable human capital. Some attorneys have surplus human capital they cannot share. Plaintiff's litigation firms provide an example.

Although we acknowledge the evidence that something "shocked" law firms into more rapid growth after 1970, we argue that shock theories are both underinclusive (because they fail to explain why firms grew before 1970 and why their growth after 1970 took its particular shape) and overinclusive (because they attempt to account for too large a portion of the growth).

Some have attributed the growth of large law firms to the general lawyer boom. One such argument assumes that large law firms simply have received their proportionate share of the growing number of law school graduates. Another emphasizes that, while the nation's law schools graduated almost 300 percent more lawyers in 1980 than in 1960, the most prestigious schools did not maintain that pace. As firms have recruited deeper into the classes of these schools and more heavily from the less prestigious schools, they demanded more hours and hired more graduates to compensate for lower average production.

Rapid growth often is traced to law firm mergers, which have increased for three reasons. An attempt by attorneys to diversify their risks by developing a full "portfolio" of specialties can explain increased vertical integration. But though income inequality within the legal profession decreased from 1949 to 1969—just what one would expect if lawyers were trying to diversify their portfolios of law-related income—it increased in the next decade. Moreover, the contemporaneous increase in the use of productivity-based compensation plans tended to defeat the purpose of risk diversification. Mergers often are explained as building internal referral markets and "one-stop shopping." But given that this incentive always existed, it cannot explain post-1970 mergers. Finally, law firms are sometimes described as reflecting or "mimicking" their clients. None of these stories, however, explains why law-firm growth accelerated in the early 1970s, before the wave of mergers.

Some contend that large law firms simply received their proportionate share of the growing demand for legal services. Between 1970 and 1985 aggregate demand nearly tripled. But the impressive industry-wide growth of 11 percent accounted for only 65 percent of the growth of big firms. Second, the theory neither explains accelerated growth after 1970 nor offers an account of causation. A more sophisticated variant suggests that the demand for *corporate* legal services increased. Business clients, which purchase most of their services from large firms, grew from 39 percent to 48.6 percent of total law firm receipts. But this fails to distinguish between the need for more corporate lawyers and the demand for larger law firms. Some, therefore, argue that legal matters have become more complex, requiring a greater mix of specialties, disciplines, and law-office locations. But there is little objective evidence of the changing scale and complexity of law firm work—for instance, increases in the size of work teams or complexity of work product.

A refinement of the internal-referral market story credits the rise of in-house counsel with accelerating law firm mergers. Rather than choose a law firm to marry for life, corporate counsel now chooses particular lawyers or firms for specific projects. We remain only partly convinced. Usually when a producer's market shrinks, it must cut back on the size of its operations. Furthermore, a law firm's need to fashion its own referral market might *decline* with the increased sophistication of its clients' purchasing agents.

Another version of the increased demand argument maintains that an increase in the number of important disputes within business and a breakdown in conditions that foster nonlitigious forms of dispute resolution forced businesses to change their use of law and lawyers. Handling any particular matter—both litigation and "deal-making"—may require larger numbers of lawyers because of short time lines, issues crossing specialties, and the enormous sums at stake.

While useful above, the assumption of unhindered growth is clearly unrealistic and, for our argument, unnecessary. As the firm grows, it converges upon a series of binding constraints: revenue or budget, the ability to find associates, and the ability to maintain quality control. As growth becomes so rapid that the firm can no longer generate new revenues sufficient to cover the costs of adding new attorneys, a "revenue gap" develops. An environment where clients have become more willing to shop for lawyers presents especially acute problems. As they gain additional leverage, clients will reduce any preexisting monopoly rents. As returns from economies of scale diminish, adding new attorneys changes the firm's historic cost structure, forcing the firm to adjust. The partners can either make less money or ask associates to bill more hours with no increase in compensation. Between 1972 and 1987, the receipts of the twenty largest firms quadrupled in constant dollar terms, but profits per partner increased only one percent per year in constant dollars.

A second strategy suggests that the firm attempt to reduce its growth rate by adjusting the ratio of associates to partners, the percentage of associates becoming partners, the length of time to partnership, and the number of partners leaving. Adjusting any of the first three variables also implies a change in the underlying structure of the firm—a transformation of the practice. All this seems to be happening: the percentage of associates becoming partners seems to be declining in some firms and the years to partnership lengthening. Firms now make wider use of non-equity partnerships, paralegals, "temporary" attorneys, "second-class" associates with no expectation of making partner, and permanent associates. Slowing down a firm's growth potential in this manner, however, creates difficulties in compensation, recruitment, motivation, and retention of productive young associates. Hiring fewer associates in a given year is an alternative means of slowing growth, but this strategy is likely to reduce partner income.

A third strategy calls on the firm to increase the demand for its services by competing for clients, marketing services, and moving into non-law businesses.

Exponential growth poses an additional problem: where will the firm find the ever-increasing number of associates? Firms that recruit lower-ranked students or graduates from less-prestigious law schools may anticipate a higher attrition rate among associates and thus hire more of them, increasing the associate-to-partner ratio. Firms increase lateral hiring, almost unheard of twenty years ago. Finally, firms can merge with others that have surplus labor.

The firm's capacity to maintain quality output places a third constraint on growth. As part of the solution to this monitoring problem, firms require attorneys to post a hostage upon becoming a partner by investing in the firm, thereby subjecting their capital to retaliation if problems arise. Firms may divide into functional subgroups and extend the tournament-based monitoring scheme to include junior partners, senior partners, members of the executive committee, managing partners, and the like. In short, the firm will become increasingly hierarchical and take on the characteristics of the proverbial "corporate ladder."

This is not to say that the classic "promotion-to-partnership" firm will become extinct. If it starts small enough and has good luck in obtaining clients, such a firm can have a long run. But we expect that greater experimentation and diversity in organization will characterize big-firm practice in the near future. We would like to speculate briefly about the near future.

The "Later" Big Firm. A host of slowing devices—two-tier hiring, permanent associates, paralegals, enhanced technology, and increases in time to partnership—would reduce the "promotion-to-partnership" core. The firm would maintain various levels of partnership and continually test performance.

The "Big Eight" Firm. Combining the shrinkage of the "promotion-to-partnership" core with the coverage-driven push toward greater size, more locations, and greater range of services lets us imagine giant national (or even international) firms that bear some resemblance to the "Big Eight" accounting firms in size and structure. Law firms might similarly rely on salaried employees and more bureaucratic systems of control, though conflict-of-interest problems might place an upper limit on the degree of possible concentration.

The "Interdisciplinary" Firm. The big law firm may increasingly supplement its core law practice with other services like management consulting, investment counseling, and lobbying. Some foresee that law firms will become diversified service firms deploying teams drawn from many disciplines.

"In-House" Law Departments. In some instances, corporate legal departments give businesses enhanced control over outside law firms; in other cases, these departments may displace the large law firm completely.

Boutiques. These firms cultivate their comparative advantage in selected specialties and suppress any push toward more general coverage in order to maintain their attractiveness for referral work from big firms.

"Mixed-Compensation" Firms. Some firms mix pecuniary and nonpecuniary rewards, such as child-rearing leaves, flextime, part-time work, sabbaticals, or time off for political or pro bono work.

Networks or Affiliation Groups. Firms may seek to obtain the benefits of size—visibility, economies of scale and scope, capacity to take on large matters—by linking themselves to others for the sharing of clients, information about management or practice development strategies, tactics, support services, and experts for litigation.

Subcontracting. Such strategies are facilitated by the growth of firms that supply temporary legal workers, both lawyers and paralegals. Other out-side suppliers provide firms with "litigation support services" that not only include computerized document retrieval but also can extend to "taking over case management, tracing the whereabouts of defendants and witnesses, writing briefs and research issues, providing expert witnesses, and making visual presentations for trial."

The transformation and displacement of the big law firm does not necessarily represent a danger to professionalism; indeed, it may present an opportunity for new forms of pursuing professional excellence.

A review essay of the book in which Galanter and Palay advanced these ideas* suggests alternative interpretations and empirical tests for choosing among them.

A LITTLE THEORIZING ABOUT THE BIG LAW FIRM: GALANTER, PALAY, AND THE ECONOMICS OF GROWTH[1]
Richard H. Sander and E. Douglass Williams

WHY LAW FIRMS ARE BIG: GILSON, MNOOKIN, AND NELSON

A logical place to begin an inquiry into the growth of law firms might be the identification and measurement of economies of scale in the practice of law and the study of how those economies have changed over time. So far as we know, no one has attempted to measure economies of scale in law firms, and those who consider the issue give such economies little weight in explaining law-firm growth. Robert Nelson, for example, comments that "law firms can achieve economies of scale at modest size, certainly at a more modest size than current levels."[2] Gilson and Mnookin suggest that economies of scale may be important in specific legal contexts where lawyer teams are important (e.g., merger and acquisition and large-scale litigation) but argue that, as a general matter, scale economies are modest and can be achieved through sharing arrangements that avoid consolidation.[3] All three authors agree, moreover, that economies of scale are declining over time.

---

* *Tournament of Lawyers: The Transformation of the Big Law Firm* (1991).

1. 17 *Law & Social Inquiry* 391 (1992). Reprinted with permission.

2. Robert L. Nelson, *Partners with Power: Social Transformation of the Large Law Firm* 10 (1988).

3. Ronald Gilson and Robert Mnookin, "Sharing among the Human Capitalists: An Inquiry into the Corporate Law Firm and How Partners Split Profits," 37 *Stanford Law Review* 313 (1985); see also "Coming of Age in the Corporate Law Firm: The Economics of Associate Career Patterns," 41 *Stanford Law Review* 567 (1989).

The Portfolio Theory of Gilson and Mnookin

Gilson and Mnookin emphasized the central importance of *human* capital—particular skills and capacities that enable an individual to produce more future income than other ordinary mortals. A senior law partner is a walking repository of human capital, full of accumulated expertise and native intelligence as well as specialized knowledge about the needs of particular clients and a reputation for competence and rectitude.

As with physical capital, the income-generating capacity of human capital is somewhat risky. But whereas a manufacturer may diversify its physical capital by selling a variety of products, it is very costly to diversify human capital in order to reduce the variability of return. The law firm, according to Gilson and Mnookin, solves this problem by serving as a kind of human portfolio. The bad news (for law firms) is that fixed profit-sharing agreements invite three forms of opportunistic behavior from members. First, partners may reduce their effort ("shirk"), since they only get a fraction of what they contribute to profits. Second, highly productive partners may jump to other firms ("leave") with clients in tow in order to get their full contribution to profits. And third, partners may simply threaten to leave unless they are fully compensated for their marginal contribution to profits ("grab"). Gilson and Mnookin suggest that professional and collegial norms within the law firm have historically mitigated such opportunistic behavior and allowed firms to obtain the benefits of risk sharing. As firms grow and these norms erode, however, partners become more likely to grab or leave, and their actions further erode the old norms.

Their theory has something to say about both the optimal scale of law firms and a mechanism for growth. First, the need to diversify a firm by including partners across several specialties, combined with certain modest economies of scale within some specialties, could account for a firm of substantial size. On the other hand, the erosion of professional norms and profit sharing and the increase of competitive pressures create centrifugal pressures on the firm, making partners more likely to leave and partnerships more likely to dissolve. Moreover, these centrifugal pressures seem likely to intensify as firms get bigger. Not only are norms of sharing harder to preserve in a large group, but the profit allocation decisions are more likely to be made by a smaller fraction of the partners.

While it seems plausible that diversification to reduce risk has played a role in firm development, it seems to us that such motives could not have played the leading role. If risk-avoiding incentives drive the emergence of big firms, they should also ultimately limit their growth. Indeed, their analysis suggests to us that average firm size should have *decreased* in the 1980s. Nor does their theory account for continuing diversity of firm size.

Nelson on Economies of Scope

Robert Nelson offers a more straightforward account of the essence of law firms and big-firm growth. He emphasizes that lawyers who represent large business firms often have durable, long-lasting relationships with their clients. This is partly because the firms have large, ongoing legal needs; but it also reflects the fact that both the lawyer and the client have an investment in the relationship. Over time, the lawyer accumulates a great deal of specific knowledge, which allows the lawyer to assess problems with a broad perspective on the firm and to solve those problems more efficiently. Thus, any long-standing lawyer–client relationship creates "sunk costs" on both sides.

These sunk costs may induce the lawyer to join efforts with other lawyers. Suppose an established client encounters a legal problem outside her lawyer's area of expertise. The client might still rely on the lawyer's trustworthiness, discretion, and knowledge of the firm (that is, his firm-specific human capital) to find and supervise a second lawyer with the requisite specialized knowledge. The first attorney may feel some ambivalence, however. The conscientious lawyer naturally wants to make sure that the client's new problem is handled well, but the lawyer may also be concerned about a new lawyer intruding on and weakening his own relationship with the client. A solution that may well satisfy both parties is for the lawyer to associate with a colleague.

On a large scale, this type of story creates what economists call "economies of scope." A diversified firm derives the advantage of being able to serve a broad array of a particular client's needs. The law firm becomes something of a "brand name." The benefits from these economies of scope provide, we think, a more compelling reason for large firms than mere diversification away from risk. But, as Nelson notes, economies of scope are no more successful in explaining the continuing growth of law firms. Indeed, Nelson suggests that these economies might be eroding over time. As more corporate clients secure in-house counsel and legal staffs, the brokering role formerly played by a big-firm partner is taken over by the corporation's lead counsel.

WHY FIRMS KEEP GROWING: GALANTER, PALAY, AND NELSON AGAIN

Galanter and Palay seek to uncover economic forces, operating within the firm, which would explain not only why firms are big, but why growth has been so consistent and continuous over the past 60 years. The promotion-to-partnership tournament is a straightforward mechanism that accounts for bigness and for rapid growth. But we are struck by two missing subplots in the story. First, what is *paying* for all this growth? Second, where is the "visible hand" of management? The revenue of individual large firms can only grow if the number of competing firms is shrinking or the demand for big-firm services is growing. Galanter and Palay implicitly reject the notion that the number of firms has declined. Their theory also implies that at some point in the past, partners made a decision to permanently fix the growth rate of the firm. But virtually every firm seems deeply engaged in debates about growth: whether to open a new branch office, close an existing one, consider a merger, or hire lateral associates.

For Nelson, the key to law-firm growth is twofold: The demand for corporate legal services has increased dramatically, and existing big firms have generally managed to capture that growth. Taking account of external demand and internal preferences for growth poses a dilemma for the tournament theory: A law firm *must* grow faster and faster, Galanter and Palay seem to say, unless it does not want to or cannot. We think the solution lies in a more modest story. Law firms that

embarked on a path of growth between 1920 and 1940 widely adopted associate tournaments as a way of binding the interests of associates to the interests of the firm. Once adopted, the tournament tended to lock the firms into fairly rigid, geometric patterns of growth, where the rate of expansion could only increase, never decrease. This expansion generally accelerated after 1970, when the demand for legal services increased, and is only now confronting its first crisis, as law firms have individually and collectively become so vast that they have finally outrun the growth of demand. The next question is whether their empirical tests successfully distinguish their model from others.

THE EMPIRICAL CASE FOR THE TOURNAMENT

Galanter and Palay argue that one of the central attractions of the tournament theory is its ability to account for geometric growth. The difficulty is that almost *any* theory of growth is a theory of geometric growth. The reason is simple: Growth happens one moment at a time, and always occurs in reference to the preceding moment. The other important empirical claim they make is that the rate of growth is essentially fixed by the tournament. The only external influence came in the late 1960s and early 1970s, when a "demand shock" boosted the need for legal services. A variety of evidence, however, suggests that law firm growth is neither universal nor fixed. Their own evidence indicates that, for some firms, the rate of growth did not rise after 1970 but *fell*.

Second, Galanter and Palay are working with a biased sample. The best way to test their theory is to examine a sample of firms that instituted the tournament in the 1920s or 1930s and track their subsequent history. Examining only the largest firms at the end of the story, in 1986, guarantees that one will only look at those firms whose growth is likely to fit the tournament story. This is not a trivial point. A table in Nelson's book, of the ten largest Chicago firms at different points over the past half-century, shows how individualized and erratic growth patterns were. The largest Chicago firm in 1935, Winston & Strawn, has grown exponentially over the past half-century but at an accelerating rather than constant rate. Kirkland & Ellis, in contrast, grew an average of 1.8 percent per year from 1935 to 1952, doubled its growth rate to 3.7 percent from 1952 to 1962, slowed down to 2.8 percent annual growth for the rest of the 1960s, and then accelerated again. Even more strikingly, four of the ten largest firms in 1935 simply disappeared from the ranks of large firms by the 1970s.

Third, the authors' own empirical tests do not produce terribly convincing results. Any trend that has lots of growth built into it will tend to correlate very closely with the passage of time. The performance of the geometric model is mediocre. On average, their predicted 1988 firm sizes missed the actual size by 68 lawyers, or 29 percent. Even when they improve their predictions by adding a kink in the geometric curve denoting faster growth from 1970, they still miss by an average of 30 lawyers, or 13 percent, and this modification is data-driven rather than theoretically derived.

Galanter and Palay measure the partnership promotion rate by calculating the ratio of each year's increase in a firm's partners to each year's total number of associates. This gives a very imprecise measure. The numerator may include new partners brought in from outside and is not adjusted for retirements or other partner departures; the denominator includes all associates, rather than just those who were eligible for promotion. A good test also should not focus on year-to-year fluctuations. A more satisfying test of the tournament theory would be an examination of how stationary (i.e., how free of drift) the promotion rate remained at individual firms over time. Consider an alternate story, which we will call a "theory of adaptive growth." Firms are constantly guessing as to the underlying trend of demand. Their growth curve over the past 60 years, then, would look like a ship trying to follow a line with a rather poor compass—they would zig north of the line, then zag south of the line. If promotion rates at large firms tend to show drift over time, that would support a theory of adaptive growth; if promotion rates show no drift, that would support a theory of fixed growth.

We examined seven firms that the authors used as exemplars of geometric growth and found three patterns that jar with the tournament. First, the year-to-year promotion rates of all the firms vary dramatically. Second, in two firms there is a statistically significant upward trend in promotion rates. Third, in four firms the five-year floating averages showed distinct cycles. This strongly suggests that promotion rates commonly drift and supports the countertheory described above.

Yet it still seems plausible that some sort of tournament plays a role in growth. If the demand for corporate legal services jumps, existing corporate law firms have an inside edge on capturing that demand. The easiest way to do so is to hire associates. And once a law firm has a large pool of talented associates, it has incentives to create a stable promotion rate. This serves other functions besides providing work incentives and mitigating opportunism by associates. It helps control lobbying by partners for the promotion of associates who have been loyal or reliable but may not be of sufficient quality. It also discourages an excessively short-term perspective on partner profits, which are lowered by promotions. If the tournament is *driving* growth, we should expect frequent occasions when firm growth follows a dip in partnership earnings, revealing that the firm is so wedded to the tournament that it simply cannot help itself. In contrast, if declines in partner income are followed by contractions in promotions to partnership or less associate hiring, that suggests that the tournament is instrumental and at the service of partners.

DISCUSSION QUESTIONS

1. Which of these theories best explains the growth patterns of large firms? Can you advance others? What is the difference between economies of scale and scope? How is portfolio theory relevant? theories of human capital? Can these theories explain shrinkage as well as growth? Nearly half the 250 largest firms contracted between 1992 and 1993.[4] An increasing number of large firms have dissolved in recent years, notably Herrick & Smith (1986), Finley, Kumble (1987), Wyman Bautzer (1991), Lord, Day & Lord, New York's "oldest" law firm (1994), Shea & Gould (1995), and Mudge Rose—Nixon's

---

4. *New York Times* C2 (9.20.93).

firm (1995).⁵ What explains these failures?

Do any of these authors offer an empirical index of human capital that is independent of the "rents" its owners enjoy? If not, the theory risks tautology. Can you devise such an index? Is the theory consistent with the increasingly common practice of requiring lateral hires—especially partners, but also associates—to bring clients in tow: an estimated $500,000 to $750,000 in billings to join a firm of 50–100 lawyers, $1 to $1.5 million for a larger firm?⁶

It has long been known that a law firm bills associates at roughly three times the hourly rate it pays them.⁷ (For instance, 2,000 billable hours at $125 per hour produces $275,000.) Another third represents overhead; the remaining third engorges the extraordinary incomes large-firm partners enjoy. Is this exploitation of associates? If so, why are partners able to appropriate this surplus? What would have to change to allow associates to retain it? Would you favor such changes? To the extent that this depends on "running up the meter," it may be changed by client refusal to pay by the hour and insistence on fixed fees, capped fees, and value-based fees.⁸

2. Why do firms deny lawyers full responsibility for clients and firm governance until they are in their late thirties or early forties? How do firms select for partnership?

3. Until very recently, large firms were unique to the common-law world and much larger in the United States than anywhere else. Can these theories explain the difference between the United States, Germany, and Japan, for instance? What else might explain it? Corporations in civil-law countries tend to have large in-house staffs (and many legally trained executives). What are the relative advantages and disadvantages of these two very different structures for delivering legal services to business?

4. How do the productive units in law differ from those in other professions and service occupations (and within each), e.g., medicine, accounting, banking, architecture, education, religion?

5. What predictions would you make about the future of the large firm:

A. respective roles of firms and corporate counsel?

B. competition among firms and its consequences? between lawyers and other advisers?

C. size: Is there an upper limit? Could law become as concentrated as accounting? (The 100 largest firms earned $14.3 billion in fiscal 1992.)⁹ Will the trend toward transnational practice continue? Will the proportion of lawyers practicing in large firms continue to increase?

D. specialization within and between firms? the future of the boutique firm?

E. hierarchy: the proliferation of strata, the growing distance between them, selection for each and mobility across them, intensification of subordination and exploitation and the emergence of new forms of resistance?

F. structural convergence between firms and their corporate clients; for instance, might firms adopt the corporate form, selling equity shares? (The SEC has allowed accounting firms to do so.)¹⁰

If you are thinking of working for a large firm, what characteristics do you find attractive? unattractive? How could the latter be changed? Anderson, Russell, Kill & Olick grew from 40 lawyers in 1984 to 120 in 1988 and 240 by 1995 on the principle that every lawyer was a partner and they divided profits by discussion.¹¹ For comparisons of large firms, see Sheila Malkani and Michael Walsh, *The Insider's Guide to Law Firms* (1993).

SUGGESTED READING

The first empirical study of large firms—typical postwar functionalist apologetics—was Erwin Smigel, *The Wall Street Lawyer* (1964). There are numerous house histories, e.g., Walter Earle and Charles Perlin, *Shearman & Sterling 1873–1973*

5. *New York Times* 17 (1.29.94), A1 (2.7.94), §1 p33 (10.2.94), B17 (2.17.95), §1 p12 (10.1.95).

6. *New York Times* §3 p11 (8.25.96).

7. E.g., A. Liebowitz and R. Tollison, "Earning and Learning in Law Firms," 7 *Journal of Legal Studies* 65 (1978).

8. *New York Times* §3 p5 (7.4.93), A1 (10.22.93).

9. *New York Times* B10 (7.9.93).

10. *New York Times* C1 (6.14.90).

11. *New York Times* (9.30.88), B17 (2.17.95).

(1973); *Simpson, Thatcher & Bartlett, The First One Hundred Years, 1884–1984* (1984); Sullivan & Cromwell, *Lamplighters: The Sullivan & Cromwell Lawyers April 2, 1879 to April 2, 1979* (1981); Robert A. Swaine, *The Cravath Firm and Its Predecessors, 1819–1947* (2 vols.) (1946); Virginia Kays Veenswijk, *Coudert Brothers: A Legacy in Law: The History of America's First International Law Firm 1853–1993* (1994). Unfortunately, there are few objective empirical studies: Robert Nelson (cited above and quoted below); John Flood, "Anatomy of Lawyering: An Ethnography of a Corporate Law Firm" (Ph.D. dissertation, sociology, Northwestern University, 1987); Elizabeth Chambliss, "New Partners with Power? Organizational Determinants of Law Firm Integration" (Ph.D. dissertation, sociology, University of Wisconsin, 1992). Two law review special issues dissect large firms, 37 *Stanford Law Review* 271–659 (1985); 64 *Indiana Law Journal* 423–600 (1988–89). There is equally little good empirical research on house counsel, e.g., C. S. Maddock, *Corporate Legal Departments* (1950); J. D. Donnell, *Corporate Counsel* (1970); Robert E. Rosen, "Lawyers in Corporate Decision-Making" (Ph.D. dissertation, sociology, University of California, Berkeley); Jeffrey S. Slovak, "Working for Corporate Actors: Social Change and Elite Attorneys in Chicago," 1979 *American Bar Foundation Research Journal* 465; "Giving and Getting Respect: Prestige and Stratification in a Legal Elite," 1980 *American Bar Foundation Research Journal* 31; "Influence and Issues in the Legal Community," The Role of a Legal Elite," 1981 *American Bar Foundation Research Journal* 141.

For additional economic analyses of law-firm growth, including other countries, see Jack Carr and Frank Mathewson, "The Economics of Law Firms: A Study in the Legal Organization of the Firm," 33 *Journal of Law and Economics* 307 (1990); R. G. Lee, "From Profession to Business: The Rise and Rise of the City Law Firm," 18 *Journal of Law and Society* 31 (1992) (England); Ronald J. Daniels, "Growing pains: The Why and How of Law Firm Expansion," 43 *University of Toronto Law Journal* 147 (1993) (Canada);

Avrom Sherr, "Of Super Heros and Slaves: Images and Work of the Legal Profession," 48 *Current Legal Problems* 327 (1995) (England).

Muckraking accounts include Martin Mayer, *The Lawyers* (1966); James C. Goulden, *The Superlawyers: The Small and Powerful World of the Great Washington Law Firms* (1972); Paul Hoffman, *Lions in the Street: The Inside Story of the Great Wall Street Law Firms* (1973); Mark J. Green, *The Other Government: The Unseen Power of Washington Lawyers* (1975); Ralph Nader and Mark Green (eds.), *Verdicts on Lawyers* (1976); James B. Stewart, *The Partners: Inside America's Most Powerful Law Firms* (1983); Mark Stevens, *Power of Attorney: The Rise of the Giant Law Firms* (1987); Nancy Lisagor and Frank Lipsius, *A Law Unto Itself: The Untold Story of the Law Firm Sullivan & Cromwell* (1988); Steven J. Kumble and Kevin J. Lahart, *Conduct Unbecoming: The Rise and Ruin of Finley, Kumble* (1990); Kim Eisler, *Shark Tank: Greed, Politics, and the Collapse of Finley, Kumble* (1990); Lincoln Caplan, *Skadden: Power, Money, and the Rise of a Legal Empire* (1993). Gossip, comparison, and law-firm profiles can be found in the "new" legal journalism, such as *National Law Journal, American Lawyer,* and *Legal Times.*

On the internationalization of law practice, see David M. Trubek, Yves Dezalay, Ruth Buchanan, and John R. Davis, "Global Restructuring and the Law: Studies of the Internationalization of Legal Fields and the Creation of Transnational Arenas," 44 *Case Western Reserve Law Review* 407 (1994); Richard L. Abel, "Transnational Law Practice," Id. 737; Yves Dezalay, "The *Big Bang* and the Law: The Internationalization and Restructuration of the Legal Field," 7 *Theory, Culture & Society* 279 (1990); "Territorial Battles and Tribal Disputes," 54 *Modern Law Review* 792 (1991); Yves Dezalay and David Sugarman (eds.), *Professional Competition and Professional Power: Lawyers, Accountants, and the Social Construction of Markets* (1995); Alan Tyrell and Zahd Yaqub (eds.), *The Legal Profession in the New Europe: A Handbook for Practitioners* (1993). You can follow the evolution of these firms in the *International Financial Law Review.*

Robert Nelson deals not only with the growth of law firms but also with their ethical environment and how this is affected by lawyer–client relations.

IDEOLOGY, PRACTICE, AND
PROFESSIONAL AUTONOMY:
SOCIAL VALUES AND CLIENT
RELATIONSHIPS IN
THE LARGE LAW FIRM[1]

Robert L. Nelson

THE LAWYER–CLIENT RELATIONSHIP

Time Devoted to Principal Client

I begin the analysis of lawyer–client relationships by examining the degree to which individual lawyers in large law firms concentrate their work on one client. These data address Smigel's argument that the diversification of law firm client bases "frees" individual lawyers from dependence on particular clients. I asked the sample 224 lawyers in four Chicago firms, stratified by seniority, what proportion of their work time during the last year was spent on the client they worked for the most. Table 1 reports the mean response by firm and field of practice. Lawyers spend a substantial proportion of their

time on the client for whom they work the most, averaging more than one-third in the sample as a whole, and almost 50 percent in the corporate field. This pattern tends to contradict Smigel's assumption. The highest concentrations are found in Becker, where lawyers spend close to half their time for one client. This pattern reflects the fact that Becker represents a number of major institutional clients and is organized around them. Lawyers working in the two broad fields most closely associated with Becker's institutional clients (the corporate area and other office fields) spend an average of almost 60 percent of their time (58.32 percent and 56.57 percent, respectively) on their principal client. In the other three firms, lawyers in the other office fields represent mostly smaller clients and individuals; they spend, on average, less than a quarter of their time on any one client.

ROLE PERCEPTIONS AND REPORTS
OF LAWYER–CLIENT CONFLICT

I asked three questions about the relationships of lawyers to clients. First, I sought to measure the respondent's perception of the breadth of the lawyer's role. A commonly mentioned concern is that specialization in large firms has narrowed the lawyer's view of her normative role, that she may no longer see it as her responsibility to gain an

---

1. 37 *Stanford Law Review* 503 (1985). Reprinted with permission.

TABLE I

Mean Percentage of Time Spent on Client for Which Lawyers Worked the Most in the Last Year by Field of Practice and Firm

Field	Firm				
	AARON	BECKER	CURRAN	DUNCAN	TOTAL
LITIGATION	47.37	42.04	32.64	35.69	38.58
(N)	(19)	(27)	(36)	(16)	(98)
CORPORATE	31.33	58.32	28.75	39.80	47.98
(N)	(6)	(25)	(4)	(10)	(45)
FINANCE	23.75	23.44	25.00	17.00	19.73
(N)	(4)	(9)	(2)	(22)	(37)
OTHER OFFICE FIELDS	25.38	56.57	18.33	21.32	27.82
(N)	(8)	(7)	(6)	(19)	(40)
TOTAL	38.58	47.98	30.21	26.09	35.38
(N)	(37)	(68)	(48)	(67)	(220)

TABLE 2

*The Opportunity to Give Nonlegal Advice
by Partnership Status, Field, and Reasons Affecting
Such Opportunities*

A. Percent Reporting Opportunity to Give Nonlegal Advice by Partnership Status and Field of Practice (Number of Cases in Parentheses)

Field *	*Partnership Status* †		
	ASSOCIATES	PARTNERS	TOTAL
LITIGATION	53 (64)	83 (36)	64 (100)
CORPORATE	95 (19)	85 (27)	89 (46)
FINANCE	65 (17)	85 (24)	88 (41)
OTHER OFFICE	76 (17)	96 (20)	76 (37)
TOTAL	65 (117)	87 (107)	75 (224)

* P < .05
† P < .01

B. How Opportunity for Giving Nonlegal Advice Arises

Responses	NUMBER OF RESPONSES	PERCENTAGE OF RESPONSES	PERCENTAGE OF CASES
CLIENT ASKS	24	11.5	14.2
LAWYERS' ROLE	10	4.8	5.9
FIELD REQUIRES IT	42	20.1	24.9
BUSINESS DECISIONS	74	35.4	43.8
PERSONAL INVESTMENT DECISIONS	19	9.1	11.2
PERSONAL ADVICE	33	15.8	19.5
PUBLIC RELATIONS CONCERNS	4	1.9	2.4
MISSING/DK	3	1.4	1.8
TOTAL	209	100.0	123.7

N = 166; 2 cases were missing information.

C. Reasons for No Opportunity to Give Nonlegal Advice

Responses	NUMBER OF RESPONSES	PERCENTAGE OF RESPONSES	PERCENTAGE OF CASES
FIELD TOO TECHNICAL	9	21.4	22.5
TOO LATE TO GIVE ADVICE	7	16.7	17.5
NO CLIENT CONTACT	20	47.6	50.0
NOT LAWYER RESPONSIBILITY	6	14.3	15.0
TOTAL	42	100.0	105.0

N = 40; 16 cases were missing information.

overview of her client's affairs or to give clients more than technical legal advice. A second and related question dealt with lawyers' opportunities to give nonlegal advice, how the opportunities arose, and whether the opportunities were accepted when presented. The opportunity for giving nonlegal advice is a useful measure of how often the division of labor in large firms allows holistic lawyer–client interactions that go beyond technical legal advice. And third, I asked whether the lawyers had "ever refused an assignment or potential work because it was contrary to your personal values." This construction was intended to include matters that violated the code of professional ethics, as well as other values not codified.

Despite specialization and growth in firms, large-firm lawyers adhere to a broad conception of their role vis-à-vis clients (see table 2). More than three-quarters of the sample (76 percent) responded that it was appropriate to act as the conscience of a client when the opportunity presented itself—a consensus of opinion that did not vary by age, firm, or field of practice. Virtually the same majority (75 percent) responded that they had the opportunity to give nonlegal advice to clients, but as panel A of table 2 indicates, there are significant differences by field and partnership status. Litigation presents practitioners with

fewer opportunities for giving nonlegal advice. As panel C of table 2 suggests, the reason is that litigation associates have little contact with clients, and, by the time a case is in litigation, it is too late to give nonlegal advice.

By far the leading reason for giving nonlegal advice (mentioned by 43.8 percent of respondents) is that a business decision is involved. The majority of other responses have a pragmatic ring as well: that the client asked for advice (14.2 percent), that the field of law required it as part of the practice (24.9 percent), that matters required personal investment decisions (11.2 percent), or

TABLE 3

*Refusals of Assignments
by Circumstances of Refusal and Reasons
for No Refusals*

A. Percent Having Refused an Assignment or Potential Work as Contrary to Their Personal Values.

	N	PERCENTAGE
HAVE REFUSED	36	16.22
NEVER HAVE REFUSED	186	83.78
TOTAL	222	100.00

2 cases were missing information. 12 cases reported 2 refusals.

B. Percent Distribution of Circumstances of Refusals

	N	PERCENTAGE
AGAINST PERSONAL VALUES	22	47.83
VIOLATIONS OF ETHICAL CODE	23	50.00
IGNORED LAWYER'S ADVICE	1	2.17
TOTAL	46	100.00

Unit of analysis is refusal. Information on 2 refusals is missing.

REASON AGAINST PERSONAL VALUES	N
Did Not Like Client or Position	10
Would Not Defend Race Discrimination	2
Would Not Defend Age Discrimination	1
Would Not Defend Organized Crime	1
Civil Rights Case	2
Would Not Defend Pollution	2
Involved Company Participating in Boycott of Israel	1
Would Not Represent Management Against Labor	1
Would Not Defend Violent Crime	1
Would Not Defend Redlining	1
TOTAL	22

❦

REASON VIOLATING ETHICAL CODE	N
Client Was Committing a Crime	10
Conflict of Interest	5
Client Was Not Being Honest	4
Client Harassing Others Through Law	2
Client Refused to Produce Documents	1
Convinced Client Not to Proceed for Ethical Reasons	1
TOTAL	23

C. Percent Distribution of Reasons For No Refusals

	N	PERCENTAGE
No Conflicts With Personal Values	158	91.9
Personal Values Should Not Dictate	14	8.1
TOTAL	172	100.0

14 cases were missing information.

that the client needed personal advice (19.5 percent). Very few of the responses suggest broader moral or social concerns. Only 2.4 percent of the respondents mentioned giving advice to address "public relations concerns," the category that would seem to come the closest to concern for the public interest. These responses make clear that lawyers and clients typically come together on business, investment, or fairly narrow legal problems, and it is on those kinds of questions that lawyers and clients most often engage in open discussion. Again, a normative model is inappropriate for the vast majority of lawyer–client interactions. When lawyers advise clients in a practical vein, questions of the greater good seldom arise.

While lawyers may not often be asked to offer advice concerning the commonweal, how often do they have conflicts with clients over the propriety or morality of client positions? Respondents were asked, "Have you ever refused an assignment or potential work because it was contrary to your personal values?" If they answered "yes," they were asked "under what circumstances?" If they answered "no," they were asked whether it was because "your work has never required you to take a position contrary to personal values or because you do not believe personal values should dictate what work a lawyer will do?" Table 3 shows the breakdown of responses.

Only 16.22 percent of the sample ever refused an assignment or potential work, and one-third of these 36 respondents had done so twice. As shown in table 3B, half the coded refusals were in response to violations of professional ethics, such as ongoing criminal conduct by clients, conflicts of interest, and the use of the law to harass other parties. To assist clients in these endeavors would have violated professional ethics and clearly went beyond offending personal values. Roughly half the other refusals implicated personal values, with several respondents refusing to defend clients against certain types of accusations. Reflecting their seniority, partners were more than twice as likely as associates (28 percent to 11 percent) to have refused an assignment. Of those respondents who had never refused an assignment, 91.9 percent had never been confronted with an assignment contrary to their personal values. Only 8.1 percent of the subset who never refused said that personal values should not dictate what a lawyer does. Hence, three-quarters of the respondents for whom I have complete data have never been faced with a conflict between their personal values and the request of a client.

DISCUSSION QUESTIONS

1. Why do large-firm lawyers so rarely perceive ethical questions concerning whom they represent or what they do for those clients? Does the lay public share their moral stance? Do rules of professional ethics address such issues?

2. Sociologist Charles Derber has suggested a distinction between two kinds of proletarianiza-tion.[2] Technical proletarianization is the kind of deskilling with which we are familiar, subordinating the worker to *means* chosen by another through progressive division of labor, substitution of computers, etc. Ideological proletarianization subordinates the worker to *ends* chosen by another. Why do lawyers seem oblivious, or indifferent, to the latter, while strongly, and successfully, resisting the former? Is this true of other professions and occupations?

SUGGESTED READING

The legal realists and New Dealers offered similar criticisms half a century earlier, e.g., A. A. Berle, "Modern Legal Profession," 9 *Encyclopedia of the Social Sciences* 340 (1933); Karl Llewellyn, "The Bar Specializes—With What Results?" 167 *The Annals* 177 (1933); "The Bar's Troubles, and Poultices—and Cures?" 5 *Law & Contemporary Problems* 104 (1938); Ferdinand Lundberg, "The Law Factories: Brains of the Status Quo," 179 *Harper's Magazine* 180 (1939); Harlan Fiske Stone, "The Public Influence of the Bar," 48 *Harvard Law Review* 1 (1934). Stone's words were echoed by a successor on the Supreme Court, William J. Brennan, "The Responsibilities of the Legal Profession," in A. E. Sutherland (ed.), *The Path of the Law from 1967* (1968); see also Jethro Lieberman, *Crisis at the Bar: Lawyers' Unethical Ethics and What To Do About It* (1978). Eve Spangler looks more generally at the tension between professionalism and employment in *Lawyers for Hire: Professionals as Salaried Employees* (1986).

---

2. Charles Derber, *Professionals as Workers: Mental Labor in Advanced Capitalism* (1982).

Chapter Six

THE EXPERIENCE OF LAW SCHOOL

Almost all students find law school overwhelming. Their self-perpetuating mythology—affirmed and reproduced in novels and television series like Scott Turow's One L *and John Jay Osborn's* Paper Chase *—analogizes the experience, hyperbolically, to Marine boot camp or the brainwashing of American POWs in North Korea. Students complain that it is intensely boring, makes impossible time demands, requires endless memorization, dehumanizes and infantilizes, undermines moral intuitions, and conservatizes politically. Robert Stover, who taught sociology at the University of Colorado while studying law at the University of Denver, used participant observation, interviews, and survey research to test these myths.*

MAKING IT AND BREAKING IT: THE FATE OF PUBLIC INTEREST COMMITMENT IN LAW SCHOOL[1]

Robert V. Stover

SINGING THE BLUES: EROSION OF PUBLIC INTEREST PREFERENCES

IT was finals week of the first quarter. I sat in the library, my feet propped up on the table, a well-used spiral notebook in my hands, memorizing the law of property. I'd been there all day, and my level of restlessness increased with each arcane rule of law my mind absorbed. As the afternoon passed, the frequency of my trips to the water fountain and rest room increased geometrically. Around four o'clock, I once again pushed back my chair, stood up, and walked out of the library into the hall. Moving as slowly as possible, I bypassed the second-floor men's room and descended the stairs.

As I pushed open the door to the first-floor restroom, I was greeted by a blues melody. Inside one of the stalls, someone was playing the har-

monica and singing, "I got the law school blues, ya dooba, wabba, doo—and I bet you got 'em too." A buoyant feeling of relief swept over me as I laughed for the first time that day. Someone's creative impulse, humor, and sense of proportionality had survived finals week! By the second verse, I recognized the voice. It was Nelson Fixx, a fellow first-year student, one of the nine with whom I was conducting in-depth interviews for my research.

I told Nelson later that listening to him sing the blues in the men's room was the high point of the first quarter of law school for me. Nelson himself was one of the high points of our class, in my opinion. Before starting law school, he'd taught kindergarten, worked as a carpenter, sold automobiles, and spent four years with a social service agency organizing the inner-city poor. He was a conscientious objector during the Vietnam War and had participated actively in the presidential campaigns of liberals George McGovern and Fred Harris. During our first quarter of law school, he organized an effort to get every first-year student to sign a sympathy card for a professor whose wife had died. He was continually collecting contributions from friends to buy birthday presents for other friends. He wore big floppy hats to parties and had a dog named Cassidy that sang when Nelson played the harmonica.

Nelson started law school planning to practice public interest law. In answering my first questionnaire, he described the job he'd most like upon graduating as employment by "an environmental planning commission for a region of Colorado—preferably a small, freewheeling team making legislative recommendations." A liberal, pro-environmental orientation was evident from his answers to other questions as well. The job from a list of twenty that he marked as most preferable was "attorney for a 'public interest lobby group' for which you did litigation, lobbying, investigative research, political organizing,

1. Evanston: University of Illinois Press, 1989. Reprinted with permission.

and public relations." His second choice was "attorney for a nonprofit 'public interest' law center that specializes in environmental and consumer law."

When I interviewed Nelson at the end of the first quarter, he told me, "I want to be able to work at something that I can feel good about on the weekends at home, so I feel that I'm using what I know in some constructive way for the greater good—if there is such a thing.... I don't want to work for corporate interests.... I don't want to work for interests that I see have given us the pollution and the Disneylands of the world—the more and more plastic that will last beyond us as many generations as we can see into the future."

But even then, in his typically honest and introspective fashion, Nelson expressed doubts about that vision. He openly volunteered the possibility that he might change his career aspirations, noting that age seems to make people more conservative and that legal education seems to corrode what once had been clear-cut moral certainties. "Sometimes, I wonder," he said. "The more law school I have, the more I wonder."

By the time he graduated, Nelson had changed his vision of the ideal first job and was seeking employment as a deputy district attorney or as a clerk for a federal judge. After passing the bar exam, he took a prestigious position as a clerk for a judge on the U.S. Court of Appeals.

Changes in Job Preferences During Law School

The shifts in preference were almost entirely in one direction. Of the 38 students expressing at least an ambiguous desire for public interest practice during the first quarter of law school, 21 shifted away. But of the students initially not expressing such a preference, only two shifted toward public interest law during their law school career.

The second method of measuring the students' desire for public interest practice used twenty job descriptions. During their first quarter of law school, 33 percent of those responding chose one of the seven public interest jobs; but by their final quarter of law school, only 16 percent chose one of the seven jobs. The questionnaire also asked students to rate each of the 20 jobs on a ten-point scale in terms of desirability as a first

job after graduation. At the beginning of the students' law school careers, three of the five most popular jobs were in public interest practice, and three of the five least popular jobs were with business-oriented private firms. By the students' final quarter of law school, only one public interest job was among the five most popular. On the other hand, "attorney for a medium-sized law firm that specializes in business and corporate law" advanced from sixteenth to third in the ratings. And "attorney for a large firm that specializes in corporate law" moved from 20th position to tenth. The number of high ratings dropped for every public interest job on the list. This drop was sharpest for jobs with a public interest law center and with a public interest lobbying group.

Values and Expectations: A First Step in Explaining Change in Job Preferences

As an undergraduate, Allison Smith had majored in social work, answered mail for the American Civil Liberties Union, served as a volunteer probation counselor for juveniles, and canvassed for liberal candidates for political office. In addition, she spent a summer working for an American Indian Center. As a law student, she participated in a Denver Bar Association program providing legal services for the poor.

Allison began law school hoping for a career serving what she described as "human/humane interests." Jobs through which she thought she might accomplish this goal included work as a public defender, American Civil Liberties Union staff attorney, or private attorney with a speciality in American Indian law. The job she considered most preferable from my list of 20 was "attorney for an organization working to protect the rights of racial minority groups, such as the Native American Rights Fund or the NAACP."

Allison's desire to practice law in the public interest hardly wavered during her years in law school. She steadily maintained her desire to work for the disadvantaged and sharpened her initial interest in Indian law. During her final year of law school she used personal contacts and the Martindale-Hubbell directory of lawyers to seek out potential employers of the type she desired. Her persistence paid off with a job clerking for the judge of a tribal court while she studied for the bar exam. After being admitted to the bar, she established a solo practice specializing in Indian law, with the tribal judge and the tribe providing her with enough work to stay afloat economically.

A useful way to understand Allison's sustained commitment to public interest law is to focus on the continuity of her values and expectations. I measured *values* using a list of 21 job attributes, including such items as "earn a high starting salary," "help persons or groups with whom you identify or sympathize," "challenge your ability," and "control your own work schedule." The stability of Allison's values over time is reflected by the fact that the attributes included in her top five did not change between her first quarter in law school and her last. Those five (in rank order from the second questionnaire) were "live in the right geographical locale," "help persons or groups with whom you sympathize," "work for desired social and political goals," "have time to satisfy off-the-job interests," and "earn at least a moderate starting salary."

In contrast to Allison, consider the case of Barbara Phillips. Like Allison, Barbara started law school planning to practice public interest law. In answering my first questionnaire, she described her ideal first job out of law school by saying that she "would like to be a partner in a small group of feminist women lawyers, using our skills and resources for the advancement of women." Her preferred job on my list of 20 was "attorney for a 'public interest lobby group' for which you did litigation, lobbying, investigative research, political organizing, and public relations." By her final quarter of law school, Barbara's responses to both my open-ended and closed-ended questions indicated that she wanted to work in the corporate department of a large law firm.

At the beginning of her law school career, Barbara's values were in many respects similar to Allison's. The five job attributes Barbara rated most highly on the first questionnaire were "help persons or groups with whom you identify or sympathize," "have time to satisfy off-the-job interests," "work for desired social and political goals," "live in the right geographical locale," and "work in a congenial interpersonal atmosphere." But Barbara's values changed in an important

respect during her years in law school. Three of her top five job attributes remained the same, but "help persons and groups with whom you sympathize" and "work for desired social and political goals" fell from the top five to be replaced by "challenge your ability" and "control your own work and work schedule."

What appears to have happened to Barbara during law school is that she found great satisfaction in conquering the intellectual challenges posed by complex legal problems. Over time, she came to value that intellectual challenge more than the chance to work for social and political goals or to help persons or groups with whom she sympathized. Interestingly, Barbara's political ideology changed hardly at all during law school; her answers to another series of questions indicated that she retained the same strong left-wing views with which she began. Thus, although her views on political issues did not change, her desire to use her position as an attorney to advance her political beliefs changed markedly. By the fall of her second year, this transformation had progressed to the point that Barbara could say, "I don't see being an attorney [as] being an expression of my political beliefs. It's [just] something I'll be good at."

Accompanying this shift in Barbara's values was a shift in her expectations. When she took the basic class in corporate law, she was surprised to find that it was her favorite course. She had imagined that corporate law would be boring but found that, more than any other area of law, it provided her the sort of tough intellectual challenge that she increasingly appreciated. Her expectations concerning the likelihood that employment by a large corporate firm would fulfill some of her most important values shifted accordingly. As Barbara explained:

> I took it [Corporations] because it's on the bar [exam], and I found that I really like the area of law. I find it very challenging, very intellectually challenging. I thought for a long time I wanted to do domestic relations, and it's a good area to go into to help people and all that, but it's basically boring.... you're basically either doing adoptions or doing divorces.... I'm not sure I really want to do that. I really think I'd get a lot of satisfaction out of it but not intellectual satisfaction—not that kind of really brain-teasing challenge. And you find that in corporate commer-

cial practice. That stuff is hard! I mean you're talking about securities work that is really hard to do!

Thus, just as Allison's continuing commitment to public interest practice can be explained by her relatively stable values and expectations, Barbara's shift away from public interest practice can be explained by her changing values and expectations.

Shifts in Values and Expectations as Reflected in the DU Questionnaire

Values. In the spring of 1977 a sample of then-enrolled DU law students answered a pilot questionnaire asking them to describe the attributes they would most like to find in their first job as an attorney. Their answers were used to construct a list of 21 job attributes later used to measure the values of my panel of respondents.

The two attributes showing the sharpest *decline* in mean rating were those involving altruistic goals. The average respondent's desire to "work for desired social and political goals" in the initial job dropped by 1.23 points between the beginning and end of law school; desire to "help persons or groups with whom you identify or sympathize" dropped by .83 points. Although at the beginning of law school these altruistic goals were rated at about the middle of the list of job attributes (10th and 12th, respectively), by the end of law school they were much nearer the bottom (17th and 16th).

Three of the four attributes with statistically significant increases in mean rating were those involving interpersonal and organizational factors. While in law school, the students became more concerned with finding a job in which they would "receive guidance from experienced attorneys" (up .99, from 14th to 5th position), "work in a congenial interpersonal atmosphere" (up .48, from 9th to 3rd), and "control own work and work schedule" (up .46, from 13th to 10th). The fourth attribute with a large increase in mean rating was "advance professionally with initial employer" (up .80, from 21st to 20th).

Expectations. The students' expectations concerning the 21 attributes were measured for eight of the 20 jobs discussed earlier. The eight jobs included five public interest jobs and three jobs

with conventional law firms. Not surprisingly, at both the beginning and the end of law school the DU students rated the eight attributes associated with salary, prestige, security, and *long-term benefits* as more likely to be found in jobs with both a medium-sized business law firm and a large corporate law firm than in jobs with a public defender, a legal aid office, a minority rights organization, or a public interest law center. However, it is noteworthy that the gap between the four public interest jobs and the two conventional jobs generally widened between Time 1 and Time 2, primarily because of decreases in the scores for the public interest jobs.

At the beginning of law school the students expected more opportunities for both altruism and craft satisfaction from the public interest jobs than from the conventional jobs. In fact all four public interest jobs were rated above both the conventional jobs on all seven of the job attributes involving altruism and craft satisfaction. But by the end of law school, important changes had occurred. The public interest jobs still were uniformly rated superior to the conventional jobs on altruism, but the magnitude of the differences had substantially declined, especially with regard to "helping persons or groups with whom you identify or sympathize." The mean scores for the altruistic job attributes declined for all four public interest jobs and increased for the two conventional jobs. Seven of these 12 individual changes were statistically significant at the .05 level, and two more were significant at the .15 level.

The change was also great for expectations of craft satisfaction. The pattern of increasing expectations of craft satisfaction from the conventional jobs was especially clear; eight of the ten individual changes were statistically significant at the .05 level. For three of the four public interest jobs (legal aid, minority rights organization, and public interest law center) there was a clear pattern of change in the opposite direction.

Values, Expectations, and Job Preference: An Analysis of Change at the Individual Level

Are the people who show a decrease in altruistic goals, and/or report changed expectations about the opportunity to realize their values in public interest jobs, the same ones who report reduced preferences for public interest jobs themselves? The importance of working for social and political goals declined markedly, while the importance of working in a congenial atmosphere increased. Three *changes in expectations* about what legal aid work would be like are important in predicting change in preference for a legal aid job: (1) the change in the expectation about the opportunity to gain valuable experience, knowledge, and contacts through legal aid work, (2) the change in the expectation that this type of work would challenge the new lawyer's ability, and (3) the change in the expectation that legal aid work would give the respondent the opportunity to help persons or groups with whom he or she sympathized. The expectation that each of these attributes would be present in legal aid work decreased during law school.

Change in preference for a job with a large firm specializing in corporate work poses a sharp contrast to the findings for public interest jobs. The most important *changes in value* are the desire to advance professionally with the initial employer, which is positively associated with change in preference for a job with a large firm, and the desire to work in a congenial interpersonal atmosphere, which is negatively associated. In the aggregate, students came to value both these attributes more highly during law school.

Three *changes in expectations* predict change in preference for a job with a large firm: (1) that the new lawyer would have a chance to advance professionally with the firm, (2) that there would be opportunities to do innovative and creative work there, and (3) that the results of work at the firm would be satisfying. In the aggregate, expectations about chances for advancement in large firms decreased somewhat during law school, but expectations about the creative opportunities and rewards of the work increased significantly.

Finally, the results for a medium-sized firm specializing in business and corporate law indicate that while change in desire to help persons or groups with whom the respondent sympathized is negatively correlated with changed preference for this job, the changed expectation that the job setting would give opportunities for altruistic work is positively correlated with changes in job preference. This job had the greatest increase in

preference rank (from 16th to 3rd) in the list of 20 jobs and the data suggest that this increase results, in significant part, from a decrease in altruistic sentiments, combined with increasing acceptance of the view that working for a medium-sized business law firm allows one to serve "ordinary people."

FIRST-YEAR CRISIS, SECOND-YEAR DISTRACTIONS: THE SOURCES OF VALUE CHANGE

At least five interrelated factors contribute to the high degree of stress felt by most beginning law students. First, the legal neophyte is confronted by the difficult task of mastering a new and confusing body of knowledge. Second, the law school environment provides only minimal feedback regarding success; uncertainty concerning how to study and how much to study remains high for much of the first year. Third, the student is faced by the challenge of the Socratic method of teaching and by the daily possibility of exposure and embarrassment that it presents. Fourth, almost all law students have known academic success throughout their prior careers; yet in law school, half of them must become accustomed to being "below average." This is especially problematic because of the importance of grades to success in the job market. Finally, the first-year students must integrate themselves into a new social environment and may attach added importance to academic performance in an attempt to win the respect of their classmates. All of these factors direct beginning students' attention toward their studies, leaving little psychic energy for long-term concerns.

I would estimate that during the first two quarters of law school, the total time devoted to attending class, reading course-related assignments, and engaging in other activities directly involving the learning of course materials averaged between 35 and 60 hours a week for the vast majority of students. A reasonable estimate would place the median at no more than 45 or 50 hours a week. To at least some extent, the complaints about workload appear to be part of the myth that the incredible difficulty of the first year affirms the professional competence of those who have withstood the "test of fire" and justifies their high monetary compensation.

The effect most relevant to the present study concerns the value placed by students on using the law to work for social and political change or to help the disadvantaged. During the course of the first quarter, I observed that students simply seemed to stop thinking about these matters as they became increasingly preoccupied with their studies. This change manifested itself both in an eventual absence of "reform-oriented" conversation during my day-to-day contacts with law school acquaintances and in the self-reports of the students I interviewed.

At the beginning of the year, Sharon Lollar had hoped to participate in a Lawyers Guild project in which law students represented needy clients in unemployment compensation hearings, but she abandoned those plans because of "lack of time." When I interviewed her near the end of the first quarter, Sharon observed that her earlier concern with pursuing a career in which she could help others had declined with her immersion in the rigors of law school:

> I'm more confused than before. It's more like I just don't think about it that much. When I first started law school, I had all these ideas about what I wanted to do, and now I just think about coming here and doing the work.

Barbara Phillips felt the same forces at work but attempted to resist them by characterizing them as a tug-of-war between students and faculty:

> I think a lot of people are just saying, "I want to get through [law school]." And I don't know whether that's just first-year panic or whether being in law school does that to you.... I find that I have to do a lot of reading and do a lot of this and a lot of that. I think a lot of it is designed to bog us down. Whether the faculty realizes that or not, I think that's what's going on. I think they're playing games with the workload—trying to make us think we're overworked. I think it's a psych game, and I think the faculty is winning.

Perhaps more important, a number of alternative—although not necessarily competing—values *were* stressed. At the most obvious level, the academic and professional importance of systematic, analytical thought was emphasized. At a more subtle level, most professors placed a repeated, if unintentional, emphasis on the pecu-

niary aspect of legal practice. Perhaps the most telling manifestation of this tendency was in the use of classroom humor. In at least four of my first-quarter courses—contracts, torts, property, and legal research—the professors joked about the relationship between legal skills and economic success. Perhaps surprisingly, this "green humor" was quite common among those professors who appeared to be the most politically liberal. One explanation for this might be that these professors were consciously or subconsciously trying to build rapport with less liberal students by emphasizing that "liberals are human, too." Another possible explanation is that they were in fact attempting to poke fun at the legal profession's excessive concern with money. But if they were, the students I interviewed did not interpret it in that way.

Law Student, Law Clerk: Professional Culture and the Decline in Professional Altruism

The difference between the first and second years has been noted by previous observers. The constant preoccupation with course work—with workload, with understanding the material, with professors and classmates—was gone. People talked about their jobs with law firms, their work on one of the student-edited legal journals, or even their personal lives. Classes were mentioned frequently, too, but usually to note flippantly that the speaker hadn't started the reading yet or to complain about a professor. Equally noteworthy was the almost total elimination of anxiety about academic performance.

Professors and Students. The way in which the law school's failure to support altruistic values affects students' choice of jobs is illustrated by Sharon Lollar's drift away from public interest practice. Conscientious and compassionate, Sharon had worked as a caseworker for a state welfare agency and had begun graduate study in social work before switching to law. In answering my first questionnaire, she had said she hoped to "become involved with the ACLU" in her first job as an attorney. When I interviewed her near the end of her first quarter of law school, she said, "I know much more what I don't want to do than what I want to do. I don't want to work for a large corporation or in business-type law, but I think

I'd like to do something that's more client-oriented. I've been thinking about legal aid-type work."

By October of her second year, Sharon's job preferences were shifting toward practice with a private law firm. In describing the job she would most like upon graduation, she said,

It's changing for me because....I'm thinking more on the lines of a small firm doing...I don't know...not necessarily any sort of specialty. But I'm getting more interested in property law—stuff like that.... I've pretty much changed my mind from doing a poverty law-type of thing to doing whatever comes in the door.

By the end of her third year, Sharon was still hoping to find a job with a small law firm with a general civil practice.

One point that Sharon emphasized was the sharp contrast between the support for altruistic values in the graduate social work program and in law school:

When I was in social work school.... it was client-centered. and you really thought about the issues that affected people, and law school just isn't oriented in those terms. And so I think you can't help realigning your thinking.

While first-year students may listen intently to a professor's occasional lapse into moral, philosophical, or policy-related issues, the second- or third-year students typically react to such a breach of conventional behavior by putting down their pens and perhaps also by rolling their eyes in disgust, whispering to a neighbor, or staring into the distance. By the second year, most students have learned that in law school legal analysis, narrowly defined, is what matters. Everything else is peripheral.

Even in the fall of the first year, about half of the altruistically oriented students I interviewed expressed the feeling that they were in a tiny minority, and by the second or third year there was universal agreement that students with a public interest orientation were vastly outnumbered by persons with more materialistic concerns. At the beginning of her second year, Sharon Lollar commented on the effect that this had on her, reporting that she did not feel comfortable discussing her preference for public interest work in front of other students. Attempts

to voice support for professional altruism outside the friendly confines of a sympathetic subculture often met with silence or other forms of subtle disapproval, perhaps because they were interpreted as displays of moral superiority. Rather than risk such disapproval from potentially unsympathetic listeners, it often was easier to remain quiet. Louie Littell's description of this phenomenon was perhaps somewhat exaggerated, but it illustrates the point.

The enemies I've made in law school probably have been the most vehement that I've ever run across in my life. I stand on the premise it's not me, it's them, and so now I have a dual existence.... I realized in coming through law school that you've got to watch your politics and watch what you say in front of certain people.... I think...that has affected the way I deal with things here. I look at school life on one hand and my outside life on the other now. And that's tricky, but it's the healthiest way I can play it.

The Impact of Part-Time Legal Work. The absence of support for professional altruism in the law school environment apparently was duplicated in the work environments of most second- and third-year students. Ninety-six of the 103 students who responded to my questionnaires held at least one law-related job outside the law school at some point in their law school careers. The students' responses to the second questionnaire included descriptions of 194 such jobs. Fifty-eight percent of these jobs were with private law firms or solo practitioners, and 75 percent of the respondents listed at least one job with a private firm or solo practitioner. Only 21 of the 194 jobs listed were with private or governmental organizations specifically devoted to the practice of public interest law.

The substance of the work that student employees are sometimes required to do may also contribute to the decline in altruistic values. Most student law clerks are not in a position to choose their cases. Thus students committed to serving the economically disadvantaged, consumers, or environmental interests sometimes found themselves working on the "other side." In the fall of their second year, Sharon Lollar, Barbara Phillips, and Nelson Fixx all expressed certain reservations about the type of work they were required to do. Barbara was affected to the point that she was concerned that her initial commitment to public interest goals could be in jeopardy.

> There are days when I think I'm wavering. I have a lot of doubts about my clerkship job, which is with a small firm that does primarily corporate practice. And I have a lot of objections about working for corporate clients. Some of the things that we do—none of them are illegal—it's things that I politically object to…. I would like to think I could stand firm on my principles, but I'm feeling I could rationalize in a way how my little part in this case couldn't hurt.

In a sense, Barbara may have already been rationalizing, as she went on to emphasize that her top-rate on-the-job training would ultimately serve interests more compatible with her political beliefs. Similarly, Nelson Fixx may have been rationalizing when he implied that after graduation he would be able to choose his own cases.

> I think that right now, not being licensed to practice law and not having enough personal or financial power to pick who I work for makes more difference…. When one thinks of only representing the good or only taking cases that one really believes in, you have to assume power to be in a position to make a choice, and the law clerk in Denver in 1978 doesn't have that. He or she is at the bottom of the pile…. You don't have any options, or not many. You have [only] an original option in deciding who you're going to work for.

But this dilemma is not unique to the student law clerk; it also exists for the young attorney seeking employment.

Support for Alternative Values. Classroom emphasis on systematic, analytical thinking continued from the first year into the second and third years with one significant change. Whereas during the first year the professors had sometimes been very explicit about the importance of analytical precision, by the second year it was simply taken for granted. Furthermore, in some cases this shift seems to have had a fairly direct impact on job preferences. For example, Sharon Lollar helped explain her shift away from public interest practice as follows:

> I think that my original choice of jobs was based on sort of a "helping the other people" attitude, and that was like the prime thing. And now it's more—I think I'm more interested in getting something that's intellectually stimulating for myself.

Students who began law school with scant background in systematic, analytical thinking and little confidence in their analytical abilities also learned the rewards of solving legal puzzles. Ellen Torgeson, for example, began law school with a sense of unease about legal reasoning, in spite of her prior work as a legal secretary for Legal Services. After the first quarter of law school she told me:

> Law school stresses a certain kind of analytical mind that they are trying to form—they are trying to mold you into. And I don't have a very analytical mind at all. I felt like that's something that makes me uncomfortable…. I've never done anything like law school. I was an art and music student, and so I wasn't even in philosophy or English. I just have a different style of thinking, and I thought they're trying to teach me this one style, and it seems like it's a narrow thing they try to push me into, but I have to do it to get through school. And I feel very rebellious about that.

By the end of her third year, Ellen's evaluation of her analytical abilities and of the value of analytical thinking had been transformed. She praised her courses on corporate law and the Uniform Commercial Code because they facilitated systematic thought. As she said with only slight caricature when describing the Uniform Commercial Code:

> I love all the little sections, how they fit together, working with them and knowing, OK, it's this, so we look under here—[Section] 7-11—and there's the remedy!

The importance of money and prestige and the career advantages attached to working for the very wealthy were more frequently conveyed more subtly. For example, illustrations drawn from professors' own law practices more often than not involved rich or powerful clients or substantial awards of monetary damages. Similarly, many of the hypothetical examples used in class implied an extremely affluent clientele. In my basic taxation class, the numbers on the chalkboard invariably were far greater than the dollar amounts likely to be encountered by the general practitioner attending to the tax needs of typical middle-class or even upper-middle-class clients. Other professors based some hypotheticals on the problems likely to be encountered by average citizens, intermittently lamenting that the rewards accruing to the client probably would not justify the hiring of an attorney in the first place.

During the three years of law school, a sometimes indistinct, but nevertheless important, academic pecking order developed. Students at the top of the class or those who held an editorial position on the *Denver Law Journal* were generally respected for their success, and a few of these students clearly considered themselves part of an emerging elite. Among the law reviewers and others at the top of the class, the pull of professional prestige was especially great. A job with a large, powerful law firm was one of the acknowledged rewards of academic success. As Barbara Phillips put it, "It's very prestigious, it really is— especially when you beat out people from Harvard." For those with a real chance at such a job, it was extremely difficult not to be caught up in the competition. One such student, seemingly firmly committed to a career serving the interests of ordinary people, surrendered to the allure of the large law firm only after failing to get an offer from his first few interviews. My impression was that had he received an offer earlier, he might have felt secure enough in his place at the top to turn it down and pursue his original interests. However, having been rejected as not good enough, he felt compelled to find a job comparable to those taken by his friends on the law review.

The importance of money, prestige, and career advancement were also conveyed to the students by the private attorneys for whom they clerked. According to Allison Smith:

> The first comment made to me, after I came back from being gone this summer, by the youngest attorney [in the law firm] was…"We really made a lot of money." The one man in this office that makes $130,000 just off his practice—plus investments, plus he is independently wealthy—loves to tell me each week how much money he makes, and this oil well is coming through well, and this client paid us this much, and that sort of thing.

REALITY AND MYTH: SOURCES OF CHANGED EXPECTATIONS ABOUT LAW JOBS

Changes in Expectations of Craft Satisfaction

Two shifts in perception appeared particularly important to the students' improved image of the amount of craft satisfaction to be found in business-oriented practice. First, as the students took business-oriented courses, they discovered that business law in general and corporate law in particular was far more intellectually and analytically challenging than they had imagined. The importance of this change was magnified by a growth in the students' appreciation for intellectual and analytical activities. Second, the students' experience both inside and outside the law school conveyed an equally appealing image of other aspects of corporate and business practice. Whereas at the outset many students conceived of the daily activities of the corporate lawyer as involving routine "paperwork," by the end of law school they were more likely to think of them in terms of the human drama involved in managing a large organization or pulling off a successful financial deal.

> [Before I took Corporations] I thought, "I never want to get involved in this; I have no need for it." I took it because it was a bar course and I figured I needed to know something about it. I'm finding it really challenging, or at least interesting. It s personally challenging because it's like little puzzles, little problems that you have to figure out. [Sharon]

> Before I took the course I thought it would probably be dull, but then when I started taking the course I realized it was very intricate, that there was a lot to deal with and it was a challenge for someone to work with it.… I think there's a lot of prestige and money in it, but it's hard. [Ellen]

The students' increasing appreciation for less cerebral attractions of corporate and business law was perhaps best captured by the classmate who told me that he had come to view corporate law as "sort of like playing Monopoly." For many students the allure of corporate law appeared to be less the opportunity to earn lots of money than the opportunity to play with lots of other people's money. Barbara Phillips explained during the middle of her second year that "you find the power really even more tempting than the money...."

The influence of work experience on changes in perception was also illustrated by Will Goodman's description of his experience as a legal intern with a medium-sized corporation.

> That internship I did with the 3M Corporation was interesting. It convinced me that I could actually probably do some kinds of corporate work where I thought before that was impossible.... I was in a situation where I could sit in on all the meetings, and I got what you might call a big picture—not only law, but management, day-to-day stuff, which was really fascinating. It's every bit as challenging as trial work or anything else—just dealing with all the regulations and the people, the organization, the management. It's all fascinating stuff. I may have found a new interest.

Rising expectations of craft satisfaction from business-oriented practice were accompanied by decreased expectations of craft satisfaction from public interest practice. Thus, by the fall of her second year, Jenny Landis's initially favorable perception of legal aid work had given way to the view that "it is more of a treadmill type of thing. You're just hit with cases and cases and cases." Similarly, Sharon Lollar had reevaluated the opportunities for intellectual stimulation presented by the altruistically oriented jobs to which she had formerly aspired. "I guess I feel that...the kind of practice I was interested in doing tends to get old real fast," she said.

Barbara Phillips's initial desire to work with a small group of feminist lawyers "for the advancement of women" faded as her perceptions of the intellectual and creative outlet provided by such work diminished. The extent of Barbara's shift in perception was illustrated at the end of her third year in law school, when she referred to her former dreams of feminist-oriented practice as no more than a previous desire "to do domestic relations" law. And that area of law, according to Barbara, is "basically boring" in "all kinds of ways." "I mean you can be creative," she explained, "but it seems to be that the legal parameters and even the social parameters of domestic relations are very limited."

There are scattered indications that firsthand contact with public interest law may have helped lower, rather than raise, students' expectations concerning the craft satisfaction available in public interest practice. For example, Jenny Landis reported that her poverty law class was "a lot more laid back" than most courses and not really very challenging. And Nelson Fixx's description of his experience as an intern for the Environmental Protection Agency, which arguably is a public interest employer, shows his disillusionment with the degree of craft satisfaction to be found there.

> I quit because I didn't feel I was being productive. That was a big change—to be working in a position that *should* have been the real me, should have been. It was a prestigious position that paid well, and it was with a young, energetic agency. And it was boring. It was terribly boring.... [T]here were a lot of factors in this, but one was the agency itself, being a big federal bureaucracy, was pretty stifling.... It didn't seem like there was much being done to change the environment, to work on the expressed goals of the agency. Instead people were more concerned about the coffee breaks, about whose daughter was going out with who. A lot of gossip time. Very little work happened. Terrible support staff.

Over all, though, I do not believe that Jenny's and Nelson's reactions to their experience with public interest law were typical. Jenny's reaction was not shared by most other students enrolled in courses with a public interest emphasis. Louie Littell spoke enthusiastically of his poverty law course, and another one of my classmates told me that his poverty law professor made a special effort to present a stiff academic challenge. My limited interview data on the subject also suggest that students enrolled in advanced civil rights and civil liberties courses viewed the work as both stimulating and challenging.

More importantly, the questionnaire data suggest that students with public interest work experience were less likely than other students to move toward negative expectations of public interest jobs. For example, for the 80 students who did not work for any type of public interest organization during law school, there was a decrease in the expectation that a legal aid job would be challenging, while it appears that for students who worked in public interest jobs outside of legal aid, the decrease was less, and for the four students who worked in legal aid positions, the expectation that the new lawyer would find this work challenging actually appears to have increased.

Consider, for example, Nelson Fixx's and Sharon Lollar's perceptions of corporate securities law. If the prospectus accompanying the issuance of a certain stock misrepresents or omits a material fact of concern to potential investors, the attorney who handled the legal work can be individually sued for the investors' losses—even if the mistake involved no negligence or fraudulent intent on the part of the attorney. Both Nelson and Sharon emphasized this point in describing the intellectual complexity of corporate law.

> [Securities law is a] highly specialized, very complicated area to which attaches, as we say in the legal profession, a lot of personal liability. In other words, if you make a bad decision as a corporate securities lawyer, you expose yourself to tremendous personal financial liability. People can take you to court and turn you into a pauper. There's big money in it. [Nelson]

> One thing I think is that there's a sort of strict liability under the federal statutes on securities so that if you violate a certain section you can be sued individually as a lawyer, so that's why I think the salaries are so high. [Sharon]

It is interesting that both Nelson and Sharon not only saw a relationship between the attorney's personal liability and the intellectual complexity or challenge of securities law, but also connected these factors to the prestige or economic rewards accruing to securities lawyers.

Both Nelson and Sharon came to law school from backgrounds in serving the underprivileged, and both entered law school intending to pursue public interest careers. But by October of the second year both showed definite signs of rejecting public interest practice for more lucrative conventional careers. And both were clearly feeling a certain amount of anxiety about that change. For example, without interruption Sharon followed her explanation of the personal liability of the securities lawyer with the following comment: "I've even started to think in terms of, like, jobs that offer more salary, you know, and that sort of thing." Then, after a brief follow-up exchange with me, she continued: "OK, I've given up this emphasis on the clients, so why shouldn't I look at myself? I mean…if I felt like I

really wanted to be helping people, I'd do it regardless of how much money I was making. I don't know. *I feel really funny saying this*" (emphasis added).

And Nelson followed up with this explanation of his growing uncertainty about his job preferences: "From what little I've seen, I don't want to just say at this point that I'll be working for the state or working for the Sierra Club, because I think a person who's environmentally conscious can do some good working for development companies, oil companies, coal companies. *I feel I should cut my tongue out for saying that*" (emphasis added).

Changes in Expectations of Opportunities for Long-Term Benefits and for Altruism

A law student was celebrating his birthday, and the guests were exuberant. Conversations around the room were animated. I was talking to a woman not in law school who was curious to learn what legal education was "really like." Attempting to impress her with my erudition, I mentioned that research at several schools had shown a decline during the law school years in students' desire for public interest practice. Overhearing my comment, a fellow law student leapt quickly into the conversation.

"So what?" he nearly shouted. "That doesn't prove anything! I don't have anything against public interest practice, but I want to work someplace where I'll get some decent training. At Legal Services, it's baptism by fire. Everybody's overworked. The quality of the practice is crummy! Lots of people just don't know that when they start law school. You can't ask people to make that kind of sacrifice!"

I was struck by the intensity of this man's concern, but not by the content of his remarks. Second- and third-year law students, I had learned, viewed the initial job after law school as a continuation of their legal training. They had little faith that law school could prepare them for the practical exigencies of legal practice, and they cared deeply about the experience, knowledge, and contacts that their first job would provide. Furthermore, during the course of their legal education they formed rather definite opinions about various employers in this regard. Large and medium-sized law firms generally were believed to be especially likely to provide new attorneys with a solid foundation of experience, knowledge, and contacts. Public interest employers were not.

Long-Term Career Benefits. Why did the DU students lose confidence in the quality of experience, knowledge, and contacts to be found in public interest practice? First, the students' perception of the resources commanded by public interest institutions appears to have declined as their earlier, media-based images of these jobs were replaced by more realistic pictures of limited budgets and heavy caseloads. For example, Sharon Lollar explained her disillusionment with the value of legal aid work as a source of additional training as follows: "I think they're really restricted as far as the time they can spend on cases—the caseloads are enormous, I think—and feeling like they don't have as good facilities as in a private firm." Similarly, Jenny Landis mentioned, in explaining her disillusionment with public defender and legal aid work, that "there's a lack of government resources. It's always going to be that way." Other students specifically contrasted the training available at the city's resource-rich larger law firms with the more limited opportunities in public interest practice.

Second, it seems likely that there was significant change in the students' judgments concerning the proximity of public interest law to the mainstream of legal practice. This shift in perceptions was probably especially important to students who initially thought of public interest jobs as way stations in careers that might later head in more conventional directions. As these students learned how few attorneys, in fact, are engaged in public interest practice, they may have worried that public interest jobs would not place them at or near the center of the informal networks helpful in building professional contacts. Similarly, as they learned how little interest some conventional law firms have in legal specialties associated with most public interest jobs, they might have concluded that a job with a minority rights organization, for example, would not provide widely marketable skills and knowledge. Anxiety about the long-term benefits of early

public interest practice was probably heightened as students learned to differentiate between the skills and knowledge appropriate to various legal specialties. For example, a beginning law student might overestimate the similarity of public defender work to conventional business practice, but a third-year student probably would not.

Third, as their contacts with the legal profession increased, the students discovered the generally low repute in which many attorneys hold public interest practice.

Opportunities to Work for Altruistic Goals. It is only a slight exaggeration to say that some of the DU students began their legal studies with a caricatured image of business-oriented practice, in which attorneys with such firms pursued starving widows on behalf of avaricious creditors, defended rich, bigoted employers against race and sex discrimination suits, and represented real estate developers hell-bent on destroying the pristine beauty of the Colorado mountainside. Clerking for a conventional law firm exploded that myth, as students discovered that business law practice is far more benign. It is not that business lawyers are never involved in disputes such as those caricatured but simply that any such activity is a much smaller part of most business law firms' practice than many students had assumed. And to the extent that the common activities of business law firms do contribute to the economic oppression of underprivileged groups, the methods are almost always more subtle.

In addition, the students' exposure to business practice led them to personalize their cognitive images of a business law firm's clientele. For example, a law clerk working on a legal problem for Smith Office Supply Co. would soon discover that the real client is a particular Ms. or Mr. Smith. The clerk might even meet the client and learn that he or she roots for the Cubs, drives a pale blue Buick, and graduated from Purdue. A surprisingly large number of the students I interviewed seemed genuinely surprised to discover that working for a small or medium-sized business law firm would allow them to help "ordinary" (upper-middle-class) people.

For example, among the students I formally interviewed, Barbara Phillips and Ellen Torgeson were particularly influenced by such changes in perception. In the fall of her second year, Barbara explained that a good deal of her "previous prejudice against working for a corporate firm was not knowing what kind of law they do." But after working as a law clerk for an eight-attorney firm specializing in corporate law, she was surprised to discover that although some of the firm's clients were "pretty vile...for the most part they're not." Furthermore, she learned that:

A lot of what we do is take...two or three people doing some kind of business venture and make corporations out of them, as much for tax and legal purposes as anything else. But I don't think that makes corporations the bad seed. So I don't feel as bad about working there.

Ellen pointed to similar changes in her perceptions of business practice as one factor important to her increased willingness to pursue such a career.

I can [now] see working with smaller businesses because I think it's valid if you want to get together with a friend and start up a business, end up with an exciting venture. And it's not like businessmen are this group of alien people.

In contrast, the students' disillusionment with the altruistic potential of public interest practice appears to have resulted from their reassessment of both the effectiveness of law as a tool for social change and the institutional capacity of public interest organizations. By the fall of her second year, Barbara Phillips had abandoned the belief that she could use her position as an attorney to work effectively for her left-wing political goals. During one short segment of an interview, she made these statements:

I don't think the law is particularly a tool for change.... I don't see being an attorney as being an expression of my politics; it's something I'll be good at.... Nothing I do as an attorney will cause radical change.

A number of students began to question whether particular public interest employers possessed the resources, institutional commitment, or organizational structure necessary to accomplish their goals. Barbara Phillips, Sharon Lollar, and Jenny Landis all made the point that heavy caseloads and limited resources severely limited the ability

of legal aid attorneys to adequately represent indigent clients. Again in Barbara's words:

I'm not sure if I recognize the validity of the whole legal services structure. I have some doubts about that.... It's just become a mill that you run people through, and some of the problems they handle, and some of them they don't.... A lot of that has to do with workload.

The Mythological Element. Consider the case of Ellen Torgeson. As Ellen became more pessimistic about the opportunities to help the environment as an attorney for the Environmental Protection Agency, she became more optimistic about the opportunities to do so as a natural resources attorney for a conventional law firm or business corporation. According to Ellen, the advantage of business-oriented practice was that it would provide a more direct opportunity for her to convince businesses to adopt environmentally enlightened policies. It is clear that the emergence of this view was in part the product of an unusual receptiveness to "good news" about business-oriented practice. In Ellen's own words:

I'm trying to open my mind towards working for corporations because there's a lot of jobs there for, well, natural resources law in a corporation, and it would be a good place to get experience. But it wouldn't be corporate law.

CONCLUSION

This essay has attempted to explain the movement toward more negative expectations for public interest jobs and more positive expectations for conventional, business-oriented jobs. These shifts appear to have been the product of two sorts of learning processes. First, lay mythology was replaced by more accurate, experientially-based perceptions of both sorts of practice. Second, to some extent lay mythology was replaced by the mythology of the legal profession.

At DU I saw little evidence that either law professors themselves, or the written material which they assigned, directly conveyed a negative image of the craft satisfaction, long-term benefits, or opportunities for altruistic action available from public interest practice. Instead, students appeared to be more frequently exposed to such sentiments by practicing attorneys or by fellow law students who themselves had acquired their views from practicing lawyers. Thus the law school seems to play a much less important role than the practicing bar in transmitting the professional myth of public interest ineptitude and marginality.

However, it would be incorrect to conclude that the law school's stance toward public interest practice was irrelevant to the students' changing expectations. Viewed from one perspective, this stance might be characterized as demand-responsive neglect: the law school would increase its meager public interest emphasis if student demand justified it. But in the meantime, students learned very little about public interest practice unless they made special efforts to interact with the small number of professors, courses, or student organizations likely to provide the relevant information. In contrast, they learned a great deal about conventional business practice, unless they made deliberate efforts to avoid the profusion of information on that subject.

DISCUSSION QUESTIONS

1. Why are law students so emphatic and unanimous that their experience is transformative? Is it more intense than being an undergraduate—when college, for many, signifies the first separation from family, independent living, crossing many new frontiers? What makes law school unique? How does it differ from medical school? Business school? Graduate school? Is it a "total environment," as Erving Goffman said of prisons and mental hospitals? Antonio Gramsci coined the term "hegemony" to describe those aspects of a culture everyone takes for granted—just the way things have to be. Does law school impose a hegemonic culture on students? If students exaggerate its influence, what is the function of this myth?

How do law schools differ from one another? And how does the student experience vary by gender, race, class, age, prior work, etc.? What preconceptions do students bring with them—about law school, law, and professional careers? What is their origin? Why do some students seem relatively immune to influence? What form does student resistance take?

2. How would you differentiate between self-selection (who chooses law school) and socialization (what law school does to students)? Can you identify the ingredients of socialization: workload, curriculum, pedagogic style, competition? What do students learn—apart from rules? What is the function of "green humor"? Can you specify the consequences: cognitive style, personality, ethics, politics, career choice? Does anxiety about performance during the first year and about jobs (summer and permanent) during the second and third serve to mask, to distract from, the transformation in ends many students experience?

A comparison with continental European legal education may highlight the idiosyncracies (and effect) of American law schools. There, law is a first rather than a graduate degree; law faculties can be huge—as large as 15,000; instruction is by lecture and attendance poor; examination may be oral; attrition is high; only a small proportion of graduates become private practitioners.

3. What is the influence of the job market? How has it varied over time? How does it differ among schools? What is the effect of summer jobs, part-time work during the school year, externships?

How do students choose jobs? How do they rationalize those choices? How do they describe the attractions and drawbacks of jobs? How do prospective employers sell themselves? What is the importance of: pay, hours, work conditions, training, career prospects, prestige, content of work? A third of the UCLA class of 1991 went to work for firms with more than 100 lawyers, receiving an average salary of $69,000; another 15 percent joined firms of 51–100 lawyers, earning an average of $63,802. By contrast, only 2 percent took public interest jobs, earning an average of $20,000.

Does a concern with means—technical craft—displace an emphasis on ends—the social, economic or political significance of lawyering? Do students move from asking "what can I do with law?" to asking "what can law do for me?" Does law school contribute to this change?

4. How would you reform law school? What opposition would you expect to encounter? If student dissatisfaction is so pervasive, intense, and enduring, why hasn't change occurred?

SUGGESTED READING

Medical sociology anticipated sociology of law in this area as in most others: Robert Merton et al., *The Student Physician* (1957); Howard Becker and B. Geer, "The Fate of Idealism in Medical School," 23 *American Sociological Review* 50 (1958); Howard Becker et al., *Boys in White* (1961); G. Psathas, "The Fate of Idealism in Nursing School," 9 *Journal of Health and Social Behavior* 52 (1968); R. Morris and B. Sherlock, "Decline of Ethics and the Rise of Cynicism in Dental School," 12 *Journal of Health and Social Behavior* 290 (1971); J. Haas and W. Shaffir, "The Professionalization of Medical Students: Developing Competence and a Cloak of Competence," 1 *Symbolic Interaction* 71 (1977); "The Fate of Idealism Revisited," 13 *Urban Life* 63 (1984); I. Simpson, *From Student to Nurse: A Longitudinal Study of Socialization* (1977); D. Light, *Becoming Psychiatrists: The Professional Transformation of Self* (1980).

There is an immense literature on the socialization of law students (see the dated overview by Kenneth H. Barry and Patricia A. Connelly, "Research on Law Students: An Annotated Bibliography," 1979 *American Bar Foundation Research Journal* 751). More recent entries include James Foster, "The Cooling Out of Law Students," 3 *Law & Policy Quarterly* 243 (1983); "Legal Education and the Production of Lawyers to (Re)Produce Liberal Capitalism," 9 *Legal Studies Forum* 179 (1985); A. Schwartz, "Law, Lawyers, and Law School: Perspectives From the First-Year Class," 30 *Journal of Legal Education* 437 (1980); "The *Paper Chase* Myth: Law Students of the 1970s," 28 *Sociological Perspectives* 87 (1985); G. Andrew, H. Benjamin, Alfred Kaszniak, Bruce Sales, and Stephen B. Shanfield,

"The Role of Legal Education in Producing Psychological Distress Among Law Students and Lawyers," 1986 *American Bar Foundation Research Journal* 225; R. K. Wilkens, "The Person You're Supposed to Become: The Politics of the Law School Experience," 45 *University of Toronto Law Review* 98 (1987); Charles Cappell and Ronald Pipkin, "The Inside Tracks: Status Distinctions in Allocation to Elite Law Schools," in P. Kingston and L. Lewis (eds.), *The High Status Track: Studies of Elite Schools and Stratification* (1990); Elizabeth Mertz, "Linguistic Constructions of Difference and History in the U.S. Law School Classroom" (American Bar Foundation Working Paper 9419); Howard S. Erlanger, Charles R. Epp, Mia Cahill, and Kathleen M. Haines, "Law Student Idealism and Job Choice: Some New Data on an Old Question," 30 *Law & Society Review* 851 (1996).

The most notorious polemic is by Duncan Kennedy, *Legal Education and the Reproduction of Hierarchy* (1983); "Legal Education as Training for Hierarchy," in David Kairys (ed.), *The Politics of Law* (1990); see also Michael Lowy and Craig Hancy, "The Creation of Legal Dependency: Law School in a Nutshell," *The People's Law Review* 36 (1980).

For participant observer studies of Harvard, which parallel Stover's of Denver, see R. Kahlenberg, *Broken Contract: A Memoir of Harvard Law School* (1992); Robert Granfield, *Making Elite Lawyers: Visions of Law at Harvard and Beyond* (1992); Robert Granfield and Thomas Koenig, "Learning Collective Eminence: Harvard Law School and the Social Production of Elite Lawyers," 33 *Sociological Quarterly* 503 (1992); "The Fate of Elite Idealism: Accommodation and Ideological Work at Harvard Law School," 39 *Social Problems* 315 (1992); "Pathways into Elite Law Firms: Professional Stratification and Social Networks," 4 *Research into Politics and Society* 325 (1992). On Yale, see Charles Goodrich, *Anarchy and Elegance: Confessions of a Journalist at Yale Law School* (1990).

Chapter Seven

WOMEN LAWYERS

Women were almost invisible in the legal profession until the 1970s—less than 5 percent of lawyers. Harvard Law School did not admit them until 1950, Washington & Lee only in 1972. Since then, however, their numbers have grown rapidly to nearly half of all law graduates. The most prestigious employers— large firms—may actually favor them in hiring.* Yet this does not guarantee that women lawyers will have equal opportunity to pursue legal careers, much less that those careers will be identical to men's. The glass ceiling is notorious. Professions like law, which demand extremely long hours and constant availability, are difficult to combine with child-rearing. Robert Nelson's data in chapter 2 showed that women are far more likely than men to interrupt their careers; in chapter 3, Carroll Seron described women choosing solo and small-firm practice to reconcile work and family. David Chambers has used quantitative and qualitative methods to study the divergent career paths and life experience of men and women Michigan law graduates.

ACCOMMODATION AND SATISFACTION: WOMEN AND MEN LAWYERS AND THE BALANCE OF WORK AND FAMILY[1]
David L. Chambers

WHEN the legal profession was almost entirely male, almost no one thought of examining the tensions between work and family. As the number of women in the legal profession has increased, now reaching about 40 percent of students finishing law school each year, interest has grown in the problems of balancing family and work, although virtually all this literature has addressed the problems for women, not men.

* David Eaves, I. P. L. Png, and J. Mark Ramseyer, "Gender, Ethnicity, and Grades: Empirical Evidence of Discrimination in Law-Firm Interviews," 7 *Law & Inequality* 189 (1989).

1. 14 *Law & Social Inquiry* 251 (1989). Reprinted with permission.

Some recent research has examined the problems of work and family of women lawyers in the nineteenth century. Before 1900, most of the few women admitted to the bar either never married at all or married an attorney and worked in his office as stenographer, clerk, and associate. Into the latter half of the twentieth century, the number of women lawyers remained very small, and although far fewer of these women worked in their husbands' offices, women who had children commonly stopped working as lawyers altogether or shifted to part-time work.

The findings reported here were gathered in three studies of the graduates of the classes of 1976–79 at the University of Michigan Law School, the first four classes in which more than 20 percent of the graduates were women. The classes were first surveyed, by mail, one class each year, between 1981 and 1984 at the point when the graduates had been out of law school 5 years. Response rates to the surveys have been consistently high.

TABLE I

Major Settings of Work for Women and Men Five Years After Graduation, University of Michigan Law School Classes of 1976–79

Work Setting	WOMEN		MEN	
	N	%	N	%
SOLO OR FIRM PRACTICE	106	44	578	70
OTHER PRACTICE	89	37	174	21
EMPLOYED OUTSIDE LAW	35	15	76	9
FULL-TIME PARENT	9	4	—	—

At the time they graduated from law school, roughly one-third of both the Michigan women and men in the classes of 1976–79 were married. Over the five years that followed, roughly half the unmarried group married for the first time. A few of the women and men lived with a nonmarital partner. In all, by the time of the five-year survey, about three-quarters of both the women and men were married or had a partner. Not surprisingly, many men but only one woman were married to homemakers. Conversely, many more women (45 percent) than men (9 percent) had partners who were lawyers. In fact, three of every five women who had married since law school married lawyers. The substantial majority of women whose partners were not lawyers had partners who were other professionals, business owners, or managers.

As the occupations of their partners suggest, the women with partners in our sample were typically linked with someone who earned about as much as or more than they did. That was true for 80 percent of the women. By contrast, the great majority of men with partners—89 percent—were linked to someone who earned much less than they or did not have a job in the labor force at all.

At the time of the five-year surveys, when the median age of the women in our sample was 31, only 37 percent of the Michigan women had any children, and only 11 percent had two or more children, a far lower number than is found among women in general in the American population. At that point, slightly more of the men—41 percent—had at least one child. In the five-year survey, we asked all respondents to rate, on a seven-point scale, how satisfied they were with their family lives. Of those with partners, 86 percent of women and 85 percent of men registered themselves as quite satisfied with their family lives, while of single, noncohabiting persons, only 35 percent of women and 37 percent of men so reported. On the other hand, among people with partners, there were no substantial differences for either women or men between the levels of satisfaction with family of those with and those without children.

The great majority of the women in our survey believed that they gave more time than men to family. Many speak of their comparatively higher involvement with children and family with pleasure, pride, or a touch of defiance:

> My family life is more important to me. (I would not have said this before I had children.)…I love my work but will not be an absentee parent. My husband (also an attorney) would not say this.

Absolutely…. I've tried the "total immersion" approach and find I cannot stay sane for very long. I must have another activity separate from "the law" where I can clear my mind of all the debris and frustrations of my job.

I know there is life outside the law firm (apart from children, which I don't have). Many men appear to be relatively blind to this (but not all).

Other women seem to experience their position less as one assumed by choice than by assignment.

> I spend far more time with my children [than most men in comparable work]. I go home three days a week to take my child home from school. I take him to school three days a week. I get the groceries and the babysitters. I take them to the doctors, etc., even though my husband and I are…both partners in the same law firm.

> I "balance" by losing myself—my free time. I have no hobbies, little time to assess who I am and where I want to go. I "balance" by forgoing social opportunities and chit-chat with peers.

> I value my marriage and my friends. I have a two-year-old and am expecting another. I am half crazy because I put in fewer hours at work than my colleagues and I feel I am falling behind.

When surveyed in 1984, 15 percent of mothers were not working in the labor force at all, and an additional 13 percent worked part time only. And among the full-time working mothers, 48 of 56 asserted they gave more effort to family than most men in comparable work. In all, 90 percent of mothers either did not work outside the home, worked part time, or worked full time, but believed they gave more effort to family than men in comparable work.

In 1986, when the classes we surveyed had been out of law school seven to ten years, nearly 70 percent of the women with children reported that, at some point since law school, they had, for three or more months, worked part time or stopped working outside the home altogether. A quarter of the women with children had taken much longer periods—at least 18 months—of either full-time parenting or part-time work. Very few men had ever taken leaves of absence or worked part time to care for children, although a few men said they were constrained by the roles expected of men from asking their employers for leaves that women were freely granted. One male associate in a private firm wrote, "I find it extremely frustrating…when I encounter the 'good old boy' attitude that I am 'out of line' or 'weak' when I express or demonstrate by action that my wife and daughter are by far my top priority. While it is accepted that females may take extended leaves to start a family, it is not accepted that males may do so."

Women with children report working, on average, about three fewer hours than other women and four fewer hours than men. The full-time working mothers reported averaging 49 hours of work per week, 49 weeks a year, while other women and men averaged about 52 hours per week. Men with children worked no fewer hours than men without children.

Five years after law school, and again in 1984, 70 percent of men in these classes but only 44 percent of women worked in private practice. When, in one of our follow-up questionnaires, we asked the respondents whether they had any explanation for this difference in work settings, the most common explanation offered by women and the second most common offered by men was that women avoided private practice because they wanted settings where they could achieve an acceptable balance between work and their family or private lives. We had expected women with children to be especially likely to avoid private practice but found them as likely as women without children to work in private practice. We had also believed that women who did work in private practice might tend to avoid the large firms where, as we have just reported, the stresses on family life are said to be most severe, but in fact, among those in private practice, a higher proportion of women than men worked in the large firms….

Five years after law school, men who were married earned somewhat more and were somewhat more likely to be working in private practice than men who were single, suggesting deliberate choices by "family" men to work in high-paying settings. In addition, among men who began law school planning to work in legal services for the poor or in "public interest" work (where earnings are lower than in firms), men who had married by the end of law school were less likely to carry through on their plans than men who were still single….

Most people were markedly less satisfied with the balance of their family and professional lives than they were, for example, with their family lives considered alone or with their incomes, their prestige in the community, or their careers overall. Women were slightly more contented than men with the balance of their family and professional lives. Moreover, women with children were somewhat more contented with the balance than single women and than married women without children, and much more contented than men with children and men who were single. When we resurveyed the same classes in 1986, seven to ten years after graduation, a slightly different pattern emerged. At this point, no significant differences appeared among the groups. Women with children were *as* satisfied, but no more satisfied, with the balance than were other women and than men with and without children….

Most of the respondents were satisfied with their careers overall….

Single persons of both sexes are again less satisfied than those who are married or have partners. In addition, women who have children are significantly more satisfied with their careers than are married or single women without children. They are also significantly more satisfied than men with and without children….

Among women, but not men, the fact of having children remained significantly related to career satisfaction after taking other factors into account and was in fact the third strongest factor we could identify. Among men, both with and without children, those who had partners or wives were slightly more satisfied with their careers than those who were partnerless or single. The fact of having children, however, bore no measurable relationship to their career satisfaction….

One pattern only was different in 1986: in the five-year survey, the women without children were somewhat less satisfied with their careers than the women with children but no less satisfied than the men; by 1986, women without children reported lower levels of career satisfaction than both women with children and men….

Thirty-six women had a first child after the five-year survey but before we resurveyed them in 1986. Even with the burdens of a first child, half the new mothers reported higher career satisfaction in 1986 than they had reported at the time of the five-year survey (when their satisfaction levels were already high), and only a quarter reported lower satisfaction. In contrast, the 94 women who remained childless after the five-year survey display the opposite pattern. More of them were less satisfied at the time of the 1986 survey than they had been at the time of the five-year survey…. For men, by contrast, having a first child (or not having children) bore no relation to changes in levels of career satisfaction between the two surveys.

DISCUSSION QUESTIONS

1. How should we understand the dramatic increase in the proportion of law students who are women, beginning in the 1970s? Does it simply reflect the increasing proportion of women in the workforce or a shift from other occupations? If the latter, from which ones? Why did it happen then? It occurred earlier in the Netherlands and has not yet occurred in Japan. Do recent women entrants differ from men in anything other than gender?

2. The proportion of women seems to have stabilized at about 45 percent, although it is higher in other countries (e.g., Scotland, England, France, Yugoslavia). What explains these differences? The character of other occupations has changed when they have "tipped"—i.e., women have become a majority. School teaching and clerical work are typical examples in the United States, medicine in Russia. Have the monetary rewards, status, and power of the legal profession declined with the entry of women? Do you expect them to do so?

3. Several recent studies have documented the different experiences of women and men law students, e.g., "Project: Gender, Legal Education, and the Legal Profession: An Empirical Study of Stanford Law Students and Graduates," 40 *Stanford Law Review* 1209 (1988); Catherine Weiss and Louise Melling, "The Legal Education of

Twenty Women," 40 *Stanford Law Review* 1299 (1988) (Yale Law School); Linda F. Wightman, *Women in Legal Education: A Comparison of Law School Performance and Law School Experiences of Women and Men* (1996). The mass media gave considerable attention to a study by Lani Guinier (whose nomination as assistant attorney general was quickly withdrawn by President Clinton) and her associates Michelle Fine, Jane Balin, Ann Bartow, and Deborah Lee Stachel, "Becoming Gentlemen: Women's Experiences at One Ivy League Law School," 143 *University of Pennsylvania Law Review* 1 (1994).[2] They found that, although women law students at Penn entered with slightly higher undergraduate GPAs, men received significantly better grades in law school; indeed, they were almost three times as likely to be in the top 10 percent in the first year and twice as likely in the next two years. Women were underrepresented on both law review and moot court. Women participated less in class discussions; open-ended questions elicited high levels of discomfort with classroom dynamics and sexist language.

Is your law school experience consistent with this description? What explains these findings? What could be done to change the situation?

4. We know from Chapter 2 that the profession is fragmented and stratified. Do men and women enter law school with different ambitions? If so, what explains those differences? Where would you expect to find women overrepresented? Underrepresented? A 1995 study of eight large New York firms found that 17 percent of men hired after 1981 were partners, compared with 5 percent of women. In 20 California firms with more than 100 lawyers, women were 31 percent of associates but only 6 percent of partners in 1984; 12 years later they were 41 percent of associates but only 17 percent of partners. A 1993 Colorado study found that though men and women in their first year of practice earned almost identical salaries ($23,636 versus $22,581), the divergence was dramatic for those who had practiced ten to twenty years ($90,574 versus $68,466). What explains these disparities? Are they troubling?

2. *New York Times* B10 (6.5.96).

What could be done to change this distribution?[3]

How important is sexual harassment? A survey of 800 lawyers in 70 firms in 14 cities found that 43 percent of women but only 9 percent of men reported observing sexual teasing, jokes, remarks, or questions; 29 percent of women but only 3 percent of men observed sexually suggestive looks or gestures. The problem gained considerable attention when a secretary won $7.1 million in punitive damages from Baker & McKenzie (the largest law firm in the world).[4]

Given the fundamental tensions between work and family, child-rearing responsibilities critically affect legal careers. Have these responsibilities been reallocated between men and women lawyers in recent years? Lawyers' spouses tend to have equally demanding jobs; whose job takes priority in decisions about where to live? Do men and women lawyers feel different responsibilities to contribute to the family economy? Do they make different contributions?

SUGGESTED READING

For overviews of the situation, problems, and prospects of women lawyers, see Deborah Rhode, "Perspectives on Professional Women," 40 *Stanford Law Review* 1163 (1988); "Symposium on Women in the Lawyering Workplace: Feminist Considerations and Practical Solutions," 35(2) *New York Law School Law Review* (1990); Barbara A. Curran, *Women in the Law: A Look at the Numbers* (1995); Bernard F. Lentz and David N. Laband, *Sex Discrimination in the Legal Profession* (1995); David N. Laband and Bernard F. Lentz, "Is There Sex Discrimination in the Legal Profession? Further Evidence on Tangible and Intangible Margins," 28 *Journal of Human Resources* 230 (1993)

For histories of early women lawyers, see Patricia M. Hummer, *The Decade of Elusive Promise: Professional Women in the United States,* 1920–1930 (1976); D. Kelly Weisberg, "Barred from the Bar: Women and Legal Education in the United States, 1870–1890," 28 *Journal of Legal Education* 485 (1977); Dorothy M. Brown, *Mabel Walker Willebrandt: A Study of Power, Loyalty, and Law* (1984); Jeanette E. Tuve, *First Lady of Law: Florence Ellinwood Allen* (1984); Karen Berger Morello, *The Invisible Bar: Women Lawyers in a Changing Society* (1985); Ronald Chester, *Unequal Access: Women Lawyers in a Changing America* (1985); Virginia G. Drachman, "'My "Partner" in Law and Life': Marriage in the Lives of Women Lawyers in Late nineteenth- and Early twentieth-century America," 14 *Law & Social Inquiry* 221 (1989), *Women Lawyers and the Origins of Personal Identity in America: The Letters of the Equity Club 1887 to 1890* (1993); Mari Matsuda, *Called from Within: Early Women Lawyers of Hawaii* (1992); "First Women: The Contribution of American Women to the Law," 28(4) *Valparaiso University Law Review* (summer 1994).

On sex equality in specific settings, see Sharyn L. Roach, "Men and Women Lawyers in In-House Legal Departments: Recruitment and Career Patterns," 4 *Gender and Society* 207 (1990); Stephen J. Spurr, "Sex Discrimination in the Legal Profession: A Study of Promotion," 43 *Industrial and Labor Relations Review* 406 (1990); Joan Norman Scott, "A Woman's Chance for Law Partnership," 71 *Sociology and Social Research* 119 (1987); Ann Gellis, "Great Expectations: Women in the Legal Profession: a commentary on state studies," 66 *Indiana Law Journal* 941 (1990–91); Paul Mattessich and Cheryl Heilman, "The Career Paths of Minnesota Law School Graduates: Does Gender Make a Difference?" 19 *Law and Inequality* 59 (1990); Richard J. Maiman, Lynn Mather, and Craig A. McEwen, "Gender and Specialization in the Practice of Divorce Law," 44 *Maine Law Review* 39 (1992); Jo Dixon and Carroll Seron, "Stratification in the Legal Profession: Sex, Sector, and Salary," 29 *Law & Society Review* 381 (1995); "Comment: The Glass Ceiling in the Legal Profession: Why Do Law Firms Still Have So Few Female Partners?" 42 *UCLA Law Review* 1631 (1995); Jennifer L. Pierce, *Gender Trials: Emotional Lives in Contemporary Law Firms* (1996). A number of states and federal circuits have investigated gender bias

---

3. On the "mommy track" and "glass ceiling," see *New York Times* §1 p1 (8.8.88), §1 p22 (8.25.88), §1 p18 (8.26.88), A15 (12.4.89), C22 (3.16.95), C2 (9.7.95), A10 (1.8.96), C2 (2.28.96); *Los Angeles Times* D1 (3.10.94).

4. *New York Times* B12 (2.25.94), B18 (10.14.94). See P. D. Coontz, "Gender Bias in the Legal Profession: Women 'See' It, Men Don't," 15 *Gender & Politics* 1 (1995).

in the profession and the courts (although the Republican majority on the D.C. Circuit withdrew its support from the Task Force on Gender, Race, and Ethnicity).[5]

For comparisons with other legal professions, see Carrie Menkel-Meadow, "Feminization of the Legal Profession: The Comparative Sociology of Women Lawyers," in Richard L. Abel and Philip S.C. Lewis (eds.), 3 *Lawyers in Society: Comparative Theories* (1989); John Hagan and Fiona Kay, *Gender in Practice: A Study of Lawyers' Lives* (1995) (Canada); Margaret Thornton, *Dissonance and Distrust: Women in the Legal Profession* (1996) (Australia).

Most studies of gender in the legal profession focus on the consequences for women of being lawyers. Carrie Menkel-Meadow* criticized the classic work, Cynthia Fuchs Epstein's Women in Law† *for its exclusive concern with those questions and urged consideration of the consequences for law of the fact that some of its practitioners are women. She pursues that inquiry here.*

PORTIA REDUX: ANOTHER LOOK AT GENDER, FEMINISM, AND LEGAL ETHICS[1]
Carrie Menkel-Meadow

LAWYERING IN A DIFFERENT VOICE: AN ETHIC OF CARE, CONNECTION, CONTEXT, AND RELATIONSHIPS

CAROL Gilligan's work as a psychologist focusing on moral dilemmas was fueled in part by a recognition that most of the critical work in developmental psychology was based on studies of male behavior. Gilligan found that women are more likely to consider others, to consider the people in the problem in relation to each other, and to seek solutions that minimize pain to all, rather than to find universal principles that reflexively determine an issue. Thus, Amy, a sixth-grade girl, believes that in the Kohlberg problem the druggist and Heinz should sit down together and try to work out an installment payment contract, or some way to resolve the problem that attempts to meet all of the parties' needs and minimize pain to all. On the other hand, Jake, a sixth-grade boy, decides the Kohlberg problem as a mathematical equation: life is worth more than property, therefore, it is permissible for Heinz to steal the drug. Hilary, a young lawyer in another one of Gilligan's studies, is upset to see an incompetent opposing lawyer not

---

* *"Women in Law?" 1983 American Bar Foundation Research Journal* 189.

† New York: Basic Books, 1981; 2d ed. Urbana: University of Illinois Press, 1993. Epstein replied to her critics, "Faulty Framework: Consequences of the Difference Model for Women in the Law," 35 *New York Law School Law Review* 309 (1990).

1. 2 *Virginia Journal of Social Policy & the Law* 75 (1989). Reprinted with permission.

use a document that would help his case, and she longs to lean across the adversarial table and help her client's opponent.

In more recent work, Gilligan uses fables to continue to test the tendencies of girls and boys to elaborate different moral languages in solving problems. In one such fable, two industrious moles have worked all summer to build themselves a shelter for the winter. When winter arrives, a less forward-thinking porcupine pleads with the moles to share their comfortable hole. In their concern, they take the porcupine in the close and small space, and then are hurt by the sharpness of the porcupine's quills.

What, subjects of the study are asked, should the moles do? Adolescents with a "rights" or "justice" orientation—more often boys in the research—suggest that the moles should throw the porcupine out because they built the shelter. Indeed, if the porcupine refuses to leave, they maintain, it would be permissible for the moles to shoot the porcupine. Those who use a "care" approach—more often girls in the studies—develop solutions like covering the porcupine with a blanket or asking the porcupine to help enlarge the hole—solutions that both seek to meet the needs and minimize the harm to all parties.

It appears that most men, and about one-third of women, reason from rational, abstract principles or rules, like a weighing of competing rights. Women are more likely, though not exclusively, to reason from a care perspective that relies on notions of responsibility, human connection, and care. They are more likely to rearrange rules or principles or to seek incrementally inclusive solutions in order to accommodate the needs of people. When asked to choose another way of resolving some of the moral hypotheticals discussed above, boys and girls demonstrated an ability to shift from one mode of reasoning to another. This suggests that both females and males are capable of reasoning from different perspectives, especially when directed to consider other approaches. Many feminists fear that valorizing women's differences will legitimate discriminatory treatment of women's difference and assign women to conventional domestic, maternal, and other "caring" roles. Yet at the same time, some

feminists claim that Gilligan's account of a different morality is derived from women's experiences, experiences that have been overlooked by moral philosophers and social scientists through the years. Some root that "experience" in oppression or exclusion, others in the physical and emotional connections of mothering, and still others in the objectification that comes from being viewed as sex objects.

LAW PRACTICE

Most simply stated, those who claim women will change the legal profession because of their gender argue that women may be more likely to adopt less confrontational, more mediational approaches to dispute resolution. They maintain that women will be more sensitive to clients' needs and interests, as well as to the needs and interests of those who are in relation to each other, for example, clients' families, or employees. They suggest that women employ different moral and ethical sensibilities in the practice of law, use less hierarchical managerial styles, and are more likely to have social justice or altruistic motives in practicing law. They believe that women will be more likely to develop greater integration between their work and family lives, seeking what the literature refers to as "horizontal," as well as "vertical," satisfaction.

THE PRODUCTION OF LEGAL KNOWLEDGE

Women lawyers have adopted a variety of strategies or patterns of arguments in advocating legal and doctrinal change. These range from utilizing conventional categories to protect women's interests, such as claims for privacy and equality, to recrafting old categories, such as the defense of consent in rape. Women lawyers are also creating new categories of analysis, such as sexual harassment and pornography, and exposing the male and white bias. They challenge assumptions of male experience in defining legal categories, such as freedom from connection in defining liberty, and they argue that women's difference will produce different legal theories and constructions thereof, such as the recognition of additional compensable wrongs. Finally, feminist scholars and lawyers are exposing how law disadvantages women, even when framed in "neutral" terms, and how arguing from a women's perspective may transform the legal emphasis from rights to needs.

The story "A Jury of Her Peers" is another example of women's production of knowledge. It has joined the canon of feminist approaches to law to demonstrate that women see things differently from men and often reach different factual, as well as moral, conclusions. The story troubles those who identify with "justice" concerns in the law more than those who focus on "care." In it a sheriff and his men are sent to investigate the murder of an isolated man. They gather evidence from the victim's home while his wife, the obvious suspect, is in jail. The sheriff's men are accompanied by a few of their wives, who are concerned that they did not pay enough attention to the lonely woman. While the men search for the obvious—artifacts of the crime or other proof of motive—their wives gather in the kitchen and, without speaking a word to each other, gradually come to understand from the broken neck of the suspect's pet bird, that the man abused his wife. The women conclude that the wife was morally justified in killing her husband. They quietly remove the bird, the only physical evidence of motive, in the hope that their act will free the jailed wife. Hence, they acquit the wife in their own moral court.

While legal scholars, lawyers, and judges may debate the justice of the women's actions, the story has evoked at least some consideration of how women reason differently and, in this case, how they connect seemingly unrelated matters to understand the situation more deeply. The women's ability to empathize with the wife enables them to see the "evidence" buried in the "non-evidentiary." Have they made a correct moral judgment? The discussion in a law school classroom or roomful of judges is most interesting: gender plays a large role.

LEGAL ETHICS/MORAL DECISION-MAKING

At least one study has expressly set out to test Gilligan's theories in moral decision-making by lawyers. Rand Jack and Dana Crowley Jack—the latter a student of Gilligan—interviewed 36 lawyers, matched by age and gender, in western Washington state to explore moral conflict and legal ethical dilemmas. A disproportionate number of women were more likely to express a care orientation, which dissipated when the professional rules or roles were clear. Men, too, expressed care and connection concerns but were clearly more comfortable with the conventional role of being a "hired gun," following the wishes of the client. At the same time, the Jacks noted that responses to ethical dilemmas were situationally based. Both male and female lawyers responded clearly with a justice or rights orientation when the ethical or professional norms were clear. For example, in criminal defense advocacy, differences emerged only when there was less clarity in the professional expectations. In the general moral-orientation portion of the interviews, women lawyers were slightly more likely to express dissatisfaction with the conventional role morality plays in the adversary system. Thus, the professional role, legal education, and an understanding of the norms of the profession could often, if not always, trump gender patterns in moral reasoning.

DOES PORTIA SPEAK IN A DIFFERENT VOICE?

The Merchant of Venice places discussions of ethics, morality, and right-doing at its center. During the trial scene, Portia, disguised as a male jurist, comes to "save" her lover Bassanio's friend, Antonio, from the demands for enforcement of the bond by Shylock the Jew. The recompense is a "pound of flesh" for failure to honor a debt. Over the years, many literary critics and legal commentators have read this scene as central to one of the major themes of the play, that "mercy should season justice." Portia is seen as the symbol of mercy and Shylock of "justice, judgment, and Law." The source of much of this commentary is Portia's first principal speech in the scene where she sets the stage by asking Shylock to consider the virtues of mercy:

> The quality of mercy is not strain'd,
> It droppeth as the gentle rain from heaven
> Upon the place beneath: it is twice blest,
> It blesseth him that gives, and him that takes,

'Tis mightiest in the mightiest, it becomes
The throned monarch better than his crown.
His sceptre shows the force of temporal power,
The attribute to awe and majesty,
Wherein doth sit the dread and fear of kings:
But mercy is above his sceptred sway,
It is enthroned in the hearts of kings,
It is an attribute to God himself;
And earthly power doth then show likest God's
When mercy seasons justice: therefore Jew,
Though justice be thy plea, consider this,
That in the course of justice, none of us
Should see salvation: we do pray for mercy,
And that same prayer, doth teach all of us to render
The deeds of mercy. I have spoke thus much
To mitigate the justice of thy plea,
Which if thou follow, this strict court of Venice
Must needs give sentence 'gainst the merchant there.

It is important to examine the rest of the scene to fully understand the complexity of Portia's role as lawyer. Shylock rejects Portia's pleas. "I crave the law," he says, "the penalty and forfeit of my bond." At that moment, Portia becomes an extraordinary, albeit conventional, lawyer. She recognizes that the law must be followed and the bond enforced because precedents must be obeyed or "many an error by the same example will rush into the state—it cannot be."

Having decided that the law must be enforced, Portia demands to see the document, the contract of debt. She gives Shylock his judgment—a pound of flesh, closest to the heart of Antonio. Then, in an act of clever lawyering and language manipulation, Portia proceeds to read the text of the law quite literally. She reports that Shylock had better find a skilled surgeon, for the bond grants him a pound of flesh, but "this bond doth give thee here no jot of blood, The words expressly are 'a pound of flesh:' Take then thy bond, take thou thy pound of flesh, But in the cutting it, if thou dost shed One drop of Christian blood, thy lands and goods Are (by the laws of Venice) confiscate Unto the state of Venice." Portia shows Shylock the law and tells him that if he urges justice, he shall have justice and, thus, must live by the law himself. Shylock capitulates and asks for the previously offered "settlement" of three times the money owed. Yet Portia, the masterful lawyer, recounts still another Venetian law in response. Because Shylock will have "justice," interpreted as the letter of the law, he must con-

template how those laws affect him as well; according to the law, any alien—Jew—who seeks to tamper with the life of a citizen shall lose his property, half to the citizen harmed and half to the state. Furthermore, his life shall be at the discretion of the Duke. The Duke and Antonio, however, show Shylock their mercy. They allow him to live, but only as a Christian, forcing him to give up his faith and identity. They condition their mercy on Shylock's promise to leave his property to his Christian son-in-law.

Has mercy triumphed over justice? No. Portia has played a clever lawyer's game and shown that she can be as manipulative of language and the law as any of her brethren. I think Portia's "disguise" is an important metaphor for what the Jacks found about the role of gender in ethical decision making. Portia's judge's robes are those of the professional role and "mantle" she must take on. Like the women in the Jacks' sample, she tries to use nonrule-based measures of morality and justice—mercy, heart, feeling, concern for others—to appeal to Shylock, but when forced to resort to law and rules, she shows herself as capable as any male lawyer. Perhaps it is Shylock's unwillingness to accept her offer of mercy that pushes Portia into the literal reading of the contract—demonstrating how hard it is, even for judges, to dislodge the desire of litigants from their self-interested "justice." Disentangling implications of gender in this play is further complicated by the fact that Portia, in Shakespeare's time, was actually played by a man disguised as a woman. Of course, all the words were written by a man. And, as some commentators have suggested, Portia's "justice" is correct—Shylock would, after all, be a murderer or at least have murderous intent.

Yet Portia still evokes a feminist aspiration for law and legal ethics. As Jane Cohen has nicely summarized, those of us who have relied on Portia as a metaphor for women's role in the legal profession see three roles for women. First, women would inhabit the role of lawyer differently from men if they could overcome men's domination of the profession. Second, women will reconstruct the profession and the legal system to be more cooperative, more contextualized, less rule-bound, more responsible to others, as well as clients, and more conscious of socially just ends. Third, women will refuse to capitulate to a "macho" ethic of law and will try to incorporate their own integration of psychosocial health and family balance into their roles as lawyers.

to clients differently? adversaries? Do they have different styles of litigation, negotiation, counseling? seek different rewards from practice? Would it be sex discrimination for a woman lawyer to refuse a male client?[3]

DISCUSSION QUESTIONS

1. Are there gendered differences in the practice of law? If so, what causes them? What are likely to be the consequences for the legal system, and society, of the increase in the proportion of the profession that is women, from less than 5 percent to nearly 50 percent? Is the adversary process distinctively male? are legal rules?

2. Do you expect women to change legal roles? or to choose or be channeled into existing roles that are more consistent with women's socialization? (Compare the incorporation of other outsiders defined by ethnicity, religion, race, or class.) What has happened to women at the pinnacles of political or economic power (e.g., Golda Meir, Margaret Thatcher, Indira Gandhi, Benazir Bhutto, Hillary Rodham Clinton)? women judges (e.g., Sandra Day O'Connor, Ruth Bader Ginsburg, Judith Kaye)? Attorney General Janet Reno? The first woman ABA president, Roberta Cooper Ramo?[2] Do women and men law teachers differ in pedagogic style? in other respects? Do women practice law differently from men when not subordinated to them, e.g., in solo practice or all-women law firms? Do they relate

SUGGESTED READING

Carrie Menkel-Meadow has developed these themes elsewhere, e.g., "Portia in a Different Voice: Speculations on a Women's Lawyering Process," 1 *Berkeley Women's Law Journal* 39 (1985); "Exploring a Research Agenda of the Feminization of the Legal Profession: Theories of Gender and Social Change," 14 *Law & Social Inquiry* 289 (1989); "Culture Clash in the Quality of Life in the Law: Changes in the Economics, Diversification, and Organization of Lawyering," 44 *Case Western Reserve Law Review* 621 (1994); see also Robert Granfield, "Contextualizing the Different Voice: Women, Occupational Goals, and Legal Education," 16 *Law & Policy* 1 (1994); see also Janet Rosenberg, Harry Perlstadt, and William R. F. Phillips, "Politics, Feminism, and Women's Professional Orientation: A Case Study of Women Lawyers," 10 *Women and Politics* 19 (1990). As Menkel-Meadow notes, Rand Jack and Dana Crowley Jack attempted to test Gilligan's hypothesis: *Moral Vision and Professional Decisions: The Changing Values of Women and Men Lawyers* (1989). For a more popular treatment, see Mona Harrington, *Women Lawyers: Rewriting the Rules* (1995).

---

2. *New York Times* B10 (2.4.94), §4 p17 (2.6.94).

3. *Los Angeles Times* B9 (2.9.96).

Chapter Eight

MINORITY LAWYERS

African Americans were estimated to be 0.5 percent of the legal profession in 1900 and 1.3 percent in 1970. No Southern law school admitted them until 1935, and the American Bar Association excluded them until 1943. We saw in Chapter 2 that racial minorities, who had been less than 5 percent of law school enrollments at the end of the 1960s, increased to 13 percent by 1990. The following table shows the disparity in the early 1990s.*

	Percent of Category		
	BLACK	LATINO	ASIAN
U.S. RESIDENTS (1992)	12.1	9.0	2.9
U.S. LAWYERS (1990)	3.0	2.4	1.5
MALE LAWYERS (1990)	2.3	2.1	1.1
LAW TEACHERS (1992–93)	6.4	2.9	1.5
PASSING CALIF. BAR (7.95)	3.6	5.5	8.7
20 CALIF. FIRMS >100 LAWYERS (1996)			
ASSOCIATES	3.3	3.4	7.6
PARTNERS	1.7	0.9	2.0

Unlike women, racial minorities are still grossly underrepresented in law school in comparison to their proportion of the population. Minority male lawyers are even more underrepresented. Racial minorities also are far less likely to occupy roles in the twenty elite California firms (where women were 40.8 percent of associates and 16.7 percent of partners).

None of this should be surprising. Racism was official American policy until a generation ago. Most African American lawyers attended the half-dozen segregated law schools and practiced alone or in small firms or worked for government. Most racial minorities continue to be disadvantaged by poverty and inferior education.

As the number of minority law graduates has increased, concern has focused on their professional

careers. The following reading considers the obstacles confronting even those endowed with superior educational credentials.

WHY ARE THERE
SO FEW BLACK LAWYERS IN
CORPORATE LAW FIRMS?
AN INSTITUTIONAL ANALYSIS[1]
David B. Wilkins and G. Mitu Gulati

FORTY years after the Supreme Court's landmark decision in *Brown v. Board of Education*, society has made substantial progress toward eradicating the kind of overtly racist policies that excluded blacks from virtually every desirable sector of the economy. For many blacks, these changes have produced a dramatic growth in income and opportunity. In recent years, however, it has become painfully clear that simply dismantling America's version of apartheid has not produced economic parity between blacks and whites. Although poor blacks have benefited the least from the civil rights revolution, "high level" jobs in business and the professions have also proved surprisingly resistant to change. The fact that blacks have made so little progress in breaking into the corporate law-firm elite—particularly at the partnership level—fits this larger pattern.

Commentators generally offer one of two explanations for this "glass ceiling" effect. The first, generally proffered by firms, posits a shortage of black applicants with both the qualifications and the interest necessary to succeed in the demanding world of elite corporate practice. The second, most often articulated by blacks, blames the slow progress on continued racism both inside corporate firms and among the clients upon whom these entities depend for their livelihood.

As we argue below, both the "pool problem"

---

* Sources: *National Directory of Legal Employers* (1996/97); III(3) *Consultant's Digest* 4 (11.93); 1990 PUMS census data; 1992 *Statistical Abstract*.

1. 84 *California Law Review* 493 (1996). Reprinted with permission.

and continuing racism against blacks play important roles in determining the employment opportunities available to African American lawyers. Standing alone, however, each explanation begs important questions. The "pool problem" explanation begs the question of whether the existing hiring and promotion criteria utilized by elite law firms to determine who is in the pool fairly and accurately predict future productivity. The racism story, on the other hand, fails to explain why firms that discriminate by refusing to hire or promote qualified black lawyers do not suffer a competitive disadvantage when those workers are employed by their competitors.

We present a stylized model of the contemporary elite corporate law firm, premised on two related features of professional work: the inherent subjectivity of quality assessments and the difficulty and expense of monitoring. In response to these realities, we posit that it is efficient for firms to adopt the following tripartite strategy: high wages to create a large pool of available workers and motivate those who are hired to work with relatively little supervision; a high associate-to-partner ratio, thus further encouraging associates to work hard in the hopes of becoming partners while at the same time allowing the firm to spread legal work among many lawyers with varying levels of knowledge and skill at the lowest possible cost; and a tracking system whereby the pool of associates is divided into those who will receive scarce training resources and those who will work on relatively undemanding assignments.

These features, we assert, disproportionately disadvantage black lawyers while also affecting whites. Two tendencies contribute to this result. First, because firms hire a large number of associates from a pool that has been artificially inflated by high salaries and ask many of them to do relatively undemanding work, these institutions have little incentive to invest in obtaining detailed information about the quality of potential employees. Hence, individuals within the firm can use race as a factor in their decision-making without hurting the firm's bottom line. The same goes for retention and promotion. Decisions to invest scarce training resources in average whites as opposed to average blacks will not hurt the

firm's chances of producing the small number of high-quality partners that it needs to guarantee its productivity in future years. As a result, firms have little incentive to root out employment decisions that, either consciously or unconsciously, prejudice blacks or favor whites.

Second, because firms have no incentive to stop these practices, black lawyers in firms (as well as those contemplating joining firms) are more likely to choose human-capital strategies that, paradoxically, decrease their overall chances of success. Since blacks reasonably believe that they face an increased risk that their abilities will be unfairly devalued or overlooked, they have an incentive to overinvest either in avoiding visible negative signals or in obtaining easily observable positive signals that clearly identify them as superstars. Both of these strategies, however, are potentially counterproductive to the extent that they diminish a black lawyer's opportunity or incentive to obtain the skills upon which success at the corporate law firm ultimately depends.

ARE BLACKS UNDERREPRESENTED IN CORPORATE LAW FIRMS?

The *National Law Journal* reported that as of 1995 there were more than 1,641 blacks working in the nation's 250 largest firms, of whom 351 were partners. Viewed against the rapid expansion in corporate firms during the last 25 years and the dramatic growth in the number of women lawyers working in this area, these numbers are a good deal less inspiring. The same survey revealed that blacks constituted just 2.4 percent of the lawyers in corporate firms and, more importantly, just over one percent of partners. These percentages have remained relatively constant for the last 15 years. Moreover, they lag behind those achieved by other legal employers. For example, minorities constitute 17.2 percent of the lawyers employed by federal, state, and local government agencies in the Chicago metropolitan area, as compared to 3.6 percent of the attorneys in large Chicago firms. Minority lawyers occupy 19.5 percent of the supervisory positions in these government offices as compared to 1.6 percent of the partnerships at large Chicago firms.

These statistics cannot answer the question of

whether blacks are underrepresented in corporate firms. One must also have some idea about the number of blacks in the pool of people qualified to become corporate lawyers. Since the mid-1970s, blacks have consistently constituted more than 6 percent of the students enrolled in law schools. Many would assert, however, that the population of all law school graduates is not the relevant pool. The claim that law firms have always employed a set of meritocratic hiring criteria that limit the eligible pool to elite law school graduates at the top of their class is belied by the historical record. Whatever the traditional patterns of law firm recruitment were, the tremendous growth in the size of these institutions during the last 25 years has resulted in a significant expansion in the schools from which firms interview and recruit. Robert Nelson's study of Chicago corporate firms found that only 18.4 percent of incoming associates between 1970 and 1974 graduated from local or regional law schools, but the proportion had more than doubled to 37.5 percent between 1975 and 1988.

"EFFICIENT" DISCRIMINATION IN HIGH-LEVEL JOBS

For two reasons, firms that employ high wages, tournaments, or some combination thereof to induce worker effort face reduced market pressures to detect and sanction employment decisions that either penalize blacks or favor whites.

First, assuming that firms face a normal bell-shaped distribution of worker talent, they should be relatively indifferent as to which average candidates are hired. Since quality is subjective and therefore difficult to evaluate, the signals applicants use to demonstrate their merit (for example, educational credentials, recommendations, work experience) will be "noisier" (that is, less reliable predictors of actual quality) the closer one gets to the mean. As a result, the firm has little reason to investigate whether those responsible for hiring systematically prefer average whites to average blacks. By definition, the firm does not lose productivity as a result of such discrimination. Furthermore, because of the inflexibility of wages, the firm will not be placed at a competitive disadvantage vis-à-vis those firms who do not discriminate, since the latter will find it difficult to hire blacks at reduced wages. Firms that utilize a tournament to separate those who are truly outstanding from the merely competent know they will be able to collect a large amount of relatively reliable information about employee performance and thus have even less incentive to make accurate distinctions among average workers at the hiring stage.

Second, because black applicants know that they face reduced opportunities unless they can clearly signal themselves to be superstars, they have an incentive to invest in human-capital strategies that, paradoxically, will on average decrease their chances for success. Firms are likely to prefer less accurate but easily observable signals over ones that are more difficult to observe or measure but ultimately better correlated with future job performance. Although black candidates who invest disproportionately in signals may increase their chances of being hired, if we make the plausible assumption that there is at least some trade-off between investing in signals and investing in skills, these workers may also have a *decreased* chance of actually winning the tournament.

The incentives that push the investment decisions of black employees in directions that decrease their chances for success are even more prevalent once the employment relationship begins, given that the same social forces that tend to lead whites to prefer average whites over average blacks are likely to continue inside firms. Some black workers may seek to minimize the adverse consequences of their employers' diminished expectations by avoiding situations where they believe that their competence might be drawn into question. Others will take the opposite tack and invest heavily in their careers at the firm by taking on difficult or risky projects. The futility of the first choice is clear. At the same time, average black workers who pursue *high-risk* strategies by taking on more than their share of difficult or risky work assignments run a substantial risk of being downgraded in the estimation of their employers if they fail to pull off all of these projects successfully.

MAPPING THE RACIAL LAW OF AVERAGES

We have supplemented the publicly available data with our own preliminary research on black Harvard Law School graduates in the classes of 1981, 1982, 1987, and 1988; a survey of 200 Harvard black alumni; a survey of 250 corporate law firms; and interviews. We divide our review of the data into two parts: recruiting and retention. Simply hiring more black lawyers is unlikely to change the racial composition of these institutions in light of the fact that virtually all of these new entrants leave before making partner. Retention, not recruitment, is therefore the key to increasing the number of black lawyers. Retention, however, is affected by the dynamics of the recruiting process. The fewer blacks a firm already has among its associates and partners, the more difficult it may be to recruit black students.

Firms now expend enormous resources on interviewing second-, third-, and even some first-year students for summer and full-time positions. Paradoxically, however, they collect little information about a student's actual substantive legal knowledge or skills, and the information they do acquire is generally ignored. The on-campus interview consists of a brief twenty-minute discussion with a single lawyer, taken up almost entirely with the applicant's general interests, background, and experience and whatever questions the applicant has about the firm. Firms make call-back decisions based on the information that appears on an applicant's resumé and transcript and this interview. Rather than ranking candidates by academic standing, firms tend to use loose grade cutoffs pegged to the academic standing of the applicant's school. More often than not, call-back interviews merely repeat this pattern. At some firms, this is a pro forma process in which most candidates receive summer offers; even firms that use call-back interviews as a screening device focus primarily on personality and fit. Although firms collect information about their summer associates, large firms in San Francisco, New York, and Chicago make permanent offers to more than 80 percent of summer associates. Many of the country's most prestigious firms extend offers to virtually all their summer associates.

The question remains why firms invest such large sums in recruiting and why they rely on a mixture of objective and subjective criteria. Elite firms also use recruiting as a means of signaling the firm's quality to potential clients, competitors, and potential recruits. Among the traditional signals are the number of former Supreme Court law clerks, law review members, and elite law school graduates. In order to win the competition for these coveted recruits, firms must both credibly signal their quality to these applicants and appear to treat applicants fairly. This helps to explain the division of the recruiting process into a "visible" stage, in which firms review a candidate's objective credentials, and an "invisible" stage dominated by subjective judgments about personality and fit. Because the call-back interview occurs out of sight, firms focus on assessing whether the applicant will fit its culture. The objective signals firms employ at the visible stage, although a highly imperfect measure of an applicant's potential, do a reasonably good job of reducing the pool and, more importantly, give clients, competitors, and law students an accessible and rankable method of rating firms.

The fact that firms rely on a few objective signals to identify qualified applicants at the visible stage and reserve the right to go behind these credentials to make judgments about personality and fit at the invisible stage doubly disadvantages black applicants. By relying on sorting devices such as law school status, grades, and law review membership, firms systematically exclude the majority of black applicants who do not have these standard signals. Thus, although blacks may be more likely to attend higher-status law schools than whites, the schools with the largest black populations are not ones from which large firms typically recruit. Even black students with superstar credentials from lower-status schools have little or no chance of being hired by a large firm. Those blacks who do attend elite schools face recognized barriers (e.g., poor primary and secondary school education, diminished expectations, hostile environments, and part-time work) to performing well in the classroom or in extracurricular activities such as law review. Given these added pressures, it is plausible that some black students who are currently admitted to elite schools would be more successful if they did not attend these academic institutions. However, given the nearly dispositive role that the status of an applicant's law school plays in the recruiting process, black students who want to have the option of working at an elite firm have little incentive to choose this option.

To the extent that firms make hiring decisions based on signals such as grade point averages, as opposed to the substantive content of the courses a student has taken, black applicants have an incentive to maximize the former at the expense of the latter. At the same time, the emphasis on personality and fit at the invisible stage (both on-campus and call-back interviews) can disadvantage black applicants with traditional signals. Although incidents such as the 1989 debacle involving a partner from Baker & McKenzie, who demanded to know a black female applicant's high school grade point average and how she would react to being called a "black bitch" or "nigger," are undoubtedly rare, they underscore the fact that outright prejudice against blacks still exists at elite firms. A consistent line of empirical research demonstrates that when whites evaluate blacks, they frequently attribute negative acts "to personal disposition, while positive acts are discounted as the product of luck or special circumstances." Pervasive myths about black intellectual inferiority combined with lower than average levels of achievement in areas such as grades and test scores tend to make white interviewers question the credentials of blacks more than those of whites. In addition, interviewers generally expect to feel less comfortable when interviewing blacks. Similarly, as we note above, interviewers frequently tend to believe that blacks are "uninterested" in corporate practice.

Since race is costless to observe, it provides a convenient mechanism, much like "personality" and "fit," for sorting applicants. Blacks, on average, have less access to influential contacts and other informal networks that allow some candidates to bypass the formal screening requirements. Consider the experiences of two students at the University of Virginia law school. Jay, a white male, and Jennifer, a black female, both had grades in the B-minus–C range. As a result, although both have strong personal qualities and

extracurricular activities, neither was able to secure an interview with a large firm in their respective cities of choice (Richmond for Jay, Atlanta for Jennifer) through the normal University of Virginia process. Nevertheless, by the end of the story, Jay is headed for three promising interviews with Richmond firms while Jennifer has no such prospects. Why? Because Jay was able to call a friend "with considerable influence in Richmond." Jennifer had no similar connections, although she was a member of the University of Virginia law review and had worked for two small firms during prior summers, one in Atlanta.

Ironically, these structural features of the recruiting process also lead us to predict that blacks who *are* hired will tend, on average, to be clustered in the superstar range. At the 73 elite firms who responded to our survey (29 percent response rate; 51 and 50 percent in New York and Washington, D.C., respectively) 5 percent more black than nonblack associates were graduates from elite schools. The black associates also tend to come from schools at the top of the elite range. Graduates from Harvard Law School constituted 24 percent of all the blacks in our law-firm survey; even if we limit the universe of qualified African American applicants to the graduates of the schools from which the firms in our survey actually hired during the year in question, this is nearly four times greater than the percentage of black Harvard graduates in the available pool. In New York firms, Harvard, Columbia, and NYU graduates were 51 percent of black associates; in the District of Columbia, Harvard, and Georgetown graduates were 52 percent.

When we look back to a period when there was less affirmative action, we find evidence that going to an elite law school was even more important for blacks. At five national law firms, 77 percent of black partners attended one of 13 elite law schools, compared with 70 percent of all white partners; the respective percentages who had attended Harvard or Yale were 47 and 33.

Because virtually all the blacks who start at a given elite law firm leave before becoming partner, we now examine how the institutional characteristics of those firms—high salaries, pyramiding, and tracking—affect a black associate's partnership prospects. Some associates report that they receive valuable training opportunities, while others do not. Once an associate acquires a reputation as being well trained, she will continue to receive training in the form of demanding work. An associate's perception about which track she is on will have a substantial impact on how long she decides to stay with the firm.

Black associates face three significant barriers to getting on the training track. First, an associate has to have mentors among the firm's partners or senior associates who can provide the royal jelly of good training. Less than 40 percent of our survey of black Harvard Law School graduates (only 24 percent of pre-1986 graduates) stated that a partner had taken interest in their work or career. Of those who did not find a mentor, 68 percent said this was a significant factor in deciding to leave the firm (79 percent of post-1986 graduates). There is reason to believe that the situation is even bleaker for black women. Chief among the factors that contribute to this problem is the bias that potential mentors have for protégés who resemble them. Because partners have little information about a new associate's actual skills, the decision about who is a superstar worthy of training will be made in the same way as it is done at the recruiting stage—based on a few easily observable signals. Blacks may also suffer from a general perception that they are "less interested" in corporate work than other lawyers. This sentiment may be reinforced by the fact that black associates appear to be more likely than their white peers to do more than the average amount of pro bono work, to hold skeptical views about the social utility of some of the goals of their corporate clients, and to leave corporate practice for jobs in the public sector. Finally, black associates will have difficulty getting onto the training track precisely because the generation of black associates before them did not.

Sociologists contend that when a group's representation in the workforce is small, individual members face increased pressures to perform and conform. Over 40 percent of our respondents reported that they were criticized more than white associates for making similar mistakes. If partners expect black associates to be average or unacceptable, then any mistake will be seen as confirming this initial assessment. Small numbers also increase the probability that group members will be tied together in the minds of members of the dominant group.

Lawyers wishing to move laterally face conflicting incentives: the longer they stay, the more they can claim to have accumulated valuable skills; but the closer they are to partnership, the greater the danger that potential employers may presume that they are leaving because they are not "good enough" to make partner. Only 15 percent of black Harvard respondents who had left their first elite firm went to another one; 33 percent went into government, 20 percent to corporate legal departments, and 17 percent to small nonelite firms. We hypothesize that the optimal time for black associates to leave firms is earlier than that for white associates.

Black associates therefore have strong incentives to choose career strategies that either minimize the danger of sending a negative signal or, conversely, maximize their opportunity for being regarded as superstars. The first requires the associate either to steer clear of demanding assignments or take fewer risks in completing the work. Only 32 percent of Harvard black alumni worked in corporate practice (24 percent of pre-1986 graduates). Only 14 percent of black partners work in general corporate practice, and less than 11 percent specialize in technical fields, such as banking (6 percent), bankruptcy (2 percent), and tax (1 percent). Anecdotal evidence also suggests that black associates may be overly cautious when performing their work. Those who study law-firm interactions report that many black associates tend to speak less in meetings (particularly with clients), ask more clarifying questions when receiving work, are more likely to check assignments before handing them in, are more reluctant to disagree with partners or express criticism of their peers, and construe their assignments more narrowly. But successfully completing "difficult" work assignments is the best way for an associate to signal quality and thus worthiness for training.

At the opposite extreme, a black associate may seek out demanding assignments in order to overcome the presumption that she is "only" average—or worse. In response to our survey, 45 percent reported specializing in litigation (52 percent of pre-1986 graduates). These percentages are higher than those in all but the most litigation-oriented firms. This has been the most successful avenue to partnership: 56 percent of black partners at elite firms are litigators. Although many kinds of corporate work are handled exclusively by elite firms, litigators are needed in many different settings, including government, small firms, solo practice, and in-house legal departments. The lower level of scrutiny in litigation, however, increases the risk that an associate will fall through the cracks. There also is a substantial amount of routine low-visibility work. These factors make litigation one of the least likely routes to partnership for associates as a whole. Moreover, the pro bono or other small cases in which a black associate might be given major responsibility often do not generate the kind of positive feedback that might justify the risk and effort. Finally, litigation is generally less stable than corporate work, and dispute-specific factual knowledge is less transferrable to future cases.

In a study of successful minority managers in corporations, David Thomas concluded that even those who ultimately make it into the top ranks do not have the same smooth, linear progression as their white peers. This pattern of slow growth followed by relatively dramatic jumps in position is virtually impossible in a world in which both firms and associates make important career decisions within the first one or two years. There is, however, a way in which black lawyers have been able to replicate the success patterns Thomas outlines, although it involves leaving the firm. A substantial percentage of all black partners in our data set first worked in government (37 percent), in-house counsel's office (28 percent), and/or academia (11 percent). Similarly in our survey, all four black Harvard graduates who had become partners in major firms first left their original firms and went into either government (three) or a small firm (one).

FINDING EFFICIENT RESPONSES TO
EFFICIENT DISCRIMINATION

So long as firms continue to generate both a small number of high-quality partners and a steady supply of hardworking associates, they have little economic reason to alter the way they structure their business. Those who wish to break this cycle must therefore alter the incentives that firms presently face. Many commentators have documented the difficulty of applying Title VII and other similar antidiscrimination laws to high-level jobs in which quality judgments are inherently subjective. Nevertheless, the threat of liability undoubtedly encourages firms to pay more attention to their employment practices. Lawrence Mungin, a black Harvard Law School graduate, successfully sued the Washington, D.C., office of Katten, Muchin & Zavis for "constructively discharging" him on the basis of his race. When Mungin, a senior associate, requested that he be evaluated along with the other associates in his class, he was working primarily on projects that would normally have been handled by second- and third-year associates. Not surprisingly, Katten's managing partner informed him that it would be impossible to make him a partner based on his current performance. Mungin's lawsuit revealed, however, that when Katten's Washington office lost most of its bankruptcy business (Mungin's area of specialization), he was told he would receive work from the Chicago main office, which never arrived. Nor was Mungin included in departmental meetings in Washington or Chicago or given a performance review during his first 18 months, even though Katten's policy was to review every associate twice a year. By shining light on the normally invisible world of law-firm staffing and work-assignment decisions, Mungin's case may encourage firms to pay more attention to whether black associates are getting access to challenging and productive work.

Formal training and mentoring programs might seem to be the ideal solution to the institutional dynamics we describe. But despite the fanfare with which firms announce their new training efforts, it is clear that those wishing to succeed must still gain access to the traditional training track. These programs say nothing about who will actually get the type of work associates need to succeed. Formal assignment systems could break these patterns, but powerful partners routinely bypass them to grab superstar associates. Similarly, formal evaluation systems, while potentially providing valuable information and feedback, can also act as a diversion that allows partners to refrain from giving real feedback in the course of the working relationship.

A growing number of elite law firms have hired diversity consultants, who attempt to educate lawyers about their colleagues by alerting them to differing and sometimes incorrect perceptions, pointing out the possibility that some minority lawyers believe that they are being discriminated against, and illustrating how stereotypes can often result in discriminatory behavior. Anecdotal reports suggest that diversity consultants tend to concentrate on exposing how racist comments, unintended slights, and cliquish social patterns marginalize black lawyers. However, less than a third of the respondents to our survey mentioned explicit racist comments made in their presence, and less than 20 percent of those who did said the incident was a major reason for leaving the firm. Although a higher proportion (56 percent) did not feel welcome in the informal social networks within the firm, nearly half (46 percent) of these did not consider this a major factor in deciding whether to leave the firm. Moreover, there is a long history of firms and courts subtly transforming informal grievance procedures into mechanisms for suppressing conflict.

In 1988, the American Bar Association initiated the Minority Counsel Demonstration Project to encourage participating corporations to retain minority firms and to ensure that minority partners in majority firms do some of their legal work. In its first three years, 133 corporations, 39 major law firms, and 21 minority-owned firms participated, generating more than $100 million in billings for minority lawyers. Moreover, the number of minority associates at the 15 majority firms reporting increased by over 50 percent during the three years, and the number of minority partners by 57 percent. Nevertheless, there is reason to be skeptical. The claim that diversity is good for a corporation's bottom line has substantial force in sectors of the economy that sell consumer products, trade internationally, or do substantial business with the government. But when AT&T is considering a new joint-venture agreement, it wants lawyers who know how to operate in the complex world of strategic planning and corporate finance, a world that is still overwhelmingly white and male. It is not surprising, therefore, that most corporate participants in the ABA Program do little more than send the same letter every year "requesting information" and dole out a few small projects that are often below the pricing structure for most major firms. Yet, anecdotal evidence suggests that black in-house lawyers are more likely to take an active interest in ensuring that work is fairly distributed to black lawyers inside firms, and black political clout has frequently been translated into opportunities for black lawyers.

At least since the 1970s, many elite firms have hired black lawyers whose rankable signals were lower than the average credentials of the firm's white associates. These affirmative action programs appear to have increased the presence of black lawyers in the elite firms. The most common objections raised to such programs—lowered standards, reduced worker effort, and stigmatized beneficiaries—do not provide persuasive grounds for abandoning them at elite firms. To the extent that goals and timetables or other affirmative recruiting measures give firms a reason to detect and prevent practices that favor whites over blacks with functionally *equal* qualifications, these measures will, in fact, serve rather than weaken the goal of "standards." Moreover, the standards critique ignores the tremendous growth in the size and quality of the law school applicant pool over the last few decades. Firms have an incentive to seek out superstars and to protect themselves against unacceptable workers. In the middle, however, they are (at least on efficiency grounds) indifferent since they know that differences among candidates in this range are not worth the trouble of investigating. Paradoxically, even in a world where some find the standards critique persuasive, the firm that hires the most black lawyers ought to be the one whose reputation among these skeptics suffers the least. Thus, firms such as San Francisco's Morrison & Foerster and New York's Cleary, Gottlieb, Steen & Hamilton can credibly claim that they are among the "best" firms for black lawyers. This, in turn, should signal to their clients, their competitors, and the general population of law students that the black lawyers they hire are likely to be the best in the available pool.

If affirmative action provides the average black associate, who today faces a low probability of success, with a somewhat greater probability, this can *only increase* her incentive to work. Associates are choosing some combination of signals and skills to help them both get a *ticket to the tournament* (where the price of the ticket is the level of signals the firm requires) and then have a chance of *winning the tournament* (where initial skills are necessary to help one be chosen by a partner for the training track). If as a result of affirmative action, blacks have to spend less of their scarce resources on purchasing the ticket, they can use those resources to acquire skills that will increase their chances of winning the tournament.

The logic of the stigma argument is straightforward and compelling. If it is widely known that at least some significant number of blacks have benefited from affirmative action, employers will rationally discount any particular black candidate's credentials by the amount they think she has benefited. The danger is that partners will choose to give routine projects to the black associates while assigning analytical-training-related ones to the white associates. The solution, however, is not to abandon voluntary affirmative action in hiring but to extend it to decisions regarding the choice of associates for projects and other internal firm decisions. Companies such as Procter and Gamble and AT&T rate their managers in terms of their success in promoting the firm's diversity goals and weigh these ratings in setting compensation and determining promotions. If elite firms were to institute policies of this kind, partners would have concrete incentives to insure that blacks make it onto the training track.

DISCUSSION QUESTIONS

1. What are the similarities and differences between women and racial minorities in their experiences of exclusion from and admission to the profession and in the professional roles they have come to occupy?[2] What are the differences among racial minorities? How has the experience

of racial minorities differed from that of ethno-religious minorities? On Jewish lawyers, see J. Young, "The Jewish Law Student and New York Jobs—Discriminatory Effects in Law Firm Hiring Practices," 73 *Yale Law Journal* 625 (1964); Jerold Auerbach, *Unequal Justice: Lawyers and Social Change in Modern America* (1970); *Rabbis and Lawyers: The Journey from the Torah to the Constitution* (1990).

2. What should be our goals with respect to the racial composition of the legal profession? How is that composition important for racial minorities? For the profession? The legal system? The larger society? Should we be equally concerned about the class background of lawyers?

3. What mechanisms should we use to achieve these goals? Why are market forces insufficient to eliminate discrimination? What changes would be necessary in practice settings other than the large firm to increase minority representation?

How does the educational system reproduce racial inequality? How did ethnoreligious minorities and the poor enter the profession earlier? What are the other barriers to entry and success in the profession? Are affirmative action policies still needed? Are they constitutional? Politically viable? If both, how should they be structured? In November 1996, by a 53.6 to 46.4 percent margin, California voters approved Proposition 209, declaring that "the state shall not discriminate against, or grant preferential treatment to, any individual or group on the basis of race, sex, color, ethnicity, or national origin in the operation of public employment, public education, or public contracting." What explains this backlash? What should public university law schools do in response?

SUGGESTED READING[3]

J. Clay Smith Jr. has written a massive history of black lawyers through World War II, *Emancipation: The Making of the Black Lawyer, 1844–1944* (1993); see also his article "In Freedom's Birth-

---

2. On women's lawsuits against accounting and law firms, see *New York Times* B14 (11.30.90), B8 (1.1.93).

3. I am grateful to Aaron Porter for several of these references.

place: The Making of George Lewis Ruffin, The First Black Law Graduate of Harvard University," 39 *Howard Law Journal* 201 (1995). Mark Tushnet is writing the history of the NAACP and Thurgood Marshall: *The NAACP's Legal Strategy against Segregated Education, 1925–1950* (1987); *Making Civil Rights Law: Thurgood Marshall and the Supreme Court, 1936–1961* (1994); see also J. L. Chestnut Jr. and Julia Case, *Black in Selma: The Uncommon Life of J. L. Chestnut Jr.* (1990). Other studies include Fitzhugh L. Styles, *Negroes and the Law* (1937); W. H. Hale, "The Career Development of the Negro Lawyer in Chicago" (Ph.D. dissertation, sociology, Chicago, 1948); J. Schuman, "A Black Lawyers Study," 16 *Howard Law Journal* 255 (1971); Harry T. Edwards, "A New Role for the Black Law Graduate—A Reality or an Illusion?" 69 *Michigan Law Review* 1407 (1971); Kenneth S. Tollett, "Black Lawyers, Their Education, and the Black Community," 17 *Howard Law Journal* 326 (1972); Marion S. Goldman, *A Portrait of the Black Attorney in Chicago* (1972); Edward B. Toles, *History of the National Bar Association* (1975); J. Clay Smith, "Career Patterns of Black Lawyers in the 1980s," 7 *Black Law Journal* 75 (1981); Geraldine Segal, *Blacks in the Law: Philadelphia and the Nation* (1983); "Symposium: National Conference on Minority Bar Passage: Bridging the Gap Between Theory and Practice," 16 *Thurgood Marshall Law Review* (1991); Steven Greer and Colin Samson, "Ethnic Minorities in the Legal Profession: A Case Study of the San Francisco Bar," 22 *Anglo-American Law Review* 321 (1993). For earlier studies of black lawyers in business law practice, see "Symposium: The Black Lawyer in America Today," 22 *Harvard Law School Bulletin* (February 1971); John T. Baker, "Black Lawyers and Corporate and Commercial Practice: The Unfinished Business of the Civil Rights Movement," 18 *Howard Law Journal* 685 (1975); John T. Baker and Jerome Davis, "Black Businesses and Their Lawyers," 8 *North Carolina Central Law Journal* 53 (1976). Elizabeth Chambliss's Ph.D. dissertation in sociology at the University of Wisconsin, "The New Partners with Power? Organizational Determinants of Law Firm Integration" (1992), dealt with women and minorities in large firms; Aaron Porter's at the University of Pennsylvania is a history of the Austin Norris law firm in Philadelphia; see also Abraham Mortimer Casson, "The Negro Law Student: His Childhood Experience, Vocational Interests, and Professional Concerns" (Ph.D. dissertation, University of Michigan, 1970); Susan Silbert, "Making It to the Top: A Study of Black Partners in Major Law Firms" (Ph.D. dissertation, sociology, University of Southern California, 1985).

On the consequences of an earlier Supreme Court decision limiting affirmative action, see John Gruhl and Susan Welch, "The Impact of the *Bakke* Decision on Black and Hispanic Enrollment in Medical and Law Schools," 71 *Social Science Quarterly* 458 (1990); Valeria Fontaine, "Progress Report: Women and People of Color in Legal Education and the Legal Profession," 6 *Hastings Women's Law Journal* 27 (1995); see also Lewis A. Kornhauser and Richard L. Revesz, "Legal Education and Entry into the Legal Profession: The Role of Race, Gender, and Educational Debt," 70 *New York University Law Review* 176 (1995); Wilma Williams Pinder, "When Will Black Women Lawyers Slay the Two-Headed Dragon: Racism and Gender Bias," 20 *Pepperdine Law Review* 1053 (1993); Deborah Jones Merrit and Barbara F. Reskin, "Sex, Race, and Credentials: The Truth About Affirmative Action in Law Faculty Hiring," 97 *Columbia Law Review* 199 (1997). For a black law professor's take on affirmative action, see Stephen L. Carter, *Reflections of an Affirmative Action Baby* (1991).

There are a number of studies of the experience of racial minorities in law school, which may help explain their representation within the profession, e.g., Leo M. Romero, Richard Delgado, and Cruz Reynoso, "The Legal Education of Chicano Students: A Study in Mutual Accommodation and Cultural Conflict," 5 *New Mexico Law Review* 177 (1975); Linda E. Davila, "The Underrepresentation of Hispanic Attorneys in Corporate Law Firms," 39 *Stanford Law Review* 1403 (1987).

If racial minority lawyers were evenly distributed throughout the profession, there would be fewer in the practice categories that have contributed most to redressing racial inequality. David Wilkins reflects on the obligations of those who have achieved the greatest professional success.

TWO PATHS TO THE MOUNTAINTOP? THE ROLE OF LEGAL EDUCATION IN SHAPING THE VALUES OF BLACK CORPORATE LAWYERS[1]

David B. Wilkins

THE week of January 18, 1993, was filled with both hope and sorrow for black lawyers. At the beginning of the week, Martin Luther King's birthday was legally celebrated in every state for the first time since it was declared a national holiday. The next day, the first president in twelve years to enthusiastically endorse the use of law as an instrument for social change took the oath of office. By week's end, however, two of the most famous black lawyers of their respective generations had died. On January 20, Reginald F. Lewis, who came to national prominence when he engineered the billion-dollar leveraged buyout of Beatrice, International, died at the age of 50. Five days later, Justice Thurgood Marshall, the guiding light of the modern civil rights movement and a tireless advocate for the rights of all Americans, died at the age of 84.

In life, these two men had a good deal in common. Both were natives of Baltimore and attended historically black colleges. From there, however, their paths diverged significantly. Marshall attended Howard Law School, where, under the stewardship of Charles Hamilton Houston, he learned the skills that would eventually make him history's most effective advocate for the legal rights of blacks. Almost forty years later, Lewis attended Harvard Law School, where he learned the skills that would propel him on his meteoric rise in the corporate world; first as an associate in a prestigious corporate law firm, then as the founder of his own Wall Street firm, and finally as chairman and chief executive officer of a multibillion-dollar corporation.

These differing paths mirror a general trend within the black bar. With few exceptions, the black lawyers of Thurgood Marshall's generation attended segregated schools and spent most of their careers providing services to black clients. Some, like Marshall, were specifically trained to combat legal segregation and devoted the majority of their professional lives to this struggle. But even those who were not full-time civil rights lawyers participated indirectly in the struggle for racial justice by helping ordinary blacks gain access to a legal system that was at best recalcitrant and at worst hostile to their interests.

Reginald Lewis's generation of black lawyers typically have a different biography. Although born before *Brown v. Board of Education*, these lawyers came of age during the civil rights movement. As a result, many were admitted to integrated colleges or law schools as part of the first wave of affirmative action programs. And, as the years passed, a growing number of blacks who graduated from the top law schools were given the opportunity to pursue careers in the previously all-white world of corporate law practice.

What difference will it make to the long-term struggle to end the legal, economic, and political subjugation of blacks in the United States that a substantial number of the most talented and best educated black lawyers are likely to spend some or all of their careers in corporate law practice? First, there are significant risks that black lawyers who devote their professional energies to serving the needs of corporate clients will often fail to reduce, and may in some instances reinforce, unjustified inequalities between blacks and whites. Second, one important strategy for minimizing this danger is for black corporate lawyers to recognize that they have moral obligations running to the black community that must be balanced against other legitimate professional duties and personal commitments when deciding on particular actions and, more generally, when constructing a morally acceptable life plan. I call this strategy the obligation thesis.

1. 45 *Stanford Law Review* 1981 (1993). Reprinted with permission.

THE PARADOX OF OPPORTUNITY:
CORPORATE LAW PRACTICE
AND THE STRUGGLE FOR RACIAL JUSTICE

Those who designed the first wave of affirmative action programs that brought bright young black students like Reginald Lewis to Harvard Law School believed that one way to address these pervasive inequalities was to increase the number of black lawyers. At the time these programs were instituted, there were no more than a handful of black lawyers in most areas of the United States. Given the relative poverty of many black communities and the unwillingness of many white lawyers to serve even those black clients who could afford legal services, most blacks had relatively little access to lawyers. For many early affirmative action proponents, this pervasive legal need was the primary justification for making special efforts to increase the number of black lawyers.

Viewed from this perspective, the fact that many of the black students who came to law school as a result of these programs will spend a substantial portion of their professional lives serving the interests of corporate clients constitutes something of a missed opportunity. The true cost of the transition to corporate practice, however, may be more than simply missed opportunity. Corporations employ a disproportionate share of the total number of lawyers, who in turn help these powerful actors plan future projects, develop strategies for obtaining maximum advantage from existing rules, lobby government officials for favorable rule changes, and defeat claims brought against them by others.

The fact that corporations use lawyers to perpetuate their absolute and relative power has two important implications for the present inquiry. First, by solidifying corporate power, corporate lawyers help to entrench the current overall distribution of wealth and power in American society. Most blacks, however, are at or near the bottom of this distribution, Moreover, this position is *unjustified* given the link to past and present racial practices. Black lawyers who assist corporations in achieving their objectives may in fact perpetuate the status quo and thereby indirectly participate in the subjugation of the black community.

Moreover, on a growing number of issues, the practices of certain large corporations and the interests of either individual blacks or the articulated concerns of the black community will be directly opposed. For example, employment discrimination litigation often pits large corporate employers against one or more blacks who assert that they have been denied employment benefits on the basis of race. A similar story is emerging with respect to many environmental and consumer issues. In these and other areas where particular blacks are challenging a given corporate practice, a black lawyer who works to sustain that practice may directly impede the cause of racial justice.

Some might assert that in light of this danger, blacks should avoid corporate law practice altogether. This argument, however, ignores the potential social justice benefits of having at least some black corporate lawyers. The claim that blacks should not be corporate lawyers must overcome a heavy presumption against closing off opportunity on the basis of race.

Furthermore, consequentialist arguments about the negative effects that black corporate lawyers will inevitably impose on the black community frequently ignore the beneficial externalities that might flow from establishing a black presence within the corporate bar. Five such benefits seem plausible. First, if nothing else, the presence of blacks within these elite ranks undermines the stereotype of black intellectual inferiority. It therefore becomes somewhat more difficult to justify policies and practices that retard black achievement on the express or implicit assumption that blacks are inherently unqualified to perform the work. Second, as a corollary to the first point, the achievements of black corporate lawyers might inspire other young black women and men to strive harder to become successful in their own right. Indeed, in addition to being passive role models, black corporate lawyers might work actively to open up additional opportunities for blacks, in law or elsewhere. Third, corporate law practice gives black lawyers access to money and other resources that can be directed toward projects to benefit the black community. Fourth, in addition to offering material rewards, corporate law practice traditionally has been a stepping-stone to politics and potential influence. As a result, black corporate lawyers may be able to translate their private power into public power in ways that benefit the black community. Finally, the very fact that corporations have such power to impose costs on the black community underscores the benefits that could accrue if black lawyers are able to persuade corporations to act in ways that are less harmful (and perhaps even beneficial) to the black community.

We are left, therefore, with a paradox. On the one hand, a primary goal of the civil rights movement was to ensure that blacks have an equal opportunity to participate in every aspect of the mainstream economy. Precisely because these new opportunities are located in the mainstream, however, they will often be closely linked with the very structures that have contributed to the oppression of blacks in the first instance. As a result, the more blacks take advantage of these new opportunities, the more they may find themselves separated from, and perhaps even opposed to, the demands of other blacks for substantive justice.

The obligation thesis offers one potential way out of this paradox. By positing that successful blacks have a duty to consider the interests of other blacks when performing their new roles, proponents of this thesis seek to ensure that the progress of individual blacks will not unduly impede the advancement of the black community as a whole.

THE CHALLENGE OF COMPREHENSIVE UNIVERSALISM

From the perspective of comprehensive universalism, the obligation thesis must answer one fundamental question: what is the *moral* justification for focusing on the obligations blacks in corporate law firms allegedly owe to other blacks? The answer begins with the fundamental fact that America was built on race. From the framework of our political order, to the origins of the capitalist enterprises that drive our economic system, to the mores and images that underlie our social and artistic lives, every contemporary American institution or practice traces at least part of its origins to the history of discrimination

against blacks. This legacy has two important consequences for the present inquiry. First, despite all of our many differences, black Americans continue to be joined by an identifiable common culture that overlaps with, but is distinct from, mainstream American culture. Moreover, and this is the second point, although individual blacks undoubtedly participate in and identify with this common cultural community in many different ways, no one can escape it altogether. In *today's* America, "race matters" in ways that go beyond individual choice. This is undeniably true with respect to how one will be perceived by others. But it is likely to affect one's self-perception as well. Almost one hundred years after DuBois's prophetic statement, the problem of the twentieth century continues to be "the color line." Neither blacks nor whites can escape this ever-present reality.

Two aspects of this reality support the move from the "is" of race consciousness to the "ought" of the obligation thesis. First, for many blacks (including some black corporate lawyers), the bonds of solidarity and community with other blacks constitute an important source of strength and well-being. In order to be sustained, however, these bonds must be nurtured for, as Stephen Carter argues, "the light of solidarity, like the light of love, will go out if not carefully tended." Second, regardless of whether one values the bonds of racial solidarity, the actions of individual blacks and the well-being of the black community are inextricably linked.

Taken together, these two consequences of contemporary race consciousness provide a moral foundation for the claim that black professionals have obligations running to other blacks. For those blacks whose membership in the black community is central to their identity, recognizing the existence of such an obligation promotes both a healthy self-love and a firm foundation for helping other blacks who are truly in need. Given the link between individual opportunity and group advancement, even those blacks who ultimately care only about their own moral right to be free from racist constraints ought to recognize a moral responsibility to participate in collective projects to end racist oppression. Moreover, moving beyond self-interest, black professionals must also recognize that they have *already* benefited from the group-based struggles of others.

Finally, morality requires that individual blacks take account of the unintended but nevertheless predictable consequences of their actions. Consider, for example, a black corporate lawyer who is asked to defend a company accused of discriminating against blacks in employment. No matter how much that lawyer protests that his race is irrelevant to the performance of his professional role, his very presence at the counsel table sends a message to the jurors (both black and white) about the merits of the discrimination claim.

At this point, opponents of the obligation thesis might raise one or more of the following six related objections to the moral arguments presented above. First, race consciousness is solely the product of race prejudice and therefore cannot give rise to any moral obligations on the part of those who are the victims of racist beliefs. Second, regardless of the current benefits of linking moral obligations to race, such thinking will inevitably perpetuate the power of these artificially created categories instead of helping to stamp them out. Third, even assuming that one should talk about race at all, it is *whites*, as the authors of this racist system, who have the sole responsibility for rectifying the situation. Fourth, moral obligations can only result from voluntary action, and the current generation of black lawyers neither asked for the sacrifices of past generations nor volunteered to be put in a leadership role. Fifth, even if the past is relevant, it is impossible to recover any specific intent from the millions of discrete individuals who participated in the relevant prior struggles. Finally, race consciousness and group solidarity, even when justified, should be avoided because of the danger that they will slip into hatred and oppression.

There are plausible grounds for rejecting all of these arguments as foundational critiques. First, moral wrongs by one person do not necessarily abrogate the moral obligations of another. Second, though it may be true that blacks focusing on race make it more likely that whites will do so as well, the opposite conclusion—that if blacks

stop focusing on race, whites will, too—seems a good deal less plausible. Without this crucial link, it is hard to see how the benefits of inching somewhat closer to race blindness outweigh the very real cost to the long-term group advancement that has in the past been the key for other groups to transcend discrimination and oppression. Third, even assuming that whites could remedy many of the unjustified harms inflicted on blacks, it is perfectly clear that they have so far failed to do so. Once it becomes apparent that the real wrongdoer does not intend to act, this reality becomes a *fact* that all other parties must take into consideration in fashioning their own conduct. Fourth, while those black lawyers who either choose to identify as members of the black community or voluntarily accept the benefits of affirmative action may incur additional obligations, even those who try to deny their racial identity cannot escape their history or their heritage. Given the dominance of race consciousness in the society at large, these lawyers cannot prevent their race from affecting the consequences of their actions. Like clean air, a less racist and hostile environment is a "public good" that black corporate lawyers cannot do without. Basic principles of fair play, reciprocity, and gratitude counsel in favor of recognizing an obligation to repay this benefit with actions that support the continued production of the public good. Fifth, although the multiple goals of the civil rights movement complicate the task of giving *content* to the obligation thesis, this diversity does not undermine the *existence* of such a duty. Whether one looks at the statements of black and white civil rights leaders, or the efforts by poor blacks to open the doors of opportunity for black professionals, it is clear that most of these participants would view the obligation thesis as a proper method for black professionals to honor the sacrifices of other blacks on their behalf. Finally, the proper response to the danger that group solidarity will slide into racism and oppression is not to hide behind a race blindness that willfully denies contemporary racism but rather to subject all group loyalties to ethical scrutiny.

MORALITY AND POLITICS: GIVING CONTENT TO THE OBLIGATION THESIS

Something more must be said about the content of the obligations if this thesis is to be anything other than a general call to arms for black corporate lawyers. Two questions lie at the heart of this task. First, what are the "interests" of the black community? Second, what are the morally acceptable strategies for "advancing" those interests?

The obligation thesis rests on two features of contemporary American life: the legacy and continuing presence of racism and pervasive black poverty. Antiracism and efforts directed at those blacks with the least opportunities are therefore a natural starting point for any attempt to define the "interests" of the black community. By themselves, however, they cannot provide a concrete blueprint for action. Consider, once again, the black lawyer asked to defend a company accused of race discrimination. What must he do to discharge his obligation to the black community? Must he refuse the case or perhaps even resign from the firm? Can he take the case so long as he has reasonable grounds to believe that the company did not in fact discriminate? Should he refrain from engaging in certain tactics (e.g., vigorously cross-examining the plaintiff) that he otherwise would be prepared to employ? What happens if he vigorously defends the case but then makes a substantial contribution to a job retraining program catering primarily to a black clientele? Or can the lawyer discharge his entire obligation by being the best lawyer that he can be, thereby continuing to shatter racist stereotypes?

CONCLUSION

In a prophetic speech the night before he was assassinated, Martin Luther King defiantly declared that he could stare death in the face because "I've been to the mountaintop.... And I've seen the promised land. I may not get there with you. But I want you to know tonight, that we, as a people, will get to the promised land." There can be no question that Thurgood Marshall, Charles Hamilton Houston, William Hastie, and the other visionary black lawyers of that generation walked the right path. As we mourn their passing, it is clear that the next generation of black leaders will in all probability walk a different one. Perhaps if we give these new black professionals a coherent and morally attractive reason to value their commitments to their community, they will not only find their way up the mountain, but finally help us to come down on the other side.

DISCUSSION QUESTIONS

1. Do racial minority lawyers have different career goals? Should they? Have the differences changed over time? Should we expect more difference across race than across gender or class?

2. Is there a relationship between expectations of community service and affirmative action programs? Should the latter be structured to encourage the former?

SUGGESTED READING

Wilkins continues to pursue the unique ethical dilemmas of minority black lawyers in "Race, Ethics, and the First Amendment: Should a Black Lawyer Represent the Ku Klux Klan?" 63 *George Washington University Law Review* 1030 (1995).

Chapter Nine
THEORIES OF THE LEGAL PROFESSION

Professions are occupational categories that have sought, and been accorded, distinctive privileges and responsibilities. Together with the military and the clergy, law and medicine are classic instances. For more than a century sociologists have analyzed the trajectory of professionalization; the following reading surveys the major approaches.

AMERICAN LAWYERS[1]
Richard L. Abel

THE study of professions encompasses three principal theoretical traditions: Weberian, Marxist, and a structural-functional approach associated with Parsons but rooted in Durkheim. Because each poses fundamentally different questions about society, they view the professions from radically divergent perspectives.

WEBERIAN THEORIES OF PROFESSIONS
IN THE MARKETPLACE

Constructing the Professional Commodity

Because professions produce services rather than goods, they confront two distinct problems in particularly acute form. First, the consumer must value the producer's services. The perception of value does not seem problematic from the perspective of contemporary medicine or even law. But if we consider the sorcerer in tribal societies or the clergy in many contemporary Western societies, the difficulties are immediately apparent. Second, consumers must be convinced they cannot produce the services themselves. Once again, consumer incompetence may be obvious if we reflect on neurosurgeons or corporate lawyers. In practice, however, we doctor, lawyer, and minister to ourselves much of the time, often resisting advice to consult an expert.

The success of producers in constructing a

1. New York: Oxford University Press, 1989. Reprinted with permission.

market for their services turns on several variables. What consumers "need" is a function of cultural beliefs, over which producers have limited influence. All they can do is amplify or dampen demand by connecting their services to fundamental values: religion with transcendental beliefs, medicine with physical well-being, and law with justice, security, or political and economic stability. Once potential consumers believe in the value of the service, professionals must persuade them to purchase it rather than simply produce it themselves. The division of labor compels this: as producers become specialized, consumers necessarily become generalized and thus dependent on others. Additional factors shape consumer dependence: professional services contain an irreducible element of uncertainty or discretion, a delicate balance between indetermination and technicality, art and science. Too much art and consumers lose confidence (as in quack medicine or investment advice); too much science and consumers can provide the service themselves or resort to nonprofessional advisers (do-it-yourself home repairs or divorces).

Other ingredients may help the profession construct a marketable commodity. The producer's expertise must appear objective, not arbitrary or idiosyncratic. For religious believers, the warrant of expertise is often tradition—a sacred text or church hierarchy—although charismatic leaders also contribute. But for most contemporary professions, the most powerful assurance of objectivity is identification with the natural sciences. Despite the efforts of lawyers to portray law as a logically deductive system, the public clearly sees it as a human construct and thus a reflection of political power. Professional knowledge must be esoteric; but aside from cherished residues of Latin and French, together with English archaisms, legal language is just ordinary language used in strange ways. Professional knowledge must reconcile stasis and change, traditional warrants of legitimacy and innovations that ensure continuing uncertainty. But whereas scientific traditions can invoke the validation of repeated experiments, ancient laws may be seen as the heavy hand of history. And whereas scientific novelty is axiomatically progress, law "reform" may be exposed as concessions to special interests. Professional knowledge is standardized; heterodoxy threatens its very foundation. At least since the triumph of the nation-state, law has been the voice of a single sovereign; but such unity may be resented as tyranny in pluralistic societies.

The relation between producers and consumers profoundly influences the construction of a marketable commodity. It is not coincidental that the two most successful contemporary professions, medicine and law, emerged by selling their services to individual consumers (as did their predecessor, the priesthood). Conversely, many occupations that entered the market more recently and sold their services either to existing professions (nurses to physicians, paralegals to lawyers) or large bureaucratic employers (social workers to government, teachers to school systems) never became more than semiprofessions. The commodity must be packaged in units consumers can afford, which may be one reason why physicians have been relatively more successful than lawyers. And it is very helpful to have exclusive access to a vital arena: hospitals for physicians, courts for lawyers, document registries for European notaries.

Efforts to construct the professional commodity are constantly being undermined. Other bodies of knowledge may challenge the hegemony of professional expertise: natural science has been eroding religious authority since at least the Enlightenment, and economics may be displacing law as the foundation of government today. Expert authority may also be unmasked as political domination: the feminist critique of medicine is a contemporary example, but law is far more vulnerable to such demystification. And the ratio of indetermination to technicality may become unbalanced. Art may be revealed as fakery: "laetrile" as a cancer cure, for instance. More dramatically, politicians and the public may lose faith in the ability of economists to forecast or manipulate macroeconomic trends. At the other extreme, technicality exposes professions to competition from paraprofessionals—as when dental hygienists practice independently—a threat that is amplified by developments in information technology.

Pursuing Social Closure

By constructing a marketable commodity, service producers become only an occupation. To professionalize they must seek social closure. This "professional project" has two dimensions: market control and collective social mobility. Although these are inextricably linked in practice, it is analytically useful to distinguish them, dealing with market control here and collective mobility later. Markets compel all occupations to compete. This may be advantageous to consumers—that is the market's fundamental justification, after all—but for producers competition is the classic zero-sum game: a consumer who buys more from one generally buys less from another. It is not surprising, therefore, that producers energetically try to escape from that freedom, notwithstanding their professed enthusiasm for markets.

Producers of goods can seek protection from market forces in a variety ways: through horizontal monopolies or cartels, vertical control over raw materials, and legal rights to technology and other intellectual inputs (patent, trademark, and copyright). Because services are not embodied in a physical form, however, their producers have only one option: control over the production of producers. Nonprofessional forms of closure include guilds, trade unions, civil service employment, academic tenure, and employment within large private bureaucracies. Weber suggests some of the permutations of closure:

> Various conditions of participation may be laid down: qualifying tests, a period of probation, requirement of possession of a share which can be purchased under certain conditions, election of new members by ballot, membership or eligibility by birth or by virtue of achievements open to anyone.

The mechanism of closure may be the object of struggle between potential competitors. "Healers" in California have sought to replace credentialing with title licensure, so that everyone could provide medical services as long as they identified themselves as physicians, nurses, chiropractors, osteopaths, podiatrists, or other healers.

Structural functionalists address this issue from a very different perspective. Closure is not a response to the market, and certainly not the conscious, self-interested strategy of producers, but simply the means by which society ensures that consumers receive quality services. Because it is so difficult for consumers to evaluate either the process of rendering services or the outcome, society maintains quality through input controls. Producers justify their obviously selfish behavior in the same way. When Los Angeles initiated a campaign against "bandit" taxicabs operating without an annual $690 permit, the city attorney proclaimed: "We're going to do everything we can to have a full frontal assault to protect our licensees *and to protect the public*" (emphasis added). And the Taxi Industry Council, representing the seven companies that cartelize the permits, denounced the "bandits" for such wrongs as having "actively advertised, solicited, cruised for fares, sat on taxi stands, hailed passengers, placed telephone ads, responded to telephone and radio orders, and otherwise sought to do business."

Weber categorically rejected this functionalist interpretation:

> When we hear from all sides the demand for an introduction of regular curricula and special examinations, the reason behind it is, of course, not a suddenly awakened "thirst for education" but the desire for restricting the supply of these positions and their monopolization by the owners of educational certificates.

Today the "examination" is the universal means of this monopolization, and therefore examinations irresistibly advance. A recent news article reported that it is virtually impossible to work as a clown in a major American circus today without a diploma from Clown College in Venice, Florida, which admitted only 60 out of 3,000 applicants in 1985.

Weberians can point to the lack of fit—or at least the failure to demonstrate any empirical correlation—between credentials and the actual work performed, whether technical qualifications and manual work or a liberal education and a white-collar job. Even if we concede that education may confer technical competence, the credentials required often far exceed the skills demanded.

It would be hard to argue that the credentials required of lawyers are necessary to the practice of law, given the national variation in legal pedagogy. Indeed, the little we know about what lawyers do suggests that they make scant use of their formal legal education.

> Scottish solicitors explained that on average they would deal with the law, in the sense of technical knowledge, for something around one hour a week. The rest of their time—taken up with handling personal relationships and business negotiations, and with consultations and meetings—involved little legal skills; either they used totally routinized legal knowledge or else they moved out of, or beyond, specifically legal work.

Jerome Carlin's study of sole practitioners in Chicago in the late 1950s came to similar conclusions:

> Time devoted to writing legal briefs and memoranda is at a minimum for all but a very few respondents. Reading legal material either for "keeping up" or on research in connection with some matter at hand accounts for only a small fraction of the individual practitioner's working day—less than a half hour a day, on the average. And only six respondents specifically mentioned engaging in any legal research.

To the extent that mandatory education serves purposes other than market control, it confers status through the university's association with high culture, socializes entrants to their professional roles, and provides warrants of loyalty and discipline.

Physicians are unusually open about their desire for social closure. In 1983, the president of the Union of American Physicians and Dentists declared that "now we find ourselves with a glut of doctors in California. In San Francisco, for example, there is one physician for every 187 citizens, or approximately three times the numbers that are needed to serve the population adequately." The following year the University of California requested no increase in funding for its medical schools, cut their budget by $7 million, and began planning to reduce enrollment between 5 and 7 percent. In 1986, the American Medical Association board of trustees issued a report urging "review" of medical school enrollments and exclusion of foreign-trained physicians. The chairman of the board noted that physicians were under "tremendous" pressure to lower their fees.

Closure strategies can be exclusionary (directed against equals or inferiors) or usurpationary (against superiors). They may emphasize either training or testing. Credentials may be demanded of individual producers or the institutions through which they become qualified or services are delivered. Closure can be achieved through exclusive rights to use a title, registration, or licensing.

Associations of producers obviously play a critical role in imposing entry requirements. Yet, paradoxically, the elite who typically organize and dominate the professional association and direct the professional "project" stand to gain few economic benefits by controlling the production of producers; they are more concerned with collective status. Closure is negotiated by the profession, the university, and the state. But despite the profession's constant invocation of the shibboleth of "independence," closure ultimately depends on the authority of the state, whose influence increases as it plays a greater role in financing training and reimbursing professionals.

A central question for a Weberian approach, and one of the most difficult, is why some occupations successfully professionalize while others do not. A number of factors may be relevant. Professions differ in the value their services promote: health and justice obviously rank high today, as salvation did in the past (and still does in many communities). Collegial control of the market is easier to attain if the clientele consists of isolated individuals. Furthermore, the homogeneity of the clientele is correlated with that of producers, which in turn affects whether a single profession emerges or several occupations continue to compete. Elite sponsorship can advance the professional project; conversely, professionalization can be hindered if many members of the occupation have disadvantaged social backgrounds (they are ethnic and racial minorities, from working-class families, or women). Elite universities can be instrumental, as in continental Europe; but England (and such former colonies as the United States, Canada, Australia, and New Zealand) clearly demonstrate that legal professions can train entrants largely or exclusively through apprenticeship.

Social closure is an elusive goal, even for the most successful professions, and must constantly be defended against threats from consumers and potential competitors, as well as the consequences of adventitious events. Success intensifies pressure for entry by aspiring professionals, jurisdictional challenges by potential competitors, and consumer complaints about excessive costs. Limitations on American medical school enrollment have driven 12,000 to 15,000 Americans a year to study outside the country, especially in nearby Mexico and the Caribbean, and then seek to have their credentials recognized in the United States. (The Reagan administration invoked the "threat" to American medical students in Grenada to justify the 1983 invasion.) The profession has responded by increasing the difficulty of the examination administered by the Education Commission for Foreign Medical Graduates (whose pass rate fell from 33 percent in 1982 to 14 percent in 1984) and persuading state boards in New York and California to reject the credentials of particular foreign schools. Those unable to obtain the necessary credentials can use political pressure to seek an individual exception, purchase a bogus diploma, attend cram courses that use previous tests, steal the examinations, or simply practice without a license—as an estimated 28,000 "physicians" are believed to do. Ideological changes and social movements can render the continued exclusion of disadvantaged groups intolerable. Demographic shifts caused by war or changing birthrates can alter both supply and demand. Changes elsewhere in the labor market can affect the relative attractiveness of a professional career. And the expansion of education—secondary schooling at the end of the nineteenth century, the tertiary sector after World War II—can lead to the inflation of credentials.

Economic Analyses of the Professions

Sociological theories of professions as closure are paralleled by economic analyses of professions as restraints on an otherwise free market. Although Adam Smith justified the exemption of professions from market forces as a means of ensuring quality, many of his twentieth-century followers have been considerably more skeptical. A strong and growing tradition sees limitations on entry to the profession and on competition among professionals as unfair to potential competitors (both outside the profession and within) and detrimental to consumers. Some economists subsume these objections within the broader critique that regulation inevitably is captured by and benefits producers at the expense of consumers. Although economists concede that licensing can increase the quality of services *delivered*, they emphasize that the quality of services *received* inevitably declines because higher prices depress demand.

Human-capital theory also seeks to justify the price of professional services as representing a reasonable return on the investment in education. Professional credentials are said to tell prospective employers the value of the employee's services. Yet there is no evidence that training correlates with either productivity or quality. Indeed, empirical studies find that the rate of return on the professional credential varies with the height of entry barriers, even when the length of educational preparation is controlled.

Finally, labor economists have noted the similarities between professions and segmented labor markets. Professions are simply a special instance of the dual labor market, although professionals' generalized skills allow them to move between employers. Economists attempt to justify these privileges, too, on the basis of informational inequality; but they remain open to the general critique of segmented labor markets.

Positive economic analyses describe not only how professions distort the market for services but also how those markets are self-correcting. Entry barriers may create monopoly rents in the short run, but these inevitably attract additional entrants who drive down the price of the professional commodity. There is evidence that the rising number of physicians has encouraged some to practice in smaller towns and forced others to reduce their fees. More generally, the use of credentials as a means of securing economic advantage and social status leads to the overproduction of those credentials and their progressive devaluation. If the 1970s was a decade of rapid professional expansion in response to supply shortfalls, the 1980s appear to have initiated a period in which excess supply discouraged entry: professional school enrollment declined in law, medi-

cine, dentistry, and veterinary medicine. Dental school enrollment in 1987 was a third lower than it had been in 1978, applications were down by two-thirds, and three of the 60 dental schools had closed.

Closure as Collective Mobility

The professional "project" is directed not only toward controlling the market but also toward enhancing professional status, an issue sociologists treat far more extensively than economists. Indeed, some sociologists define professions in terms of status—the quality and degree of respect enjoyed by virtue of an occupational role. Collective mobility appears to be a central objective of American teachers, who long have been organized in unions but now are preparing to seek a national credential based on examinations and apprenticeship. This interpretation is consistent with the fact that professional elites, whose economic privileges are secure, energetically pursue (and often initiate) efforts to raise the status of the entire occupational category. Even occupations that cannot achieve market control persist in seeking professional status.

The relationship between economic privilege and social respect is complex. Although inequality always requires justification, entrepreneurs seem to view success within the "free" market as self-legitimating, whereas professionals, who visibly control their markets, feel compelled to offer additional explanations. The exhausting training professionals must complete might better be understood as conspicuous sacrifice justifying future privilege, rather than inculcation of technical skill; such an interpretation helps explain the relative poverty endured by students, the tedium of study, the long hours and indignities of apprenticeship, the anxiety inflicted by examinations, and the postponement of full adulthood (including marriage). Medical internships and large law-firm associateships are familiar examples.

The status of a profession is affected by two principal factors (aside from its economic rewards): membership and clientele. Limitations on entry—the foundation of market control—inevitably influence the profession's composition as well as its numbers, whether or not this is intended. When American physicians excluded "persons of inferior ability, questionable character and coarse and common fiber" by implementing the reforms ultimately embodied in the Flexner report, the proportion of women medical graduates declined from 4.3 percent between 1880 and 1904 to 3.2 percent in 1912. Sociologists categorize entry barriers in terms of whether: (1) professional status is ascribed or achieved, (2) the warrant is aristocratic or modern, (3) entry is based on particularistic or universalistic qualities, and (4) mobility is sponsored or contested. Both the classic elite professions (like the English bar) and those occupations that successfully professionalized only in the nineteenth century (like Scottish accountants) appear to have benefited from their members' high status by birth. Professions shifted from ascribed to achieved status during the nineteenth and twentieth centuries as higher education, particularly within the university, came to confer prestige. Some professions resisted this transformation, however, fearing that barriers based on achievement would admit entrants from lower social backgrounds. And many have noted that previously male occupations, such as teaching and clerical work, lost status (and pay) when they were feminized during this period. But it is important not to allow meritocratic ideology to conceal the fact that even "achieved" qualifications disproportionately exclude those disadvantaged by class, race, or gender. Whatever mobility does occur tends to be found within the middle class rather than between classes.

Professions also gain and lose status from their clients. The classic professions of law and medicine clearly benefited from their historical association with aristocratic patrons. On the other hand, the failure of occupations like teaching and social work to professionalize during the twentieth century may be partly a result of their association with low-status clients.

Although professions are defined by the fact that the status of their members is collective—conferred on all entrants and enhanced by mobility of the entire category—internal status differences inevitably persist. These, too, may be a function of the characteristics of the particular member (ascribed or achieved) or the member's clients. But whereas collective mobility tends to solidify the professional category, intraprofessional mobility can impair it, as lower strata challenge those above them or higher strata seek to immunize themselves from taint by their inferiors.

Controlling Production by Producers

Controlling entry—the production *of* producers—is only the first step in the professional project. An occupation that seeks to professionalize also must control production *by* producers, both to increase its earnings and to enhance its status. This may be difficult: the American Psychological Association, unable to prevent members from seeking publicity or offering "instant therapy" on radio and television, repealed the rule prohibiting such practices.

Weber, again, surveys the range of possible restrictions:

> Closure within the group as between the members themselves and in their relations with each other may also assume the most varied forms. Thus a caste, a guild, or a group of stock exchange brokers, which is closed to outsiders, may allow to its members a perfectly free competition for all the advantages which the group as a whole monopolizes for itself. Or it may assign every member strictly to the enjoyment of certain advantages, such as claims over customers or particular business opportunities, for life or even on a hereditary basis.

Restrictions may be formal or informal, visible or invisible. Although their principal object is to protect members from competition with each other as well as with outsiders, such restraints may also enhance the profession's status by conferring an aura of disinterest. The image of professionals as *honoratiores* is reinforced by such devices as the academic hood (into which students put the fees paid to professors at medieval universities), Pooh-Bah's characterization of bribes as "insults" in *The Mikado*, and the widespread convention (now obsolete) that lawyers and physicians do not discuss fees in advance. British barristers are an extreme example: their clerks negotiate their fees, and they cannot sue clients who fail to pay.

Neoclassical economics discussed and criticized these forms of market control (as well as the entry barriers described earlier). Economists have found empirical confirmation for the theoretical prediction that advertising bans, fee schedules, prohibitions on interprofessional partnerships, and other anticompetitive rules increase consumer prices. Recent studies by the Federal Trade Commission, for instance, have shown that commercial optometrists sell contact lenses for about 35 percent less than ophthalmologists and that laws in 36 states limiting the number of automobile dealerships cost consumers $3.2 billion in 1985.

Yet just as professions have found it difficult to construct and defend their monopolies against external attack, so these restrictive practices, too, are very fragile. Psychiatrists and psychologists have been unable to prevent the proliferation of social workers and marriage and family counselors offering psychotherapy, whose numbers multiplied from 43 percent of providers in 1975 to 55 percent in 1985. Subordinated occupations constantly seek to expand their markets and increase their autonomy: pharmacists now can sell drugs that fall within a category intermediate between prescription and over-the-counter medicines; dental hygienists, dental assistants, and denturists have fought to enlarge their authority and gain the right to practice independently.

Demand for Professional Services

Theories of professionalism as closure focus on the nature and extent of occupational control over the *supply* of services. This is particularly true of economic analyses, which view demand as an exogenous variable independent of supply. Explanations of demand must be specific to the service, although demographic changes in the size and age distribution of the population affect most services.

Many factors influence the demand for legal services. Because all law is intimately associated with property rights, the demand for lawyers varies with the distribution of wealth and income. Thus, the rise of the bourgeoisie, the diffusion of home ownership, the growth of pension funds, the concentration of capital, and the proliferation of state welfare benefits all affect that demand. Within the private sector, the mix of economic activities (between the production of goods and services, for instance) can influence the level of demand. As portions of the economy are nationalized, administration may displace law, and econ-

omists or other technocrats may substitute for lawyers. Indeed, when the growth of the state antedates the accumulation of private capital, lawyers become civil servants rather than independent practitioners. Because law is state social control, it varies inversely with other forms of institutional control. Trends such as the increase in geographic mobility, attenuation of kinship bonds, declining salience of residential communities, weakening class identification, and secularization may augment the demand for legal control. Whenever the state subjects new areas of social life to legal regulation, the demand for lawyers increases—a notable contemporary example being laws that address the dissolution of marriage. Changes in existing law can have the same effect: the 1987 revision of federal income tax law increased demand for accountants by as much as 25 percent. Finally, cultural approval of recourse to law differs among societies and across time.

But demand is not a given to which professions simply react. Economists have argued theoretically and sought to demonstrate empirically that physicians create demand for their own services. One strategy is the development of new capabilities: physicians increase their ability to preserve or restore health or to prolong life by expanding their scientific knowledge and technological armory; and lawyers expand the benefits they can confer with every legal innovation—or complication. More than 80 percent of American dentists now perform "cosmetic" dentistry, which was estimated to have earned the profession half its $32 billion in annual revenue.

Professions also seek to rationalize and expand their markets by using intermediaries in both private and public sectors. Private insurance, frequently a benefit of employment or union membership, has dramatically affected the markets for medical services in the United States and legal services in Germany. Public subsidies have been even more important to the professions, particularly when the state reimburses private practitioners rather than employing professionals. Medicare payments to American physicians now exceed $20 billion a year—more than a third of the income of those who participate. The consequences of these forms of "demand creation" extend far beyond the economic benefits they confer on professionals. They create the potential for abuse and fraud.

In response, those who pay the bills insist on "mediative" control over the production and distribution of professional services, which increases the heterogeneity of consumers, stratifies the profession, and alters the relationship between producers and consumers. Medicare has drafted a "preferred provider" program, which would reimburse a higher proportion of medical costs if patients consult designated physicians whose charges remain within government guidelines. Physicians deeply resent governmental cost-containment measures that place a ceiling on their fees or circumscribe the care for which they may be reimbursed. Private employers, whose fringe benefits pay for about $100 billion a year in medical care, are requiring second opinions and insisting that many medical procedures be performed on an outpatient basis. Third-party payment may also affect the profession's collective status, perhaps enhancing it as a larger proportion of the population enjoys the services but also possibly lowering it if demand creation is seen as professional greed.

MARXIST THEORIES OF PROFESSIONS IN THE CLASS STRUCTURE

If Weberian theories address horizontal relations among occupational categories competing for market shares and social status, Marxist theories are concerned with the location and behavior of professions within the vertical hierarchy of classes defined by relations of production. Yet Marxists encounter difficulties in placing professionals. They could be capitalists—but they clearly do not own the means of production. They could be workers—but the tasks they perform, the rewards they garner, and their relations with subordinates and superiors are vastly different from those of most workers. And they could constitute a third category—but that would require a fundamental reworking of Marxist theory.

Marx seems to have expected the professions either to disappear or to be incorporated into one of the two great class adversaries. At times, however, both he and later Marxists recognized that the increasing concentration of capital would

require the expansion of a category of functionaries representing the owners of capital in their interactions with other capitalists, financiers, and workers.

Orthodox Marxism: Professionals and Relations of Production

Marx defined classes in terms of their relationship to the means of production, arguing that all societies have exhibited the opposition of two major classes, one of which exploits the other by extracting surplus value from its labor. This criterion leaves the class identity of lawyers as ambiguous as ever. Much of their work involves reproduction rather than production (e.g., family law, inheritance, or the transfer of unproductive property such as homes). Even within the capitalist enterprise, lawyers are more involved in distributing surplus among capitalists (e.g., through struggles over corporate control) than extracting it from workers. The basic unit for the production of legal services—the law firm—contains both associates who produce surplus value and partners who consume it.

Some authors have construed Marxism in functional terms, distinguishing the "global" functions of capital and labor and assigning members of society to one category or the other on the basis of the functions they perform. The global functions of capital include ideological inculcation, political repression, and the management and supervision of the working class. By this definition, physicians and engineers are members of the dominant class. Lawyers are even more intimately associated with such global functions as social control (criminal law), structuring the relations of production (labor law), exchange among capitalists (commercial law), and ownership of capital (corporate law). Yet such an expansive definition of capital subsumes a large proportion of the population, leaving the working class a minority, the outcome of class conflict a foregone conclusion, and history static.

Erik Olin Wright has argued that the Marxist concept of class is structural and therefore cannot be understood in such functionalist terms. Consequently, he and his associates have refined the basic categories by acknowledging that a number of crucial actors occupy contradictory class locations: semiautonomous wage earners (e.g., law-firm associates and the lower ranks of house counsel) between the proletariat and the petty bourgeoisie, small employers (e.g., partners in smaller law firms) between the petty bourgeoisie and the bourgeoisie, and managers (perhaps senior partners in larger firms and corporate general counsel) between the bourgeoisie and capitalists. This more nuanced picture highlights the ambiguity of professions in the class system, but in rejecting functionalism it conflates professionals who perform very different roles.

Professional Expertise as Power

Ever since Berle and Means noted the increasing separation of ownership and control within the capitalist enterprise, analysts have had to assess whether the technical expertise acquired by managers (on the job) and professionals (in the academy) renders them servants of power or enhances their autonomy. A large, diverse group of observers embrace the latter conclusion, although they disagree about whether technocrats will use their power for selfish or unselfish ends. If these analysts are correct and professionals do enjoy some autonomy, class analysis tells us relatively little about their behavior.

Working Conditions and the Proletarianization of Professionals

The third variant of Marxist theory predicts that professionals will become members of the proletariat as a result of changes in their working conditions. Indices of proletarianization include ever more detailed specialization and specification of tasks, speedups, subordination to external authority, and the entry of disadvantaged categories into the profession. Eliot Freidson is most vehement in rejecting the proletarianization thesis, noting that professions have suffered no decline in either their knowledge base or their social status—indeed, both have increased.

Derber makes a useful distinction between ideological and technical proletarianization. Technical proletarianization reflects the progressive separation of mental and manual tasks, the substitution of computers for workers, and the growth of a reserve labor force. Professionals avoid this fate by embracing ideological proletar-

ianization. They remain autonomous in selecting their means but only by allowing others to determine their goals. Extrinsic rewards (pay, career advancement, working conditions), which are often lavish, displace intrinsic satisfaction, which is limited to the exercise of technical skill. Lawyers have actually elevated their plight into an ethical mandate: the "cab rank" rule, which requires English barristers to represent any client who seeks their services (and can pay their fees); and the "principle of nonaccountability," which categorically rejects any moral identification of lawyers with the clients they represent.

What Does Class Analysis Tell Us?

Frank Parkin maintains that "those who monopolize productive property and credentials share for the most part a broadly similar political and ideological stance." There is evidence that educated workers are increasingly discontent with their conditions and rewards. They have joined unions in greater numbers and displayed more militant opposition to private and public employers. At the same time, professionalism fosters individualism, status consciousness, and preoccupation with technical autonomy. "New class" theorists emphasize the autonomy of professional ideology, noting the apparent diversity of lawyers' political attitudes. But if professionals do not constitute a class "for themselves," with a unitary program, then class analysis may not throw much light on the behavior of lawyers.

STRUCTURAL FUNCTIONAL THEORIES
OF PROFESSIONS AND THE SOCIAL ORDER

Whereas the problem for Weberians and neoclassical economists is the market and the problem for Marxists is class, the problem for structural functionalists is the social order: what holds together an aggregation of egoistic individuals? At least since Durkheim, professions have been an important part of the answer.

Professions in the System of Stratification

While Marxists conceptualize inequality as dividing society into two discrete and opposed classes defined by a single criterion (relations of production), structural functionalists stress continuous differences along a multiplicity of variables—including wealth, income, occupation, education, religion, ethnicity, race, gender, and parental background. They emphasize the heterogeneity of the professions in terms of background, training, function, clientele, rewards, and politics. The hierarchic ordering, and the location of professions at or near the top, encourages competing for rewards within the system instead of challenging it.

Threats to Professional "Autonomy"

An essential foundation of structural functional theories of the professions is the belief that, if protected from outside interference, they will use their expertise for the general good. Talcott Parsons exemplified this approach in writing about lawyers:

> His [the lawyer's] function in relation to clients is by no means only to "give them what they want" but often to resist their pressures and get them to realize some of the hard facts of their situations, not only with reference to what they can, even with clever legal help, expect to "get away with" but with reference to what the law will permit them to do.

The first question raised by such a theory—the extent to which the "independent" professional actually pursues client interest rather than personal interest and elevates the public interest above both—is rarely investigated empirically. Instead, structural functionalism simply assumes that independent professionals exhibit such desirable traits and then explores the threats to their hypothetical autonomy. The danger most commonly posited is employment, followed closely by third-party reimbursement. This threat is the functionalist version of what Marxists characterize as the proletarianization of professionals. There can be no doubt that employment is increasing, more rapidly outside the older professions originally organized around independent practice (primarily medicine and law) but also within them.

Typically the problem is framed as a tension or conflict between professionalism (equated with fee-for-service production) and bureaucracy. Whether as employers or paymasters, private and public bureaucracies control professionals through decisions about hiring, promotion, and retention and through the allocation of resources, especially technology. Professionals increasingly do find themselves working in bureaucratic settings. Between 1980 and 1985, the number of physicians in group practices increased by 43 percent, while the number in solo practice increased only 18 percent. Other service industries have concentrated much more rapidly: the five largest advertising agencies in the world billed nearly $25 billion in 1985 as a result of recent mergers.

This literature has stimulated a revisionist reply, which questions the tension between professionalism and bureaucracy. Critics note that the "autonomy" of private practitioners is not only empirically unsubstantiated but also theoretically dubious. First, market pressures to find and retain clients powerfully influence professionals even when they collectively have succeeded in limiting entry and internal competition. Second, professionalism is not "autonomy" but simply another form of control, one that is particularly appropriate when tasks require a high level of technical discretion and work is discontinuous and relatively unpredictable. Professionalism may differ from bureaucracy, but it is no less constraining. If bureaucracy controls work through rules and constant supervision, professionalism does so by selecting those predisposed to comply with authority and subjecting them to a lengthy socialization process. Third, external authorities, whether bureaucratic superiors or third-party payers, may be concerned with the organization of work and its cost, but they usually leave technical execution to the professional.

Professions as Communities

Community remains an attractive but elusive goal in a mass society in which ideologies of individualism, universalism, and efficiency constantly undermine strong, multiplex, enduring personal bonds. It is against this backdrop that structural functionalism sees professions as a powerful and valuable source of community. Members of a profession are united by a common role definition, an esoteric language, and fairly clear social boundaries. Membership is attained only after a long and painful initiation rite and usually is a permanent status. Finally, professions do engage in self-governance.

But there are serious problems with the notion of profession as community. Other communities based on kinship, race, ethnicity, class, religion, gender, locality, friendship, or politics are far more salient to most people most of the time. To the extent that professions do become communities, they often secure the loyalty of their members by excluding those disadvantaged by class, gender, or race—forms of discrimination that are no longer acceptable in the workplace. All professions are riven by major internal divisions between practitioners, administrators, and teachers or researchers. And as an increasing proportion of professionals become employees, especially of large private or public bureaucracies, their community tends to be limited to their fellow workers rather than encompassing the entire profession.

Lawyers have even fewer communal characteristics than other professionals. In an inegalitarian society, professionals necessarily reflect the stratification of their clients. An extreme example within medicine is the social distance between psychiatrists employed by a public mental hospital and those who treat private outpatients, despite the fact that they share common credentials and possess similar expertise. Specialties also diverge dramatically: in 1983, the median income of anesthesiologists was more than twice that of physicians concerned with industrial and occupational health. Even within private practice, the clienteles of lawyers diverge more dramatically than those of physicians, varying from the poorest individual to the wealthiest corporation. The divisions within the legal profession— among employed, employing, and independent private practitioners and between them and judges, prosecutors, civil servants, house counsel, and law teachers—are more numerous and deeper than those within medicine, even disregarding subject-matter specialization. Partly for this reason, and partly because lawyers have traditionally practiced within a single jurisdiction (though this is changing), legal knowledge is more localized and particular than knowledge in other professions, such as medicine. Certainly lawyers agree less about the meaning of their ultimate value— justice—than physicians do about health. Thus, although groups of lawyers may form particular

communities, the legal profession as a whole is a weak community.

Self-Regulation

If structural functionalism had to distinguish professions by means of a single characteristic, self-regulation would be a prime candidate. Because professions emerge out of the division of labor between producers and consumers, mechanisms are needed to ensure that producers are technically qualified and do not abuse the power they derive from their specialized knowledge. Powerful consumers—aristocratic patrons in the past, large public or private entities today—may be able to command the loyalty and competence of producers. But most consumers must rely on other protections.

Professions are adamant that they, not the state or the consumer, must exercise regulatory authority. In one of his weekly advertisements in the *New York Times*, entitled "Professionalism Under Fire: Power vs. Knowledge in St. Louis," Albert Shanker, president of the American Federation of Teachers, attacked the use of student performance on standardized tests to rate teachers. School boards have recently battled attempts by religious groups to exclude certain books from the curriculum and excuse children from classes in which objectionable books are used. Journalists in Latin America have opposed laws requiring them to obtain licenses to work. The president of the American Institute of Certified Public Accountants boasted of his organization's success in resisting federal regulation: "Congress never laid a glove on us because we worked pretty hard to keep that glove off." And Florida neurosurgeons have refused to treat patients in order to protest increases in medical malpractice insurance premiums.

Professions rest their argument for self-regulation on two grounds. First, they insist that only fellow professionals possess the necessary expertise to judge performance. Even if true, this is self-serving, since the profession deliberately constructed the monopoly of expertise in the first place. Second, they point to the profession's independence from the state; but this assumes that the profession is more solicitous than the state of client (and other public) interests and will defend them against the state—empirical propositions for which there is no evidence. Furthermore, despite its emphasis on autonomy, the profession necessarily derives its regulatory power from the state.

Professions do not fulfill their regulatory responsibilities very effectively. Although they claim to dedicate their technical skills to serving society, Weber notes that self-interest frequently dampens their ardor for reform.

> Whenever legal education has been in the hands of practitioners, especially attorneys, who have made admission to practice a guild monopoly, an economic factor, namely their pecuniary interest, brings to bear a strong influence upon the process not only of stabilizing the official law and of adapting it to changing needs in an exclusively empirical way but also of preventing its rationalization through legislation or legal science.

Like all professionals, lawyers also display their altruism by providing free or low-cost services; but the magnitude of such charity seems to vary with the publicity it receives—conspicuous production being the necessary complement of conspicuous consumption. Although professions portray self-regulation as a means of reducing client uncertainty, they deliberately draft ethical rules in vague and ambiguous language to preserve the indeterminacy that is a foundation of professional power. Many ostensibly "ethical" rules serve the Weberian objective of market control rather than the Parsonian goal of protecting clients and society. Rules focus on professional technique but ignore the ends to which it is directed. Enforcement is weak. Client confidentiality is invoked to obstruct external surveillance of professional misconduct. Larger productive units resist professional control over their members or employees. And the goal of self-regulation often appears to be to protect the inept members of the profession rather than the society they ostensibly serve. One reason for systematic underenforcement of ethical and technical norms is that control of misconduct and incompetence readily becomes an arena for intraprofessional conflict, which threatens the very community that self-regulation purports to symbolize. Consequently, self-regulation may be more comprehensible as an assertion of status than a form of social control.

The visible failure of self-regulation, however, could lead to assertions of control by clients and external bodies, such as legislatures, courts, and administrative agencies. The Federal Trade Commission has announced its intent to abrogate optometry industry rules and practices that limit the number of branch offices, ban offices in shopping malls, prohibit the use of trade names, and restrict employment by drug and department stores and optical chains. Congress has discussed increased regulation of the scientific research institutes it funds because of its dissatisfaction with their choice of subjects and results. The American Institute of Certified Public Accountants is requiring its members to look actively for financial fraud in every client, partly to protect themselves from the rising number of malpractice claims.

CONCLUSION

Any attempt to understand lawyers must address the Weberian questions of how they constructed their professional commodity (legal services) and sought to control their market and raise their collective status by regulating the production *of* and *by* producers and stimulating demand, the Marxist question of the class location of lawyers as defined by the structures within which legal services are produced, and the structural functional questions about lawyers in the system of stratification, professional autonomy, self-governance, and self-regulation.

DISCUSSION QUESTIONS

1. What difference does it make whether an occupation is a profession? To put it differently, why do occupations seek to professionalize? Should professions enjoy these differences?

2. How do we know whether an occupation is a profession? What characteristics enhance or detract from an occupation's claims to professional status? Two French sociologists have suggested that professions require a delicate mix of technicality and indetermination. Too much technicality and they become mechanical, capable of being performed by anyone (including the service recipient); too much indetermination and

they become art or magic, incapable of warranting quality.[2] How does this apply to law?

We might approach the question by arraying occupations along a continuum from the least to the most professional. Where would you put the following: travel agent, financial adviser, interior decorator, personal trainer, massage therapist, spiritual counselor, gourmet chef, astrologer, beautician? London's Public Carriage Office administers a test of The Knowledge—468 routes within six miles of Charing Cross and the names of 25,000 streets, buildings, parks, monuments, apartment blocks, pubs, and hotels. Candidates for a "black taxi" license prepare for an average of 2–3 years, many studying 12–14 hours a day, often helped by cram schools. Those who win one of the 20,000 licenses will earn about $17 per hour. Are they professionals?[3]

Where on the continuum did you put lawyers? What characteristics determine location on the continuum? Consider such variables as: knowledge, clientele, training, payment, visible distinctions, entry barriers, unity or divisions, background and homogeneity of entrants? How do lawyers compare to other occupations along each variable? Are its entry barriers justified? Steven M. Welchons worked as a public defender in Madison County, New York, counseling more than 1,000 clients over two years without complaints before it was revealed he had never attended law school or even graduated from college.[4]

3. How do service occupations emerge? How did lawyers convince clients to hire them rather than perform lawyerly functions themselves? How did lawyers convince clients they needed legal services at all?

How do occupations professionalize? How do contemporary trajectories differ from earlier ones? If we put aside law and medicine for the moment, can you think of other occupations that presently are seeking to professionalize? How are they going about it? Do you expect them to succeed? What explains success and failure?

How do occupations fight turf wars? Should chiropractors be able to give physical examinations for school athletics?[5] Should dental hygienists and denturists be able to work without the supervision of a dentist?[6] Banks sell insurance policies?[7] Optometrists treat glaucoma, prescribe medication, or perform laser keratectomy?[8] Lay midwives deliver babies?[9] Folk healers prescribe medicine?[10] Pharmacists, psychologists, and nurses do so?[11] Should nurses be able to manage chemotherapy in hospitals? provide preventive health care for women and children? do psychotherapy?[12] Should the American Psychoanalytic Association be able to require medical degrees of aspiring psychoanalysts?[13]

Should paralegals be able to practice without a lawyer? What should they be able to do: uncontested divorces, domestic violence temporary restraining orders, real estate closings, relatives seeking custody of abused children, name changes, wills, personal bankruptcies, eviction defense? Should the National Association of Independent Paralegals, representing more than 7,000 individuals and organizations, seek to professionalize? The National Association of Legal Assistants offers a certificate; is that a step toward professionalization? Nolo Press in Berkeley and Help Abolish Legal Tyranny in Washington, D.C., champion non-professional lawyering.[14]

---

2. H. Jamous and B. Peloille, "Professions or Self-Perpetuating Systems? Changes in the French University-Hospital System," in J. A. Jackson (ed.), *Professions and Professionalization* (1970).

3. *New York Times* A1 (10.15.92).

4. *New York Times* B6 (6.15.95).

5. *Los Angeles Times* §2 p1 (10.2.89), A1 (4.7.94).6. *Los Angeles Times* A41 (10.26.89); *New York Times* §1 p10 (8.21.94).

7. *New York Times* A1 (5.4.95).

8. *New York Times* A1 (4.8.96), A14 (4.25.96).

9. *New York Times* A15 (11.6.95).

10. *New York Times* A5 (4.11.94); *Los Angeles Times* B3 (4.13.94).

11. *Los Angeles Times* E1 (9.7.93).

12. *New York Times* A19 (3.11.93), A1 (11.22.93); *Los Angeles Times* A1 (1.1.94).

13. *New York Times* B6 (8.19.92).

14. *New York Times* B12 (10.12.90), B12 (7.16.93), B6 (10.12.94), B18 (2.3.95).

4. How do professions deprofessionalize?[15] Can you think of examples? Are lawyers undergoing proletarianization? Should doctors feel threatened by the Clinical Computer, a software program facilitating self-diagnosis?[16] By third-party payers who regulate what they can do?[17] By HMO employers that limit what they can tell patients or create incentives to limit treatment?[18] Confronted with competition and squeezed by third-party payors, doctors are selling their practices to managed care companies and becoming employees.[19] Their incomes fell more dramatically in 1994 than they had since the Great Depression.[20] Some are joining unions in response.[21]

5. Is there any necessary relationship between the characteristics that distinguish professions from occupations and professional commitment to self-governance, self-regulation, and altruism?

SUGGESTED READING

Eliot Freidson transformed the sociology of professions with his *Profession of Medicine: A Study of the Sociology of Applied Knowledge* (1970), the first of his many books (the latest being *Professionalism Reborn: Theory, Prophecy, and Policy* [1994]). Magali Sarfatti Larson drew on Weber and Marx in her comparison among professions and across nations, *The Rise of Professionalism: A Sociological Analysis* (1977); I synopsized her argument in "The Rise of Professionalism," 6 *British Journal of Law and Society* 82 (1979). Freidson and Larson inspired my theorization above; I replied to those who criticized my use of it in "Revisioning Lawyers," in Richard L. Abel and Philip S. C. Lewis (eds.), *Lawyers in Society: An Overview* (1995). One strand of criticism can be found in Michael Burrage and Rolf Torstendahl (eds.), *Professions in Theory and History: Rethinking the Study of Professions* (1990); Rolf Torstendahl and Michael Burrage (eds.), *The Formation of Professions: Knowledge, State and Strategy* (1990). Other theorizations can be found in: Richard L. Abel and Philip S. C. Lewis (eds.), *Lawyers in Society*, vol. 3: *Comparative Theories* (1989); Robert Nelson, David Trubek, and Rayman Solomon (eds.), *Lawyers' Ideals/Lawyers' Practices* (1992); Maureen Cain and Christine B. Harrington (eds.), *Lawyers in a Postmodern World: Translation and Transgression* (1994). On the tension between professionalism and employment, see Eve Spangler, *Lawyers for Hire: Salaried Professionals at Work* (1986). If you liked Charles Derber's distinction between ideological and technical proletarianization, you might want to look at Charles Derber, William A. Schwartz, and Yale Magrass, *Power in the Highest Degree: Professionals and the Rise of a New Mandarin Order* (1990); Steven Brint, *In an Age of Experts: The Changing Role of Professionals in Politics and Public Life* (1994).

Andrew Abbott attempted the most ambitious, if not entirely convincing, re-theorization of the professions in terms of their knowledge bases: *The System of Professions: An Essay on the Division of Expert Labor* (1988). It has influenced subsequent work on lawyers and related professions, e.g., Ronen Shamir, "Professionalism and Monopoly of Expertise: Lawyers and Administrative Law, 1933–1937," 27 *Law & Society Review* 631 (1993); Yves Dezalay and David Sugarman (eds.), *Professional Competition and the Social Construction of Markets* (1994); Abbott recently surveyed the field, "The Sociology of Work and Occupations," 19 *Annual Review of Sociology* 187 (1993); for an earlier overview, see Thomas Brante, "Sociological Approaches to the Professions," 31 *Acta Sociologica* 119 (1988). A study of the emergence of the subspecialty of international arbitration, using Bourdieu's theory of cultural capital, is Yves Dezalay and Bryant G. Garth, *Dealing in Virtue: International Arbitration and the Construction of a Transnational Legal Order* (1996).

---

15. See, e.g., George Ritzer and David Walczak, "Rationalization and the Deprofessionalization of Physicians," 67 *Social Problems* 1 (1988).

16. *New York Times* B9 (11.3.92).

17. *New York Times* §1 p1 (1.24.93), A14 (5.29.94), C1 (3.20.95), A17 (1.17.96).

18. *New York Times* A1 (12.21.95), D1 (12.22.95), C2 (1.6.96) A1 (12.25.96); *Los Angeles Times* A1 (1.17.96), A1 (12.26.96).

19. *New York Times* A1 (9.1.93), 9 (6.25.94), A1 (5.15.96).

20. *New York Times* A1 (11.17.95).

21. *New York Times* A1 (5.30.96), A1 (10.25.96).

An earlier chapter mentioned the pervasive nostalgia for a legal profession that never was: Anthony Kronman, *The Lost Lawyer: Failing Ideals of the Legal Profession* (1993); Mary Ann Glendon, *A Nation Under Lawyers: How the Crisis in the Legal Profession is Transforming America* (1994); Sol M. Linowitz, *The Betrayed Profession: Lawyering at the End of the Twentieth Century* (1994); Carl T. Bogus, "The Death of an Honorable Profession," 71 *Indiana Law Journal* 911 (1996); Professionalism Committee, ABA Section of Legal Education and Admissions to the Bar, *Teaching and Learning Professionalism* (1996). For critiques, see Russell G. Pearce, "The Professionalism Paradigm Shift: Why Discarding Professional Ideology Will Improve the Conduct and Reputation of the Bar," 70 *New York University Law Review* 1229 (1995); Marc Galanter, "Lawyers in the Mist: The Golden Age of Legal Nostalgia," 100 *Dickinson Law Review* 549 (1996).

Chapter Ten
USING THE THEORIES:
COMPARING LEGAL PROFESSIONS

Theories of professions, although usually presented as universal, inevitably are drawn from and colored by the concrete historical and social environments the theorist knows best. This is particularly true of conceptions of legal professions, which differ fundamentally across time and space. Professions located in the Muslim, former Communist, and third worlds obviously are shaped by the role of religion,* the relationship between state and economy,† and the underdevelopment of the economy.‡ But there also are fundamental differences within advanced capitalism. The conventional division is between common-law countries, whose legal systems were influenced by England, and the civil-law countries of continental Europe and their former colonies (as well as borrowers like Japan and Turkey). The comparative project I co-directed, which examined legal professions in 18 countries, began with a strong common-law bias. In the following essay I explore the most striking differences between civil and common lawyers.

🙖

---

* See, e.g., Farhat Jacob Ziadeh, *Law and Liberalism in Modern Egypt* (1968).

† See Louise I. Shelley, Lawyers in Soviet Work Life (1984); "Lawyers in the Soviet Union," in Anthony Joneds (ed.), *Professions and the State: Expertise and Authority in the Soviet Union and Eastern Europe* (1991); Eugene Huskey, *Russian Lawyers and the Soviet State: The Origins and Development of the Soviet Bar 1917–1939* (1986).

‡ See, e.g., C. J. Dias, R. Luckham, D. O. Lynch and J. C. N. Paul (eds.), *Lawyers in the Third World: Comparative and Developmental Perspectives* (1981); Dennis O. Lynch, *Legal Roles in Colombia* (1981); Richard J. Wilson, "The New Legal Education in North and South America," 25 *Stanford Journal of International Law* 375 (1989).

LAWYERS IN THE CIVIL LAW WORLD[1]
Richard L. Abel

WHAT IS A LEGAL PROFESSION?

THE civil-law world is dramatically different from its common-law counterpart in every respect. The common-law folk concept of "lawyer" has no synonym in European languages, except through such awkward literal translations as *homme de loi*. Instead, civil-law countries recognize two categories, one more inclusive than the common-law concept and the other less so. The first is the jurist: to acquire a university degree in law is to attain an honored status (if one devalued by credential inflation in recent decades). Many such graduates (sometimes a majority) pursue occupations unrelated to law, however, and possession of a degree does not constitute a corporate group. The second category is the private practitioner—a concept with clear equivalents in all European languages and sharply defined boundaries. But it emphatically is not the core of any notional legal profession. Rather, other subsets of law graduates take precedence—historically, numerically, and ideologically. These include the magistracy (judges and prosecutors, often combined in a way that is inconceivable to the common-law), civil servants, law professors, and lawyers employed in commerce and industry. In some civil-law countries the list of "legal occupations" includes roles performed in the common-law world by those with little legal training: notaries everywhere, police chiefs in Norway and Brazil, and bailiffs and process servers in France.

---

1. In Richard L. Abel and Philip S. C. Lewis (eds.), *Lawyers in Society*, vol. 2: *The Civil Law World* (Berkeley: University of California Press, 1988). Reprinted with permission.

Comparisons between common- and civil-law worlds thus become acutely problematic. One illustration of this difficulty is the repeated tendency of Western observers to exaggerate the population per lawyer in Japan—10,056 in 1982—by counting only *bengoshi* (private practitioners who have graduated from the Institute of Legal Training and Research). If the calculation is expanded to include all those who perform lawyerly functions in Western countries—law professors, judges, public prosecutors, in-house counsel, judicial scriveners, administrative scriveners, patent attorneys, tax attorneys, and foreign lawyers—the ratio becomes 1,239:1, which is not very different from that of Western European countries.

The historical dominance of common-law professions by private practitioners is symbolized by the appointment of their most senior and respected members to the bench. England represents the most extreme example: privately practicing barristers are briefed as prosecutors by the government (even the attorney general and solicitor general retained their private practices until the end of the nineteenth century); practicing barristers and solicitors did most of the law teaching in both university law faculties and private courses designed to prepare students for the professional examinations until after World War II; and privately practicing barristers often serve as part-time judges.

In much of the civil-law world, by contrast, lawyers were state employees first and private practitioners only later. Japan, for instance, created a judiciary and a prosecutorial staff in the nineteenth century, which had to undergo rigorous training and examinations. By contrast, private practitioners were required to pass a much easier examination only in 1893, they received no practical training, and many qualified under a grandfather clause; not until 1933 did they take the same examination as judges and prosecutors, and not until after World War II did they receive the same training.

Even after private practice acquired a distinct identity within civil-law systems, states monitored it closely, fearful of challenges to their sovereignty. Throughout the eighteenth and nineteenth centuries, the German states restricted the number of advocates, who formally were part of the judicial service. Prussia even abolished private practice between 1780 and 1783, appointing civil servants to a quasi-judicial role to advise litigants.

The relative significance of private practitioners is suggested by the ratio between them and other categories. Throughout the common-law world there are between two and seven judges per 100 private practitioners. The ratio is higher everywhere in the civil-law world except Spain, generally many times higher. In Germany in 1962, there were ninety judges for every 100 private practitioners—more than twenty times the American ratio. In Britain and the United States, the ratio of lawyer civil servants to private practitioners never exceeds 20:100; in most civil-law countries for which I have statistics, the two categories are roughly equal. Finally, there are fewer than ten lawyers employed in business for every 100 private practitioners in the common-law world (except the United States, which had sixteen in 1980); however, the ratio was far higher throughout the civil-law world, where lawyers employed in business usually outnumbered private practitioners.

In the civil-law world, the judiciary (and to a lesser degree prosecutors and civil servants) are at least the equals of private practitioners in prestige and income and generally their superiors. In the common-law world, successful private practitioners always earn far more than judges, prosecutors, or civil servants and often are reluctant to relinquish these material rewards, even for the status and power enjoyed by the highest positions in the judiciary or the executive. Throughout the civil-law world, only those law students with the best academic records can enter the judiciary.

The common-law world offers lawyers considerable mobility among practice categories. In the civil-law world, by contrast, law students make a fairly irrevocable decision about which category to enter soon after graduation. In many countries they then receive additional formal training or a specialized apprenticeship, and subsequent career changes are rare.

CONTROL OVER ENTRY

In the common-law world, private practitioners formed voluntary associations, a central goal of which was to control entry into and competition within the profession. In the civil-law world, by contrast, the state historically controlled entry into the core of the profession by appointing judges, prosecutors, state attorneys, and civil servants. Many other legal occupations, although economically dependent on client fees rather than state salaries, were protected by a *numerus clausus* (admission quota). In Germany, some states controlled the number of private practitioners (*Anwälte*) until 1879. In Italy, the office of *procuratore* was governed by a numerus clausus as late as 1950. In many European countries, a clause still limits the size of the notariat and the number of lawyers qualified to appear before the highest courts. France preserved the most elaborate restrictions. The state controls the numbers of all *officiérs ministériels*, *avoués* (official representatives of parties responsible for procedural formalities in courts of appeal), *notaires* (notaries), *huissiers* (bailiffs), and *greffiers* (court clerks). The holder of such an office can sell it on retirement; greffiers have been able to obtain as much as eight times their annual incomes in such sales. Another public institution—the university—mediates entry to private practice in civil-law countries. Here, again, the divergence between the two worlds is marked. Common lawyers traditionally qualified through apprenticeship. By contrast, a university law degree long has been essential for almost all legal occupations in civil-law countries. Law (together with theology and medicine) was one of the first faculties established by European (and Latin American) universities, many of which are very old—Bologna celebrated its nine-hundredth anniversary in 1988. Requiring this credential substantially limited entry because only a tiny proportion of the population traditionally attended the elite secondary schools that prepared for university and had the financial resources to survive the many years it took to obtain a university degree. If universities in the civil-law world were exclusive until the 1960s, law was one of the least selective subjects. Because law faculties did not offer vocational training for private practice but rather granted a degree that conferred generalized status and entry to public and private administration, they attracted a large proportion of undergraduates.

University legal education in the two worlds differs in content as well as numbers. Everywhere in the civil-law world it is an undergraduate degree, whereas in the United States it is exclusively graduate, and in Canada, Australia, and New Zealand it generally is combined with undergraduate education in another subject. The organized legal profession (i.e., the association of private practitioners) strongly influences the content of legal education in the common-law world, either directly or by controlling professional examinations. In the civil-law world, the state plays a much larger role in determining the curriculum, even in private universities. In northern Europe, law professors earn high salaries and receive the highest prestige of any legal professional. In southern Europe and Latin America, they also enjoy considerable status but must augment their low salaries by spending most of their time in private practice. Yet, paradoxically, the full-time academics in common-law faculties offer a fairly vocational training, whereas the full-time practitioners who teach part time in civil-law faculties are intensely theoretical (perhaps because the former see themselves preparing students for private practice, whereas the latter educate for the magistracy and civil service).

Whereas the student/faculty ratio in most common-law faculties is about 20:1, it is more than 100:1 in Germany, whose law faculties range from 1,200 to 4,000 students; and other civil-law faculties are incredibly large: 14,476 in Madrid in 1978–79; 11,559 in Barcelona; 16,290 in Naples in 1974; 15,275 in Rome; 11,163 in Bari; and 8,870 in Palermo. All these students could not attend class even if they wanted. In Austria, fewer than half regularly attend classes. Three-quarters of Brazilian students work six to eight hours per day to support themselves, at jobs usually unrelated to law. The reasons for this lack of academic commitment are also pedagogic: students find the lectures uninteresting and unrelated to the examinations they must pass, for which they rely heavily on private crammers.

Until the mid-1960s (outside the United States) entry to university was limited to the tiny socioeconomic elite who attended academic secondary schools. The educational reforms of that decade opened the university to *all* secondary school graduates, greatly expanding existing universities and establishing new ones. In Germany, for instance, 25 percent of the relevant age cohort attended university in 1981, compared to only 2–4 percent in 1960. Because these institutions vary much less in prestige than those in the United States or England, most students attend the one nearest their home in order to minimize living expenses. Yet if admission to university law faculties is not a barrier, many students fail to complete their degrees—often because of lack of interest rather than academic difficulties, sometimes for economic reasons.

In common-law countries, associations of private practitioners successfully campaigned for entrance examinations, required by the state but administered by the profession. In civil-law countries, examinations play a different role. Given the importance of the university as gatekeeper, further examinations often were superfluous. Law graduates did not have to take professional examinations until 1925 in Switzerland and 1963 in Brazil. In the Netherlands, Belgium, Spain, and Colombia there still are no requirements beyond a university law degree. Where examinations are required, they are administered by the university itself (as in Norway or the first examination in Germany) or by the state, not the profession. There is substantial national variation in the difficulty of the examinations. Although half of German law students drop out before the first state examination, 75–80 percent of those who take it pass the first time, half the failures repeat, and half the repeaters also pass, so that nearly 85 percent ultimately pass. Japan represents the other extreme: even after completing a law degree and preparing for an additional three to five years, only 2 percent of those taking the entrance examination for the Institute of Legal Training and Research (ILTR) are admitted (and can become judges, prosecutors, or private practitioners).

In the common-law world, apprenticeship with a private practitioner long performed the gatekeeping and training functions. Given the centrality of the university in the civil-law world, it is not surprising that apprenticeship is less important and structured quite differently. In France, the Netherlands, and Austria apprenticeship is the point at which legal careers diverge: judges and prosecutors take one path and private practitioners another. Even when several legal occupations share a common apprenticeship, magistracy dominates the experience. In Germany, where all those who pass the first state examination are eligible for a two-and-one-half-year paid apprenticeship (*Referendarzeit*) administered by the state, most of the time is spent in civil and criminal courts, with prosecutors, and as civil servants and only a small portion with private practitioners. Universities resist efforts to expand apprenticeship—Brazilian law schools successfully opposed the Brazilian Bar Association's campaign to require apprenticeship, and there is a tendency to formalize postuniversity training—French *avocats* copied the institute created by the magistracy.

The last obstacle to entering the profession is actually beginning to work. England, again, is the most extreme example of control by private practitioners. Barristers must obtain a tenancy in an existing chambers; the scarcity of physical space within the Inns of Court in London poses a major obstacle for all; women and racial minorities also encounter discrimination. Solicitors must be employed as assistants for at least three years before setting up practice on their own or in partnership. In the civil-law world, the number of entry-level positions as judges, prosecutors, and civil servants represents the single greatest constraint. As we will see below, civil-law countries have had a strong (and distinctive) ideological antipathy to both large partnerships and the employment of private practitioners. Consequently, law graduates often enter private practice on their own, although they remain dependent on referrals from established lawyers (with whom they may share office space).

THE STRUCTURE OF PRIVATE PRACTICE

Private practice in all professions emerged as a collection of individuals. The contemporary civil-law world recalls the high proportion of solo practitioners in the nineteenth-century common-law world—everywhere more than half, some places more than 80 percent. This does not reflect economic forces so much as persistent loyalty to the ideology of professional "independence" and the desire of private practitioners to differentiate themselves from employed lawyers. Consequently, whereas solo practitioners generally occupy the base of the professional hierarchy in common-law countries, they often constitute the elite in the civil-law world.

All common lawyers (other than barristers) always have been able to form true partnerships. Civil lawyers were allowed to do so only recently: local professional organizations could permit associations of up to five lawyers in France in 1954, but true partnerships without a numerical ceiling were allowed only in 1972; Italian lawyers could not form loose professional associations until 1939 or partnerships until 1973.

Even after the relaxation of formal restrictions, civil lawyers have been slow and cautious in forming partnerships. Most associations share only expenses, not profits: only 9 percent of Japanese lawyers in the 1980s belonged to true partnerships. Furthermore, most partnerships remain very small: 36 percent of Italian lawyers in Lombardy in 1978 were associated with only one or two others, while only 13 percent were in larger firms (the rest practiced alone). The largest firms remained small by common-law standards: no more than about 20 in Lombardy in 1978, a maximum of 20 by law in Spain, only three Tokyo firms with more than ten lawyers in 1962, the largest of which contained 15, no firm larger than nine in Germany in 1967 and only 42 that large in 1985. One reason for the slow growth is principled opposition to the employment of private practitioners. Yet economic forces appear to be eroding this aversion to growth.

Private practitioners in the civil-law world are concerned, even obsessed, with a need to demonstrate their independence from the state, perhaps because it seems so dominant. They do this, typically, by emphasizing their role as advocates, particularly criminal defense counsel. This ideological identification is consistent with the distribution of work across substantive areas: French *avocats* in 1973–74 devoted 18 percent of their time to family law, 14 percent to personal injuries, 14 percent to commercial law, 10 percent to criminal law, and 8 percent to labor law; Japanese bengoshi spend more than a quarter of their

time on debt collection and another 14 percent on damage claims. Few lawyers are able to specialize. Individuals and small businesses form a relatively large proportion of their clientele.

This powerful self-conception of private practitioners as advocates affects their relations with competing occupations. On one hand, they have sought to oust potential competitors from advocacy, especially during periods when the supply of lawyers has been increasing. In contrast, civil lawyers have allowed competitors to encroach on functions that fall outside their narrow self-definition. In France, nonlawyers dominate the labor court and justices of the peace; in Germany, they may appear in tax, administrative, social insurance, and labor courts. Everywhere private practitioners have lost the counseling function to others: notaries in all countries, *Syndici* (house counsel) in Germany, *conseils juridiques* and *juristes d'entreprise* in France, bachelors of commerce and accountants in Norway, *dottori commercialisti* in Italy, *despachantes* in Brazil, and a host of occupations in Japan—judicial and administrative scriveners, patent and tax attorneys, and even illegal accident specialists.

CONTROL OVER THE MARKET
FOR LAWYERS' SERVICES

In the civil-law world, advocacy is the core of private practitioners' monopoly, vigorously defended against intruders. Indeed, countries like Germany, France, Italy, and Venezuela compel litigants to retain a qualified advocate in most matters, prohibiting self-representation. Because civil lawyers have chosen to defend the core of advocacy while surrendering the periphery of advice, powerful competitors have occupied the latter realm. Although French conseils juridiques were only a third as numerous as avocats, they could assume a corporate form much earlier, and many of these firms became quite large, whereas avocats only recently began to form small partnerships; *sociétés fiduciaires* of conseils juridiques could have branch offices in the principal French cities, whereas even professional civil associations of avocats were limited to a single office. In Japan, as we have seen, bengoshi have exclusive rights of audience in court, but outside it they confront numerous competitors. In both these countries, the competing occupations have sought to professionalize. The 1971 reform of the French legal professions gave conseils juridiques the exclusive right to use that title, while requiring them to obtain the same law degree as an avocat (license) and complete a similar three-year apprenticeship; it also disqualified them from commercial activities. In Japan, many of the competing occupations are almost as exclusive as bengoshi. Judicial scriveners, for instance, must take an examination whose pass rate is only 2 percent, are limited to a single office, and were allowed to form partnerships only in 1967.

Categories of practitioner sometimes seek to eliminate competition through unification. The division between barrister and solicitor did not survive export to the United States, Canada, Australia, or New Zealand (although it has been revived in the last two). The civil-law distinction between those who draft pleadings and take formal responsibility for the proceedings (avoués, *procuratori, procuradores)* and those who argue in court (avocats, avvocati, *abogados*) also has weakened. The former category has disappeared everywhere except in the higher French courts and in Spain. Yet the role of notary, which is almost vestigial in the common-law world, remains a wholly independent and powerful profession throughout the civil-law world. In addition, the ambitious attempt to merge all the French legal professions, begun in the 1950s, succeeded in 1971 only in incorporating the avoués in lower courts and the *agréés* in commercial courts, although conseils juridiques and avocats finally merged in 1992.

Restrictions on competition among domestic lawyers appear to be directed almost as much to maintaining a "professional" self-image and preserving social status as they are to securing economic gains. The constraints on "incompatibility" are most striking to an observer from the common-law world, where they limit the bar only in divided professions. In the civil-law world, by contrast, they apply to all private practitioners and are far more extensive. In Italy in the 1950s and 1960s, private practitioners could not enter any form of employment or be notaries, members of the clergy, merchants, business exec-

utives, journalists, judges, prosecutors, or civil servants. A second important restriction is geographic. In federal common-law polities (the United States, Canada, and Australia), lawyers can practice only in the states or provinces to which they have been admitted, a limitation justified by local variation in the law. In the unitary civil-law polities, similar restrictions lack even this weak justification. In Germany, a lawyer could appear only in a single *Landgericht* and the *Amstgerichte* subordinate to it. In France, lawyers could appear only before the courts of the *barreau* to which they belonged. Lawyers in France, Germany, Denmark, and Japan had to practice from a single office situated within the local bar to which they belonged.

THE CREATION OF DEMAND

In the common-law world, the erosion of control over supply (discussed below) coincided with growing interest in stimulating demand, by both private and public means. Although it was the state that initiated legal aid programs, suspicious professions soon became enthusiastic supporters. Civil lawyers have been far more conservative about creating demand, just as they have been about other aspects of private practice. No professional association has engaged in collective advertising, and no country has liberalized the rules prohibiting individual advertising. With some notable exceptions, civil lawyers have been equally reluctant to seek state subsidies for demand. Here the reasons are more complex and various. Many third world countries lack either the resources or the political will to ensure legal representation for the vast mass of the population too poor to purchase services on the market. In those predominately Catholic countries where divorce was either illegal or socially disapproved (Italy, Spain, and Latin America), the staple of legal aid practice was unavailable. Several constituencies have been not only indifferent to legal aid but actually hostile. The legal profession has several reasons for suspicion. French lawyers feared that they would lose the "symbolic capital" they generated by offering their services charitably—a burden they were willing to sustain because it had been declining (few clients sought such services) and fell mostly on apprentices. French lawyers also feared that state control of legal aid payments would lead to state control over the fees paid by private clients. When private practitioners do endorse legal aid, they naturally want the work themselves; the state, by contrast, often prefers to employ lawyers, which facilitates fiscal and political control. Spain and many Latin American countries already have "public attorneys" with a vested interest in representing the members of dependent groups (the poor, women, children, and ethnic minorities). In the absence of effective systems of state legal aid, trade unions, political parties, and churches advise their members and help them obtain legal representation. These institutions may oppose state action as a threat to the political loyalty that their own assistance engenders. Some of the most innovative programs were established by students and political activists, who remain intensely suspicious of state intervention.

PROFESSIONAL ASSOCIATIONS

In the common-law world, the association of private practitioners was the indispensable mechanism for limiting entry, enhancing status, restricting competition, and asserting a claim to self-regulation. In the civil-law world, by contrast, professional associations are far less salient to the core of the legal profession—judges, prosecutors, and civil servants—or to the numerous law graduates employed in business, all of whom have their own organizations. In the civil-law world, associations of private practitioners began as local guilds and retained this form long after powerful national bodies had emerged in the common-law world. In some instances these local organizations were created by and subordinated to the state. National associations emerged late.

The structure of professional associations shaped the regulation of private practitioners. Local associations used largely informal mechanisms that remained fairly effective as long as those bodies were small. With the gradual shift of authority from local private bars to national official associations, regulation has been formalized. Furthermore, the state plays a larger role than it does in the common-law world.

THE POSTWAR TRANSFORMATION: ARE CIVIL-LAW AND COMMON-LAW PROFESSIONS CONVERGING?

The Numbers Explosion

Legal professions in almost all capitalist nations have experienced rapid growth in the last two decades. The rate of expansion is particularly noteworthy because it follows a long period of stasis. Although the university made a major contribution in both worlds, the reasons were somewhat different. In most common-law countries, the university displaced apprenticeship as the gatekeeper to practice only after World War II. In the civil-law world, where the university always had responsibility for legal education, entry was extended from graduates of elite academic secondary schools to all secondary-school graduates. Public universities charged little or no tuition, and most countries provided means-tested support for living expenses. The rate of increase in law student enrollments often exceeded that in the university as a whole because more popular subjects imposed quotas, forcing many to study law as a second or third choice.

In the common-law world, the increase was most dramatic in those countries experiencing a rapid shift from apprenticeship to the university. Yet even these high rates of increase were dwarfed by those in the civil-law world. In both worlds, entrants rapidly expanded the number of private practitioners. Because most law graduates in the common-law world already were engaged in private practice, the rate of increase there was lower. In the civil-law world, the number of places in the magistracy and the civil service remained fairly constant, forcing private practice (and private employment) to expand more rapidly.

The rapid increase in entry inevitably stimulated those already admitted to seek tighter controls over supply. In the common-law world, mechanisms to do so already were in place: limits on enrollment in law faculties and sometimes in postgraduate vocational training programs; professional examinations (controlled by private professional associations); and limits on the number of places for apprentices and on the initial jobs or practice opportunities for those fully qualified. In the civil-law world, the situation may have been more acute because the fiscal crisis of the state precluded any expansion of public-sector employment. University enrollments also ceased to grow, less because places were limited than because students lacked the financial means or the economic incentive to earn a degree that offered *no* job. Where enrollment was capped, the moving force was not private practitioners protecting their economic interests but university professors seeking to maintain educational quality.

Yet there were precedents for private practitioners to seek to control entry. In Germany, associations of private practitioners had responded to the Great Depression by supporting the expulsion of Jewish attorneys and urging a numerus clausus and the expulsion of women, younger and older attorneys, and socialists and communists. Even during the postwar boom, when the number of German law students nearly doubled between 1954 and 1959, bar associations mounted a leaflet campaign exaggerating the problem of overcrowding and the low incomes of Anwälte, which resulted in a 69 percent decline in the size of the entering class in 1960. Rapid growth since the 1960s has excited similar responses. In France in 1981, the pass rate on the entrance examination for the vocational year required of all private practitioners fell to 20 percent, reducing the number of entrants by half. The 1983 biannual meeting of the Deutsche Anwaltsverein focused on the "flood of Anwälte," and the association began circulating pamphlets warning school leavers against studying law. The Dutch bar association (unsuccessfully) has sought the introduction of a state examination and a mandatory postgraduate course. The Brazilian bar association persuaded the Federal Council of Education to disapprove the establishment of any law faculties and to freeze the number of places at existing schools.

Demographic Changes

The rapid rate of growth was accompanied by changes in the composition of the legal profession. By far the most dramatic was the entry of women. Because civil-law faculties offered a liberal arts education rather than the more voca-

tional training found in common-law faculties, women entered the former earlier than the latter. Women represented 8 percent of students in the Faculty of Law and Political Science in Paris in 1953–54 and 26 percent as early as 1967. Women represented 21 percent of law students in the Netherlands in 1969. Women's success in gaining entry to law faculties, however, does not ensure they will be equally distributed across professional roles. In both common- and civil-law worlds, women appear to prefer employment over private practice (because the hours are limited) and the public sector over the private (because of its greater universalism). Consequently, they remain severely underrepresented in the more prestigious and rewarding forms of private practice: they constituted only 2 percent of Dutch notaries in 1979; there were practically no women avoués in Paris in 1960, when women constituted a quarter of all avocats. The judiciary lies at the other extreme because of its fixed hours and generous leave policies and, most of all, because recent graduates are appointed on the basis of academic performance in the civil-law world (whereas in the common-law world judicial appointments reward success in private practice and political connections). Women constituted 32 percent of Dutch apprentice judges in 1979 and 56 percent of the graduates of the Ecole Nationale de la Magistrature in 1984 and 1985. The fact that as many as half the positions in law faculties have been filled by women has further narrowed the class recruitment of the profession for two reasons: the social obstacles women still must overcome are more easily surmounted by those from privileged backgrounds, and the intensified competition for entry and advancement advantages those with better educational credentials, which are correlated with class background.

Changes in the Distribution of Law Graduates and the Structure of Private Practice

In both the common- and the civil-law worlds, the increased number of graduates has compelled some to enter less favored sectors of the profession, thereby enlarging their relative size. In the common-law world, intense competition for positions in private practice (employment in law firms and seats in barristers' chambers) has encouraged many to seek employment in private industry or government. In the civil-law world, the pressure of numbers has had the opposite effect. Jobs for law graduates outside private practice have grown slowly, if at all. In no country has the number of judges kept pace with population increases, much less with the more rapid growth of the legal profession. The fiscal crisis of the state has frozen or reduced the number of lawyers in the civil service, which had risen dramatically until the 1970s. Although large private enterprises have hired many law graduates since World War II, further growth in this sector is unlikely. The disproportion between the number of law students (even allowing for attrition) and the number of private practitioners in Scandinavian countries in 1980—4,000 to 2,500 in Denmark, 3,600 to 2,000 in Norway, 10,000 to 1,400 in Sweden—strongly suggests that private practice will continue to expand rapidly. Although the civil-law world retains its strong ideological attachment to independent practice, change may be occurring there as well. The power of environmental forces to overcome inherited traditions is suggested by the fact that private practice in Quebec resembles that in English-speaking Canada more than that in France, in terms of the proportion of law graduates in private practice, the size of law firms, and the amount of time devoted to advice rather than advocacy.

Lawyers as a Political Force

We saw above that civil-law professions did not create the powerful, private, voluntary, self-interested, self-regulating associations characteristic of the common-law world. Instead, associations of private practitioners were created and dominated by the state, their competence and interests were limited, and membership was compulsory. In recent decades, this began to change dramatically in several ways. First, local organizations have sought to form national coalitions or to take concerted action. Second, some associations of law graduates have adopted a syndicalist form. This began in Italy and France in the 1960s among the younger and more radical magistrates, but it gradually extended to private practitioners. The change reflected a profession that rapidly

was growing more youthful (44 percent of French judges were less than 35 years old in 1982), the political radicalization of the period, and disenchantment with local bar associations. Third, outside competitors also are organizing to advance their economic interests and enhance their social status: judicial scriveners in Japan, conseils juridiques in France, and house counsel in Japan, Belgium, and Norway. Finally, private practitioners are forming coalitions with the other categories of law graduates and other free professionals to promote their common concerns, particularly in negotiations with the state.

A partial explanation for the historical weakness of civil-law professional associations may have been the prominence of law graduates in legislatures, where they were able to influence state action. At the end of the nineteenth and the beginning of the twentieth centuries, law graduates (some of them private practitioners) constituted nearly three-fourths of the Italian legislature, three-fifths of the French, half or two-thirds of the Dutch, a third of the German, and a fourth of the Norwegian. They were equally dominant in Brazil and Venezuela. In most of Europe, their representation has declined markedly, although no decrease in the historically high proportion of lawyer-legislators is found in the common-law world.

CONCLUSION

No one entering a law faculty today would have any difficulty identifying the world in which it was located, even before a word had been spoken. The magistracy and the civil service play very different roles and attract different recruits in the two systems. Private practice still is structured differently and relates differently to large corporate clients— and professional associations are viewed differently by their members and interact with the state in different ways. Yet legal professions in both systems are being transformed by forces that operate across national boundaries. Some of these are social: the expansion of higher education (a response to the need for skilled personnel, the drive for mobility within the middle class, and the inflation of credentials) and the entry of women into the labor force. Some are economic: progressive concentration within industry and commerce, the expansion of the service sector, and the internationalization of business (accelerated by the European Union). Some are political: the increased role of the state in all economies, the growth of welfare programs, and the emergence of movements to oppose the growing dominance of the state and to equalize access to law. Some are cultural: the availability of divorce and the demand by women and racial and ethnic minorities for equal opportunity. Just as national cultures, languages, polities, and economies have been losing their distinctiveness, so national legal professions necessarily will converge, even if they never will become identical.

DISCUSSION QUESTIONS

1. Why do the proportions of lawyers in private practice and in state and corporate employment differ so greatly among national professions? Why do those categories differ in status and rewards? in mobility across categories? in the ratio of private practitioners to judges? of private practitioners to population? in the boundaries and structure of voluntary associations among legal professionals? What is the significance of those differences? of the fact that prosecutors and judges are closely related in civil-law professions? that all English judges are chosen from senior barristers?

2. What are the relative roles of apprenticeship and formal education? What are the consequences of law being a first or graduate degree? taught through lectures or Socratic dialogue? by practitioners or academics? in small classes or large? oriented toward practice or part of liberal education?

3. How do the strategies of supply control differ among professions? What are the roles of the state, university, professional association, courts? of entrance and final examinations, professional examinations, apprenticeship, employment, numerus clausus, cost?

4. Why is private practice organized so differently across countries? Where has solo practice survived and flourished and why? What is the justification for limitations on partnerships? Why did the large firm arise first in the United States, spread to the common-law world, and only recently emerge in the civil-law world? Who are the competitors of lawyers in different countries, and how have they divided up the work? What are the formal divisions among private practitioners, and what explains their survival and transformation? Can their restrictive practices be justified?

5. Why do professions seek to stimulate demand? What market mechanisms do they use? what state mechanisms? How do professions differ in this respect?

6. What explains the growth of legal professions? changes in demography? the redistribution of lawyers among subcategories?

SUGGESTED READING

Philip Lewis and I edited three volumes of essays, *Lawyers in Society* (1988–89). The first surveys the common-law world: England and Wales, Scotland, Canada, the United States, Australia, New Zealand, and India. I updated the English essay in "Between Market and State: The Legal Profession in Turmoil," 52 *Modern Law Review* 285 (1989); my book-length account is *The Legal Profession in England and Wales* (1988). For India, see 3(2) *Law & Society Review* (1968) (special issue); J. S. Gandhi, *Lawyers and Touts: A Study in the Sociology of Legal Profession* (1982); H. Nagpaul, "The Legal Profession in Indian Society: A Case Study of Lawyers at a Local Level in North India," 22 *International Journal of the Sociology of Law* 59 (1994). On Australia, see David Weisbrot, *Australian Lawyers* (1990).

The second volume samples the civil-law world: Belgium, Brazil, West Germany, France, Italy, Japan, the Netherlands, Norway, Spain, Switzerland, and Venezuela; see also Hannes Siegrist, "Professionalization with the Brakes On: The Legal Profession in Switzerland, France, and Germany in the Nineteenth and Early Twentieth Centuries," 9 *Comparative Social Research* 267 (1986). The German essay is updated to account for unification in *Lawyers in Society: An Overview* (1995); other treatments include E. J. Cohn, "The German Attorney," 9 *International and Comparative Law Quarterly* 580 (1960), 10 *ICLQ* 103 (1961); Walter Weyrauch, *The Personality of Lawyers: A Comparative Study of Subjective Factors in Law, Based on Interviews with German Lawyers* (1964); Dietrich Rueschemeyer, *Lawyers and Their Society: A Comparative Study of the Legal Profession in Germany and the United States* (1973); Jürgen R. Ostertag, "Legal Education in Germany and the United States—A Structural Comparison," 26 *Vanderbilt Journal of Transnational Law* 301 (1993); Kenneth F. Ledford, *From General Estate to Special Interest: German Lawyers, 1873–1933* (1996). On French lawyers, see René David and Henry P. de Vries, *The French Legal System: An Introduction* (1958); Peter Herzog and Brigitte Ecolivet Herzog, "The Reform of the Legal Professions and of Legal Aid in France," 22 *International and Comparative Law Quarterly* 462 (1973); Lucien Karpik, "Lawyers and Politics in France, 1814–1950: The State, the Market, and the Public," 13 *Law & Social Inquiry* 707 (1988); *Les Avocats entre l'état, le public e le marché: XIIIe–XXe siècles* (1995); Yves Dezalay, *Marchands du Droit* (1992); Jean-Paul Poisson, *Notaires et Société: Travaux d'histoire et de sociologie notariales* (2 vols.) (1985; 1995); Ezra Suleiman, *Private Power and Centralization in France: The Notaries and the State* (1987); David Avrom Bell, *Lawyers and Citizens: The Making of a Political Elite in Old Regime France* (1994). On Italian lawyers, see Mauro Cappelletti, John Henry Merryman, and Joseph M. Perillo, *The Italian Legal System: An Introduction* (1967); G. Leroy Certoma, *The Italian Legal System* (1985).

The third volume contained theoretical and comparative essays on topics like education, gender, the "new class," the state, revolution, and neo-corporatism. There is a long, and rather unilluminating, tradition of comparative law scholarship offering snapshots of national legal professions or global generalizations about differences, e.g., John Henry Wigmore, *A Panorama of the World's Legal Systems* (3 vols.) (1928); René David and John E. C. Brierly, *Major Legal Systems in the World Today: An Introduction to the Comparative Study of Law* (1968; 1978; 1985); "International Association of Legal Sciences Symposium," 25(2) *Case Western Reserve Journal of International Law* (Spring 1993); Alan Tyrrell and Zahd Yaqub, *The Legal Professions in the New Europe* (1993). A few comparisons do illuminate the role of lawyers, e.g., Mirjan Damaška, *The Faces of Justice and State Authority: A Comparative Approach to the Legal Process* (1986); John Henry Merryman, *The Civil Law Tradition* (1969).

Chapter Eleven

USING THE THEORIES: THE HISTORY OF
AMERICAN LEGAL EDUCATION

*We can test and refine sociological theories of profes-
sionalism by examining the emergence and transformation of the American legal profession after the
Civil War. The following reading is by an Oxford-
trained barrister, subsequently a Yale law professor
and American university president. Contrast this
"professional project" with the trajectory of professionalism in civil-law countries.*

LAW SCHOOL:
LEGAL EDUCATION IN AMERICA
FROM THE 1850s TO THE 1980s[1]
Robert B. Stevens

HARVARD DECREES THE
STRUCTURE AND CONTENT

SUCH success as American legal education
had had before the Civil War had been
achieved through proprietary schools such as the
Litchfield Law School. The law school that
Christopher Columbus Langdell inherited, as
dean, in 1870 was an adjunct of what was to
become Harvard University, but it had no relation to Harvard College. During Langdell's
deanship, which lasted until 1895, Harvard not
only became the preeminent law school in the
country, but institutionalized legal training was
established as *de rigueur* for leaders of the profession. Langdell and Eliot found the Harvard Law
School a two-year operation, at best, with students free to start at any point. Langdell, as dean,
at once established first- and second-year
courses—what became known as the graded curriculum. The long-term goals, however, were far
grander. In addition to the development of a system of teaching that emphasized the analysis of
appellate cases, it was Langdell's goal to turn the
legal profession into a university-educated one—

1. Chapel Hill: University of North Carolina Press, 1983.
Reprinted by permission.

and not at the undergraduate level but at a level
that required a three-year post-baccalaureate
degree. The proposed three-year degree became a
reality before law was recognized as a graduate
study. By the beginning of World War I, only
Harvard and Pennsylvania had established any
serious claim to have the law curriculum treated
as a graduate one, and at least at the University of
Pennsylvania, the assumption was that law
school and clerking in an office would be done
concurrently. Nationwide, the chief change in the
early part of the twentieth century was to bring
admissions standards at the law schools up to the
level of other undergraduate programs. This was
not always easy to achieve even at schools with
well-known names. For instance, in 1899 when
Cornell moved to apply to the law school the
admissions standards by then applied elsewhere
in the university, namely, four years of high
school, the entering class fell from 125 to 62.

Harvard, however, continued to be both the
market leader and professional exemplar, and
Harvard's innovations concerned not only its student body but also its faculty. The appointment
of James Barr Ames in 1873 as an assistant professor of law was considered a milestone. He was the
first of a new breed of academic lawyer, a law
graduate with limited experience of practice who
was appointed for his scholarly and teaching
potential. Ames, a recent Harvard Law graduate
who had scarcely practiced law, was exactly the
type of professor Langdell demanded: "A teacher
of law should be a person who accompanies his
pupils on a road which is new to them, but with
which he is well acquainted from having often
traveled it before. What qualifies a person, therefore, to teach law, is not experience in the work of
a lawyer's office, not experience in dealing with
men, not experience in the trial or argument of
cases, not experience, in short, in using law, but
experience in learning law."

At many schools there appeared to be a gulf between rhetoric and reality, springing from the reception that the law schools, designed for professional or even vocational training, were given by the universities, which were increasingly seeing themselves as centers of scholarship. In the 1890s, for instance, President Welling of Columbian (George Washington) University liked to talk of the Columbian Law School as a School of Comparative Jurisprudence. The truth was that it was a successful night school helping government clerks get through the bar examination. Georgetown, which was packing in nearly 1,000 part-time students in its only program—the night school—in the 1890s, still went through the pretense of insisting that it was especially interested in "nonlegal" subjects like legal ethics, legal philosophy, and legal history. A problem with having a standard national curriculum soon manifested itself in the less-prestigious local law schools. Albert Kales of Illinois suggested in 1909 that, since between 65 to 95 percent of law students at the University of Illinois intended to practice locally after graduating, a standard curriculum based on the development of legal reasoning was less pertinent to the career goals of such students than learning the law of their particular jurisdiction. With respect to the core curriculum, however, virtually all these schools had accepted the Harvard model by 1920.

HARVARD SETS THE STYLE

Just as there was to be a "scientific" base for history, the classics, and politics, the spirit of science was to invade the law. The spirit at Harvard during these years is perhaps best exemplified in the words of John Fiske, professor of philosophy in Harvard College: "The truth of any proposition, for scientific purposes, is determined by its agreement with observed phenomena, and not by its incongruity with some assumed metaphysical basis." Moving from lectures and quizzes about rules to the examination of cases was the law schools' apparent passport to academic respectability. The case method proved to be a brilliant and effective vehicle for the "imaginative activity" of the law. Generations of law students were to be weaned on determining relevant facts,

making arguments to a law professor masquerading as a court, and justifying or destroying judicial opinions in terms of legal "rightness" and, later, in terms of the nonlegal desirability of some principle or another.

Harvard's most obvious area of dominance was its teaching approach. The case method, although not an original creation of Langdell's, became known as his by virtue of his determined and systematic application of the approach. Intellectually, Langdell shared with Dwight the assumption that law was a science: "If law be not a science, a university will best consult its own dignity in declining to teach it. If it be not a science, it is a species of handicraft, and may best be learned by serving an apprenticeship to one who practices." Langdell, however, had already concluded that:

> Law, considered as a science, consists of certain principles or doctrines. To have such a mastery of these as to be able to apply them with constant facility and certainty to the ever-tangled skein of human affairs, is what constitutes a true lawyer…and the shortest and the best, if not the only way of mastering the doctrine effectually is by studying the cases in which it is embodied…. Moreover, the number of legal doctrines is much less than is commonly supposed.

Teaching at Harvard Law School under Langdell's influence consisted of the professor and a large number of students analyzing appellate decisions, primarily in terms of doctrinal logic. He explained that he was attempting by his example to put American law faculties in much the same position as that of faculties in continental Europe. "To accomplish these objects, so far as they depended upon the law school, it was indispensable to establish at least two things—that law is a science, and that all the available materials of that science are contained in printed books." Langdell's confusion between science as an empirical and as a rational activity was to continue. In his confusion, however, Langdell never wavered in his view that law was a science and that the center of legal education was the library: "We have also constantly inculcated the idea that the library is the proper workshop of professors and students alike; that it is to us all that the laboratories of the university are to the chemists and physicists, the museum of natural history to the zoologists, the botanical garden to the botanists."

Eliot, in his inaugural address, announced that "the actual problem to be solved is not what to teach, but how to teach." He may have been somewhat unfair in saying of the earlier system that "the lecturer pumps laboriously into sieves. The water may be wholesome but it runs through," yet Ames's view of the earlier recitation method was equally unrelenting. It was not "a virile system. It treats the student not as a man, but as a school boy reciting his lines."

This machismo view of the case method was neatly caught in the *Centennial History of the Harvard Law School.* The student, it suggested, "is the invitee upon the case system premise, who, like the invitee in the reported cases, soon finds himself fallen into a pit. He is given no map carefully charting and laying out all the byways and corners of the legal field, but is left, to a certain extent, to find his way by himself. His scramble out of difficulties, if successful, leaves him feeling that he has built up a knowledge of law for himself. The legal content of his mind has a personal nature; he has made it himself." Ames and Louis Brandeis were enthusiastic about Langdell's teaching, but others were more reserved. Of the course in equity practice, Roscoe Pound said: "It was a curious course.... Langdell was always worried about 'Why?' and 'How?' He didn't care particularly whether you knew a rule or could state the rule or not, but how did the court do this? And why did it do it? That was his approach all the time." Joseph Beale commented that Langdell had been "too academic; and many of his students said, if they did not really feel, that his teaching was magnificent, but was not law." Although Langdell had set out to teach law as a series of definable, objective, and interrelated rules, the genius of his system appeared to be to emphasize methodology by examining the irrational and the discretionary.

Methodology rather than substance became the nub of the system. Indeed, led by Ames, a new type of casebook, embodying this rather different approach, was developed. In Ames's nine casebooks, the cases were grouped by subjects and had been chosen for their "striking facts and vivid opinions" instead of being printed chronologically as were Langdell's (so that students might trace "by slow steps the historical development of legal ideas"). The lasting influence of the case method was to transfer the basis of American legal education from substance to procedure and to make the focus of American legal scholarship—or at least legal theory—increasingly one of process rather than doctrine. Langdell set the style when he moved from examination questions in essay form, calling for the systematic exposition of rules, to a primitive problem method. By this move he not only outraged many students, but ensured that American law would take the atomistic rather than the unitary approach that distinguishes it from other common-law systems today.

If the leading universities had "received the faith" by 1891, the American Bar Association had not. That failure was not entirely surprising. The fashionability of the case method was in so many ways ironic, for that was the period when the leadership of the profession was passing from courtroom lawyers to the office lawyers who sought to avoid litigation. Meanwhile, the law schools were favoring a system that appeared designed to produce litigators. The leaders of the bar were men who thought that "jurisprudence," even if they did not quite understand what it meant, was a "good." Similarly, studying civil-law systems based on Roman law, with which Langdell would not have been comfortable, was also attractive to them, and at ABA meetings there was a good deal of talk about the need for more social science in the legal curriculum.

Practitioners had always had some doubts about the case method, both intellectually and politically. As early as 1876 the *Central Law Journal* had condemned the system "which we understand to involve a wide and somewhat indiscriminate reading of cases—some of them overruled." Even John Chipman Gray was forced to admit that "given a dunce for a teacher, and a dunce for a student, the study of cases would not be the surest mode to get into the Bar.... it does need a fairly moderate amount of intelligence." This was the point the opponents of the case method pressed. Henry Wade Rogers of Michigan insisted that "it was quite unsuited to the average student," and Theodore Dwight refused to concede that the case method was better "for any student," but he was clear it was "inferior to true teaching in its effects upon those of average powers."

The leaders of the bar might be confused about what was "scientific," but "they knew what they liked." They were especially attracted to the high formalism of the English judiciary, a formalism that had grown higher with each succeeding expansion of the parliamentary franchise. Although Langdell might talk the language of "scientism," many in the bar rightly feared that what Langdell was up to would undermine the elegant symmetry that they sought as they gave their support to organizations like the National Conference of Commissioners on Uniform State Laws, which operated under the umbrella of the ABA after 1892.

It was in this context that the 1891 report of the ABA Committee on Legal Education attacked the heart of the Harvard system. Having announced "it would be beneath the dignity of the Association or even of its humblest committee to take part, however incidentally, in controversies which must become more or less personal," the committee proceeded to oppose the attempt to make law a graduate study and attacked the case method as "unscientific." The report argued that the ideal work of the lawyer was to be done by knowing the rules and keeping clients out of court. Teaching decisions without systematically instilling rules led to the "great evil" manifested by young lawyers who were all too willing to litigate, did not restrain their clients, cited cases on both sides in their briefs, and left all responsibility to the court.

As it turned out, the ABA meetings of 1891 and 1892 were the last serious doubts the legal establishment expressed about the case method. The fashionability of the Langdell system grew with remarkable rapidity. For a short time, it was a phenomenon largely confined to certain elite schools, but once such schools as Columbia had fallen to the trend, others followed in quick succession. Wigmore's and Abbott's appointments at Northwestern in 1893 and Beale's at Chicago in 1900 were further signals of the change. President Eliot opined to Wigmore, "I congratulate you on having got into a missionary diocese. On the whole, missionary work is the most interesting part of the teachers' function, and there is great need for it in the teaching of law."

When William Howard Taft, then district judge in Ohio and dean of the law school of the University of Cincinnati on the side, reorganized the school in 1895, he did it on the basis of the case method. By 1900, the newly created five full-time faculty members at Stanford all used the Harvard system, citing William Keener as their role model. The leading state universities were just as anxious to import the Harvard technique. The 1890s saw the case method arrive in Madison, Wisconsin, when President Charles Adams brought in Charles Gregory as associate dean. Edwin E. Bryant, the dean, who had been running the Wisconsin Law School as an "ideal law office," attacked the case method as "narrow, slow and unprofessional." When Harry Richards became dean in 1903, however, the case method had finally won, and Richards was able to address himself to what he perceived as more important issues, such as how to Harvardize other schools and prevent the "less worthy" from "creeping into the legal profession." The pattern was similar at most university-affiliated law schools, including the less prestigious, which saw the innovation as a way of gaining academic recognition. Hastings Law School adopted the Harvard case method with the arrival of Warren Olney and dropped the Pomeroy case method. Moreover, the appearance of the case method was almost invariably linked with rising admissions standards as well as longer law programs. Tulane succumbed to the case method in 1906 when Monte Lemann and Ralph Schwarz, just returned from Harvard, joined the law faculty as lecturers. Only a year after they introduced the case method, a high school diploma was required for admission to the school, and the law course was extended to three years.

Law professors undoubtedly relished their increasing power and influence in the classroom and happily made the change from treatise-reading clerk to flamboyant actor in a drama. Moreover, the law student felt the appeal, too. By the 1890s, going to law school was no longer a rarity; a law student who wanted product differentiation sought out a case-method school.

Even with all these features in its favor, the case method system also held a trump card—finance. The vast success of Langdell's method enabled the establishment of the large class.

Although numbers fluctuated, Langdell in general managed Harvard with one professor for every 75 students; the case method combined with the Socratic method enabled classes to expand to the size of the largest lecture hall. Its Socratic aspect justified the abandonment of the recitation and the quiz, the "exercises" used at good schools relying on the lecture method. Indeed, the lecture had been merged with the quiz in a teaching method that expanded the personalized aspects of earlier methods to classes that could compete with the largest lectures. The case method was thus both cheaper as well as more exciting for both teacher and student.

THE MARKET EXPLODES

The ABA's urge to upgrade the legal profession, a revived intellectual interest in law and related disciplines, and the emergence of the modern university closely paralleled one another. It was during this period that the new law school industry became more clearly integrated with the burgeoning universities. For the leading law schools this move was probably made for reasons of social prestige and, in economic terms, for reasons of market differentiation. When Mrs. Stanford and President David Starr Jordan were building the Leland Stanford, Jr., University, they began by bringing Nathan Abbott from Northwestern in 1893, but there was no full legal program until 1899. Iowa Law School, on the other hand, had begun in 1865, and it became a part of the state university in 1868. By the 1880s, the school was producing the majority of lawyers in the state and was cautiously arguing in favor of higher standards. Michigan rapidly established itself as the premier school in the Midwest, averaging 200 students a year by the late 1860s.

Some schools, like Cornell, set out to be "scholarly," calling for "a resident faculty of competent men whose duty is to give their predominant energies to the labor of imparting education," while encouraging students to take courses in the School of History and Political Science. Boston University, on the other hand, founded in 1872 by those who disagreed with the appearance of the case method at Harvard, claimed to teach "the science of law with a view to its application" and, unlike Harvard, to keep students in touch with practicing attorneys.

Part-time law schools opened up a whole new sector of the legal education market. The first of these was established in the 1860s for students who had full-time jobs—and not by any means always jobs in law offices. They began in Washington, D.C., where the size of the civil service had grown rapidly during the Civil War. Columbian College (George Washington) led the way in 1865 with a program designed to serve federal employees whose workday then ended at three in the afternoon. In 1870, new rivals—Georgetown and National—grew up in the District of Columbia. The movement spread rapidly. Whereas Washington had a predominantly white, Anglo-Saxon population, in the late 1880s part-time schools began to spring up in the cities with heavy immigrant populations. Moreover, immigrant groups early saw the importance of both education and of law in America as well as the need and advantage of being a lawyer. Northwestern College of Law was opened in Portland, Oregon, in 1884. The year 1888 saw the establishment of evening law divisions at Metropolis Law School in New York City (later absorbed by New York University) and Chicago College of Law (later Chicago-Kent). Then the University of Minnesota opened a night school in 1892 in an effort to increase the size of its student body. Baltimore University (later absorbed by the University of Maryland) began its part-time program in 1889. The nineties were to see an even more dramatic expansion.

During the period 1889–90, there were six full-time schools with three- or four-year courses, with some 1,192 students, one mixed day and night school with 134 students, and nine night schools with 403 students, as contrasted with 51 "pure" day schools with 3,949 students. The 55 part-time and short-course schools had 3,294 students. By 1899–1900, the 24 full-time full-course schools could claim 3,992 students. The 74 other schools, however, had some 7,631 students. In 1870 there had been 1,200 law students in 21 law schools (or four law students per 100,000 of population). This figure had risen to 4,500 students in 61 law schools (or seven per 100,000 of population) by 1890. The explosion, however, produced the antithesis of uniformity.

By 1916, there were 24 "high entrance full-time schools" with 4,778 students, 43 "low entrance schools offering full-time courses of standard length" with 7,918 students, 50 "part-time schools offering courses of standard length" with 7,464 students, and 23 "short-course schools" with 2,043 students. The law school movement had remarkable success; by 1917, only seven states did not have a law school. Perhaps equally important, legal education had become urbanized. By 1917, 59 percent of cities over 100,000 had law schools: Chicago had nine, Washington eight, New York five, and St. Louis and San Francisco four each.

As the lesser law schools emerged, however, commercial or neocommercial arrangements were frequent. The Blackstone Law School, organized in Denver in 1888, entered into a contract with the University of Denver in 1892 to become its law faculty. Not only was the faculty paid through fees, but until the 1920s, the books in the library were owned by the professors. There were equally complex arrangements regarding other law schools. Union College of Law originally opened in 1859 as the law department of the (old) Chicago University, beating out Northwestern, which had hoped to have the school affiliated with it. In 1873, Chicago University and Northwestern became joint managers of Union. When the Chicago University closed in 1886, Northwestern took over sole management, and, in 1891, Union College of Law became the official law school of Northwestern University. In rather the same way St. Louis Law School, founded in 1867, after a series of vicissitudes ultimately became the law school of Washington University.

St. Lawrence University, a liberal arts college in northern New York State, provided a particularly intriguing example of the "can-do" period of legal education. Its own law school lasted only two years (1869–71), and for the next 30 years the right to grant law degrees remained dormant. In 1903, Norman Hefley, running a highly successful proprietary business school in Brooklyn, decided to branch out into law. His school possessed no power to grant degrees, something he appreciated only after he had been running the law school for a year. The dean of the Brooklyn Law School, however, discovered in the catalog of St. Lawrence that it had the unexercised power to grant law degrees. St. Lawrence, a liberal arts college catering mainly to WASP families in upstate New York, then got together with Brooklyn Law School, catering to immigrant families from the ghettoes, and the law school became a "branch" of the college 360 miles to the north. By 1929, with 3,312 students, Brooklyn was the second-largest school in the nation, serving a predominantly immigrant student body. The historian of St. Lawrence coyly noted: "The School also prospered financially; a sizeable surplus was accumulated and the community [i.e., St. Lawrence] was compensated for its sponsorship and educational guidance."

Sometimes the intellectual "success" of a university law school was the inspiration for the establishment of a proprietary or at least a nonelite school. In Wisconsin, the state university, founded in 1848, followed the usual pattern of four basic undergraduate divisions: academic, education, medicine, and law. It took some 20 years to get the law school started, and until this century its costs were expected to be borne by student fees. At first, the law school saw itself as supplementing office training, although it did obtain the diploma privilege (its degree granted admission to the state bar). Later, in the 1890s and the following decade Wisconsin became Harvardized and grew in national reputation. This elitist development created a need for a different type of law school for a different clientele. In response, Marquette Law School, which traded in "practicality" and served mainly immigrants and the poor, opened in 1908. So, too, when, in 1911, the University of Minnesota Law School appointed a dean from Yale (William Reynolds Vance) with a mission to "raise standards," he responded by phasing out the night program at the university. The result was predictable: the St. Paul College of Law, founded in 1900 as a night school, flourished, and two more proprietary schools—Minneapolis College of Law (1912) and Minnesota College of Law (1913)—appeared.

Boston, for instance, was the locus of fierce competition. With Harvard next door in Cambridge, and Boston University firmly planted in the middle of the city, probably only the most intrepid would open a proprietary school. Early in this century, however, two schools took up the challenge: the Boston YMCA Law School and Gleason Archer's Suffolk Law School. From its beginnings, the Boston YMCA Law School received favorable treatment from the establishment. In 1897, the Lowell Institute began to offer its classes through the YMCA, including such subjects as elementary electricity, advanced electricity, and law. The following year, the YMCA founded its own Department of Law, with James Barr Ames, the dean of Harvard Law School, on the podium as the first lecture was delivered. The YMCA's educational work prospered, and it was later segregated into Northeastern College. The faculty included many leading practitioners— Brandeis, for example, taught there in the evenings. By 1917, the YMCA Law School had a branch in Worcester and, by 1921, branches in Springfield and Providence.

Although YMCA schools prospered in Boston and around the country, other proprietary schools did not achieve success as easily. Gleason Archer's Suffolk Law School in Boston had to compete with Northeastern's more elite faculty without any help from the profession, which saw his school as an encouragement to the "unworthy" poor. Archer, who wrote his first autobiography at age 35 in 1915, saw two main dangers in society: the "reds" (Communists) and the "crimsons" (Harvard). Opening law schools to the poor was his attempt to establish bulwarks against the encroachment of both these sinister forces. Beginning in 1906, Suffolk taught a highly practical course, mainly by the pedagogical technique of the lecturer dictating notes. Archer had no hesitation in battling President A. Lawrence Lowell of Harvard, and in 1914 succeeded in obtaining a state charter despite Harvard's opposition. After that, expansion was rapid—to 460 students in 1915; 1,512 in 1922; and 2,018 in 1924. By 1928 Archer could still claim that Suffolk was the largest school of law in the world, boasting nearly 4,000 students.

It thus became increasingly possible for white males, even poor immigrants, to qualify for the legal profession. The portals were far narrower for blacks and women. Although blacks seem to have entered the legal profession in this country sooner than women, their success was more limited. Already facing social ostracism, they fought white middle-class prejudice against blacks practicing law. There are few recorded stories of black lawyers in the nineteenth century; the law journals of the time were clearly not comfortable with the subject. The career of John Mercer Langston was exceptional. The son of a Virginia planter and a half-black, half-Indian slave, he entered Oberlin, one of four colleges in the country then admitting blacks, in 1849. After studying theology and then clerking under Philemon Bliss, he received a license to practice from an Ohio court in 1854. (Some have attributed his success in this endeavor to his appearance, which allowed him to pass as white.) He eventually went on to be the first dean of Howard Law School, which opened in 1868, and later acted as president of Howard University. Howard's Law School ought to have increased the number of black lawyers quickly, and for a while it did flourish because of the absence of admission requirements, a two-year program, and a reasonable supply of government clerks to fill its evening program. Then it fell on harder times. In 1877, the District moved to require three years of training for lawyers. In 1879, Congress announced that none of its appropriation might be used for Howard's professional schools. In 1887, Howard had 12 law students (eight blacks), and it almost went out of business in the financial panic of 1893. Census figures show that although black lawyers nationwide, at one point, outnumbered women lawyers, reaching 431 in 1890, the Jim Crow system took its toll. By 1900, their number was only 728, below that for women.

Arabella Mansfield was probably the first woman in modern times to be allowed to join the bar when she was admitted in Iowa in 1869, and Lemma Bankaloo, admitted to the Missouri bar the following year, was probably the first woman to try a case, in St. Louis in March 1870. In that same year the first woman on record to have received a law degree was Ada Kepley from Union College of Law in Illinois (Northwestern). The federal courts, however, were less willing to admit women, denying admission in 1869 to Myra Bradwell, the successful editor of the *Chicago Legal News*, who wished to join the Illinois bar. The U.S. Supreme Court upheld the exclusion with Mr. Justice Joseph Bradley giving his notorious opinion that "the natural and proper timidity and delicacy which belongs to the female sex evidently unfits it for many of the occupations of civil life.... The paramount destiny and mission of women are to fulfill the noble and benign offices of wife and mother. This is the law of the creator. And the rules of civil society must be adapted to the general contribution of things, and cannot be based on exceptional cases." In 1878, Belva Lockwood, however, completed her successful campaign to have the federal courts opened to women attorneys.

Despite the intimidation from the Supreme Court, women fought for their right to be lawyers. As early as 1869 the University of Iowa admitted women law students. The chief justice of the state, Austin Adams, declared that their presence so enhanced "the cause of liberal education that women of society in Dubuque entered the Law School to encourage, by their presence, the young women students, and give them countenance." Michigan soon followed Iowa's lead and in 1872 Boston University Law School admitted women. In 1878 two women successfully sued to be admitted to the first class at Hastings Law School. The elite law schools, however, remained hostile. A Yale Law School alumnus opined in 1872, "In theory I am in favor of their studying law and practicing law, provided they are ugly." In 1886 Alice Ruth Jordon actually registered at the Yale Law School, arguing accurately that "there isn't a thing in your catalogue that bars women." That very year the Yale Corporation hastened to include the words, "It is to be understood that the courses of instruction are open to the male sex only." In 1883, the Trustees of Columbian (George Washington) University in the District had been prepared to admit women, but the law faculty, which included two Supreme Court justices, held that "the admission of women into the Law School was not required by any public want. In the whole history of the institution, only one woman has applied for admission and her wants were adequately supplied by the Law School of Howard University in

this city." By the turn of the century, this intransigence had led Ellen Spencer Mussey and Emma Gillett to found the Washington Law School for women and men. Overall, the census reported five women lawyers in the United States in 1870. As of 1880, it listed 75 and, by 1900, there were 1,010.

The rise of the suffragist movement increased the pressure on the law schools. In 1899 the Women Lawyers' Club of New York was founded, and in the same year a major effort was made to have the Harvard Law School thrown open to women. There was a bitter faculty debate, with Langdell opposing the admission of women and Thayer expressing the prevailing view that "he should regret the presence of a woman in his classes, because he feared it might affect the excellence of the work of men; but he could not deny the inherent justice of the claim." The faculty thereupon agreed to admit women if Radcliffe would admit them as graduate students. Radcliffe was willing, but the Harvard Corporation vetoed the idea. Partly, but only partly, in response to this, in 1908, Portia Law School was founded in Boston. The genesis of the only law school with an all-women student body was more complex. It was the brainchild of Arthur W. MacLean, Gleason Archer's law partner. The evidence suggests that it was begun as a commercial enterprise—MacLean gaining the women's market and Archer the men's. Certainly their friendship withered when MacLean finally admitted men to the LL.B. In the meantime, however, a significant number of high school graduates in the Boston area gained a law school education at Portia.

THE ESTABLISHMENT ATTEMPTS TO CONTROL THE MARKET

At its first meeting in 1879, the ABA Committee on Legal Education and Admissions to the Bar not only urged national comity for lawyers of three years' standing—its original chore—but it began the crusade for an expansive program for standardization. The committee accepted as axiomatic that bar standards had declined between 1840 and 1870, and it was equally adamant that "membership in a great and learned profession like the law ought to carry with it presumption of merit; and experience and distinction are of right entitled to distinctions." The committee had no doubt, since "education is the parent of public and private virtue," that the improvement should take place in law schools where law would be studied "scientifically." Not that the committee was satisfied with the majority of law schools that did exist; their courses of study were too short, they were too concerned with enrollments, examinations were shallow, and degrees were "thrown away on the undeserving and the ignorant." Law schools needed to be brought closer to the profession and to "submit to restraints which the necessity of the case make indispensable." The model was to be the scientific training of France and Germany. There was a need for "a full scientific course upon the Roman civil-law," and allegations were made that constitutional history and political science were neglected. At all costs the "proneness" of law students "to be practical" had to be "combatted." The outcome of all of this was that, in addition to the comity practices, the committee resolved that there should be "public maintenance" of law schools with at least four well-paid and efficient teachers, written examinations for graduation, the requirement of a law degree before practice, the recommendation by state and local bars of graded (i.e., sequential) law school programs for three years. It was not until 1881 that the association as a whole became involved in what was to be a century-long crusade. In that year, the ABA House of Delegates passed a resolution recommending (not attempting to require) attendance at law school for three years, although it also urged law schools to let students complete the work in less than three years. It further recommended that all states give credit toward apprenticeship for time spent in law school.

The annual meeting of the ABA in 1891 was spent discussing data on admissions to the bar and bar examinations. The need to return to serious bar examinations had been encouraged partly by the temper of the times and partly as a response to the diploma privilege of which the ABA disapproved. As the diploma privilege declined, the bar examination necessarily became a more serious activity, if only to justify removing

such authority from the schools. Written bar examinations appeared in some counties of Massachusetts in 1870 and in New York in 1877. Local bar associations, both for prestige and for competitive reasons, generally fought hard to have the states impose strong bar admission requirements. After 1878 the ABA added its voice. Slowly, the boards of examiners, normally controlled by local bar associations, replaced the supreme courts as the examining authorities. Beginning with New Hampshire in 1876, statewide boards were established that financed themselves out of applicants' fees.

The 1891 ABA annual meeting was, however, an opportunity once again to emphasize the importance of attending law school. It was of considerable concern to the Committee on Legal Education that only one-fifth of the lawyers admitted each year had been to law school, that no state required attendance at law school, and that there was little chance of the latter being achieved "within the present generation." The resolution on the 1891 report came on for discussion at the poorly attended 1892 annual meeting of the ABA. It was to prove to be the most important such discussion thus far. The association passed a resolution calling for two years of legal education, with the assumption that those years would be in law school. Although there was agreement that only two years could be required, there was also agreement that postgraduate courses should be provided for those who could stay longer. Commercial schools and the diploma privilege were officially deprecated, and the resolution that bar exams should be run by the highest court in the state was finally passed. It was again recommended that law schools be maintained by the states and have at least one full-time faculty member. The strength of interest in the 1891 committee report led to the founding of the first ABA section in 1893, the Section of Legal Education and Admissions to the Bar. The section immediately took up the issue of the length of law school and, as part of this general trend, in 1895 the section approved a resolution, which it sent on to the House of Delegates, calling for a mandatory three years of law school. Although the resolution was sent back to the Committee on Legal Education, positions were hardening.

Despite all the rhetoric and resolutions, the ABA had, at best, the power of persuasion, and by 1895, it had had virtually no impact in raising the educational standards of lawyers. As a result of these efforts by the organized bar, it is true that time spent in law school came to be counted as time spent in a law office, as states gradually increased (or restored) the requirement for some kind of apprenticeship or clerkship. Yet no state required attendance at law school, and the majority of lawyers in the 1890s had seen the inside neither of a college nor of a law school.

In 1896, the ABA approved the requirement of a high school diploma and two years of law study for bar admission. By 1897, the period of study required was lengthened to three years, with the hope that state legislatures would not only approve but also restrict the method of study to that of attending law school. In 1908, the association was discussing a requirement of two years of college before law school, although its official requirement was still a high school diploma (and would remain so until 1921). In 1899, the ABA, under pressure from the new breed of academic lawyer, called for the establishment of an organization of "reputable" law schools, which came into being in 1900, with 25 members, as the Association of American Law Schools. Membership was open to schools rather than individuals, and the schools were required to meet certain minimum standards; students were to have a high school diploma, courses had to be two years long (30 weeks a year), and students were required to have access to a library with *U.S. Reports* and local state reports. The association raised the minimum requirement for membership to a three-year law school program in 1905, and after 1907 two-year schools were denied membership. By 1912, the AALS would no longer accept members with day and night sessions of equal length.

By 1916, the AALS was prepared to go further still and debate a resolution not to recognize any night work after 1920. Although the resolution was ultimately referred to the Executive Committee, positions were hardening. It was in that debate that Eugene Gilmore, a law professor at Wisconsin, later to be president of the University of Iowa announced: "The universities can turn out all the lawyers the country needs; we don't

have to sit up nights to find ways for the poor boy to come to the Bar." At that same meeting, the association adopted a requirement of three "substantially" full-time faculty members, despite the threats of Marquette and Pittsburgh that "if you adopt it to take effect at once, we shall withdraw."

Although the ABA undoubtedly contained the leaders of the profession, it represented only a tiny proportion of the bar as a whole. In 1900, only 1.3 percent of lawyers were members; by 1920, a little over 9 percent were members. The AALS was in a similar position. In the first two decades of this century, it was representing a steadily smaller proportion of the total law school population, partly through losses as member schools, which could not keep up with requirements, were dropped, but mainly through the growth of nonmember proprietary and part-time schools.

In response to this open market, different schools looked for methods to minimize or eliminate competition. An early example of this was the diploma privilege, which gave legislative approval to individual law schools to determine the quality of student needed to pass the bar. Although the privilege was abolished locally by some jurisdictions, little major action took place nationally, until 1892, when the ABA began an outright attack. The system declined more rapidly after the ABA assault. In 1917, the numerous California and Minnesota schools lost the privilege, although 22 schools in 15 states still enjoyed its advantages. (Even in 1965 four states had some form of diploma privilege.) By the 1920s, however, the end of the privilege as a major force was in sight.

As with the abolition of the diploma privilege, the initiation of state bar examinations by legislatures was predominantly the result of the activities of the ABA and local bar associations. By 1917, centralized boards of bar examiners existed in 37 jurisdictions. At the same time, the number of jurisdictions requiring some formal period of training—either in law school or a law office—rose rapidly. In 1860, only nine out of 39 jurisdictions required it. In 1890, the requirement had risen to 23 out of 49. By 1917, the requirement had reached 36 out of 49, with 28 demanding a three-year period. Even in 1917, however, there was no state that required attendance at law school.

The leaders of the bar shared the then current assumptions about the ethnic superiority of native white Americans. In 1909, ignoring a plea from John Henry Wigmore that "we had better recognize cosmopolitan conditions and not for the sake of a theory have a rule which would prevent us in the next 20 years from doing a little more justice to our great foreign populations," the Section of Legal Education of the ABA adopted a requirement that lawyers had to be American citizens. An ABA delegate from West Virginia argued forcefully in favor of prelaw college training "where proper principles are inculcated, and where the spirit of the American government is formed." The "influx of foreigners" into the cities consisted of "an uneducated mass of men who have no conception of our constitutional government." A New York delegate defended the college requirement of prelaw training with even less sophistication: it was "absolutely necessary" to have lawyers "able to read, write and talk the English language—not Bohemian, not Gaelic, not Yiddish, but English." In 1922, the Yale Board of Admissions was deeply concerned about "the Jewish problem." In that same year, a Yale psychologist warned the state bar association that "this invasion of foreign stock" was undermining "the finer professional spirit and feeling which characterizes the professional training of the typical American lawyer." Dean Swan of the Yale Law School suggested to the state bar in 1923 that students with foreign parents should be required to remain longer in college than native-born Americans before being admitted to law school. At a Yale faculty meeting in the same year, Swan argued against using grades as the basis of limiting enrollment to the law school, because such a development would admit students of "foreign" rather than "old American" parentage, and Yale would become a school with an "inferior student body ethically and socially."

RISING STANDARDS FOR THE MANY

The 1920s were to begin with the ABA and the AALS moving vigorously to raise standards from the bottom up. In 1921, the ABA put its seal of approval on the requirement of two years of prelegal college work for all prospective law students while approving either four-year part-time or three-year full-time programs in law schools. As an entirely voluntary body, the ABA's only weapon in promoting conformity to its standards was, in theory, logic but, in practice, the art of persuasion. This did not always work, although there were some successes. In 1922, the ABA-sponsored meeting of local and state bar associations (the Conference of Bar Association Delegations) generally approved these decisions. At the conference, however, certain variations from the ABA model, as envisaged by the Root report, surfaced. Although the delegates did not accept the basic two years of prelegal college training (which the Reed report had also called for), they approved a requirement of "equivalent training" as an alternative.

In 1923, the ABA issued its first list of approved schools. In 1924, the AALS established a requirement of one full-time teacher for each 100 students, tightened the definition of part-time education yet again, and raised the library requirements that had originally been set in 1912. The next year, the AALS requirement of two years of prelegal education went into effect; the ABA in its turn adopted the AALS faculty requirement and dropped its category of provisionally approved schools. In 1926, the ABA again adopted an earlier AALS requirement by demanding two years of prelegal college work, and the AALS rescinded the rules allowing law students to take limited college work concurrently with their law studies. The AALS, having set new library standards only three years before, raised them once again in 1927, establishing a minimum of 7,500 volumes with an annual minimum maintenance of $1,000. At the same time, it shook off virtually all alternatives to two years of prelaw college work. In 1928, the ABA followed the AALS once more and demanded of its members a minimum of three full-time instructors and 7,500 volumes in the library.

All of this was, however, "like the action of acid on metal." ABA standards were met by only about half the country's law schools (there were 65 ABA-approved schools in 1927) and only about one-third of law students were in AALS schools (34 percent in 1928), representing a rapid drop since the beginning of the decade. More important, however, was the fact that, in 1927, of the 49 jurisdictions (the 48 states and the District of Columbia), 32 still had no formal legal requirement for prelaw studies, and 11 required merely high school graduation or its equivalent. Only six required two years of college or its equivalent. In 1927, none required attendance at law school. On the other hand, during the 1920s, there had been a significant rise in the requirement for some formal legal training. By 1928, every jurisdiction except Indiana had a compulsory bar examination. Nine jurisdictions still had no requirements for any law training, but the tide had turned. By 1930, four states had come to require attendance at law school (three years in West Virginia, two years in Colorado, one each in Kentucky and Wyoming). Moreover, in the remaining 45 jurisdictions, law school and law-office training had become alternatives, and only four states still insisted on some office training for all students. All other states allowed the alternative of a preparation exclusively done at a law school, and a few—including Illinois, Michigan, Minnesota, New York, Ohio, Washington, and Wisconsin— were actually ready to offer three years of law school as an alternative to four of apprenticeship.

It was in this atmosphere of rising standards and increasing conformity that Reed's second report appeared. His major concern by 1928 was the rapidly accelerating homogenization of law schools, which pressures from the ABA and the AALS were promoting. The only major exception to the pattern was the "four-year part-time" proviso that had saved the "better" evening schools. Reed was indeed back to his perennial theme—the misleading assumptions underlying the supposed homogeneous bar in America. This time he called for only two types of law schools, with his model by then more clearly the English barrister and solicitor.

The potential conflicts between the different types of law schools were abundantly evident at the meeting of the ABA Section of Legal Education in 1929. That year's meeting of the section was probably one of the most unpleasant on record. All the questionable aspects of the policy of raising standards were brought to the surface and expounded upon at length. The supporters of ABA-AALS policy were no less vocal in their

defense of their point of view. The two approaches were typified, on one hand, by William Draper Lewis, the chairman of the section, and on the other, by Gleason Archer, the dean of Suffolk Law School, the largest in the country. The former was able to boast that "progress" had been so rapid that 14 states were "now" complying with ABA regulations. When Archer's turn came, he announced his address under the title, "Facts and Implications of College Monopoly of Legal Education," and the content matched its title. After noting that the ABA had given the section $15,000 to use during Lewis's chairmanship, Archer asked:

> Now, what is the Section of Legal Education doing with this lavish contribution from our treasury?… The present Chairman of this Section, but for twenty years the guiding spirit of the Association of American Law Schools, and in 1924 its President, has hired H. Claude Horack, the present President of the Association of American Law Schools, at a $10,000 a year salary as field agent to capture the various states of the Union for the college monopoly.

James Brennan of Massachusetts backed Archer's charges of the suppression of the nonelite: "this great big organization now is attempting to divide our schools into groups, using, may I say, the blacklist—one of the most damnable and dangerous things in American life—the blacklist and the boycott." Edward T. Lee, the dean of the John Marshall Law School in Chicago, also refused to back down before the section:

> A group of educational racketeers—deans and professors in certain endowed and university law schools of the country—have used the American Bar Association as an annex to the Association of American Law Schools, a close corporation of "case law" schools, entirely irresponsible to the American Bar Association, and…they have been boring from within our Association in the interest of their own, unmindful of two fundamental objects of our Association, to uphold the honor of the profession of the law and encourage cordial intercourse among the members of the American Bar.

At least within the organized bar, however, the forces of "standardization" and "progress" were in the ascendant. The idea of a legal profession without standards was as unacceptable as a hospital without asepsis. Henry Drinker from Philadelphia said the majority of complaints received by the grievance committee of that city's bar association concerned "Russian Jew boys" and that requiring a college education from such people would "allow" them to "absorb American ideals." Xenophobia, economic concerns, and professional vanity, coupled with a genuine concern for the public interest, were more than strong enough to resist Archer's and Lee's spirited attacks. Pluralism was apparently on the wane, and all the ABA standards were reaffirmed at the 1929 meeting.

The 1930 meeting was almost as tense. Archer prefaced his remarks this time with the query: "Is this to be a deliberative meeting, or are we to have shock troops rushing in at the last minute and outvote those who have heard the debates?" The ABA responded by passing a resolution against commercially operated schools. Archer was not to be cowed into submission, and he renewed the attack by proposing that one-half of each law school faculty be composed of practicing lawyers. The resolution caused a storm and, although it received considerable support, was ultimately defeated handsomely. The scholar-lawyers could still rely on the support of successful practitioners. Archer and Lee managed only to have a vague recommendation passed calling for personal contact between law students and established practitioners.

Despite higher standards promulgated by the association, in 1928 part-time and mixed schools contained 60 percent of the total number of law students, but the net was closing. In 1930 the ABA sponsored a new organization—the National Conference of Bar Examiners—led by Will Shafroth, who had succeeded Claude Horack as adviser to the ABA Section of Legal Education. Some saw this new organization as a way of maintaining educational diversity. Reed, for instance, was optimistic. The initial list of objectives of the conference, however, indicated a different orientation, namely toward standardizing legal education and admissions to the bar nationally. The National Conference of Bar Examiners rapidly became part of the vehicle of the middle-grade AALS law schools' march toward uniformity, and a major effort was launched to convince bar examiners that, as far as possible, they should set exam questions that looked like exam questions in the "better" law schools.

By 1932, no fewer than 17 states required two years of prelegal college training—nearly three times the number four years earlier. Moreover, 33 states required at least three years of law study, although that was generally allowed either in law school or by way of apprenticeship. Between 1928 and 1935, the number of students in ABA schools actually increased by 5,000, represented only partly by an increase in the number of such schools from 66 to 68; the enrollment in unapproved schools fell by 10,000, and the number of such schools remained constant at 107. In percentage terms, the approved schools' share of the student body rose from 32.2 percent to 48.8 percent. In 1935, when the ABA took over from the Carnegie Foundation the publication of the *Annual Review of Legal Education*, the main article was by Will Shafroth, the new adviser to the ABA Section of Legal Education. After discussing "overcrowding" and the importance of "good moral character," Shafroth noted, without complete condemnation, that the Philadelphia Bar Association had voted to limit the number of practicing lawyers in its jurisdiction.

Perhaps Shafroth was not overly worried about the action of the Philadelphia bar because the organized bar, in fact, did have other methods in mind. Once again the medical profession, as it had in the time of Flexner, provided the precedent for the two-pronged attack: "This control has been accomplished by securing the adoption of rules and regulations in forty-four states requiring the applicant for a medical license to be a graduate of a school approved by the American Medical Association. Substandard medical schools have been eliminated and in the last thirty years the number of medical schools have been cut in two." The ABA was determined to emulate this achievement. By 1937, it adopted the requirements of two years of college study and three years of full-time or four years of part-time study at a law school that had a library of at least 7,500 volumes, a minimum of three full-time professors, and a student/faculty ratio of no more than 100 to one.

Each year during the 1930s, three or four states moved to a requirement of two years of prelegal college education. Isolated states went so far as to require three years of prelegal work. Pennsylvania, among other states, used stiffer character requirements as a means of curbing the number of lawyers, and other boards of bar examiners steadily raised the minimum passing grade. Increasingly, the states required law school training and required that training to be in ABA schools; and, increasingly, the students went to those schools. In 1937, California, for instance, delegated the accrediting of law schools to the state bar and required students in unaccredited schools to take a special qualifying exam after one year. By 1938, there were 101 ABA-approved schools with 63.7 percent (23,827) of the national law school student body. By that year there were only eight states that did not require two years of college education before law school, and the ABA cheerfully noted a drop in the number of law students: "This decline is likely to continue as the effect of the adoption of the two-year college requirements in Massachusetts, California, and the District of Columbia, as well as in other states, continues to be felt." Overall numbers were falling. In 1939 there were 34,539 students, 3,000 less than there had been the year before, "undoubtedly...due in most instances to the increased entrance requirements." The following year the president of the AALS referred to his organization as an "accrediting agency" and announced that "in the competition between schools for students, the non-member carries a heavy handicap." Either the depression or the AALS appeared to have become the savior of legal education.

DISCUSSION QUESTIONS

1. Who were the principal actors in the formation of the American legal profession? What were their interests? Whose interests prevailed?

2. Why was apprenticeship replaced by formal education? Why did it happen so much earlier in the United States than in other common-law countries? What were the consequences for the size of the profession? its composition? Would you favor a formal requirement of apprenticeship today? Is there a functional equivalent? Why did medicine include clinical training long before law? Why does medicine take such training far

more seriously? Should legal education be more clinical?

3. Why was an undergraduate degree required and law made a graduate degree? Should this requirement be relaxed? No country other than Canada has made law a purely postgraduate degree.

4. Why did American legal education develop the case and Socratic methods? What are the consequences of this pedagogic choice? Why has it never spread beyond North America?

What explains the extraordinary homogeneity of American legal education? Can you point to or recommend pedagogic innovations?

5. Part-time night schools, which enrolled more than half of all students in the 1920s, almost disappeared by the 1950s. Should they be encouraged today? Similarly, proprietary freestanding law schools gave way to university faculties. Should the former be encouraged today? Contrast the social mobility through entry to the profession afforded the sons of Eastern and Southern European immigrants before World War II with the obstacles confronting racial minorities who have sought entry since the 1960s.

Why do the ABA and AALS regulate legal education so intensely, but cram courses for the bar are proprietary and wholly unregulated? How does this compare with the SAT/LSAT and organizations like the Princeton Review?

Should the ABA be accrediting law schools? Should the AALS be imposing requirements for membership? In 1993 the ABA denied accreditation to the Massachusetts School of Law, which filed an antitrust action and asked the U.S. Department of Education to withdraw the ABA's accrediting authority. The school's dean argued that it kept its tuition at $9,000 per year by using adjunct professors from practice and electronic databases in lieu of a hard-copy library.[2] Under attack from the antitrust division of the Justice Department, the ABA agreed in 1995 not to collect data on or set standards concerning law school salaries and not to deny

2. *New York Times* B10 (2.4.94), A13 (2.9.94).

accreditation to for-profit institutions.[3] Should these accreditation functions be performed by state legislatures? supreme courts? Should some or all of the regulation be eliminated?

The Reed report proposed that the profession acknowledge it was divided into two tiers, whose members came from different backgrounds, attended different kinds of law schools, and performed different kinds of services for different clients. As we saw in Chapter 2, Heinz and Laumann documented the persistence of the two hemispheres half a century later. Should Reed's recommendations have been followed in the 1920s? Should they be followed today?

6. A few states still grant the "diploma privilege"—graduation from an in-state law school offers admission to the bar without further examination. What are the arguments for or against such a rule? In a few states, the bar exam is the *only* requirement for entry. In California, you need not graduate from college, attend an ABA-accredited law school or, indeed, any law school at all. Should other states adopt this approach? Why do so few entrants take that route? How effective is the bar examination in protecting clients from incompetence? Should there be other protections?

7. Is there any justification for other entry barriers, such as citizenship and state residence (both invalidated by the U.S. Supreme Court) or "character" examinations?

8. Why was supply control successful between 1930 and 1950? Why did it fail in the 1960s and 1970s? Look back at the statistics on the size of the profession in Chapter 2.

9. What predictions would you make about the future of the American legal profession with respect to: entry barriers, demand for entry, locus and content of legal education, locus of authority to regulate the profession? What would you like to see change? If selectivity is essential, when should it occur and by what mechanisms?

Entering classes at 76 of the 177 ABA-accredited law schools were smaller in 1994 than 1993. The University of Oklahoma decided to cut its incoming class from 670 to 500 over three years; Oklahoma's bar passage rate recently dropped 10 percent.[4] Although applications to medical schools reached record levels in 1993, 60 percent higher than five years earlier, a year later the Pew Health Professions Commission recommended that medical school enrollments be cut 20-25 percent over ten years. A few months after that an Institute of Medicine Committee recommended that residency programs be curtailed to reduce the number of new doctors, especially those trained abroad, and American medical school graduates be given preference. The AMA promptly backed the latter recommendation. The *New York Times* praised a Clinton administration proposal to pay New York hospitals approximately $120 million to train 2,000 fewer physicians over six years. The A.M.A., the Association of American Medical Colleges, and four other medical groups urged that production of doctors be cut by at least 20 percent.[5] Who should be making these decisions?

SUGGESTED READING

Although Stevens offers the most comprehensive and provocative history, there are other good overviews: J. Willard Hurst, *The Growth of American Law: The Law Makers* (1950); Lawrence M. Friedman, *A History of American Law* (1973); M. H. Bloomfield, *American Lawyers in a Changing Society, 1776–1876* (1976); "Symposium: Legal Education," 91(8) *Michigan Law Review* (August 1993); William P. LaPiana, *Logic and Experience: The Origin of American Legal Education* (1994); Robert M. Jarvis, *History of Legal Education in the United States* (1996). You may want to look at the two reports by A. Z. Reed: "Training for the Public Profession of the Law" (1921) and "Present Day Law Schools in the United States and Canada" (1928). For a sense of what used to pass for history, see Charles Warren, *A History of the American Bar* (1911); F. R. Aumann, *The Changing*

---

4. *ABA Journal* 26 (12.95).

3. *AALS Newsletter* (4.95); *AALS Newsletter* 4 (8.95); *New York Times* A1 (6.28.95).

5. *New York Times* A26 (9.1.93), C2 (11.17.95), C20 (1.24.96), A16 (2.28.97), 6(3.1.97).

American Legal System: Some Selected Phases (1940); Albert J. Harno, *Legal Education in the United States* (1953); Roscoe Pound, *The Lawyer from Antiquity to Modern Times, with Particular Reference to the Development of Bar Associations in the United States* (1953); A. H. Chroust, *The Rise of the Legal Profession in America* (2 vols.) (1965); Charles Haar (ed.), *The Golden Age of American Law* (1965). For earlier periods, see A. M. Smith, "Virginia Lawyers, 1680–1776: The Birth of an American Profession" (Ph.D. dissertation, history, Johns Hopkins University, 1967); George Gawalt, "Massachusetts Lawyers: A Historical Analysis of the Process of Professionalization, 1760–1840" (Ph.D. dissertation, history, Clark University, 1969); Charles R. McCurdy, "Lawyers in Crisis: The Massachusetts Legal Profession, 1760–1790" (Ph.D. dissertation, history, North western University, 1969); D. R. Nolan (ed.), *Readings in the History of the American Legal Profession* (1980). For more specific studies, see A. E. Sutherland, *The Law at Harvard: A History of Ideas and Men, 1817–1967* (1967); Jerold S. Auerbach, "Enmity and Amity: Law Teachers and Practitioners, 1900–1922," in Donald Fleming and Bernard Bailyn (eds.), *Law in American History* (1971); George Gawalt, "Massachusetts Legal Education in Transition, 1866–1940," 17 *American Journal of Legal History* 27 (1973). For an economic analysis of the professional project, see Harry First, "Competition in the Legal Education Industry," 53 *New York University Law Review* 311 (1978), "Competition in the Legal Education Industry II: An Antitrust Analysis," 54 *New York University Law Review* 1074 (1979). On the bar examination, see Robert M. Jarvis, "An Anecdotal History of the Bar Exam," 9 *Georgetown Journal of Legal Ethics* 359 (1996).

Chapter Twelve

BEYOND MARKET CONTROL:
PROFESSIONAL ASSOCIATIONS AND
THE PUBLIC INTEREST

If functionalist theories of professionalism (discussed in Chapter 9) can be apologetics for self-interest (as in the limitations on advertising discussed in Chapter 16), they also contain essential insights. Professions are concerned with the public interest, engaging in self-regulation (Chapter 13), documenting "unmet need" (Chapter 15), offering services "pro bono" (Chapter 17), supporting public and privately funded legal services for the unrepresented (Chapters 18 and 19), and seeking social change (Chapter 20). This chapter considers the role of professional associations in reforming the legal system and how this is affected by the stratification and segmentation we observed in Chapter 2.

ELITE PROFESSIONALISM IN MODERN SOCIETY: ITS PERSISTENCE AND ITS LIMITS[1]
Michael J. Powell

FOLLOWING his visit to the United States in the early nineteenth century, Alexis de Tocqueville projected that lawyers and judges would come to constitute the aristocracy of the New World. Viewing lawyers and judges as inherently conservative and antidemocratic in their commitment to the rule of law, Tocqueville anticipated that the members of the new aristocracy would defend order against change, thereby limiting the negative consequences of excessive democratization. Clearly Tocqueville was not referring to all lawyers and judges, but rather to an elite segment of the bench and bar represented by figures such as Boston's Daniel Webster, who capped his successful legal career with high political office.

1. In *From Patrician to Professional Elite: The Transformation of the New York City Bar Association*, chapter 7 (New York: Russell Sage Foundation, 1988). Reprinted with permission.

If any group of American lawyers inherited the Tocquevillean mantle, it was the New York legal elite of the late nineteenth and early twentieth centuries. At first composed of renowned courtroom advocates such as William Evarts, Samuel Tilden, David Dudley Field, the Choate brothers, and James Carter, and then of highly successful corporate lawyers, such as Elihu Root, William Howard Taft, Charles Evans Hughes, John W. Davis, and William D. Guthrie, this WASP legal aristocracy played the Tocquevillean role in grand style. They were not only eminent New York lawyers but also prominent national figures, many of whom sought and held high national political office.

They led the American bar during the critical period of professionalization from the turn of the century until World War II. This Tocquevillean aristocracy created and maintained the Association of the Bar of the City of New York (ABCNY) as a patrician legal association with membership requirements akin to those of the upper-class clubs with which they were so familiar. Holding to patrician notions of professionalism, and generally opposed to democratic tendencies within the bar, they advocated higher entry standards and character and fitness requirements for practice, and led the opposition to the movement to establish statewide, compulsory-membership bar associations. The patrician model dominated the ABCNY until the 1960s, when it was seriously challenged for the first time by significant changes in the surrounding bar and its wider societal context, which required major adaptation on the part of this aristocratic association.

By what means can elite associations such as the ABCNY maintain their distinctiveness and yet retain their legitimacy in the face of egalitarian pressures and democratizing tendencies? If they are able to survive as distinctively elite associations, what is the extent of their power and influence? Are these strategic elites actually able to shape the main contours of their particular institutional domains, as has been suggested by various elite theorists? Are the resources available to elite associations superior to those of nonelite groups so that the elite associations are able to exercise determinative influence over the outcomes of broader policy making and statutory change?

We have seen that the ABCNY did persist as an elite association in the midst of an increasingly heterogeneous bar. It did not follow the path taken by the Chicago Bar Association (CBA) decades earlier and become a mass voluntary bar association, fully representative of the surrounding bar. Indeed, despite rapid membership growth in the 1960s and 1970s, the ABCNY still, in 1980, included fewer than one out of every three New York lawyers. Graduates from the elite national law schools and large-firm lawyers continued to be overrepresented in its membership, and the powerful president's office remained firmly in the hands of the corporate legal elite. By 1980, there still had not been a president elected from the personal-plight hemisphere of legal practice.

Although the ABCNY remained an elite association, it was less closely identified with the WASP establishment than previously. Fewer of its leaders belonged to the exclusive clubs of the city than in the interwar years, and the anti-Semitism that had earlier characterized the American upper class, and was clearly viewed as a hurdle for Jewish lawyers seeking to play an active role in the ABCNY during this time, was no longer apparent. If Jewish and Catholic lawyers remain underrepresented in the ABCNY, as they appear to be, it is not because of ABCNY admissions policies or procedures but because they continue to be underrepresented in the prestigious large firms from which the ABCNY still recruits a high proportion of its members. Similarly, once completely excluded from membership in the ABCNY, female lawyers are well represented in the 1980s. There was certainly greater diversity in the social backgrounds and ascriptive characteristics of members in the late 1970s compared to the early 1950s.

If the ABCNY opened up its doors in the 1970s, welcoming instead of scrutinizing membership applications, why did not lawyers from the nonelite segments of the bar flood into the ABCNY, thereby radically changing its character? Relatively high initial fees and annual dues, the operation of differential levels of admission (representation, inclusion, and incorporation), and the retention of an elite organizational structure with small, exclusive committees all contributed to discouraging the massive entry of lawyers from the personal-plight bar and permitted the maintenance of the ABCNY's elite character. For many graduates of local law schools, practicing alone or in small firms, the ABCNY offered little more than the status of membership. Its location was inconvenient (a long way from the courts and City Hall), committee appointments were hard to come by, and it lacked a dining room for business lunches. It did not promise to be a good source for referrals, except, perhaps, for the white-collar criminal defense lawyers who regularly get work from the large corporate firms. These disincentives tended to outweigh the incentives of access to excellent library facilities and status conferral that the ABCNY offered. Consequently, the leadership of the large-firm elite was not seriously challenged by an influx of nonelite lawyers.

On top of these disincentives, the atmosphere at the ABCNY remained overwhelmingly elitist, dominated as it was by large-firm lawyers. The personal-plight lawyers in small firms and solo practice and the corporate lawyers of the large firms live and practice in two quite separate worlds. At least in Chicago, lawyers from the two hemispheres met in the CBA. In contrast, in New York the ABCNY was almost exclusively identified with the corporate hemisphere, whereas the New York County Lawyers Association (NYCLA) and the local bar associations provided meeting places for personal-plight practitioners.

Although the ABCNY did not undergo fundamental democratization, its more diverse membership brought new ideas and values into the association. New committees were founded, and older committees drew from a wider pool of lawyers. Greater membership diversity resulted in increased dissensus, especially following the co-optation of young reformist lawyers and consumer advocates into new committees in areas of law defined as much by ideology as by substantive legal content. The higher level of conflict was manifested not only in members' meetings replete with contention but also in disagreements within and between committees. On occasion this internal conflict spilled over into the public arena as committees disseminated their conflicting reports, thereby undermining any unified collective influence the ABCNY might have had over policy making on the issues at stake. Even without the premature publication of conflicting reports, the difficulties the ABCNY experienced in reaching early agreement on controversial professional issues hindered its ability to intervene expeditiously in ongoing policy debates.

Yet, notwithstanding this higher level of internal conflict, the ABCNY was still able to reach decisions on controversial matters even if only after lengthy debate. Furthermore, these decisions were not all of the "lowest common denominator" variety, as tended to be the case in fully representative professional associations, but on occasion were decisions that advocated major changes in long-standing professional or public policy. The ABCNY successfully utilized various organizational strategies to manage conflict, including channeling discontent into peripheral sections or relatively isolated subunits; creating new ad hoc committees to bypass extant committees regarded as too unpredictable or conflictual; respecting the relative autonomy of highly technical standing committees; and strengthening hierarchical, centralized authority over committee actions.

Furthermore, the newcomers to the ABCNY were not all that different from the old guard in terms of their educational and professional backgrounds and practice interests. Although the old patrician leadership undoubtedly disapproved of some of the proposals for legal reform emanating from some of the new committees, by and large these proposals did not conflict with their real material interests. Rather, the real opposition remained outside the ABCNY in the wider New York bar, where the sharpest differences in pro-

fessional values and interests were to be found. Thus there was little conflict within the ABCNY over the recommendation of a true no-fault law in the early 1970s; vigorous opposition came from segments of the bar not at all included in the ABCNY. Similarly, relaxation of the norms governing lawyer advertising sought by consumer advocates within the ABCNY met its strongest opposition in state bar politics and in the state courts where the small-firm and solo practitioners who stood to be negatively affected by such a policy had considerable influence.

Elite theorists, whether of society as a whole or of particular institutions, emphasize the continued power of cohesive, integrated elites to determine important policy outcomes. Jerold Auerbach, for instance, contends that the stratification of the bar historically enabled "relatively few lawyers, concentrated in professional associations, to legislate for the entire profession and to speak for the bar on issues of professional and public consequence." These few lawyers were typified for Auerbach by the WASP corporate elite of the ABCNY.

Certainly, the ABCNY historically had attempted to shape the modern legal profession as it emerged in twentieth-century New York. It developed discipline committees, established a judiciary committee to screen candidates for the bench, engaged in periodic campaigns against ambulance chasers, and led the movement for stiffer qualifications for admission to the bar. Yet in all these areas the ABCNY was less than successful: its discipline committee merely touched the tip of the iceberg of unethical practice; its campaigns failed to rid the city of ambulance chasers; and its attempt to act as a gatekeeper to the local and state benches was notably unsuccessful. Perhaps of greater importance than the extent of its actual instrumental authority over the bar and the legal system was the symbolic significance of its efforts in these areas. The ABCNY, and through it the corporate elite of the New York bar, became identified with legal reform and professional regulation, thereby imbuing its initiatives with considerable moral force.

There is a further question, however, that arises from the ABCNY's postwar transition from patrician to elite professionalism. Did the admission of lawyers from more diverse social and ethnic backgrounds improve the ABCNY's ability to exercise effective leadership in the profession and the wider society? In *The Protestant Establishment*, Digby Baltzell held that an open upper class or elite, incorporating within its ranks rising elites of achievement, would be able to exercise more effective moral leadership than a closed or caste-like upper class because it would be more representative of the wider society and therefore enjoy greater legitimacy. Following Baltzell's logic, then, we could anticipate that the ABCNY's influence capabilities would have been strengthened by its movement away from a caste-like WASP solidarity.

Examination of the ABCNY's activities in the postwar period, however, shows that it was not any more successful than before in implementing the professional and legal-system reforms it initiated. Indeed, it lost its century-long control over lawyer discipline in 1980, and was unable to prevail with its advocacy of radical changes in professional policies governing admission to the bar, lawyer advertising, and no-fault automobile insurance. The newcomers to the ABCNY in the 1960s and 1970s were not, by and large, graduates of local law schools who practiced alone or in small firms, and the reform proposals the newcomers espoused did not bring the ABCNY closer to the local nonelite bar groups. Indeed, there was an interesting inversion of roles in the 1970s, with the nonelite local lawyers defending traditional professional restrictions and regulations against attacks brought by elite reformers seeking fundamental changes.

Even when the leadership of the ABCNY made a special effort to ensure representativeness on major projects, it could not readily escape its large-firm identity. When the ABCNY decided to tackle seriously the massive problems of the criminal justice system in New York City in the late 1970s, it created a special committee to study the situation and recommend changes to the relevant statutory and judicial bodies. Although a wide variety of lawyers and laypersons representing all the diverse interests in the criminal justice area were appointed to this committee, it was still viewed as reflecting the interests of the large-firm

elite. Thus its recommendations were greeted with great suspicion and skepticism by criminal justice practitioners and policy makers. Labeled in this way, the ABCNY's special committee, although broadly representative, found it very difficult to make any headway against the intractable opposition of special interests in the criminal justice system. The continued accurate perception of the ABCNY as an organization of the large-firm legal establishment militated against its effective leadership within the sharply differentiated New York legal system.

In addition, the professional and practice interests of most leaders of the ABCNY were directed overwhelmingly toward Washington, D.C., the federal courts, and national political and economic developments. Consequently, the ABCNY was much more effective on the national and federal levels, where the natural interests and connections of its leaders were found, than it was at the local and state levels. Not well integrated into local and state political networks, its leaders generally lacked strong local connections and political clout. Large-firm lawyers may enjoy high social standing but they do not get the vote out. Cyrus Vance was an exception, and his strong local political ties proved important to the eventual achievement of a modicum of judicial reform. In comparison, solo and small-firm practitioners frequently appeared in the local courts before the local and state judiciary and were more likely to belong to local political clubs and develop close ties to state legislators, many of whom had once been local lawyers themselves. Moreover, they were embedded in community and ethnic relations that overlapped with political and professional ties and therefore were in a position to mobilize local political opposition to elite reform initiatives that threatened their interests. Many of the important professional and legal system reforms sought by the ABCNY required the action of state judicial or legislative bodies with which local nonelite bar groups had strong connections and therefore could exercise countervailing influence.

It is clear that even after the ABCNY became more of an open elite organization, there remained limits to its authority and its ability to determine professional policy and reform the

New York legal system. Unable to prevent elite reform initiatives, local bar interests could effectively neutralize and limit their reach. They could do this within the inclusive and representative metropolitan or state bar association before issues ever reached the public, as in the case of the CBA, or through representations in local and state decision-making arenas where their influence resources have particular utility. Furthermore, metropolitan bars are embedded in highly differentiated urban political systems that make it difficult for any one group, whether a class or functional elite, to control decision-making processes and outcomes.

If the elite association is unable to exercise a determinative influence in the making of professional policy notwithstanding its considerable resources, what is its role? The elite association generally has access to the resources necessary to undertake major studies of problem areas upon which it can then base reform proposals. The ABCNY frequently utilized its access to foundations to fund such studies and to academics and experts to staff them. Many of its research projects were published in book form and received wide circulation, contributing significantly to the flow of information and ideas on issues of local and national policy concern. Furthermore, because of the relative homogeneity and economic security of its members, the elite association may well be able to consider and support quite radical changes that would be inconceivable for heterogeneous and representative associations. Thus the ABCNY was able to tackle, and provide decisive leadership for, controversial professional issues such as federally funded neighborhood legal clinics, lawyer advertising, and no-fault automobile insurance because those segments of the bar that stood to lose most from changes in these areas were not incorporated into its membership. In contrast, fully representative associations, such as the CBA and ABA, had to satisfy multiple and conflicting internal constituencies and therefore found it very difficult to adopt positions welcoming change at all.

The distance of the leadership of the ABCNY from local ethnic groups also facilitated its national leadership in the civil rights movement of the 1960s. Not only did it provide a platform for Martin Luther King Jr. in New York, but it also was an early and strong supporter of federal civil rights legislation. Its substantial, and widely cited, report on the 1964 Civil Rights Act provided detailed argumentation supporting its constitutionality and defending its necessity. In contrast, the CBA, with its more conservative leadership and close connections to local white ethnic communities, was very reluctant to endorse major civil rights legislation and provided only lukewarm support for the Civil Rights Act itself.

Similarly, the elite association's prestige and legitimacy may endow it with greater autonomy from political authorities and therefore enable it to be more outspoken in opposition to repression or violations of rights. Although elite corporate lawyers scarcely rushed to represent unpopular political defendants during the height of McCarthyism in the early 1950s, the ABCNY did intervene in an attempt to protect individual rights in the face of abuses by congressional investigating committees. It first issued in 1948 a widely circulated and influential report on the procedures of congressional investigations that recommended the adoption of due-process protections for those under investigation. Several years later, it was one of the very few bar associations to oppose publicly the ABA's proposal that all lawyers should be subject to loyalty oaths, and in 1954 it established a national committee to inquire into the federal loyalty-security program. Reflecting the tenor of the times, this report did not reject the program as a whole but rather sought to restrict its scope and improve the fairness of its procedures. Published as a book in 1956, the ABCNY's report contributed to the growing doubts about the usefulness and fairness of the entire loyalty-security effort. Although in retrospect it is clear that the ABCNY did too little too late, it went farther than any other local association, or the ABA, in attempting to insert some reason and procedural protections into the national anticommunist witch-hunt of the time. Moreover, the ABCNY was usually successful in getting its reform proposals on the agendas of the relevant decision-making bodies. That the elite ABCNY was constantly bringing merit selection of the judiciary before legislators and the public facilitated its eventual partial adoption when the time was ripe.

What about the elite bar's influence over broader public policy issues, over the direction and content of legal change? When professional associations move outside their primary spheres of influence—in this case, the legal profession and the court system—into the wider public policy arena, they have to contend with not only competing professional interests but also multiple other organized interests. Some commentators have suggested that the collective influence of lawyers, even elite lawyers, in the public policy-making arena is very limited indeed. Heinz, for example, contends that the collective action of lawyers "does not bring about an allocation of the society's scarce resources that differs in any substantial way from the distribution that would have been willed by the lawyers' clients or by the polity" quite apart from that action. First, he argues that sharp internal divisions prevent the organized bar from taking decisive stands on any but the most inconsequential of issues; and, second, he finds little evidence to indicate that lawyers are able or willing to support policies that run contrary to the interests of their clients.

Internal veto groups were not a serious problem for the ABCNY, even after its membership became more diversified. Rather than obstructing bar association action from within, the opposition of local bar groups to ABCNY reform proposals surfaced in the external political process, as demonstrated in the debate over no-fault automobile insurance. But the eventual outcome was the same whether the debate took place within or outside the bar association: the collective influence of the bar was significantly impaired by intraprofessional dissensus. On many other issues that had either a positive or a negligible impact on the interests of specific segments of the bar, however, there was no significant opposition from diverse bar groups to ABCNY proposals. A more telling judgment is that lawyers, individually or collectively, are rarely willing to challenge the policy interests of their clients and therefore are unable to make an independent professional contribution to legal change on major issues affecting the distribution of wealth and political power.

If this lack of separation between client and professional values characterizes the practices of individual lawyers and their firms, what about their collective representations through their professional associations? The bar association represents an arena of professional action quite separate from that of daily practice where client interests must prevail. Thus the ideology of the organized bar stresses that lawyers leave their clients at the door when they enter the bar association and participate in its deliberations. In large part, of course, the validity of the claim of the organized bar to be more than just another interest group depends upon public acceptance of this professional ideology. That is, the bar association must not only appear to be above narrow partisan politics but its deliberations must also reflect the disinterested application of autonomous professional expertise to legislative change. Only then can its recommendations be taken as representing independent professional judgment in the public interest.

Basic to Terence Halliday's thesis that the collective action of lawyers makes a significant contribution to modern governance is his contention that bar associations are able to transcend sectional professional and client interests in bringing expert knowledge to the service of the embattled state. His detailed analysis of the CBA's contribution to judicial and constitutional change in Illinois assumes the independent application of autonomous professional knowledge to the determination of which legislative proposals further the public good. In other parts of his analysis, however, Halliday leans toward a rather different argument, which accepts the close identity of lawyers with their client and practice interests in their bar association activities. His contention that bar associations are still able to exercise influence comes to rest, paradoxically, on the very heterogeneity of the bar that Heinz finds so debilitating. The presence of diverse groups of lawyers within the inclusive association necessitates its reaching compromises or transcending narrow professional or client interests. He found this to be the case in the CBA's active involvement in the revision of the revenue article of the Illinois Constitution. The initial position adopted by the CBA was seen to be too closely aligned to particular economic interests and was opposed by representatives of other interests within the CBA, leading to the eventual modification of the CBA's original position. To exercise any influence on the shape of the new revenue article, the CBA had to reconcile or transcend the competing interests within it.

Charles Cappell also demonstrates the close similarity between positions supported within the CBA and the practice and client interests of its members. Identifying the typical clients and practices of members of the CBA's board of governors, Cappell found that "the advocacy profiles of board members were partisan for the most part, and in most instances, consistent with the board member's set of clients and practice characteristics." It was the absence of relevant client ties that freed a board member to take a more general, nonpartisan approach to an issue. There was not much evidence of the disinterested application of autonomous professional knowledge to proposals for legislative change within the CBA.

ABCNY committees also tended to recommend policies or adopt positions in line with the interests of the clients of their members. For instance, perceiving that the time had come to revise the New York State corporation law in the late 1950s, the ABCNY and NYCLA established a joint committee largely composed of corporate lawyers, which pressed the legislature to replace the existing regulatory approach with an enabling act that would encourage incorporation in the state rather than discourage businesses with burdensome requirements and excessive liabilities. Its position was clearly pro-business and did not take into account the interests of labor and consumers. Notwithstanding the cumulative expertise of this joint committee, and the support of the business community, the bar committee failed to dissuade the legislature from retaining the regulatory orientation in the revised corporation law.

Similarly, the report of an ad hoc committee established by the ABCNY in the mid-1970s to examine proposed legislation imposing sanctions on corporations making illegal foreign payments was consistent with the interests of the giant corporations. There was strong sentiment in Congress to impose not only reporting requirements

with civil penalties on offending corporations but also criminal sanctions on corporate leaders. The ABCNY's committee questioned the need for additional legislation at all, but in the eventuality of legislation strongly opposed the inclusion of criminal penalties.

In both these instances of proposed legal change, ABCNY committees advocated positions in line with the general interests of the corporate clients of their members. In the mid-1970s, the Committee on Trade Regulation did begin to diverge from its traditional pro-business stance and supported increased sanctions for violations of the antitrust laws. This apparent aberration, however, is explained by the changing composition of this committee. It reflected not corporate antitrust lawyers taking positions contrary to the interests of their clients but rather the increased presence of law professors, government lawyers, and lawyers who represented consumer groups.

Without question, the preponderance of the evidence suggests that lawyers even in their collegial associations find it difficult to distance themselves from their clients' interests. I do not wish, however, to advance a crude interest theory of collective professional action. The explanation lies less in the proclivity of lawyers to advance consciously their clients interests in their professional associations than in their close identification with, and sharing in, those interests. Although lawyers may leave their immediate clients at the door of the bar association committee room, they are unable to leave behind the common culture and values they share with their clients in general.

Nelson's research on large-firm lawyers in Chicago finds that they strongly identify with the economic interests of their clients even to the point of putting clients' long-term interests over their own short-term interests. Thus, large-firm lawyers will support deregulation of an area of business activity even if it ultimately threatens to reduce substantially their own legal work because deregulation is in the long-term interests of their clients and they share with their clients a general distaste for government regulation.

In this sense there would seem to be ample grounds to support Heinz's ready dismissal of any independent collective influence of the bar over important allocative decisions. However, his test of lawyers' collective influence is framed too narrowly. For one thing, it ignores the broader institutional and ideological roles of the organized bar. Nelson argues persuasively that large law firms have a considerable impact "not because they bring about an allocation of society's scarce resources which differs from that willed by clients, but precisely because they maintain and make legitimate the current system for the allocation of rights and benefits." The same argument could be made even more strongly for major bar associations such as the ABCNY, which are not involved in the immediate adversarial representation of clients. Their support for, or opposition to, particular legislative proposals is presented as the considered opinion of independent, disinterested legal experts, thereby garbing the positions represented in those proposals in the symbols of justice and the language of rights.

Furthermore, Heinz does not consider the influence of the organized bar on important issues that do not directly involve major distributive questions. Yet Halliday recounts the CBA's active defense of individual rights through its emphasis on procedural protections and its consistent efforts to rationalize the Illinois court system. He also points out that the Illinois legislature delegated virtually complete responsibility for the revision and codification of the Illinois criminal law to a joint committee of the Chicago and Illinois bar associations in the 1950s.

The contributions of the ABCNY to general law reform were no less noteworthy. The ABCNY played a critical role in the 1960s in the substantial revision of New York's mental health and divorce laws. A decade later, it did so again in the evaluation and revision of the New York drug laws. Joining forces with the Drug Abuse Councils, Inc., the ABCNY undertook an examination of the impact of the harsh drug laws enacted during Governor Rockefeller's administration in New York in 1973. Popularly known as "the nation's toughest drug law," the Rockefeller laws imposed stiff mandatory sentences on those convicted of drug offenses. Funded by the Law Enforcement Assistance Administration, a joint committee of the ABCNY and the Drug Abuse

Council studied the effect of these laws on drug use and availability, and on the arrest, conviction, and sentencing of drug offenders. After three years of research, it reported that the tough laws did not seem to have the intended deterrent effect. The use and availability of drugs were not reduced, and the already overburdened New York courts were further overloaded because those charged with offenses had no motivation to plead guilty as they faced severe mandatory prison sentences. Shortly after the publication of the joint committee's report, the legislature revised the New York drug law, reducing the mandatory penalties considerably. The widely reported study initiated by the ABCNY provided the data and justification for significant legislative reform in a very sensitive area of the criminal law.

In these successful excursions into law reform, the bar associations mobilized their organizational, financial, and knowledge resources to initiate and inform statutory change. Despite the apparent importance of these law reform efforts to the social control powers of the state, the bar associations experienced relatively little opposition. Although New York psychiatrists made representations with respect to reform of the mental health law, they approved its general direction, and there was no organized group of mental health lawyers with vested interests in the status quo to oppose it. Neither law enforcement agencies nor the judiciary opposed the relaxation of the draconian Rockefeller drug laws which had placed the entire criminal justice system of New York under extra pressure. Once the ABCNY–Drug Abuse Council report demonstrated the apparent failure of the laws to achieve their stated goals, thereby providing legitimacy for their revision, the legislature was quite willing to amend them.

While the success of the bar on these issues does not provide a good test of its ability to have its way despite the mobilized opposition of others, these were not inconsequential issues and in each instance involved more than mere technical law reform. Halliday suggests that as the boundaries are blurred between what is technical and what is normative in the law, "the legal profession has an unusual opportunity to exercise moral authority in the name of technical advice." This might have been the case in the revision of the Illinois criminal law but was certainly not so in the other examples, where the normative and substantive implications of changes proposed by the bar were apparent. Reform of the New York drug law promised to increase judicial discretion over sentencing and reduce the severity of penalties for drug offenses; the new mental health law would take commitment proceedings out of the courtroom and place them completely in the hands of medical experts; and revision of the New York divorce law offered to make divorce more readily available. The statutory changes in the criminal, divorce, and mental health laws advocated by the ABCNY had important, and apparent, consequences for social behavior and for the social control powers of the state.

Although this study indicates that the collective influence of the elite bar was generally unable to prevail over strong, organized opposition even in areas in which the elite bar had considerable expertise, it was able to get its proposals onto decision-making agendas in the first place and thereby influence the discourse of legal change. It was also able to initiate and shape legislative developments in important areas upon which there was agreement about the need for, and the general direction of, change. The existence of a broad consensus on the need for change does not guarantee that change will in fact occur, however, or determine the direction of change. There first need to be change agents who take up the cause of reform and mobilize support for change.

In the revision of New York's mental health, divorce, and drug laws, committees of the ABCNY initiated the process of legal change, either by undertaking research and publishing its results or by actually drafting new statutes and having them introduced into the state legislature. In the case of divorce law reform, the ABCNY committee worked closely with legislative leaders in guiding the reform through the legislature and in mobilizing support at critical junctures.

Critical views of the collective action of the modern professions emphasize either its self-interested monopolistic intent or its subservience to the interests of powerful clients or patrons. In the first view, the collective entities of the profession seek to expand or protect its boundaries,

exclude outsiders, and stimulate demand for its services. Codes of ethics, for instance, are seen as merely ideological camouflage that legitimate the profession's self-interested exploitation of its market. In the second view, the profession's collective action reflects the dominant client interests of the bar's leadership.

Although it could be argued that some of the ABCNY's activities advance the generalized interests of the clients of its members, others clearly do not. The reform of the criminal, divorce, and mental health laws were not issues from which any immediate professional or client advantages could be inferred. Similarly, the immense energy expended by the organized bar over the last forty years in court reform activities does not have any immediate apparent advantage to lawyers or particular client interests. Why, then, does the organized bar commit its resources to such reform efforts? In particular, why would the elite ABCNY expend considerable resources on reformist activities in areas of law in which few of its members and none of its leaders practice? Mental health, divorce, and drug law were far removed from the practices of the corporate legal elite of the ABCNY, as were the local criminal, civil, and domestic relations courts. Yet it committed its prestige, money, and organizational resources to reform in these areas throughout the postwar period.

One possible answer to this paradox of elite collective action in nonelite areas of practice is what might be described as moral displacement on the part of the elite bar. Developed to explain the enthusiasm the Victorian middle and upper classes exhibited for the moral improvement of the lower classes, all the while ignoring their own moral lapses, the displacement theory suggests that it is easier, and indeed even therapeutic, for elites to reform the institutions and behaviors of the nonelite than of their own. Accordingly, elite corporate lawyers, unwilling or unable to address problems in their own practices, displace their reformist energies onto nonelite activities where the need for reform is only too apparent and the implications for their own conduct negligible.

A more likely, although not unrelated, explanation would hold that the paradoxical involvement of the elite bar in nonelite reform was one way by which the elite emphasized its separation from the lower and dirtier world of ambulance chasing, contingent fees, plea bargaining, and custody fights. Andrew Abbott argues that the status of a particular specialty or area of practice within a profession is largely a function of its distance from the more unpleasant professional tasks. Thus lawyers who deal with the rarified, abstracted legal problems of corporate law enjoy higher standing within the bar than their colleagues who defend nasty criminals or represent parties to messy divorces.

By directing its reform efforts at nonelite areas of practice, the large-firm elite of the bar was suggesting that this was where reform was most needed and at the same time implying that its own areas of practice were characterized by rationality and integrity. The ABCNY committed much more energy to the reform of local and state courts and procedures than to the reform of the federal system. The clear implication was that federal practice, the practice of the elite of the bar, was morally superior to local and state practice, which was infested with political, particularistic, and commercial considerations. From this perspective, the symbolic significance of the ABCNY's reform efforts is what is critical.

There clearly is some basis to these accounts of elite lawyers' reform interests, but they fail to explain why the ABCNY committed so much of its time and energy to reform activities. Surely, it could have achieved the same end with periodic forays in the direction of reform that did not require the expenditure of vast amounts of its scarce resources. Yet it devoted considerable effort to judicial reform over a large number of years, far in excess of what would have been necessary for merely symbolic purposes. Similarly, the ABCNY did not simply wave a symbolic flag at divorce law reform but made two major attempts spanning almost twenty years until a new divorce law was enacted in 1966. Certainly, the ABCNY benefited from its identification with reform, which usually enabled it to occupy the high moral ground, and allowed its members to bask in its reflected glory; but the extent of its commitment to achieving actual legal change far exceeded that required for mere symbolic purposes.

An alternative explanation is that of civic professionalism proffered by Halliday, who argues that established professions such as law and medicine are in a position to contribute their expertise to the service of the state. On the one hand, mature professions no longer need to focus their collective energies on monopolistic concerns and are able to commit their resources in other areas; on the other hand, governments increasingly suffer from overload and crisis and look to the professions for assistance in meeting the many demands made upon them. According to Halliday, the professions can, and do, contribute to the adaptive upgrading of state agencies and institutions by "bringing their knowledge to the service of power."

The legal profession is particularly suited to bring its talents to the aid of the state because it is partly a "state-constitutive" profession, straddling the boundary between the state and civil society. Halliday suggests it is motivated to offer its services because of the "civic consciousness" of bar elites and a collective sense of obligation. Halliday tempers this idealist view with the recognition that the strain toward materialist self-interest is always present, but the overall impression is of a profession collectively animated by concerns of public service.

Civic professionalism requires that the professions do not simply respond to state requests for assistance but actually precipitate state action by drawing attention to the areas in which adaptation is required and by presenting specific proposals to state agencies calling for change. The proactive legal profession reviews existing statutory law and initiates reform in areas where it appears to be archaic, inconsistent, disorganized, or otherwise ineffective in achieving its ends. Utilizing their concentrated expertise, and professing disinterested motives, bar committees draft and propose rationalized legislation for enactment. Thus the Illinois bar associations initiated the codification of the Illinois criminal law and drafted a new criminal code that then became the basis for debate and eventual legislative action. Similarly, the ABCNY determined that the statutes governing divorce and commitment procedures for the mentally ill were archaic and needed substantial revision. It established special committees to study the existing law and draw up recommendations for reform. In so doing, the ABCNY drew the legislature's attention to the need for legislative change in these areas and developed proposals upon which the legislature could act.

Halliday's depiction of a proactive profession eagerly coming to the aid of an overburdened state may appear rather Pollyanna-ish at first glance, endowing the organized bar with too much civic virtue, but it does provide a tenable explanation for the initiation of legislative change by the organized bar on issues that are irrelevant to its collective self-interest and immaterial to the interests of its clients. Moreover, some of the initiatives of the bar have undoubtedly contributed to the adaptability and legitimacy of state institutions and agencies. The revised federal conflict-of-interest statutes, modeled on those the ABCNY proposed, greatly facilitated the movement of experts between the private and public sectors, enabling the state to draw more effectively on expertise from the private sector. By launching an examination of the impact of the harsh Rockefeller drug laws, the ABCNY was able to present the legislature with the data necessary to justify revision of the controversial laws, thereby relieving it of the burden of undertaking such research itself. These are instances of the ABCNY's contributing its resources and expertise to the strengthening and adaptation of the state.

Civic professionalism provides a timely corrective to the popular debunking of professionalism as mere ideology, masking occupational self-interest. One must take seriously the ideal interests of bar elites as well as their materialist concerns, as Robert Gordon suggests in his examination of the tension between the ideal and the actual in the professional lives of the elite New York lawyers who founded the ABCNY. A solely materialist, or monopolistic, interpretation of the collective action of the profession cannot explain the full range of reform activities of the ABCNY.

Of course, the ABCNY could afford to be in favor of professional or legal change on issues that did not affect in any way the interests of its members or their clients. It could afford to support proposals for federal funding of legal services, neighborhood legal clinics, and lawyer advertising because these changes in the provision of legal services involved little risk for the large-firm elite, whereas they impinged directly on the practices of solo and small-firm general practitioners. It could also afford to support vigorously civil rights legislation since its leaders were safely ensconced in corporate law firms and affluent suburbs where integration was not likely to have much of an impact. Yet lack of an interest at stake in these proposed changes is not in itself an adequate explanation of the ABCNY's action. Although it might, perhaps, explain lack of opposition on the part of the elite ABCNY to proposed changes such as these, it does not elucidate its strong, positive support. The ABCNY did not simply withhold opposition to federal funding of legal services for the indigent, or civil rights legislation. It actively campaigned for them. Nor does the absence of interest help us understand why the ABCNY involved itself in the revision of the New York divorce and mental health laws. Narrow interest theories, then, are not sufficient to explain the law reform activities of the large-firm elite of the bar.

Ultimately driving civic professionalism in the bar, according to Halliday, are strongly held collective value commitments to an efficient and rational legal system, to the legitimacy of law as an institution, and to the merits of procedural justice. Undoubtedly, members of the bar hold to these values to varying degrees, but one need not have recourse to ultimate values to understand the elite bar's reform agenda. The ABCNY's considerable involvement in law and legal system reform certainly reflects the high value its leadership places on the rule of law, but it may be more usefully viewed as a manifestation of the large-firm elite's perception of its responsibility for the maintenance of the larger system of which it is part and from which it ultimately benefits.

The leadership of the ABCNY was very much aware of its prominent place in the profession and the wider legal system. Representing the large-firm elite of the bar, the leaders of the ABCNY clearly felt they had a particular responsibility for the moral order of the profession and the legitimacy of the legal system. Such a view was a recurring theme in presidents' reports and innumerable bar association speeches. Advocates of particular issues of concern to the bar and the legal system more generally would refer to this obligation as a means of mobilizing the ABCNY. The ABCNY's ongoing concern with questions of professional self-regulation reflects this elite self-perception, and its reform activities can be understood as attempts by the elite to shore up the legal system and restore respect for the law. Thus its vigorous support for civil rights legislation reflected the general apprehension that the continued denial of rights to a substantial minority of the American population undermined the legitimacy of the law; its advocacy of federal funding of legal services represented its concern about the consequences of lack of access to justice; and its sustained efforts to achieve divorce law reform revealed its awareness that a law so out of touch with social reality as New York's outmoded divorce law engendered widespread disrespect for the law in general.

Representing an important strategic elite in contemporary American society, the leadership of the ABCNY committed its resources to uphold the legitimacy of the law and to improve the efficiency of the legal system. Ultimately, the advantaged position of the corporate legal elite, and of lawyers in general, depends on the continued recognition and acceptance of legal institutions as effective and necessary integrative mechanisms in the political economy and social order.

DISCUSSION QUESTIONS

1. Powell draws on Tocqueville's famous observation: "If I were asked where I place the American aristocracy, I should reply without hesitation that it is not among the rich, who are united by no common tie, but that it occupies the judicial bench and the bar."[2] Do you find this equally persuasive a century and a half later?

2. What are the interests of elite lawyers? Of their clients? Do those interests coincide? Do elite lawyers ever act against self-interest? Client interest? Are there actions of elite lawyers that cannot be attributed to self or client interest?

2. *Democracy in America*, vol. 1, p. 288 (1958).

What about nonelite lawyers? Are there self-interested explanations for even the most altruistic behavior? Are you persuaded of the existence of "civic professionalism"? Do elite lawyers share common values?

3. Powell mentions positions taken or reports written on such topics as divorce, criminal justice, and automobile no-fault. What about topics that more directly affect elite lawyers and their clients, such as corporations, tax, and regulation? Lawyer advertising or fees?

4. Can and should bar associations take positions on contentious topics about which they can claim no expertise, such as gun control, the death penalty, discrimination against gays and lesbians, or legalization of drugs? Is there a clear distinction between technical and normative issues? After the ABA House of Delegates approved an abortion-rights resolution 276–168, more than 3,000 of its 370,000 members resigned in protest. The conservative Federalist Society enjoyed an upswing of support in response to this decision and the ABA decision to give an award to Anita Hill. In February 1997, over the objection of the U.S. Deputy Attorney General, the ABA House of Delegates voted 280–119 to call for an immediate suspension of the death penalty on the ground that its administration is marred by "a haphazard maze of unfair practices." The *New York Times* praised the action as fulfilling "the legal profession's duty to act boldly against serious wrongs in the justice system."[3] How are these issues different from earlier controversies over the New Deal, the labor movement, McCarthyism, civil rights, or legal services?

Does your answer turn on whether association membership is voluntary or compulsory? See Theodore J. Schneyer, "The Incoherence of the Unified Bar Concept: Generalizing from the Wisconsin Case," 1983 *American Bar Foundation Research Journal* 1; Bradley A. Smith, "The Limits of Compulsory Professionalism: How the Unified Bar Harms the Legal Profession," 22 *Florida State University Law Review* 36 (1994).

5. Should bar associations play a role in judicial

3. *Los Angeles Times* A32 (11.4.92), A1 (2.4.97); *New York Times* 16 (2.22.97).

selection? Can they do so in a nonpartisan fashion? See Joel Grossman, *Lawyers and Judges: The ABA and the Politics of Judicial Selection* (1965); R. A. Watson and R. G. Downing, *The Politics of the Bench and Bar: Judicial Selection under the Missouri Nonpartisan Plan* (1969). Despite the State Bar of California's "unqualified" rating, the state Commission on Judicial Appointments affirmed Governor Wilson's nomination of Janice Rogers Brown as the first African American woman on the state Supreme Court. Senate Judiciary Committee chair Orrin Hatch (R-Utah) has threatened to end the ABA's role in reviewing federal judicial appointments.[4]

SUGGESTED READING

There are a number of earlier, often "official" or commissioned, histories of bar associations, e.g., W. W. Robinson, *Lawyers of Los Angeles: A History of the Los Angeles Bar Association and the Bar of Los Angeles County* (1959); G. Martin, *Causes and Conflicts: The Centennial History of the Bar Association of the City of New York, 1870–1970* (1970); H. Kogan, *The First Century: The Chicago Bar Association, 1874–1974* (1974); M. Radin, "The Achievements of the American Bar Association: A Sixty-Year Record," 25 *ABAJ* 903, 1007 (1939), 26 *ABAJ* 19, 135, 227, 318, 358 (1940). For accounts of anti-establishment bar associations, see Esther Lucille Brown, *Lawyers and the Promotion of Justice* (1938) (National Lawyers Guild); Michael Powell, "Anatomy of a Counter-Bar Association: The Chicago Council of Lawyers," 1979 *American Bar Foundation Research Journal* 501.

For more critical accounts, see M. L. Rutherford, *The Influence of the ABA on Public Opinion and Legislation* (1937) (opposition to the New Deal); B. N. Twiss, *Lawyers and the Constitution* (1942) (ibid.); John P. Heinz, Robert W. Gettleman, and Morris A Seeskin, "Legislative Politics and the Criminal Law," 64 *Northwestern University Law Review* 277 (1969) (Chicago and Illinois bar association influence on criminal law reform); Jerold S. Auerbach, *Unequal Justice: Lawyers and Social Change in Modern America* (1976); John P. Heinz, Edward O. Laumann,

Charles L. Cappell, Terence C. Halliday, and Michael H. Schaalman, "Diversity, Representation, and Leadership in an Urban Bar: A First Report on a Survey of the Chicago Bar," 1976 *American Bar Foundation Research Journal* 725; Alfred P. Melone, *Lawyers, Public Policy, and Interest Group Politics* (1977); Andrew Abbott, "Status and Status Strain in the Professions," 86 *American Journal of Sociology* 819 (1981); Charles L. Cappell and Terence C. Halliday, "Professional Projects of Elite Lawyers, 1950–1974," 1983 *American Bar Foundation Research Journal* 291; Terence C. Halliday, *Beyond Monopoly: Lawyers, State Crises, and Professional Empowerment* (1987) (Chicago Bar Association); Rayman Solomon, "Five Crises or One: The Concept of Legal Professionalism, 1925–1960," in Robert Nelson, David Trubek, and Rayman Solomon (eds.), *Lawyers' Ideals/Lawyers' Practices* (1992); Robert L. Nelson and David M. Trubek, "Arenas of Professionalism: The Professional Ideologies of Lawyers in Context," in Id.; Terence C. Halliday, Michael J. Powell, and Mark W. Granfors, "After Minimalism: Transformations of State Bar Associations from Market Dependence to State Reliance, 1918–1950," 58 *American Sociological Review* 515 (1993); Quintin Johnstone, "Bar Associations: Policies and Performances," 15 *Yale Law & Policy Review* 193 (1996). On the role of elite lawyers in the greatest governmental experiment of the twentieth century, see Ronen Shamir, *Managing Legal Uncertainty: Elite Lawyers in the New Deal* (1995); see also Mark C. Miller, *The High Priests of American Politics: The Role of Lawyers in American Political Institutions* (1995); Terence C. Halliday and Lucien Karpik, "Politics Matter: A Comparative Theory of Lawyers in the Making of Political Liberalism" (American Bar Foundation Working Paper 9522); Terence C. Halliday and Lucien Karpik (eds.), *Politics Matter: Lawyers and the Rise of Western Political Liberalism* (forthcoming).

❦

---

4. *Los Angeles Times* B7 (5.21.96); *New York Times*, A11 (2.19.97).

Chapter Thirteen

SELF-REGULATION: PROMULGATING AND ENFORCING ETHICAL RULES

Although regulation of lawyers is entrusted in the first instance to state supreme courts, they often delegate it to state bar associations, which have relied on the American Bar Association to draft and revise ethical rules. The last major effort was the Kutak commission, whose final draft was issued in May 1981.* The following article analyzes conflicts within the ABA and between it and other groups over the content of the new rules.

PROFESSIONALISM AS POLITICS: THE MAKING OF A MODERN LEGAL ETHICS CODE[1]
Theodore J. Schneyer

THE commission's draft of 25 January 1979 provided that a lawyer presenting a case to a tribunal must disclose facts adverse to the client's case if "disclosure...would probably have a substantial effect on the determination of a material issue of fact." This departed from the traditional view that lawyers should inform a tribunal of adverse legal authority, but not of adverse evidence, which may be left to one's adversary to present or not to present. The same draft (and later ones) revived Louis Brandeis's famous concept of the "lawyer for the situation," allowing lawyers to act as "intermediaries" between clients, even at some risk that a conflict of interest might later materialize. The August 1979 draft barred lawyers from drawing up or negotiating for a client an agreement containing terms a reasonable lawyer would know to be unconscionable as a matter of law. This duty to third parties went well beyond the code's rule that lawyers may not

counsel or assist a client in conduct they know is criminal or fraudulent. The Model Rules process gave little attention at any stage to the distribution of legal services. But, responding to critics, the August 1979 draft did require lawyers to devote forty hours a year, or the dollar equivalent, to improving the legal system or providing legal services to those who cannot afford them.

Once the discussion draft was published, bar groups had to decide how to respond. They could try to influence matters directly by participating in the ABA process, thereby confirming the ABA's status as a fountainhead of ethics; or they could react through other channels. The most important decisions to "go outside" were those of ATLA (Association of Trial Lawyers of America) and the NOBC (National Organization of Bar Counsel, who enforce the rules), organizations fairly new to bar politics and anxious to become more visible. Like other specialty groups, they found it easier to reach a consensus on ethics than the general-purpose state and local bars did. But neither had a strong voice in the ABA House of Delegates. NOBC members thought the discussion draft contained many provisions that would let lawyers "equivocate [enforcers] to tears." Also, since they used the Code of Professional Responsibility constantly, they had invested more time than most lawyers in learning it and were afraid of losing their expertise.

ATLA's decision to "go outside" was more momentous. Founded in 1946, ATLA consists mostly of plaintiffs' personal injury lawyers, a substantial percentage of whom are the urban, ethnic, solo, and small-time practitioners that the conflict critics of earlier ABA codes of ethics considered a professional underclass. Though its present membership of more than 60,000 is only about a sixth of the ABA membership, ATLA is the second-largest national bar organization and lately has been growing at a faster rate than the

---

* *ABA Model Rules of Professional Conduct.*

1. In Robert L. Nelson, David M. Trubek and Rayman L. Solomon, eds., *Lawyers' Ideals/Lawyers' Practices: Transformations in the American Legal Profession* (Ithaca: Cornell University Press, 1992). Reprinted with permission. A more detailed version appeared in 14 *Law & Social Inquiry* 677 (1989).

ABA. ATLA brought a conscious ideology to the subject. The creed has two tenets. One is consumerism—the customer is always right. The discussion draft of ATLA's code, for example, abandoned the traditional rule allowing lawyers to use client confidences to recover a fee. The second tenet in the ATLA creed, suggested by the description of a code of legal ethics as a clients' "bill of rights," is (liberal) constitutionalism, that form of legalism which grounds the lawyer's ethical duties in clients' (generously defined) constitutional rights. This tenet extends the imagery and values associated with criminal defense work to other forms of law practice, especially civil litigation. There was no greater gulf between the discussion drafts of the Model Rules and the Code of Conduct than on the issue of confidentiality. For example, the Model Rules draft required lawyers to disclose a client's confidences to prevent him from killing or seriously injuring someone, and permitted disclosure to prevent, or rectify the consequences of, a client's "deliberately wrongful act." The American Lawyer's Code of Conduct took two positions on the issue, but even the less extreme had no provisions requiring disclosure, and they permitted it only to avert imminent loss of human life.

It was clear by fall 1982 that the Model Rules process would produce a new code. Hazard, Meserve, and Kutak (until his death in January 1983) sought support among the delegates by accommodating a number of "special interests." A seemingly key accommodation involved Rule 1.13, on which the commission had been negotiating with the Evans committee from the beginning. When he announced the Corporation Section's endorsement of the Rules in August 1982, Loeber Landau of the committee called Rule 1.13 one of the "most important rules our Section had a hand in shaping." He was pleased with the rule's new attention to the special problems of representing organizations, with its clear statement that the lawyer for an organization represents the entity and not its various constituents, and with its careful hedging in, but not complete removal, of the lawyer's discretion to blow the whistle outside the corporation on managerial wrongdoing that jeopardized company interests.

Negotiations produced language responsive to the special pleading of many other groups, some of them quite small. For example, an organization of state attorneys general succeeded in having passages included that made it clear that government lawyers are often authorized to make choices that in private practice must be left to the client—such as whether to sue or whether to accept a settlement offer. Similarly, the ABA Administrative Law Section negotiated more latitude in case selection for former government lawyers and their private firms.

There were still other issues, touching on confidentiality, which not only had to be decided by house vote but also set up a showdown between the Kutak commission and the group that ultimately emerged as its most formidable antagonist—the American College of Trial Lawyers (ACTL). ACTL membership is by invitation. Most ACTL members concentrate on civil litigation, where they often represent insurers and other companies against clients represented by ATLA lawyers. Though ACTL has no direct representation in the ABA House of Delegates, Robert Meserve, himself an ACTL fellow, estimates that one-sixth of the delegates are members. He also thinks the House defers to the ACTL fellows far more than their numbers might suggest. ACTL found the Rules "permeated by a philosophy that is inimical to the adversary system and to effective legal representation." ACTL was worried about four rules above all, each touching on confidentiality. One was Rule 1.6. As proposed by the commission, Rule 1.6 allowed lawyers to disclose otherwise protected information to prevent a client from committing a crime or fraud likely to cause substantial bodily harm or substantial injury to financial interests or property; it also allowed lawyers to make disclosures to rectify the consequences of a crime or fraud that their services had been used to further. ACTL argued that so broad a hedge on confidentiality would make clients less candid and thus reduce lawyers' opportunities to discourage client wrongdoing (an argument, notice, based on public rather than client interests). At the February 1983 ABA meeting, ACTL proposed an amendment allowing disclosure only to prevent crimes likely to cause "imminent death or substantial bodily harm" (crimes ACTL lawyers apparently do not *want* a chance to discourage!). The House adopted the amendment 207 to 129. The second key rule ACTL sought to amend was 1.13. Rule 1.13(c), discussed earlier, permitted a lawyer in unusual circumstances to reveal confidential information to outsiders in order to protect the organization, even over the objection of the organization's highest authority. ACTL considered it presumptuous for lawyers ever to "play God" by disclosing information the highest authority in the corporation was determined to keep confidential. If counsel is troubled by the board's resolution of a legal problem, ACTL argued, let counsel withdraw.

The other troubling section was 1.13(a), which provided that the lawyer for an organization represents the organization "as distinct from" its directors, officers, employees, members, shareholders, or other constituents. ACTL considered "artificial" the distinction between the organizational client and its various constituents, especially management, since most lawyers who represent companies are retained by and work closely with management. Lawyers in this position are often expected to treat management if not precisely as the client then at least as the most vivid embodiment of the client. That is precisely why the Evans committee welcomed Proposed Rule 1.13(a). ACTL, however, sought to change "as distinct from" to "including," implying that the lawyer for an organization should normally think of him or herself as representing its various constituents as well. The House adopted both ACTL amendments to Rule 1.13, this time by a vote of 185–113.

The other two provisions of special interest to ACTL were Proposed Rules 3.3 and 4.1. These concerned the lawyer's rights and duties upon learning that the client has used the lawyer's services in perpetrating a fraud on a tribunal (3.3) or a person (4.1). The Code of Professional Responsibility had required lawyers to take steps to remedy both kinds of fraud. As first promulgated, it did not indicate how the duty to rectify could be squared with the duty to keep a client's confidences. A 1974 ABA amendment (adopted in only a minority of states) made it clear that confidentiality overrode the duty to rectify. The Kutak commission addressed the problem in two separate rules because it was committed to structuring the Model Rules according to the lawyer's various roles, something the Code had only begun to do. Fraud on a tribunal involved the lawyer's duties as advocate; fraud on a person involved the lawyer's duties as drafter or negotiator. In each case, the commission proposed that the duty to rectify frauds should override the duty of confidentiality. And in both cases, ACTL members or their allies proposed amendments subordinating the duty to rectify to the duty of confidentiality. The commission won by a 209 to 101 vote on Rule 3.3 but lost by a 188 to 127 margin on 4.1.

Only a month or so before the showdown in New Orleans, the *New York Times* and *Wall Street Journal* printed stories about a multimillion-dollar business fraud involving a computer-leasing firm (OPM). Perhaps unwittingly, a New York law firm—Singer, Hutner, Levine, and Seeman—had helped OPM close many fraudulent deals, so many that for several years OPM accounted for 60 percent of the firm's billings. Eventually, the firm withdrew from further representation. But it did not tell OPM's new law firm why it had withdrawn. Perhaps as a result, there were additional fraudulent transactions.

The news stories dwelt on Singer, Hutner's seemingly willful blindness to fraud and its later refusal to share its concerns with the successor firm. Ethical questions were raised: When is a law firm on notice of a client's wrongdoing? To what lengths should it go to monitor a client's conduct? At what point should it resign? When should it blow the whistle on a client who has used the firm's services to perpetrate frauds? The *Times* indicated that the ABA was in the throes of an "acrimonious debate" on these issues and would take action at an upcoming meeting.

In its response to the ACTL amendments in New Orleans, the Kutak commission was as sensitive to the press coverage of the OPM scandal as it had been to coverage in the first stage of the Model Rules process. It supported on the House floor an amendment to its proposed Model Rule 1.16 that made it clear that a lawyer may withdraw from representing a client who has used his services to carry out a crime or fraud. Geoffrey Hazard also drafted comments that weakened the thrust of the ACTL amendments to Rules 1.6 and 4.1. Those amendments, remember, took away the lawyer's *right* to disclose confidences in order to rectify a fraud in which his services had been used, and subordinated the lawyer's *duty* to rectify a client's out-of-court fraud to the duty of confidentiality. Hazard's commentary permits a lawyer, when he withdraws from representing a client who has used his services for purposes of fraud, to publicize the withdrawal and "disaffirm" any opinion or document he prepared for the client. Although the lawyers for future OPMs would not be permitted to blow the whistle on their clients, they could "wave the red flag."

The House of Delegates, however, responded to the OPM publicity with indifference, adopting the ACTL-sponsored amendments to Rules 1.6 and 4.1 by a substantial margin. "Forced to choose starkly between models of the lawyer as client's mouthpiece and as caretaker of the law," barked a follow-up *New York Times* editorial, the ABA House of Delegates "has opted for mouthpiece."

DISCUSSION QUESTIONS

1. To what extent is the content of legal ethics different from ordinary law or morality? Are the exhortations intended to be regulatory or merely aspirational? To what audience are they directed? Is anybody listening? How has the content changed over time? Are there ethical issues the profession ignores?

2. How do the divisions within the legal profession shape its ethical rules? Do the ethical rules reinforce the divisions? Do groups or institutions outside the profession influence the content of those rules? Should others participate in formulating those rules? How could they be involved? When do the media become interested in these issues?

3. Most of the conflicts involved tension between lawyers' loyalties to their clients and lawyers' duties to the legal system or society. Why is this such a central and intractable issue? How do you think it should be resolved? How do you think it is resolved in practice? What would have to be done to make these rules effective?

SUGGESTED READING

For critiques of the content of professional ethics, see Philip Shuchman, "Ethics and Legal Ethics: The Propriety of the Canons as a Group Moral Code," 37 *George Washington Law Review* 244 (1968); Richard L. Abel, "Why Does the ABA Promulgate Ethical Rules?" 59 *Texas Law Review* 639 (1981); Theodore L. Schneyer, "Policymaking and the Perils of Professionalism: The ABA's Ancillary Business Debate as a Case Study," 35 *Arizona Law Review* 363 (1993); Amy R. Mashburn, "Professionalism as Class Ideology: Civility Codes and Bar Hierarchy," 28 *Valparaiso University Law Review* 657 (1994).

Courts and bar associations have exclusive authority to promulgate ethical rules. But lawyers are responsible to a wide range of regulators, as the following article outlines.

WHO SHOULD REGULATE LAWYERS?[1]

David B. Wilkins

ENFORCEMENT proposals can be grouped into four models: disciplinary controls, liability controls, institutional controls, and legislative controls.

1. *Disciplinary Controls.* The reference point for this model is the current disciplinary system, in which independent agencies acting under the supervision of state supreme courts investigate and prosecute violations of the rules of professional conduct. The basic structure resembles a criminal prosecution. To avoid the appearance of favoritism or bias, disciplinary enforcement is consciously set apart from the day-to-day performance of legal work. The process is conducted almost exclusively *ex post* by independent officials who have no prior association with the case. These officials are instructed to reach their judgments solely on the basis of the evidence presented at a formal hearing in which the accused lawyer is accorded a full panoply of due process protections. In keeping with the criminal justice analogy, disciplinary agencies primarily focus on punishment and deterrence. Compensation, although allowed under limited circumstances, remains a secondary goal.

2. *Liability Controls.* Injured clients, and to a limited extent third parties, have traditionally had the right to sue lawyers under a variety of statutory and common-law theories. Although bar leaders and others have tried to separate "malpractice" from "discipline," these efforts have been largely unsuccessful. Recent developments are likely to blur the distinction even further. For example, the Resolution Trust Company has filed a number of lawsuits alleging that several promi-

nent law firms committed malpractice when, in conjunction with the managers of various savings and loans, they prevented regulators from discovering massive financial improprieties at these federally insured institutions. Similarly, as courts and legislatures relax the traditional restrictions against suits by nonclients, a growing number of third parties are suing lawyers for breaching ethical duties. As a result, litigation is now a viable alternative to professional discipline.

Like the disciplinary model, liability controls operate on the basis of *ex post* complaints by injured parties. A victorious claimant, however, is entitled to full compensatory and even punitive damages. Restrictions on the lawyer's right to practice law, on the other hand, are generally not available.

3. *Institutional Controls.* Lawyers work either directly in, or in the shadow of, state institutions. With increasing frequency, these institutions are expressly taking responsibility for uncovering and sanctioning lawyer misconduct. For example, Federal Rules of Civil Procedure Rule 11 now authorizes judges to impose sanctions for certain kinds of litigation-related misconduct. Similarly, several federal administrative agencies, including the Securities and Exchange Commission, the Office of Thrift Services, and the Internal Revenue Service, are now seeking to sanction lawyers who do not properly advise their clients about their duties under these regulatory regimes.

These and similar efforts share a common goal: to locate enforcement authority inside the institutions in which lawyers work. A judge, for example, will know if a lawyer has failed to file a pleading. Because the enforcement official and the lawyer to be disciplined are involved in a continuing relationship, sanctions can be imposed either immediately or after a separate hearing. Finally, the substantive jurisdiction of these institutional enforcement officials is likely to be confined to the area in which the institution operates.

4. *Legislative Controls.* Certain public officials and commentators have proposed a new administrative agency that would have sole responsibility for investigating and prosecuting lawyer mis-

1. 105 *Harvard Law Review* 799 (1992). Reprinted with permission.

conduct. Although such an agency might be patterned after the agencies that currently regulate doctors in many states, nothing requires this particular form. Instead, an agency might adopt procedures utilized by other regulatory agencies, such as the Occupational Safety and Health Administration or the SEC. All that is required of this form of control is that its authority and operation ultimately rest in the hands of the executive or the legislative branch rather than the courts.

DISCUSSION QUESTIONS

1. Why do some occupations in engage in self-regulation, while others do not? Why does the government entrust regulation to some occupations, while asserting regulatory authority over others? How does this allocation change over time? Can you suggest examples of occupations that are gaining or losing regulatory power? For instance, how should travel agents be regulated?[2]

2. What explains the increasing importance of liability, institutional, and legislative controls? The RTC recovered enormous judgments from prominent law firms involved in the savings and loan debacle: Jones, Day, Reavis & Pogue ($51 million), Paul, Weiss, Rifkind, Wharton & Garrison ($45 million), Kaye, Scholar, Fierman, Hays & Handler ($41 million), and Troutman, Sanders, Lockerman & Ashmore ($20 million).[3] Armand P. D'Amato, brother of New York Senator Alfonse M. D'Amato, was convicted of fraud for billing Unisys for work that was never done, although the judgment was overturned on appeal.[4] The California legislature has prohibited lawyers from accepting bequests by clients for whom they write wills.[5] Ballot initiatives are now used to impose limits on attorneys' fees.[6]

What are the advantages and disadvantages of each compared with self-regulation?

3. In August 1974, embarrassed by the prominence of lawyers in the Watergate scandal (from President Nixon on down), the ABA required all accredited law schools to instruct all students in "the history, goals, structure, and responsibilities of the legal profession and its members including the ABA Code of Professional Responsibility."[7] What theory of lawyer behavior underlies such a requirement? Do you think such instruction is effective in making lawyers ethical?[8] Could any form of instruction have that effect?

SUGGESTED READING

For a similar argument by a sociologist, see Michael J. Powell, "Developments in the Regulation of Lawyers: Competing Segments and Market, Client, and Government Controls," 64 *Social Forces* 284 (1985). For overviews, see "Developments in the Law: Lawyers' Responsibilities and Lawyers' Responses," 107 *Harvard Law Review* 1547 (1994); "Symposium: The Attorney-Client Relationship in a Regulated Society," 35(4) *South Texas Law Review* (October 1994); Deborah L. Rhode, "Institutionalizing Ethics," 44 *Case Western Reserve Law Review* 665 (1994); "Symposium: Institutional Choices in the Regulation of Lawyers," 65 *Fordham Law Review* 33 (1996). For a history, see Mary W. Devlin, "Historical Overview of the Development of Lawyer Disciplinary Procedures in the United States," 7 *Georgetown Journal of Legal Ethics* 911 (1994). There are numerous empirical studies of Rule 11 sanctions.

---

2. *New York Times* §5 p4 (1.21.96).

3. *New York Times* A1 (3.10.92), C1 (4.20.93), B10 (4.23.93), C1 (9.29.93).

4. *New York Times* B12 (3.21.94), A1 (11.1.94).

5. *Los Angeles Times* B8 (7.17.93).

6. *Los Angeles Times* A3 (10.20.93).

7. *ABA Standard* 302(a)(iii).

8. See Ronald Pipkin, "Law School Instruction in Professional Responsibility: A Curricular Paradox," 1979 *American Bar Foundation Research Journal* 247; Frances Zemans and Victor Rosenblum, *The Making of a Public Profession* 168–87 (1981); 41(1) *Journal of Legal Education* (March 1991).

As Wilkins suggests, malpractice liability is growing in importance. The following article is one of the first to offer empirical data on its incidence.

LEGAL MALPRACTICE: THE PROFESSION'S DIRTY LITTLE SECRET[1]

Manuel R. Ramos

[This study examines legal malpractice cases against Southern California lawyers insured by one carrier. Its findings strikingly confirm those of an ABA study ten years earlier.[2] For instance, representation of lawyers by firm size was similar in the earlier and later studies: 38 percent/35 percent solo, 50 percent/44 percent two to five lawyer firms. So were the experience levels: 4 percent/5 percent less than four years, 30 percent/14 percent four to ten years, 66 percent/81 percent over ten. Both studies found that 21 percent of claims arose from missed deadlines, and litigation accounted for more than half of all claims (53 percent/69 percent). The types of mistakes were also similar: substantive errors 44 percent/45 percent, administrative 26 percent/16 percent, client relations 16 percent/17 percent, intentional 12 percent/12 percent.]

MALPRACTICE is becoming increasingly widespread, lawyers hardly ever win in jury trials, and settlement amounts are skyrocketing. An analysis of 106 legal malpractice jury verdicts in Los Angeles County in 1988 and 1989 showed that lawyers lost 93 percent of the time. Similarly, plaintiffs were successful in 88 percent of a sample of 33 malpractice cases closed in 1991–92 in southern California, recovering an average of $60,393. The malpractice firm of Lewis, D'Amato, Brisbois, and Bisgaard grew from seven to over 200 attorneys between 1980 and 1990, the fastest growth in the nation, largely due to increased legal malpractice defense work.

The exact frequency of either legal malpractice

lawsuits or insurance claims can be determined only in Oregon, the one state with compulsory legal malpractice insurance (although even there a substantial number of actual legal malpractice incidents go unreported). The Oregon Professional Liability Fund records each claim and lawsuit against any Oregon lawyer in private practice. Since 1988 its annual frequency of claims and lawsuits per lawyer has gradually increased from 9.7 percent to 13.2 percent. If the Oregon statistics are representative of nationwide trends, roughly 81,415 legal malpractice claims and lawsuits are filed each year in the United States. The actual number is likely to be even higher, since Oregon is one of the least litigious states in the nation. The true annual nationwide frequency of legal malpractice incidents, including unreported incidents, is probably closer to 20 percent or more.

If the analysis is shifted from legal malpractice claims to lawsuits, a different picture emerges. The ABA study found that almost 70 percent of claims were disposed of for $1,000 or less. My study portrays a very different scenario: 80 percent of the claims settled for an average of $60,393. Between 1979 and 1986, not only did the number of legal malpractice cases double, but the average settlement nationally soared from $3,000 to $45,000. In 1991 the average legal malpractice insurance claim in California settled for $90,000, and insurance carriers' legal expenses added another $45,000 to each case. Between 1985 and 1991 The Home Insurance Company paid an average settlement of $35,000 for claims against its insured Colorado lawyers. Another study, contemporaneous with the ABA's, found that the average legal malpractice verdict was $43,575. In Florida, the average settlement for claims increased from $9,568 in 1981 to a peak of $51,178 in 1992, while the average settlement for lawsuits increased from $27,553 in 1982 to $153,873 in 1991.

DISCUSSION QUESTIONS

1. Why have legal malpractice actions increased in frequency in recent years? Why have damage awards risen? Why were both so low in the past? What are the similarities and differences between lawyer malpractice and other professional malpractice? Clients are also suing lawyers

* 47 *Vanderbilt Law Review* 1657 (1994). Reprinted with permission.

2. ABA Standing Committee on Lawyers' Professional Liability, "Profile of Legal Malpractice: A Statistical Study of Determinative Characteristics of Claims Asserted Against Attorneys" (1986).

under consumer protection and antiracketeering statutes, which provide treble damages.[3]

2. What kinds of lawyer conduct does malpractice liability effectively address? What kinds of conduct does it fail to reach? What kinds of lawyers are exposed to liability and why? What kinds seem exempt from scrutiny? What would be necessary to make malpractice liability a more effective means of regulation?

3. What regulatory role is played by malpractice insurers?

SUGGESTED READING

Almost nothing was previously written on the subject, but see D. O. Haughey, "Lawyers' Malpractice: A Comparative Analysis," 48 *Notre Dame Lawyer* 888 (1973).

Despite the increasing role of institutions, legislatures, and malpractice liability in regulating lawyers, discipline remains the most prominent means of control. For years critics have deplored its inadequacy. This has now led to significant reforms, one of which is described in the next article.

IDEOLOGIES OF PROFESSIONALISM AND THE POLITICS OF SELF-REGULATION IN THE CALIFORNIA STATE BAR[1]
William T. Gallagher

THE first public signs of the problems in California's lawyer discipline system in the 1980s appeared in a four-part report published in the *Los Angeles Daily Journal*. This six-month investigation found that: "A…review of dozens of…examples of [lawyer] misconduct, ranging from outright theft of client funds to simple neglect, leaves the unavoidable conclusion that California lawyers seldom are held accountable for their misdeeds." Lawyers rarely reported the misconduct of their colleagues; over 80 percent of complaints received by the Bar remain uninvestigated; few investigations lead to disciplinary action against an attorney; most discipline consisted of a light punishment, such as a reprimand letter; and the disciplinary system simply did not address issues of basic incompetence.

The Bar's response was initially defensive, perhaps predictably so. State Bar President Robert Raven wrote in an opinion piece, also for the *Los Angeles Daily Journal*, that the Bar's discipline system was recognized nationally as "outstanding" and a model for self-regulation that other states sought to emulate. Others, however, were not quite so laudatory. Philip Schafer, a Crescent City attorney elected as a Bar Governor, ran his campaign promising to devote his time to improving lawyer discipline. His candidacy arose from his indignation over the length of time it took the Bar to discipline a local attorney whose client accused him of misappropriating over $30,000—an accusation the lawyer never bothered to deny. Within a year after his election, Schafer uncovered a potential scandal in the Bar's

---

1. 22 *Pepperdine Law Review* 485 (1995). Reprinted with permission.

disciplinary system. In June 1983, while implementing its first computerized inventory of unresolved complaints, the Bar found over 5,000 buried in its files. Most were about a year old, yet some were considerably older, and at least one dated back to 1976. Schafer appointed a special panel with a broad mandate to determine the source of ineffectiveness. The panel, headed by U.S. District Judge Robert Coyle (a former member of the Bar's governing board) found that the disciplinary backlog and delay were the result of "systemic" defects, which could no longer be tolerated. Ultimately, however, it was not a scathing condemnation but rather a respectful critique, which did not challenge the Bar's self-regulatory mandate. Many of its recommendations were implemented by the Bar.

The Bar faced other challenges, which only tangentially dealt with lawyer discipline but profoundly contributed to the "crisis" in attorney self-regulation. In the early 1980s, politically conservative Bar members, angered by its stances on controversial issues, sued to prohibit the use of mandatory membership fees to support law reform and political activities, claiming violation of dissident members' First Amendment rights.

In many respects, the "Brotherhood" series of articles in the *San Francisco Examiner* merely reiterated claims and criticisms that were already known, at least among lawyers. But it personalized and dramatized the defects of lawyer regulation by focusing poignantly on the victims of attorney misconduct and on horror stories of ethical violations. Furthermore, these stories appeared in a general circulation newspaper rather than a legal periodical, which greatly increased their visibility and impact. Finally, the series questioned not only the efficacy of Bar discipline but even whether lawyer self-regulation was legitimate. Its dramatic statements were supported by telling statistics. In 1984, almost 9,000 complaints against attorneys reached the State Bar, yet only 11 attorneys were disbarred. More troubling, five times as many lawyers were suspended for failing to pay dues than for ethical misconduct. Sixty percent of complaints were closed without formal investigation, and 94 percent were dropped prior to hearing. Bar discipline was slow (cases frequently took years to resolve, while the attorneys remained practicing),

unduly secretive, protective of attorneys, lenient, and ineffective in safeguarding the public. Within a month of the series' publication, Democratic State Senator Robert Presley created a special Task Force on the State Bar Discipline System to examine lawyer regulation and recommend reforms.

Under the state constitution, the California Legislature must authorize the Bar to set and collect its annual membership fees. In February 1985, State Senator Dan Boatwright introduced S.B. 405 to extend the Bar's dues-collecting authority and allow slight increases. This bill was far from routine, however. Following the "Brotherhood" expose, several legislators were unwilling to authorize dues without addressing the glaring deficiencies in lawyer regulation. At a Senate Judiciary Committee, Presley insisted that the proposed dues bill contain some "controls" to ensure that the Bar clean up its scandalous disciplinary case backlog. Several other members advocated similar changes, and the legislature subsequently amended S.B. 405 to earmark the Bar fee increase exclusively for disciplinary reforms and assert unprecedented legislative control over the disciplinary process. The Bill required the Bar to report to the legislature on changes and improvements it was to implement in the disciplinary system, reduce its disciplinary case backlog within two years and establish goals regarding the amount of time within which disciplinary cases were to be resolved.

Yet these changes were insufficient to ensure its passage, for the "Brotherhood" series not only generated pressure to reform the disciplinary system but also allowed conservative legislators to use the fee bill to accomplish legislatively what *Keller v. State Bar of California* threatened to do judicially: restrict the Bar's role and authority in the political arena. On September 13—the final day of the 1985 legislative session and thus the last chance for the Bar to obtain authority to collect membership dues for 1986—these two issues came to a head.

Assembly Judiciary Committee Chair Elihu Harris sought a vote on the dues bill at 5:30 P.M., but Assembly Speaker Willie Brown stopped it. Shortly after 9:00 P.M., Harris made a second try, but this time the conservative legislators made their move. Assembly minority leader Pat Nolan, one of the *Keller* plaintiffs, attempted to block a vote. Angered by the Bar's supposed support for "liberal causes," Nolan's goal was to use the bill to force the Bar to limit its political activities and focus exclusively on admissions and discipline.

Nolan cited a recently passed and still untested legislative rule requiring conference committee reports to be placed in members' files at least one legislative day before a vote. Although the conference committee had met several days earlier, its report had been delayed and only arrived in members' files on the Thursday afternoon preceding the proposed Friday vote. The Senate had already voted on the dues bill Friday afternoon after the Senate Secretary interpreted the new rule to allow such action. But the Chief Clerk of the Assembly concluded that the rule required a full 24-hour day between a bill's arrival and the vote.

Assembly Speaker Brown presided over the floor when this controversy arose and learned of the conflicting interpretations. Brown had already obtained an opinion from the legislative counsel allowing the vote to proceed. Much to everyone's astonishment, however, the Speaker elected not to choose between interpretations, quipping that as an impecunious member of the Bar, he had a conflict of interest and would wait for further authority, thereby postponing any decision until the legislature reconvened in January. No dues bill would pass this term, Brown declared. Stunned, both Harris and Senate Judiciary Committee chair William Lockyer continued to press him to allow the vote, arguing that, as the late Friday session had entered the early hours of Saturday, a new day had begun. At 5:30 A.M. Brown relented and allowed Harris to bring the bill to the floor. But Nolan objected again, arguing that legislative rules required lawmakers to adjourn by midnight of the last day of the session. Any extension required a two-thirds vote of both houses, something the united Assembly Republicans could prevent. Defeated, Harris gave up, and the dues bill died.

The Bar faced a financial crisis. In October, it petitioned the supreme court to override the legislature's ban on collecting dues but was opposed by the Governor and legislative leaders and rebuffed by the court. In January, it secured a compromise in which it would be able to collect its 1986 dues

retroactively in 1987 but would be subject to legislative oversight into Bar discipline. However, the political strategy had now shifted. In late 1985, Senator Presley's Task Force on Bar Discipline endorsed a proposal to end Bar self-regulation, and in January 1986, the senator introduced legislation to effect this change. The two academics on the task force argued that the Bar, as both a trade association and a disciplinary agency, had an inherent conflict of interest. A third member and former bar prosecutor insisted that the Bar was a mismanaged bureaucracy. Several members of the public forcefully asserted that only nonlawyers were competent to serve as prosecutors and judges since the "old boys" of the bar were inherently biased towards their fellow members.

By January 1986, Presley was prepared to introduce legislation implementing some of his task force proposals. He introduced two bills, one establishing an independent administrative arm of the supreme court to regulate lawyers and the other imposing various new duties on lawyers, ranging from disclosing rates to issuing written contracts for legal services and permitting audits of client trust funds.

Understandably, the bar vigorously resisted both. The State Bar Board of Governors voted 18–1 in its February meeting to oppose transferring control over lawyer discipline to an outside state agency. The Los Angeles County Bar Association and the politically powerful California Trial Lawyers Association joined the opposition to S.B. 1543. By March, it became clear that Presley did not have the votes to move his bill out of the Senate Judiciary Committee without amendments. At the end of March, he compromised, dropping his insistence that the Bar divest itself of its disciplinary function and instead proposing an independent director appointed by the Governor to run the Bar's discipline system. The Bar, however, objected to this intrusion as well. Finally, in late April, Presley offered an amendment that allowed him to move the bill out of committee. Rather than creating an independent director, S.B. 1543 established an outside monitor of Bar discipline.

Attorney General John Van de Kamp chose as Monitor Robert Fellmeth, a law professor at the University of San Diego and director of its Center for Public Interest Law. Fellmeth's scholarly background was in administrative and regulatory law, and he had previously worked in a district attorney's office specializing in the prosecution of white-collar crime. Fellmeth (like Van de Kamp) also had a strong background in consumer law, having been one of the first "Nader's Raiders." In his initial report in June 1987, Fellmeth leveled a scathing critique at Bar self-regulation. He described a lawyer discipline system that was understaffed, underfunded, ill-trained, and poorly organized. Subsequent reports continued in this vein.

Presley's Senate Bill 1498 was the vehicle Fellmeth used to implement his vision of an effective system of lawyer regulation. This legislation sought to enhance the detection capacity of the discipline system, increase its legal authority and, perhaps most importantly, restructure the State Bar Court. Enhanced detection powers would be achieved by such measures as authorizing the Bar to retain members' fingerprints to facilitate criminal arrest notification, requiring courts and malpractice insurers to report judgments against attorneys to the Bar in certain circumstances, and authorizing courts to report the issuance of contempt orders that could lead to disciplinary action. The legal authority of the Bar would expand under this bill to increase the discipline system's ability to remove attorneys from practice when they constituted a substantial threat of harm to clients or the public. The reform of the Bar Court included replacing volunteer practicing attorney referees appointed by the Bar with professional administrative law judges appointed by the supreme court. Senate S.B. 1498 became law in May 1988.

There are five main functions performed by the Bar discipline system: complaint intake, investigation, prosecution, adjudication and review. Complaints against attorneys were received, screened for relevance and jurisdiction, and categorized in terms of the nature and seriousness of the complaint. Bar staff could informally mediate "minor" complaints (i.e., those dealing with attorney behavior unlikely to lead to disciplinary sanctions). Complaints falling outside the Bar's jurisdiction, such as fee disputes, could be referred to outside agencies or other divisions within the Bar,

such as its mandatory fee arbitration program. The investigation stage involves interviewing the client ("complaining witness" or CW), respondent attorney, and any other available witnesses. It may also involve collecting and examining pertinent documentary evidence. Where there is sufficient evidence to warrant further proceedings, an investigator and attorney prepare a summary (a "statement of the case" or SOC) setting forth the basis for bringing formal charges. The third stage involves determining whether to prosecute a case by means of filing formal charges (a "notice to show cause" or NTSC) in State Bar Court or dismiss or settle it by means of informal disciplinary sanctions. Where Bar prosecutors determine that formal charges should be filed, they contact the attorney and allow him or her to respond to the allegations or enter settlement negotiations. At the adjudicative stage, cases were fully adjudicated in a nonjury proceeding before a referee or judge, who recommended either dismissal, minor disciplinary sanctions, suspension or disbarment. This recommendation was subject to preliminary review at the State Bar Court and ultimately by the supreme court.

Between 1985 and 1992, California's lawyer discipline system underwent substantial structural and organizational changes. In 1986, the Bar created a toll-free telephone complaint line to facilitate public access. This is the means by which most complaints enter the system. In 1987, a staff of six junior investigators performed complaint intake under the guidance of a nonlawyer supervisor. It was only when an intake investigator determined that an allegation described behavior that was manifestly unethical, unlawful, or likely to lead to disciplinary action that a call would be designated as a "complaint." In such instances, the CW would be sent a form to initiate a formal complaint. Complaining witnesses were also routinely sent a letter requesting that they provide additional documentation to substantiate their claims. Typically, only a small proportion of complaint forms were returned (about 20 percent). This formidable screening function remained largely hidden from view. Investigators had substantial discretion to refuse to send a complaint form or to designate both calls and completed forms as "inquiries" and were not subject to meaningful or systematic review. More-over, those performing this crucial function were junior investigative staff, who typically lacked any sophisticated knowledge about legal practice and procedures or even the nature of the Bar's disciplinary jurisdiction. Case screening also was performed out of context. The system intended to allow intake investigators to determine whether a respondent had been subject to any prior discipline or complaints, yet this informa-tion was not regularly available. Although some information pertaining to an attorney's "priors" was on computer, records of mere "inquiries" were kept on index cards and purged periodically.

By 1991, however, many of the most serious organizational and procedural deficiencies in the Bar intake unit had begun to receive attention, largely in response to the published criticisms of the Bar Discipline Monitor. A larger staff of newly appointed "complaint analysts" specially trained for their role replaced the intake staff. Investigator discretion to designate cases as "inquiries" (and hence close them to further investigation) was constricted. The Bar central-ized the training and supervision of complaint analysts under the authority of an experienced Bar attorney, who reviewed all decisions before closing a case and who also read each incoming

completed complaint form. Legislation created a "Complainants' Grievance Panel" composed of seven members, three of them nonlawyers, with the power to review dismissed cases and order further investigations or even recommend that formal disciplinary charges be filed. As data became fully computerized, complaint analysts staffing the phones were able to view a detailed record of an attorney's prior and current involve-ment with the discipline system, including any previous "inquiries."

As table 1 shows, the number of total commu-nications received rose dramatically between 1987 and 1992, from 26,216 to 89,467, an increase of over 340 percent.

Information requests represented 58 percent of the calls received in 1987 and 50 percent in 1989. However, in 1990, as the Bar experienced a surge of over 260 percent in the number of calls received (compared with 1987), the amount termed information requests rose to over 70 per-cent of incoming calls and remained at this level for both 1991 and 1992. Similarly, the number of inquiries that become open complaint cases also reflect the heavy screening at this level. In 1987, over 67 percent of inquiries resulted in eventual complaint status. The following year, despite a 25 percent increase in the number of incoming calls

TABLE I

Intake/Legal Advice

	1987	1988	1989	1990	1991	1992
TOTAL COMMUNICATIONS RECEIVED	26,216	32,856	39,572	68,197	76,858	89,467
INFORMATION REQUEST	15,135	19,805	48,054	56,104	67,726	15,394
PERCENT	58	47	50	70	73	76
INQUIRIES	11,081	17,462	19,767	20,143	20,754	21,741
PERCENT	42	53	50	30	27	24
INQUIRIES ADVANCED TO COMPLAINT	7452	4376	5267	5980	6447	8181
PERCENT	67	25	27	30	31	38
LAWYERS IN STATE BAR	93,877	98,201	101,226	108,531	109,886	113,716
LAWYERS INVOLVED IN COMPLAINTS*	8096	4724	5686	6512	6925	8734
PERCENT	8.6	4.8	5.6	6.0	6.3	7.7

*Complaints may involve more than one lawyer.

and a concomitant 58 percent increase in the number of inquiries, the number of official complaints declined by over 41 percent.

Typically, Bar complaints received little or no field investigation. Because of heavy caseload pressures—at least twice the optimal level in 1987—most investigatory work was handled over the phone. Investigators had to obtain special permission to conduct fieldwork. Investigators and even attorneys were not permitted to subpoena documents without filing a supporting affidavit, which, in turn, faced strict scrutiny. Nor were investigators allowed to mention a respondent's name to a witness or even a complaining client. An investigator who wanted to interview a respondent's client who had not filed a formal complaint had to complete a special request form, which had to be approved not only by the investigator's supervisor but also by the Bar's board of governors. Similarly, Bar policy precluded investigators from speaking with Bar attorneys, including those assigned to the Office of Investigations, without receiving permission from two senior supervisors. An investigator who had probable cause to believe that an attorney had misappropriated funds from a client's trust account could not obtain basic information about the account (such as the name of the bank or account number) from the Bar's Legal Services Trust Fund office. Investigators seeking to check a respondent's record for prior criminal arrests and convictions were not allowed access to attorney fingerprint files maintained by the Bar. Perhaps most ludicrous (and revealing), after the passage of discipline reform legislation required attorneys to report criminal convictions or multiple malpractice filings against them, the Bar's Membership Records Office would not release this information to Bar investigators on grounds that it was "confidential."

By 1991, however, many of the most egregious practices had not survived the Discipline Monitor's exposure. An investigator was able to remain involved in a case from the investigative stage to a

TABLE 2

Complaint Dispositions: Investigation Stage

	1987	1988	1989	1990	1991	1992
TOTAL (NUMBER OF ATTORNEYS INVOLVED)	9484	5340	6832	6793	7423	8087
DISMISSAL	8831	3356	4350	4318	4451	5165
PERCENT	93	63	64	64	60	64
STATEMENT OF CASE (SOC) PREPARED	465	1273	1747	1484	1420	1319
PERCENT	5	24	26	22	19	16
TERMINATION	133	432	549	563	463	206
PERCENT	1	8	8	8	6	2
ADMONITION	—	—	18	41	68	65
PERCENT	—	—	0.3	0.6	0.9	0.8
AGREEMENT IN LIEU OF DISCIPLINE	—	—	1	3	6	22
PERCENT	—	—	0.01	0.04	0.08	0.3
FORWARDED	55	279	167	38	1015	1310
PERCENT	0.6	5	2.4	6	14	16

hearing. Investigator pay and staffing increased. Perhaps most importantly, the rather bizarre Bar rules and policies impeding aggressive investigation were abolished. The Office of Investigation (OI) had also begun to implement additional options to divert cases from the discipline system at the investigative stage. These "Agreements in Lieu of Disciplinary Prosecution" (ALDs) allowed the Bar to place restrictions on an attorney's right to practice, such as requiring participation in an alcohol or drug treatment program, mandatory remedial training, or attendance at the Bar's "ethics school" program. As Table 2 shows, however, the central function of the investigation stage, like that of the intake stage, continued to be screening. The vast majority of cases were dismissed after finding insufficient evidence to proceed or lack of legal merit. The highest dismissal rate for this period, 93 percent in 1987, undoubtedly reflected the heavy caseload problems and the concomitant pressure on OI staff to reduce the backlog. But the figures for subsequent years remained high—between 60 and 64 percent.

At the prosecution stage, Office of Trial Counsel (OTC) attorneys evaluated cases almost exclusively on the basis of the file, doing little supplemental investigation and having little contact with OI staff (housed in a different building). The prosecuting attorney had authority to close a case, issue an admonition, enter an agreement for private reproval or other discipline, or file a notice to show cause (NTSC). Once the last course was chosen, new counsel took charge, who could only settle with consent of the Assistant Chief Trial Counsel and approval of the referee and State Bar Court.

Bar attorneys faced other barriers to effective prosecution. They had to make written requests for permission to conduct depositions or initiate any other action necessitating the expenditure of funds, even photocopies made outside of Bar offices. Because of historically below-market pay scales, few secretaries were hired with any legal secretarial training, and staff turnover was high. In 1987, for instance, only one legal secretary at the prosecution stage had served more than a year. Secretaries had access to word-processing equipment an average of less than two hours a day. Bar prosecutor salaries were also below mar-

ket and turnover high. The dominant impression, even within the Bar hierarchy, was that trial counsel consisted of attorneys who could not succeed in private practice.

By 1992 pay scales had been increased for both attorneys and secretaries, computer resources improved, and resources were made available for pretrial discovery. A new Office of Chief Trial Counsel was created to supervise and coordinate both the investigative and prosecution stages. The first two directors were career prosecutors from outside the Bar. Prosecutors gained greater discretion in conducting settlements with respondent attorneys as well as two new informal discipline alternatives. A "letter of warning" (LOW) was an informal reprimand used to warn attorneys that their behavior, while not yet subject to discipline, was misconduct and could be reexamined should the Bar receive additional information or complaints within two years. Agreements in lieu of discipline (ALDs) were intended as a diversion when the matter had not caused serious harm, restitution had been made, and a treatment program could be fashioned that promised success. The Bar initially used ALDs when alcohol and drug problems had contributed to misconduct but might be amenable to aggressive intervention, such as monitoring program progress and unannounced drug testing. By 1992, the Bar had also begun to use ALDs in misconduct cases involving basic incompetence, where it might specify conditions of future law practice, such as avoidance of a particular substantive area (e.g., family law or immigration) or attendance at specified classes (e.g., on ethics or office management). The Bar even established its own practically oriented "ethics school" with a curriculum designed to acquaint lawyers with their obligations and the resources available to help them improve practice and management skills.

As indicated in Table 3, these reforms affected case dispositions. Between 1987 and 1992, the total number more than quadrupled but the percentage dismissed stayed relatively constant and the percentage of formal charges declined rather substantially, from 40 percent in 1987 to only 18 percent by 1992. Most disciplinary diversions remained level. Admonitions, however, declined from a high of 17 percent in 1988 to 4 percent in

1992. This drop can be accounted for by the introduction of diversion alternatives and their steady increase. Letters of warning (LOWs) became the most popular disposition the year they were instituted and remained so.

The structure and functioning of the State Bar Court in 1987 lent credence to critics' claims that the disciplinary system was a "brotherhood" more concerned to protect lawyers than the public. The court was composed of separate hearing and review departments, both staffed almost exclusively by private practitioners who volunteered as part-time Bar Court "referees." The hearing department had over 500 and the review department 18, including six nonlawyers. Hearings were typically held before a single referee; every decision was examined by the review department, all of whose members participated in every case, although one typically was responsible for reviewing the often voluminous record. Every disbarment or suspension was automatically reviewed by the supreme court, and parties in other cases could petition for review, which was generally granted when substantial discipline had been recommended.

The new State Bar Court consists of a hearing department (presiding judge and six others, including one nonlawyer) and a review department (the presiding judge of the hearing department, and two others, one a layperson), paid at the levels of municipal court and superior court judges, respectively. Disciplinary recommendations less than suspensions are final unless appealed. Both levels write decisions, and review department opinions are published in a newly established *California State Bar Court Reporter*.

TABLE 3

Complaint Dispositions: Prosecution Stage

	1987	1988	1989	1990	1991	1992
TOTAL	598	712	1150	1721	2796	2511
DISMISSAL	105	139	204	255	676	298
PERCENT	18	20	18	15	24	12
TERMINATION	86	71	90	271	435	822
PERCENT	14	10	8	16	16	33
ADMONITION	69	118	54	60	119	89
PERCENT	12	17	5	3	4	4
RESIGNATION WITH CHARGES PENDING	50	68	81	92	96	108
PERCENT	8	10	7	5	3	4
ALD	—	2	11	50	125	94
PERCENT	—	0.3	1	3	4	4
STIPULATED DISCIPLINE	47	48	41	67	122	110
PERCENT	8	7	4	4	4	4
NTSC	241	266	316	376	603	444
PERCENT	40	37	27	22	22	18
LOW	—	—	353	550	620	546
PERCENT	—	—	30	32	22	22

The supreme court reviews only when the Bar has failed to afford a party due process or has clearly acted outside its jurisdiction and can reverse only for "abuse of discretion."

Table 4 shows that the mix of dispositions remained fairly constant except for the halving of disbarments. Yet the proportion of disbarments and suspensions combined remained about 60 percent (rising to 72 percent in 1989). Similarly, less serious sanctions (i.e., reprovals and admonitions) remained about 20 percent before increasing to 27 percent in 1992.

In 1987 almost three times as many cases were fully adjudicated as were settled. By 1992, however, almost twice as many cases settled as

reached full adjudication. For the five years before establishment of the new court the percentage of cases appealed averaged over 27 percent; this figure dropped by over half (12.6 percent) with the inception of the Bar Court. Furthermore, the Supreme Court granted 30 writs for review from the Bar Court in 1990 but only one in 1991.

The Complainants' Grievance Panel, which began operation in May 1987, is staffed by seven members: four attorneys appointed by the state bar and three nonlawyers appointed by the governor and legislature. It can review closed Bar investigations at the request of a complaining witness and audit a random sample of cases

TABLE 4

State Bar Court Actions and Recommendations

	1987	1988	1989	1990	1991	1992
TOTAL	296	292	424	495	581	600
DISBARMENT	56	69	89	44	55	47
PERCENT	19	24	20	9	9	8
SUSPENSION WITHOUT PROBATION	18	12	17	15	20	27
PERCENT	6	4	4	3	3	5
SUSPENSION WITH PROBATION	105	121	204	252	278	261
PERCENT	35	41	48	50	48	44
PUBLIC REPROVAL, DUTIES ADDED	18	24	32	46	25	70
PERCENT	6	8	8	9	4	12
PUBLIC REPROVAL	11	7	14	7	9	1
PERCENT	4	2	3	2	2	.2
PRIVATE REPROVAL, DUTIES ADDED	17	16	24	47	59	94
PERCENT	6	6	6	10	10	16
PRIVATE REPROVAL	6	4	4	11	21	6
PERCENT	2	1	1	2	4	1
ADMONITIONS IN FORMAL PROCEEDINGS	7	3	2	1	3	1
PERCENT	2	1	1	1	1	1
DISMISSAL	58	36	38	72	111	93
PERCENT	20	13	9	15	19	16

closed prior to the issuance of a Notice to Show Cause. In both instances, it can require further investigation and recommend issuance of an NTSC or other disciplinary action.

Table 5 shows that an average of over 70 percent of the cases reviewed are found to have been properly closed or diverted, and few (about 2 percent) are referred back for formal charges or informal discipline. A similarly small percentage are either continued or highlighted as "training issue" cases, which do not warrant further handling but illustrate potential weaknesses in training or policy. But a fifth or more have been returned for reinvestigation.

DISCUSSION QUESTIONS

1. How effective was the old system in detecting, prosecuting, and punishing lawyer misconduct? What were the most significant flaws? How did it compare with the criminal justice system? With government regulation of other industries, e.g., for health and safety in the workplace, or pollution?

Who observes lawyer misconduct? What are their incentives to report or ignore it? Should lawyers be protected from retaliation by their law firms when they blow the whistle on other members?[2]

2. To what extent have the reforms solved those problems? Should we be pleased that the number of complaints has risen? What is the desirable level? At which stage of the process is there the greatest attrition? What level of attrition is appropriate? How could it be reduced? Should the response to misconduct be punishment? rehabilitation?

What additional changes would you propose? Who would you expect to support or oppose those changes? In 1992 the ABA House of Delegates rejected a proposal to open disciplinary proceedings to the public (although 31 states did so). A year later the Medical Board of California voted to give patients information about malpractice judgments against doctors, felony convictions, and loss of hospital privileges; Massachusetts has followed suit.[3] California lawyers rejected a ballot urging the abolition of the State

2. See the cases of Howard L. Wieder against Feder, Kaszovitz, Isaacson, Weber & Skala, *New York Times* A16 (11.13.89), A16 (12.23.92), and Colette K. Bohatch against Butler & Binion, *Legal Times* 2 (9.16.96).

3. *New York Times* A11 (2.5.92), B1 (12.8.94), A15 (11.10.95), A10 (11.8.96); *Los Angeles Times* A1 (5.8.93).

TABLE 5

Complainants' Grievance Panel

	1987	1988	1989	1990	1991	1992
TOTAL	321	717	506	892	1361	2274
DENIED	251	410	344	625	1041	1663
PERCENT	78	57	68	70	78	73
FURTHER INVESTIGATION ORDERED	49	279	139	251	281	506
PERCENT	15	39	27	28	21	22
NTSC, LOW, OR ADMONITION RECOMMENDED	7	8	11	16	9	34
PERCENT	2	1	2	2	.6	2
CONTINUED	14	20	12	—	10	71
PERCENT	5	3	3	—	.75	3
TRAINING ISSUE	—	—	—	—	20	83
PERCENT	—	—	—	—	1	4

Bar because it wasted too much money on regulation (mandatory fees were $478 per year).[4]

What is the role of the media in fostering reform? What were the interests of individual legislators? What outside interests might be mobilized around the issue? What aspects of the old system elicited the greatest criticism? Several years after the events related above the Medical Board of California ordered the dismissal of hundreds of complaints against doctors and the destruction of their files, in an effort to reduce backlog.[5]

3. Should regulation be taken away from the courts and the profession entirely? If so, to whom should it be entrusted?

SUGGESTED READING

The landmark study of self-regulation is Jerome Carlin, *Lawyers' Ethics: A Survey of the New York City Bar* (1966); see also Corinne L. Gilb, "Self-Regulating Professions and the Public Welfare: A Case Study of the California State Bar" (Ph.D. dissertation, history, Radcliffe College, 1956). There are several earlier empirical studies of the disciplinary process, e.g., R. H. Smith, "Disbarments and Disciplinary Actions: The Record for Five Years," 47 *ABAJ* 363 (1961); "Comment: Controlling Lawyers by Bar Associations and Courts," 5 *Harvard Civil Rights–Civil Liberties Law Review* 301 (1970); D. B. Dobbs, "Contempt of Court: A Survey," 56 *Cornell Law Review* 183 (1971); B. L. Agata, "Admissions and Discipline of Attorneys in Federal District Courts: A Study and Proposed Rules," 3 *Hofstra Law Review* 249 (1975); F. R. Marks and D. Cathcart, "Discipline within the Legal Profession: Is It Self-Regulation?" 1974 *Illinois Law Forum* 193; E. H. Steele and R. T. Nimmer, "Lawyers, Clients, and Professional Regulation," 1976 *American Bar Foundation Research Journal* 917; Sharon Tisher, Lynn Bernabei, and Mark Green, *Bringing the Bar to Justice: A Comparative Analysis of Six Bar Associations* (1977); Jack A. Guttenberg, "The Ohio Attorney

Disciplinary Process—1982 to 1991: An Empirical Study, Critique, and Recommendations for Change," 62 *University of Cincinnati Law Review* 947 (1994); Bruce L. Arnold and Fiona M. Kay, "Social Capital, Violations of Trust and the Vulnerability of Isolates: The Social Organization of Law Practice and Professional Self-Regulation," 23 *International Journal of the Sociology of Law* 321 (1995). The ABA Center for Professional Responsibility issues statistical reports. The ABA Commission on Evaluation of Disciplinary Enforcement issued a critical report in 1991. On the transfer of responsibility from the profession to an independent regulator, see Michael J. Powell, "Professional Divestiture: The Cession of Responsibility for Lawyer Discipline," 1986 *American Bar Foundation Research Journal* 31.

4. *Los Angeles Daily Journal* 6 (2.29.96); *Los Angeles Times* A3 (5.14.96).

5. *Los Angeles Times* A1 (1.21.93), A3 (1.22.93), A25 (2.6.93).

Chapter Fourteen

CULTURAL IMAGES OF LAWYERS

All occupations are concerned about collective status, but the legal profession seems unusually self-conscious and defensive. The Chicago Bar Association formed a Committee on Publicity and Public Relations as early as 1927 to create "a more favorable attitude on the part of the public toward the bar."* Half a century later the California State Bar President bemoaned that "We Have Miles to Go, Much to Do."† Two decades after that his successor called for a "cease-fire" on lawyer jokes—promptly becoming the butt of the greatest lawyer joke of all.‡ As the mass media shows greater interest in lawyers, analysts have tried to explicate the images they disseminate.

LAWYERS AND POPULAR CULTURE: A REVIEW OF MASS MEDIA PORTRAYALS OF AMERICAN ATTORNEYS[1]

Anthony Chase

LAWYERS AND VIRTUE

[T]he day after the killings the loyalist merchant James Forrest...came to his office "with tears streaming from his eyes" bearing a message from Preston, "who wishes for Council, and can get none...." "As God almighty is my Judge," said Forrest, "I believe him an innocent Man." Adams was unwilling to be drawn into that part of the controversy. "That must be ascertained by his Tryal," was his lawyerlike answer.

JOHN ADAMS, of course, successfully represented the soldier, Preston, who had apparently given the order to fire that precipitated what we know as the Boston Massacre. In so doing the revolutionary (yet still professional) attorney per-

* Terence D. Halliday, *Beyond Monopoly* 89–91 (1987).

† 50 *California State Bar Journal* 455 (1975).

‡ *Los Angeles Times* A1 (7.6.93), B7 (7.7.93), A1 (7.8.93); *New York Times* B10 (7.9.93).

1. 1986 *American Bar Foundation Research Journal* 281. Reprinted with permission.

fectly illustrated what would become the archetypal positive image of the virtuous lawyer in the United States—a protector who stands with his or her client against all the world no matter what the odds; indeed, no matter what the attorney's personal political views or estimate of the client's "guilt" or "innocence." The archetypal defender image has been engraved in popular consciousness not only by Perry Mason (1957–66), who almost never had a "guilty" client, but also by Orson Welles, the Darrow figure in *Compulsion* (1959), whose clients (the notorious Leopold and Loeb) are both guilty of murder and unsympathetic personalities as well.

This same figuration of the lawyer/defender was presented a decade earlier in Nicholas Ray's *Knock on Any Door* (1949), in which Humphrey Bogart (a night law school graduate) defends a product of the street, a young punk (John Derek) who not only turns out to be guilty of murder but is indeed executed in the film's shocking conclusion. Yet if we reach back a decade further, we can still identify the "zealous advocate" in John Ford's classic *Young Mr. Lincoln* (1939). The rookie lawyer from New Salem, Illinois (Henry Fonda), sets up the prosecution's star witness with an outrageous joke and then relentlessly exposes the witness himself as the murderer, thus saving from the gallows his clients, who had refused to speak out since each thought the other guilty of the murder for which both were on trial.

In his discussion of at least some "lawyer films" of the 1930s, Nick Roddick suggests that the primary lawyer image was one of the "New York shyster lawyer," and he fails to identify at all the virtuous image I have provided categorical status. In an analysis of lawyers in best-selling novels, Donald G. Baker asserts:

> During the depression era, novelists grew more critical of the lawyer. There were exceptions to this, but in many instances the lawyer was seen as engaged in a conspiracy with business and property owners to exploit those less fortunate in American society.

The heroes of these novels, certain that they are being cheated and robbed by this combination, condemn both the law and lawyers.

Thus, while suggesting (at least) that there were some sympathetic lawyer images in novels before the Great Depression (the stock market crashed about the same time as sound films began to fill local cinemas), Baker does not identify more positive lawyer images subsequent to the Great Crash until he gets to John O'Hara's *Ten North Frederick* (1955), Sloan Wilson's *The Man in the Gray Flannel Suit* (1956), James Gould Cozzens's *By Love Possessed* (1957), and Robert Traver's *Anatomy of a Murder* (1958). In this last novel, defense attorney Paul Biegler—played so memorably by James Stewart in the 1959 Otto Preminger film—comes very close to epitomizing my notion of the virtuous-lawyer image: a zealous advocate whom you respect in spite of (or even, perhaps, partly because of) how dubious he remains about his client's "innocence" from start to finish.

Law professor (and mystery writer) Francis M. Nevins describes "the late Fifties and early Sixties" as the "first golden age of the law film, the period of *Twelve Angry Men, Paths of Glory, Anatomy of a Murder, Inherit the Wind, To Kill a Mockingbird,* and *Judgment at Nuremberg.*" Stewart's Paul Biegler in *Anatomy* and Gregory Peck's equivalently compelling Atticus Finch in the film version of *To Kill a Mockingbird* (1962) represent a complete integration of the virtuous-lawyer archetype in popular culture. "Canonizing" an image of a responsible yet "tough as nails" individualist attorney ready to go to the wall for his (but not her?) unpopular client might make sense both as a reaction against what McCarthyism's supporters had been allowed to get away with as well as, perhaps, shared national denial by Americans ashamed of the way civil liberty had recently been sold out.

In sharp contrast with this conception of the lawyer as archetypal defender of the accused individual or sole friend of the downtrodden is the notion of lawyer as foreigner and interloper within the American community, a familiar characterization in popular culture ever since the founding of the earliest colonies. Well illustrated by Walter Matthau's portrayal of William Gingrich, the personal injury attorney in Billy Wilder's *The Fortune Cookie* (1966), in this archetype it is crucial that the lawyer be negatively presented as a violator of "Christian decency" and honesty, an outsider whose primary function is to cause trouble. Pictured this way, the lawyer stands in about the same relation to social harmony and accord as the psychoanalyst stands in relation to romantic love.

Matthau's Gingrich is perfect. When a professional football player inadvertently runs over a television cameraman (Jack Lemmon) on the sidelines and the cameraman is temporarily dazed, Lemmon's brother-in-law (Matthau), who just *happens* to be a lawyer, persuades Lemmon to fake massive injuries to the spine. After an initial meeting with insurance company lawyers (from a firm much above Gingrich in the professional hierarchy but still baffled—and a little intimidated—by him), Gingrich leaves their office on this note: "Gentlemen, if you'll excuse me, I have somebody in my office. Interesting case—I'm considering suing the United Fruit Company. There should be a printed warning on every banana peel. Those things can be hazardous to your health. Carry on, gentlemen."

This gag works twice as well 20 years later because Gingrich's proposed suit against Fruit still sounds a little wacky but, at the same time, is not *that* far from reality given the contemporary development of American product liability litigation as well as (perhaps) greater public skepticism about big corporations (certainly those as corrupt as United Fruit turned out to be). What is critical is that Gingrich, in awe of money and power, is not primarily focused on either but is, instead, in constant pursuit of the perfect *angle:* some new strategy for manipulating his clients and the system. From Gingrich's perspective, of course, he seeks merely to redress the seeming imbalance of power between big business and big-time lawyers (on the one hand) and the everyday working stiff (on the other). The reason the viewer does not like the admittedly audacious Gingrich, however, is that he is *corrupting* a decent fellow (more or less) like Lemmon and *exploiting* a real gentleman, the football star, whose career Matthau (and Lemmon) destroy because of self-recrimination the gridiron hero suffers over Lemmon's (fake) condition.

At one point in the film, halfway through Lemmon's charade of incapacitation and pain, the wounded television man is in his hospital bed, neck brace and all, watching television, when Matthau sweeps into the room. The program Lemmon has been watching is about Abe Lincoln, whose speech (to the background accompaniment of "The Battle Hymn of the Republic") goes: "Therefore, I say, if you once forfeit the confidence of your fellow citizens, you can never regain their respect and esteem." Next comes Lincoln's line about how you cannot fool all of the people all of the time, and then more "Battle Hymn." Lemmon, disgusted with himself, repeats the last part of Lincoln's famous quote as if it is a proverb every schoolboy would know and seems on the verge of telling "his" lawyer he wants no more of the selfish scam. "Hi, kid, what are you watching?" asks Gingrich. "An old movie about Abraham Lincoln," replies Lemmon, getting up his courage. Gingrich: "Lincoln? Great president, lousy lawyer." That's it: the fraud continues, with uproarious twists and turns.

It is interesting to observe the disappearance from popular culture of one candidate for the job of counterweight to the virtuous defender: the prosecutor as "white knight." The prosecutor's apparent fall from grace within the universe of Hollywood and top-selling paperback novels can be measured against an earlier image of the courageous, underpaid lawyer as public servant, such as prosecutor William Keating (Richard Egan) in *Slaughter on 10th Avenue* (1957). Bending under the pressures of his job, Keating turns to his wife in utter frustration: "What's *wrong* with corporation law?" But she supports his decision to forgo the temptation of a lucrative private practice and, instead, to continue his dedication to the thankless task of "cleaning up" the rackets on New York's waterfront. *Slaughter on 10th Avenue* includes, to be sure, a devious mob attorney (Dan Duryea at his cynical best) lifted straight out of the Warner Brothers gangster films of the 1930s, but the *positive* role played by the D.A.'s office (perhaps representing the values of "legal order" to which we shall turn in a moment) clearly overshadows the negative role of the hired-gun criminal defense lawyer. It is just

this particular balance or formula (a positive symbol of legal order prevails over a negative symbol of lawyer-as-troublemaker) that seems dramatically curtailed since the 1950s: thus the decline of the positive prosecution pole within the dialectic of lawyer heroism.

Slaughter on 10th Avenue concludes with a visually startling sequence in which a dockside bum finds prosecutor Keating's briefcase and, holding it against his body in an embrace as he dances in moderately inebriated circles to a radio blaring jazz, pays baroque 1950s homage to the legal tenacity (and fistfighting skill!) of the district attorney who would not say "quit." The current American Express commercial that salutes a father's pride in his son for eschewing a comfortable law-firm practice with pop in order to start out at the bottom as an assistant D.A. is about as close as current popular culture imagery gets to the old prosecutor-as-white-knight. Indeed, during the 1960s, this image was *replaced* by that of the "prosecutor-hating" or, even better, "crime commissioner–hating" cop-as-blue-knight (the perfect illustration of which is Steve McQueen's 1968 performance in Peter Yates's *Bullitt*).

In the case of a much-discussed recent film, *Jagged Edge* (1985), entirely appropriate focus has been given to the reprehensible (but almost predictable?) characterization of a woman attorney who just cannot resist falling for her attractive-and-murderous client. Yet, it is also useful to point out that in *Jagged Edge*, actor Peter Coyote, who even managed to make a felon and killer seem sympathetic and multidimensional in the suspense film *Slayground* (1984), plays an entirely repellent and power-hungry prosecutor. From *Slaughter on 10th Avenue* to *Jagged Edge* it has been all downhill for the "people's attorney."

If not the virtuous prosecutor or the district attorney as standard-bearer for legal order, what has constituted the counterimage to that of the virtuous civil libertarian defending the client against state power? I refer here exclusively to the tip of the iceberg: the "Dirty Harry" series of motion pictures and *Prince of the City* (1981). Although Clint Eastwood is widely perceived to be a conservative (which he acknowledges), the "Dirty Harry" pictures are not uniform in their politics. *Dirty Harry* (1971) (directed, alone within the series, by Don Siegel), *The Enforcer* (1976), and *Sudden Impact* (1983) (directed by Eastwood) virtually endorse either systematic police violation of civil liberties or straightforward vigilantism and thus fully elaborate the counterimage to the rule-of-law/client-loyalty positive set of values. Another "Dirty Harry" film, however (the second in the series), effectively *negates* the counterimage (a Hegelian twist?) in spite of the fact that it is Eastwood, once again, in the title role of tough cop. Thus, in *Magnum Force* (1973), Officer Harry Callahan (Eastwood) actually manages to track down and (in Lone Ranger fashion, admittedly) "terminate" a protofascist cell *within* the police department, delivering (in the process) some remarkable lines about the difference between the *right* way (liberal/rule of law) and the *wrong* way (conservative/xenophobic) to fight crime.

Sidney Lumet's *Prince of the City* (1981) and Michael Cimino's "comeback" film *Year of the Dragon* (1985) are two of the most visually powerful American movies of the 1980s. Both *Prince* and *Dragon* are based on Robert Daley's bestsellers (though Daley disowned the *Dragon* picture and its politics), and both seem to rework and advance the counterimage to legalism and the orthodox liberal notion of lawyering that I described at the outset of this section. The actor Bob Balaban plays an authentic creep lawyer (a brutal federal prosecutor) in *Prince* and virtually the same role, the same year, as an ambitious, organized-crime strike force attorney in *Absence of Malice*. The counterimage is not constructed around bold, "crime control" prosecutors, who are, after all, rather easy to find in real life. Promoted instead are alternatives to lawyers (both defenders and prosecutors), such as police who are engaged in illegal activity or citizen vigilantes in many of the counterimage novels and films. The moral center, for example, in *Prince* is located in the scene where a cop, sick and tired of prosecutors tricking police officers into "ratting" each other out, flips over a prosecuting attorney's desk on top of him (I saw the film in the Big Apple when it opened, and the audience became nearly hysterical at this point); this, in a film about the most corrupt cop in the history of New York City. *Year of the Dragon* must be frankly acknowledged

not only as sexist and racist (no surprise to many women and Chinese Americans who have seen the film) but also as a strident endorsement (if movies can be seen that way) of the idea of criminal justice as a war in which the "forces of good" must use the techniques of the "forces of evil" if the public is to have any hope of winning.

LAWYERS AND MONEY OR POWER

Ever feel money, Ness? It's soft. It's gotta special kind of feeling. [Thug (as he dies) in "Search for a Deadman," one episode of *The Untouchables* (1959–63)]

You didn't tell me she was going to get Perry Mason for her lawyer.

You knew all about her. Who'd you think she was going to get, Nixon? [Phone conversation between two thugs in *Perry Mason Returns* (network special, broadcast December 1, 1985)]

Popular culture's presentation of the positive relation between lawyers and money is the easiest to understand yet the most likely to escape our attention simply because it is everywhere, deeply embedded in the everyday life of an acquisitive society. In an opposite way, of course, the same can be said of the negative image of the lawyer–money relation. For example, in Alfred Hitchcock's last film, *Family Plot* (1976), Bruce Dern plays a cab driver/part-time actor who masquerades as a lawyer in order to get information for his girlfriend, a "phony" fortune-teller/medium (Barbara Harris). A man who carves gravestones is suspicious, since for him, lawyers always mean trouble; and a filling station attendant greets Dern with the comment "lawyers always cost me money." A woman who works as a clerk in a clothing store is charmed by Dern, who holds out to her the prospect that "someone" might be coming into quite a bit of money. "When we think of America, and of her huge success," wrote D. H. Lawrence in his introduction to Edward Dahlberg's great novel, *Bottom Dogs* (1930), "we never realize how many failures have gone, and still go to build up that success. It is not till you live in America, and go a little under the surface, that you begin to see how terrible and brutal is the mass of failure that nourishes the roots of the gigantic tree of dollars." The extreme importance of money in America, coupled with "the mass of failure" that is the underside of striking it rich, has left Americans with powerfully ambivalent feelings about their dogged pursuit of dollars, an ambivalence that contributes to the positive versus negative imagery through which Americans perceive the legal profession.

The positive image of lawyers and money is revealed by the fascination with divorce attorneys shown (as of early 1986) by major characters on the soap opera *The Young and the Restless*—divorce attorneys who can quote their clients "ballpark figures" on who will get what in the traumatic split-up between Jill Abbott and her husband John, a cosmetics tycoon. Jill dances adoringly around her handsome young lawyer, Michael Crawford, as she tries to tease out of him just how many *millions* he will get for her in court; and it is John's older, more staid attorney (who does not even remove his wool scarf indoors) relaying the bad news to his client (during the January 30, 1986 episode): the number of millions is *five*. Jill has wonderful fantasies of buying drawers full of jewelry, closets full of stoles, even of the haughty Mrs. Chancellor having to do *Jill's* nails! It is the lawyers on these shows who have about them, to borrow another film title, "the sweet smell of success."

The odor that rises, however, from the negative version of the lawyer–money relation is not so sweet. In Orson Welles's brilliant *Lady from Shanghai* (1948), the sailor and veteran of the Spanish civil war (Loyalist side), Michael (played, by Welles himself, as an Irishman), tells the corrupt high-powered San Francisco attorney, Arthur Bannister (Everett Sloan) that he (Michael) has "always found it very sanitary to be broke." Bannister ridicules this point in a speech on why money is the only important thing, a speech surely calculated by the director to make his audience's skin crawl. Later, when Bannister and his wife (played by Rita Hayworth, actually married to Welles at the time the film was made), and Bannister's law partner, George Grisby, are drinking and viciously insulting each other at an expensive, all-night beach party, Michael makes a little speech of his own:

Is this what you folks do for amusement? Do you know, once off the hump of Brazil, I saw the ocean so darkened with blood it was black and the sun fainting away over the lip of the sky. We put in at Fortaleza and a few of us had lines out for a bit of idle fishin'. It was me had the first strike—a shark it was—then there was another, and another shark again, 'till all about the sea was made of sharks and more sharks still and no water at all. My shark had torn himself on the hook, and the scent, or maybe the stain it was, and him bleeding his life away drove the rest of 'em mad. Then the beasts took to eating each other. In their frenzy they ate at themselves. You could feel the lust and murder like a wind stinging your eyes, and you could smell the death reekin' up out of the sea. I never saw anything worse until this little picnic tonight. And you know, there wasn't one of them sharks in the whole crazy pack that survived.... I'll be leavin' now.

This makes for a truly eerie moment, with the youthful Welles's face held in medium-shot, silhouetted against the dark ocean and sinister night sky. Then Bannister, reclining in a 1940s lounge chair and holding a cocktail, looks at his partner and says: "George, that's the first time anyone ever thought enough of you to call you a shark. If you were a *good* lawyer, you'd be flattered."

The positive image of lawyers in relation to power often presents attorneys as ethically superior to the dog-eat-dog values of a competitive business system as well as economically "market proof"—as thoroughgoing professionals who are the beneficiaries of a genteel security. It is especially in soap operas, in such films as the endlessly fascinating *The Young Philadelphians* (1959), and in the novels of writers like Cameron Hawley and Louis Auchincloss that we are most likely to discover the extraordinary power of attorneys emanating from their aloofness toward the hurly-burly of working for a living that presumably plagues those in nonprofessional (including business) occupations.

There is also the negative version of the lawyer–power nexus—a striking example is provided by the film *The Caine Mutiny* (1954). Attorney Barney Greenwald (José Ferrer), having successfully defended his Navy clients from being convicted of mutiny in a full-blown court martial, turns on them and (with the help of several cocktails) gives this lecture:

I got a guilty conscience. I defended you, Steve, because I found the wrong man was on trial. So I torpedoed Queeg for you. I had to torpedo him. And I feel sick about it. You know something? When I was studying law, and Mr. Keefer here was writing his stories, and you, Willy, were tearing up the playing fields of dear old Princeton, who was standing guard over this fat, dumb, happy country of ours, eh? Not us. Oh, no. We knew you couldn't make any money in the service, so who did the dirty work for us? Queeg did and a lot of other guys. Tough, sharp guys who didn't crack up like Queeg.

A final negative portrayal of lawyers in their relation to power reveals the legal profession's neurotic desire for absolute control. The December 7, 1985 episode of *Saturday Night Live* (1975–) (hosted by John Lithgow), for example, included a comedy sketch in which a doctor is cataloging symptoms of the malady "bug up the ass." He inquires of the patient: "Do you have a policy on loaning tools? Do you see a coat on the floor and walk on it because it shouldn't be there? Do you have car covers for each of your cars? Do you get angry when a stupid person wins the lottery? Are you an attorney?" The concluding line climaxes the routine and brought down the house in its live performance on network television.

LAWYERS AND ORDER

Justice? That's not even an issue here. [Prosecutor in *The Onion Field* (1979) based on Joseph Wambaugh novel]

The negative conception of the relation between lawyers and order can be effectively located within the criminal justice system. From the liberal angle, an obvious negative image is revealed by the prison film. From *Mayor of Hell* (1933, juvenile institution) and *I Am a Fugitive from a Chain Gang* (1932, southern rural institution) through *Brute Force* (1947, urban institution), *Escape from Alcatraz* (1979, "true story" film about illegal departure from the Rock) and *Escape from New York* (1981, island of Manhattan transformed into maximum security facility, ca. 1997), the American prison movie has systematically presented a picture of the legal order as an absolute nightmare.

Another negative conception of legal order (seen from a liberal perspective) was the basis for one of the most popular prime-time television series, *The Fugitive* (1963–67). Although there is a kind of bitterness and anger running through the "outlaw" genre in popular culture *(Bonnie and Clyde* [1967] is a good example), there is also a characteristic fatalism, a sense of predestination that tends to undercut political critique of "the system" that produces outlaws. But David Janssen's Dr. Richard Kimble was one of television's most decent and admirable characters ever, a man who unquestionably had not received justice from the legal system and yet seemed trapped in a hopeless effort to catch up with a ghostlike one-armed man before Lieutenant Gerard caught up with Kimble. The trap is familiar, but Kimble's innocence and his refusal to give up presented viewers, week after week for four years, with a running condemnation of an order that relentlessly sought to execute a doctor who had lost his wife to a killer and yet would constantly risk being captured in order to provide emergency medical care to those who (invariably) required his services. Even William Gingrich would not have sued *this* doctor. Kimble was often repaid for his sacrifice of personal security by law-abiding citizens who would systematically obstruct police efforts to detain Kimble once they became convinced of the doctor's fundamental moral quality. *The Fugitive* rarely, if ever, showed individuals prosecuted for helping Kimble defeat the good soldiers of legal order.

From a conservative perspective, there is an equally disturbing negative image of legal-order-as-nightmare. *The Onion Field* seems to me to be a different kind of film from, say, the "Dirty Harry" pictures. It does not so much convey a personalized attack on defense attorneys, liberal judges, or "constitutional baloney"—let alone contribute to the development of counterimage cowboys; rather, it expresses a sense of tragic inequity (told from a prosecuting attorney's perspective!) at the results the legal order achieves. Delay in the trial and appellate process, the absence of support systems for victims of crime, and vagaries in sentencing produce results that can only be seen as part of a bad dream. "Campbell's forgotten," says the assistant district attorney, "he may as well never have lived. Hettinger's a ghost. Only the legal process has meaning. I've got to get away." So much for a police officer who was randomly shot to death in an onion field.

There are also, needless to say, very positive images of the lawyer–order relation in popular culture, which should come as no surprise if we accept the notion that fear of disorder is one of the most deeply felt social emotions. Again, in the classic Ford film *Young Mr. Lincoln*, we get a mass culture archetype: the lawyer who intervenes to impose (or reimpose) sanity and civilization. Here Lincoln's youthful clients are about to be lynched by a mob in the streets, and the incredibly low-keyed Lincoln (Henry Fonda) takes individual members of the mob through their paces, convincing them they should be deeply ashamed of what they are doing and about to do. The lawyer's magic works; Lincoln's clients make it to trial, where he achieves another miracle. In Fritz Lang's *Fury* (1936), the "lynched" victim is, indeed, *innocent* (wrongly jailed for a crime he did not commit, Spencer Tracy is trapped in his cell while a crazed mob burns the building down trying to kill him). Once the tables are turned, however, and it develops that Tracy actually survived the fire and thus holds in his own hands the lives of those convicted of murdering him (he remains in hiding while his tormentors are convicted at trial despite the absence of a corpse), he chooses the order of law/truth as against that of self-help/revenge and dramatically reveals to a stunned courtroom that he is alive.

Finally, there remains a positive conception of the relation between law, lawyers, and order that can best be approached through application of contemporary feminist criticism. Just as some feminist critics have raised the question, "Is science sexed?" so Catherine MacKinnon raises the same question with respect to law. *The Birds* is precisely what most serious critics have realized: "a dark, lyric poem about the fragility of our supposedly ordered world, and the chaos which is ready to burst in and shatter our expectations." In another way, *The Birds* is a perfect illustration of how the discourses of law, rationality, order, and maleness silently converge within our social system. A successful (and handsome) San Francisco criminal lawyer, Mitch Brenner (Rod Taylor), places the attractive socialite and "spoiled rich kid," Melanie Daniels (Tippi Hedren), on the

defensive in the film's first scene. In a bird shop, Mitch allows Melanie to pretend she is a shop salesperson (demonstrating, in the process, that she doesn't know her birds); then teases her because he knows who she really is (from the newspapers—her father owns one); and finally puts down her recent practical joke in a Roman fountain that led to a court appearance: "I merely believe in the law, Miss Daniels, I'm not so keen on practical jokes." You can argue that she has been shabbily treated by a complete stranger, yet Melanie's hooked: she goes after Mitch, perceiving him as powerful and seductive (though she would not admit it at this stage).

Even before the birds make their savage move, it is clear that all the women in the film—Mitch's mother and little sister, an old flame who lives near Mitch's weekend home on Bodega Bay just to be near him, and gradually the "stuck-up" Miss Daniels—have come to depend on Mitch in some crucial way. He is the center of their lives and, at least since his father died, his mother's and sister's essential support. Melanie comes to dinner, and as Mitch, mom, sis, and Melanie enter the house, they debate whether to call the local feed salesman since the chickens won't eat.

> Mitch says, "What good is that gonna do?"
> "He sold me the feed, didn't he?" replies Mom.
> "Caveat emptor, mother," says Mitch, "let the buyer beware."
> She comes back, "Whose side are you on?"
> "Merely quoting the law, dear."
> "Never mind the law," she says.

But you can ignore neither the law (order/Mitch/rationality) nor the horrible threat to it posed by chaos and fear, which are already drilling their ugly little beaks through the front door in the form of this inexplicable problem: Why won't the chickens eat? (In the trailer for the film, Hitchcock invites you to see his latest work while sitting at a dining table eating an elegant chicken entree!)

On the one side, then, there is order and the male point of view; on the other side is "the fragility of our supposedly ordered world." In the middle, with no hope of survival save in the powerful grasp of male protection/values, reside women. The extraordinary extent to which law, what it represents, and Mitch's legal personality are subtly interwoven with order and rationality in scene after scene makes *The Birds* a prime candidate for the application of MacKinnon's feminist perspective. After the most horrifying bird attack to date (on the restaurant and gas station), Mitch saves Melanie from being pecked to death while trapped in one of those special "claustrophobia boxes" (a phone booth), and they repair to the restaurant, where a shocked group of people are huddled in silence, utterly terrified by what they have just witnessed. A woman, who nearly (but not quite) escaped with her children before the attack, hysterically begins to blame *Melanie* and her arrival in Bodega Bay for the inexplicable bird attacks. In a genuinely stunning visual moment, Melanie reaches out and slaps the woman across the face. Suddenly, order (civilization) is restored, *exactly as in the* Young Mr. Lincoln–*type antilynching sequences* from countless films. Mitch puts his arm around Melanie in a show of solidarity. His opinion of her is definitely improving.

What is critical is that we understand how dependent Melanie and all the other women remain on Mitch; indeed, after she is trapped with hundreds of birds in an upstairs room back at the farmhouse and is mauled, Melanie becomes catatonic and more dependent than ever. It isn't even a message, really, just an awesome "point of viewlessness," as MacKinnon would say, which unites the inevitability of legal order with the virtue of male rationality as the only hope for salvation that women have in this world. And the specific image of legal order, in which Melanie acts out the male role of imposing rationality to shut up a hysterical woman who is nearly as helpless as her children, thus plays a rather sophisticated double function. On the one hand, Melanie imposes a high-level legal order value on the situation (presence of mind versus panic, rules versus riot, and so forth). On the other hand, in so doing she experiences a rite of passage into the universe of genuine rationality— truly a man's world within which she is now free to become a total dependent and live in the shade provided by Mitch's reassuring shadow. Perhaps the only saving grace (from this perspective) to *The Birds* is its somewhat flat and unexpected conclusion: even Mitch is revealed as having almost no idea what he is doing.

WOMEN LAWYERS IN CELLULOID: WHY HOLLYWOOD SKIRTS THE TRUTH[1]
Carole Shapiro

AFTER more than half a century with only a few movies about women lawyers, Hollywood made more than 20 films from 1979 until 1993 in which women lawyer characters played some speaking part. Of the contemporary films I have located in which women lawyers play a significant role, most of them are litigators. Of those, 13 are involved in criminal work, eight are defense lawyers, and the rest are prosecutors.

How these films depict the personal lives of female lawyers is critical to their ultimate message: woman has a continuing need for a man. To make their point, consciously or otherwise, they need to focus on the women's failure in intimate relations. The films blame the women for this situation—often focusing on their "unnatural" interest in their work. While the majority of women lawyers are—or at least have been— married, not one of this crop in backlash era films is currently married, and only six of them have ever been. Of that latter group, five have been divorced, and one is widowed. Moreover, almost none of them has children. The plight of women like that, who are desperate to get married but just never seem to succeed, despite their often frantic and frequent best efforts, may even become the source of comedy. While this humor may be poignant in tone, it may simultaneously make the woman the butt of jokes. *The Big Chill* takes such an approach with its unmarried lawyer character, who is depicted as desperately trying to get pregnant.

In this film, Meg, the attorney Mary Kay Place plays, is a nice but plain woman with a great sense of humor, "sitting on her biological clock." She has been unsuccessful with men, despite as she says "dating for the last twenty years." The movie presents the plight of this unmarried lawyer, who, having given up on finding a husband, has decided to become a single mother. While her

---

1. 25 *University of Toledo Law Review* 955 (1995). Reprinted with permission.

male friends are clearly fond of plain Meg, we see that none of them has any interest in accommodating her desire. This is shown in a series of amusing but painful rebuffs, through which the audience pities her for her failure to find even one interested man. But perhaps the solution to the problem is the most humiliating part: She gets her man only when one of the happily married characters convinces her own husband that he should father Meg's child.

Unlike Mary Kay Place's character in *The Big Chill*, the lawyers' physical unattractiveness in most other films is not generally the explanation for their being single. It would be difficult to draw that conclusion when actresses like Cher, Jessica Lange, Ellen Barkin, Demi Moore or Rebecca DeMornay are the attorneys. Whatever appearance problems they do have, the spectator knows that these women with just a little help could drastically improve their looks. Most often, it is a question of making their dress softer and more becomingly feminine. For example, Sean Young in *Love Crimes* plays a crusading assistant district attorney in Atlanta. Her hairstyle at the beginning of the film is very short and severe. It echoes the severity of her dress and emphasizes the off-putting harshness of her manner. Yet, the audience ultimately sees that she can choose to be more appealing in her appearance. Indeed, the change, when it comes, is dramatic as Young makes both her hairdo and her clothing more feminine for a self-initiated undercover assignment. The appearance of the angular Glenn Close in *Jagged Edge* is similarly transformed when her straight hair miraculously becomes softer and therefore more feminine after a romantic interlude.

Many of the other lawyer characters also need to be made to look more feminine as their unwomanliness rather than their physicality is the real problem. Paradoxically, however, that severity of appearance, while making them initially less attractive, also serves in some of these films as a challenge to the male protagonist. That is the case in *The Big Easy*, in which Ellen Barkin plays Ann Osborne, a New Orleans assistant district attorney assigned to investigate corruption in that city's police department. Barkin is presented as uptight, dressed in classic "old maid" fashion: man-tailored suit, blouse closed at the

neck, big glasses, hair severely pulled back. While the lawyer initially tells Dennis Quaid, playing a police homicide detective, "let's keep this professional," Quaid pursues the reluctant Barkin, who despite her misgivings, eventually succumbs to his charms. Predictably—in this genre—she becomes a much more desirable woman as she literally and figuratively lets down her hair.

It may also be that these lawyers have become unwomanly while still physically attractive as a result of excessive devotion to job and professional ambition. This type of character fits a commonly occurring prototype in cinema. According to feminist film critic Mary Ann Doane, she uses her femininity as one might wear a mask in a "masquerade," putting it on and taking it off at will. This exaggeration of femininity is designed to hide her real masculinity and, according to this theory, prevent her from being punished for it. The contradiction between the woman's female appearance and her male essence offers danger to men who may succumb to the temptation of her wiles, not knowing what lurks beneath. "This type of masquerade, an excess of femininity, is aligned with the *femme fatale* and…is necessarily regarded by men as evil incarnate."

Such is the case with the prosecutor that Greta Scacchi plays in *Presumed Innocent*, a film based on the best-selling novel of that name. In that film, Scacchi's character is the divorced Caroline Polhemus, a gorgeous blonde prosecutor, zealous in devotion to her work. However, she is equally devoted to cultivation of men with rising professional stars. She seduces the married Harrison Ford, a straight-arrow colleague with a promising career beyond his number-two spot in the district attorney's office. It is clear to the audience that he does not have a chance against the maneuvering and irresistible Scacchi because he is blind to the danger she represents.

The audience has a similar feeling about Glenn Close's divorce in *Jagged Edge*. She goes out to dinner with her estranged husband, who is also depicted as close to their children. Close, on the other hand, seems to be less concerned about them than about herself. The film makes the audience infer that a bad mother would also be a bad wife. Likewise Barbara Hershey in *Defenseless* seems to imply that she, a woman characterized in college as "never having time for the boys," was responsible for the break-up with her ex-husband.

Defective women lawyers not sufficiently devoting themselves to pursuit and/or maintenance of home and hearth often possess a companion trait: unbecoming sexual aggressiveness in their dealings with men. We see this phenomenon in the film *Wild Orchid*, in which two female lawyer characters prominently figure. Jacqueline Bisset, playing the older and more experienced of the two, has never married although it appears that she has had numerous affairs. She acts sexually provocative, for example, insuring the presence of a recalcitrant male principal at the consummation of a big real estate deal by bringing him in on a leash. Moreover, Bisset is the kind of unwomanly woman who could become so sexually obsessed with a man that she could in her own words become "out of control" and go after him. Having such feelings for Mickey Rourke's character, Bisset describes her unbecomingly aggressive pursuit, confessing that she had "dresse[d] up as a maid to get into his room."

Predictably, the notably unprudish Rourke ends up not choosing the attractive Bisset but her younger, more sexually innocent colleague. The vampish character Greta Scacchi plays in *Presumed Innocent* is likewise ultimately unacceptable in her behavior, even if sexually exciting. She starts to seduce the excruciatingly straight, married Harrison Ford character after they have won a case, telling him, in the first mention of sex between them, "It's going to be so good." Later, when they get to her office, she pulls him to her, kisses him and takes off her earrings, jacket and skirt while he remains fully dressed. When he finally takes off his jacket, she initiates the action by kissing him hard. What follows ultimately leads to her punishment: death.

In a similar vein, Glenn Close's sin in *Jagged Edge* of pursuing her desires is compounded by her being a mother. In the first *Jagged Edge* incident, Close, playing a divorced mother of two, kisses her client in her own home where her young son witnesses them. She is so selfish that they do it again even after she knows the boy has seen her. The son, disturbed by what he sees, reports the incident to his father. The latter con-

veys his anger to Close, explaining the impact of her behavior on their child, thereby showing his concern in marked contrast with her lack of feeling. The second incident involves her staying over at her client's house the night they begin their affair. While Close initially tells him she cannot stay because her children expect her home, she ultimately telephones her daughter to say she will not be home that night. Of course, Close's punishment comes when she discovers the truth in earlier warnings that her client, played by Jeff Bridges, is a psychopathic killer, and he subsequently attempts to take her life.

An alternative model to the *femme fatale* lawyer is the woman whose career has made her deny her own femininity and therefore has exiled her (at least until the movie begins) from the charmed circle of a happy family life. For this repressed lawyer prototype, overwork may have made the lawyer a burned-out case, good only for her job. Like Cher, playing a Washington, D.C., public defender in *Suspect*, this type of female character may be able to say about herself:

> I don't have a life. The only time I listen to music is in my car. The last time I went to the movies, it was like a year ago. I don't date. I'd like to have a child but I don't even have a boyfriend so how can I have a child? I spend all my time with murderers and rapists.... I'm tired, I'm really tired.

Moreover in *Class Action* Mary Elizabeth Mastrantonio, like Cher, is too busy working to have time for a vacation. Uptightness, humorlessness and sexual failure or inexperience do not make a woman more likely to find a man unless she is a character in one of the romance films. In that case, the films stress the hero's seeing the real woman beneath the dowdy exterior and his subsequently saving her from a miserable life. Or in the words of the inimitable Cary Grant, uttered as he works on the stern judge Myrna Loy plays in the 1949 film *The Bachelor and the Bobbysoxer*, the pursuing male knows "[you can't] judge a book by its cover."

Part of what is missing from the miserably lonely lives of these screen lawyers is friendship, particularly with other women. Where the movies do show some kind of relationship between the protagonist and another woman, the friendship almost invariably involves someone of lower professional status. This is the case for example in *Love Crimes*, where Sean Young is friendly with an African American woman police officer who works with her. When Young tells the officer she is her best friend, the woman responds, "I'm your only friend." Similarly, Jessica Lange's only contact with a woman in *Music Box*, either in the office or out of it, is with an African American legal assistant. And the blonde Rebecca DeMornay's one connection with a woman in *Guilty as Sin* is with her brown-haired secretary. The latter is decidedly less glamorous than the lawyer and provides her with no competition, either professionally or personally.

At first glance, *Defenseless* appears to have broken this mold and shown a real friendship between two women, but in the end the difference is illusory. In this film, Barbara Hershey, as T. K. Katwuller, a Los Angeles criminal defense lawyer, meets her former college roommate, Elly, after a 20-year hiatus. While they initially reminisce about old times at Smith College, by the end of the film Hershey tells her that she never really did like her, and that she always made her "feel guilty." Conversely, Elly attacks Hershey by telling her that in college she was just "Miss Smarty Pants" and that she "hadn't changed a hair since then." Is it any wonder, then, that Elly ends up framing Hershey for the murder of her husband, a murder that she herself committed? Even apparent friendship between two women, however rarely portrayed in these films, is chimerical and moreover can be dangerous.

While the legal success may not have won happiness for the lawyer personally, in the worst-case scenario the victory results in destruction to her dear ones. Jessica Lange's sorry plight in *Music Box* is typical of the negative results that professional victories can bring for these women lawyers. Lange, a criminal lawyer, has successfully defended her father against deportation proceedings. This action is based on the efforts of Hungary, his birth country, to extradite him for war crimes he had committed as an SS agent during World War II. Despite her initial belief in his innocence, she ultimately discovers that he has committed the brutal acts of which he was accused. Her legal victory, while a triumph against the odds, is hollow because she has dis-

covered her father's guilt by meddling in matters not her business.

Glenn Close, like Jessica Lange, wins a tough case in *Jagged Edge* with an acquittal for her client, Jeff Bridges. The triumph of her victory is also far from complete. In setting the tone, the movie shows its bitter fruits—and not its sweet success—as Close leaves the courthouse. Rather than making a statement of victory to the assembled throng of expectant journalists waiting for her, Close implicates herself for her inadvertent use of perjured evidence in an earlier case she has prosecuted. As if her statement to the press had not sufficiently dampened her hard-earned victory, Close then discovers Bridges really had murdered his wife, and she must defend herself against his efforts to kill her.

The unhappy results of Close's success signify the danger of victory, a message echoed in *Guilty as Sin*. Like Glenn Close's attorney character, Rebecca DeMornay discovers that Don Johnson, her cute but psychopathic client, is actually guilty although she has won an acquittal for him. After this legal victory, Johnson wreaks havoc on the two men who love DeMornay. He brutally assaults her boyfriend and then kills her devoted detective friend who had unstintingly assisted her on the case in response to her pleas for help. Moreover, paralleling the successful *Jagged Edge*, Johnson then starts stalking DeMornay. While she does not die in the struggle with her former client, she does fall many stories from a hotel balcony onto a concrete floor below. Carted off on a stretcher and bleeding from her mouth as the movie closes, her character also strongly indicates the price of winning may be too high.

Compounding this theme, in two of these movies the woman's victory in the courtroom causes her misery through the ensuing loss of a significant relationship with a man. In *Music Box*, this loss involves a break in a daughter's formerly close relationship with a father. Moreover, because she discovers through her investigation that her father was a war criminal, she severs her young son's connection with him as well. Or, in an alternative model, the woman lawyer's victory may be no consolation since she continues being alone and, therefore, unhappy. Consistent with this theme is Barbara Hershey's situation in

Defenseless. In this film, while Hershey first wins an acquittal defending her former college roommate and then beats murder charges brought against her, the movie ends with her sitting alone in her stalled car.

While none of the women lawyers is married at the beginning of these movies, they often are united with the male protagonist at the end. The progression of this movie group is generally romantic, although not always so. For example, in *Class Action*, the woman is reconciled with a man who is her father rather than with a love interest. As the plot develops, the lawyer comes to understand, in the words of the 1950s television series classic, that "father knows best." In this movie, Mary Elizabeth Mastrantonio plays a corporate attorney in the highly unlikely position of opposing Gene Hackman, her father, a crusading public interest lawyer, on a $30-million product liability case. This lawsuit has Mastrantonio defending the manufacturer of a car with a defective electrical system, which severely injured Hackman's client.

During the course of the case, Mastrantonio discovers that her boyfriend, a partner at the law firm where she too is trying to achieve that status, has concealed evidence that would have shown the car company's knowledge of its defective design. She leaves this man whom she discovers, despite his surface charm, represents everything her father despises and has warned her against. She ultimately quits her firm and the case to help her dad win on behalf of his wronged client.

The majority of these films, however, involve romantic love. When this is the case, the woman lawyer's romantic involvement follows a prototypical pattern. Whatever the woman's particular situation, she is initially indifferent, if not outright hostile, to the male protagonist. In the romances, he is the one who pursues her as she tries to pull away. However, he persists in his efforts, often helping her win her case and then winning her. This plot pattern is an embodiment of the myth that a woman's "no" really means "yes." This pattern is clear in *The Big Easy*. Ellen Barkin, as the repressed, all-business prosecutor, initially resists Dennis Quaid's advances, but with the audience rooting for Quaid, she ultimately succumbs to his charms. Moreover, view-

ers and Quaid know how good it would be for Barkin if she just let him make her happy by waving his magic wand.

Their first prolonged encounter in the movie exemplifies this push-pull approach to romance. In it, Quaid has persuaded Barkin to go out to dinner, telling her if she does, he will give her information for her corruption investigation. Despite her judgment that it would be improper to do so as, since Quaid might be a target of her investigation, she succumbs to curiosity. At the restaurant, she is initially dismayed to see there is music, which signifies their meeting is a social occasion rather than the business meeting she had intended. However, he persuades her to dance with him, although she initially declines because she says she does not know how. At the table, as Quaid takes her hand and strokes it, she palpably relaxes but then becomes businesslike again.

After their meal, she refuses dessert because she "ha[s] to get up early." While he is driving her home, she jumps out of the car because she does not like his making light of police corruption. She refuses to allow him to wait for her as she makes a stop on her way home, but he follows her anyway. As circumstances have it, after a stop at the grocery store, Barkin is knocked down as she unsuccessfully tries to help capture the robber of a woman passerby. Luckily Quaid, who is at the scene despite her wishes, rescues her and catches the thief, saying "good thing I'm such a pushy guy." The romance of the movie continues, in a similar pursue/avoid/succumb fashion, until it culminates in their wedding in the final scene.

The busy Dennis Quaid also must use all of his powers of persuasion on Cher in *Suspect*, in which he plays a juror hearing a murder case with Kathleen Riley playing the public defender. She initially resists his assistance in proving her client's innocence and tells him, "If you really want to be helpful you should leave me alone." Predictably, she eventually welcomes his help—and him. He puts his own body on the line, as he did with the reluctant Ellen Barkin in *The Big Easy*, when he again makes sure he is in the right place at the right time. This time, he saves Cher from the knife of a psychotic witness by taking the blow himself. The audience sees her defense against him start to crumble as she dresses his wound and tells him he is not as "big an asshole" as she had thought. While she accepts but does not participate in his good-night kiss that night, the audience knows it is just a matter of time before she welcomes it.

Consistent with this premonition, several days further into the trial and their joint investigation, the movie shows Quaid unexpectedly appearing at Cher's door. She first coldly tells him she is tired, but after he upbraids her for her failure to appreciate his efforts, she finally screams that she "wants [him] to go." Quaid, moving strategically, takes that opportunity to grab her for a kiss. Cher, despite the hostile front the audience has just seen, responds passionately to his embrace. His subsequent triumphant smile and good night to her mark the beginning of the audience's certainty that Quaid has conquered the formerly indifferent Cher and they will live happily ever after. While he needs to save her life one more time, the audience's faith is vindicated in the final scene.

When a female lawyer character is explicitly inexperienced with men, as well as reluctant, she provides a special challenge to the pursuing male protagonist. For example Emily, the innocent character Carre Otis plays in *Wild Orchid*, drives Mickey Rourke into hot pursuit. In the film, she is a young law school graduate, hired by a big New York firm. That she has never before left the Midwest signifies to the audience, as well as Rourke, her purity and wholesomeness. Indeed the predictably debauched but ultimately redeemable Mickey Rourke tells Otis in the early part of the film that he "bets she sang in the Presbyterian church choir and picked berries."

Moreover, while Emily is clearly gorgeous as well as bright, she has no idea of her own potential attractiveness to men or her power over them. She does not, therefore, hold the same danger for them as does her man-eater colleague Jacqueline Bisset or other such characters, including Greta Scacchi in *Presumed Innocent*. While the less-than-wholesome Rourke is attracted to her purity as an antidote to his own debauchery, he simultaneously attempts to initiate her sexually. Despite her initial reluctance to play these games, she finds herself responding to them and to him.

Not only does she become the woman of his dreams, but in a final stroke of male luck, she loves the orphaned Rourke so unconditionally and perfectly, she can heal his psychic wounds. She fulfills the male fantasy of the beautiful virgin who becomes the eternal wife. That he is the one man to penetrate her formerly impenetrable sexual veil speaks to his special manhood.

Interestingly, in several of the romances, the attraction between the female lawyer and the male protagonist develops through his helping her solve the case on which she is working. While in each of the above movies, the women lawyers are supposedly intelligent and professionally competent, the male partner is critical to the solution of the mystery. She may participate in the process by coming up with good ideas, but he is always the one, consistent with movie traditions, who makes the key moves toward the solution. The films may show the male protagonist publicly humiliating the woman lawyer, either before or during their work together.

This jousting and male victory occur early in *Suspect*. Cher, playing a public defender on a murder case, voir questions dires Dennis Quaid as a prospective juror. Her tone is tart as she questions him. She begins the dialogue by saying, "You say you're a congressional adviser. Is that another word for lobbyist?" He ups the ante by responding, "I don't know. It's like calling a lawyer a mouthpiece." After some additional repartee, she cuts him off and tells him to turn around to face the back of the courtroom. To make a point about witness observation, Cher asks Quaid the color of her hair. He answers "brown" although she is playing the role of defense lawyer Kathleen Riley with raven locks. Falling into his trap, she asks him whether her hair looks brown. Springing it, he responds, "I thought you wanted the real color." The *voir dire* continues until Cher accepts Quaid for her jury, but the point of the exchange is Quaid's humiliation of Cher by calling attention to her dyed hair.

Similarly, in *Physical Evidence*, Burt Reynolds humiliates Theresa Russell, who plays his legal aid attorney, during their first meeting. He asks her, "Who dresses you in the morning?" He also comments on her Rolex watch and tells her to send him "someone who works for a living" rather than a "wealthy chick," whose defense of him "seems dangerously like a hobby." She tells him: "I'll be damned if you're going to pass on me for the way I dress. That's not me. This is me—guts and brains. You can't do any better." His response: "Oh, a Vassar version of Tarzan." This answer gives him the last word. While Russell smartly answers Reynolds, he still sets the pace with the debasing, personal comments he makes.

In *Legal Eagles*, Robert Redford also demeans the woman lawyer, played by Debra Winger, with whom he comes to live happily ever after. He plays a New York City district attorney who is prosecuting Winger's attractive client on an art fraud case. She entices him into the case through a series of attention-getting maneuvers and then becomes interested in Redford. After they start working together on an investigation, she asks him plaintively whether "there's anything" about her he likes. He can only say, "Your eyes, very warm eyes." That night, he allows Winger's client to seduce him, and, for various reasons, the press finds him in bed with the attractive, exotic blonde the next morning. This becomes front-page news, much to Winger's chagrin. She then sorrowfully asks Redford, "Why'd you have to sleep with her?...Did you have to make your conquest public?"

But Redford's humiliation of Winger is professional as well as personal. The first moment of the former occurs early in the film, when defense lawyer Winger is pitted against prosecutor Redford. She has devised a ludicrous, almost comical, defense for her client, who is charged with possession of stolen property. She explains to the jury that he had 14 stolen television sets in his home because his relatives were helping him to realize his dream of a "media room, just like the president of the United States."

During summation, Redford destroys Winger's defense. She has previously seemed pleased with its ingenuity, but she slumps in her seat as Redford cuts it to shreds. When she sees him afterward in the courthouse, he tells her she should have pleaded the client guilty at arraignment, something any criminal attorney knows is the obvious approach in such a bad case. Winger's response, "that everyone is entitled to a defense," is an embarrassing answer for the experienced criminal lawyer she is supposed to be.

Her effort to convince Redford of the innocence of her performance artist client ("a client I can believe in") is met with his skeptical response. It prompts Redford, given Winger's performance earlier that day, to put her down by saying, "like Howard Marshak?" (the man of the aforesaid television sets).

Dennis Quaid follows the same pattern in *The Big Easy*. He ultimately wins Ellen Barkin's heart as well as her body. But he humiliates her several times even after they begin their affair and are working together on an investigation of several murders in New Orleans. At one point, Barkin is assigned to prosecute Quaid, a New Orleans homicide detective, for bribe-taking. It is a case that even other prosecutors consider entrapment. Still, she pursues it with a vengeance, in part because of her fury at Quaid for betraying her. She ultimately is forced to withdraw the charges in an announcement made to a jubilant courtroom audience filled with Quaid supporters. In a prosecutor's nightmare, she abashedly admits to the judge that the destruction of the key piece of evidence has made it impossible to proceed. Her loss to Quaid, humiliating to the fervent Barkin, is compounded by her sureness that he personally engineered it. Indeed the audience knows that her suspicion is well-founded.

This incident does not end the power politics between them. When Barkin, still smarting from the sting of her courtroom defeat, refuses to speak to Quaid, he arranges for a policeman relative to pick her up on a false charge as she jogs. He then brings her in the police car to a Quaid family party, at which his relatives and friends are celebrating the dismissal of the charges against him. Barkin is brought into this hostile situation in shorts and tank top, dripping wet from her run, so that Quaid can talk to her and soften her attitude toward him. In the meantime, though, she is the object of scrutiny and derision by the other party guests, mostly family members and police officers, who scorn her.

Barkin's embarrassment is heightened by being caught in clothes that highlight her vulnerability. Because her scanty outfit exposes her body, and all the other guests are fully attired, their gaze, in cinematic terms, has additional power. Quaid's mother's question to her as she sees the sweaty, disheveled Barkin is, "Did he get you out of the bath or something [to bring you here?]"

In these three above-mentioned romances, the working partnership is the focal point of the plot. The viewer, however, sees the male protagonist's superiority in dealing with the central mystery of the film. This pattern is most pronounced in *Suspect*. Cher is portrayed as an experienced, albeit overworked, public defender, who is enthusiastic about her work. Although an otherwise hostile judge says, "I've heard good things about you," she appears not to have done even elementary investigation in the murder case that is the film's focus. Nor are her instincts in court any better. Dennis Quaid, as a juror on her case, helps her by starting to secretly feed her the results of his investigation. He also provides creative ideas that allow her to find the real murderer and exculpate her client. In fact, each step toward the solution is a result of his initiative alone.

In his first effort at helping Cher win her case, Quaid anonymously telephones her and suggests she consider whether her client is left- or right-handed. With this critical suggestion, Cher starts to build the defendant's case by establishing that he is left-handed, while the killer was right-handed. He helps Cher locate a critical witness she has been unable to find on her own, gets the license plate numbers of other cars in the parking lot the night the murder victim was killed there, and makes the connection between what looks like a random street murder and a larger conspiracy, which turns out to be the key to Cher's client's victory. Moreover, as is the pattern in many of these films, Quaid saves her life twice during the course of their joint investigation.

In *Legal Eagles*, what also at first appears to be a work partnership between equals who become romantically involved turns out to be, like *Suspect*, quite different. When Redford resigns from the district attorney's office after being found in flagrante delicto with Winger's client, whom he is investigating, Winger asks him to join her on the case. As the two attorneys work together, however, he becomes the moving force. This is so despite the fact that her enthusiasm and ingenuity had gotten him involved in the matter. Moreover, it is her far superior knowledge of modern art that is critical to their successful defense.

Consistent with movie conventions, however, Redford becomes the active member of the team. He is the one discovering and assembling the pieces of the mystery. When Winger does initiate some of the action, she generally gets them into trouble, from which he extricates them. For example, she persuades him to follow a suspect into his warehouse. Although they find important information there, they discover the place has been wired with dynamite, and the timer indicates it is about to explode. While Winger instigated their being there, she commands Redford to "do something!" As he yells at her to "move," he takes the initiative for their rescue. He drives a forklift, and with her as passenger, they break through the door as the warehouse explodes. He then directs her to "jump" as they head off the pier toward New York Harbor. Finally, he pulls her from the water, since he has crawled out first.

Redford rescues Winger from death twice more in their film partnership, and, just as important for this analysis, he saves the case. As the trial begins and the defense prospects look dim because of new evidence the prosecutor reveals, Redford persists in believing their client is innocent. Of course, viewers later learn she is, but in the meantime Winger dismissively calls her defense "the most preposterous explanation." Subsequently Redford is trial counsel, while Winger sits worshipfully at the defense table, observing his courtroom performance. Their ultimate victory, as his former boss says about Redford, makes him "the hottest legal property in the city." Amid these accolades for Redford, viewers see only the most fleeting glimpse of Winger. Indeed that is fitting because her case has in fact become his, along with the victory. Redford finally decides to remain Winger's partner "because he is happy there," rather than return to his former prosecutor's job. It seems, however, that he will be the dominant of the two partners, both professionally and personally.

In most of the romances, the lawyer wins her case as well as her man. However, if she wins the man but loses the case, the movie may still have a happy ending. For example, *Other People's Money* ends well for the woman lawyer, played by Penelope Anne Miller, even though her client loses. She represents her mother's boyfriend, a decent factory owner (played by the ever upright Gregory Peck), against a hostile takeover attempt by her shark-like opponent (Danny DeVito). By the end, not only has she lost the case for the sentimental favorite but also, symbolically, she has allowed the defeat of the "little people" at the hands of greedy capitalists. Despite the loss, however, *Other People's Money* ends happily because the lawyer succumbs to the charms of her irresistibly smarmy adversary.

Moreover, at a time of challenged male egos, these films show that any man can win over these professional, seemingly unreachable women. He can be a corrupt police detective; a short, fat, vulgar, heartless takeover artist; a womanizing, manipulative lobbyist; a dissolute, drunk, defrocked police detective; a questionably honest but rags-to-riches business success; or an endearingly disorganized and insomniac district attorney. Even Gene Hackman, as the womanizing, self-involved father in *Class Action*, ultimately proves to be a worthy father for his angry lawyer daughter.

Some of these movies also strike class notes in constructing this pantheon of victorious men. Although there are some professionals in this group, it also includes a number of working-class heroes. The notion that only one of these real men can satisfy a tough professional woman is central to the plot in *Physical Evidence*. In that film, the glamorous and intelligent Theresa Russell dumps her wealthy, obnoxious fiancée and falls for her client, Burt Reynolds. The audience understandably approves her leaving the first man because, as a stockbroker, he epitomizes the unappealing 1980s yuppies. But how can the audience understand the fastidious Russell falling for the alcoholic, brawling, penniless slob that Reynolds plays? His character seems terminally unappealing until the audience remembers that Burt Reynolds signifies the macho man with a good heart who is also a regular guy.

The change in her dress after Russell announces her feelings for him supports this conclusion. Throughout most of the movie, she has worn severely tailored but attractive suits to work, with her long hair tied back in a knot. But her style changes in the final moments of *Physical Evidence* when, after Russell has moved out of her fiancée's

luxurious apartment and into Reynolds' life, she wears her hair long with a soft V-necked dress. For the first time, she also shows a little cleavage.

Whatever their other problems, these women lawyers are portrayed as intellectually sharp and professionally successful. For example, Glenn Close in *Jagged Edge* says she won every case as a prosecutor. Don Johnson wants to hire Rebecca DeMornay in *Guilty as Sin* as his defense lawyer because "they say [she's] the best." About Sean Young in *Love Crimes*, playing an Atlanta prosecutor, it was said, "If [she] was a man, they'd be lining up to give her medals." Then there's the aforementioned Phi Beta Kappa, Barbara Hershey in *Defenseless*.

But in the movies, the intelligence of these women lawyers is a two-edged sword. The films seem to stress this attribute so they can point out their many other inadequacies. Their personal failures range from not being able to drive to being a terrible housekeeper to being unable to cook. They may also be sexually inept and unable to dance.

More disturbingly, however, they often show themselves as unethical or at least exhibit poor judgment in connection with their work. For example, despite their intellectual acumen, many of them make terrible decisions in their choice of clients or become involved with them and subsequently suffer for either of those missteps. Often others—most notably men around them—point out the woman's mistake. But when a man gives the warning, she willfully ignores this sage advice entirely or until it is too late. The women are punished for this hubris in daring to believe in themselves.

For example, Jessica Lange in *Music Box* decides to take on her father's deportation case, albeit reluctantly at first. She only agrees after her father convinces her that he is innocent and in real danger of being sent back to Hungary. However, from the beginning, others question her choice and are eventually proven correct. Before she has made her decision, even her ex-husband advises her not to represent her father. He tells her rightly, "It's not just another case." When she leaves her law practice because she has accepted her father's defense, one of her male associates echoes this sentiment. He asks her "why [she] doesn't get someone else to represent [her] father." Even her prosecutor adversary gives her similar advice, albeit in a sneering fashion: "Get a real lawyer to represent your father, one who isn't emotionally involved."

Talbot, her former father-in-law, who is a lawyer, also gives Lange advice which she initially rejects but ultimately accepts as correct. At one point, when he offers to help her, she says, "I can handle my own case. I don't need help." Unlike Lange, the viewer knows Talbot is right when he tells her that she "needs all [she] can get." He is equally perceptive when he suggests, contrary to Lange's initial convictions about her father's innocence, that her parent may well have committed the atrocities of which he is accused. In fact, he says, the war criminals he questioned for the U.S. government after World War II "weren't monsters but salt-of-the-earth types like your old man." As her father's case develops and she begins to think he's culpable, Lange says to Talbot, "I don't know how to fight this." He responds, "I thought you didn't need help." Humbled at last, she must swallow her pride and ask for his assistance.

As the story unfolds, the audience sees the increasing toll of Lange's misjudgment. Viewers observe her becoming increasingly uneasy about the accusations against her father and hear her say the case is making her "sick." Viewers watch her drinking alone at home and see her teary in court as she hears testimony about her father's brutality. Ultimately, of course, viewers witness the destruction of her family as she discovers that her father is indeed the war criminal the government alleged.

Another woman lawyer's professional misjudgment involving her father is critical to the plot in *Class Action*. In that film, Mary Elizabeth Mastrantonio's character is also headstrong, taking a case she should have refused by any professional standards. The moral of the story hinges on the daughter's becoming the father's adversary—a situation that is, by definition, conflict. Exacerbating her misjudgment is Mastrantonio's role in seeking the case. The audience has previously seen her plead with a partner in her law firm to assign her to this lawsuit because it is a "partnership express." After her assignment, she even

asks her father whether she should pass up a "great case at the firm" because of "extreme conflict." Her father tells her that she should, that the firm is merely "using" her by giving her the case. When her mother, one of the movie's sympathetic characters, suggests it would be better if she "dropped" it, the young lawyer, in a snit, refuses. She responds, "This is the first time where I can beat [dad], where he doesn't make the rules. I'm sick and tired of not being good enough, of being afraid."

In *Jagged Edge*, Glenn Close acts equally unprofessionally in a murder case involving Jeff Bridges as her client. Playing a criminal defense lawyer, she decides to represent Bridges, accused of brutally murdering his wife. She does so only because, having ultimate faith in her ability to tell who is lying (wrongly, it turns out), she believes him innocent. Not only does she become his attorney but also, compounding her earlier poor decision, his lover. As if their becoming sexually involved were not bad enough, this occurs practically on the eve of trial. Close's character acts imprudently despite the wise warning of Sam, her trusted investigator. Likewise, *Guilty as Sin* shows a female criminal attorney exercising spectacularly poor judgment in the face of warnings against taking the handsome Don Johnson as a client. "Feeling her oats" after first turning down his request for representation, she is convinced she "can get him off" and reverses her previous refusal. When Johnson begins to terrorize DeMornay, once again it becomes excruciatingly clear that a female attorney has exercised poor judgment.

Moreover, consistent with the pattern of these films, DeMornay's trusted investigator and surrogate father figure is more perceptive about the situation than the attorney. This character, played by veteran actor Jack Warden, tells DeMornay that Johnson "has been toying" with her. At that point, she is ready to turn in her own client because she is convinced he is a killer. However, Warden convinces her not to because she "would kiss her career good-bye." DeMornay then says, "I need your help, Moe." He gives it to her but at the cost of his life.

In the romance films, the male protagonist may not be in a position to warn the female lawyer about the consequences of her action. However, he does extricate her from the results of her own unethical or improper decision. While this man may not even be an attorney, his assistance, often unsolicited, is invaluable in helping the woman find a way out of her predicament. For example, in *Wild Orchid*, Jacqueline Bisset and Carre Otis play two lawyers attempting to close a real estate deal in Rio de Janeiro with Hong Kong investors. Viewers know early in that film that Bisset is trying to arrange the transaction, although she has flagrantly ignored a problem with her client's rights to the property, something that the beautiful and naive Otis is shocked to hear. In the end, the wealthy Mickey Rourke, who has fallen in love with Otis, rescues the damsels in distress— i.e., the lawyers—by buying the property. He gives the deed to Otis, who tells the surprised Bisset that with Rourke's help maybe they can "save the deal"—and Bisset's skin—after all.

Viewers see smart, accomplished women who deviate from movie norms through their intellect as much as their profession. Being smart and accomplished signifies they are also cold and self-centered. The woman lawyer in *Three Men and a Baby*, in a minor role as the girlfriend of one of the three men, seems to be in the film just to make the point about the unfeelingness of this group. That, of course, is predictable in a film where a mother abandons her baby, and the three male characters ultimately show how loving they are despite their initial incompetence and indifference as caretakers. The woman lawyer is interested primarily in herself. For example, she refuses to stay with her boyfriend on his birthday and even leaves his party early, despite his entreaties, because she has "to be up at seven for a pretrial meeting." She later refuses to stay with the same character, played by Ted Danson, even though there is a crisis with his baby. Instead she goes on a date with another man.

Love Crimes' prosecutor, Sean Young, also exemplifies a woman who is heartless, albeit in a professional setting. She is unconcerned that she may hurt others as she pursues her goals, worthy though they may be. In an early scene, Young sets up a decoy operation to trap corrupt police officers who are preying on prostitutes. One of the decoys is a police officer, Young's close friend,

whom Young personally endangers by not stopping the operation earlier. The angry officer confronts Young afterward, saying, "You just don't care about anyone," and the audience sees that she is absolutely correct.

DISCUSSION QUESTIONS

1. Why have lawyers become so prominent in the mass media in recent decades? Is the public as interested in lawyers as filmmakers, television networks, authors and publishers, reporters and newspapers, and politicians assume? Is this a passing fad?

2. In what ways are the media portrayals selective? How do they distort what you know about lawyers? Why? Does the media idealize or demonize lawyers—or both?[2] How do media portrayals differ from the image individual lawyers and professional associations seek to convey?

3. What is the relationship between media images and public perceptions and attitudes? How else does the public obtain information and images of lawyers?

4. Can you offer examples of media treatment of the following:

    A. The lawyer as hired gun and the lawyer's personal responsibility for taking positions

    B. Vigorous advocacy versus scrupulous legality

    C. Lawyer–client relations

    D. Gender, race, ethnic, and class stereotypes of lawyers

    E. The structure of law practice: law firms, public defender and prosecutor offices

    F. The relationship of lawyers to money, power, and justice

    G. The content of lawyers' work

    H. Lawyer personality and character

2. For additional accounts, see *New York Times* §2 p21 (9.2.90), §2 p9 (7.4.93), A13 (7.12.93).

SUGGESTED READING

Although a relatively recent genre, studies of lawyers in the media are burgeoning. For inventories, see Paul J. Mastrangelo, "Lawyers and the Law: A Filmography," 3 *Legal Reference Service Quarterly* 31 (1983), 5 *LRSQ* 5 (Winter 1985–86); "Lawyers and the Law: A Television Filmography," 8(3/4) *LRSQ* 135 (1988). For analyses, see Anthony Chase, "Toward a Legal Theory of Popular Culture," 1986 *Wisconsin Law Review* 527; Steven D. Stark, "Perry Mason Meets Sonny Crockett: The History of Lawyers and the Police as Television Heroes," 42 *University of Miami Law Review* 229 (1987); Robert C. Post, "On the Popular Image of the Lawyer: Reflections in a Dark Glass," 75 *California Law Review* 379 (1987); Robert Eli Rosen, "Ethical Soap: *L.A. Law* and the Privileging of Character," 43 *University of Miami Law Review* 1229 (1989); Norman Rosenberg, "Hollywood on Trials: Courts and Film," 12 *Law and History Review* 341 (1994); Paul Bergman and Michael Asimow, *Reel Justice: The Courtroom Goes to the Movies* (1996). On other forms of popular culture, see Stewart Macaulay, "Images of Law in Everyday Life: The Lessons of School, Entertainment, and Spectator Sports," 21 *Law & Society Review* 185 (1987); "Symposium: Popular Legal Culture," 98(8) *Yale Law Journal* (June 1989); 7(1) *Focus on Law Studies* (Fall 1991); David Ray Papke and Paul T. Hayden (eds.), "Law and American Culture," 15(1) *Journal of American Culture* (Spring 1992); David L. Gunn (ed.), *The Lawyer and Popular Culture* (1993); Marc Galanter, "Predators and Parasites: Lawyer-Bashing and Civil Justice," 28 *Georgia Law Review* 633 (1994); Thomas W. Overton, "Lawyers, Light Bulbs, and Dead Snakes: The Lawyer Joke as Societal Text," 42 *UCLA Law Review* 1069 (1995). For recent fictional treatments of lawyers, see Scott Turow, John Grisham, Steve Martini, Grif Stockley, and George V. Higgins. There is an older tradition of literary criticism that looks at portrayals of law and lawyers, e.g., Robert A. Ferguson, *Law and Letters in American Culture* (1984); *Cardozo Studies in Law and Literature* (1989–); Richard H. Weisberg, *Poethics and Other Struggles of Law and Literature* (1992); Daniel H. Lowenstein, "The Failure of the Act: Conceptions of Law in *The Merchant of Venice*, *Bleak House*, *Les Misérables*, and Richard Weisberg's *Poethics*," 15 *Cardozo Law Review* 1139 (1994).

Chapter Fifteen

IS THERE "UNMET LEGAL NEED"?

In a capitalist society, legal services are distributed by the market according to fluctuations in supply and demand. But justice is not just a commodity. Both the state and the profession feel some obligation to make representation available to those who cannot afford it. This raises the threshold question of how legal services should be redistributed: quantity, content, and target population. The following article explores how sociological research might help answer that question.

INSTITUTIONS OF REPRESENTATION: CIVIL JUSTICE AND THE PUBLIC[1]
Leon H. Mayhew

A limited but informative example will illustrate the complexity of the problem of measuring the demand for legal services. What portion of the American population could benefit from legal services in connection with problems of divorce, alimony, child support, and other domestic matters? In 1967 I undertook a survey of the attitudes about and experiences with law among a random sample of the citizens of the Detroit metropolitan area. Among the previously unpublished findings of this study was the pattern of response to the query, "Have you ever wanted to go to a lawyer but didn't for some reason?" Nineteen percent of our respondents answered in the affirmative.

Of those who answered "yes," less than 6 percent said that their problem involved some aspect of domestic relations. Divorce, alimony, child support, and domestic problems accounted for about 9 percent of contacts with lawyers and ranked sixth in frequency among all categories of legal problems brought to lawyers. This pattern did not vary by the income of the respondents. Fourteen percent of the sample had seen attorneys about such matters.

Let us compare this pattern of perceived need

for legal services in domestic relations with the experience of legal aid agencies. About 40 percent of the clients of legal aid and neighborhood law offices are seeking help with domestic difficulties. From the relatively minuscule proportion of the Detroit sample who reported an unfulfilled need for legal counsel in this area, we could not easily predict that domestic matters would represent such a considerable proportion of legal aid cases.

Patterns of use reflect an interaction between the needs of the population and the social organization of the distribution of legal services. Any given legal agency, be it a private law firm, a neighborhood law office, or a civil rights commission, in part receives and in part generates a clientele. The agency has a public definition, including a reputation for various competencies and incompetencies.

Neither surveys of the experiences of the public nor the patterns of cases brought to legal agencies produce a particularly valid measure of the "legal needs" of the citizenry. Needs for legal services and opportunities for beneficial legal action cannot be enumerated as if they were so many diseases or injuries in need of treatment. Rather, we have a vast array of disputes, disorders, vulnerabilities, and wrongs, which contain an enormous potential for the generation of legal actions. Whether any given situation becomes defined as a "legal" problem, or even if so defined, makes its way to an attorney or other agency for possible aid or redress, is a consequence of the social organization of the legal system and the organization of the larger society—including shifting currents of social ideology, the available legal machinery, and the channels for bringing perceived injustices to legal agencies.

For example, less than 1 percent of the women interviewed in the Detroit study said they had ever been discriminated against by reason of their sex—this despite both a general query and repeated questions about several forms that such

34. 9 *Law & Society Review* 401 (1975). Reprinted with permission.

discrimination might have taken! A good example of the impact of the organization of the agency on the shape of the caseload is found in the experience of the Buffalo Citizen's Administrative Service. This agency achieved an interesting reversal of the usual pattern of relative exclusion of low-income and minority groups from access to representation. The BCAS operated an ombudsman-like service without any limitations on the income or race of the client. Complaints could be brought to a central office or generated in the neighborhood. By employing a staff of black and Puerto Rican "neighborhood aides" (case finders, really), the agency produced over 1,000 complaints in a little over a year; 66 percent of the clients were black, 8 percent were Puerto Rican and 60 percent received less than $5,000 per year income.

The usual survey of legal needs, the actuarial approach to estimating the demand for legal services, and the typical attack on class bias in the law all assume, apparently, that there exists a set of felt needs within a population that is experiencing difficulties of one sort or another. It is further assumed that there are professional advocates (the bar) capable of representing these needs. Given these two assumptions, it is an easy step to a third: that the problem of distribution and delivery of legal service is a problem of facilitating the access of persons experiencing legal difficulties to qualified professionals. The main barriers to access, poverty and ignorance, are usually said to derive from low social status.

I wish to propose an alternative approach. (1) There exists in the population an aggregate of interests and claims and potential problems; some are well understood by the members of the population, while others are perceived dimly or not at all. (2) The legal system is institutionally organized and includes a set of institutions of representation. An institution of representation is an organized, established, routinized method of providing advocacy, representation, or other legal services to those who have legal needs, interests, and claims. (3) Each institution of representation possesses a peculiar set of biases; it is more likely to stimulate and provide for the representation of some claims than others.

This essay is founded on a particular conception of the process of institutionalization. The word institution refers to a practice or norm that is *established*. A pattern of conduct is institutionalized when it is built into social organization— into the routine expectations, habits, interests, and relationships within a social group. In previous studies I have suggested that a norm becomes institutionalized when the following conditions are met: (1) *specific rules* or expectations governing conduct develop; (2) these rules or expectations are supported by a set of *ideological beliefs;* (3) people come to have an *interest* in conforming to these expectations; (4) agents of the collectivity come to have *access* to the conduct of those who follow or violate the norms.

Applying this analysis to legal representation, there are four conditions for the institutionalization of representation for any given right, claim, or interest:

(1) The right must be specified in such a way as to be palpable to those who possess it, experience its violation, and advocate or protect it.

(2) Such persons must also define the right as substantial, defensible, and remediable if violated.

(3) There must be a set of persons with an interest in vindicating the right and another set of persons having an interest in the skilled legal representation of the former.

(4) The two groups, let us call them the bearers and the representors, must have access to each other. Access is controlled by many factors other than income. For example, if any sphere of conduct (let us say the purchasing of homes in a given jurisdiction) is legally organized, then the participants (in this case buyers and sellers) will routinely come into contact with attorneys. Thus, transactions in real property, wills, and estates accounted for nearly half of all citizen–lawyer contact in the Detroit study.

Specification. The first condition of institutionalization is adequate specification of the right that is to be represented. Recognition of this forms one of the foundations for the militant stance within some legal assistance programs: to represent the poor is not just to give them assistance with their individual problems; it is necessary to develop rights and actions that can be used repeatedly on behalf of other potential claimants.

Specification is a necessary but not a sufficient condition of institutionalization. It is bootless, for example, to attempt to control the process of plea bargaining by specifying a series of explicit waivers of rights to be made in the presence of the trial judge. Waivers do not, in fact, ensure that false or irrelevant pleas will be excluded.

Ideology. The second condition of institutionalization is a belief among participants in the legal process that the right in question can and ought to be represented. For attorneys, the sense of what is utopian and what can be attempted is, in turn, entwined with ideas about the professional role. Adherence to a traditional professional model implies severe limitations to legal action: the attorney must tell the client what can and cannot be done and must serve the client's interests by helping and encouraging him to be realistic—to settle for the possible or the expedient. The "new breed" lawyer, who seeks reform and the redress of injustice, emphasizes the creative side of law—the possibility of specifying new rights as a foundation for new institutions.

The Detroit study produced evidence suggesting that the biggest obstacle to more use of lawyers is not inadequate income but an absence of the perception that seeing a lawyer would be useful or appropriate. Those who felt the need to see a lawyer usually found one. It is true that 19 percent of the sample reported an occasion when they wanted to see a lawyer but did not. Nevertheless, the ratio of situations wherein a lawyer was actually used to situations of perceived failure to use a lawyer was 9:1 among both low- and middle-income respondents.

For example, 35 percent of the Detroit sample reported one or more problems with government agencies. Among those who considered one of these problems to be among the two most serious they had experienced (in the realm of problems we studied), only 13 percent had consulted a lawyer. However, only 1 percent of the entire sample reported that they had wanted to see a lawyer about this type of problem but had not! This handful constitutes less than 4 percent of those who experienced problems with public organizations.

Interests. Representation of a class of legal claims requires a set of interested parties and a set of professionals with an interest in providing service. The principal source of complexity arises from the distinction between the concrete, pressing problems of individuals—problems arising from events in their daily lives—and the interests of various groups and segments of society. The interests of individuals are often less broad, abstract and long-term than the interests implied in conceptions of social justice. Citizens were asked to recount their worst problems in five possible areas of difficulty—relations in the neighborhood, landlord–tenant relations, the purchase of expensive objects, relations with public agencies (including the police), and discrimination. Respondents were asked how they had wanted to see the problem settled. Very few answered that they sought justice or the recognition of their rights (2, 0, 4, and 9 percent respectively, in the first four categories); only in discrimination cases did 31 percent seek justice. Even when given (in a closed-ended question) an opportunity to choose directly between the law and expedience in explaining the grounds of their satisfaction or dissatisfaction with the outcomes of their problems, respondents chose practical rather than legal terms by ratios varying from 1.7:1 to 7.1:1, depending on the area involved.

Access. Rights are represented only when there are channels linking the representer and the represented. The most important sociological insight into access is captured in Donald Black's distinction between reactive and proactive legal action. The various proactive approaches produce caseloads which reflect such features as the organizational capacities and ideological appeal of claimant groups who, in turn, may or may not represent the most pressing needs or the most oppressed victims. The reactive or passive approach relies upon the channels that exist within an established social structure, producing a caseload shaped by everyday troubles and the established rules of legal practice. Few cases are produced that might challenge institutionalized conceptions of the normal and feasible uses of lawyers.

The conservative features of the passively created caseload are found in the work of specially designed enforcement agencies as well. I found that blacks brought cases alleging discrimination against firms that were already integrated. Fisher

TABLE I

*Percentage of All Residents Who Wanted to but
Did Not See a Lawyer by Family Income*

INCOME	ALL RESPONDENTS	WHITE MALES ONLY
0 TO $2,999	14	12
$3,000 TO $4,999	14	10
$5,000 TO $6,999	15	32
$7,000 TO $9,999	26	26
$10,000 TO $14,999	21	21
$15,000 TO $24,999	20	14
OVER $25,000	12	18
ALL INCOME GROUPS	19	20

N = 34

and Ivie found that the vast bulk of cases brought to both traditional legal aid offices and OEO Legal Services offices in three cities were far removed from the "cutting edge of poverty law." Hallauer found that the participants in a (union-organized) prepaid legal services plan used such services primarily to resolve questions of property rights.

Given the repetition of a similar basic problem in the various components of institutionalization, we should not be surprised to find that the components interact to produce two diverse

TABLE 2

*Percentage of Respondents Who Attribute
Lack of Legal Counsel to Lack of Funds, by Income*

INCOME	ALL RESIDENTS	THOSE WANTING TO SEE LAWYER
0 TO $2,999	8	56
$3,000 TO $4,999	5	36
$5,000 TO $6,999	5	35
$7,000 TO $9,999	7	26
$10,000 TO $14,999	6	30
OVER $15,000	0	0
ALL INCOME GROUPS	5	29

N = 136

cycles of representation. On the one hand, there is a cycle of *complacency*. An ideology defining the lawyer as part of an institution for professional service calls for a passive stance, allowing the cases to come as determined by established social structure. In consequence, few cases are other than routine. Those that are not are easily perceived as outside of the established set of legal protections and can be refused as cranky or utopian. "Experience" then shows that the legal system is doing a good job.

On the other hand, there is the cycle of *controversy*. The militant lawyer seeks strategic footholds and joins (or creates) an organized network for finding important cases. In consequence, clients become involved in issues and conflicts transcending their own immediate needs and, perhaps, the obligation to provide service in regard to daily problems is slighted. Attacks upon established patterns of legal practice involve the attorney in confrontations with established power. The consequent rebuffs confirm the sense that important rights are ignored and that great segments of the population are excluded from the corridors of power.

Let us consider the equities of free legal services in connection with some data from the Detroit study. As stated earlier, 19 percent reported that they had wanted to go to a lawyer but, for some reason, had not. The distribution of respondents on this variable by income is shown in table 1. Note that the percent who wanted but did not receive legal counsel rises sharply at $7,000 per year ($5,000 for white male respondents), and is *higher* for middle-income groups than low-income groups. Table 2 shows the distribution by income for the reason given for not seeking legal advice. Note that the proportion of those wanting to see a lawyer but not doing so because of a sense of inadequate funds is highest at the poverty level, drops at low to moderate income levels, and falls to zero at $15,000. As income rises, respondents begin to attribute their failure to see a lawyer to other things: "The need just wasn't pressing enough" or "it wasn't worth the cost." Apparently, as income rises, the respondent is forced to make the calculation as to whether legal services will bear the cost. It is difficult to construct a justification for the organization of legal services around the principle of distribution by pure economic calculation in some strata and free distribution in others.

1. What explains the existing distribution of legal services? Legal services are expensive because lawyers undergo a lengthy education (and because the profession has actively sought to restrict the supply). They can only be efficiently deployed when substantial value is at stake, when capital (including human capital) is aggregated. Government, private corporations, and other collectivities do this. When do individuals aggregate capital? Contrast birth and death, marriage and divorce, leasing and buying housing, road and workplace injuries, serious and petty crimes, tourism and immigration. Do people look to law for principled vindication rather than material gain? If so, when?

2. In 1978 the Greater Manchester (England) Legal Services Committee distributed 30,000 copies of a leaflet in English, Bengali, Gujarati, Hindi, Punjabi, and Urdu through hospitals, public libraries, and advice agencies, urging accident victims to consult solicitors and offering a referral and free initial interview. A subsequent survey found that the scheme greatly increased use of the legal system by previously underrepresented groups: women, elderly, un- and underemployed, and those in the lower socioeconomic categories. It also encouraged injured in settings other than roads and workplaces—who otherwise were very unlikely to claim. Nearly two-thirds of users had never previously consulted a solicitor. Four-fifths of those consulting a solicitor ended up taking some action to obtain compensation. Only 16 percent of those doing so abandoned their claims. Both users and their solicitors were highly satisfied with the scheme.[2]

Should we emulate this experience (which resembles that of the Buffalo Citizen's Administrative Service)? Is it appropriate for public institutions to take a partisan, activist role in identifying victims and injuries? How can such schemes respond to the accusation that the population is already too litigious? What is the desirable level and mix of litigation?

3. All schemes for redistributing legal services assume there is something wrong with the market distribution. Is there? Why do we have doubts about the market here but not with respect to other goods and services? Can you construct a spectrum of goods and services, with those for which the market is ideal at one end and those for which the state or private philanthropy is ideal at the other? Where would you locate legal services?

Efforts to redistribute legal services are fairly recent: charitable legal aid began about the turn of the century and government intervention after World War II (first in Britain, then the Netherlands, and only later in the United States). How did people understand and justify the market distribution of legal services in the past? Should the state entirely displace the market? Nineteenth-century Norway and twentieth-century Cuba, Tanzania, and Mozambique "nationalized" their legal professions. How should such state lawyers allocate their services?

If we do not rely on the market, where can we find criteria for the appropriate distribution of legal services? Although champions of legal aid often advocate "equality"—drawing support from the slogan "equal justice under law"—such a goal is unattainable in a capitalist society.[3] Who should be making allocative decisions?

If we are unhappy with the distribution of legal services, why not just redistribute income and let people buy what they want with it—including legal services?

See also Alan Barton and Saul Mendlovitz, "The Experience of Injustice as a Research Problem," 13 *Journal of Legal Education* 24 (1960); Leon Mayhew and Albert J. Reiss Jr., "The Social Organization of Legal Contacts," 34 *American Sociological Review* 309 (1969); F. Raymond Marks, *The Legal Needs of the Poor: A Critical*

---

2. Hazel Genn, *Meeting Legal Needs? An Evaluation of a Scheme for Personal Injury Victims* (1982).

3. Richard L. Abel, "Socializing the Legal Profession: Can Redistributing Lawyers' Services Achieve Social Justice?" 1 *Law & Policy Quarterly* 5 (1979).

Analysis (1970). For a similar critique of a Dutch study, see John Griffiths, "The distribution of legal services in the Netherlands," 4 *British Journal of Law and Society* 260 (1977). For arguments that the legal system inevitably shapes consciousness of wrongs and decisions to claim, see William L. F. Felstiner, Richard L. Abel, and Austin Sarat, "The Emergence and Transformation of Disputes: Naming, Blaming, Claiming...," 15 *Law & Society Review* 631 (1980–81); Lynn Mather and Barbara Yngvesson, "Language, Audience, and the Transformation of Disputes," Id. 775. For early redistributive arguments, see Reginald Heber Smith, *Justice and the Poor* (1919); Eliot Cheatham, *A Lawyer When Needed* (1963); Jerome E. Carlin and Jan Howard, "Legal Representation and Class Justice," 12 *UCLA Law Review* 381 (1965); Jerome E. Carlin, Jan Howard, and Sheldon Messinger, *Civil Justice and the Poor* (1967); Marvin E. Frankel, *Justice: Commodity or Public Service* (1978). For counterarguments about the limitations of redistribution, see Geoffrey C. Hazard Jr., "Social Justice through Civil Justice," 36 *University of Chicago Law Review* 699 (1969); "Law Reforming in the Anti-Poverty Effort," 37 *University of Chicago Law Review* 242 (1970).

Mayhew's caution notwithstanding, a number of studies have explored existing patterns of lawyer use as a foundation for public or private efforts to change it. The following is the most comprehensive.

THE LEGAL NEEDS
OF THE PUBLIC[1]
Barbara A. Curran

THRESHOLD questions in assessing the legal needs of the public are: What legal problems do people encounter and how do they handle such problems? The analyses are based on experiences and behavior recounted by survey respondents in reply to inquiries about 29 problem situations covering the following subject matter areas: real property, employment, consumer, estate planning and settlement, marital, governmental, torts, constitutional violations, crimes, and juvenile matters.

The mean number of problems reported, including all multiple occurrences of any one problem type, was 4.8 per respondent. There were, however, wide differences among respondents: while 1 percent had more than 20 problems each, 8 percent reported having had none. The mean number of problems per respondent was greater among successively older age groups up to age 55. The mean number of problems reported by males was 5.2, compared to 4.5 for females. On the average, whites reported five problems to every four reported by blacks and Latinos. For each age group, the higher the amount of 1973 discretionary family income, the greater the mean number of problems reported. The relationship between incidence and education was even stronger.

Aggregate frequency of problems is but a first step in measuring incidence. Real property and serious tort matters were the most widely experienced; over 50 percent of the population had at least one real property problem, and 50 percent had at least one tort problem. Consumer matters ranked third, with 27 percent reporting at least one serious consumer problem. At the next level were problems with government, employment

---

1. Chicago: American Bar Foundation, 1989. Reprinted with permission.

problems, and marital difficulties, each of which was experienced by between 10 and 25 percent of the population. Similar proportions had encountered estate matters: 23 percent had made some kind of effort at estate planning, and 10 percent had been confronted with the death of a spouse. Less than 10 percent of the population had been faced with criminal charges or with violations of their constitutional rights or problems involving their children and juvenile authorities.

There is substantial variation in lawyer use by problem type: only 1 percent of persons faced with job discrimination consulted a lawyer about the most recent occurrence of this difficulty, compared to 30 percent of those whose wages had been garnished, 69 percent of those who were involved in divorce proceedings, and 85 percent of those undertaking estate planning. Property acquisitions had the highest resource use in the real property category (63 percent of problem-havers) as well as the highest proportion of lawyer consultations among resource users (62 percent). Job discrimination problems had the lowest resource use (15 percent of problem-havers) and the lowest lawyer use (4 percent of resource users). Estate planning with a ratio of 790 lawyer consultations per 1,000 most recent occurrences and marital problems with 670 had the highest proportions of lawyer use. These two categories far outstripped the real property category, which had the third highest ratio of lawyer use to incidence—370. Problems with governmental agencies ranked seventh among the 10 problem categories with a ratio of 150. Consumer matters tied with constitutional problems for the next to lowest ratio, 120. The lowest ranking was that involving employment difficulties, with only 40. Job discrimination matters, which accounted for 61 percent of occurrences in the employment category, had the lowest ratio, 10.

The overall ratio was 340 for women, compared to 280 for men, and 320 for whites, compared to 250 for blacks and Latinos (but in torts problems and juvenile offenses the ratio was higher for blacks and Latinos than for whites). The mean 1973 discretionary family income for problem-havers who consulted lawyers was about the same as that for those who did not consult lawyers ($10,600 versus $10,200). While higher mean income may be observed for lawyer users in real property matters, difficulties with governmental agencies, and settlement of spouse's estate, it was lower for lawyer users in torts and juvenile offenses. The two groups had substantially the same mean income for estate planning, marital matters, consumer problems, and constitutional problems. Mean education was the same for those who did and did not use lawyers, although there were differences for particular problems. For spouse's estate, marital, and constitutional matters, those consulting lawyers were better educated. For consumer, estate planning, torts, and juvenile delinquency, those consulting lawyers were less well educated.

Nearly two-thirds of respondents (64 percent) had had at least one nonbusiness professional contact with a lawyer in their lives; the mean number of cases among those who used lawyers was 2.15; only 40 percent had used lawyers more than twice, and only 7 percent more than four times. Lawyer use was less common among women than men (61 versus 68 percent), blacks and Latinos than whites (53 versus 66 percent), and black and Latina women than white women (43 versus 62 percent). At almost all ages, users had higher incomes and more education than nonusers. Multiple use was even more strongly correlated with income and education. The number of problems taken to lawyers per 1,000 population ranked in descending order from real property through estate planning, marital, estate settlement, car accidents, consumers, other torts, employment, to crimes.

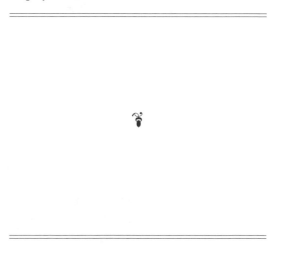

Curran updated her survey a decade later, finding some evidence that law was more "accessible" but that demographic differences remained.

1989 SURVEY OF THE PUBLIC'S USE OF LEGAL SERVICES[1]

Barbara A. Curran

AS of 1989, a larger proportion of the adult population had consulted lawyers for personal, family matters than was the case in 1974 (72 versus 64 percent). Although this was true across all income groups, income still correlated strongly with lawyer use within the previous three years (27 percent in lowest decile, 49 percent in highest quartile). The proportion of adults having wills increased from 27 to 43 percent, explaining a good part of the increase in lawyer use. The proportion ever divorced also rose (from 15 to 21 percent), although a smaller proportion of them were using lawyers to do so. The lowest decile was substantially more likely to have encountered a serious consumer problem in the previous three years (16 versus 11 percent for all income groups). Although respondents in the lowest 10 percent and highest 50 percent were more likely to report at least one problem, those having problems in the lowest 10 percent were also least likely to consult a lawyer (41 versus 66–67 percent in the top 50 percent).

DISCUSSION QUESTIONS

1. Does legal need research help to answer such questions as: whether to redistribute legal services, how much to redistribute, which services, to which people, through what mechanisms? Could any empirical research be relevant to these questions?

2. Were you surprised by infrequency with which Americans consult lawyers? How do you reconcile that with criticism of American "litigiousness"? What is the "right" frequency of usage? Are there situations where Americans use lawyers and should *not* do so? For $7.95 per month the Legal Services Plan of America offers

telephone and office consultation, letter writing and telephoning, wills, advice on government programs, and "reduced charges" for services like adoption, name change, and uncontested divorce. How would you expect this to change patterns of lawyer use? Would such changes be desirable?

Why does lawyer use sometimes vary *inversely* with income? Why do women sometimes use lawyers more than men? Racial minorities more than whites?

Were you surprised by the number of legal "problems" people recognized? Is this an accurate reflection of the "real" number of problems they encountered? If not, why is it lower or higher? What should we do to change the frequency of problem recognition or lawyer usage? Did Curran ask the right questions—are there other problems for which lawyers could be useful?

3. Do the statistics offer guidance as to which clients should be targeted? Which subject matter? How would you restructure legal services to reach those clients or deal with those subjects? Are there obstacles other than cost?

4. Suppose we started with a different question— not how people presently use lawyers but what problems people recognize, why they perceive these and not others, how they define them, and the resources they use to solve them. How relevant would legal services be to problems such as: housing, employment, education, or medical care?

SUGGESTED READING

Although the rash of "legal need" studies coincided with, and were provoked by, the expansion and transformation of government legal aid programs in the 1960s (see Chapter 18), there were a few antecedents, e.g., ABA Special Committee on the Economic Condition of the Bar, *The Economics of the Legal Profession* (1938); Charles E. Clark and Emma Corstvet, "The Lawyer and the Public: An A.A.L.S. Survey," 47 *Yale Law Journal* 1272 (1938) (both stimulated by the depression and falling demand for legal services); William F. Riley, "The Lay Opinion Survey of Iowa

---

1. Chicago: American Bar Foundation, 1977. Reprinted with permission.

Lawyers, Courts, and Laws," 33 *Journal of the American Judicature Society* 38 (1947); Iowa State Bar Association, Committee on Public Relations, *Lay Opinion of Iowa Lawyers, Courts, and Laws: A Survey of Iowa Adults* (1949); State Bar of Michigan, *Report on a Pilot Study to the State Bar of Michigan* (1949); Earl L. Koos, *The Family and the Law: The Report of a Study of Family Needs as Related to Legal Services* (1952); Missouri Bar/Prentice-Hall Survey: *A Motivational Study of Public Attitudes and Law Office Management* (1963); Preble Stolz, *The Legal Needs of the Public: A Survey Analysis* (1968).

Other studies contemporaneous with Mayhew and Curran include "The Legal Problems of the Rural Poor," 1969 *Duke Law Journal* 495; Gresham M. Sykes, "Legal Needs of the Poor in the City of Denver," 4 *Law & Society Review* 255 (1969); "Comment: Legal Services Survey Report," 49 *Nebraska Law Review* 875 (1970); Felice Levine and Elizabeth Preston, "Community Resource Orientation among Low Income Groups," 1970 *Wisconsin Law Review* 80; Barlow F. Christensen, *Lawyers for People of Moderate Means: Some Problems of Availability of Legal Services* (1970); State Bar of Texas, "Bar Attitudinal Study," 34 *Texas Bar Journal* 13, 105, 208, 304 (1971); Philadelphia Bar Association, Delivery of Legal Services Committee, *A Survey of the Delivery of Legal Services to People of Low and Middle Incomes* (1974); June Louin Tapp and Felice J. Levine, "Legal Socialization: Strategies for an Ethical Legality," 27 *Stanford Law Review* 1 (1974); Boston Bar Association, *Action Plan for Legal Services to the Poor* (1977); W. D. Popkin, "The Effect of Representation in Non-Adversary Proceedings—A Study of Three Disability Programs," 62 *Cornell Law Review* 989 (1977); Y. Avichai, "Trends in the Incidence of Legal Problems and the Use of Lawyers," 1978 *American Bar Foundation Research Journal* 289; Kenneth P. Fisher and G. S. Humphreys, "Costly Misconceptions of Law and Legal Services: The Small Business Owner vs. the Chicago Personal Property Tax," 1978 *American Bar Foundation Research Journal* 545.

Interest in prepaid legal service plans, primarily for unionized workers, spawned another set of studies, e.g., *Group Legal Services: Proceedings of the Conference on Prepaid and Group Legal-Aid Plans* (1970); Robert Paul Hallauer, "Low Income Laborers as Legal Clients: Use Patterns and Attitudes Toward Lawyers," 49 *Denver Law Journal* 169 (1972); "Shreveport Experiment in Prepaid Legal Services," 2 *Journal of Legal Studies* 223 (1973); F. Raymond Marks Jr., Robert Paul Hallauer, and Richard R. Clifton, *The Shreveport Plan: An Experiment in the Delivery of Legal Services* (1974); National Conference on Prepaid Legal Services and Beyond (1974); P. J. Murphy, R. N. Jackson and D. Chandler, *Lawyers for Laborers: The Shreveport Plan of Prepaid Legal Services After Four Years, 1971–1974* (1975); Lillian Deitch, David Weinstein, Harold S. Becker, and William Renfro, *Prepaid Legal Services: Socioeconomic Impacts* (1976).

For comparative studies in other countries, see Pauline Morris, Jeremy Cooper, and A. Byles, "Public Attitudes to Problem Definition and Problem Solving: A Pilot Study," 3 *British Journal of Social Work* 301 (1973); Brian Abel-Smith, Michael Zander, and Rosalind Brooke, *Legal Problems and the Citizen: A Study in Three London Boroughs* (1973); Pauline Morris, Richard White, and Philip Lewis, *Social Needs and Legal Action* (1974) (UK); David Otto, *Prepaid Legal Service in Alberta: The Survey of Albertans on the Matter of Prepaid Legal Service Plans* (1974); Kees Schuyt, Kees Groenendijk, and Ben Sloot, *De Weg Naar Het Recht* (The Road to Justice) (1976), "Access to the Legal System and Legal Services Research," 1977 *European Yearbook in Law and Sociology* 98 (Netherlands); Mauro Cappelletti (ed.), *Access to Justice* (4 vols.) (1978); "Surveys of Users and Non-users of Legal Services in England and Wales," in *Royal Commission on Legal Services, II Final Report* 173 (1979); "Survey of Users and Non-users of Legal Services in Northern Ireland," in Id. 705; "Legal problems and legal services: Public attitudes and experience," in *Royal Commission on Legal Services in Scotland, II Report* 39 (1980).

Chapter Sixteen

HOW DO PEOPLE GET LAWYERS AND LAWYERS GET BUSINESS?

Although lawyers openly solicited business well into the twentieth century, one of the earliest "ethical" rules promulgated by the new professional associations was a ban on advertising. When the U.S. Supreme Court finally subjected lawyers to antitrust laws in 1975, outlawing minimum fee schedules,* the stage was set to attack the rules against advertising two years later.

BATES V. STATE BAR OF ARIZONA[1]

APPELLANTS John R. Bates and Van O'Steen are attorneys licensed to practice law in the State of Arizona. As such, they are members of the appellee, the State Bar of Arizona. After admission to the bar in 1972, appellants worked as attorneys with the Maricopa County Legal Aid Society.

In March 1974, appellants left the Society and opened a law office, which they call a "legal clinic," in Phoenix. Their aim was to provide legal services at modest fees to persons of moderate income who did not qualify for governmental legal aid. In order to achieve this end, they would accept only routine matters, such as uncontested divorces, uncontested adoptions, simple personal bankruptcies, and changes of name, for which costs could be kept down by extensive use of paralegals, automatic typewriting equipment, and standardized forms and office procedures. More complicated cases, such as contested divorces, would not be accepted. Because appellants set their prices so as to have a relatively low return on each case they handled, they depended on substantial volume.

After conducting their practice in this manner for two years, appellants concluded that their

practice and clinical concept could not survive unless the availability of legal services at low cost was advertised and, in particular, fees were advertised. Consequently, in order to generate the necessary flow of business, that is, "to attract clients," appellants on February 22, 1976, placed an advertisement in the *Arizona Republic*, a daily newspaper of general circulation in the Phoenix metropolitan area…offering "legal services at very reasonable fees," and list[ing] their fees for certain services.

Appellants concede that the advertisement constituted a clear violation of Disciplinary Rule 2-101(B). "A lawyer shall not publicize himself, or his partner, or associate, or any other lawyer affiliated with him or his firm, as a lawyer through newspaper or magazine advertisements, radio or television announcements, display advertisements in the city or telephone directories or other means of commercial publicity, nor shall he authorize or permit others to do so in his behalf."

[A Special Local Administrative Committee recommended six months' suspension, which the Board of Governors reduced to one week and the Arizona Supreme Court upheld against constitutional challenge.]

The heart of the dispute before us today is whether lawyers…may constitutionally advertise the prices at which certain routine services will be performed.

1. *The Adverse Effect on Professionalism.* Appellee places particular emphasis on the adverse effects that it feels price advertising will have on the legal profession. The key to professionalism, it is argued, is the sense of pride that involvement in the discipline generates. It is claimed that price advertising will bring about commercialization, which will undermine the attorney's sense of dignity and self-worth. The hustle of the marketplace will adversely affect the profession's service orientation, and irreparably damage the delicate

---

* *Goldfarb v. Virginia State Bar,* 421 U.S. 773 (1975).

1. 433 U.S. 350 (1977).

balance between the lawyer's need to earn and his obligation selflessly to serve. Advertising is also said to erode the client's trust in his attorney: Once the client perceives that the lawyer is motivated by profit, his confidence that the attorney is acting out of a commitment to the client's welfare is jeopardized. And advertising is said to tarnish the dignified public image of the profession.

[W]e find the postulated connection between advertising and the erosion of true professionalism to be severely strained. At its core, the argument presumes that attorneys must conceal from themselves and from their clients the real-life fact that lawyers earn their livelihood at the bar. We suspect that few attorneys engage in such self-deception. And rare is the client, moreover, even one of the modest means, who enlists the aid of an attorney with the expectation that his services will be rendered free of charge. Moreover, the assertion that advertising will diminish the attorney's reputation in the community is open to question. Bankers and engineers advertise, and yet these professions are not regarded as undignified. In fact, it has been suggested that the failure of lawyers to advertise creates public disillusionment with the profession. The absence of advertising may be seen to reflect the profession's failure to reach out and serve the community: Studies reveal that many persons do not obtain counsel even when they perceive a need because of the feared price of services or because of an inability to locate a competent attorney. Indeed, cynicism with regard to the profession may be created by the fact that it long has publicly eschewed advertising, while condoning the actions of the attorney who structures his social or civic associations so as to provide contacts with potential clients. In this day, we do not belittle the person who earns his living by the strength of his arm or the force of his mind. Since the belief that lawyers are somehow "above" trade has become an anachronism, the historical foundation for the advertising restraint has crumbled.

2. *The Inherently Misleading Nature of Attorney Advertising.* It is argued that advertising of legal services inevitably will be misleading (a) because such services are so individualized with regard to content and quality as to prevent informed comparison on the basis of an advertisement, (b)

because the consumer of legal services is unable to determine in advance just what services he needs, and (c) because advertising by attorneys will highlight irrelevant factors and fail to show the relevant factor of skill.

We are not persuaded that restrained professional advertising by lawyers inevitably will be misleading. The only services that lend themselves to advertising are the routine ones: the uncontested divorce, the simple adoption, the uncontested personal bankruptcy, the change of name, and the like—the very services advertised by appellants. The appellee, State Bar itself sponsors a Legal Services Program in which the participating attorneys agree to perform services like those advertised by the appellants at standardized rates. Indeed, until the decision of this Court in *Goldfarb v. Virginia State Bar...*the Maricopa County Bar Association apparently had a schedule of suggested *minimum* fees for standard legal tasks. Advertising does not provide a complete foundation on which to select an attorney. But it seems peculiar to deny the consumer, on the ground that the information is incomplete, at least some of the relevant information needed to reach an informed decision. If the naïveté of the public will cause advertising by attorneys to be misleading, then it is the bar's role to assure that the populace is sufficiently informed as to enable it to place advertising in its proper perspective.

3. *The Adverse Effect on the Administration of Justice.* Advertising is said to have the undesirable effect of stirring up litigation. The judicial machinery is designed to serve those who feel sufficiently aggrieved to bring forward their claims. Advertising, it is argued, serves to encourage the assertion of legal rights in the courts, thereby undesirably unsettling societal repose.

But advertising by attorneys is not an unmitigated source of harm to the administration of justice. It may offer great benefits. Although advertising might increase the use of the judicial machinery, we cannot accept the notion that it is always better for a person to suffer a wrong silently than to redress it by legal action. As the [ABA] acknowledges, "the middle 70 percent of our population is not being reached or served adequately by the legal profession." Among the reasons for this underutilization is fear of the cost, and an inability to locate a suitable lawyer. Advertising is the traditional mechanism in a free-market economy for a supplier to inform a potential purchaser of the availability and terms of exchange. A rule allowing restrained advertising would be in accord with the bar's obligation to "facilitate the process of intelligent selection of lawyers, and to assist in making legal services fully available." ABA Code of Professional Responsibility EC 2-1 (1976).

4. *The Undesirable Economic Effects of Advertising.* It is claimed that advertising will increase the overhead costs of the profession, and that these costs then will be passed along to consumers in the form of increased fees. Moreover, it is claimed that the additional cost of practice will create a substantial entry barrier, deterring or preventing young attorneys from penetrating the market and entrenching the position of the Bar's established members.

These two arguments seem dubious at best. Neither distinguishes lawyers from others, and neither appears relevant to the First Amendment. The ban on advertising serves to increase the difficulty of discovering the lowest cost seller of acceptable ability. As a result, to this extent attorneys are isolated from competition, and the incentive to price competitively is reduced. Although it is true that the effect of advertising on the price of services has not been demonstrated, there is revealing evidence with regard to products; where consumers have the benefit of price advertising, retail prices often are dramatically lower than they would be without advertising. It is entirely possible that advertising will serve to reduce, not advance, the cost of legal services to the consumer.

The entry-barrier argument is equally unpersuasive. In the absence of advertising, an attorney must rely on his contacts with the community to generate a flow of business. In view of the time necessary to develop such contacts, the ban in fact serves to perpetuate the market position of established attorneys. Consideration of entry-barrier problems would urge that advertising be allowed so as to aid the new competitor in penetrating the market.

5. *The Adverse Effect of Advertising on the Qual-*

ity of Service. It is argued that the attorney may advertise a given "package" of service at a set price, and will be inclined to provide, by indiscriminate use, the standard package regardless of whether it fits the client's needs.

Restraints on advertising, however, are an ineffective way of deterring shoddy work. An attorney who is inclined to cut quality will do so regardless of the rule on advertising. And the advertisement of a standardized fee does not necessarily mean that the services offered are undesirably standardized. Indeed, the assertion that an attorney who advertises a standard fee will cut quality is substantially undermined by the fixed-fee schedule of appellee's own prepaid Legal Services Program. Even if advertising leads to the creation of "legal clinics" like that of appellants—clinics that emphasize standardized procedures for routine problems—it is possible that such clinics will improve service by reducing the likelihood of error.

6. *The Difficulties of Enforcement.* Finally, it is argued that the wholesale restriction is justified by the problems of enforcement if any other course is taken. Because the public lacks sophistication in legal matters, it may be particularly susceptible to misleading or deceptive advertising by lawyers. After-the-fact action by the consumer lured by such advertising may not provide a realistic restraint because of the inability of the layman to assess whether the service he has received meets professional standards. Thus, the vigilance of a regulatory agency will be required. But because of the numerous purveyors of services, the overseeing of advertising will be burdensome.

It is at least somewhat incongruous for the opponents of advertising to extol the virtues and altruism of the legal profession at one point, and, at another, to assert that its members will seize the opportunity to mislead and distort. We suspect that, with advertising, most lawyers will behave as they always have: They will abide by their solemn oaths to uphold the integrity and honor of their profession and of the legal system. In holding that advertising by attorneys may not be subjected to blanket suppression, and that the advertisement at issue is protected, we, of course, do not hold that advertising by attorneys may not be regulated in any way. We mention some of the clearly permissible limitations on advertising not foreclosed by our holding.

Advertising that is false, deceptive, or misleading of course is subject to restraint....the leeway for untruthful or misleading expression that has been allowed in other contexts has little force in the commercial arena. In fact, because the public lacks sophistication concerning legal services, misstatements that might be overlooked or deemed unimportant in other advertising may be found quite inappropriate in legal advertising. For example, advertising claims as to the quality of services—a matter we do not address today— are not susceptible of measurement or verification; accordingly, such claims may be so likely to be misleading as to warrant restriction. Similar objections might justify restraints on in-person solicitation. We do not foreclose the possibility that some limited supplementation, by way of warning or disclaimer or the like, might be required of even an advertisement of the kind ruled upon today so as to assure that the consumer is not misled.

As with other varieties of speech, it follows as well that there may be reasonable restrictions on the time, place, and manner of advertising. And the special problems of advertising on the electronic broadcast media will warrant special consideration.

Shortly after deciding Bates, *the Supreme Court confronted the issue of solicitation of business from individuals. The first case concerned nonprofit public interest lawyers, the second a private practitioner seeking a personal injury case.*

IN RE PRIMUS[1]

WE consider on this appeal whether a State may punish a member of its Bar who, seeking to further political and ideological goals through associational activity, including litigation, advises a lay person of her legal rights and discloses in a subsequent letter that free legal assistance is available from a nonprofit organization with which the lawyer and her associates are affiliated. Appellant, a member of the Bar of South Carolina, received a public reprimand for writing such a letter.

Appellant, Edna Smith Primus, is a lawyer practicing in Columbia, S.C. During the period in question, she was associated with the "Carolina Community Law Firm," and was an officer of and cooperating lawyer with the Columbia branch of the American Civil Liberties Union (ACLU). She received no compensation for her work on behalf of the ACLU, but was paid a retainer as a legal consultant for the South Carolina Council on Human Relations (Council), a nonprofit organization with offices in Columbia.

During the summer of 1973, local and national newspapers reported that pregnant mothers on public assistance in Aiken County, S.C., were being sterilized or threatened with sterilization as a condition of the continued receipt of medical assistance under the Medicaid program. Concerned by this development, Gary Allen, an Aiken businessman and officer of a local organization serving indigents, called the Council requesting that one of its representatives come to Aiken to address some of the women who had been sterilized. At the Council's behest, appellant, who had not known Allen previously, called him and arranged a meeting in his office in July 1973. Among those attending was Mary Etta Williams, who had been sterilized by Dr. Clovis H. Pierce after the birth of her third child. Williams and her grandmother attended the

---

1. 436 U.S. 412 (1978).

meeting because Allen, an old family friend, had invited them and because Williams wanted "[t]o see what it was all about...." At the meeting, appellant advised those present, including Williams and the other women who had been sterilized by Dr. Pierce, of their legal rights and suggested the possibility of a lawsuit.

Early in August 1973 the ACLU informed appellant that it was willing to provide representation for Aiken mothers who had been sterilized. Appellant testified that after being advised by Allen that Williams wished to institute suit against Dr. Pierce, she decided to inform Williams of the ACLU's offer of free legal representation. Shortly after receiving appellant's letter, dated August 30, 1973—the centerpiece of this litigation—Williams visited Dr. Pierce to discuss the progress of her third child who was

---

2. Written on the stationery of the Carolina Community Law Firm, the letter stated:

August 30, 1973

Mrs. Marietta Williams
347 Sumter Street
Aiken, South Carolina 29801

Dear Mrs. Williams:

You will probable [sic] remember me from talking with you at Mr. Allen's office in July about the sterilization performed on you. The American Civil Liberties Union would like to file a lawsuit on your behalf for money against the doctor who performed the operation. We will be coming to Aiken in the near future and would like to explain what is involved so you can understand what is going on.

Now I have a question to ask of you. Would you object to talking to a women's magazine about the situation in Aiken? The magazine is doing a feature story on the whole sterilization problem and wants to talk to you and others in South Carolina. If you don't mind doing this, call me collect at 254-8151 on Friday before 5:00, if you receive this letter in time. Or call me on Tuesday morning (after Labor Day) collect.

I want to assure you that this interview is being done to show what is happening to women against their wishes, and is not being done to harm you in any way. But I want you to decide, so call me collect and let me know of your decision. This practice must stop.

About the lawsuit, if you are interested, let me know, and I'll let you know when we will come down to talk to you about it. We will be coming to talk to Mrs. Waters at the same time; she has already asked the American Civil Liberties Union to file a suit on her behalf.

Sincerely,
s/Edna Smith
Edna Smith
Attorney-at-law

ill.[2] At the doctor's office, she encountered his lawyer and at the latter's request signed a release of liability in the doctor's favor. Williams showed appellant's letter to the doctor and his lawyer, and they retained a copy. She then called appellant from the doctor's office and announced her intention not to sue. There was no further communication between appellant and Williams.

Unlike the situation in *Ohralik* [see below]... appellant's act of solicitation took the form of a letter to a woman with whom appellant had discussed the possibility of seeking redress for an allegedly unconstitutional sterilization. This was not in-person solicitation for pecuniary gain. Appellant was communicating an offer of free assistance by attorneys associated with the ACLU, not an offer predicated on entitlement to a share of any monetary recovery. And her actions were undertaken to express personal political beliefs and to advance the civil-liberties objectives of the ACLU, rather than to derive financial gain. The question presented in this case is whether, in light of the values protected by the First and Fourteenth Amendments, these differences materially affect the scope of state regulation of the conduct of lawyers.

In *NAACP v. Button* [we held that] "the activities of the NAACP, its affiliates and legal staff shown on this record are modes of expression and association protected by the First and Fourteenth Amendments which Virginia may not prohibit, under its power to regulate the legal profession, as improper solicitation of legal business violative of [state law] and the Canons of Professional Ethics." [T]he record does not support the state court's effort to draw a meaningful distinction between the ACLU and the NAACP. From all that appears, the ACLU and its local chapters, much like the NAACP and its local affiliates in *Button*, "[engage] in extensive educational and lobbying activities" and "also [devote] much of [their] funds and energies to an extensive program of assisting certain kinds of litigation on behalf of [their] declared purposes." We find equally unpersuasive any suggestion that the level of constitutional scrutiny in this case should be lowered because of a possible benefit to the ACLU. It is conceded that appellant received no compensation for any of the activities in question. It is also undisputed that neither the ACLU nor any lawyer associated with it would have shared in any monetary recovery by the plaintiffs in *Walker v. Pierce.*

Contrary to appellee's suggestion, the ACLU's policy of requesting an award of counsel fees does not take this case outside the protection of *Button.* [I]n a case of this kind there are differences between counsel fees awarded by a court and traditional fee-paying arrangements which militate against a presumption that ACLU sponsorship of litigation is motivated by considerations of pecuniary gain rather than by its widely recognized goal of vindicating civil liberties. Counsel fees are awarded in the discretion of the court; awards are not drawn from the plaintiff's recovery, and are usually premised on a successful outcome; and the amounts awarded often may not correspond to fees generally obtainable in private litigation.

South Carolina's action in punishing appellant for soliciting a prospective litigant by mail, on behalf of the ACLU, must withstand the "exacting scrutiny applicable to limitations on core First Amendment rights...." The record does not support appellee's contention that undue influence, overreaching, misrepresentation, or invasion of privacy actually occurred in this case. The transmittal of this letter—as contrasted with in-person solicitation—involved no appreciable invasion of privacy; nor did it afford any significant opportunity for overreaching or coercion. Moreover, the fact that there was a written communication lessens substantially the difficulty of policing solicitation practices that do offend valid rules of professional conduct. Nor does the record permit a finding of a serious likelihood of conflict of interest or injurious lay interference with the attorney–client relationship. Admittedly, there is some potential for such conflict or interference whenever a lay organization supports any litigation.

The State's interests in preventing the "stirring up" of frivolous or vexatious litigation and minimizing commercialization of the legal profession offer no further justification for the discipline administered in this case. And considerations of undue commercialization of the legal profession are of marginal force where, as here, a nonprofit organization offers its services free of charge to individuals who may be in need of legal assistance and may lack the financial means and sophistication necessary to tap alternative sources of such aid. The State is free to fashion reasonable restrictions with respect to the time, place, and manner of solicitation by members of its Bar.

OHRALIK V. OHIO STATE BAR ASSOCIATION[1]

[After Ohralik learned that Carol McClintock, a casual acquaintance, had been injured in a car accident, he called her parents and suggested he visit her in hospital. When he stopped by their home first, at their request, they told him she had been driving the family car and been hit by an uninsured motorist, and they expressed concern that her passenger, Wanda Lou Holbert, might sue them. He explained that the automobile guest statute would preclude this and suggested they hire a lawyer. They replied that the decision was up to Carol, who was 18. At the hospital, where she was in traction, he inquired about her condition and learned that a hospital administrator was recommending a lawyer. Ohralik offered to represent her and proffered a retainer, but she said she would have to talk to her parents. He tried to see Wanda, but she had been released. He took some photographs at the accident scene, picked up a tape recorder, which he concealed under his raincoat, and returned to the McClintocks, where he re-examined their policy, whose uninsured motorist clause covered both Carol and Wanda for up to $12,500. Mrs. McClintock told him that "Wanda swore up and down she would not" sue, but Carol had phoned to say he could "go ahead" with her representation; two days later she signed a retainer. Ohralik also visited Wanda at home, concealing his tape recorder, and offered her the "little tip" that the McClintocks' policy might give up her to $12,500. She replied she really did not understand what was going on. He offered to represent her, and she said "O.K." When he telephoned her the next day, her mother sought to repudiate the retainer, saying they did not want to sue anyone and, if they did, would consult their own lawyer. He insisted the agreement was binding. A month later Wanda repeated her repudiation in writing and asked that Ohralik tell the McClintocks' insurer he was not representing her, because they would not pay her while he claimed a contingent fee. He replied he was entitled to $2,466.66, one third of his "conservative" estimate of her claim. Although Ohralik told the disciplinary hearing he would relinquish

this claim, he sued Wanda for it afterwards. Carol also fired Ohralik and was represented by another lawyer in her claim against her insurer; nevertheless she paid him one-third of the $12,500 she recovered. Both Carol and Wanda filed grievances. The disciplinary board found violations and recommended a public reprimand; the state Supreme Court increased this to indefinite suspension.]

WE have not discarded the "common-sense" distinction between speech proposing a commercial transaction, which occurs in an area traditionally subject to government regulation, and other varieties of speech. In-person solicitation by a lawyer of remunerative employment is a business transaction in which speech is an essential but subordinate component. [T]he Disciplinary Rules are said to have limited the communication of two kinds of information. First, appellant's solicitation imparted to Carol McClintock and Wanda Lou Holbert certain information about his availability and the terms of his proposed legal services. In this respect, in-person solicitation serves much the same function as the advertisement at issue in *Bates*. But there are significant differences as well. Unlike a public advertisement, which simply provides information and leaves the recipient free to act upon it or not, in-person solicitation may exert pressure and often demands an immediate response, without providing an opportunity for comparison or reflection. The aim and effect of in-person solicitation may be to provide a one-sided presentation and to encourage speedy and perhaps uninformed decision-making; there is no opportunity for intervention or counter-education by agencies of the Bar, supervisory authorities, or persons close to the solicited individual.

It also is argued that in-person solicitation may provide the solicited individual with information about his or her legal rights and remedies. In this case, appellant gave Wanda Lou a "tip" about the prospect of recovery based on the uninsured-motorist clause in the McClintocks' insurance policy, and he explained that clause and Ohio's guest statute to Carol McClintock's parents. But neither of the Disciplinary Rules here at issue prohibited appellant from communicating

43. 436 U.S. 447 (1978).

information to these young women about their legal rights and the prospects of obtaining a monetary recovery, or from recommending that they obtain counsel. DR 2-104(A) merely prohibited him from using the information as bait with which to obtain an agreement to represent them for a fee. The Rule does not prohibit a lawyer from giving unsolicited legal advice; it proscribes the acceptance of employment resulting from such advice. Appellant does not contend, and on the facts of this case could not contend, that his approaches to the two young women involved political expression or an exercise of associational freedom, "employ[ing] constitutionally privileged means of expression to secure constitutionally guaranteed civil rights." A lawyer's procurement of remunerative employment is a subject only marginally affected with First Amendment concerns.

The state interests implicated in this case are particularly strong. In addition to its general interest in protecting consumers and regulating commercial transactions, the State bears a special responsibility for maintaining standards among members of the licensed professions. "The interest of the States in regulating lawyers is especially great since lawyers are essential to the primary governmental function of administering justice, and have historically been 'officers of the courts.'" While lawyers act in part as "self-employed businessmen," they also act "as trusted agents of their clients, and as assistants to the court in search of a just solution to disputes."

As is true with respect to advertising, it appears that the ban on solicitation by lawyers originated as a rule of professional etiquette rather than as a strictly ethical rule. "[T]he rules are based in part on deeply ingrained feelings of tradition, honor, and service. Lawyers have for centuries emphasized that the promotion of justice, rather than the earning of fees, is the goal of the profession." But the fact that the original motivation behind the ban on solicitation today might be considered an insufficient justification for its perpetuation does not detract from the force of the other interests the ban continues to serve. While the Court in *Bates* determined that truthful, restrained advertising of the prices of "routine" legal services would not have an adverse

effect on the professionalism of lawyers, this was only because it found "the postulated connection between advertising and the erosion of true professionalism to be severely strained." The *Bates* Court did not question a State's interest in maintaining high standards among licensed professionals. Indeed, to the extent that the ethical standards of lawyers are linked to the service and protection of clients, they do further the goals of "true professionalism."

[A]ppellant has conceded that the State has a legitimate and indeed "compelling" interest in preventing those aspects of solicitation that involve fraud, undue influence, intimidation, overreaching, and other forms of "vexatious conduct." [That] would end this case but for his insistence that none of those evils was found to be present in his acts of solicitation. Appellant's argument misconceives the nature of the State's interest. The Rules prohibiting solicitation are prophylactic measures whose objective is the prevention of harm before it occurs. The detrimental aspects of face-to-face selling even of ordinary consumer products have been recognized and addressed by the Federal Trade Commission, and it hardly need be said that the potential for overreaching is significantly greater when a lawyer, a professional trained in the art of persuasion, personally solicits an unsophisticated, injured, or distressed lay person. Such an individual may place his trust in a lawyer, regardless of the latter's qualifications or the individual's actual need for legal representation, simply in response to persuasion under circumstances conducive to uninformed acquiescence. Although it is argued that personal solicitation is valuable because it may apprise a victim of misfortune of his legal rights, the very plight of that person not only makes him more vulnerable to influence but also may make advice all the more intrusive. Thus, under these adverse conditions the overtures of an uninvited lawyer may distress the solicited individual simply because of their obtrusiveness and the invasion of the individual's privacy, even when no other harm materializes. Under our view of the State's interest in averting harm by prohibiting solicitation in circumstances where it is likely to occur, the absence of explicit proof or findings of harm or injury is immaterial.

Having drawn a bright line between advertising and solicitation, the Supreme Court still found it necessary to respond to the repeated efforts by state bars to restrict advertising.

ZAUDERER V. OFFICE OF DISCIPLINARY COUNSEL[1]

[Seeking to augment his practice, Zauderer ran a small ad in the local Columbus, Ohio, paper in 1981 promising clients that "Full legal fee refunded if convicted of DRUNK DRIVING." When the Office of Disciplinary Counsel (ODC) of the Supreme Court of Ohio told him this violated the ban on contingent fees in criminal cases, he withdrew it immediately, promised not to accept clients who responded, and apologized. A few months later he put an ad in 36 Ohio papers offering to represent women who had used the Dalkon Shield (which it pictured), describing the potential injuries, and promising "no legal fees" if no recovery. He received more than 200 inquiries and filed suits on behalf of 106 of those responding to the ad. The ODC now charged him for both for the earlier drunk driving ad and the IUD ad, complaining that it contained illustrations and impermissible information and was not "dignified." A panel of the Board of Commissioners on Grievances and Discipline found that the drunk driving ad might deceive clients unaware that a guilty plea to a lesser offense would leave them liable to attorney's fees. It found the IUD ad objectionable because of the illustration and the failure to disclose client liability for costs even if the claim failed. The panel recommended public reprimand; the Board affirmed the findings and recommended indefinite suspension. The Supreme Court of Ohio imposed a public reprimand.]

THE advertisement's information and advice concerning the Dalkon Shield were, as the Office of Disciplinary Counsel stipulated, neither false nor deceptive.... The State's power to prohibit advertising that is "inherently misleading" thus cannot justify Ohio's decision to discipline appellant for running advertising geared to persons with a specific legal problem. It is appar-

1. 471 U.S. 626 (1985).

ent that the concerns that moved the Court in *Ohralik* are not present here. Although some sensitive souls may have found appellant's advertisement in poor taste, it can hardly be said to have invaded the privacy of those who read it. [A] printed advertisement is a means of conveying information about legal services that is more conducive to reflection and the exercise of choice on the part of the consumer than is personal solicitation by an attorney. Nor does the traditional justification for restraints on solicitation—the fear that lawyers will "stir up litigation"—justify the restriction imposed in this case. [W]e cannot endorse the proposition that a lawsuit, as such, is an evil. That our citizens have access to their civil courts is not an evil to be regretted; rather, it is an attribute of our system of justice in which we ought to take pride. The State is not entitled to interfere with that access by denying its citizens accurate information about their legal rights.

We need not...address the theoretical question whether a prophylactic rule is ever permissible in this area, for we do not believe that the State has presented a convincing case for its argument that the rule before us is necessary to the achievement of a substantial governmental interest. The State's argument proceeds from the premise that it is intrinsically difficult to distinguish advertisements containing legal advice that is false or deceptive from those that are truthful and helpful, much more so than is the case with other goods or services. This notion is belied by the facts before us: appellant's statements regarding Dalkon Shield litigation were in fact easily verifiable and completely accurate. Nor is it true that distinguishing deceptive from nondeceptive claims in advertising involving products other than legal services is a comparatively simple and straightforward process. The value of the information presented in appellant's advertising is no less than that contained in other forms of advertising—indeed, insofar as appellant's advertising tended to acquaint persons with their legal rights who might otherwise be shut off from effective access to the legal system, it was undoubtedly more valuable than many other forms of advertising.

The use of illustrations or pictures in advertisements serves important communicative functions: it attracts the attention of the audience to the advertiser's message, and it may also serve to impart information directly. Accordingly, commercial illustrations are entitled to the First Amendment protections afforded verbal commercial speech.... [A]lthough the State undoubtedly has a substantial interest in ensuring that its attorneys behave with dignity and decorum in the courtroom, we are unsure that the State's desire that attorneys maintain their dignity in their communications with the public is an interest substantial enough to justify the abridgment of their First Amendment rights. Even if that were the case, we are unpersuaded that undignified behavior would tend to recur so often as to warrant a prophylactic rule. [N]owhere does the State cite any evidence or authority of any kind for its contention that the potential abuses associated with the use of illustrations in attorneys' advertising cannot be combated by any means short of a blanket ban.

The State's application to appellant of the requirement that an attorney advertising his availability on a contingent-fee basis disclose that clients will have to pay costs even if their lawsuits are unsuccessful...easily passes muster....

SHAPERO V. KENTUCKY BAR ASSOCIATION[1]

[Shapero sought approval from the Kentucky Attorneys Advertising Commission to send a letter to prospective clients who had foreclosure suits filed against them, offering "FREE information on how you can keep your home. Call NOW, don't wait. It may surprise you what I may be able to do for you." The Commission found the letter violated a Kentucky Supreme Court rule against mailing "precipitated by a specific event...or relating to the addressee...as distinct from the general public." The court itself, however, found the rule inconsistent with *Zauderer* and replaced it with ABA Rule 7.3, which prohibited solicitation "in person, by telephone, or telegraph, by letter or other writing, or by other communication directed to a specific recipient, but does not include letters addressed...to persons not known to need legal services...."]

LIKE print advertising, petitioner's letter—and targeted, direct-mail solicitation generally—"poses much less risk of overreaching or undue influence" than does in-person solicitation. Neither mode of written communication involves "the coercive force of the personal presence of a trained advocate" or the "pressure on the potential client for an immediate yes-or-no answer to the offer of representation." Unlike the potential client with a badgering advocate breathing down his neck, the recipient of a letter and the "reader of an advertisement...can 'effectively avoid further bombardment of [his] sensibilities simply by averting [his] eyes.'" A letter, like a printed advertisement (but unlike a lawyer), can readily be put in a drawer to be considered later, ignored, or discarded. In short, both types of written solicitation "conve[y] information about legal services [by means] that [are] more conducive to reflection and the exercise of choice on the part of the consumer than is personal solicitation by an attorney." Nor does a targeted letter invade the recipient's privacy any more than does a substantively identical letter mailed at large. The invasion, if any, occurs when the lawyer discovers the recipient's legal affairs, not when he confronts the recipient with the discovery.

---

1. 486 U.S. 466 (1988).

Respondent identifies two features of the letter before us that, in its view, coalesce to convert the proposed letter into "high pressure solicitation, overbearing solicitation," which is not protected. First, respondent asserts that the letter's liberal use of underscored, uppercase letters (e.g., "Call NOW, don't wait"; "it is FREE, there is NO charge for calling") "fairly shouts at the recipient…that he should employ Shapero." Second, respondent objects that the letter contains assertions (e.g., "It may surprise you what I may be able to do for you") that "stat[e] no affirmative or objective fact," but constitute "pure salesman puffery, enticement for the unsophisticated, which commits Shapero to nothing."

A truthful and nondeceptive letter, no matter how big its type and how much it speculates can never "shou[t] at the recipient" or "gras[p] him by the lapels," as can a lawyer engaging in face-to-face solicitation. The letter simply presents no comparable risk of overreaching. And so long as the First Amendment protects the right to solicit legal business, the State may claim no substantial interest in restricting truthful and nondeceptive lawyer solicitations to those least likely to be read by the recipient.

These cases seemed to offer the state little leeway to regulate lawyer advertising. Then the Court took the further step of protecting solicitation by accountants.

EDENFIELD V. FANE[1]

RESPONDENT Scott Fane is a CPA licensed to practice in the State of Florida by the Florida Board of Accountancy. Before moving to Florida in 1985, Fane had his own accounting CPA practice in New Jersey, specializing in providing tax advice to small and medium-sized businesses. He often obtained business clients by making unsolicited telephone calls to their executives and arranging meetings to explain his services and expertise. This direct, personal, uninvited solicitation was permitted under New Jersey law.

When he moved to Florida, Fane wished to build a practice similar to his solo practice in New Jersey but was unable to do so because the Board of Accountancy had a comprehensive rule…that a CPA "shall not by any direct, in-person, uninvited solicitation solicit an engagement to perform public accounting services…where the engagement would be for a person or entity not already a client of [the CPA], unless such person or entity has invited such a communication."

The rule, according to Fane's uncontradicted submissions, presented a serious obstacle, because most businesses are willing to rely for advice on the accountants or CPAs already serving them. In Fane's experience, persuading a business to sever its existing accounting relations or alter them to include a new CPA on particular assignments requires the new CPA to contact the business and explain the advantages of a change. This entails a detailed discussion of the client's needs and the CPA's expertise, services and fees.

Fane sued the Board in the United States District Court for the Northern District of Florida, seeking declaratory and injunctive relief on the ground that the Board's anti-solicitation rule violated the First and Fourteenth Amendments. Fane alleged that but for the prohibition he would seek clients through personal solicitation and would offer fees below prevailing rates.

1. 507 U.S. 761 (1993).

In response to Fane's submissions, the Board relied on the affidavit of Louis Dooner, one of its former chairmen. Dooner concluded that the solicitation ban was necessary to preserve the independence of CPAs performing the attest function, which involves the rendering of opinions on a firm's financial statements. His premise was that a CPA who solicits clients "is obviously in need of business and may be willing to bend the rules." Dooner also suggested that the ban was needed to prevent "overreaching and vexatious conduct by the CPA."

In the commercial context, solicitation may have considerable value. Unlike many other forms of commercial expression, solicitation allows direct and spontaneous communication between buyer and seller. A seller has a strong financial incentive to educate the market and stimulate demand for his product or service, so solicitation produces more personal interchange between buyer and seller than would occur if only buyers were permitted to initiate contact. Personal interchange enables a potential buyer to meet and evaluate the person offering the product or service, and allows both parties to discuss and negotiate the desired form for the transaction or professional relation. Solicitation also enables the seller to direct his proposals toward those consumers who he has a reason to believe would be most interested in what he has to sell. For the buyer, it provides an opportunity to explore in detail the way in which a particular product or service compares to its alternatives in the market. In particular, with respect to nonstandard products like the professional services offered by CPAs, these benefits are significant.

To determine whether personal solicitation by CPAs may be proscribed under the test set forth in *Central Hudson* we must ask whether the State's interests in proscribing it are substantial; whether the challenged regulation advances these interests in a direct and material way; and whether the extent of the restriction on protected speech is in reasonable proportion to the interests served. [O]ur cases make clear that the State may ban commercial expression that is fraudulent or deceptive without further justification. But where, as with the blanket ban involved here, truthful and nonmisleading expression will be

snared along with fraudulent or deceptive commercial speech, the State must satisfy the remainder of the *Central Hudson* test by demonstrating that its restriction serves a substantial state interest and is designed in a reasonable way to accomplish that end. Likewise, the protection of potential clients' privacy is a substantial state interest.

The Board's second justification for its ban [is] the need to maintain the fact and appearance of CPA independence and to guard against conflicts of interest.... In the Board's view, solicitation compromises the independence necessary to perform the audit and attest functions, because a CPA who needs business enough to solicit clients will be prone to ethical lapses. The Board claims that even if actual misconduct does not occur, the public perception of CPA independence will be undermined if CPAs behave like ordinary commercial actors. We acknowledge that this interest is substantial. [However,] the Board has not demonstrated that, as applied in the business context, the ban on CPA solicitation advances its asserted interests in any direct and material way. It presents no studies that suggest personal solicitation of prospective business clients by CPAs creates the dangers of fraud, overreaching, or compromised independence that the Board claims to fear. [Twenty-one] States place no specific restrictions of any kind on solicitation by CPAs, and only three States besides Florida have enacted a categorical ban.

The Board directs the Court's attention to a report on CPA solicitation prepared by the American Institute of Certified Public Accountants in 1981. The Report contradicts rather than strengthens the Board's submissions. The AICPA Committee stated that it was "unaware of the existence of any empirical data supporting the theories that CPAs (a) are not independent of clients obtained by direct uninvited solicitation, or (b) do not maintain their independence in mental attitude toward those clients subjected to direct uninvited solicitation by another CPA." Louis Dooner's suggestion that solicitation of new accounts signals the need for work and invites an improper approach from the client ignores the fact that most CPA firms desire new clients. With respect to the prospect of harassment or overreaching by CPAs, the Report again acknowledges an "absence of persuasive evidence that direct uninvited solicitation by CPAs is likely to lead to false or misleading claims or oppressive conduct." It appears from the literature that a business executive who wishes to obtain a favorable but unjustified audit opinion from a CPA would be less likely to turn to a stranger who has solicited him than to pressure his existing CPA, with whom he has an ongoing, personal relation and over whom he may also have some financial leverage. [A]s applied in this context, the solicitation ban cannot be justified as a prophylactic rule. Unlike a lawyer, a CPA is not "a professional trained in the art of persuasion." A CPA's training emphasizes independence and objectivity, not advocacy. The typical client of a CPA is far less susceptible to manipulation than the young accident victim in *Ohralik*. Fane's prospective clients are sophisticated and experienced business executives who understand well the services that a CPA offers. In general, the prospective client has an existing professional relation with an accountant and so has an independent basis for evaluating the claims of a new CPA seeking professional work. The manner in which a CPA like Fane solicits business is conducive to rational and considered decision-making by the prospective client, in sharp contrast to the "uninformed acquiescence" to which the accident victims in *Ohralik* were prone. While the clients in *Ohralik* were approached at a moment of high stress and vulnerability, the clients Fane wishes to solicit meet him in their own offices at a time of their choosing. If they are unreceptive to his initial telephone solicitation, they need only terminate the call. Invasion of privacy is not a significant concern.

If a prospective client does decide to meet with Fane, there is no expectation or pressure to retain Fane on the spot; instead, he or she most often exercises caution, checking references and deliberating before deciding to hire a new CPA. Because a CPA has access to a business firm's most sensitive financial records and internal documents, retaining a new accountant is not a casual decision. The engagements Fane seeks are also long-term in nature; to the extent he engages in unpleasant, high pressure sales tactics, he can impair rather than improve his chances of obtaining an engagement or establishing a satisfactory professional relation. The importance of repeat business and referrals gives the CPA a strong incentive to act in a responsible and decorous manner when soliciting business. "Broad prophylactic rules in the area of free expression are suspect. Precision of regulation must be the touchstone in an area so closely touching our most precious freedoms." Even under the First Amendment's somewhat more forgiving standards for restrictions on commercial speech, a State may not curb protected expression without advancing a substantial governmental interest. Here, the ends sought by the State are not advanced by the speech restriction, and legitimate commercial speech is suppressed. For this reason, the Board's rule infringes upon Fane's right to speak, as guaranteed by the Constitution.

Shapero and Edenfield *seemed to open the door for attorneys to contact potential clients who might be in particular need of legal services, as long as they did not solicit business in person. If so, the Court slammed it shut two years later.*

FLORIDA BAR V.
WENT FOR IT, INC.[1]

[In late 1990, following a two-year Florida Bar study of the effects of lawyer advertising on public opinion, the state Supreme Court adopted recommended rules prohibiting lawyers from written solicitations of personal injury victims for 30 days after an accident. G. Stewart McHenry, who owned the lawyer referral service Went For It, Inc., sought to invalidate these rules. When McHenry was disbarred for unrelated reasons, another lawyer was substituted. The District Court rejected a magistrate's recommendation of summary judgment for the defendant and granted summary judgment for the plaintiff; the Court of Appeals affirmed.]

JUSTICE O'Connor [who had dissented vigorously in *Shapero*] delivered the opinion of the Court.

[W]e engage in "intermediate" scrutiny of restrictions on commercial speech. The Florida Bar asserts that it has a substantial interest in protecting the privacy and tranquility of personal injury victims and their loved ones against intrusive, unsolicited contact by lawyers. This interest obviously factors into the Bar's paramount (and repeatedly professed) objective of curbing activities that "negatively affec[t] the administration of justice." Because direct mail solicitations in the wake of accidents are perceived by the public as intrusive, the Bar argues, the reputation of the legal profession in the eyes of Floridians has suffered commensurately. The regulation, then, is an effort to protect the flagging reputations of Florida lawyers by preventing them from engaging in conduct that, the Bar maintains, "'is universally regarded as deplorable and beneath common decency because of its intrusion upon the special vulnerability and private grief of victims or their families.'"

1. 115 S. Ct. 1792 (1993).

We have little trouble crediting the Bar's interest as substantial. The Florida Bar submitted a 106-page summary of its two-year study of lawyer advertising and solicitation to the District Court. That summary contains data—both statistical and anecdotal—supporting the Bar's contentions that the Florida public views direct-mail solicitations in the immediate wake of accidents as an intrusion on privacy that reflects poorly upon the profession. As of June 1989, lawyers mailed 700,000 direct solicitations in Florida annually, 40% of which were aimed at accident victims or their survivors. A survey of Florida adults commissioned by the Bar indicated that Floridians "have negative feelings about those attorneys who use direct mail advertising." Fifty-four percent of the general population surveyed said that contacting persons concerning accidents or similar events is a violation of privacy. A random sampling of persons who received direct-mail advertising from lawyers in 1987 revealed that 45% believed that direct-mail solicitation is "designed to take advantage of gullible or unstable people"; 34% found such tactics "annoying or irritating"; 26% found it "an invasion of your privacy"; and 24% reported that it "made you angry." Significantly, 27% of direct-mail recipients reported that their regard for the legal profession and for the judicial process as a whole was "lower" as a result of receiving the direct mail.

The anecdotal record mustered by the Bar is noteworthy for its breadth and detail. With titles like "Scavenger Lawyers" (The Miami Herald, Sept. 29, 1987) and "Solicitors Out of Bounds" (St. Petersburg Times, Oct. 26, 1987), newspaper editorial pages in Florida have burgeoned with criticism of Florida lawyers who send targeted direct mail to victims shortly after accidents. The study summary also includes page upon page of excerpts from complaints of direct-mail recipients. For example, a Florida citizen described how he was "'appalled and angered by the brazen attempt'" of a law firm to solicit him by letter shortly after he was injured and his fiancée was killed in an auto accident. Another found it "'despicable and inexcusable'" that a Pensacola lawyer wrote to his mother three days after his father's funeral. Another described how she was "'astounded'" and then "'very angry'" when she received a solicitation following a minor accident. Still another described as "'beyond comprehension'" a letter his nephew's family received the day of the nephew's funeral. One citizen wrote, "'I consider the unsolicited contact from you after my child's accident to be of the rankest form of ambulance chasing and in incredibly poor taste.... I cannot begin to express with my limited vocabulary the utter contempt in which I hold you and your kind.'"

[The Court distinguished *Shapero* on three grounds: the ban was not based on privacy; it had no time dimension; and the state offered no empirical data in support. It also distinguished *Bolger*, which invalidated a federal ban on direct-mail advertising of contraceptives, holding that "[r]ecipients of objectionable mailings...may 'effectively avoid further bombardment of their sensibilities simply by averting their eyes.'" The "'short, though regular, journey from mail box to trash can...is an acceptable burden, at least so far as the Constitution is concerned.'"] Here, in contrast, the harm targeted by the Florida Bar cannot be eliminated by a brief journey to the trash can. The purpose of the 30-day targeted direct-mail ban is to forestall the outrage and irritation with the State-licensed legal profession that the practice of direct solicitation only days after accidents has engendered. The Bar is concerned not with citizens' "offense" in the abstract, but with the demonstrable detrimental effects that such "offense" has on the profession it regulates. Moreover, the harm posited by the Bar is as much a function of simple receipt of targeted solicitations within days of accidents as it is a function of the letters' contents. Throwing the letter away shortly after opening it may minimize the latter intrusion, but it does little to combat the former. The Bar's rule is reasonably well-tailored to its stated objective of eliminating targeted mailings whose type and timing are a source of distress to Floridians, distress that has caused many of them to lose respect for the legal profession. [T]he record contains considerable empirical survey information suggesting that Floridians have little difficulty finding lawyers when they need one.

Justice Kennedy, with whom Justice Stevens, Justice Souter, and Justice Ginsburg join, dissented.

I take it to be uncontroverted that when an accident results in death or injury, it is often urgent at once to investigate the occurrence, identify witnesses, and preserve evidence. Vital interests in speech and expression are, therefore, at stake when, by law, an attorney cannot direct a letter to the victim or the family explaining this simple fact and offering competent legal assistance. Meanwhile, represented and better informed parties, or parties who have been solicited in ways more sophisticated and indirect, may be at work. Indeed, these parties, either themselves or by their attorneys, investigators, and adjusters, are free to contact the unrepresented persons to gather evidence or offer settlement.

It would oversimplify to say that what we consider here is commercial speech and nothing more, for, in many instances, the banned communications may be vital to the recipients' right to petition the courts for redress of grievances. The problem the Court confronts, and cannot overcome, is our recent decision in *Shapero*. In assessing the importance of the interest in that solicitation case, we made an explicit distinction between direct in-person solicitations and direct mail solicitations. *Shapero*, like this case, involved a direct mail solicitation, and there the State recited its fears of "overreaching and undue influence." We found, however, no such dangers presented by direct mail advertising. We reasoned that "[a] letter, like a printed advertisement (but unlike a lawyer), can readily be put in a drawer to be considered later, ignored, or discarded." To avoid the controlling effect of *Shapero* in the case before us, the Court seeks to declare that a different privacy interest is implicated. As it sees the matter, the substantial concern is that victims or their families will be offended by receiving a solicitation during their grief and trauma. But we do not allow restrictions on speech to be justified on the ground that the expression might offend the listener. [I]n *Zauderer*, where we struck down a ban on attorney advertising, we held that "the mere possibility that some members of the population might find advertising...offensive cannot justify suppressing it. The same must hold true for advertising that some members of the bar might find beneath their dignity." It is only where an audience is captive that we will assure its protection from some offensive speech.

In the face of these difficulties of logic and precedent, the State and the opinion of the Court turn to a second interest: protecting the reputation and dignity of the legal profession. While disrespect will arise from an unethical or improper practice, the majority begs a most critical question by assuming that direct mail solicitations constitute such a practice. The fact is, however, that direct solicitation may serve vital purposes and promote the administration of justice, and to the extent the bar seeks to protect lawyers' reputations by preventing them from engaging in speech some deem offensive, the State is doing nothing more than manipulating the public's opinion by suppressing speech that informs us how the legal system works. [W]hat the State has offered falls well short of demonstrating that the harms it is trying to redress are real, let alone that the regulation directly and materially advances the State's interests. The parties and the Court have used the term "Summary of Record" to describe a document prepared by the Florida Bar, one of the adverse parties. This document includes no actual surveys, few indications of sample size or selection procedures, no explanations of methodology, and no discussion of excluded results. There is no description of the statistical universe or scientific framework that permits any productive use of the information the so-called Summary of Record contains. The majority describes this anecdotal matter as "noteworthy for its breadth and detail," but when examined, it is noteworthy for its incompetence. [T]he relationship between the Bar's interests and the means chosen to serve them is not a reasonable fit. The Bar's rule creates a flat ban that prohibits far more speech than necessary to serve the purported state interest. There is, moreover, simply no justification for assuming that in all or most cases an attorney's advice would be unwelcome or unnecessary when the survivors or the victim must at once begin assessing their legal and financial position in a rational manner. With regard to lesser injuries, there is little chance that for any period, much less 30 days, the victims will become distraught upon hearing from an attorney. Even as to more serious injuries, the State's

argument fails, since it must be conceded that prompt legal representation is essential where death or injury results from accidents. The accident victims who are prejudiced to vindicate the State's purported desire for more dignity in the legal profession will be the very persons who most need legal advice, for they are the victims who, because they lack education, linguistic ability, or familiarity with the legal system, are unable to seek out legal services. [T]he Court neglects the fact that this problem [of intrusiveness] is largely self-policing: Potential clients will not hire lawyers who offend them. And even if a person enters into a contract with an attorney and later regrets it, Florida, like some other States, allows clients to rescind certain contracts with attorneys within a stated time after they are executed.

It is most ironic that, for the first time since *Bates v. State Bar of Arizona*, the Court now orders a major retreat from the constitutional guarantees for commercial speech in order to shield its own profession from public criticism. Obscuring the financial aspect of the legal profession from public discussion through direct mail solicitation, at the expense of the least sophisticated members of society, is not a laudable constitutional goal. There is no authority for the proposition that the Constitution permits the State to promote the public image of the legal profession by suppressing information about the profession's business aspects.

DISCUSSION QUESTIONS

1. Is advertising appropriate for some goods and services but not others? If so, what are the differences? Should prescription drug manufacturers advertise directly to potential consumers, bypassing the doctors who must prescribe their products?[2]

We are bombarded by "personalized" letters, phone calls (including those made by computers), faxes, and people knocking on our doors. Why is that permitted for some goods and services but not others, such as law? What is wrong with a lawyer sending a wreath to a funeral parlor, offer-

2. *New York Times* §1 p17 (3.3.91), §4 p2 (4.10.94), C7 (1.9.95).

ing both condolences and legal services?[3] Why did the Supreme Court distinguish between profit and non-profit lawyering? How clear and persuasive is its commercial-noncommercial speech distinction? The Court said Ohralik could offer free advice—he just could not accept a subsequent paid retainer. Are lawyers likely to make use of this opportunity? Aside from solicitation, what else did Ohralik do wrong?

Many people are troubled by the unseemly interest of personal injury lawyers in mass torts: bus and airplane crashes, hotel fires (San Juan, Las Vegas), defective products, the egg-swapping case against UC Irvine fertility doctors, environmental disasters (Bhopal).[4] The Texas, Louisiana, and Florida bar associations collaborated in a sting operation seeking to uncover lawyers who solicited business from the victims of the ValuJet crash.[5] What is wrong with lawyers soliciting such clients? How will they assert their legal rights otherwise?

The market has spawned numerous occupations linking producers and consumers: real estate agents, travel agents, theater ticket agents, stockbrokers, agents for writers, entertainment stars, and athletes. Should we allow for-profit intermediaries between lawyers and clients? (Bar associations already provide free lawyer-referral services.) Should California permit United Reporting of San Diego to offer attorneys its "Jail Mail" service: "Using a powerful computer network, daily arrest information is compiled, sorted and selected for you based on your specific criteria. This information is converted into personalized letters on your letterhead, and sent to the home of those recently arrested...making your phone ring off the hook!"[6]

What is the difference between the letter to clients approved by the Court in *Shapero* and the communications outlawed by Florida with the Court's approval in *Went For It*? What is the difference between solicitation by accountants,

approved in *Edenfield* and that by lawyers, disapproved in *Went For It*? Could lawyers ever come within the rationale of *Edenfield*? Which of O'Connor's justifications do you find persuasive? What other restrictions on free speech would they support?

2. Critics of advertising (notably Justice O'Connor) insist it is inconsistent with professionalism. What does that mean? Civil-law professions resisted advertising longer than common law, and England longer than the United States. Were the holdouts more professional? Is the professionalism of occupations other than law impaired by advertising?

3. Why was the ban on advertising enacted in the early twentieth century? Why was it eliminated in the 1970s? Does it surprise you that the American Trial Lawyers Association prohibited members from contacting potential clients or even visiting the scene of an accident unless requested?[7] The California Trial Lawyers Association sponsored a bill that treated as presumptively false or misleading any reference to money or case outcome. The California State Bar President supported it: "Too many of the ads give the justice system a wrong image and a bad image. It really is time to do something before we reach a situation where there is high distrust of the legal profession." This legislation was provoked in part by television ads featuring a prominent personal injury lawyer with clients who declared: "Larry Parker won me $2.1 million, and I'm sure enjoying it." Yet at least four states explicitly allow client endorsements.[8] If advertising is to be regulated, who should do so? What kinds of regulation would you favor? Should there be restrictions on advertising prices? experience? win/loss ratios and recoveries? client testimonials? Should any information be mandated? O. J. Simpson's hot-line for "important leads" on the murder, offers of expert testimony, and those who wanted to write him in jail attracted as many as 100 calls a minute its first day; it also offered a message center for those "seeking legal representation from

---

3. *New York Times* B14 (6.7.91).

4. E.g., *New York Times* A1 (1.18.90) (Alton, Texas, school bus crash), B18 (9.16.94) (USAir crash in Pittsburgh, killing 132); *Los Angeles Times* A3 (7.24.95) (fertility doctors).

5. *New York Times* §1 p7 p42 (9.15.96).

6. *Los Angeles Lawyer* 10 (9.93).

7. *New York Times* B11 (5.25.90).

8. *New York Times* B11 (3.1.94); *Los Angeles Times* A3 (2.22.93), A3 (8.22.94), E1 (4.10.95).

the law offices of Robert L. Shapiro."[9] Should this be allowed? A New York personal injury lawyer advertised his telephone number as 1-800-EX-JUDGE. How is this different from renaming a Wall Street law firm Nixon, Mudge, Rose after the former Vice-President joined it?[10] After *Zauderer*, which restrictions will survive First Amendment scrutiny?

Which lawyers would you expect to favor or oppose continued limitations on advertising?[11] Which would you expect to make extensive use of advertising? The National Law Firm Marketing Association had over a thousand members in 1995. Firms produce brochures and newsletters, hire public relations officers, and issue press releases.[12] How do you expect the legal profession to change as a result of advertising?

4. How do people decide whether to consult a lawyer? Which lawyer to consult? How do these decisions differ across lawyers and clients? subject matters? How are they different from the purchase of other goods and services (including other professional services)? What are the consequences for potential clients and society of lawyer advertising?

SUGGESTED READING

Several student projects antedated or followed *Bates*, e.g., "Note: Advertising, Solicitation and the Profession's Duty to Make Legal Counsel Available," 81 *Yale Law Journal* 1181 (1972); "Comment: Bar Restrictions on Dissemination of Information about Legal Services," 22 *UCLA*

---

9. *New York Times* A4 (7.22.94).

10. *New York Times* B9 (4.3.93).

11. See, e.g., Terence Shimp and Robert Dyer, "How the Legal Profession Views Legal Service Advertising," 42(3) *Journal of Marketing* 74 (1978); Robert Dyer and Terence Shimp, "Reactions to Legal Advertising," 20(2) *Journal of Advertising Research* 43 (1980); Donald E. Stem Jr., Dante Laudadrio, and Jeff T. Israel, "The Effects of Attorney Seniority on Legal Advertising Practice and Attitudes," in Kenneth Bernhardt et al., *The Changing Marketing Environment: New Theories and Applications* (1981).

12. *New York Times* B11 (3.26.93), A17 (4.21.95).

Law Review 483 (1974); "Student Project: Attorney Advertising: *Bates'* Impact on Regulation," 29 *South Carolina Law Review* 457 (1978). While state bar associations continued to discipline lawyers for advertising, investigators documented and questioned the benefits to consumers, e.g., Jack Ladinsky, "The Traffic in Legal Services: Lawyer-Seeking Behavior and the Channeling of Clients," 11 *Law & Society Review* 207 (1976); S. R. Cox, W. C. Canby Jr., and A. C. Deserpa, *Legal Service Pricing and Advertising* (1979); Timothy J. Muris and Frederic S. McChesney, "Advertising and the Price and Quality of Legal Services: The Case of Legal Clinics," 1979 *American Bar Foundation Research Journal* 179; Larry Lang and Ronald B. Marks, "Consumer Response to Advertisements for Legal Services: An Empirical Analysis," 8 *Journal of the Academy of Marketing Science* 357 (1980); Larry T. Patterson and Robert A. Sherdlow, "Should Lawyers Advertise? A Study of Consumer Attitudes," 10 *Journal of the Academy of Marketing Science* 314 (1982); Murdock and White, "Does Legal Service Advertising Serve the Public's Interest? A Study of Lawyer Ratings and Advertising Practices," 8 *Journal of Consumer Policy* 153 (1985); see generally "Delivery of Legal Services," 11(2) *Law & Society Review* (1976).

On Justice O'Connor's claim that advertising impairs the image of lawyers, see Jeffrey M. Kallis and Dinoo J. Vanier, "Consumer Perceptions of Attorney and Legal Service Advertising: A Managerial Approach to the Delivery of Legal Services," 14 *Akron Business and Economics Review* 42 (1983); ABA Commission on Advertising, *Report on the Survey on the Image of Lawyers in Advertising* (1990); William E. Hornsby Jr. and Kurt Schimmel, "Regulating Lawyer Advertising: Public Images and the Irresistible Aristotelian Impulse," 9 *Georgetown Journal of Legal Ethics* 325 (1996). On the widespread practice of solicitation, see Kenneth J. Reichstein, "Ambulance Chasing: A Case Study of Deviation and Control within the Legal Profession," 13 *Social Problems* 3 (1965). On lawyer behavior under the new regime, see *Lawyer Advertising News*.

Chapter Seventeen

WHEN DO AND SHOULD LAWYERS RENDER PRO BONO LEGAL SERVICES?

A crucial element of the functionalist conception of professionalism is an altruistic concern for the public good. We have already seen this manifested in collective efforts to reform the legal system (see Chapter 12). Lawyers, like other professionals, have also felt an obligation to provide charitable services. In England, for instance, judges claimed authority to assign indigent accused to any barrister who happened to be in court during a hearing. In recent decades, political conservatives like President Reagan's Attorney General Edwin Meese have argued that charity could fulfill all the unmet legal needs of the public. The following article is one of the few empirical studies of which lawyers actually provide what services to which clients.

THE NO-FEE AND LOW-FEE LEGAL PRACTICE OF PRIVATE ATTORNEYS[1]
Philip R. Lochner Jr.

IN order to probe the nature of no-fee and low-fee (NF/LF) law practice, 154 lawyers practicing in one upstate New York county were interviewed. Half were solo practitioners, while a fourth belonged to firms with three or fewer lawyers and the rest to larger firms.

HOW NO-FEE AND LOW-FEE CLIENTS COME INTO CONTACT WITH ATTORNEYS

Solo Practitioners

Few claimed to have actively sought out NF/LF work on a regular basis. Since many solo practitioners had to struggle to earn a living, it should not be surprising that their interest in cases that would not generate a fee was relatively slight. As one solo practitioner said:

---

1. 9 *Law & Society Review* 431 (1975). Reprinted with permission.

I don't have time to go looking for those [no-fee and low-fee] cases. Even if I did have the time, I'd be crazy to use it that way.... My first obligation is to support my family, not to some person I don't even know.

Given the disinclination of solo practitioners to seek out NF/LF work, and given the barriers potential NF/LF clients faced in getting to an attorney, how did NF/LF cases find their way into lawyers' offices? A two-step process was involved: first, prospective NF/LF clients made contact with a class of persons to be referred to here as "intermediaries," and then the intermediaries initiated contact with attorneys. One attorney characterized the system this way:

There is always somebody in the middle.... Most of these people [who need help] don't know any [attorney] or they don't want to go to the [attorneys] they know. So they find somebody or ask a friend to recommend [an attorney].... How else'd they know who to call?

Intermediaries were the potential NF/LF client's doctor or employer, local union officer or city councilman, neighbor or friend, fellow Elk or brother-in-law. Compared to the clients themselves, attorneys described the intermediaries as being better off financially, more likely to be professionals, white-collar workers, or small businessmen, and better educated than the NF/LF clients.

Sometimes the prospective NF/LF clients had problems—not defined as legal problems at this early stage—and they turned to intermediaries for general help or advice. The intermediaries saw the problems as legal ones and persuaded the individuals to see attorneys. As one lawyer observed:

Half the time clients don't even know what's wrong. Somebody who knows me will send them over...[the intermediary] will know more about what the problem is than the client. It happens all the time.

Sometimes the prospective clients went to the intermediaries hoping they would be able to solve the problem themselves; hoping, in short, they would not be intermediaries. Only after the intermediary failed to solve the problem was an attorney's help suggested. A solo practitioner described one situation:

> This lady went to see her minister first. She wasn't sure [her marital difficulties] couldn't be worked out…. They must have tried about forty reconciliations. After a while, I guess maybe they all just got tired of trying. So this minister, he sent her to me.

Intermediaries, in turn, knew attorneys either because of some professional contact, or because of some social relationship. For example, judges very occasionally served as intermediaries. One solo practitioner described his contacts with a judge-intermediary:

> Judge [A] is an old friend. We graduated from [B law school] together and I've known him ever since. Sometimes we used to play a little golf together…so when [the judge] gets something like this [a potential no-fee or low-fee client], he'll send it on to me. He knows I'll help.

Small businessmen served as intermediaries, too, since they were likely to have professional and business ties to attorneys. Politicians also played the intermediary's role.

About half of the intermediaries were professional and business contacts of the attorneys. The other half knew attorneys in nonbusiness situations; they were the friends, neighbors, and relatives of the attorneys. One attorney recalled:

> My brother-in-law works at [a newspaper]…. He meets all sorts of people. So he'll call me up when someone needs a little help.

Ministers or doctors who knew attorneys socially also served as intermediaries. Occasionally, the attorneys might not know the intermediaries very well at all. One lawyer told of a client who called for an appointment:

> I asked him where he'd gotten my name. He said [C] had given it to him. I didn't say anything but I didn't know [C] from Adam…. I must have met him at a party or the [club].

What motivated individuals to play the intermediary role? There were some specific rewards that might have impelled the intermediaries to play this role; the psychological and personal ones that came from helping someone in trouble. In other instances the rewards might simply be getting bothersome applicants out of their lives. A solo practitioner said:

> Judge [D] gets these types all the time. They come to him because they know his name. He's too nice to kick them out the door so he sends them over here.

For still others, men in politics and business, the favors done for the prospective clients in helping them find attorneys were, no doubt, expected to be returned. Most intermediaries did no more for the prospective NF/LF clients than to offer the names of attorneys who might be helpful or to telephone an attorney to let him know that a prospective client might call. A few intermediaries saw the attorneys first, explained the problems in some detail, and made virtually all the necessary arrangements for having the prospective clients meet the attorneys. One or two even carried their role further, sitting in on conversations between attorneys and clients and following up later events. One lawyer remembered a case in which the intermediary…

> …drove the client down here and sat in on the conference. He was helpful because he'd keep on reassuring [the client] and add pieces of the story [the client] had left out.

Sometimes chains of intermediaries existed; one would phone a second who would recommend a third, who, finally, would recommend an attorney. But in the vast majority of instances, only one intermediary stood between the prospective client and the attorney.

The more common pattern, however, was that a given intermediary would direct only one or two NF/LF clients to a given solo practitioner. Some intermediaries, of course, did not come into contact with enough people who needed NF/LF legal services to have the opportunity to play the intermediary role more than once. Other intermediaries seemed to believe that they ought not to put a given attorney too often in the position of being asked to give free help. Still other intermediaries feared that they would "wear out their welcome."

Firm Attorneys

Unlike many solo practitioners, many firm attorneys sought out nonremunerative work, though many also refused to do any NF/LF work at all. Firm attorneys volunteered their services to civil liberties organizations and other groups that used their legal skills to help the disadvantaged. Other firm attorneys, though not active volunteers, were widely known in the community as willing to donate their legal skills to those who were unable to pay for them. One respondent described one such attorney:

> [E] has been around since the year one. He's got lots of money and plenty of clients. He's not young anymore and he can afford to please himself, so he takes a break every now and then and will take on an interesting case [without charge]. He's taken an interest in a good number of public issues which have wound up in court.

More typical were the firm attorneys who, like the solo practitioners, did not seek out NF/LF legal work. When one firm attorney was asked about his NF/LF clients he said:

> I don't do that work. I don't have time. The regular [paying] clients come first and there's plenty of work that needs to be done…. That's what they are paying us for…. When I have free time I spend it with my family.

Prospective NF/LF clients of firm attorneys seemed, according to the attorneys interviewed, to have a better idea of what it was that they needed, and why, than did the prospective clients of solo practitioners. As a result, intermediaries performed more limited functions and often intruded less forcefully into the client–attorney relationship.

The firm attorney intermediaries were more likely to be made up of those who knew attorneys professionally rather than socially. Older firm attorneys, partners in established firms, were likely to count among their professional acquaintances individuals who were associated with substantial institutions—corporate executives, educational administrators, and so forth. It was these institutionally situated persons who often served as intermediaries for firm attorneys.

Also considerably more evident as firm attorney intermediaries were individuals who were professional representatives of those who needed the NF/LF legal services. One firm attorney gave an example:

> [G] calls me once every couple of months…. He's president of [charitable organization]. He's always got somebody who needs help.

Lawyers themselves served as intermediaries for other lawyers. This is especially true when a specialist in one area of law came into contact with someone who needed help but whose problem demanded subject matter expertise in a different area of law.

WHY LAWYERS HELP NO-FEE AND LOW-FEE CLIENTS

Solo Practitioners

What motivated lawyers to take NF/LF cases? Occasionally, attorneys believed that the stories their clients told them showed that justice had not been done, and trying to right these wrongs was reward enough. In a few other cases, the attorneys' motives were charitable ones; that is, attorneys were motivated to take the cases less because of the nature of the wrongs done than because of the dire need of the specific client. One client had been out of work for a year and had no savings. His marriage then began to disintegrate. The attorney took the case because

> I felt sorry for the guy. He had nothing left. Everything was gone. And now his wife walks out on him. Somebody had to help the guy.

Since most NF/LF clients were not destitute, however, this charitable motive rarely accounted for the willingness of attorneys to help. Nor did political or ideological motives surface very frequently. There were instances in which attorneys claimed they were striking a blow for the poor, the dispossessed, or the downtrodden but such cases were rare for several reasons. First, the NF/LF cases that attorneys took usually could not, without taxing the imagination, be made to yield great ideological issues. Middle- and lower-middle-class clients were involved, the equities lay on both sides, and legal questions—if any—were often relatively well settled. Second, even if NF/LF cases could be seen as having ideological or political undercurrents, the lawyers interviewed were not, by and large, inclined to notice them. These lawyers saw their job as winning what they could for their particular clients, and most clients, the lawyers maintained, did not want Supreme Court cases which bore their names; they wanted specific problems solved and if a trial could be wholly avoided, so much the better. The inclination of the attorneys was, typically, to settle their NF/LF cases and get back to the important paying business.

Very few attorneys questioned took NF/LF cases because they believed that to do so was to fulfill professional obligations that all attorneys had to help those who could not afford legal services. This is not to say that the attorneys had no sense of professional obligation. But many attorneys believed work performed for the bar association or in community service fulfilled that obligation. One attorney said:

> I am on the [H] Committee of the [local] bar association. It is time-consuming and there are meetings constantly…. I'm doing my part [in fulfilling professional obligations].

Other attorneys thought their professional obligations were fulfilled by being honest and careful lawyers in their normal legal practice. One lawyer argued:

> An attorney's duty is to practice law, to represent his client the best he knows how…. Nothing is as important as that.

Indeed, more common than a sense of professional obligation as a motive for doing NF/LF work was a sense of obligation to the community or to a group to which the attorney belonged. This was especially the case among ethnic attorneys who believed they "owed" something to those with the same ethnic backgrounds. An attorney said:

> Sure I've got professional duties. [They are] to help people who are honest and hardworking, the kinds of people…who…live in the old neighborhood where I grew up. Those are the people who need my help.

If a sense of community obligation explained only a part of the attorneys' willingness to give of their services, what explained the rest? The primary reasons for taking NF/LF cases developed

out of the need to get and keep paying clients.

The central problem faced by young attorneys who tried to establish a solo practice or who joined with a law school classmate or two to open a law office was how to draw and retain clients. Some of the most common ways of drawing clients were not open to them at the very start of legal practice. Unlike successful politicians, young lawyers could not survive on the business brought by clients who were drawn by their names. Unlike other successful attorneys, young attorneys could not count on referrals by satisfied customers because, as yet, they had no customers, satisfied or otherwise. Referrals from other lawyers came only after attorneys had acquired some expertise and after they became relatively well known in the legal community. For all these reasons, young underemployed attorneys welcomed NF/LF clients: their problems gave the attorneys something to do; more important, the attorneys got chances to learn how law was practiced; it was an occasion to meet the County Clerk and the clerks in the Surrogate's Court offices; it was an occasion to learn to negotiate; it was an occasion to build professional self-confidence and to begin to become known in the legal community.

Equally important to young attorneys as a reason for taking these cases was the hope that current NF/LF clients might eventually become paying clients. This hope especially accounted for willingness to perform trivial legal tasks and small odd bits of work for younger NF/LF clients. Today's impoverished unmarried graduate student, after all, might well turn out to be tomorrow's solidly middle-class university faculty member and family man with taxes to be paid, wills to be written, and homes to be purchased. An older attorney said:

> People remember you and your helping them out. When they can do [you] a favor, they remember [you]. Some clients I can't even remember helping have come back years later with some business for me.

Other attorneys hoped for more short-term benefits from an NF/LF case. Such a case might generate some favorable publicity for the attorney, which would attract other clients. What at first appeared to be an NF/LF case might blossom into a fee-generating one as the facts unfolded. One attorney remembered an NF/LF case involved a complaint against a landlord, which, after a full investigation…

> …turned out to be a case of invasion of privacy, harassment, and defamation. The landlord settled and I got a piece of the settlement…. I'd never have guessed it when [the client] first showed up that I'd get a nickel out of the case.

Thus the ban on advertising and many other forms of self-promotion, which particularly affect young attorneys, encouraged the taking of NF/LF clients.

But what of the majority of attorneys who were middle-aged and older? They were likely to be more skilled, to have existing paying clients, and to have established reputations within the legal community. Because of these factors, their need for NF/LF clients ought to have been reduced. These older attorneys, however, also regularly took NF/LF clients primarily to aid their practice. Why was this so? In part, older attorneys saw NF/LF work as a way to create client loyalty. Attorneys cast their bread upon the waters in hope, but without firm conviction, that rewards might follow.

In many instances, the legal services provided without charge were not trivial, nor was it to be expected that the clients who were helped would later return with paying business. Even in such cases, well-established practitioners took the cases. Here the primary concern was with pleasing intermediaries. It was more than occasionally true that the NF/LF clients were referred to an attorney by intermediaries who were existing, paying clients, or who were intermediaries who had steered paying clients to the attorney in the past.

Among attorneys who performed NF/LF work primarily for clubs, civic organizations, charitable institutions, and the like, a sense of duty was sometimes evident. An attorney said:

> I worked hard for five or six years getting this [organization] going and it's doing good work…. I feel that I'm doing my duty by helping [it].

But business rather than personal motives tended most often to explain why it was that attorneys took such organizations as NF/LF clients. One hope was that doing legal chores for an organiza- tion would serve to publicize the existence of a qualified lawyer to the organization's member- ship. Doing NF/LF work, then, became a form of advertising. It was also hoped that if some NF/LF work was performed for these organiza- tions then, at some later date when the organiza- tions needed legal services for which they were willing and able to pay, the organizations would turn to the attorneys who had done favors for them in the past. Attorneys would also take orga- nizations as NF/LF clients to please paying clients or other intermediaries who had put the attorneys and organizations into contact.

Sometimes, however, attorneys became con- vinced that no paying business was likely to be generated by organizations that had been pro- vided NF/LF legal services. Even in such cases, attorneys might continue to serve the organiza- tion without fee since, once the organizations and their leaders began to expect attorneys to provide free services, and once attorneys had begun to receive social rewards in recognition for their help, they could not refuse to continue to work without a fee without upsetting existing social relationships and cutting off important nonmonetary benefits. As one attorney put it:

> There's no way I could stop [helping the organiza- tional client for free]…. I'd have to quit the [organi- zation] in shame.

An additional reason for doing NF/LF work arose from the nature of office-management practices and of legal work. Though attorneys often spend much of their time on relatively major pieces of legal work—tort cases, divorces, and so forth—they also work at many lesser tasks. These latter problems, in many instances narrow and specific, could often be solved in a few moments' time. Sometimes, cases that at first looked as though they might involve major liti- gation later collapsed into rather minor concerns. In one case, for example, a client came to an attorney after having been served with a sum- mons and complaint in an action arising out of an employment relationship. A major piece of liti- gation appeared to be in the offing. Before the day was out, however, the attorney had discov- ered that the statute of limitations had run and, shortly thereafter, the suit was dropped.

These kinds of problems—ones that could be dealt with in a few minutes or looked major at the outset but turned out not to be problems at all— were very often the kinds that became NF/LF work. Frequently in such cases lawyers would not bill clients, in part, because it was not worth the effort to do so. An attorney said:

> If I billed every time I gave somebody a piece of advice, I'd be doing nothing but sending bills. I'd never have time for anything else.

Firm Attorneys

Unlike young solo practitioners, young firm associates had enough paying legal work to keep them busy. Thus, there were no immediate economic advantages to such associates in working for NF/LF clients. Furthermore, it was intrafirm reputation and not reputation within the legal community that was important in associates' careers at their earlier stages. Thus, there was no need to take NF/LF cases to build a reputation. Associates, indeed, were wary of taking on too much NF/LF work for fear of seeming "dilettantish" in the eyes of seniors in their firms. In spite of these conditions, young firm attorneys worked on NF/LF cases. This was because partners occasionally accepted NF/LF clients and asked associates to do the work. In such instances, of course, the associates' motives for doing the work—a desire to please a superior—might be quite different from the motives that led the partners to accept the cases in the first place. In general, if partners accepted the cases but expected the associates to do the work, the cases were likely to have been accepted to please clients or other intermediaries. If the partners both accepted the cases and worked on them themselves, the cases were likely to have been accepted for reasons personal to partners: outrage at a miscarriage of justice, the desire to do a good deed, and so forth.

WHO ARE THEN NO-FEE AND LOW-FEE CLIENTS?

In order to be helped by an intermediary to make contact with an attorney, prospective NF/LF clients had, first, to know the sorts of persons who were likely to be intermediaries. Intermediaries were characterized by the attorneys interviewed as being mostly middle-class persons. The social contacts of such persons were likely to be limited to those who, like themselves, were relatively well-educated, middle- and lower-class men and women. This class makeup of the intermediary group may explain the reasons why NF/LF clients were largely middle-class persons. As one attorney nicely summarized it:

> I do a good deal of [no-fee or low-fee] work.... I've never had a [no-fee or low-fee] client on welfare.... [My no-fee and low-fee clients aren't] poor or anything, but they're not rich either; they're in-between.

With the exception of the two black attorneys interviewed, no solo practitioners had more than a very occasional black NF/LF client, despite the presence in the county of a substantial black community. The intermediary system, in fact, was not likely to promote contacts between attorneys and a variety of individuals and groups with needs for NF/LF legal services, such as the relatively young and the relatively old.

NF/LF legal services offered by solo practitioners were provided, by and large, to members of the middle class. The attorneys interviewed characterized these individuals as high school or junior college educated persons who held clerical jobs or jobs as skilled or unskilled manual laborers. Often they had a steady income but no savings out of which a lawyer might be paid. Rather than serving the chronically poor, solo practitioners served the temporarily disadvantaged. One case might serve as an example: a construction worker who had been out of work for months, and who had made several large credit purchases while employed, found himself hounded by one creditor and threatened with repossession by another. He was referred by a friend to a lawyer who quickly and easily worked out an arrangement with the creditors. No attorney's fee was charged.

Solo practitioners also served some who were currently poor but whose long-range economic prospects were excellent. In one case an attorney charged a fraction of the going rate for an uncontested divorce. The couple had been married for only a year and had no children. The wife was working and the husband was just finishing graduate school. Both were likely to find well-paying careers in the long run but neither had much money currently available to pay legal fees.

Solo practitioners also served those in the ethnic communities. The central city had relatively homogeneous, and extensive, Italian and Polish communities, as well as other smaller ethnic enclaves, and many solo practitioners had come from these communities. Connections between these attorneys and their ethnic communities often remained strong over long periods of time; early ties arising out of childhood, family, and neighborhood friendships were frequently reinforced by memberships in fraternal organizations and by political associations. Ethnic intermediaries often directed ethnic NF/LF clients to attorneys of the same ethnic origin.

The NF/LF clients served by solo practitioners included organizations as well as individuals. It is important to realize, however, that work for such organizations was performed only for organizations with middle-class memberships and not for organizations that might represent the poor or the disadvantaged. Solo practitioners did NF/LF legal work for clubs, fraternal organizations, and so forth because they were members and knew other members.

THE NATURE OF THE NO-FEE AND LOW-FEE CASE

What kinds of problems did NF/LF clients bring to their attorneys? About one-third, the single largest category, involved matrimonial issues: divorces, separations, adoptions, child-custody questions, maintenance and support orders, and so forth. The second most common type of problems—about 15 percent of the total—involved debtor–creditor disputes: disputes with creditors about how much was owed, with banks about loans, with merchants about whether or not various items had been bought or paid for, with repairmen about charges or repairs or the quality of work done, and so on. About 15 percent concerned landlord–tenant questions; whether the rent had been paid on or before the date penalties began to run, what repairs were promised and/or delivered, what charges could be made for leaving the premises in an untidy condition, and what obligations there were for keeping common halls

clean or lawns mowed. About 10 percent involved criminal actions: shoplifting, assault, theft, dealing in stolen property, and the like. The remaining 25 percent included a variety of legal subjects: wills and estates, contracts, real property, naturalization and immigration, and taxation.

Some types of problems were conspicuous by their absence. Because attorneys were willing to take tort cases on a contingency-fee basis (and willing to absorb whatever cash outlay was needed) virtually no tort cases were taken by attorneys on an NF/LF basis. There were, however, some minor injury cases in which attorneys collected very small sums for their clients—$50 or $75—and took no-fee, contingent or otherwise, for doing so. Another type of problem infrequently reported was the dispute with an official or governmental body. The relative absence of civil rights and civil liberties problems might be explained by the class origins of NF/LF clients. In summary, the types of problems dealt with for NF/LF clients did not differ significantly, at least according to the testimony of the lawyers involved, from the types of problems individual paying clients brought to their offices.

The legal problems of NF/LF clients were usually settled with dispatch. Over 40 percent of the problems took five or fewer hours for the attorneys to deal with and another 20 percent took fewer than ten. Attorneys were virtually unanimous in claiming that less time was invested in dealing with the legal problems of NF/LF clients than in the problems of paying clients. This may be in part because lawyers also were disinclined to take very difficult or highly complex cases on an NF/LF basis.

In only a very few cases did lawyers institute legal action in the name of an NF/LF client, and in no cases did disputes go to trial. The suits initiated for NF/LF clients were filed not to obtain a decision on the merits but to put clients in better bargaining positions. As one attorney noted:

> If you slap a summons on the other party, it scares the hell out of them, unless they've been around.... then the other guy has to go to a lawyer, and then he begins to see what it's going to cost to be stubborn.

Attorneys did, occasionally, make brief, pro forma appearances before judges in divorce proceedings, for example, but even these were exceptional. There was an utter absence of those two stalwarts of recent writings about legal practice for those who cannot pay for legal services—the test case or the class action. Little of the attorneys' time was spent in legal research. Older attorneys especially tended to rely for the legal learning necessary to settle a question on their general knowledge, or on consultations with fellow attorneys experienced in a given field. Fact research was one task on which the attorneys spent considerably more time. Lawyers also spent a good deal of time advising NF/LF clients. At times the advice was explicitly legal, but much advice was of a more personal nature. One attorney, for example, attempted to persuade his client to try a reconciliation with a spouse she had just deserted. The advice had legal implications, of course, but it was also advice based on human considerations and the attorney's belief that this was the advice "the client wanted to hear." Attorneys also spent time educating clients to realities they might have been unwilling to face. One attorney noted, "There are times when you can't do anything and the guy is just going to have to take it…. You have to let him know."

One type of work, however, was more likely to be performed, or performed earlier in the game, than it was for paying clients—negotiating. The first impulse of many attorneys, given an NF/LF client with a problem, was to go to the other party and try to negotiate a solution. Often only a phone call, a meeting, and a brief conversation were needed to reach a settlement. Rarely did the negotiations involve more than the two parties' attorneys, and, not infrequently, they involved only the attorney of the NF/LF client and the other party. One lawyer pointed out:

> Bargaining is the fastest way to get a case finished, once you know what the problem is. Everyone is willing to talk about the problem, and once you've got them talking you can begin to say, "All right, let's forget about whose fault it is. If he does this, now, will you do that?" Sometimes you're dealing for both sides, just trying to find a middle ground.

Sometimes attorneys were needed not because of the law they knew or because of their bargaining skills but so that the clients could impress on the other parties how seriously the clients felt about the issues at stake.

Few resources other than the attorney's time were needed to deal with the legal problems of NF/LF clients. In 40 percent of the instances the attorneys incurred no out-of-pocket expenses—such as filing fees, copying costs, travel, and so forth—on behalf of NF/LF clients, nor did they even consume any secretarial time. And, in half the cases where such additional costs were incurred, their estimated value was less than 25 dollars.

THE QUALITY OF NO-FEE AND LOW-FEE LEGAL SERVICES

In some cases, the attorneys serving such clients would not extend themselves very far. Attorneys who were negotiating on behalf of NF/LF clients, for example, might be likely to accept a settlement that was not the maximum that could have been attained if the attorneys were willing to delay, harass, and, in general, use all the other tactics available in law. Furthermore, the busier an attorney was with his paying clients, the more inclined he was to give short shrift to the problems of NF/LF clients. One attorney put it this way:

> You do what you can for [NF/LF clients]…. It will depend on how much time you've got, what else you've got [to do]…how important [the problem] is.

There were also factors that pushed attorneys to expend extra effort on behalf of their NF/LF clients. These included the attorneys' needs for self-development, the clients' potential for becoming paying clients in the future, and the attorneys' concerns for their reputations. More important than any of these factors in persuading attorneys to do more than the minimum work necessary for NF/LF clients, however, was the importance to the attorneys of their networks of intermediaries.

Institutional NF/LF clients tended to be better served than individual NF/LF clients. The reasons for this appeared to be two-fold. First, institutional NF/LF clients typically came to attorneys for legal help primarily in non-adversarial situations. Furthermore, the work they brought was likely to be relatively uncomplicated. In one case in which a church asked an attorney to close a land transaction, the attorney needed only to make sure the papers were properly made out, the various filings were made, and so forth. No complex judgments or extra research efforts were required. Thus, the attorney was able to provide his best efforts at a relatively low cost to himself. Second, and more important, since the attorneys were usually members of the organizations for which they were providing NF/LF services, they had added reasons for not wanting things to go badly. Not only could they lose the respect of professional colleagues or damage their intermediary networks, but also they could damage their relationships with fellow members of the organizations which they were helping.

Lochner's article demonstrates that the existing incentive structure provides limited amounts of service, in specific kinds of cases, to only certain clients. In recent decades, the profession has debated whether all lawyers should be obligated to provide a minimum amount of pro bono services and, if so, how that obligation should be defined and enforced.

YOUR MONEY OR YOUR LIFE: A MODEST PROPOSAL FOR MANDATORY PRO BONO SERVICES[1]
Mary Coombs

THE objections to mandatory pro bono fall into several categories. First, some contend that there is no substantial need for more pro bono legal services for the poor. Second, there are the constitutional/policy objections that it is wrong to require lawyers to do legal work they do not choose to do: opponents have asserted that it violates the First, Thirteenth, and Fourteenth Amendments. Third, there are equality arguments. Some complain that the obligation falls disproportionately on certain lawyers, such as busy solo practitioners. Others object because certain categories of lawyers, such as corporate lawyers or government lawyers, are excluded. Although including them is very impractical, excluding them may seem unfair to the lawyers who are burdened. Fourth, opponents contend that mandatory pro bono may harm potential clients because most lawyers are untrained in the areas of law relevant to poor peoples' needs. Mandatory pro bono work, then, may result in a higher incidence of malpractice. Alternatively, it is claimed that it is inefficient to require every lawyer to become proficient in such arcane areas as public benefits or eviction law in order to do a modest amount of legal work for the poor. Finally, there are arguments that mandatory pro bono is inconsistent with the values underlying voluntary pro bono: it erodes the sense of volunteerism and the psychic value to the lawyer while reducing the legal services available for other good causes not included within the scope of the mandatory pro bono program.

1. 3 *Boston University Public Interest Law Journal* 215 (1993). Reprinted with permission.

The objections mentioned above seem largely unpersuasive. Every study has shown that the poor have significant unmet legal needs. Similarly, the simultaneous general public obligation to provide legal services to the poor does not vitiate the particular pragmatic or moral justifications for requiring lawyers to do so. One could argue that the need for legal services, like the need for food or housing or medical care for the poor, is a general social obligation to be met by taxes. Certainly, such general societal subsidization of the legal needs of the poor is appropriate. It seems extremely unlikely, however, that the government will fully fund legal services.

The central feature of this proposal is a monetary opt-out provision designed to make the lawyer's choice between time (20 hours per year) and money as unconstrained as possible. Its primary benefits are the freedom it provides to lawyers (compared to other mandatory pro bono plans) and the value it provides to beneficiaries. Simultaneously, the poor will benefit more under a plan with a buy-out option than under a straight time obligation, because they will receive either work performed by those who choose to do such work or an equal or larger quantity of services from public interest lawyers funded through monetary contributions. The funds generated by attorneys exercising the monetary option can support other lawyers—providing more legal services—in moderately paid full-time legal services work. Assume, for example, that it costs $50,000 a year to support a beginning legal services lawyer ($25,000 salary and $25,000 to cover overhead expenses) who can provide 2,000 hours in legal work for the poor. The monetary contributions of 12.5 lawyers earning $200 per hour would support that lawyer, though they would have directly provided only 250 hours of such services.

The desirability of a "time-or-money" form of pro bono is particularly evident when we examine the constitutional objections raised against mandatory pro bono. Opponents have suggested three constitutional problems, that it: amounts to involuntary servitude prohibited by the Thirteenth Amendment; is a taking without compensation under the Fourteenth Amendment; and is a forced expression of belief (in the value of pro bono causes) contrary to an individual's conscience forbidden by the First Amendment. Whatever validity these argu-

ments might have in the context of a different program, they are inapplicable to a time-or-money option. Since the obligee is wholly free to provide money, the Thirteenth Amendment argument collapses of its own weight. The notion that mandatory pro bono is a taking is equally untenable. In effect, it is a tax on a profession, a variant on traditional income taxes and franchise fees, with a service alternative to the monetary obligation. Finally, mandatory pro bono, especially in the form proposed here, does not require the lawyer to profess or support any particular belief and thus raises no First Amendment problem. The obligation can be met by providing any form of legal work to indigent persons or monetary support to any organization doing such work. It is difficult to imagine anyone claiming that she has a belief system that is offended by providing any legal assistance to any group of poor people.

This proposal also provides the best response to the pragmatic objection that some lawyers may lack the competence to do poverty law and that forcing them to do so will induce malpractice. It seems unlikely that many attorneys lack any skills and knowledge that can be applied to the legal problems of the poor. Corporate and tax specialists, for example, can help structure nonprofit organizations designed to provide food, housing, or other services to the poor. Whatever plausibility such an argument might otherwise have, however, wholly evaporates when, as here, an attorney who is unable or unwilling to develop the competence to carry out some form of legal work for the poor can simply choose the monetary option. The monetary option also allows the imposition of the obligation on various categories of lawyers who may find it difficult or impossible to provide direct legal services, such as in-house corporate counsel, government attorneys, legal aid lawyers, and law professors. This proposal could also permit the extension of the pro bono obligation to legal services attorneys; the employing organization would be free to recognize the money contributed by a general increase in compensation levels and/or to structure their employees' workload specifically to include work designated to meet the pro bono obligation.

The proposal advocated here also differs from many by restricting eligible mandatory pro bono work to legal services to the poor, while simultaneously imposing only a quite modest obligation of 20 hours per year. This aspect of the proposal similarly is designed to meet or reduce the force of objections to any mandatory pro bono scheme, often put forth by those who are themselves seriously committed to such work, that it may negatively affect existing, voluntary pro bono. First, it might reduce the psychic value to the lawyer from having volunteered her services. Second, it might reduce the supply of pro bono legal services to causes and individuals not within the scope of the mandatory program. In considering the costs of "diverting" lawyers from other pro bono work, we must distinguish between genuine pro bono work directed toward causes other than the legal needs of the poor and activities claimed as pro bono but arguably "mislabeled." Legal work done without charge for one's relatives or friends may be a normal and appropriate part of a lawyer's workload, but it is not particularly deserving of the moral approbation that is the current "payment" for pro bono work nor legitimately a basis for the Bar's institutional claim of commitment to public interest. Similarly, unpaid legal work, i.e., for the local symphony or community chest, is more appropriately accounted as "business development." Potentially more troubling is the effect of a mandatory pro bono proposal, such as this one, on traditional pro bono legal work that would fall outside its boundaries, such as most of the environmental, international human rights and reproductive rights litigation that has been a staple of large-firm pro bono practice.

Because the level is set low, it is relatively easier for those who wish to volunteer, and especially for those who wish to volunteer for causes not included in the mandatory program, to do so with additional time. A significant portion of the legal community—what may be called the volunteers—currently provides, in voluntary pro bono work, closer to 40 hours per year or more. Meanwhile, another large group does little or nothing. By setting the mandatory level between these two peaks, we can significantly increase available legal services from the group that has been undercontributing, while limiting the negative consequences on the work currently being done by the volunteers.

There is no apparent reason not to permit a law firm to pool its obligation, arranging to have one or a small group of its attorneys do the legal work required of all. The monetary equivalent to the 20-hour-per-year obligation is determined based on an attorney's own hourly rate. If obligations are pooled, they should be measured in dollars and then translated back into a time obligation. That time obligation, in turn, should be measured by the time value of the attorney doing the pro bono work on behalf of the firm. It is more dubious whether groups should be permitted to form solely for the purpose of pooling mandatory pro bono obligations. One likely benefit would be to permit an attorney not associated with a large firm to take on a substantial pro bono project by, in effect, selling his additional pro bono time to other attorneys. However, such a desire can frequently be accommodated by provisions for a carry-forward of excess pro bono hours.

DISCUSSION QUESTIONS

1. What are the arguments in favor of a pro bono obligation for lawyers? Why is it felt more now than in the past? Why does it seem to be of greater concern in the United States than in other countries? Is there a constitutional problem with compelling such service?[2] If so, is it solved by Coombs's "buy-out" alternative?

How do lawyers compare with other professions in their sense and performance of this obligation? Consider the ebb and flow of charitable work by doctors.[3] Is there a relationship between the sense of obligation and the state's willingness to provide minimal levels of service? Lochner observed that some lawyers took pro bono cases because they could not advertise; would you expect the spread of advertising to reduce the amount of service rendered?

How do our charitable expectations about professions and occupations differ? Do we expect banks to give away money, supermarkets or restaurants to give away food? Do our expectations vary with disparities and aggregations of wealth? Should national service be expected or required of everyone—in school or soon after graduation?[4]

2. See, e.g., letters to the editor in *New York Times* A14 (5.18.90).

3. *New York Times* B7 (1.31.89).

4. See William F. Buckley Jr., *Gratitude* (1990).

2. What are the motivations for individual lawyers or law firms to provide pro bono services? Do law students ask about opportunities to do pro bono work when they interview? Did they ever do so? If so, why then and not now? What explains the level of services rendered by different lawyers? How could it be increased? Which clients (both individuals and collectivities) receive such services? How could the client base be expanded and diversified? What functions do lawyers perform? How could they be changed? What is the quality of services rendered? How could it be improved? In what kinds of matters is service rendered? How could that be diversified? Should the role of intermediaries be institutionalized? As we saw in Chapter 16, the legal profession has outlawed commercial intermediaries between lawyers and paying clients.

Compare pro bono legal services along each of these dimensions with state-funded legal aid and charitably funded public interest law, described in the next two chapters. How do their incentive structures and motivations differ? Until South Africa abolished the death penalty in the 1990s, most of those charged with capital offenses were represented "pro deo" (the civil-law equivalent of pro bono) by recently qualified advocates handling their first cases. Should death penalty defense in the United States be handled pro bono?[5]

3. What is the best way of structuring lawyers' pro bono obligation? Should it be mandatory or hortatory? Bar associations with the power to coerce have restricted themselves to exhortation; a few voluntary associations have required service of members; a few local judges have required it of local lawyers.[6] If we rely on moral suasion, how can it be maximized? What is the effect of bar associations and the legal press publishing the amounts contributed by law firms?[7] Should lawyers have a choice between service and payment? Would it be better to levy a tax on lawyer income, or a sales tax on legal services, and use

the funds to support legal aid? Should law students be required to perform public service as a condition of graduation? Should law graduates be required to do an internship in a public interest setting as a condition of entry to the profession? How should the quantity be determined? Which lawyers should be included? Should firms be able to pool and reallocate their obligations? How should the obligation be enforced? What kinds of service should satisfy it? How can quality be monitored and maintained?

SUGGESTED READING

Although lawyers have always performed some pro bono services, the profession began to discuss the obligation collectively and experiment with ways to fulfill it in the late 1960s. See, e.g., "Note: Structuring the Public Service Efforts of Private Law Firms," 84 *Harvard Law Review* 410 (1970); Dorothy L. Maddi and Frederic R. Merrill, *The Private Practicing Bar and Legal Services for Low-Income People* (1971); Douglas Rosenthal, Robert A. Kagan, and Debra Quatrone, *Volunteer Attorneys and Legal Services: New York's Community Law Office Program* (1971); F. Raymond Marks, Kirk Leswing, and Barbara Fortinsky, *The Lawyer, the Public, and Professional Responsibility* (1972); Alan Ashman, *The New Private Practice: A Study of Piper & Marbury's Neighborhood Law Office* (1972); Joel F. Handler, Ellen Jane Hollingsworth, and Howard S. Erlanger, *Lawyers and the Pursuit of Legal Rights* chapters 5–6 (1978); Richard L. Abel (ed.), "Lawyers and the Power to Change," 7(1) *Law & Policy* (1985). For empirical confirmation that little has changed since Lochner's study, see D. Weston Darby, "It's About Time: A Survey of Lawyers' Timekeeping Practices," 4(3) *Legal Economics* 39 (fall 1978); Carroll Seron, *The Business of Practicing Law: The Work Lives of Solo and Small-Firm Attorneys* chapter 8 (1996). There is a large prescriptive literature on mandatory pro bono, on which Coombs draws, e.g., David Luban, "A Workable Plan for Mandatory Pro Bono," 5(1) *Report from the Center for Philosophy & Public Policy* 10 (Winter 1985); Roger C. Cramton, Mandatory Pro Bono," 19 *Hofstra Law Review* 1113 (1991); Robert A. Katzmann, ed., *The Law Firm and the Public Good* (1995).

---

5. See *New York Times* A13 (12.30.94).

6. E.g., Knoxville, Tennessee, *New York Times* B10 (1.17.92).

7. E.g., the *American Lawyer*, see *Los Angeles Times* E5 (8.2.90).

Chapter Eighteen

REPRESENTING THE POOR

Legal aid programs emerged in the United States as efforts by municipalities and philanthropies to assist recent immigrants in the late nineteenth century. They remained small, and timid, until Lyndon Johnson's War on Poverty involved the federal government in 1965, expanding national expenditure from less than $5 million to more than $300 million at the end of the Carter Administration. The following excerpt describes the experience of being a legal services lawyer; elsewhere the book contrasts that with legal aid before 1965.

POOR PEOPLE'S LAWYERS IN TRANSITION[1]
Jack Katz

POOR PEOPLE'S CONFLICTS
AND LAWYERS' WORK PROBLEMS

Confinement to Proximate Social Environment

THE setting for civil legal work for the poor contrasts dramatically with the setting in which lawyers work for wealthy corporate and individual clients. Whatever their own inclinations and abilities, lawyers for wealthy clients are expected, assisted, and at times formally directed to treat their work as significant. This expectational environment has its fundamental source not in client preferences but in the social networks that attend wealth and other sources of power. Conversely, lawyers for the poor, regardless of their competence and values, confront an everyday environment that treats their work as routine by assuming, suggesting, and at times demanding that it ought to be regarded as insignificant. Lawyers for large corporations, unions, and government agencies represent representatives. The lawyer's actions will signify broadly; they will ramify in implications throughout the social relations that create their

clients' social status. More important, so will the lawyer's inaction. In some of the most remunerative civil legal practices, it is unusually easy to treat work as unusually difficult. Lawyers for clients with significant interests often create a collegial environment in which each encourages the other to see complexity in the situation at hand. There is typically no elaborate social network attending problems when they are presented to legal assistance lawyers.

The poor seek out lawyers for assistance with personal troubles that are often in or near a crisis state: having been denied public aid, having received an eviction notice, having had utilities shut off, having had a violent domestic argument. Often the situation is within or at the edge of litigation, the client with court papers or "final" dunning letters in hand. This context of personal conflict initially gives the work of the legal assistance lawyer a very local setting. Poor clients may insist their problems are of unsurpassed importance, and their lawyers may agree; but the latter will not be urged to that opinion by adverse parties and opposing counsel. Adversaries are not likely to treat conflicts with the poor as worth much investment. Courts often follow suit. When legal services lawyers began bringing unprecedented questions of law to state courts, they found judges dominated by local perspectives and geared to summary treatments. Dramatic conflicts sometimes followed. As indicated in the following report by a Chicago Legal Services lawyer of his experience in 1968, the reason for judicial hostility may not be antipathy to the poor so much as an insistence on everyday predictability.

> I went into [Judge] Hermes' court with a motion, not a long one but the longest one he had on his desk, and he rolled it up into a ball and threw it at me. *Literally?* Yes. A hundred lawyers in the courtroom were laughing. They would decide things without ever reading them. He just wasn't going to do that kind of work in his court. Later, when I came back down from the Supreme Court with an order, he enforced it without hesitation. That was

1. New Brunswick, N.J.: Rutgers University Press, 1982. Reprinted with permission.

the normal order of work he was used to. But on that motion he said, "If you want this decided, take it to the Supreme Court."

On what definitions of the lawyer's role do clients leave the office peacefully? First, they often accept "eligibility rules" as precluding further service. Prospective clients may be induced to leave by the citation of rules limiting eligibility by income or organizational priorities. As examples of the latter, the Chicago programs in the early 1970s officially refused to perform bankruptcies for the unemployed and to prosecute uncontested divorces where there were no minor children in the family.

Poor people also often accept "hard realities" as a reason they should not expect to receive elaborate legal assistance. They may be told, "You need more evidence," "You haven't been damaged enough," or simply, "It's not fair, but there's no legal remedy." If the legal assistance lawyer accepts the client's objective as within the organization's competence and advises that something can be done about it, the client will often be content with the advice that not much need be done. Poor people are often content to leave legal assistance offices without receiving commitments for far-reaching or long-lasting service, provided they obtain an indication that the end of the current contact does not end the relationship. Legal assistance lawyers quickly learn that an effective way to overcome a client's reluctance to leave is to announce open-ended conditions for another contact.

Discontinuities Between Cases

In any contact with a client, a lawyer may have to negotiate an understanding of what the client wants, determine what the relevant facts are, and convey comprehensible advice. For lawyers who have long-term relations with clients, the accomplishment of these tasks on any given occasion is also an investment in subsequent work. The requests for help typical at legal assistance offices center on crises; the urgency implies that the lawyer–client relation will be short term or one-shot. Moving from one short-term client to the next, legal assistance lawyers experience problems in making work on one problem useful for the next.

Large organizations and wealthy people often place their lawyers "in house" or on retainer. In such relations, the lawyer may provide service without the client even perceiving a need for it; for extended periods of work, the lawyer may avoid the need to negotiate a definition of service with the client. In contrast, the stream of personal crises brought to legal assistance offices makes the task of learning what the client wants an everyday experience. The following excerpt is taken from an intake interview conducted by a lawyer who at the time had two years of experience in legal assistance. It indicates how idiosyncrasies in perception and style of expression limit the ability to use the experience of one client interview in the next.

> Cl. enters L.'s office with the standard intake card. It has been filled out by a secretary, and it indicates that his problem is "social security." His income is a bit over scale, there's one in his family, and he's 66.
>
> L. at first assumes Cl. has a social security problem. Cl., realizing that L. is basing his questions on a reading of the card, says: "No, I don't care what she puts down there." L. finds Cl. difficult to understand, as do I. He mumbles and seems to be talking on irrelevant tacks about his family, his first and second wives, and their relatives. Social security seems somehow relevant; he keeps referring to what "the man at Social Security" told him. L. keeps asking, "What's the problem?" Cl. keeps saying, "I don't have a problem. I'm here because you white folks have common sense, and I don't."
>
> Cl. mentions something about being taken for less than 65 at Social Security. He is 65, he insists, although his birth certificate shows him to be younger. L. pursues this, trying to pin down his age and what was determined about his age at Social Security. But Cl. frustrates this line of questioning. He indicates that he's got a job for the next few months, and then he'll be 65 even according to his birth certificate.
>
> Cl. also mentions that he got married without divorcing his first wife. His second wife died. The Social Security guy told him he was a bigamist. He doesn't want to break the law, and he realizes that bigamy is illegal. He never has broken the law, and "I don't want you white folks to throw me in jail." At first L. brushes this aside as irrelevant but then tries the idea that divorce is the reason he came in. But no, he doesn't want a divorce.
>
> Now L. is enjoying this fellow and the struggle to figure out why he came in. He asks a series of questions on family history and status. At least that's a line of questions he can pursue in an orderly fashion, and it seems somehow relevant. At various

points, L., concerned that he's misinterpreting Cl., reads back his interpretation of Cl.'s statements: "OK, now look, you're married now, you've got two kids, you never were divorced from the first marriage.... Right?"

Finally L. figures that when Cl. went to Social Security, someone jokingly told him he was a bigamist. Cl., afraid of being a "criminal," came in to see if he needed a divorce to avoid jail. L. reads this back. Cl. nods "yes." L. tells him there's nothing to fear, that he should return if he wants to remarry but otherwise "there's no problem." As Cl. is leaving, L., thinking of claims that the first wife might make against him, asks if he has any property. Cl.: "Just the clothes on my back. Thank you, white folks."

Discontinuities Within Cases

Pressed by expectations to remain within a local social environment, hemmed in by difficulties in making efforts on one case relevant to the next, legal assistance lawyers run into still tighter restrictions on their work: extraordinary risks that investments made in the initial or preparatory stages of cases will never be realized. Short-term relations preclude supervision of how clients use advice beyond the office doors. I interviewed L. after he completed his first month in a neighborhood office.

I feel a tremendous pressure to do something that'll be of value for people who come in. I feel I'm not doing my job if I just tell them that there's nothing to do. Maybe they've been waiting for weeks for an appointment, or an hour in the waiting room; they've spent some money to get here, or they're taking the time off work and losing money that way. So I do a lot of social work.... But then if I don't make a case out of it, when they leave the office I don't know how their lives are going to be affected. I don't even know if they understood me. You know, sometimes I'll be going on, telling them where to go and what to do to handle something on their own, and then when they're smiling, about to leave, I'll ask them something and it's clear they never knew what I was talking about. And—I thought of this for a while—I guess it's not my place to call them up and find out what happened. That's too paternalistic.

Legal assistance lawyers believe that their clientele contains a sizable percentage of "crazies." Whether or not they are crazy before coming to legal assistance offices, poor people often *appear* crazy when they leave before the lawyer is able to grasp their perspective; and given the pattern of short-term relations with unscreened clients, this is a frequent event. For the lawyer, the upshot is a sense—sometimes bitter, sometimes absurd—of wasted effort. The lawyer may render his experience of incomprehensibility and absurdity comprehensible and rational by imputing craziness to clients. As the effort to identify client objectives may be rendered futile by "crazy" clients, so the effort to establish facts may be undercut by "clients who lie." Several lies are said to be typical: a husband's insistence that he cannot pay support because he is unemployed; the claim by a defendant in an auto accident damage suit that his car was stolen on the fateful day and later returned, all mysteriously; a tenant's claim that he did not receive the notice required by statute to initiate an eviction.

Whether or not poor people do lie to lawyers with unusual frequency, the legal assistance lawyer is in a relatively impotent position for protecting himself against client deceit. In contrast to "clean" law practices, which arrange the use of organizational property or power on the basis of documentary evidence, legal assistance lawyers primarily handle "dirty" work. They can be suddenly and visibly stained by an unexpected appearance of client immorality.

BECOMING A POVERTY LAWYER

Making Cases Significant

Legal assistance lawyers have attempted to make their work significant to audiences beyond their proximate social environment through a variety of reform strategies. These include using class actions; bringing law reform cases, which illuminate doctrinal issues for a broad legal community; representing militants whose actions are symbolic to supporters and opponents; and coordinating complaints into campaigns to put notorious merchants out of business. The common methodology is to redefine an individual client's problem as it has been narrowly defined by an adversary so that it impinges upon greater interests. These strategies raise the stakes for Legal Services practice, with the result that work experience literally becomes more challenging.

Rates of turnover have been consistently higher in neighborhood offices, where lawyers must respond to requests by individual clients to handle their problems, than in "downtown" positions, where lawyers are expected to concentrate on reform litigation. I interviewed a lawyer working in the Family Division of the Legal Aid Bureau:

> Are there some cases that you've had that have been more memorable than others? Yes, my free-transcript case. That's where I changed the law. How did that come about? I took a crappy case and developed a side issue from it. [The issue is a free transcript for appeals in divorce cases for "paupers." The Legal Aid director has spoken of L.'s success with great pride, emphasizing to me how excited L. was over handling the case—the most excited he'd ever seen L. in his work.] It was my first appeal in five and a half years [at Legal Aid.] [L. describes the case in detail and with an enthusiasm that exceeds his response to any other topic I've raised in this two-hour interview.]

Even more telling are accounts in which involvement is seen to fluctuate with periods of participation in reform litigation.

> I'd always been concerned with professional growth, that there wasn't any on this job. Then it seemed from time to time something would happen to give me renewed hope.... From the [client] interviews, some things came up that developed into appeals. Like this case against the debt-pooling outfit. It's a class-action. It's not like the kind of trivia you usually get.... We've been working nights and weekends on it. We've done a lot of work on it. We put in a 55-page complaint.... I got in with A. [another lawyer] on [this] case, and later into the voter's rights case [on the provision of election instructions in Spanish in voting booths]. I did the brief in support of the TRO [temporary restraining order], and the direct examination in federal court. For the first time, I felt that the Spanish-speaking people felt that I was doing something useful. Oh, you always get individual signs of gratitude, from individual cases. But we got a lot of response from people not directly involved.

Achieving Autonomy

Recent graduates saw their poverty litigation experience as extraordinary relative to the opportunities their law school peers were finding.

> One day we were going down to Springfield to argue a Supreme Court of Illinois case. I said, let's go over the arguments that you [a more experienced and older Legal Services lawyer] will make. He said, "What do you mean, I'll make? You'll do the oral

argument." I said, "But you could do it better." I'd just been admitted a month before. I was just 24 years old. My friends hadn't even made it to traffic court yet. He said, "Don't worry, they won't listen anyway." After I was out [of Legal Services], friends would call me all the time on how to do things. I'd been in every court from the municipal court to the Supreme Court; I'd been in the newspapers and on TV. I knew I could do anything that I wanted.

Several of the most consistent law reform litigators fought program leaders for control of their "big" cases.

> The odd nature of this business, it's totally different from private practice, in that in private practice the work comes in from the top. If it's my client, I'm the senior man. The client comes to me and tells me what the problem is. I have the client contact; I know what the client wants; I go to the meetings with the client; you work for me. In this business, the client comes in on the bottom. You know what the client wants.

A recent law graduate who had entered the LAB expressly to prepare for a move to a neighborhood office recalled using various strategies to achieve autonomy on his "desk."

> I forced that desk to get into interesting issues. It had been a nonlitigating desk, but it was the greatest vehicle for litigation. But there were all these limits: $300 maximum recovery; no punitive damages; and class actions were hard to bring off. I had to work on [LAB officials] for changes in these rules.... What changes did you press for, and which did you get? Changes in the type of case. For example, they had a rule—or no rule that you wouldn't take a case if it was worth less than $50. I got that [prohibition] in. I wouldn't take any plaintiff's case for less than $50. I had to scream and yell for that, but I finally convinced [the officials].... I started to take different kinds of cases: the first employment discrimination that had been taken off that desk.... I was getting into utility cases, which was supposed to be J.'s area. But I'd write it up so that I'd get it.

Elaborating a Culture of Significance

The third condition of involvement is the symbolic transformation of moral pressures toward routine into themes of transcending significance. Downtown lawyers in Legal Services Programs characteristically have been relieved from intake responsibilities. In contrast, neighborhood staff lawyers have faced a routinely discouraging environment. The maintenance of peer relations that could provide a collective forum for the expression of a transcendent culture was an uncommon and unstable achievement.

Neighborhood lawyers who described themselves as demoralized spoke as isolated individuals. One was discouraged by a supervisor who identified with the local professional environment.

> I [would] frequently…talk about leaving. A. [his office supervisor] would always say, "You're doing all right, fine. You're too hard on yourself."…She would say, "You get good pay, you're a good lawyer, things aren't going badly." Her competence is different from mine, in terms of what she'd be satisfied with. I combine law reform with top quality. She emphasizes top quality but isn't that oriented to changes in the system. She has accepted the court system as it is, and most of the statutes she works with. She tries to win the cases on the facts. She gets along fine, fits right in with the p.i. [personal injury] bar.

Conversely, career interviews showed the quick development of involvement when a collegial relation that expressed this culture was struck up. The supervisor of one office emphasized the impetus he received from the supervisor of another office on a jointly handled case.

> One of my problems…is that I can't sustain B.'s rage, a rage in self-righteous terms…. You must dehumanize the opposition, identify yourself completely with the client, and believe completely that the other side is really bad. You must be brutal, unrelenting. B. is good at this; he can sustain a tremendous indignation and energy…. How did this Credit Systems case develop? A year and a half ago, I had a case through intake…. I knew the defenses if we'd be sued, so I just sat on it. Then I talked to people in other offices, to B. and C., and they had clients who had problems with Credit Systems too, so we decided to file a class action.

Entering and leaving a collective culture of significance was closely related to the rise and decline of involvement. From 1966 to 1974, there were six dyads containing lawyers who maintained an involvement in reform litigation during careers of two or more years in Chicago's neighborhood offices. The members of each of these pairs shared "latent culture," background characteristics formally irrelevant to their jobs, which they drew on to form close friendships. The lawyers in five of the pairs broke down the distinction between "job" and "personal life," regu-larly seeing each other and talking about work after hours and outside of the office. In each of these pairs, when one member moved out of the office, the other soon left as well. Significantly, the members of the dyads did not always practice together on litigation. They helped each other sustain a posture; they did not necessarily help one another with professional tasks. In some of the pairs, one supplied technical knowledge, the other moral outrage.

How does the culture of significance work to sustain involvement? At least three themes in the culture can be isolated. The first theme is that problems that would otherwise mean frustration can be transformed into resources for reform. Every instance of significant litigation expresses this theme. Individuals who have suffered a harm that legal assistance lawyers previously had been unable to remedy are cast as representatives of others in a judicial drama that promises to turn moral discouragement into exemplary reform. Reform litigation contains a paradoxical principle. Its excellence depends on the depths of misery of its beneficiaries.

> [While I am interviewing A. in his office, B. comes in and asks] "How do you find out if a property is FHA financed?" [B. has a client whose rent has been raised. The financing information may indicate some way to gain leverage over the owner. A., realizing it will not be easy to get the information, wonders if the effort will be worthwhile. He asks:] "One client, or the whole building?" [B. laughs]: "Oh, there are hundreds of people in this building."

By expecting cases to be handled according to their routines, judges, adversaries, and opposing counsel imply that the interests at stake are insignificant. Given the right perspective, the more outrageous these pressures, the more easily they can be transformed into resources for reform. A stupid decision by a state judge may be taken as an occasion for mounting a general attack on the lower court systems. To this end, an otherwise unremarkable issue for appeal may be phrased as an indictment:

> [From CLC (Community Legal Counsel) activity reports] A. and I presented a motion on [misdemeanor defendant's] behalf to obtain a free transcript of the proceedings for appeal. The motion was based on the U.S. Supreme Court case of *Williams v. Oklahoma City*, which is directly in

point. Magistrate Jankowski denied the motion because the U.S. Supreme Court's interpretation of the U.S. Constitution is not the law of Illinois, and he will follow the law of Illinois. We then went to Judge Lahowski and asked him to reverse Jankowski. He refused to make any decision and said the magistrates could use their own discretion. [In a subsequent report]: The question to be reviewed [in the U.S. Supreme Court] and which Magistrate Jankowski and the Illinois Supreme Court needs [sic] the U.S. Supreme Court to answer is: "Whether the decision of the U.S. Supreme Court in *Williams*…is applicable in the State of Illinois and binding on the Circuit Court of Cook County." [This was celebrated by its inclusion in numerous reports, which were circulated through the organization.]

In the same spirit, unethical behavior by opposing counsel may be made a basis for a disbarment effort. Deceitful and harassing methods of collection may be described in a counterclaim for punitive damages that is added to the defense of a debt suit. And "incompetent" representation by an opposing counsel that makes "unnecessary" work for the poverty lawyer may be argued as a basis for charging the adversary with the costs and attorney's fees of the litigation.

Dramatic instances of unbending militance in the face of restraints received extensive collegial review. Several versions circulated of the following demonstration of involvement under fire.

> Another hilarious scene: King got assassinated,…I remember it got real quiet. I went outside, and you could hear a pin drop. The next day they started rioting in the morning. I was in the office with L. and G. [two staff lawyers]. L. was having a big controversy with this guy who represented some models, and I remember hearing L. say, "Fuck you, you son of a bitch," and he hung up. And oh, about a minute later C. [the opposing counsel] calls back, and they engage in more heated debate, and L. ends it again with, "Oh fuck you, you son of a bitch," and hangs up again. Two minutes later A. [director] calls up. C. had called him. They used to do that all the time, report us to the higher ups, and A. would never back us up. So A. calls back and he'd just hear L.'s end of it, and they engage in a heated debate on it, and L. hangs up on him. A. had apparently said, "you're fired," and L. had said, "You can keep your goddamn job." Wham. [Laughs] It didn't bother him. He was working; he was writing a brief or something. And these calls would come in—"fuck you, you son of a bitch"—and he'd keep writing. The guy's really composed. It's just remarkable. He's

really composed. Then A. calls back again. Then he unfires him. Then he fires him again. And while all this is going on, they're burning down the West Side. Incredible. You hear gunfire out there [laugh].

A second cultural theme is that the lawyers may distance themselves from pressures toward routine with incredulous outrage and humorous ridicule. These techniques can be used to sustain an impetus toward reform in the face of an infinite number of frustrations. By expressing incredulity at judicial or adversarial conduct, a lawyer can assume a posture of righteous superiority. Incredulity implies the disruption of naivete, but its use is not limited to new or inexperienced lawyers. On the contrary, it can be practiced most effectively by experienced lawyers. The emphatic assertion that behavior is extraordinarily improper requires confident assumptions about what is ordinary and proper. Performing one's first professional expression of incredulity with flawless self-confidence is a significant status passage in the career of a poverty lawyer.

Incredulity guards a perspective on significance cautiously. By refusing to expect the identity that others expect of them, poverty lawyers take care not to assume it. Various ridiculing devices are also used to set oneself off from the person others expect. One lawyer cast his frequent opposing counsel in the characters of Snow White's dwarfs and gave them roles in allegorical comedy routines he borrowed from the professional comedian, George Carlin. Many mimicked adversaries, judges, and clients to resist identification:

> [Jim gets off the phone with an opposing counsel, laughs, and says], "Hey Jimmy, [chewing an imaginary cigar], whaddayasay we make a deal?"

The functional value of ridicule was articulated for me by a consumer protection litigator who enjoyed an unexcelled reputation for venting outrage. Each of the six or so times I had been in his office, I had witnessed mocking activities. He would describe angrily the conduct of an adversary to another staff lawyer, who would supply heavy sarcasm and transform the atmosphere to one of ridicule. The two had apparently been doing variations on this ritual virtually every day for over four years.

The main way we work together…his main virtue and the main virtue of the job to me, is that it lends itself to a lot of laughs. It's like reading a good novel—very humorous—that exposes human frailties, foibles, idiocies, human greed. It's a wonderful position to observe all this in: co-workers, clients, judges, opposing counsel, people working for the schlock companies. But most people don't appreciate it to the full if they don't have a sense of humor. Our clients, they're of course not to be laughed out of the office, but there's an opportunity for a lot of laughs. And we are able to laugh at it…the collection lawyers, a bunch of phonies, going in for sham continuances, the threats they use, making fools of themselves in court, shouting at us for the benefit of their client, making facetious arguments before judges, posturing. I love it all. It's like one of those British movie comedies, or like a sarcastic Dickens novel. Or Alice in Wonderland. Honestly, I really love this job.

A final theme in the culture of significance exploits the possibilities for irony in the reform litigator's work. Rich contrasts may be drawn between the abstract, promissory stature of reform suits and their immediate implications for concrete clients. A theme of the absurd simultaneously portrays futility and promotes involvement. The portrayal responds to discouragement by tacitly affirming a transcendent spirit. An accomplished act of describing absurdity paradoxically presumes the rationality, meaningfulness, and value of its own creation. It denies absurdity by celebrating it.

A final example shows how poverty lawyers can create a culture for involvement by appreciating dearly a client whose personal struggles cast their own as insignificant. By dwelling on the pathos of the client, the lawyers can celebrate their work as an absurd yet therefore heroic attempt to achieve significant results with makeshift means against apparently hopeless odds.

[Cl. comes in, and A. introduces him to me as "the third-largest manufacturer of cornhusk brooms in Chicago." Cl. is an old man, without teeth, who mumbles with a heavy black accent. His clothes are crumpled and dirty: an old beret; pants which were once part of a suit but are now thread-worn work clothes. He has huge fingers that appear extremely arthritic. A. later tells me that that's from the bones breaking repeatedly when working machines.]

[They talk about corporate business forms and financing. I'm wondering: This man owns a business? A. later tells me that his brooms are of excellent quality and much desired, but by a decreasing number of people. He had a chance to make or break himself for good a few years ago when a deal with Sears was in the works, but he couldn't meet their volume. Some time ago A. and B., another staff lawyer, worked on his case. He defaulted on a $10,000 loan from the Small Business Administration (SBA) and is now persona non grata there. He's been literally keeping his business going on shoestrings and other waste materials.]

[A. is determined he can keep him going by pursuing credit under the right facade. Cl. and A. talk about a legal shell that will disguise Cl.'s control enough so that he can get credit, but not so much that it will pass control to the friend whose credit reputation will be the key to the scheme.]

[B. comes in, and now both he and A. have great fun with Cl.] B.: I was over around your place the other week, and the wreckers were there, working next door. And the construction guy said to me, pointing to your place, "We could take the ball and go over there next."

Cl.: They ought to. It's a terrible building.

A.: That's not a rough neighborhood, is it Cl.?

Cl.: It's getting rougher. I've got to move. They did [this and this] to me. It's getting too rough for me.

[They all laugh. It's been incredible for years that he could stay there, given the crime and economic dangers. When Cl. says he's moving, B. asks if he can move his equipment without it falling apart in the move. This occasions laughter from A. and B., and, after a pause, from Cl.]

B.: How's your rooster?

Cl.: Fine.

[Then A. recounts] when [Cl.] defaulted on the SBA loan, IRS men were sent out to padlock his building and equipment. From fear of the neighborhood, they were constantly looking over their shoulders. One said, "I've got to get out of here, this place is too rough for me."

Then they got inside and found that [Cl.] has chickens around that eat the droppings from the corn that goes into the brooms. And he has a rooster there. It is ferocious and it attacked one of the IRS men as he was trying to padlock [Cl.'s] equipment. [On Cl.'s way out, B. and then A. repeat]: Whatever you do, don't send anything into SBA with your name on it. It'll be thrown right out again. They've got your file, and when they see your name, they'll check their files and will pull out your old one. So if you send anything to the SBA, don't put your name on it. Put your friend's, else it will come right back at you. [A. and B. laugh again and again at this.]

DISCUSSION QUESTIONS

1. Outside the United States, most legal aid is delivered by private lawyers reimbursed by the government—a scheme Americans call "judicare" (by analogy to Medicare). Why did we choose salaried full-time poverty lawyers instead? Britain is moving toward "franchising" a limited number of solicitors firms to provide the bulk of legal aid. What are the relative advantages of the two systems with respect to the following:

   A. clients (eligibility, access)

   B. subject matter covered

   C. cost

   D. quality (including caseload)

   E. tactics

   F. commitment

   G. political support

   H. amount

   I. personnel

2. In the late 1960s and early 1970s legal services attracted "the best and the brightest." Does it still? If not, why? Should and could anything be done about this? What factors other than salary affect the choice of such a career? Should we be concerned about high turnover in such jobs? Should we require a post–law school internship in legal aid or some other public interest organization as a condition of bar admission?

3. The U.S. Supreme Court has never centrally addressed the question of a constitutional right to *civil* legal services.[2] Can you make such an argument? What should be the content of the right?

4. Many observers, both supporters and critics, see legal aid as inescapably "political." Can you offer an apolitical justification? Should the state be involved in funding political activity? Are there any kinds of activities in which legal aid lawyers should *not* be involved? Who should be making the decisions about hiring, which clients to serve, which cases to take, which strategies to follow? How could we insulate legal aid programs from political "interference"? Now that the federal government has placed severe restrictions on what the lawyers it funds can do, where should legal services look for alternative funding?[3]

SUGGESTED READING

For histories of legal aid, both before the federal government became involved in 1965 and after, see R. Abrahams, "Law Offices to Serve Householders in the Lower Income Group," 42 *Dickinson Law Review* 133 (1937–38); "The Neighborhood Law Office Experiment," 9 *University of Chicago Law Review* 410 (1942); "The Neighborhood Law Office Plan," 1949 *Wisconsin Law Review* 634; "The New Philadelphia Lawyer," 185 *Atlantic Monthly* 72 (April 1950); "Twenty-five Years of Service: Philadelphia's Neighborhood Law Office Plan," 50 *ABAJ* 728 (1964); E. Brownell, *Legal Aid in the United States* (1951); "Neighborhood Law Offices: The New Wave in Legal Services for the Poor," 80 *Harvard Law Review* 805 (1967); H. H. Weisman (ed.), *Justice and the Law in the Mobilization for Youth Experience* (1969); Jerome E. Carlin, "Store-front Lawyers in San Francisco," 7 *Transaction* 64 (1970); F. Raymond Marks, *Military Lawyers, Civilian Courts, and the Organized Bar: A Case Study of the Unauthorized Practice Dilemma* (1972); R. Pious, "Congress, the Organized Bar, and the Legal Services Program," 1972 *Wisconsin Law Review* 418, "Policy and Public Administration: The Legal Services Program in the War on Poverty," in Ira Katznelson et al. (eds.), *The Politics and Society Reader* (1974); R. W. Ide III and L. L. Thompson, "The Organized Bar—Yellow Brick Road to Legal Services for the Poor," 27 *Vanderbilt Law Review* 667 (1974); Earl Johnson Jr., *Justice and Reform: The Formative Years of the*

---

2. *Meltzer v. C. Buck LeCraw & Co.*, 402 U.S. 954 (1971). A few state supreme courts have interpreted state constitutions to require representation of prisoners and those threatened with paternity or loss of children, e.g., *Salas v. Cortez*, 154 Cal. Rptr 529 (1979); *In re Jacqueline H.*, 145 Cal. Rptr. 548 (1978); *Payne v. Superior Court*, 553 P.D2 565 (1976).

3. On the categorical limitations and budget cuts, see *New York Times* 8 (11.25.95), §1 p9 (1.21.96), §1 p8 (1.28.96), §1 p8 (4.28.96), §1 p47 (9.15.96); *Los Angeles Times* B9 (9.19.95), B9 (11.29.95), A1 (12.29.95), A1 (12.30.95).

OEO Legal Services Program (1974); Marjorie Girth, *Poor People's Lawyers* (1976); W. E. George, "Development of the Legal Services Corporation," 61 *Cornell Law Review* 681 (1976); P. J. Hannon, "From Politics to Reality: An Historical Perspective on the Legal Services Corporation," 25 *Emory Law Journal* 639 (1976); S. K. Huber, "Thou Shalt Not Ration Justice: A History and Bibliography of Legal Aid in America," 44 *George Washington Law Review* 754 (1976).

For more about the experience of legal aid lawyers, see Howard S. Erlanger, "Social Reform Organizations and Subsequent Careers of Participants: A Follow-up Study of Early Participants in the OEO Legal Services Program," 42 *American Sociological Review* 233 (1973), "Lawyers and Neighborhood Legal Services: Social Background and Impetus for Reform," 12 *Law & Society Review* 253 (1978); Joel F. Handler, Ellen Jane Hollingsworth, and Howard S. Erlanger, *Lawyers and the Pursuit of Legal Rights* chapters 3, 7, 8 (1978).

For political critiques, some emphasizing the ethical dilemmas of legal aid lawyers, see Spiro T. Agnew, "What's Wrong with the Legal Services Program," 58 *ABAJ* 930 (1972); "Lawyers versus Indigents: Conflict of Interest in Professional–Client Relations in the Legal Profession," in Eliot Freidson (ed.), *The Professions and Their Prospects* (1973); J. R. Bolton and S. T. Holzer, "Legal Services and Landlord–Tenant Litigation: A Critical Analysis," 82 *Yale Law Journal* 1495 (1973); Harry Brill, "The Uses and Abuses of Legal Assistance," 31 *Public Interest* 38 (1973); Charles Rowley, *The Right to Justice: The Political Economy of Legal Services in the United States* (1991). On conservative attempts to curb legal aid, see Harry P. Stumpf, "The Legal Profession and Legal Services: Explorations in Local Bar Politics," 6 *Law & Society Review* 47 (1971), *Community Politics and Legal Services: The Other Side of the Law* (1975); Richard Blumenthal and M. I. Soler, "The Legal Services Corporation: Curtailing Political Interference," 81 *Yale Law Journal* 231 (1971); J. B. Falk Jr. and S. R. Pollak, "Political Interference with Publicly Funded Lawyers: The CRLA Controversy and the Future of Legal Services," 24 *Hastings Law Review* (1973).

For descriptions and evaluations, see Theodore Finman, "OEO Legal Service Programs and the Pursuit of Social Change: The Relationship between Program Ideology and Program Performance," 1971 *Wisconsin Law Review* 1101; K. P. Fisher and C. C. Ivie, *Franchising Justice: The Office of Economic Opportunity Legal Services Program and Traditional Legal Aid* (1971); P. J. Hannon, "National Policy versus Local Control: The Legal Service Dilemma," 5 *California Western Law Review* 223 (1969), "The Leadership Problem in the Legal Services Program," 4 *Law & Society Review* 235 (1969), "Law Reform Enforcement at the Local Level: A Legal Services Case Study," 19 *Journal of Public Law* 23 (1970); Alan Widiss et al., "Legal Assistance for the Rural Poor: An Iowa Study," 56 *Iowa Law Review* 100 (1970); Anthony M. Champagne, "An Evaluation of the Effectiveness of the OEO Legal Services Program," 9 *Urban Affairs Quarterly* 466 (1974), "The Internal Operation of OEO Legal Services Projects," 51 *Journal of Urban Law* 649 (1974), *Legal Services: An Exploratory Study of Effectiveness* (1975), "Lawyers and Government Funded Legal Services," 21 *Villanova Law Review* 860 (1976); Mark Kessler, *Legal Services for the Poor: A Comparative and Contemporary Analysis of Interorganizational Politics* (1987); Roger Cramton, "Delivery of Legal Services to Ordinary Americans," 44 *Case Western Reserve Law Review* 531 (1994).

For descriptions and evaluations of the few "judicare" schemes in this country, see George F. Cole and H. L. Greenberger, "Staff Attorneys vs. Judicare: A Cost Analysis," 50 *Journal of Urban Law* 705 (1973); Samuel J. Brakel, *Judicare: Public Funds, Private Lawyers, and Poor People* (1974); H. Wolf and H. Hissam, "Legal Aid to the Poor in West Virginia: A Comparative Analysis," 14 *Journal of Family Law* 405 (1975).

For comparisons of legal aid in other societies, see Mauro Cappelletti, James Gordley, and Earl Johnson Jr., *Toward Equal Justice: A Comparative Study of Legal Aid in Modern Societies* (1975); Frederick Zemans (ed.), *Perspectives on Legal Aid: An International Survey* (1979); Bryant Garth, *Neighborhood Law Firms for the Poor: A Comparative Study of Recent Developments in Legal Aid and in the Legal Profession* (1980); Erhard Blankenburg (ed.), *Innovations in the Legal Services* (1980); Mauro Cappelletti (ed.), *Access to Justice and the Welfare State* (1981); Jeremy Cooper, *Public Legal Services: A Comparative Study of Policy, Politics, and Practice* (1983); Richard L. Abel, "Law Without Politics: Legal Aid under Advanced Capitalism," 32 *UCLA Law Review* 474 (1985); "Legal Aid," 5(2) *Maryland Journal of Contemporary Legal Issues* (1994).

Because the U.S. Supreme Court held in 1938 that the federal government was constitutionally obligated to provide free representation to indigent criminal defendants and, in 1963 and 1972 respectively, that states were required to do for those charged with felonies or crimes punishable by imprisonment, both levels of government have had to create mechanisms to ensure criminal defense. This article describes the experience of public defenders. *

THE PUBLIC DEFENDER: THE PRACTICE OF LAW IN THE SHADOWS OF REPUTE[1]
Lisa J. McIntyre

"WE ARE THE BASTARD CHILDREN OF COOK COUNTY"

WHEN I asked current public defenders what had surprised them about the job, almost all responded by saying that one of their biggest surprises (and disappointments) had been the lack of respect. Some put this assessment quite succinctly: "We have a reputation as crummy lawyers"; "Everybody thinks the Public Defender's Office is just dreck." "There is a notion," another lawyer said, "that public defenders are an inferior breed compared to real lawyers."

Although some public defenders believe that many judges are prosecution minded, they seem to regard this as inevitable, if not entirely fair. What the lawyers find less easy to accept is that judges often treat them as second-class lawyers. In some courtrooms, this merely meant that judges are more considerate of private attorneys, calling their cases before calling the public defenders' cases—so that private defense attorneys do not have to "hang around all morning to get through their call." "There is good reason," one public defender allowed, "for calling the public defender's cases last: time is money for the private attorney." "But still, the private attorney walks in and gets his cases called and he's out of

---

* *Johnson v. Zerbst,* 304 U.S. 458 (1938); *Gideon v. Wainwright,* 372 U.S. 335 (1963); *Argersinger v. Hamlin,* 407 U.S. 25 (1972).

1. Chicago: University of Chicago Press, 1987. Reprinted with permission.

there. The public defender's cases don't get called sometimes until 11:00 or 11:30. After a while, something as small as that can really gall you."

If something is going to hurt a client's case, the lawyers said, they must object. One told me, for example, of a case in which he had actually pursued his objection to the Illinois Supreme Court, where he sought and received a writ of mandamus. Over and over I was told that when a judge refuses to let you argue a motion that is important to your case, you must object; when the judge allows into evidence what you believe to be incompetent or improper material, you must object: "There are times when you have got to say, 'Come on, judge, let's take off our coats, and let's get it on.' You have to do that sometimes and *of course* it's scary. Now I have been scared, and I've backed down sometimes when I shouldn't have. But I go back in there the next day and start all over again, because I will have gone home that night and chewed myself out for backing down." But when a judge's treatment of a lawyer merely reflects a disregard of the lawyer's dignity, the lawyers feel that to fight back will *hurt* their client: "Everything you do is going to affect your client, you know? If I'm acting like an asshole, if I'm being a jerk, *or if I'm taking myself too seriously*, I've got a client who's going to suffer. As opposed to sometimes, if I can shuffle or tap-dance a little bit, if I get my client to walk out with no criminal record, or time served, or whatever. And it never bothered me to do that, never. [Pause] Well, as I'm getting older perhaps it *is* starting to bother me a little bit." So, public defenders learn not to take themselves too seriously, to "laugh at a lot of dumb jokes that judges make."

Ironically, it is the clients who tend to be among the most dismissive of the lawyers' claims to respect. Two-thirds of the former public defenders interviewed agreed with the statement, "My clients often seemed to doubt my ability as a lawyer just because I was a public defender." As many of the current public defenders told it, many of their clients even refused to recognize the public defenders as lawyers: "I was *really* surprised by the way my clients felt about me—the clients' attitude can be summed up by what we heard again today: 'I don't want a PD, I want a real lawyer.' That happens all the time."

ORGANIZING PROFESSIONALS

In Cook County, with rare exceptions, different attorneys related the same kind of stories about their first days on the job. However flattered they may have been, most were horrified to discover that they were to be treated as if they were actually qualified. Memories of their first days still evoked feelings of discomfort; during the interviews, stories about those days were typically accompanied by a great deal of nervous laughter and punctuated with such disclaimers as "You won't believe this," "It was crazy," "I couldn't believe it," or "It was awful!" How do public defenders get trained? "I got trained by showing up there and they handed me a file and said, 'You are starting trials.' There was supposed to be, I remember [laugh] a lawyer there [laugh], but he wasn't there. I think he had already quit the office [laugh]; he never showed up." Other attorneys related similar experiences: one said that he did not know what to do and that there was no one there to tell him: "No one ever told what they wanted. In fact, when I was sent to the branch court, I was plopped right down in the middle of the courtroom with a heavy call. I was the only public defender there. In the courtroom next door there were two in there, and they were able to answer some questions, but I was all alone. Can you believe this?"

Most of the other attorneys said that they had had some support from partners, but to many this seemed inadequate; in several instances either the partner left after a short time or was himself also relatively new. One lawyer recalled his introduction to the misdemeanor court in which he began his career as a public defender: "I had a partner for one week and then I was put on my own. It was crazy, we used to do fifteen bench trials a day and I had, on average, forty clients a day."

In theory, professional competency belies the need for supervision, and, in fact, supervisors in the public defender's office are treated as if they are redundant. When I asked, "What do supervisors do?" the answer from nonsupervisors usually began with a chuckle and ended with "nothing" or "not much." When prodded, some of the attorneys explained.

The way this office is run—insofar as it can be said to be run—you're pretty much on your own. There is a supervisory structure, but mainly there is nobody, there is nobody looking over your shoulder, no one evaluating, no one correcting you, no one giving you feedback on what you do.

There are supervisors in charge of sneezing on Tuesday or Thursday. They read the newspaper or they play bridge or whatever. They are supposed to take an interest in what their supervisees are doing; a lot don't. They collect their salaries.

Your supervisors are there for support, research, that sort of thing. They are backup. You can ask them, "What would you do in this type of situation?" But I don't have to talk to anybody about what I am going to do.

Good supervisors just happen to be around when you have a problem or a question. But, in general, a lot of them don't do that. They just show up for work.

All six of the supervisors seemed to be uncomfortable with the idea that they were actually in charge of anyone. The first with whom I spoke turned out to be quite typical in this respect:

Q: What does a supervisor do that a regular public defender does not?

R: I do less [laugh]. It's not defined, it's not defined. It is whatever you make of it. I don't see myself as a cop. I don't see myself as an administrator, shifting papers and seeing that everyone is doing what they are supposed to be doing, being what they are supposed to be, that they are disposing of the right number of cases, or anything like that. I don't think that's our job.

Similar theories seemed to circulate on how one gets promoted to supervisor—a move that usually does mean a salary increase for the lawyer. When I asked non-supervisors, I was told that such promotions were usually the result of *anything but* merit:

Q: How does someone get to be a supervisor?

R: [Laugh] Well, I don't know [laugh]. I don't know. It's not the result of automatic tenure, it's office politics.

It's very mysterious, it's probably political. You probably have to be here a while. [pause] I guess I really don't know.

In some cases they are made supervisors because there is a need to get them out of a courtroom—or because they won't do any work. Well, maybe not very often, but sometimes.

Supervisors themselves seemed equally unsure of—or perhaps reluctant to explain—how one generally gets promoted to a supervisory position, except that most of them said that it does take time.

I think what happens is that some people leave at a crucial point and others stay on. And the ones that stay on beyond the crucial point, whatever that crucial point is, become supervisory material. And then you kind of wait your turn. Of course, there is politics. Does Justice [the first assistant public defender] know who you are? Have you caused any trouble in the past? Then you are not going to be a supervisor.

How did I get to be a supervisor? I think, longevity. Well [pause], maybe, if I want to pride myself, I'd say it's also because you do a good job. But more than anything else, I think it's just being there. I was made a supervisor sooner than others who have been here longer, but I think maybe that's just luck.

One supervisor frankly admitted that his promotion came as a result of clout—and that this was true not only in his own case:

R: I know someone six months out of law school who was promoted to supervisor. Now he was connected.

Q: Clout can make that much difference?

R: [Laugh] Now Lisa, what do you think? This is Chicago!

The myth of competency embraces public defenders from the moment that they are appointed to the office. Although there is a hierarchical structure in place, it is treated as if it is for purposes of show only: supervisors are believed to be redundant; public defenders work as a company of equals. Even when supervision or teaching and the like do occur, they are carefully done in a way that nurtures the myth and allows it to go unchallenged. Similarly, the lack of general policy identified by these lawyers suggests that, as far as they are concerned, the organization's hand rarely intrudes into their professional autonomy—and that when it does intrude, it does so without interfering with the lawyers' claim that they are a company of equals: it transfers and promotes without rhyme or reason—and so, the official judgments that the office makes about who ought to be moved and who ought to be promoted are regarded as having little credibility by the lawyers.

"BUT HOW CAN YOU SLEEP NIGHTS?"

All of the current public defenders with whom I spoke and nearly all (93 percent) of the former assistants interviewed in my research agreed that people "constantly" ask public defenders, "How can you defend those people?" The overwhelming majority (97 percent) of former public defenders interviewed agreed that they had believed that they were putting their legal skills to good use by working as public defenders. Only five (8 percent) said that they would not join the office if they had it to do over again.

How can you defend people whom you know are guilty? Public defenders usually respond in a manner that is more weary than indignant:

> Oh God, *that* question! How do you represent someone you know is guilty? So you go through all the things. You know, "he's not guilty until he's proven guilty, until a judge or a jury say he's guilty, until he's been proved guilty beyond a reasonable doubt." I think everyone deserves the best possible defense, the most fair trial he can get. It's a guarantee of the Constitution, no more, no less.

Without exception the public defenders whom I interviewed all had spiels prepared for that question.

Under some circumstances, mere empathy with the client's situation permits lawyers to feel justified when defending someone whom they know is factually guilty:

> Especially when I was in misdemeanor courts, I could see myself as a defendant. Sometimes you get angry enough at somebody to take a swing at them—if you had a gun, to take a shot at them. I could see myself doing that.... Just because somebody was arrested and charged with a crime doesn't mean they are some kind of evil person.

> Look, kids get into trouble, some kids get into serious trouble. I can understand that. In juvenile court our job isn't to punish, the result is supposed to be in the best interests of the minor. Here you've got to keep them with their family and give them all the services you can so they don't do this again.

While the differences between attorney and client mean that the attorney sometimes has a hard time understanding his or her client (and especially the client's motive), *it does not mean* that the client cannot be defended:

> A guy hits somebody over the head and takes a wallet—no problem. A guy that gets into a drunken brawl—no problem. I understand that. Somebody that goes out in the street and commits a rape—I still don't know what goes on in his mind. No, it doesn't make it harder to defend. There is never any excuse for a rape, but you don't have to understand what makes a rapist tick to defend him effectively.

> Sometimes I would question their motives—if it [the crime] seemed senseless, if it seemed particularly brutal or something like that. Then I realized that those were really, for me, irrelevant questions. I still wonder, of course, but I don't ask anymore.

But the alien character especially of the crimes that their clients are alleged to have committed—and the sorts of attributions that they make about their clients because of their crimes—often mean that "you have to care more about your clients' rights than you can usually care about your clients."

> Why do I do it? I do it because the day that I start laying down and not doing my job is the day that people who aren't guilty are going to be found guilty, and that person might be you because the whole system will have degenerated to the point where they can arrest and convict you on very little evidence. So I am protecting you. I am protecting the middle class.

On the surface, what a defense lawyer does is simply protect the client's rights. But many lawyers transform the nature of the battle. They are not fighting for the freedom of their client per se but to keep the system honest:

> It doesn't mean that I want to get everybody off. It means that I try to make sure the state's attorneys meet up to their obligations, which means that the only way they can prove someone is guilty is beyond reasonable doubt, with competent evidence, and overcoming the presumption of innocence. If they can do that, then they get a guilty. If they can't do that, then my client deserves to go home.

They do not defend simply because their clients have rights but because they believe that those rights have been, are, or will be ignored by others in the criminal justice system. That their adversaries often cheat is taken for granted by public defenders. As one put it, "I expected a fairly corrupt system, and I found one. Here I am representing people who cheat, lie, and steal, and I find the same intellect represented in the police who arrest them, in some of the prosecutors and some of the judges as well." Even when not asked to provide examples, every public defender with whom I spoke offered examples of cheating. There was cheating by the police:

> When I was [working] in the state's attorney's office, I would have cops walking up to me as I was preparing a case and I would say, "Officer, tell me what happened." And they would say, "Well, how do you want it to have happened?"

> The biggest form of police dishonesty was this street files thing. They were hiding evidence that would get people off—or get the correct person. But they had decided in their own minds, "This guy is the guy I'm going after," instead of letting the court system decide who was right.

And there was cheating by the state's attorneys:

> Sometimes you know it; sometimes you just suspect that they are kinking the case. One guy, fairly high up in the state's attorney's office, described one of their lawyers as naive because he'd been shocked to find a state's attorney had kinked the case. He said of the lawyer, "He thinks this is for real?"

> Q:Kinked the case?

> R:You might call it suborning perjury; you might call it jogging the memory.

> Q:Are you saying that state's attorneys are sometimes a little unprofessional?

> R: Yes, yes, yes! Lying, having witnesses lie; they lie themselves on the record, they make inferences that I'm lying. It's just a basic matter of cheating, of not being professional. Because they feel they must win the case and will do anything to win the case.... Their obligation is not to win; it is to make sure the law is upheld—and to make sure that my client gets a fair trial. And to them, that is a fallacy.

> I remember in that case the prosecutor basically pulled every trick she could; she argued things that were outside the record; she told the jury that [my client] had a record, that he had put a contract out on the witness. She would stop at nothing to win.

Public defenders in Cook County seem to be of two minds about their judges. On the one hand, they seem willing to trust the judges to do the right thing. "We get what we think the case is worth in most of our bench trials." On the other hand, one gets a definite impression that what public defenders trust about judges is not their fair-mindedness and goodwill but rather the judges' desire not to get into trouble by being overturned by a higher court. In any case, many public defenders told me that they just do not trust the judges' "instincts":

> Knowing legal theory is important, I guess, but it doesn't do any good in Cook County courts, because the question is not—Does the law apply? but—Can you get the judge to obey it, even though his instincts are to fuck you?

> Oh, I wised up real quick and found that judges don't care about the law; they don't always follow the law.

> Q: Do they know the law?

> R: Sometimes....

> Q: But there's always a public defender there to teach them?

> R: Yeah [laugh], but they don't usually care.

> I view judges as another state's attorney. I see judges as essentially enemies I have to deal with…most of them are just bangers.

> Q: Bangers?

> R: Someone who gives heavy sentences—oftentimes regardless of the facts of the case.

Public defenders do feel as if they are often mugged—by the legal system. There is a lot of real and passionate anger: "Some people said I'd become cynical after a while. Well, I might be more cynical about some things, but I don't think I have really changed my attitude. If anything, I might have become a little more gung ho. You see that there really is an awful lot of injustice. It becomes very real and it's scary. I find myself becoming very angry in this job, all the time."

Public defenders often said that they like the trial work more than any other part of their job. Each one will admit, however, that there are some who do not feel that way. These were pointed out to me as examples of bad public defenders or "kickers."

> Sometimes we get a public defender that does not work. He'll force his guy to take a plea, finally on the last day before trial: "Listen guy, you can take a plea which is the best thing you could do or you can go to trial. But I'm not prepared for trial and you're going to lose because you are supposed to lose this case—you know that too."

Some public defenders are labeled as bad lawyers because they cannot hack it in the courtroom, allegedly out of fear. As many pointed out, being "on trial" is scary. One veteran lawyer told me: "We lost a lot of public defenders because they can't handle being on trial."

But all of them, even the lawyers who love trial work, are ambivalent about it. Trial work is as terrifying as it is exhilarating.

> You know [a lawyer now in private practice]? Now he is one of the better trial lawyers. But he used to throw up before final arguments. Once he did it right in front of the jury; he just went over to the wastebasket and threw up.

> Trials? That's when I can't sleep well at night; I'm too busy thinking. A trial is not one issue, it's many. It's win or lose; it's deadlines, organizing things, making sure your witnesses are ready, looking good in front of the jury, looking confident in front of the judge, watching everything you are doing, being alert, keeping a lot of things in your mind at once. And remembering that your client's freedom depends on your polish, how well you can bring it off.

Public defenders are quick to admit that they usually *do not* ask their clients whether they are guilty or innocent.

> Q: Don't you ever ask your clients if they are guilty or innocent?
>
> R: Never!
>
> Q: Why is that?
>
> R: Because, in the first place, it is irrelevant. It's not my role to decide whether they are guilty—in our sense of the term guilt.
>
> Q: What about the "second place"?
>
> R: Well, it is my role to fashion a defense and to be creative. If the person says to me "This is how I did it," it's pretty hard for me to come around and try to do something for them. In general, I fence around with some of my questions. I ask them about an alibi or something like that. But the more I think they are guilty, the less I will ask.

Public defenders do not begin their relationship with a client by asking awkward questions because once the client admits guilt, it limits what the public defender can ethically do:

> I don't ask them because you put them at a disadvantage if you ask them and they say they did it.
> I had a client once who was charged with battery,

and he said, "Yea, I hit him, and I've been meaning to hit him for a long time. But it's just his word against mine, and I'm gonna say I didn't do it."

And I said: "Not with me as your lawyer you're not! You are not going to say anything like that."

So it's important to get the transcripts [from the preliminary hearing] and look at the police reports and say "Look, this is the evidence against us," and then let him make up his own story. It's the only way to do it.

Being honest, ethical and "scrupled" in a system that many of them believe is corrupt is very important to the lawyers with whom I spoke.

Public defenders try not to go into a trial with cases that cannot be won. Unfortunately, most of their cases are of this type—loser (or "dead-bang loser") cases, cut-and-dried situations in which the client was caught red-handed and "the state has everything but a videotape of the crime." In large part, being competent is being able to convince a client that it is not in his or her best interests to insist on a trial that cannot be won. One lawyer explained how he had learned this lesson back when he was assigned to a preliminary hearing court:

> "Well, pal, listen. They caught you inside this guy's home, this guy held you down while his wife called the police. You are not going to get a chance to beat this case. You say you were drunk, but being drunk just isn't a good excuse anymore. It's up to you. The state is making you an offer and if you take it, you'll be better off than if you go upstairs [to the trial court]."

> Everybody told you to say things like that and sure enough, when I got up to the trial courts, I realized it was true. The offers are much better in preliminary hearing courts.

> But to confront those guys with that decision. It was incredible, it was so hard.

> Now I can do it fairly routinely because I have been doing it long enough to have confidence in what I'm saying. I know it is true. And I learned that you aren't doing anyone a favor when you bring a loser case upstairs—it's no good for the client, it's no good for the lawyer. But then I felt incredibly guilty.

Once it is decided that they have a loser case, different attorneys have different ways of trying to "cool out" clients who want to go to trial. However, all of the attorneys with whom I spoke and all of the public defenders that I observed with clients seemed uncomfortable with the idea of forcing anyone to take a plea. Most emphasized that they always tried to reason with their clients:

> Most of our clients do feel that if you are a public defender you are not going to give it your all, because you have so many cases, or you just don't care, or whatever. They feel that you are just there to cop them out.
>
> But my partner and I sit down with a guy and say: "Look, we are lawyers, and we are paid to analyze facts. After we have analyzed the facts, we might say to you, 'we don't think you have a good case and we think you should cop out.' If you don't feel that way, it's up to you."
>
> *We* let *them* make the decision.

But, public defenders admitted, reasoning with a client does not always produce the desired result. One lawyer, now a supervisor, admitted that occasionally he would resort to a little "bullying." What did he mean by that?

> I would come in, and I would say things like, "You know, you are a damn fool if you don't take this deal, because this is the best you are going to get. If you go on trial, in my opinion, you are going to be found guilty and you are going to get more time." And then people would say—not often, but occasionally, the person would say—"I don't care; I didn't do it, and I want a trial!" And I would say, "Okay, okay. If that's your attitude, let's go to trial!"

Ask any public defender "What was your worst case?" and chances are you will hear about a case that was a loser. Understanding the nature of a loser case is crucial, for embedded in the concept—and in the distinctions that lawyers make between losers and other sorts of cases—is the clue to what makes public defenders tick.

> The worst case is where the state has an overwhelming amount of evidence and there is nothing you can do with it…. It's a case where you get beat up in court. And that is just no fun.

> You are so relieved when a guy pleads out on a case that you know you can't win and you are going to get your head beaten on, and the jury is probably going to throw rocks at you when you make the closing argument.

> My worst case was a very hopeless case, a rape and armed robbery, and the persons were captured by the police and they were contending that they were the wrong guys.

Q:Why was that your worst case? You've defended people accused of murder before.

R: The fact that the individuals were given reasonable offers and they should have copped pleas, because there wasn't a chance of their being acquitted. And they were going through the ordeal because they opted for a jury trial. It was just a very painful process; it was just an absurd situation.

Q: Was it a particularly awful crime?

R: No. Well, he just beat up his girlfriend; he didn't kill her or anything. The evidence was just overwhelming against him. He should have pleaded, and he wouldn't. He made me go to trial.

The opposite of a loser case is not necessarily a winner. It is a fun case, which in turn must be distinguished from a boring case.

> I don't like armed robberies because they are boring. There are only one or two issues—either the guy did it or he didn't—and that doesn't make for very interesting work.
>
> The case I am trying…right now is a murder that is really a lot of fun.
>
> Listen to me! "A murder is a lot of fun." How can I say that? [Laugh] It's a murder of a baby, and here I am with my two little kids and you would think that I would feel terrible about that, wouldn't you?
>
> But it's an interesting case because the facts are such that they [the state] don't really have much evidence in the case—a lot of people could have done it. It's all circumstantial evidence. That's fun. It's something for me to get excited about and get into, whereas a lot of cases—there are just no issues and that makes them boring.

> I don't know if I have a favorite kind of case, there are some that are a lot more fun to do—if you just think of it in those terms. I may sound horrible, but, just because of the circumstances, usually murder cases are kind of fun.
>
> Usually what kills you in a case is somebody is on the witness stand pointing a finger at your client, saying "that guy robbed me with his gun." Whereas in a murder case you don't have a victim.

Q:What you mean is that you don't have a victim who can come to testify in court, right?

R: Right, he's not there in court. And all the evidence—well, oftentimes you have a totally circumstantial case which gives you a lot to do…. And rape cases. I hate to say it, but there's a lot to play with in a rape case: identification, consent, much more so than in your average armed robbery. You never, for example, you never have the issue of consent in armed robbery.

Talcott Parsons once commented: "The fact that the case can be tried by a standard procedure relieves [the attorney] of some pressure of commitment to the case of his client. He can feel that, if he does his best then having assured his client's case of a fair trial, he is relieved of the responsibility for an unfavorable verdict." One of the attorneys with whom I spoke seemed to confirm Parsons's hypothesis: "There is a certain consolation of going to trial with a loser case. If I lose, what the hell. I gave it my best shot. If I lose, *it was a loser*. If I win, it's amazing."

Most of the attorneys, however, were not so sanguine and could not detach themselves from the outcomes of their cases so easily. Even losing a loser case, most of them said, is incredibly hard on the attorney.

> It's hard, you know? You can tell someone the facts of the case, and they say, "What did you expect? It was a loser." But that doesn't make me feel any better when I lose a loser. I want to win.
>
> Ah, idealistically I've talked about why I'm a public defender, about how I want to keep the state on the straight and narrow. and I could go home and say, "Well, I forced the state to prove their case beyond a reasonable doubt," but, ah, I still, that isn't what I really feel when I lose. What I really feel is just that I lost this case and I wanted to win this case.

The attorneys are not much comforted by the fact that the client was guilty—or probably guilty, anyway.

> Q: When you feel bad about losing a case, doesn't it help to know that the client was probably guilty, anyway?
>
> R: Yea [pause], maybe. But in the middle of the trial, it's you, you know? You are trying to make them believe what you are trying to sell them, and, if you don't win, it means that they don't believe you. That's probably one of the reasons that it doesn't help.
>
> There was a case, not too long ago, that I really came to believe that they had no evidence on my man, and I fought very hard for him. We lost, and I felt very bad about that.
>
> Afterward, he just fell apart, started screaming at me back in the lockup. We had this big fight. And I yelled at him: "You know, I really put myself on the line, too, and I did everything I could for you, and what are you doing yelling at me? Cause I really believed, and I worked hard."
>
> And then I misspoke myself, because I said, "And I really believed that you didn't do this."
>
> And he said, "Would it make you feel any better if I told you that I did do it?" [Laugh]

> Q: How did you answer him?
>
> R: Laugh] I said, "I don't want to know; don't tell me!" I still don't want to know, and that's how it is.

Most telling is how these lawyers talk about doing trial work. They do not say, "I'm doing a trial now"; they do not ask, "Are you doing a trial this week?" They say, "I'm on trial"; they ask, "Are you on trial?"

Lawyers hate to lose because, although reason tells them a case is a loser, sentiment says that justice favors not the stronger case but the better lawyer. What makes losing any case, even a loser, so bad is their belief that, in the hands of a *good* attorney, there is really no such thing as a dead-bang loser case. One attorney told me: "Fewer and fewer of my cases are losers.... Because I am a better and better lawyer." Most of the attorneys seemed to feel the same way:

> One of the maxims I've learned is that the evidence is always better than the way it looks on paper. There is always some goof-up of a witness, something that comes up in the trial, so that you always have something to work with. Invariably that is so.
>
> By the time I walk into the courtroom, even if rationally I sat down when I first heard the case and said "Well, there is no way I can win," by the time I walk into the courtroom I will figure out some way to argue to the judge or the jury that I think I can convince them. By that time, I believe I can win the case.

Even when they know that their client was factually guilty, public defenders are likely to feel, "I let my client down."

> You go home and you have those "ah, shit! God damn, why didn't I? If I only would have, if I only would have spent ten more minutes, if I only would have asked him this, if I would have gone out and asked, or done more investigations.... Your mistakes? Your mistakes go to jail.

The stress of being on trial and the pain of losing are compounded on those rare occasions when the lawyer believes the defendant is innocent. For this reason, although the lawyers will say, "I don't care if he's guilty or innocent," their claim to neutrality is often a lie. When they say, "I don't care if my client is guilty," what they usually mean is, "I *prefer* my clients to be guilty."

Most defense attorneys would rather not have a client they think is innocent, because it's just irrelevant. Because it's your job to fight the state's case, no matter what. You hate to lose, and you are worried about losing just because it's your job to win. And if you think he's innocent, you worry more. And that is just aggravation, which is really irrelevant to your job.

Losing is one of the costs of being an attorney; losing a lot (I was told) is one of the costs of being a public defender:

> You must try to convince the judge or the jury that what you are saying must be followed. But as a public defender, you get the realization that no matter how hard you do this, no matter how well you do this, you are probably not going to get it across. Or, even if you do, the judge or the jury is going to say no. You cannot be afraid to lose, because mostly it's a lost cause. You cannot have a personality where you must win or it's going to screw you.

> When you lose a few in a row, you question yourself. And then it becomes real hard to go back into court and try again.

Even when there is no way to mitigate the client's guilt or to partly win, there is such a thing as an almost win. Those count too—at least they are counted by the attorneys, especially if the case had seemed to be open and shut. There is a certain measure of satisfaction that can be drawn, for example, from keeping the jury out longer than could have been expected. Even when they lose, public defenders search for evidence that they did a better job, that they "out-tried" the state's attorneys.

Perhaps the most important way in which they cope with losing is knowing that they do not always lose. When I asked one attorney "How do you keep going when you lose?" he said: "Always remembering that there is a flip side of that—you feel great when you win. There is no feeling like it. And *that* wouldn't feel as good if it weren't so hard to win."

Failure is something with which every professional must cope. But implicit in the question, "How can you defend those people?" is the idea that public defenders ought to have trouble coping with winning. The lawyers are protected by the fact that they rarely win cases for clients who are horrible criminals. But however rarely it occurs, the possibility of winning big someday

and then having your client kill again exists in the future of every defense lawyer. One admitted:

> I am mindful of one public defender; I think one of the reasons he left was that he managed to get a guy acquitted on a murder and the guy went out and committed another murder. That really got to him. And I watched him suffer with that, and I wondered if I would suffer like that, and I came to no conclusion.

A few of the lawyers admitted that they had come close to winning cases that, deep down inside themselves, they had not wanted to win:

> I've never felt bad about winning a case. The last jury trial I did I almost won, and I was worried about that. It really bothered me. But all of it has to do with the relationship you have with your client. He was a real asshole and hard to deal with, and he was a mean son of a bitch.

Often it seemed that one of the things that helps the lawyer not to feel too bad about winning is one of the things that makes it so hard to lose—that is, their relationship with the client. Most of the lawyers said that usually, especially when they go to trial, they end up liking their clients. In most cases, the lawyers spoke with some affection about their "guys."

> There is in any human being a soul you can reach. [Pause] Now I use language like this hesitantly, you know; people usually look at you like you're crazy when you talk like this. But if you are willing to take the risk and open up your heart and reach into their hearts, you will reach it.
> You need to do that for yourself. You need to do that, too, because if you are going to try the case for either a judge or a jury…you have to make that person human. They are not some black or brown face—or what face, for that matter. They are someone. And that is what costs. 'Cause every time you do that, you are giving something of yourself away. You get something, sure, but you give away a lot.

Two of the lawyers with whom I spoke had experience what one called the "defense lawyer's nightmare." Only one would speak about it:

> Once on a case with ———, he came up with a brilliant idea about collateral evidence, and I wrote a brilliant brief. It persuaded the judge to dismiss the indictment—just unheard-of.
> And three months later, he killed three other people. He participated in a gang killing—didn't actually do the killing, but he was definitely part of it. That, of course, is the defense lawyer's nightmare.

There are people who can—for example, my partner—who can say, "That's not my concern," but that is bullshit. That is why he is losing his hair and I'm not. You feel bad. You *have* to feel bad.

However, the constitutional proposition was correct, and it made some important law in Illinois; and I would do it again. But I would not represent [that client] again. Because we could not wholeheartedly represent him zealously, we were let off representing him.

"How can you live with that?" I asked. "You either leave, stay and repress it, or you stay and cope. Sure you feel bad, but you deal with it by knowing that, hopefully, you're doing enough good to make you feel good about what you are doing."

DISCUSSION QUESTIONS

1. Why do public defenders suffer low status? Is that true of all public-sector lawyers in the United States? In other countries? Is it disturbing? What could be done about it?

2. What are the incentives and disincentives of legal aid lawyers and public defenders to engage in vigorous advocacy? Do they differ from those of private lawyers?

3. How do the supervisory and training hierarchies of legal services lawyers and public defenders differ from those of other lawyers, e.g., prosecutors, government lawyers, and large private firms?

4. How do public defenders deal with the strain of representing those charged with crimes? Of winning? Of losing? On behalf of those they think are guilty? Innocent? Are public defenders' coping mechanisms different from those of private lawyers?

What cases do public defenders enjoy most? Are there parallels with civil legal services lawyers?

SUGGESTED READING

For studies of private criminal defense lawyers, see A. L. Wood, *Criminal Lawyer* (1967); H. A. Lowenberg, *Until Proven Guilty: Forty Years as a Criminal Defense Counsel* (1971); Janet A. Gilboy, "The Dilemma of Seeking Bail and Preparing a Defense in Murder Cases: Perspectives and Practices of Chicago Defense Lawyers," 67 *Journal of Criminal Law and Criminology* 259 (1976), "Replacing Lawyers: A Case Study of the Sequential Representation of Criminal Defendants," 70 *Journal of Criminal Law and Criminology* (1979); P. B. Wice, *The Endangered Species: America's Private Criminal Lawyers* (1978); Kenneth Mann, *Defending White-Collar Crime: A Portrait of Attorneys at Work* (1985). There is an enormous literature on plea-bargaining, by far the commonest disposition of criminal cases, e.g., Abraham S. Blumberg, "The Practice of Law as a Confidence Game: Organizational Cooptation of a Profession," 1 *Law & Society Review* 15 (1967); Albert W. Alschuler, "The Defense Attorney's Role in Plea-Bargaining," 84 *Yale Law Journal* 1179 (1975); "Plea-Bargaining" 13(2) *Law & Society Review* (winter 1979). On "How can you defend these people?" see J. Mills, "I Have Nothing to Do With Justice," in J. J. Bonsignore, E. Katsh, P. D'Errico, R. Pipkin, and S. Arons (eds.), *Before the Law: An Introduction to the Legal Process* (1974).

For additional studies of the public defender, see E. E. Cott, "Public Defender System: The Los Angeles Story," 45 *Minnesota Law Review* 715 (1961); David Sudnow, "Normal Crimes: Sociological Features of the Penal Code in a Public Defender Office," 12 *Social Problems* 255 (1965); C. M. Lytle, *The Public Defender in Arizona: A Case Study of State Policy-Making* (1969); Gerald M. Caplan, "Career Inhibiting Factors: Problems of the Public Prosecutor and Defender," in J. R. Klonoski and R. I. Mendelsohn (eds.), *The Politics of Justice* (1970); C. Vasiliadis, "The Allegheny County Public Defender Office: A Study," 32 *University of Pittsburgh Law Review* 533 (1971); "Symposium: The Denver Public Defender," 50(1) *Denver Law Journal* (1973); Anthony Platt and R. Pollack, "The Channeling of Lawyers: The Career of Public Defenders," 9 *Issues in Criminology* 1 (1974).

For a comparison of public defenders and court-appointed counsel, see B. F. Willcox and E. J. Bloustein, "Account of a Field Study in a Rural Area of the Representation of Indigents

Accused of Crime," 56 *Columbia Law Review* 551 (1956); Lee Silverstein, *Defense of the Poor in Criminal Cases in American State Courts: A Field Study and Report* (3 vols.) (1965); M. R. Summers, "Defending the Poor: The Assigned Counsel System in Milwaukee County," 1969 *Wisconsin Law Review* 525; Michael McConville and Chester L. Mirsky, "Criminal Defense of the Poor in New York City," 15 (4) *Review of Law &* *Social Change* (1986–87). R. Hermann, E. Single, and J. Boston, *Counsel for the Poor: Criminal Defense in Urban America* (1977).

For the viewpoints of accused, see Jonathan D. Casper, *American Criminal Justice: The Defendant's Perspective* (1972); S. O'Brien, S. Peterson, M. Wright, and C. Hosticka, "The Criminal Lawyer: The Defendant's Perspective," 5 *American Journal of Criminal Law* 283 (1977).

Chapter Nineteen

LAWYERS AND SOCIAL CHANGE: INSTITUTIONS

Private lawyers have always tried to change the rules for the benefit of their clients. The ACLU and the NAACP sought to adapt such strategies to unrepresented interests: the poor and disadvantaged, the unorganized, and the inchoate. Public interest law rapidly expanded in the 1970s, when government, foundations, organizations, and individuals provided financial support.

LIBERTY AND JUSTICE FOR ALL: PUBLIC INTEREST LAW IN THE 1980s AND BEYOND[1]

Nan Aron

INTRODUCTION

IN a 1984 precedent-setting case involving the Erwin nuclear processing plant in Tennessee—a facility that was leaking hazardous PCBs, cyanide, and mercury into the surrounding environment—the Natural Resources Defense Council forced the Department of Energy to comply with federal hazardous waste laws at all national nuclear weapons facilities.

In a significant 1986 case, *Meritor Savings Bank v. Vinson*, the Supreme Court ruled that businesses may be held liable for sexual harassment by supervisors, even if the company has not been informed of the conduct and the harassment has no economic impact on the victim. The case was championed by public interest groups such as the Women's Legal Defense Fund and the National Women's Law Center.

In 1982, as a result of an administrative petition filed by Public Advocates, Inc., the Food and Drug Administration and the Department of Health and Human Services required manufacturers of infant formula to place pictorial instructions on formula packages. The pictures enabled illiterate parents to prepare the formula and helped eliminate infant health problems associated with its improper use.

In a petition filed with the New York State Attorney General's office, the Center for Science in the Public Interest called on the state to enforce ingredients-labeling laws with regard to fast-food chains. The petition served as the catalyst for announcements by McDonald's and Burger King in 1986 that they would disclose ingredients information in their restaurants. The Attorney General's office described the decision as "unprecedented" and an essential public health measure.

The National Organization for Women (NOW) Legal Defense and Education Fund joined the State of Minnesota in persuading the Supreme Court in 1984 to allow full membership to women in the Jaycees. Before the Court issued its opinion in *Roberts v. U.S. Jaycees*, the Jaycees had limited women to second-class membership and did not permit them to vote or hold office. The decision set an example for other clubs throughout the country.

A 1984 study by the Children's Defense Fund revealed that one out of three American children lives in poverty. The story received widespread coverage in leading newspapers and magazines, fueling public debate on the welfare of children and mapping out legal strategies for the future.

HISTORY OF PUBLIC INTEREST LAW

The American Civil Liberties Union

Founded as a citizens' lobby designed to call public and governmental attention to violations of the First Amendment rights of pacifists and conscientious objectors during World War I, the ACLU is a direct antecedent of the public interest law firm. From the beginning, it relied on a variety of strategies—lobbying, litigating, grass-

---

1. Boulder: Westview Press, 1989. Reprinted with permission.

roots organizing, educating the public, and using personal influence on sympathetic leaders—to oppose encroachments on the constitutional rights of individuals in cases primarily involving "sensitive issues of free speech, privacy, and due process."

Working mainly through volunteer attorneys and often limited to an _amicus_ or "friend of the court" role, the ACLU nonetheless has built a semi-autonomous network consisting of local affiliates in every state. The affiliates focus on local disputes that involve important questions of federal law and social policy, and this emphasis on national issues has become a major characteristic of subsequent public interest law organizations. The ACLU has also promoted the idea that government needs a watchdog, an outside citizen's organization to monitor its functions and guard against corruption and abuses of power.

The NAACP Legal Defense and Education Fund

In the 1930s, the NAACP, founded two decades earlier, took a significant step in the evolution of public interest law. It initiated "a comprehensive campaign against the major disabilities from which Negros suffer in American life—legal, political, and economic." The NAACP developed a legal strategy, a long-term litigation campaign that concentrated on eliminating racial segregation in education, employment, and housing based on the notion that the "separate but equal" doctrine was unworkable because separate facilities are inherently unequal. The NAACP/LDF, established as a separate entity in 1939, worked in concert with its parent organization to win the precedent-setting school desegregation decision, _Brown v. Board of Education_, before the Supreme Court in 1954. Brown was used to build a chain of decisions that eventually eliminated the legal basis for segregation in public facilities.

These legal victories in turn fostered a political climate that permitted the establishment of a federal Commission on Civil Rights in 1958 and the passage of the Civil Rights Act of 1964, which created a statutory basis for the federal enforcement of equality in education, employment, and public accommodations.

Another landmark case, _NAACP v. Button_ (1963), removed potential legal obstacles to the practice of public interest law. The Supreme Court rejected attempts by the State of Virginia to prevent attorneys working with the NAACP/LDF from seeking out and providing representation on questions with clear political importance. _Button_ made it possible for civil rights groups and later public interest lawyers to seek out clients and openly use litigation as a part of a broad strategy of reform. It also made it easier for subsequent public interest law centers to treat the law strategically.

To organize and perform its work, raise funds, and institutionalize victories, the NAACP/LDF developed an organizational model that today is used in one form or another by virtually all public interest law endeavors. The main features of this model are as follows:

Like legal aid societies, the organization uses a full-time salaried staff of highly qualified lawyers rather than relying on volunteers or counsel hired on an ad hoc basis.

Unlike legal aid societies, but like the ACLU, the organization does not handle routine "service" cases in which the matter is of concern only to those who are directly affected by the question at issue.

The organization rejects a reactive or defensive posture in representing the client's interest, instead assuming an active role in the strategic accomplishment of goals. Litigation serves as a primary tool for initiating changes in the way in which political and social institutions deal with minority interests.

The organization depends for its primary financial support upon a widespread national membership of concerned citizens that gives small sums to support the work of the organization, even though it serves a very special, relatively poor interest group. The organization rejects the simple accumulation of big cases in favor of a series of incremental victories that create a favorable legal climate while fostering a public concern that may convert victories in the courts into a change in public policy.

The organization works through a self-generated network of cooperating private attorneys to follow up victories achieved to convert theoretical statutory rights into practical substantive benefits.

Expansion of Public Interest Law

The late 1960s and the early 1970s saw a great proliferation of public interest law activity. This growth was fostered by the increase in foundation support; previously the philanthropic community had been hesitant to venture into granting funds to law-related programs. Foundations began to fund civil rights organizations and a whole spectrum of consumer, environmental, and multi-issue public interest law firms. The willingness of philanthropists to support organizations that proposed to use the law to advance new causes was crucial to the rapid development of new public interest law centers such as the Center for Law and Social Policy, the Center for Law in the Public Interest, the Citizens Communication Center, the Institute for Public Representation, the Natural Resources Defense Council, Public Advocates, Inc., and the Sierra Club Legal Defense Fund.

A PROFILE OF PUBLIC INTEREST LAW BASED ON THE 1983–84 SURVEY

Despite a hostile political climate and unusually adverse economic circumstances over the past few years, public interest legal organizations as a whole kept apace. An extensive survey of 158 groups carried out by the Alliance for Justice in 1983–84 shows, in general, an upward trend in public interest legal activity since surveys in 1975 and 1979. The number of groups has increased, the number of staff attorneys has grown, and there is greater variety in the issues these organizations address, the types of clients they serve, and the strategies they employ.

Of the 158 centers surveyed, 41 percent were classified as "cause-defined" and 59 percent as "client-defined." Multi-issue and civil rights/civil liberties groups were the most numerous of the cause-defined type, accounting for 13 percent and 10 percent, respectively, of all organizations surveyed. Centers concentrating on environmental issues made up about 8 percent of the survey group. Among the client-defined groups, those serving the poor were the most numerous, accounting for about 15 percent of all centers surveyed. Groups serving the disabled constituted 9 percent; women, 10 percent; children, 8 percent; and prisoners, 4 percent. The survey demonstrates that public interest legal centers are now more likely than in past years to focus on a specific issue or type of client.

Up to 1969, there were only 23 public interest

law centers, staffed by fewer than 50 full-time attorneys. By the end of 1975, the number of centers had increased to 108, with almost 600 staff attorneys. In 1984, there were 158 groups employing a total of 906 lawyers. The 1970s saw tremendous growth in the number of public interest legal organizations, with 111 groups established, an average of 11 per year. Since that time, the rate of growth has slowed considerably, with only nine new groups forming between 1980 and 1984.

Between 1969 and 1975, the first groups serving consumers, minorities, the elderly, prisoners, workers, and gays and lesbians emerged. Since 1975, there has been an increase in the number of organizations concerned with protection of the disabled and with international human rights. The number of multi-issue groups such as the Center for Law and Social Policy (CLASP), the Center for Law in the Public Interest (CLIPI), and New York Lawyers for the Public Interest also grew during this period.

Public interest law centers remained concentrated in the Northeast: 62 percent of the groups in the 1983–84 survey were headquartered there, almost the same proportion as reported in the 1975 survey. Twenty-three percent were located in the West, 8 percent in the Midwest, and 7 percent in the South. The cities with the most organizations were Washington, D.C. (45 groups), New York (30), San Francisco (13), Los Angeles (nine), and Boston (nine). Still, about one-third of the centers, many of them working at the state or regional level, practiced outside these urban centers in locales as diverse as Eugene, Oregon; Walthill, Nebraska; Austin, Texas; and Gainesville, Florida. A significant change from 1975 was that the proportion of groups headquartered in Washington, D.C. fell from 44 to 29 percent.

The annual budgets of those surveyed ranged from $16,000 to $10 million, with most organizations (64 percent) in the $100,000 to $999,999 range. Only four groups, the American Civil Liberties Union (ACLU), the NAACP Legal Defense and Education Fund (NAACP/LDF), the Natural Resources Defense Council, and California Rural Legal Assistance, reported 1983 budgets of $4 million or more; the largest, the ACLU, had an annual budget of $10.7 million.

The number of full-time public interest attorneys increased from fewer than 50 in 1969 to 600 in 1975, to 906 in 1984. But this increase was the result of the inclusion of new centers, not a sign that organizations were expanding. Indeed, the proportion of organizations with more than five full-time attorneys on staff shrank from 46 percent in 1975 to 28 percent in 1984; 38 percent had three to five lawyers, and 33 percent employed one or two. Poverty and civil rights firms employed the largest number of full-time attorneys. The median number of attorneys was four, again indicating that the large offices of such groups and the ACLU, the NAACP/LDF, and the Natural Resources Defense Council were the exceptions rather than the rule. Civil rights centers accounted for 10 percent of all organizations but employed 17 percent of all attorneys; poverty law firms, representing 15 percent of the survey group, employed 25 percent of the total number of lawyers. At the other end of the scale, women's law organizations constituted 8 percent of the total but employed only 4 percent of the attorneys.

Much of the legal work of public interest organizations was performed not by the full-time staff attorneys but rather by cooperating attorneys. Over three-fourths of the groups called upon outside counsel to handle some of their litigation, with more than half of these attorneys working on a voluntary basis. Outside attorneys performed 28 percent, on average, of the legal work of surveyed groups. The Women's Legal Defense Fund, for example, retained approximately 60 volunteers in its Emergency Domestic Relations program and offered them periodic training sessions and a manual on defending battered spouses. Some of these attorneys worked for government or corporations, while others were recent law school graduates seeking public interest experience.

For several decades the NAACP/LDF has operated a cooperating attorney program which retains 40 to 60 lawyers each year. These attorneys pursue civil rights cases in cooperation with the Fund, either as volunteers or as part of their private practice. Cooperating lawyers are brought together at a yearly conference to discuss current civil rights issues. In addition, NAACP/LDF's Capital Punishment Program augments its small staff with a network of well over 100 volunteer

attorneys handling cases on behalf of death row inmates. The Sierra Club Legal Defense Fund has approximately 60 lawyers in its outside counsel program.

In addition to staff and outside attorneys, almost 1,500 law students participated annually in internship programs, about twice the 1979 number. Some of these internships are in-house, while others are clinical legal education programs operated in cooperation with public interest firms. These interns continue to be an important legal resource for many organizations. Some, such as the Lawyers' Committee for Civil Rights Under Law, pay their interns a stipend during the summer.

The 1983–84 survey identified 906 full-time staff attorneys working for public interest legal organizations. About one-fifth were experienced lawyers who had been practicing 12 years or more. On the other hand, more than one-third had been at the bar for five years or less, and many were just entering the field. Public interest attorneys received comparatively modest salaries. Almost half earned $30,999 a year or less, and another one-fourth earned between $31,000 and $40,999. Only one-tenth earn $50,000 or more. In dramatic contrast, a recent graduate starting out in a large New York firm in 1984 could have expected to receive a salary of $50,000.

The financial support of individuals, through donations and member dues, was the largest single source of funding, accounting for 31 percent of all income. (Of this figure, 20 percent came from charitable contributions and 11 percent from membership dues.) Foundation grants were the second most important source of income, supplying 24 percent of total revenues, while the federal government supplied only 18 percent. Together, these three sources accounted for 73 percent of aggregate income. The remaining 27 percent was supplied by the following: court-awarded attorneys' fees (9 percent); corporate donations (3 percent); state and local government grants (3 percent); sales of materials (2 percent); Combined Federal Campaign contributions (1 percent); and income from a variety of sources, such as interest on bank accounts, speaker fees, and luncheons and conferences (7 percent). Church contributions, funds from the private bar, lawyer trust fund accounts, and loans made up the remaining 2 percent of total income.

The overall funding picture showed a 51 percent increase in total resources between 1975 and 1983, from $70,107,500 to $105,588,110. However, the increase in aggregate funding has not kept pace with the growth in the number of groups, from 86 in 1975 to 158 in 1983. The budget of the average group in the 1983–84 survey was $776,383, a drop from the 1975 average of $815,203. Between 1975 and 1979, the number of groups increased by 28 percent, while overall funding remained static, resulting in a decrease in the budget of the typical group. However, between 1979 and 1983, the increase in aggregate funding outpaced the growth in number of groups, and average group income increased 23 percent. The most dramatic change was in the amount supplied by sources other than the "big three" (foundations, government, and public contributions): alternative funding increased from $2.8 million in 1975 to over $105 million in 1983. For the typical center, which experienced a decline in the amount of funding from traditional sources, the amount supplied by other sources increased from approximately $33,000 to over $200,000.

Foundation support for public interest law remained constant between 1975 and 1983. However, because the number of groups increased by 58 percent during the same period, the average group actually experienced a 36 percent decline. With the election of Ronald Reagan in 1980, government funding for social and legal services was slashed. It rose slightly between 1975 and 1979 and then plummeted between 1979 and 1983, the aggregate by 12 percent and the average group by 29 percent. Attorneys' fees awarded by the courts to prevailing parties in public interest cases provided a substantial amount of income for public interest legal centers. In the 1983–84 survey, 98 groups reported applying for awards, and 67 actually collected fees, most of them computed at market rate, totaling over $9.2 million. This represented a 200 percent increase over the $3 million collected in 1979. Nearly half of all attorneys' fee awards in the 1983–84 survey went to civil rights and minority defense organizations, a higher proportion than in 1979. Poverty groups received almost 10 percent of the total, ten times

more than they did in 1979. Senior citizens' and children's advocates also won more fee awards.

SOCIAL CHANGE STRATEGIES

During the 1960s and early 1970s, public interest law organizations relied on forums such as the courts and administrative agencies to protect the rights of unrepresented persons and groups and to enforce public health and civil rights statutes. During the past two decades, environmental, civil rights, consumer, children's, and senior citizens' organizations have lobbied Congress to enact or strengthen public health and civil rights laws. The classic stereotype of the Washington lobbyist who engages in influence peddling and runs up huge entertainment bills while supposedly "working" social contacts has been joined by a new, less monied, but more serious breed. Once accustomed to playing a behind-the-scenes role, preparing legal memoranda for use by citizen lobbies, public interest organizations are themselves taking up legislative advocacy.

Veteran public interest lawyers are now widely recognized for their expertise in environmental, civil rights, and consumer law. They are regularly consulted by members of Congress and congressional staff for information and advice. Over the years such interaction has put some of the "tools of the trade" of the lobbyist—an extensive set of personal contacts on the Hill, knowledge of who the decision-makers are, and an understanding of the policy-making process—in the hands of public interest lawyers. For the public interest community, lobbying is largely an aspect of coalition work. Some formal coalitions, such as the Leadership Conference on Civil Rights, are supported by dues-paying member organizations to coordinate lobbying strategies on civil rights issues. Public interest centers often serve as the legal arm and adviser to coalitions. The National Senior Citizens Law Center (NSCLC), for example, works with the American Association of Retired Persons, the National Council on the Aging, the National Council of Senior Citizens, and other organizations in the Leadership Council of Aging Organizations, a coalition that has emerged as a powerful voice for the elderly. Similarly, the Institute for Public Representation served as coordinator and chief legal adviser to the 55-member Voting Access Coalition that lobbied in support of the Voting Accessibility for the Elderly and Handicapped Act. Passed in 1984, the Act requires all polling places and a reasonable number of voter registration facilities to be accessible to elderly and disabled voters.

Unusual alliances may develop in the course of such legislative advocacy. For example, in 1981, the steel industry and environmental groups jointly asked a Senate committee to act quickly on legislation to give businesses three additional years to meet clean air standards. The proposal allowed companies to spend antipollution monies on modernizing plants, rather than on installing pollution control devices on outmoded equipment. In another unusual alliance, this time in the regulatory arena, the Environmental Defense Fund (EDF) joined several large oil companies in 1982 in opposing efforts by the Environmental Protection Agency (EPA) and small oil refiners to raise the acceptable level of lead in gasoline. Together, EDF and the oil companies presented scientific studies showing that airborne lead can cause brain damage in children and persuaded EPA to forgo changes in the existing regulations.

Legislative advocacy and litigation often go hand in hand. Cases won in the courts may be in danger of being overturned by laws later enacted by Congress. For example, in 1970 the Center for Law and Social Policy successfully challenged in the courts the construction of the Alaska gas pipeline. After this victory, Congress passed a bill permitting construction to continue. On the other hand, cases lost in the courts may spur remedial congressional action. In 1985 the National Wildlife Federation unsuccessfully challenged in court the Department of Interior's sale of coal leases in Montana and Wyoming at less-than-market rates. The Federation argued that this practice of underselling had resulted in the loss to the federal treasury of millions of dollars and was threatening precious natural resources with destruction. By bringing these practices to light, the court action, although unsuccessful, sparked a furor in the press and focused public attention and Congressional scrutiny on the government's coal leasing pro-

gram. Members of Congress consulted with the Federation in designing legislative action to stop the sales. A commission was established to evaluate the government's coal leasing program and a moratorium on future sales was passed.

The publications of legal groups provide advocates with information that is not easily obtainable elsewhere and present it in a format that laypersons can understand and use. For example, the *Citizen Handbook on Groundwater Protection*, published by the Natural Resources Defense Council (NRDC), gives citizens and public officials background material on current issues so that they may act as informed advocates for better groundwater protection policies. Another NRDC publication, *Children's Art Hazards*, alerts teachers and parents to the health hazards posed by commonly available art materials. The Mental Health Law Project, the Food Research and Action Center, and other legal services support centers compiled a handbook on federal and state entitlement programs for use by operators of charitable soup kitchens, emergency shelter providers, and other advocates for homeless people.

A broad range of newsletters, from *Youth Law News* of the National Center for Youth Law to *Nutrition Action Health Letter* of the Center for Science in the Public Interest, keeps members and friends abreast of an organization's current activities, upcoming government actions, and emerging issues in the field. Sometimes these newsletters become important tools in mobilization efforts. For example, in a 1982 issue of its newsletter, *Update*, the Mental Health Law Project described a newly adopted Social Security Administration policy that terminated the benefits of many mentally ill people by classifying them as capable of supporting themselves through paid employment. The story drew a tremendous response from newsletter readers, who told the project about cases of benefits being terminated under this dubious rationale. Some of these newsletter story contacts eventually became plaintiffs in a successful challenge brought by the project to what it termed a "clandestine policy" to change eligibility criteria. A federal appeals court in New York ordered the federal government to restore benefits that had been denied to 50,000 mentally ill people in the state, and a few months later Congress passed the Disability Benefits Reform Act of 1984, which forbade such cutoffs.

The Women's Legal Defense Fund receives more than 6,000 calls a year for legal assistance. Equal Rights Advocates in San Francisco has instituted an advice and counseling program to respond to the hundreds of calls each year from women who believe they have been victims of sexual discrimination and need information and guidance. Some organizations have installed hotlines to handle the volume of public inquiries. The Center for Public Representation in Madison, Wisconsin, developed the Medigap hotline, which counsels senior citizens on the purchase of supplemental health insurance. The program proved so popular that the Board on Aging and Long Term Care was founded to continue it. The Natural Resources Defense Council maintains a toll-free Toxics Hotline, which provides information about hazardous substances to anyone concerned about possible exposure or seeking accurate information on toxic substances.

Litigation remains the crucial weapon in their arsenal. The ability to sue is the great equalizer among parties to a public interest law case. Even if no lawsuit is brought, it is often the record of past litigation successes that puts "teeth" into these other strategies. Much of public interest litigation aims simply to enforce existing laws. The vast bulk of environmental and consumer cases deal with day-to-day issues such as monitoring public health statutes, and even a substantial portion of civil rights litigation is of the watchdog variety: keeping businesses operating within the law, or trying to make federal and state regulatory agencies perform their functions.

Public interest litigation complements the legislative process in several ways. Judicial decisions that follow the passage of new legislation often serve to interpret its provisions. Even when unsuccessful, a public interest case may dramatize and publicize loopholes or injustices in existing law, thus spurring legislators to rethink public policy and pass new legislation to address the needs raised in trial.

The evolution of the Voting Rights Act of 1975 illustrates this process. In 1982, a major civil rights case, *City of Mobile v. Bolton*, contested Alabama's election system as discriminatory and therefore illegal. The trial court upheld the claim of discrimination and the Court of Appeals affirmed the decision, but the Supreme Court reversed it. The justices argued that, in order to prevail, the civil rights plaintiffs would have had to prove an intent to discriminate under Section II of the Voting Rights Act of 1965. As a direct result of this ruling, Congress clarified its policy in its reauthorization of the Voting Rights Act in 1982, stating that both intentional and de facto voting discrimination were illegal. A similar process led to the passage of the Pregnancy Discrimination Act in 1982. A large coalition of women's labor, civil rights, and abortion groups joined together to persuade Congress to pass a bill reversing the Supreme Court's decision in *General Electric v. Gilbert*, which had denied pregnant women the same protections guaranteed other working women under Title VII of the Civil Rights Act of 1964.

Public interest court cases not only raise social issues, they also bring out the facts involved and stimulate public debate involving all concerned parties. Through discovery proceedings, public interest lawyers can obtain information that the ordinary citizen would have great difficulty in procuring, including on-the-record interviews with public officials, relevant documents of public agencies, and records of actions taken by participants. Often, the expertise of public interest groups reveals obscure facts.

Bringing hidden conditions to light was crucial in the three-year court case in which the New York Civil Liberties Union and the Mental Health Law Project struggled to improve conditions in Willowbrook State School, a scandal-ridden institution for the mentally retarded. Courtroom evidence of neglect, injuries, and even deaths in this home for mentally retarded children and adults sufficiently aroused public consciousness to cause state officials to work toward a consent decree to ameliorate conditions for residents. The well-publicized case also educated the public about the rights of retarded people to as normal a life as possible and about the importance of providing care in smaller, community-based facilities.

The petition brought before the Nuclear Regulatory Commission by Ellyn Weiss for the Union of Concerned Scientists significantly increased public awareness. In 1977, six months after the Three Mile Island incident, the petition focused public attention on the inadequacies of the evacuation plan for communities around the Indian Point Nuclear Power Plant in New York. It pointed out that Indian Point was within 50 miles of New York City, a location chosen in the 1950s, before siting standards were written, and at a time when "the implicit assumption was that there would be no nuclear power plant accidents," recalls Weiss. The New York Public Interest Research Group joined the case, contacting local groups and public officials. A total of 150 witnesses—local government officials, police, school officials, and citizen groups—testified at the hearing, an unprecedented number for the Nuclear Regulatory Commission. Although the petition failed in its attempt to shut down the Indian Point plant, better emergency planning procedures were adopted, and community consciousness of nuclear safety issues was raised.

Another example of the public education role of litigation involved the New York Lawyers for the Public Interest's (NYLPI) successful case to restore the jobs of ten mentally disabled Postal Service workers. Employees of ten years' standing, they were fired when the managers who had hired them were replaced by new supervisors. NYLPI sued, the cases were settled out of court, and the postal workers were rehired. According to former director Jean Murphy, NYLPI took full advantage of the public education aspects of the case, making it into "an opportunity to do some consciousness-raising about disabled people" with both union and Equal Employment Opportunity Commission officials.

Taking major public interest cases to court is costly and growing more so. Indeed, it is difficult to predict the total costs of a case at the outset. The NAACP Legal Defense and Education Fund has found that the costs of civil rights cases, which involve a great deal of fact finding and discovery, have tripled over the past five years. To litigate an average employment discrimination case cost $65,000. The price of litigation, however, can go much higher: the costs of one Kansas desegregation case rose to $800,000.

In litigation, the focus of the court proceeding frequently shifts from whether something should be done to address the grievance of the plaintiff to more complex questions of what remedies might be appropriate or what compensation would be adequate for an entire class of people affected. However, working out such an affirmative decree may be time-consuming and complex.

Perhaps the greatest frustration of litigation for those who practice public interest law is that "individual victories require constant monitoring so that they don't become paper victories" resulting in very little change. The difficulties experienced by the Prison Project in persuading courts to issue remedial orders, particularly when the public is hostile or apathetic, extend to the entire civil rights community. Advocates for deinstitutionalization have witnessed an even more ironic turn of events. The movement achieved great legal victories in obtaining the release of many mental patients from prison-like institutions. However, without the establishment of sufficient community-based care facilities, many former mental patients may go untreated and experience severe relapses, often ending up destitute and homeless.

DISCUSSION QUESTIONS

1. Why did public interest law emerge when and where it did? Although the United States was slow in institutionalizing a national legal aid program, and remains niggardly in funding, compared to other advanced capitalist nations, it has always been preeminent in public interest law. What explains this?

2. How do public interest lawyers select cases and clients? What criteria should they use? Who else should influence them: Individual and collective donors? Activist organizations? Bar associations?

3. What resources can public interest law mobilize? What are its greatest weaknesses? How do you explain its victories? Defeats? To what extent can the models of the ACLU and NAACP be generalized? What are the relative advantages and disadvantages of public and private interest lawyers? How do public interest law and legal aid compare with respect to: goals, strategies, struc-

ture, limitations, and vulnerabilities? Should legal aid emulate the use by public interest law of volunteer attorneys? Law students?

Why did public interest law expand in the 1960s and 1970s? What are its prospects today? How could public interest law expand its resources? What new constituencies have sought to use public interest law? How has their success compared with earlier efforts?

4. Public interest law is not the exclusive domain of those on the left of the political spectrum. Conservative groups have challenged environmental regulation as takings and affirmative action as discriminatory.[2] What are the relative advantages of "liberal" and "conservative" public interest law firms and campaigns?

SUGGESTED READING

On the history of public interest lawyering before the 1970s, see Mark Tushnet, *The NAACP's Legal Strategy against Segregated Education, 1925–1950* (1987), *Making Civil Rights Law: Thurgood Marshall and the Supreme Court, 1936–1961* (1994); Jack Greenberg, *Crusaders in the Courts* (1994).

On the explosion of public interest lawyering in the 1970s, see "Comment: The New Public Interest Lawyers," 79 *Yale Law Journal* 1069 (1970); "Symposium: The Practice of Law in the Public Interest," 13(4) *Arizona Law Review* (1971); Ford Foundation, *The Public Interest Law Firm: New Voices for New Constituencies* (1973); Council for Public Interest Law, *Balancing the Scales of Justice: Financing Public Interest Law in America* (1976); Ford Foundation and American Bar Association Special Committee on Public Interest Practice, *Public Interest Law: Five Years Later* (1976); Charles R. Halpern, "The Public Interest Bar: An Audit," in Ralph Nader and Mark Green (eds.), *Verdicts on Lawyers* (1976); Robert L. Rabin, "Lawyers for Social Change: Perspectives on Public Interest Law," 28 *Stanford Law Review* 207 (1976); Joel F. Handler, Ellen Jane Hollingsworth, and Howard S. Erlanger, *Lawyers and the Pursuit of Legal Rights* chapter 4 (1978); Burton A. Weisbrod, Joel F. Handler, and Neil K. Komesar (eds.), *Public Interest Law: An*

Economic and Institutional Analysis (1978). Nan Aron, whose report is reproduced above, directs the Alliance for Justice, a Washington, D.C., umbrella group of public interest law firms, which tracks and supports their activities.

That the form is politically neutral is shown by Lee Epstein, *Conservatives in Court* (1985). On the phenomenon in Britain, see Jeremy Cooper and Rajeev Dhavan (eds.), *Public Interest Law* (1986).

2. *New York Times* A13 (12.30.94).

The previous chapter examined legal aid and public defender offices from the perspective of the lawyers themselves. Now we turn to the structural limits on what government-funded lawyers can achieve. Unlike privately funded public interest lawyers, most of their cases are routine and repetitive; both kinds of lawyer operate under restrictions that derive from their funding. But there are also structural limitations on what they could accomplish, even with adequate funding and fewer strings attached.

LAW WITHOUT POLITICS: LEGAL AID UNDER ADVANCED CAPITALISM[1]
Richard L. Abel

THE core of legal aid consists of three main areas: reproducing labor power, disciplining capital and the welfare bureaucracy, and restraining state coercion.

Family law dominates all legal aid programs. It represents as much as 90 percent of the work of private practitioners under judicare schemes, and even in staffed offices it frequently is the single largest topic. This is neither surprising nor likely to change. Indeed, legal aid lawyers who complain about such dominance are both ahistorical and ungrateful, for civil legal aid might never have been created but for the dramatic rise in the divorce rate in the last half century. In part, the mix of cases simply results from legal aid lawyers' inability to perform several of the functions that preoccupy private practitioners. They cannot transfer, protect, or invest property because their clients have none, and they cannot redress civil wrongs because of the jealousy of private practitioners. The dominance of family matters also reflects the growing role of the state within the domestic sphere. All societies must devise ways to support those members who are not directly involved in production because they are too young, too old, or too disabled, or are caring for such a person, and who therefore cannot appropriate the resources they need. Most societies rely on kinship obligations for this purpose, but private relationships no longer perform that function adequately under advanced capitalism. The

state therefore creates a variety of legal rights and remedies so that "nonproductive" members of society may claim support from those held responsible: the elderly from their descendants and especially wives and children from husbands and fathers. Because the party who is socially, economically, and politically weaker is asserting a claim against one who is stronger, the state also furnishes the claimant with legal representation. As long as a sexual division of labor continues to characterize the performance of essential tasks of nurturance, state intervention will be a necessary adjunct of social reproduction. There can be no doubt that state support for the legal representation of wives and mothers makes a significant contribution toward equalizing the conflict between estranged spouses.

Yet the limitations of this function also must be recognized. Although I do not wish to underrate the importance of redressing sexual inequalities, providing women with legal representation in family matters at most effects a horizontal or intraclass transfer of resources without altering class differences. Indeed, dividing the already inadequate resources of working-class families between two households may aggravate income inequalities. Furthermore, the state, not the wife (or descendant), actually seeks redress from the defaulting husband (or ascendant) because it is the state that has advanced welfare benefits and wants to recover them. Finally, there is some danger that alleviating a wife's dependency on her former husband through the intervention of a (usually male) lawyer may subtly reinforce sexual stereotypes. These last two reservations require further thought. What is the desirable relationship between spouses and between parents and children after divorce? How could women assert legal claims without relying on lawyers?

A second function of legal aid is to discipline both capital and the welfare bureaucracy. Because market failure arguably is more common in the provision of goods and services to the poor, the state has sought to regulate capital, for instance, in transactions involving rental housing or credit. And because regulations are not self-enforcing, lawyers must assert claims on behalf of the poor. But it is the state that responds to market failure, primarily by taking direct responsibility for redis-

1. 32 *UCLA Law Review* 474 (1985). Reprinted with permission.

tributing income and for distributing goods and services in kind. The bureaucracy that delivers these benefits is vast and highly decentralized. Although the federal government finances welfare, it relies on state and local officials, private philanthropy, entrepreneurs, and professionals to deal with the ultimate recipients. Legal aid is just one of many mechanisms—including internal hierarchy and external review by ombudsmen, politicians, and the media—that promote adherence to rules. Certainly legal aid lawyers secure real and significant economic benefits for their clients: better housing, greater security of tenure, less usurious credit, relief from debts, higher welfare benefits, etc. Perhaps as important, they help poor people assert these rights with greater dignity. Yet, again, there are serious limitations. Lawyers enforce existing private and public law rights. They may be able to compel landlords to render an apartment habitable, but they cannot make them lease it at a rent poor people can afford; they can prevent lenders from discriminating on grounds of race or gender, but they cannot make them lend to people who are bad credit risks by reason of their poverty. They can require the welfare system to grant benefits mandated by law, desist from unconstitutional discrimination, and observe due process, but they cannot determine the amount and content of welfare entitlements. As in family matters, there is some danger that what is gained for one poor person may be taken from another.

There also are problems with the limited goals lawyers can pursue. First, since they cannot assert every legal claim the poor conceivably might make against capital and the state, the disciplinary effect of those they make must depend on some theory of deterrence: the belief that the particular capitalist or public official whose conduct is challenged will observe the law in the future and others will conform for fear of being challenged. But this assumption is implausible and unsubstantiated. Joel Handler has analyzed incisively what he calls the "bureaucratic contingency" and has demonstrated the numerous obstacles to implementation of rules. Clearly the legal order—statutory, regulatory, or judicial—is just the beginning of the enforcement process, not the end. The likelihood is infinitely small that subsequent deviance

by that actor or another will be sanctioned. To the extent that legal aid lawyers seek to discipline public rather than private bureaucracies, they cannot even mobilize the profit motive as a source of leverage. Legal aid lawyers cannot translate the promises of the regulatory/welfare state into reality because these promises never were intended to be fulfilled. From the point of view of both capital and the state, paying off would be far too expensive—an enormous vertical transfer of surplus that would reduce capital accumulation and fuel inflation. Therefore, when poor people begin to assert legal rights with greater frequency (even if nothing like that of their middle-class counterparts), we hear complaints about "litigiousness" and a "rights explosion." Legal rights under capitalism are luxury goods, which are cheapened when everybody has them.

Resisting state coercion is the third major task of legal aid. Just as the high visibility of coercion in criminal prosecutions explains why the accused is the first "litigant" to be granted legal aid, so it also explains why criminal defense attracts dedicated practitioners. The assertion of rights within the family, regulatory enforcement, and the claim of welfare benefits rarely generate comparable drama. Every criminal defense reenacts the bourgeois revolution in miniature by asserting the citizen's right under the rule of law to be protected against state coercion. When that right is denied or begrudged—when success is most difficult, for example, in countries that repudiate liberal ideals or curtail them for defendants unpopular by reason of race, political belief, or the acts of which they are accused—then defense is truly heroic. Indeed, at certain moments, collective identification with and defense of an accused assumes revolutionary significance.

Yet the actual practice of criminal defense rarely exhibits these qualities. The lawyer may long for a principled confrontation that tests the state's commitment to formal justice, but clients usually want an acquittal or lenient sentence. Lawyers actually pursue and obtain the same gains for their criminal clients that they seek for their civil clients: a somewhat better deal than the client would get without a lawyer. Although in some countries legal aid represents the majority of accused (compared with a much smaller fraction of civil litigants), it does so only at trial, not during the preliminary interaction with police or during the subsequent incarceration. Furthermore, just as due process and equal protection can tolerate inadequate family budgets, poor housing conditions, and low welfare benefits, so they can tolerate long sentences, atrocious prison conditions, and a convict population composed disproportionately of ethnic minorities.

Thus far I have dealt with the strengths and weaknesses of legal aid as they pertain to the particular tasks that legal aid lawyers commonly perform. Some of the limitations are generic. Contrasting the conditions under which lawyers act for individual paying clients provides one method of uncovering the limitations. By virtue of the professional monopoly that lawyers have secured and defend, they are able to charge very high fees. They can extract those fees only when the amounts at stake are sufficiently large to justify and absorb such expense. Thus, lawyers make their services useful, indeed indispensable, in situations concerning the aggregate resources of many people (i.e., a business) or those resources that an individual has accumulated over time. Lawyers are involved in the preservation and transfer of property (both *inter vivos* and intergenerational), including residences, trusts, marital dissolution, and estate planning and administration; on the other hand, they rarely handle residential tenancies because the property interest is temporally limited rather than aggregated and thus insufficiently valuable. Similarly, lawyers assert and defend personal injury claims that aggregate labor value (lost wages), experience outside work (pain and suffering), and medical expenses over time, but lawyers are less involved in workers' compensation cases, in which payments are periodic and there is no remedy for pain and suffering. As long as the profession exercises control over the market for legal services, the cost will disproportionately outweigh the monetary value of poor people's problems. Therefore, it is inevitable that private lawyers will be reluctant to undertake legal aid work for the poor, and the state will be equally reluctant to spend scarce resources on salaried lawyers.

That poor people react to law rather than use it facilitatively, just as they react to life, also constrains legal aid. I do not mean to invoke the justly criticized concept of a culture of poverty. I am arguing, instead, that the poor use their only resource—poverty—as a source of strength. In politics they are apathetic; this simultaneously undermines democratic ideology and conveys the implicit threat that their vote, if ever exercised, would significantly alter the configuration of power. This fear is evidenced by Republican opposition to Democratic efforts to expand voter registration rolls. In the market, poverty signifies underconsumption and the problems this creates for capitalist economies; when the poor do buy, they rely on credit, threatening to default on particular debts and declare bankruptcy for the totality. In law, their modal response again is exit. The legal system would collapse if the poor claimed all the rights to which they are entitled. In the meantime, they respond to legal demands with passive noncompliance—for example, failing to pay alimony and support, or repay welfare benefits, or appear in response to a summons—knowing that the cost of enforcement usually outweighs the benefit to the claimant.

Even if lawyers were prepared to work for poor clients at price levels commensurate with the matters at stake and clients were eager to employ them, legal aid still would encounter significant obstacles. Law and lawyers are most effective in mediating interaction among strangers, severing existing relationships, and shaping arm's-length transactions in anticipation of future rupture: consider property transactions, contract formation or breach, torts, and inheritance. When people are involved in an ongoing relationship they typically use political, economic, social, or psychological means to adjust it and to resolve conflict. But legal aid clients lack those other sources of influence and are forced to use law in ongoing relationships: within the family (before it has been formed, while it is intact, and after dissolution) and between landlord and tenant, creditor and debtor, state and welfare beneficiary. Perhaps most important, legal aid operates almost entirely within the sphere of reproduction and exchange—the family, the market, and public distribution of goods and services—leaving relations of production wholly untouched. Most of those eligible for legal aid are not productive workers; among the few who are, many look to unions, not legal aid, for support in workplace struggles. Thus, legal aid contributes to an image of legal equality in the only sphere where such a myth is credible, just as money conveys the appearance of freedom and equality in the market, and the vote does so in politics, while all three preserve unaltered the central source of inequality—relations of production.

If legal aid is limited in what it can do, it also is constrained by fears of success shared by both ends of the political spectrum. Conservatives resent the fact that law, once the exclusive province of the elite, now is claimed by the masses. Radicals attack law in the name of their own communitarian vision. The diverse and often antagonistic ideas inspiring this latter movement are embodied in the creation of "alternatives" to legal and judicial institutions, which offer the poor therapy, negotiation, and mediation in place of rights and adjudication in family conflict, landlord–tenant disputes, small-claims courts, the administration of welfare benefits, tort claims, and criminal prosecutions.

The enthusiasm for alternatives expresses not only an aversion to both conflict and the legalistic assertion of rights (if the distaste is highly selective) but also the pressures of an ever-increasing and apparently limitless caseload. Of course, case overload is not peculiar to legal aid or even the legal system; it afflicts all public-sector delivery of goods and services. In the private sector, increased demand signifies success, stimulating a responsive increase in supply through the reinvestment of retained surplus, technological innovation, enhanced productivity, and the entry of new producers. In the public sector, increased demand portends disaster. The satisfaction of some demands stimulates the expression of others, by both new clients seeking conventional services and old clients seeking new ones. But this demand does not elicit a comparable increase in funding: Welfare budgets almost never grow as fast as the rate of inflation. Nor do gains in productivity make up the difference. All service providers have been slow to adopt new technology, and public legal service providers have been

slower still. The constant pressure on welfare programs to display heightened "efficiency" through lower unit costs can be satisfied only by lowering quality. But lawyers as professionals seek intrinsic rewards from their work and therefore resist such a solution. This tension between the state's obsession with "efficiency" and professional concern for "quality" is an inescapable predicament of welfare services.

Given the structural constraints on legal aid—a series of tasks that must be performed within the inherent limitations of public funding—does the experience of the last half century offer any lessons about how programs should be structured? I will suggest three. A number of commentators have argued that legal aid would be strengthened by extending its eligibility ceiling to include the middle class. Welfare programs that serve a middle-class constituency as well as the poor attract broader political support and thus enjoy higher levels of funding: compare public education (especially the tertiary sector) or social security in the United States, or the National Health Service in Britain, or highways anywhere, with food stamps, or public housing, or AFDC in the United States, or prisons anywhere. The legal aid programs that have secured the most generous funding are those that serve a majority of the population, as in Britain, the Netherlands, and Sweden. These programs also may elicit and sustain greater lawyer enthusiasm because the clientele is more diverse, lawyers find it easier to identify and communicate with middle-class clients, and the problems of the latter appear more significant because they involve larger amounts of money. Yet there are dangers associated with this strategy, whether it succeeds or fails. The middle class always consumes more than its share of public services, diverting resources away from the poor. On the other hand, if the middle class views the quality of public services as inadequate, it will buy private substitutes (as is happening in American education and British medicine), quickly changing a supportive constituency into rebellious taxpayers. Because the middle-class clientele no longer appears to be truly "needy," the program may be attacked as inviting abuse by "welfare scroungers." Finally, to the extent that the legal problems of the poor diverge from those of the middle class, lawyers who serve both may gain variety at the expense of specialized expertise in poverty.

A second strategic choice opposes salaried lawyers to judicare programs. Full-time legal aid lawyers offer higher-quality services, more closely attuned to the particular concerns of poor people, with greater potential for structural change, at lower unit costs. If the political climate were sympathetic to further expansion of their budgets, I would oppose any diversion of public resources to private practitioners. But given the conservative turn in a number of leading capitalist states, I think a qualified case can be made for a mixed system. Clients seem to prefer private lawyers for many of their most common legal needs, such as divorce and its aftermath, residential land transactions, wills and estates, and criminal defense. Even if the basis for this preference is suspect—private lawyers are not technically more competent but develop a better "bedside manner" because they enjoy lower caseloads and have an economic incentive to seek business—I see no reason to deny private practitioners the chance to compete with staffed offices for clients. Their success, to whatever extent, would free salaried lawyers from the routine drudgery and case overload that contribute to burnout and allow them to work on matters with greater potential for structural change. A mixed program also would enable salaried lawyers who leave staffed offices for private practice to continue representing poor clients, thereby retaining their accumulated expertise. Such a program also stands a better chance of enlisting the organized legal profession's support; indeed, some concession to judicare may be the price of the higher eligibility levels advocated above, which otherwise would engender intolerable jealousy among private practitioners. Perhaps because judicare potentially involves the entire legal profession, it is subject to fewer political constraints than staffed offices. Allowing private practitioners to advertise and thus generate the mass clientele that permits economies of scale may alleviate the tension between price and quality. Judicare harnesses professional self-interest in creating demand for legal services to the task of expanding representation of poor clients.

Yet the dangers and drawbacks of judicare should not be overlooked. If private lawyers handle the kinds of legal problems the poor share with the middle class, their availability may reduce the urgency to provide additional services for problems unique to the poor. Furthermore, the routine services furnished by private practitioners are unlikely to identify recurrent problems that might best be handled by law reform litigation, lobbying, or community organization. Regardless of the relative quality of the legal services offered by private and salaried lawyers, clearly there is less control over the former: little hierarchical supervision or selectivity in hiring and even less scope for the play of market forces. There is real danger, therefore, that low levels of remuneration combined with freedom to advertise will produce judicare mills that offer low-quality services while defrauding the state. If judicare makes private lawyers into legal aid supporters, it is a tenuous alliance. Most practitioners earn too little from the program to have a significant financial stake in its funding. On the other hand, those specializing in legal aid matters are concerned only with judicare; they see staffed offices as irrelevant, at best, and rivals when the two delivery systems compete for business. Private lawyers reimbursed by legal aid may suffer fewer political constraints, but they seem to make little use of their greater freedom to challenge the state. Though private lawyers may have an economic incentive to enlarge the scope of legal services rendered under legal aid, there is no guarantee that these additional activities will benefit their clients.

A third innovation also seeks to increase the legal resources of the poor. In the United States today, more than half of all legal services are devoted to advising and representing businesses rather than individuals. In countries with judicare systems, the vast majority of private practitioners do little or no work under the legal aid scheme. In countries with staffed office programs, salaried lawyers comprise less than one percent of the profession. Furthermore, most of them leave the program after a few years. This minimal involvement in legal aid contrasts sharply with findings that a substantial proportion of law students—considerably more than half according to some studies—choose a legal career because they want to help people, especially the disadvantaged and oppressed. They abandon this ideal only because they cannot find jobs in which to pursue it. Some have attributed these altruistic motives to the temporary imbalance between supply and demand for lawyers in the 1960s, combined with the political ferment of that period, but the commitment to legal aid has a much longer history. Law students have volunteered to work in its offices throughout this century, and I see increasing social commitment, undoubtedly connected with the greater proportions of women, minority, and mature students.

How can we tap this reservoir of idealism? First it is necessary to accept burnout as an inevitable concomitant of full-time salaried legal aid work: high caseloads, great emotional intensity, and repeated defeats. Legal aid programs share these characteristics with other occupations displaying high turnover, such as elementary and secondary school teaching, nursing, and social work (although these traditionally female occupations also inflict on their work forces the tension between job and family). Widespread turnover is not an unalloyed benefit, for it undermines the accumulation of expertise. But the greater dedication of law students and recent graduates more than offsets their relative inexperience. Therefore, I would like to see law schools require every student to take a clinical course in poverty law; even the reluctant may be influenced by what is likely to be their first contact with the legal problems of poor people. A postgraduate internship should follow, in a staffed office legal aid program or a private practice that handles legal aid work under a judicare scheme and meets minimum requirements of quantity and quality; this should be mandatory or at least encouraged by strong incentives (for instance, loan forgiveness). The requirement is amply justified by the 19 years of free or heavily subsidized education that every law graduate has received. Of course, most lawyers would leave such a practice at the end of their internship. But some who otherwise never would have considered this work might join staffed offices or continue to represent poor clients under a judicare scheme. All lawyers would acquire greater sensitivity to the legal problems of the poor, inevitably making these lawyers more sympathetic to legal aid programs. And the enormous cohort of students and new entrants to the profession involved in these programs would increase the resources of legal aid severalfold.

Legal aid cannot end patriarchy within the family before or after divorce, but it can alter the balance of power between men and women. It cannot transform capitalist relations of production, but it can regulate the market and discipline the welfare state. It can mitigate, if not eliminate, the pain of the criminal process. Legal aid will be most effective in promoting these vitally important, though limited, goals if it draws upon the best features of the national programs we have examined. Eligibility ceilings should be raised to include the bulk of the population, thus ending the segregation of the poor and creating a politically powerful legal aid constituency. Programs should combine staffed offices with judicare: the former should be increased whenever there is the political will; if it is lacking, the latter should be expanded in order to recruit the legal profession as an ally against conservative administrations eager to cut state funding. The idealism that inspires lawyers everywhere, because it is inherent in law, should be mobilized by making exposure to legal aid an intrinsic part of professional socialization.

DISCUSSION QUESTIONS

1. How should we understand the emergence of legal aid, first as a charitable activity, then as a municipal enterprise, and finally as a function of national government? Can we explain why each phase occurred when it did? Why does the state ever subsidize lawyers to challenge it? Why does capital? What limitations would you expect to arise from this contradiction? What are the interests of the several actors in the legal aid enterprise: private philanthropy, the three branches of government, capital, labor, social movements, individual clients, various kinds of lawyers, bar associations?

How should we understand attacks on and limitations of legal aid? Could it be eliminated entirely? How can it resist partisan efforts to restrict lawyers' functions? Attacks in the 1970s prohibited legal aid lawyers from handling cases involving desegregation, abortion, and selective service, encouraging strikes, pickets, boycotts, or demonstrations, seeking to influence legislation, initiatives, or executive orders, or participating in voter registration or community organization. In 1988 President Reagan's chairman of the Legal Services Corporation deplored that his grantees were…

> …expanding the "reproductive freedom" of children, arguing that children have a "constitutional right of privacy to engage in voluntary sex." Other centers have participated and/or co-counseled in cases with organizations such as the American Civil Liberties Union and Planned Parenthood…. one support center challenged [Florida's] requirement that high school seniors pass a literacy exam before receiving a diploma…. Legal services attorneys have fought the Department of Labor's H-2 worker program because it allegedly permits immigrants to take farm jobs from U.S. citizens. A crop of L.S.C. lawyers are fighting research in California to improve farm production.[2]

Reagan proposed zero funding for the Corporation in each of his eight years in office. In 1996 legal aid lawyers were forbidden to challenge reapportionment or the census, represent prisoners, defend evictions from public housing based on drug use, or file class actions. The budget was cut 30 percent. At the behest of an LSC lawyer, a New York judge has ruled that Congress cannot control how LSC offices use non-LSC funds. Valerie Bogart, who had brought a class action on behalf of thousands of homebound seeking accessible hearings to appeal the denial of Medicaid and welfare benefits, protested: "I was told by Congress that I could not be the lawyer for my own clients anymore…."[3] How do you expect legal aid to fare during periods of fiscal crisis? What claims can it make for scarce public resources?

2. What difference does legal aid actually make to: women, children, criminal defendants, welfare recipients, tenants, consumers, workers, the undocumented, the homeless? What are the contributions, and limitations, of legal challenges to poverty, exploitation, discrimination, and governmental abuse? Under what circumstances can legal aid lawyers change rules? Implement rules? obstruct government? What can they do proactively? Reactively?

3. How could legal aid be strengthened against political attack? Would you favor an extension of eligibility? A mix of salaried lawyers and "judicare" reimbursement of private practitioners? Compulsory service as a condition of entrance to the profession?

SUGGESTED READING

There is a large literature on the power of law, lawyers, and courts to effect social change. For theoretical approaches, see Stuart A. Scheingold, *The Politics of Rights: Lawyers, Public Policy, and Political Change* (1974); Harrell R. Rodgers Jr., and Charles S. Bullock III, *Coercion to Compliance* (1976); Kristin Bumiller, *The Civil Rights Society: The Social Construction of Victims* (1988); Gerald N. Rosenberg, *The Hollow Hope: Can Courts Bring About Social Change?* (1991).

On the civil rights movement, see Clement E. Vose, *Caucasians Only: The Supreme Court, the NAACP, and the Restrictive Covenant Case* (1959); Leon Friedman (ed.), *Southern Justice* (1965); Jonathan D. Casper, *Lawyers Before the Warren Court: Civil Liberties and Civil Rights, 1957–1966* (1972); Richard Kluger, *Simple Justice: The History of Brown v. Board of Education and Black America's Struggle for Equality* (1975); Derrick A. Bell Jr., *And We Are Not Saved* (1987), *Faces at the Bottom of the Well* (1992); Taylor Branch, *Parting the Waters: America in the King Years, 1954–1963* (1988); J. L. Chestnut Jr. and Julia Cass, *Black in Selma: The Uncommon Life of J. L. Chestnut Jr.* (1990); Richard Couto, *Ain't Gonna Let Nobody Turn Me Round: The Pursuit of Racial Justice in the Rural South* (1994); Stephen Wasby, *Race Relations Litigation in an Age of Complexity* (1994); David J.

---

2. *New York Times* A14 (11.22.88).

3. On the attack, see *Los Angeles Times* A5 (2.15.95), B3 (9.1.95); *New York Times* A28 (3.31.95), A1 (9.5.95), A9 (9.14.95), A6 (10.7.95), A12 (10.11.95), A14 (5.6.96), A16 (7.16.96), A14 (8.1.96), A11 (12.27.96).

Armor, *Forced Justice: School Desegregation and the Law* (1995); Stephen C. Halpern, *On the Limits of the Law: The Ironic Legacy of Title VI of the 1964 Civil Rights Act* (1995); Fred Gray, *Bus Ride to Justice: Changing the System by the System* (1996); Davison M. Douglas, "The Limits of Law in Accomplishing Racial Change: School Segregation in the Pre-*Brown* North," 44 *UCLA Law Review* 677 (1997).

For comparative perspectives, see Frank K. Upham, *Law and Social Change in Postwar Japan* (1987); Carol Harlow and Richard Rawlings, *Pressure Through Law* (1992) (UK); William A. Bogart, *Courts and Country: The Limits of Litigation and Social and Political Life of Canada* (1995);

Richard L. Abel, *Politics by Other Means: Law in the Struggle Against Apartheid, 1980–1994* (1995).

On other struggles, see Susan Olson, *Clients and Lawyers: Securing the Rights of Disabled Persons* (1984); Susan E. Lawrence, *The Poor in Court: The Legal Services Program and Supreme Court Decision Making* (1990); Martha F. Davis, *Brutal Need: Lawyers and the Welfare Rights Movement, 1960–1973* (1993); David J. Garrow, *Liberty and Sexuality: The Right to Privacy and the Making of* Roe v. Wade (1994); Michael W. McCann, *Rights at Work: Pay Equity Reform and the Politics of Legal Mobilization* (1994); Helena Silverstein, *Unleashing Rights: Law, Meaning, and the Animal Rights Movement* (1996).

Chapter Twenty
LAWYERS AND SOCIAL CHANGE:
STRATEGIES

The previous chapter considered the structures through which legal services are delivered to the unrepresented and how those structures shape legal strategies. Now we turn to theorizations of law and social change, especially those influenced by critical legal studies and critical feminist and race theory.

BUILDING POWER AND BREAKING IMAGES: CRITICAL LEGAL THEORY AND THE PRACTICE OF LAW[1]
Peter Gabel and Paul Harris

MOST lawyers on the left have a pessimistic view of their own political role in bringing about fundamental social change. Some think that the law is simply a tool used by the ruling class to protect its own economic interests, a view which by definition means that no important gains can be won in the legal arena. Those who believe this tend to relegate themselves to the role of protecting oppressed people against the worst abuses of an unjust system while awaiting the development of a revolutionary movement "at the base." Others graduate from law school believing that meaningful reforms can be won through legislative and judicial action and often devote several years of hard work for little pay to the goal of getting people more rights. But they then discover that the expansion of legal rights has only a limited impact on people's real lives, and that even these limited gains can be wiped out by a change in the political climate. The consequence is that by their mid-thirties many lawyers have either lost their early idealism or have had their original cynicism confirmed. And even the most committed find themselves at a loss as to how to integrate their politics with their everyday work as lawyers.

We argue that the legal system is an important public arena through which the State attempts—by manipulation of symbols, images, and ideas—to legitimize a social order that most people find alienating and inhumane. And yet precisely because the hierarchies of the legal system are sustained only by people's belief in them, legal conflicts of every type can become opportunities to crack the facade of legitimacy that these hierarchies project. The state's strategy of legitimation dictates a counter-strategy of delegitimation, or what Gramsci called "counter-hegemonic struggle."

A POWER-ORIENTED APPROACH TO LAW PRACTICE

A first principle of a "counter-hegemonic" legal practice must be to subordinate the goal of getting people their rights to the goal of building an authentic or unalienated political consciousness. This obviously does not mean that one should not try to win one's cases; nor does it necessarily mean that we should not continue to organize groups by appealing to rights. But the great weakness of a rights-oriented legal practice is that it does not address itself to a central precondition for building a sustained political movement—that of overcoming the psychological conditions upon which both the power of the legal system and the power of social hierarchy in general rest. In fact, an excessive preoccupation with "rights-consciousness" tends in the long run to reinforce alienation and powerlessness, because the appeal to rights inherently affirms that the source of social power resides in the state rather than in the people themselves. A "power" rather than a "rights" approach to law practice should be guided by three general objectives that are as applicable to minor personal injury cases as to major cases involving important social issues.

1. 11 *NYU Review of Law and Social Change* 369 (1982–83). Reprinted with permission.

First, the lawyer should seek to develop a relationship of genuine equality and mutual respect with her client. Second, the lawyer should conduct herself in a way that demystifies the symbolic authority of the state as this authority is embodied in, for example, the flag, the robed judge, and the ritualized professional technicality of the legal proceeding. Third, the lawyer should always attempt to reshape the way legal conflicts are represented in the law, revealing the limiting character of legal ideology and bringing out the true socioeconomic and political foundations of legal disputes.

Although a central objective of this article is to argue that all legal cases are potentially empowering, the classic political case remains one which receives widespread public attention because it emerges from a social conflict that has already achieved high visibility in the public consciousness. Precisely because the state's objective is in part to defuse the political energy that has given rise to the case, the legal issue is often one that deflects attention from and even denies the political nature of the conflict.

The Chicago Eight Trial

Perhaps the clearest example of this "deflection" was the so-called "conspiracy" trial of the Chicago Eight, in which the issue as defined by the prosecutor was whether the defendants who had helped to organize the antiwar demonstrations outside the Democratic National Convention in 1968 had conspired to cross state lines with the intent to incite a riot. The political meaning of the demonstrations was to challenge the morality of the Vietnam War and the political process that served to justify it, but this meaning was, of course, legally irrelevant to the determination of whether the alleged conspiracy had taken place.

Using a case like this to increase the power of an existing political movement requires a systematic refusal to accept the limiting boundaries which the state seeks to impose on the conflict. Had the lawyers and clients in the Chicago Eight

trial presented a legal defense in a normal professional way, they would have deferred to the authority of Judge Hoffman and politely tried to show, perhaps with success, that the defendants did not "intend" to incite a riot or did not "conspire" to cross state lines to do so. But the lawyers and clients understood very well that even a legal victory on these terms would have meant a political defeat for their movement. They understood that the prosecutor's real purpose was to channel the political struggle in the streets into an official public chamber, to recharacterize the protesters as hooligans, and to substitute a narrow and depoliticized legal description of the meaning of the Chicago events for their true meaning. In this context state power consists not so much in the use of direct force as in the use of the sanctity of the legal process to recast the meaning of the disruption that took place.

In concert with their courageous clients, William Kunstler and Leonard Weinglass were able to reverse the government's strategy and cause it to backfire, seizing upon the media's coverage of the trial to strengthen the resistance that had begun in the streets. By openly flouting the hierarchical norms of the courtroom and ridiculing the judge, the prosecutor, and the nature of the charges themselves, they successfully rejected the very forms of authority upon which the legitimacy of the war depended. As Judge Hoffman gradually lost the capacity to control "his" room, he was transformed on national television from a learned figure worthy of great respect into a vindictive old man wearing a funny black tunic. In the absence of an underlying popular movement, the tactic of showing continuous contempt for the proceedings might simply have been an unproductive form of "acting out." But within its concrete historical context, this tactic was the most effective way to affirm to millions of supporters following the trial that their version of the meaning of the Chicago protests was right and could not be eroded by the state's appeal to a mass belief in authoritarian imagery.

The Inez Garcia Trial

The importance of this kind of symbolic resistance was demonstrated in a somewhat different, although equally powerful, way in the two murder trials of Inez Garcia, which took place almost ten years later during an intense period in the rise of the women's movement. Inez Garcia shot and killed one of the men who helped to rape her. Twenty minutes after the rape, she looked for and found the two men; as one pulled out a knife, she killed him and shot at the other as he was running away. At her first trial facing a first-degree murder charge, she was represented by an excellent male criminal lawyer. He defended her on the grounds of "impaired consciousness," a psychiatric defense which argued that Garcia was suffering from a temporary loss of conscious control over her behavior. If successful, such an approach provided a complete defense to murder. The trial strategy was secondarily aimed at achieving a conviction on a lesser included offense, such as second-degree murder or manslaughter. This strategy was somewhat successful from a legal point of view, since Garcia was found guilty of second-degree murder and given a sentence less severe than she would have received for a first-degree conviction.

Politically, however, the defense was a failure: It contradicted the defendant's belief in the rightness of her own act, and it failed to place Garcia's conduct in the context of a rising women's movement that was demanding recognition of the violent effect of rape and sexual harassment upon women. In her defensive and apologetic posture, Garcia was humiliated by psychiatric testimony that exposed her personal life in a denigrating way, and offended by the argument, made in her defense, that she was "sleepwalking" and unconscious of what she was doing. The contradiction between this legal characterization of her conduct and her true feelings erupted on the stand when she testified: "I took my gun, I loaded it, and I went out after them.... I am not sorry that I did it. The only thing I am sorry about is that I missed Luis." Earlier in the trial, Garcia had reacted violently to the judge's decision to disallow testimony about the emotional trauma of rape. She leaped up from the counsel table and said: "Why don't you just find me guilty? Just send me to jail.... I killed the fucking guy because he raped me!" Obviously, after that, the jury could not accept the attempted portrayal of Garcia as a demure and innocent woman who was so overcome that she could not be held responsible for her acts.

Garcia's conviction was reversed on appeal because of an improper jury instruction. In the retrial, she was represented by radical-feminist attorney Susan Jordan. The defense was a creative combination of the traditional rules of self-defense and the historical reality of the victimization of women by men. The task Jordan faced was to translate the male-oriented rule of self-defense into a form that would capture the real experience of a woman facing possible attack by a man. She also had to combat, within the confines of the courtroom, the sexist myths that would influence the jurors.

The rule of self-defense is based on one's right to use reasonable force if, and only if, one reasonably perceives that there will be an imminent attack. The heart of the defense is the defendant's state of mind—it is necessary to convince a jury that the defendant acted in a reasonable manner given the circumstances.

In Garcia's situation, the jurors' understanding of whether Garcia acted "reasonably" would almost certainly be influenced by cultural myths about the act of rape. The rape myths are that women invite it, that they encourage it, and they like it, and that, ultimately, the rape is their own fault. Jordan directly confronted these stereotypes by the creative use of *voir dire*. The jurors were questioned individually, one by one in the judge's chambers. Each juror was asked questions designed to bring out any underlying sexist stereotypes. Although this was a painful process, initially opposed by the judge, and irritating to some jurors, it paid off. The final jury of ten men and two women was able to view the rape not as a sexual act caused by male–female flirting, but rather as a violent assault. This view of rape as an act of violence was key to the acceptance of the self-defense theory.

Jordan also faced the problem of Garcia's obvious anger at the men who raped her. If this anger was viewed by the jury as the motive for her shooting, then it would negate self-defense and lead to a verdict of manslaughter. The defense, therefore, attempted to show that the anger was a justified and reasonable response to her rape. Expert witnesses testified to the psychological effects of rape, especially a rape committed on a Latina, Catholic woman. Instead of the traditional tactic of trying to hide the woman's anger, the defense affirmed this anger and explained it in human terms, which broke through the male prejudices embodied in the law's traditional view of the reasonable person. The result was a complete acquittal.

The two trials of Inez Garcia demonstrate that in the right circumstances it is possible to win a case with a political approach when a more conventional legal approach would fail. Inez Garcia took the action that she did at a time when the women's movement was actively challenging the forms of patriarchal domination characteristic of man–woman relations throughout the social structure, and the central symbol of this domination was the act of forcible rape itself. With a male attorney in her first trial in effect apologizing for her action and the anger that produced it, Garcia was separated from the movement supporting her, and indeed from her own self. In pleading "impaired consciousness," she was forced to deny the legitimacy of her own action and simultaneously the legitimacy of the "unreasonable" rage that women throughout the country were expressing in response to their social powerlessness in relation to men. The form of the first trial turned Garcia into an isolated object of the legal system, a mere "defendant" requesting mercy from a "masculine" legal structure. Even a victory in the first trial would have had negative political consequences because it would have affirmed the wrongness of both her action and the feeling that provoked it, while legitimizing the authority of a benevolent state.

The most important feature of the second trial was that it reversed the power relations upon which the first trial was premised. The defense both affirmed the validity of Garcia's action and allowed Jordan to join Garcia as co-advocate for a vast popular movement, to speak to the jury not as a state-licensed technician "representing" an abstract "defendant," but as a woman standing together with another woman. Together, the two women were able to put the act of rape itself on trial and address the jurors, not as "jurors" but as human beings, about the meaning of being a woman in contemporary society. The effect of this was to transform the courtroom into a popular tribunal and to divest the prosecutor and the judge (who, as men, could not abstract themselves entirely from the evident signs of their own gender) of some of the symbolic authority upon which the legitimacy of the "legal form" of the proceeding depended. This shift in the vectors of power within the room also allowed the jurors to escape their own reification, to discover themselves as politically responsible for making a human, rather than a merely formal, decision based on an application of existing law. Thus the conduct of the second trial, coupled with the widespread publicity attendant to it, served to expand the power of the movement from which the political basis of the case derived and to delegitimate the apparent necessity of existing legal consciousness.

COUNTER-PRESSURE IN LOW-VISIBILITY POLITICAL CASES

In 1971 the Latin community in San Francisco's Mission district was experiencing "brown power" and intense organizing by radical and liberal groups. The most effective radical organization was called "Los Siete" ("The Seven"), named after seven young men who had been acquitted of murdering a policeman after a long, contested trial. Los Siete ran a community clinic, organized a formidable labor caucus, pushed for community control of police, and published a community newspaper.

Los Siete's members were often harassed by police who operated out of the then infamous Mission police station. On a busy shopping day, two of Los Siete's most active members, a Latino man and a black woman, were selling their newspaper *Basta Ya* on the sidewalk in front of the largest department store in the Mission. The store manager called the police. When the police arrived they berated the young man, called him "wetback" and told him to go back to Mexico. The police confiscated the papers and arrested both the man and the woman for trespass, obstructing the sidewalk, and resisting arrest.

There was no publicity of the arrest. The store owners saw the arrest as a vindication of their right of private property. The police viewed it as a demonstration of their power in the Mission district and a warning to community groups. The district attorney's office treated the case as a routine misdemeanor. The defendants felt the arrests had been an act of intimidation and racism. The woman was treated as a prostitute at the City Jail, examined for venereal disease, and put in quarantine for two days while awaiting the results of the test. The excuse given for such treatment was that she had been charged with obstructing the sidewalk, an offense associated with prostitution.

Los Siete asked the Community Law Collective, a local law office that acted as "house counsel" to many community organizations, to defend their members and to help them develop a legal-political analysis of the case. The attorneys explained that although there was a First Amendment issue present, it was doubtful that such a right could be vindicated at the lower court level. At trial, it would be the defendants' testimony against the testimony of two policemen, a security guard, and possibly the store manager. Even though the defendants had sold their newspapers on the sidewalk without harassing store customers, the state's witnesses would place them on store property obstructing customers, and the police would swear the Latino man had pushed them and refused arrest. The jury would be almost all white and predisposed toward the state's witnesses. If the trial was before one of the few liberal municipal court judges, the defendants might receive thirty days in jail if convicted; if before one of the many conservatives, the sentence would probably be six months in jail. If, on the other hand, the defendants were to plead guilty, the district attorney would drop all the charges except trespass, and would offer a 60-day suspended sentence.

If the lawyers had acted as apolitical professionals in this situation, they almost certainly would have advised their clients to plea-bargain. First, it makes sense to accept probation in the face of a likely jail sentence. Second, preparation and trial would be quite time-consuming, and remuneration would be small. But for the lawyers to have given such "normal" advice in this context would have made them mere extensions of the system. It is not in the interests of the state in this situation to send defendants to jail and risk an increase of organized anger in the community. Rather, the state's strategy is to break the spirit and limit the options of the community movement. It is the plea-bargain that best accomplishes this purpose, by simultaneously vindicating the police, legitimating the store owner's property rights, and making community activists feel powerless and humiliated. Moreover, in offering defendants a six-month suspended sentence, the State is also offering them a two-year probation period, the obvious effect of which is to inhibit any future activism. In this context the plea bargain becomes the iron fist in the velvet glove, and the defense lawyer who passively participates in arranging such an outcome becomes partly responsible for its consequences.

Understanding the dangers of "copping a plea," the lawyers and clients attempted to define what was really at issue and to explore a radical approach to the case. The issue was the exercise of political power, in the form of selling *Basta Ya* on the streets of the Mission community. Selling the newspaper served three purposes. First, the person-to-person contact was an effective organizing tool for Los Siete, helping them to build support for their community programs. Second, the street-corner sales were the primary means of distributing the paper and therefore of getting the information in the paper out to the community. Third, the very act of selling their paper in the streets of the Mission district made the activists feel some power in the face of overwhelming police authority, and the sight of young Latinos passing out their radical newspaper helped to create a vague but important sense of indigenous power in the community residents as well. To maintain this sense of power it seemed necessary to reject the psychological defeat inherent in the plea bargain and to risk a trial.

The tasks facing the lawyers in this case were, first, to empower their clients and Los Siete as an organization and, second, to win the trial. Both goals would be furthered by an overtly political defense: the first, because political defense would insist that the defendants were right to be reaching out to the community; the second, because this particular trial could only be won by challenging the narrow "legal" definition of their action as criminal obstruction and trespass.

The lawyers' first tactic was to go on the offensive by filing a motion to suppress the seized newspapers on the grounds that the arrest and seizure violated the First Amendment. This tactic was no different from one that any good defense lawyer would use once plea-bargaining had been rejected, but here the purpose was not so much to vindicate a legal right as such as to force the state to defend its actions. Surprisingly, the municipal court granted the motion, much to the irritation of the district attorney, who was then forced into the defensive posture of filing an appeal. The defense lawyers asked a young corporate attorney interested in "pro bono" work to prepare the appeal. The coalition of community lawyers and corporate lawyer increased the ideological pressure on the district attorney's office. Although the corporate attorney wrote an excellent brief and argued the case, the municipal court decision was reversed.

Next came the trial plan. The first strategic issue was whether to try to pack the courtroom with community people. Traditional lawyers are wary of this tactic for fear that the presence of third world and "radical" people will frighten the jury and create subconscious hostility. However, lawyers can often use crowded courtrooms to their advantage by dealing with the jury's anxiety and hostility toward the community presence in *voir dire* and by openly discussing any negative preconceptions the jurors might have in opening and closing arguments. Due to a lack of publicity, it was not possible, in this case, to fill the courtroom with community supporters, but enough were present to prevent the defendants from feeling isolated.

The second issue related to the clients' participation in the preparation and conduct of the trial. In the traditional view of the lawyer–client relationship, the lawyer is defined as the professional who "handles" all legal aspects of the case without client participation. By treating the client as someone who cannot understand the conduct of her own trial, the traditional approach increases the client's sense of powerlessness in the face of the intimidating spectacle going on in the courtroom. In this case, the lawyers took the opposite approach, asking the clients to take an active part in all aspects of the case where prior legal training

was not absolutely required. Thus, the defendants wrote *voir dire* questions and assisted in the selection of jurors. The lawyers discussed each aspect of the case, explaining their tactics and incorporating many of the suggestions of the clients. In this manner the clients began to feel some control over the process into which the state had forced them.

As for the trial itself, a traditional approach would have been to argue the client's version of the facts against the State's version, relying on a reasonable doubt defense and keeping the content of the newspaper itself out of evidence. A more liberal approach would have been to focus on the First Amendment aspects of the case, emphasizing the abstract right of dissenters to freedom of speech. The radical approach was to stress the political realities involved; to admit and defend the true nature of *Basta Ya*, and to expose the police department's racism and its attempts to harass and intimidate members of Los Siete.

The two young lawyers in the *Basta Ya* trial had a combined experience of less than four trials. Their clients faced only misdemeanors and there was very little visible community support in the courtroom. An extensive *voir dire* in this context may have been viewed as overkill. However, it was simple to ask a few questions, which had the effect of setting a political tone to the trial. For example, the first juror was asked the following: "The community newspaper that was being passed out was called *Basta Ya*, which means 'Enough Already!' Have you ever heard of it?" Since the juror's answer was no, the next question, spoken with enough clarity and strength to grab the attention of all the jurors, was, "*Basta Ya* has articles very critical of the police for harassing Latinos and Mission residents. Would that prejudice you against Raul Flores?" By the fourth or fifth juror, this question became shortened to, "Would the articles criticizing police brutality make it hard for you to evaluate the evidence with an open mind?" One of the jurors, an older Italian man, was asked the following series of questions: "Mr. Flores speaks both English and Spanish. Are you familiar with people who have the ability to speak two languages?" Answer: "Of course; in my family, my wife and I, and son do." Question: "Do you take pride in your heritage, your cul-

ture?" Answer: "Very much. It's important."
Question: "Would you think badly of Mr. Flores
if, when he testifies, he speaks with a heavy Spanish accent?" Answer: "No, not if I can understand
him." These types of questions give jurors some
understanding of the racial and political issues
behind the formal charges.

In an opening statement, one need not give a
political lecture to the jury, nor are most judges
likely to allow such an approach. However, a few
sentences can inform both the jury and the judge
as to the actual nature of the case. For example,
the following was one of two or three political
comments in the *Basta Ya* opening statement:
"Raul Flores will take the stand and testify. You
will see that he is 23 years old, married, with one
small child. He has been active for many years in
community groups, militantly organizing against
police abuse and brutality in the Mission district." At the very least, this type of statement
puts the jury on notice of the political context of
the trial.

Cross-examination is the most overrated
aspect of the trial. In a low-visibility case it is
quite difficult for a lawyer to be able to expose the
racism and bias of police officers. Consequently,
one must try to shed light on that bias rather than
attempt to tear the mask off:

> *Question*: Officer, you are assigned to the Mission
> police station, correct?
>
> *Answer*: Yes.
>
> *Question*: For two years you have worked out of the
> Mission station, right?
>
> *Answer*: That's right.
>
> *Question*: You've seen people selling Basta Ya up and
> down the streets of the Mission, haven't you?
>
> *Answer*: Yes, I have.
>
> *Question*: And you have seen Basta Ya in the little
> newsboxes on the corners?
>
> *Answer*: I've noticed them occasionally.
>
> *Question*: Before you arrested Sr. Flores and confis-
> cated his papers, you were aware that the front-page
> photo and headline were about police brutality in
> the Mission, weren't you?
>
> *Answer*: No, I don't think I was aware of that.

These questions gave the jury some insight into

the political motivations of the police, even
though they did not fit the romanticized notion
of a great political cross-examination.

The trial ended successfully for the defendants, despite the judge's persistent attempts to
ridicule the attorneys and to prohibit any mention of the First Amendment. Instead of feeling
that they had won by disguising their politics
through either the traditional or liberal approach,
the defendants felt a sense of power and truth
because the political meaning of their actions had
been presented and vindicated. After the trial,
the defendants went back with other members of
Los Siete to distribute newspapers in the same
location, while the police and store owner looked
on. "Basta Ya" means "Enough Already." The case
delivered to the arresting officers, the local police
station, and the conservative merchants a clear
message: if you mess with Los Siete, they have
the spirit and resources to hit back.

COUNTER-PRESSURE IN "NONPOLITICAL" CASES

The vast majority of legal cases do not, however,
have this immediate potential for public impact.
The experience of minor lawsuits is one of
the few times that most people actually encounter the public sphere directly, and the experience almost always intensifies the alienation
they already feel. We propose three principal
approaches to politicizing nonpolitical cases,
which we believe will enable both lawyers and
clients to begin to overcome this alienation. They
are: 1) the disruption of the State's attempt to
individualize and isolate such cases by discovering the inherent political content of common
types of cases and using this political content
to build community organization; 2) the politi-
cization of local courtrooms and other "legal"
public spaces that are currently colonized by government officials; and 3) the de-professionaliza-
tion of the lawyer–client relationship at a widespread level.

Discovering the Common Thread

In a landlord–tenant practice, which primarily
consists of fighting evictions on a case-by-case
basis, lawyers can politicize cases by encouraging

organizing efforts among tenants and by simply suggesting that people discuss their common difficulties as tenants. Such a suggestion helps reveal that the political issue at the root of land-lord–tenant conflicts is not whether tenants "need more rights" but rather what the destructive effects of the housing market itself are on people's communities and home lives. Moreover, if efforts are made to link newly formed groups of tenants to an existing local tenants' organizing committee, it becomes easier for people to overcome the isolation and frustration that is brought about by the sense that they alone face eviction lawsuits or have trouble with their landlord.

A great many lawyers make it part of their political work in every kind of case to "gently" deconstruct the courtroom in their local communities and, in so doing, contribute to eroding the symbolic power of the State's authority from the bottom up. The courtroom is a symbolically organized public space designed to reproduce, through repeated visible rituals, a collective obedience to political authority. lawyers can recognize the legitimacy of officials and the authoritative facade by acting in accordance with an authentic human morality against which this facade, because it is constructed upon images, is always powerless. In forcing the actors in their false drama to recognize them as actual and ordinary persons, lawyers are able, however briefly, to transform the courtroom, with all of its choreographed style and pretense, into a mere room inhabited only by other ordinary people.

The Politicization of the Courtroom

It is not an exaggeration to say that the single most powerful collective image of political authority is that of the courtroom. The robed judge who sits elevated from the gathering, the official and hushed character of the legal proceeding, the architecture of the room, the complex procedural technicalities—all of these and many other features of the courtroom ritual serve to reinculcate the political authority of the State and through it the legitimacy of the socioeconomic order as a whole.

Several years ago Stephanie Kline, a radical health worker, was falsely charged with murder and possession of explosives. Bail was set at \$75,000, and her lawyer moved to have it reduced. In the Oakland Municipal Court there is a "prisoner's dock" adjoining the holding cell, located to the right or left of the judge's elevated bench. At a bail hearing crowded with Kline's supporters, the bailiff escorted Kline to her dock to the right of the judge. Several yards away, to the front-left of the judge, sat her defense lawyer. Between them was the district attorney's table, located to the front-right of the judge. The defense lawyer asked the judge to allow the defendant to come over and sit with him. The judge refused. Defense counsel then got up and walked between the district attorney and the judge to the prisoner's dock. Neither the bailiff nor the judge stopped him. He argued for reduction of bail standing next to his client, a location which required the judge to turn to her right to hear the plea. The district attorney argued from his table.

Two co-defendants in San Francisco pleaded guilty to marijuana smuggling. One was represented by a young National Lawyers Guild attorney, the other by a prestigious New York dope lawyer. At the sentencing hearing, the young lawyer arrived with his client's wife and children, aged seven and ten. When they walked into the courtroom, the bailiff ordered the children to leave, stating that it was a standing rule of the judge that children were not allowed in the courtroom. This would be the children's last opportunity to see their father before he began serving his sentence. The lawyer explained to the bailiff that the children were not babies and argued that they had a right to be there based upon constitutional guarantees to privacy of family relationships and to a public trial. The bailiff replied that they were dealing with a standing rule. The lawyer told the wife and children to stay and asked the bailiff to inform the judge of his position, which the bailiff did. The judge then entered without ever raising the issue. No motion had to be made to allow the children to stay, and the children were not forcibly removed. The other defendant's children remained in the outside hall, never seeing their father because his lawyer obeyed the standing rule.

The Deprofessionalization
of the Lawyer–Client Relationship

Once the lawyer *becomes* a professional and the client *becomes* a helpless layperson, the potential for oppositional energy that is produced by legal conflict will be dissipated, and the system will be the winner whatever the outcome of the case. The first step in combatting this process is to politicize the lawyer–client relationship by ridding it of its official and professionalized characteristics.

A description of a landlord–tenant lawyer's practice helps to reveal the lawyer's potential for creating a new kind of relationship. When a tenant first comes to the lawyer's office, the lawyer attempts to discuss what the tenant can do for himself. The lawyer does this, first, in order to resist the client's tendency to see himself as powerless and to see her (the lawyer) as his savior and, second, because she wants him to understand her whole situation—to understand, for example, that she is a working person who must be paid for her time. She may ask, for example, if the tenant has met with other tenants in his building to discover their common problems in relating to their landlord, if he is aware of the work of the local tenant union, and so forth.

Assuming that the client succeeds in organizing a meeting with other tenants in his building, he will have already taken a political action more threatening and more empowering than any he may have taken in his entire life. The most important political message a client may receive arises from the fact that a legal conflict *forces* the client to come into contact with the public sphere, a sphere that in his imagination is controlled by government officials endowed with virtually magical authoritarian powers. The maintenance of this imaginary sphere through symbols of psychological terror is the state's principal weapon against the formation of a radical political consciousness, because it has the effect of privatizing people's experience of their own daily lives; it functions to imprison people within isolated worlds and to depoliticize people's understanding of their true social and economic situations. A lawyer who merely handles her clients' cases can only serve to reinforce the imaginary boundary that exists in the client's mind

between public and private life, and in so doing to reinforce the client's conditioned passivity; regardless of the outcome of the case the client will be grateful to the lawyer for having championed him in the terrifying public arena.

The client's discovery that he is capable of taking a public action on his own behalf is therefore extremely important psychologically because this action *of itself* can make the "public sphere" vanish. By acting on his situation instead of being a function of it, the client may see "the state" dissolve before his eyes into a mere group of other persons who are trying to silence him. Such an experience can have a powerful politicizing impact on the client's view of his entire life, even if the legal outcome of the specific case is unfavorable.

For the lawyer, the experience of deprofessionalization can be equally significant because it requires giving up the pseudo-power that the state has bestowed upon her in exchange for the actual power of discovering a way of working that is expressive of her true political being. The notions held by many lawyers that one should feel guilty about being a professional, that political change must be brought about by others, that lawyers "can't do anything"—all of these are merely expressions of a false consciousness resulting from a sense of powerlessness. To transcend this image is to transcend the split between one's authentic being and one's social self, which is the universal basis of alienation, and to side with the power of desire against the forces which perpetually attempt to contain it.

DISCUSSION QUESTIONS

1. What are the progressive theories of law and social change? What are the skeptical critiques of those theories? What is the difference between strategies guided by rights and by power?

2. What lessons can we draw from the high-visibility political cases? What are the preconditions for such a strategy? Can you identify similar cases in the recent past? Do you approve of the tactics in the Chicago Eight trial? in the Inez Garcia trial? What did they achieve? at what cost? In what situations might you use similar tactics? What were the alternatives?

3. What lessons can we draw from low-visibility political cases? What were the preconditions for those strategies? Do you approve of them? What did they achieve? at what cost? What were the alternatives? Can you suggest similar strategies in other low-visibility settings?

4. What strategy is proposed in nonpolitical cases? What is the theory of the lawyering function? the lawyer–client relationship?

5. What theory of political consciousness underlies all of this? Are you persuaded by it? How could we test it empirically?

⸙

SUBORDINATION, RHETORICAL SURVIVAL SKILLS, AND SUNDAY SHOES:NOTES ON THE HEARING OF MRS. G.[1]
Lucie E. White

IN 1970 the Supreme Court decided *Goldberg v. Kelly*. The case, which held that welfare recipients are entitled to an oral hearing prior to having their benefits reduced or terminated, opened up a far-reaching conversation among legal scholars over the meaning of procedural justice. All voices in this conversation endorse a normative floor that would guarantee all persons the same formal opportunities to be heard in adjudicatory proceedings, regardless of such factors as race, gender, or class identity. Beyond this minimal normative consensus, however, two groups of scholars have very different visions of what procedural justice would entail. One group, seeing procedure as an instrument of just government, seeks devices that will most efficiently generate legitimate outcomes in a complex society. Other scholars, however, by taking the perspective of society's marginalized groups, give voice to a very different—I will call it a "humanist"—vision. According to this vision, "procedural justice" is a normative *horizon* rather than a technical problem. This horizon challenges us to realize the promise of formal procedural equality in the real world.

I begin this essay by assuming that the meaningful participation by all citizens in the governmental decisions that affect their lives—that is, the humanist vision—reflects a normatively compelling and widely shared intuition about procedural justice in our political culture. The essay explores a disjuncture between this vision and the conditions in our society in which procedural rituals are actually played out. Familiar cultural images and long-established legal norms construct the subjectivity and speech of socially subordinated persons as inherently inferior to the speech and personhood of dominant groups. Social subordination itself can lead disfavored groups to deploy verbal strategies that mark their speech as deviant when measured against dominant stylistic norms. These conditions—the web

1. 38 *Buffalo Law Review* 1 (1990). Reprinted with permission.17.8 10.0 10.3

of subterranean speech norms and coerced speech practices that accompany race, gender, and class domination—undermine the capacity of many persons in our society to use the procedural rituals that are formally available to them. Furthermore, bureaucratic institutions disable *all* citizens—especially those from subordinated social groups—from meaningful participation in their own political lives.

This disjuncture between the norm of at least *equal*—if not also *meaningful*—participation opportunities for all citizens and a deeply stratified social reality reveals itself when subordinated speakers attempt to use the procedures that the system affords them. The essay tells the story of such an attempt—a story of enforced silence, rhetorical survival, and chance, as a poor woman engages in an administrative hearing at a welfare office.

THE STORY

Mrs. G. is 35 years old, black, and on her own. She has five girls, ranging in age from four to fourteen. She has never told me anything about their fathers; all I know is that she isn't getting formal child support payments from anyone. She lives on an AFDC grant of just over $300 a month and a small monthly allotment of food stamps. She probably gets a little extra money from occasional jobs as a field hand or a maid, but she doesn't share this information with me and I don't ask. She has a very coveted unit of public housing, so she doesn't have to pay rent. She is taking an adult basic education class at the local community action center, which is in the same building as my own office. I often notice her in the classroom as I pass by.

The first thing that struck me about Mrs. G., when she finally came to my office for help one day, was the way she talked. She brought her two oldest daughters with her. She would get very excited when she spoke, breathing hard and waving her hands and straining, like she was searching for the right words to say what was on her mind. Her daughters would circle her, like two young mothers themselves, keeping the air calm as her hands swept through it. I haven't talked with them much, but they strike me as quite self-possessed for their years.

At the time I met Mrs. G., I was a legal aid lawyer working in a small community in south-central North Carolina. I had grown up in the state but had been away for ten years and felt like an outsider when I started working there. I worked out of two small rooms in the back of the local community action center. The building was run-down, but it was a storefront directly across from the Civil War Memorial on the courthouse lawn, so it was easy for poor people to find.

There were two of us in the office, myself and a local woman who had spent a few years in Los Angeles, working as a secretary and feeling free, before coming back to the town to care for her aging parents. Her family had lived in the town for generations. Not too long ago they, and most of the other black families I worked with, had been the property of our adversaries—the local landowners, businessmen, bureaucrats, and lawyers. Everyone seemed to have a strong sense of family, and of history, in the town.

In the late 1960s, the town had erupted into violence when a local youth who had read some Karl Marx and Malcolm X led some 5,000 people down the local highway in an effort to integrate the county swimming pool. He had been charged with kidnapping as a result of the incident and had fled to Cuba, China, and ultimately Detroit. My colleague would talk to me about him in secretive tones. Her father was one of those who sheltered him from justice on the evening of his escape. I think she expected that one day he would come back to take up the project that was abandoned when he fled.

Since World War II, the town had been a real backwater for black people. People told me that it was a place that was there to be gotten out of, if you could figure out how. Only gradually, in the 1980s, were a few African American families moving back into the area, to take up skilled jobs in chemicals and electronics. But the lives of most blacks in the county in the early 1980s could be summed up by its two claims to fame. It was the county where the state's arch-conservative senior senator had grown up. Locals claimed that the senator's father, the chief of police at one time, was known for the boots he wore and the success he had at keeping black people in their place. It was also the county where Steven Spiel-

berg filmed *The Color Purple*. By the time Spiel-
berg discovered the county, the dust from the
1960s had long since settled, and the town where
I worked had the look of a sleepy Jim Crow vil-
lage that time had quite entirely passed by.

Mrs. G. and two daughters first appeared at our
office one Friday morning at about ten, without
an appointment. I was booked for the whole day;
the chairs in the tiny waiting room were already
filled. But I called her in between two scheduled
clients. Mrs. G. looked frightened. She showed
me a letter from the welfare office that said she
had received an "overpayment" of AFDC benefits. Though she couldn't read very well, she knew
that the word "overpayment" meant fraud. Reagan's newly appointed United States Attorney,
with the enthusiastic backing of Senator Jesse
Helms, had just announced plans to prosecute
"welfare cheats" to the full extent of the law. Following this lead, a grand jury had indicted several
local women on federal charges of welfare fraud.
Therefore, Mrs. G. had some reason to believe
that "fraud" carried the threat of jail.

The "letter" was actually a standardized notice
that I had seen many times before. Whenever the
welfare department's computer showed that a
client had received an overpayment, it would kick
out this form, which stated the amount at issue
and advised the client to pay it back. The notice
did not say why the agency had concluded that a
payment error had been made. Nor did it inform
the client that she might contest the county's
determination. Rather, the notice assigned the
client a time to meet with the county's fraud
investigator to sign a repayment contract and
warned that if the client chose not to show up at
this meeting further action would be taken. Mrs.
G's meeting with the fraud investigator was set
for the following Monday.

At the time, I was negotiating with the county
over the routine at these meetings and the word-
ing on the overpayment form. Therefore, I knew
what Mrs. G could expect at the meeting. The
fraud worker would scold her and then ask her to
sign a statement conceding the overpayment,
consenting to a 10 percent reduction of her
AFDC benefits until the full amount was paid
back, and advising that the government could
still press criminal charges against her.

I explained to Mrs. G. that she did not have to
go to the meeting on Monday or to sign any
forms. She seemed relieved and asked if I could
help her get the overpayment straightened out. I
signed her on as a client and, aware of the other
people waiting to see me, sped through my
canned explanation of how I could help her.
Then I called the fraud investigator, canceled
Monday's meeting, and told him I was representing her. Thinking that the emergency had been
dealt with, I scheduled an appointment for Mrs.
G. for the following Tuesday and told her not to
sign anything or talk to anyone at the welfare
office until I saw her again.

The following Tuesday Mrs. G. arrived at my
office looking upset. She said she had gone to her
fraud appointment because she had been "afraid
not to." She had signed a paper admitting she
owed the county about $600 and agreeing to
have her benefits reduced by $30 a month for the
year and a half it would take to repay the amount.
She remembered I had told her not to sign anything; she looked like she was waiting for me to
yell at her or tell her to leave. I suddenly saw a
woman caught between two bullies, both of us
ordering her what to do.

I hadn't spent enough time with Mrs. G. the
previous Friday. For me, it had been one more
emergency—a quick fix, an appointment, out the
door. It suddenly seemed pointless to process so
many clients, in such haste, without any time to
listen, to challenge, to think together. But what
to do, with so many people waiting at the door? I
mused on these thoughts for a moment, but what
I finally said was simpler. I was furious. Why had
she gone to the fraud appointment and signed
the repayment contract? Why hadn't she done as
we had agreed? Now it would be so much harder
to contest the county's claim: we would have to
attack both the repayment contract and the
underlying overpayment claim. Why hadn't she
listened to me?

Mrs. G. just looked at me in silence. She finally
stammered that she knew she had been "wrong"
to go to the meeting when I had told her not to
and she was "sorry."

After we both calmed down I mumbled my
own apology and turned to the business at hand.
She told me that a few months before she had

received a cash settlement for injuries she and her oldest daughter had suffered in a minor car accident. After medical bills had been paid and her lawyer had taken his fees, her award came to $592. Before Mrs. G. cashed the insurance check, she took it to her AFDC worker to report it and ask if it was all right for her to spend it. The system had trained her to tell her worker about every change in her life. With a few exceptions, any "income" she reported would be subtracted, dollar for dollar, from her AFDC stipend.

The worker was not sure how to classify the insurance award. After talking to a supervisor, however, she told Mrs. G. that the check would not affect her AFDC budget and she could spend it however she wanted.

Mrs. G. cashed her check that same afternoon and took her five girls on what she described to me as a "shopping trip." They bought Kotex, which they were always running short on at the end of the month. They also bought shoes, dresses for school, and some frozen food. Then she made two payments on her furniture bill. After a couple of wonderful days, the money was gone.

Two months passed. Mrs. G. received and spent two AFDC checks. Then she got the overpayment notice, asking her to repay to the county an amount equal to her insurance award.

When she got to this point, I could see Mrs. G. getting upset again. She had told her worker everything, but nobody had explained to her what she was supposed to do. She hadn't meant to do anything wrong. I said I thought the welfare office had done something wrong in this case, not Mrs. G. I thought we could get the mess straightened out, but we'd need more information. I asked if she could put together a list of all the things she had bought with the insurance money. If she still had any of the receipts, she should bring them to me. I would look at her case file at the welfare office and see her again in a couple of days.

The file had a note from the caseworker confirming that Mrs. G. had reported the insurance payment when she received it. The note also showed that the worker did not include the amount in calculating her stipend. The "overpayments" got flagged two months later when a supervisor, doing a random "quality control"

check on her file, discovered the worker's note. Under AFDC law, the insurance award was considered a "lump sum payment." Aware that the law regarding such payments had recently changed, the supervisor decided to check out the case with the state quality control office.

He learned that the insurance award did count as income for AFDC purposes under the state's regulations; indeed, the county should have cut Mrs. G. off welfare entirely for almost two months on the theory that her family could live for that time on the insurance award. The lump sum rule was a Reagan Administration innovation designed to teach poor people the virtues of saving money and planning for the future. Nothing in the new provision required that clients be warned in advance about the rule change, however. Only in limited circumstances was a state free to waive the rule. Without a waiver, Mrs. G. would have to pay back $592 to the welfare office. If the county didn't try to collect the sum from Mrs. G., it would be sanctioned for an administrative error.

I met again with Mrs. G. the following Friday. When I told her what I had pieced together from her file, she insisted that she had asked worker's permission before spending the insurance money. Then she seemed to get flustered and repeated what had become a familiar refrain. She didn't want to make any trouble. She hadn't meant to do anything wrong. I told her that it looked to me like it was the welfare office—and not she—who had done something wrong. I said I would try to get the county to drop the matter, but I thought we might have to go to a hearing, finally, to win.

Mrs. G. had been in court a few times to get child support and defend against evictions, but she had never been to a welfare hearing. She knew that it was not a good idea to get involved in hearings, however, and she understood why. Fair hearings were a hassle and an embarrassment to the county. A hearing meant pulling an eligibility worker and several managers out of work for a few hours, which—given the chronic under-staffing of the welfare office—was more than a minor inconvenience. It also meant exposing the county's administrative problems to state-level scrutiny.

Front-line eligibility workers were especially averse to hearings because the county's easiest way to defend against its own blunders was point to the worker as the source of the problem. As a result, the workers did all they could to persuade clients that they would lose, in the end, if they insisted on hearings. The prophecy was self-fulfilling, given the subtle and diffuse retaliation that would often follow for the occasional client who disregarded this advice.

I could tell that Mrs. G. felt pressure from me to ask for a hearing, but she also seemed angry at the welfare office for asking her to pay for their mistake. I said that it was her decision, and not mine, whether to ask for a hearing, and reassured her that I would do my best to settle the matter, whatever she decided. I also told her she could drop the hearing request at any time, for any reason, before or even after the event. When she nervously agreed to file the hearing request, I didn't second-guess her decision.

My negotiations failed. The county took the position that the worker should have suspended Mrs. G.'s AFDC as soon as the client had reported the insurance payment. This mistake was "regrettable," but it didn't shift the blame for the overpayment. Mrs. G.—and not the county—had received more welfare money than she was entitled to. End of discussion. I then appealed to state officials. They asked if the county would concede that the worker told Mrs. G. she was free to spend her insurance award as she pleased. When county officials refused, and the details of this conversation did not show up in the client's case file, the state declined to intervene. Mrs. G. then had to drop the matter or gear up for a hearing. After a lot hesitation, she decided to go forward.

Mrs. G. brought all five of her girls to my office to prepare for the hearing. Our first task was to decide on a strategy for the argument. I told her that I saw two stories we could tell. The first was the story she had told me. It was the "estoppel" story, the story of the wrong advice she got from her worker about spending the insurance check. The second story was one that I had come up with from reading the law. The state had laid the groundwork for this story when it opted for the "life necessities" waiver permitted by federal reg-

ulations. If a client could show that she had spent the sum to avert a crisis situation, then it would be considered "unavailable" as income, and her AFDC benefits would not be suspended. I didn't like this second story very much, and I wasn't sure that Mrs. G. would want to go along with it. How could I ask her to distinguish "life necessities" from mere luxuries, when she was keeping five children alive on $300 a month and when she had been given no voice in the calculus that had determined her "needs"?

Yet I felt that the necessities story might work at the hearing, while "estoppel" would unite the county and state against us. According to legal aid's welfare specialist in the state capital, state officials didn't like the lump sum rule. It made more paperwork for the counties. And, by knocking families off the federally financed AFDC program, the rule increased the pressure on state- and county-funded relief programs. But the only way the state could get around the rule without being subject to federal sanctions was through the necessities exception. Behind the scenes, state officials were saying to our welfare specialist that they intended to interpret the exception broadly. In addition to this inside information that state officials would prefer the necessities tale, I knew from experience that they would feel comfortable with the role that story gave to Mrs. G. It would place her on her knees, asking for pity as she described how hard she was struggling to make ends meet.

The estoppel story would be entirely different. In it, Mrs. G. would be pointing a finger, turning the county itself into the object of scrutiny. She would accuse welfare officials of wrong and claim that they had caused her injury. She would demand that the county bend its own rules, absorb the overpayment out of its own funds, and run the risk of sanction from the state for its error.

As I thought about the choices, I felt myself in a bind. The estoppel story would feel good in the telling but at the likely cost of losing the hearing and provoking the county's ire. The hearing officer—though charged to be neutral—would surely identify with the county in this challenge to the government's power to evade the costs of its own mistakes. The necessities story would force Mrs. G. to grovel, but it would give both county and state what they wanted to hear—another "yes sir" welfare recipient.

This bind was familiar to me as a poverty lawyer. I felt it most strongly in disability hearings, when I would counsel clients to describe themselves as totally helpless in order to convince the court that they met the statutory definition of disability. But I had faced it in AFDC work as well, when I taught women to present themselves as abandoned, depleted of resources, and encumbered by children to qualify for relief. I taught them to say yes to the degrading terms of "income security," as it was called—invasions of sexual privacy, disruptions of kin ties, the forced choice of one sibling's welfare over another's. Lawyers had tried to challenge these conditions, but for the most part the courts had confirmed that the system could take such license with its women. After all, poor women were free to say no to welfare if they weren't pleased with its terms.

As I contemplated my role as an advocate, I felt again the familiar sense that I had been taken. Here I was, asking Mrs. G. to trust me, talking with her about our conspiring together to beat the system and strategizing together to change it. Here I was, thinking that what I was doing was educative and empowering or at least supportive of those agendas, when all my efforts worked in the end only to teach her to submit to the system in all of the complex ways that it demanded.

In the moment it took for these old thoughts to flit through my mind, Mrs. G. and her children sat patiently in front of me, fidgeting, waiting for me to speak. My focus returned to them and the immediate crisis they faced if their AFDC benefits were cut. What story should we tell at the hearing? I wondered out loud. How should we decide? Mechanically at first, I began to describe to her our "options."

When I explained the necessities story, Mrs. G. said she might get confused trying to remember what all she had bought with the money. Why did they need to know those things anyway? I could tell she was getting angry. I wondered if two months of benefits—$600—was worth it. Maybe paying it back made more sense. I reminded her that we didn't have to tell this story at the hearing, and in fact, we didn't have to

go to the hearing at all. Although I was trying to choose my words carefully, I felt myself saying too much. Why had I even raised the question of which story to tell? It was a tactical decision—not the kind of issue that clients were supposed to decide. Why hadn't I just told her to answer the questions that I chose to ask?

Mrs. G. asked me what to do. I said I wanted to see the welfare office admit their mistake, but I was concerned that if we tried to make them, we would lose. Mrs. G. said she still felt like she'd been treated unfairly but—in the next breath—"I didn't mean to do anything wrong." Why couldn't we tell both stories? With this simple question, I lost all pretense of strategic subtlety or control. I said sure.

I asked for the list she had promised to make of all the things she bought with the insurance money. Kotex, I thought, would speak for itself, but why, I asked, had she needed to get the girls new shoes? She explained that the girls' old shoes were pretty much torn up, so bad that the other kids would make fun of them at school. Could she bring in the old shoes? She said she could.

We rehearsed her testimony, first about her conversation with her worker regarding the insurance award and then about the Kotex and the shoes. Maybe the hearing wouldn't be too bad for Mrs. G., especially if I could help her to see it all as strategy, rather than the kind of talking she could do with people she could trust. She had to distance herself at the hearing. She shouldn't expect them to go away from it understanding why she was angry, or what she needed, or what her life was like. The hearing was their territory. The most she could hope for was to take it over for a moment, leading them to act out her agenda. Conspiracy was the theme she must keep repeating as she dutifully played her role.

We spent the next half hour rehearsing the hearing. By the end, she seemed reasonably comfortable with her part. Then we practiced the cross-examination, the ugly questions that—even though everyone conceded them to be irrelevant—still always seemed to get asked...questions about her children, their fathers, how long she had been on welfare, why she wasn't working instead. This was the part of these sessions that I disliked the most. We practiced me objecting and her staying quiet and trying to stay composed. By the end of our meeting, the whole thing was holding together, more or less.

The hearing itself was in a small conference room at the welfare office. Mrs. G. arrived with her two oldest daughters and five boxes of shoes. When we got there the state hearing officer and the county AFDC director were already seated at the hearing table in lively conversation. The AFDC director was a youngish man with sandy hair and a beard. He didn't seem like a bureaucrat until he started talking. I knew most of the hearing officers who came to the county, but this one, a pale, graying man who slouched in his chair, was new to me. I started feeling uneasy as I rehearsed how I would plead this troubling case to a stranger.

We took our seats across the table from the AFDC director. The hearing officer set up a portable tape recorder and got out his bible. Mrs. G.'s AFDC worker, an African American woman about her age, entered through a side door and took a seat next to her boss. The hearing officer turned on the recorder, read his obligatory opening remarks, and asked all the witnesses to rise and repeat before God that they intended to tell the truth. Mrs. G. and her worker complied.

The officer then turned the matter over to me. I gave a brief account of the background events and then began to question Mrs. G. First, I asked her about the insurance proceeds. She explained how she had received an insurance check of about $600 following a car accident in which she and her oldest daughter had been slightly injured. She said that the insurance company had already paid the medical bills and the lawyer; the last $600 was for her and her daughter to spend however they wanted. I asked her if she had shown the check to her AFDC worker before she cashed it. She stammered. I repeated the question. She said she may have taken the check to the welfare office before she cashed it, but she couldn't remember for sure. She didn't know if she had gotten a chance to talk to anyone about it. Her worker was always real busy.

Armed with the worker's own sketchy notation of the conversation in the case file, I began to cross-examine my client, coaxing her memory about the event we had discussed so many times

before. I asked if she remembered her worker telling her anything about how she could spend the money. Mrs. G. seemed to be getting more uncomfortable. It was quite a predicament for her, after all. If she "remembered" what her worker had told her, would her story expose mismanagement in the welfare office, or merely scapegoat another black woman, who was not too much better off than herself?

When she repeated that she couldn't remember, I decided to leave the estoppel story for the moment. Maybe I could think of a way to return to it later. I moved on to the life necessities issue. I asked Mrs. G. to recount, as best she could, exactly how she had spent the insurance money. She showed me the receipts she had kept for the furniture payments and I put them into evidence. She explained that she was buying a couple of big mattresses for the kids and a new kitchen table. She said she had also bought some food—some frozen meat and several boxes of Kotex for all the girls. The others in the room shifted uneasily in their chairs. Then she said she had also bought her daughters some clothes and some shoes. She had the cash-register receipt for the purchase.

Choosing my words carefully, I asked why she had needed to buy the new shoes. She looked at me for a moment with an expression that I couldn't read. Then she stated, quite emphatically, that they were Sunday shoes that she had bought with the money. The girls already had everyday shoes to wear to school, but she had wanted them to have nice shoes for church too. She said no more than two or three sentences, but her voice sounded different—stronger, more composed—than I had known from her before. When she finished speaking the room was silent, except for the incessant hum of the tape machine on the table and the fluorescent lights overhead. In that moment, I felt the boundaries of our "conspiracy" shift. Suddenly I was on the outside, with the folks on the other side of the table, the welfare director and the hearing officer. The only person I could not locate in this new alignment was Mrs. G.'s welfare worker.

I didn't ask Mrs. G. to pull out the children's old shoes, as we'd rehearsed. Nor did I make my "life necessities" argument. My lawyer's language couldn't add anything to what she had said. They would have to figure out for themselves why buying Sunday shoes for her children—and saying it—was indeed a "life necessity" for this woman. After the hearing, Mrs. G. seemed elated. She asked me how she had done at the hearing and I told her that *I* thought she was great. I warned her, though, that we could never be sure, in this game, who was winning, or even what side anyone was on.

We lost the hearing and immediately petitioned for review by the chief hearing officer. I wasn't sure of the theory we'd argue, but I wanted to keep the case open until I figured out what we could do.

Three days after the appeal was filed, the county welfare director called me unexpectedly, to tell me that the county had decided to withdraw its overpayment claim against Mrs. G. He explained that on a careful review of its own records, the county had decided that it wouldn't be "fair" to make Mrs. G. pay the money back. I said I was relieved to hear that they had decided, finally, to come to a sensible result in the case. I was sorry they hadn't done so earlier. I then said something about how confusing the lump sum rule was and how Mrs. G.'s worker had checked with her supervisor before telling Mrs. G. it was all right to spend the insurance money. I said I was sure that the screw-up was not anyone's fault. He mumbled a bureaucratic pleasantry and we hung up.

When I told Mrs. G. that she had won, she said she had just wanted to "do the right thing" and hoped they understood that she'd never meant to do anything wrong. I repeated that they were the ones who had made the mistake. Though I wasn't sure exactly what was going on inside the welfare office, at least this crisis was over.

THE ROUTE TAKEN: EVASIVE MANEUVERS OR
A WOMAN'S VOICE?

If we measure Mrs. G.'s hearing against the norms of procedural formality, it appears to conform. The hearing appears to invite Mrs. G. to speak on equal terms with all other persons. Yet within the local landscape of her hearing, Mrs. G.'s voice is constrained by forces that procedural

doctrine will neither acknowledge nor oppose. Each of these forces attaches a specific social cost to her gender and race identity. The caste system implements race and gender ideology in social arrangements. The "fraud issue" revives misogynist and racist stereotypes that had been forced, at least partly, underground by the social movements of the 1960s and 1970s. And the welfare system responds to gender- and race-based injustice in the economy by constructing the poor as Woman—as an object of social control. Given the power amassed behind these forces, we might predict that they should win the contest with Mrs. G. for her voice.

Yet to detect these forces, we have read the story through a structuralist lens, which shows only the stark dichotomy of subordination as social control. It is ironic that this lens, which works so well to expose the contours of Mrs. G.'s silence, also leaves her—as a woman actively negotiating the terrain in which she found herself—entirely out of focus. If we recenter our reading on Mrs. G., as a woman shaping events, unpredictably, to realize her own meanings, we can no longer say with certainty what the outcome will be. We cannot tell who prevailed at the hearing, or where the power momentarily came to rest. Rather, what we see is a sequence of surprising moves, a series of questions. Why did Mrs. G. return to the lawyer after meeting with the fraud investigator to sign the settlement agreement? Why did she depart from the script she had rehearsed for the hearing, to remain silent before her own worker and to speak about Sunday shoes? And why did the county finally abandon its claim to cut her stipend?

Why Did Mrs. G. Return to the Lawyer?

The lawyer [the author] thought she understood the answer to this question. In her view, Mrs. G.'s life had taught her that to be safe, she must submit to her superiors. Mrs. G. was faced with conflicting commands from the welfare agency and the legal aid office. So, like the archetypical woman, shaped to mold herself to male desire, Mrs. G. said "yes" to everything the Man asked. She said yes when the lawyer asked her to go through with a hearing, yes again when the fraud investigator asked her to drop it, and yes once more when the lawyer demanded her apology. In the lawyer's view, this excess of acquiescence had a sad, but straightforward meaning. It marked Mrs. G.'s lack of social power: this woman could not risk having a point of view of her own.

Yet the lawyer was not situated to see the whole story. Though she aspired to stand beside Mrs. G. as an equal, she also sought to guard her own status—and the modicum of social power that it gave her. She saw Mrs. G. as a victim because that was the role she needed her client to occupy to support her own social status. For if Mrs. G. was indeed silenced by the violence around her, she would then be dependent on the lawyer's expertise and protection and therefore compliant to the lawyer's will. With such clients, the lawyer could feel quite secure of her power and complacent about the value of her work.

But Mrs. G.'s survival skills were more complex, more subtle, than the lawyer dared to recognize. There might be another meaning to Mrs. G.'s ambivalence about what she wanted to do. Perhaps she was playing with the compliance that all of her superiors demanded. By acquiescing to both of the system's opposed orders, she was surely protecting herself from the risks of defiance. But she was also undermining the value— to them—of her own submission. By refusing to claim any ground as her own, she made it impossible for others to subdue her will.

Self-negation may not have been the only meaning that Mrs. G. felt positioned to claim. She finally came back to the lawyer, repudiated the settlement, determined to pursue her case. Was this merely one more move between two bureaucrats, searching them both for strategic advantage while secretly mocking the rhetoric of both spheres? Or did Mrs. G. finally get fed up at the unfairness of welfare and at her endless submission? When she returned to the lawyer, she was offered a bargain. She might get money, and some limited protection from welfare, if she went along with the hearing plan. But she might also have heard the lawyer promise something different from this *quid pro quo*. In her talk of rights and justice, the lawyer offered Mrs. G. not just money but also vindication. In going forward with the hearing, was Mrs. G. simply making a street-wise calculation to play the game the

lawyer offered? Or was she also giving voice to a faint hope—a hope that one day she might really have the legal protections she needed to take part in the shaping of justice?

Why Did Mrs. G. Depart from Her Script?

The lawyer had scripted Mrs. G. as a victim. That was the only strategy for the hearing that the lawyer, within the constraints of her own social position, could imagine for Mrs. G. She had warned her client to play the victim if she wanted to win. Mrs. G. learned her lines. She came to the hearing rehearsed in the lawyer's strategy. But in the hearing, she did not play. When she was cued to perform, without any signal to her lawyer she abandoned their script.

The lawyer shared with Mrs. G. the oppression of gender but was placed above Mrs. G. in the social hierarchies of race and class. The lawyer was paid by the same people who paid for welfare, the federal government. Both programs were part of a social agenda of assisting, but also controlling, the poor. Though the lawyer had worked hard to identify with Mrs. G., she was also sworn, and paid, to defend the basic constitution of the status quo. When Mrs. G. "misbehaved" at the hearing, when she failed to talk on cue and then refused to keep quiet, Mrs. G. pointed to the ambiguity of the legal aid lawyer's social role. Through her defiant actions, Mrs. G. told the lawyer that a conspiracy with a double agent is inevitably going to prove an unstable alliance.

The lawyer had tried to "collaborate" with Mrs. G. in devising an advocacy plan. Yet the terms of that "dialogue" excluded Mrs. G.'s voice. Mrs. G. was a better strategist than the lawyer— more daring, more subtle, more fluent—in her own home terrain. She knew the psychology, the culture, and the politics of the white people who controlled her community. She knew how to read, and sometimes control, her masters' motivations; she had to command this knowledge— this intuition—to survive. The lawyer had learned intuition as a woman, but in a much more private sphere. She was an outsider to the county and to Mrs. G.'s social world. Mrs. G.'s superior sense of the landscape posed a subtle threat to the lawyer's expertise. Sensing this threat, the lawyer steered their strategic "discussion" into the sphere of her own expert knowledge. By limiting the very definition of "strategy" to the manipulation of legal doctrine, she invited Mrs. G. to respond to her questions with silence. And, indeed, Mrs. G. did not talk freely when the lawyer was devising their game plan. Rather, Mrs. G. waited until the hearing to act out her own intuitions. Although she surely had not plotted those actions in advance, she came up with moves at the hearing that threw everyone else off their guard and may have proved her the better legal strategist of the lawyer–client pair.

The disarming "strategy" that Mrs. G. improvised at the hearing was to appear to abandon strategy entirely. For a moment, she stepped out of the role of the supplicant. She ignored the doctrinal pigeonholes that would fragment her voice. She put aside all that the lawyer told her the audience wanted to hear. Instead, when asked to point a finger at her caseworker, she was silent. When asked about "life necessities," she explained that she had used her money to meet *her own* needs. She had bought her children Sunday shoes.

Her Silence Before Her Caseworker. When the lawyer asked Mrs. G. about the conversation with her caseworker regarding the insurance payments, Mrs. G. had nothing to say. The lawyer, smarting from her own rejection, felt that Mrs. G. was protecting a vulnerable black sister with her silence—at her own, and her lawyer's, expense. But perhaps something else was going on. Unlike Mrs. G., the caseworker had earned self-respect in the system. Mrs. G. and her like— desperately poor, with no formal schooling, burdened by too many children, "abandoned" by their men—cast a stigma on this woman because of the common color of their skin. Did this woman command a different kind of power over Mrs. G. from that of the white masters—a power that felt like shame, rather than fear? Perhaps Mrs. G. was not willing to flaunt her own degradation before this woman, as the lawyer demanded. Perhaps she was not willing to grovel—pointing fingers, showing off tattered shoes, listing each of her petty expenses—before this distant, disapproving sister. Perhaps Mrs. G.'s silence before this other black woman,

and her talk about Sunday shoes, expressed a demand—and an affirmation—of her own dignity.

Her Talk about Sunday Shoes. When Mrs. G talked about Sunday shoes, she was talking about a life necessity. For subordinated communities, physical necessities do not meet the minimum requirements for a human life. Rather, subordinated groups must create cultural practices through which they can elaborate an autonomous, oppositional consciousness. Without shared rituals for sustaining their survival and motivating their resistance, subordinated groups run the risk of total domination—of losing the *will* to use their human powers to subvert their oppressor's control over them. Religion, spirituality, the social institution of the black church, has been one such self-affirming cultural practice for the communities of African American slaves and remains central to the expression of black identity and group consciousness today. By naming Sunday shoes as a life necessity, Mrs. G. was speaking to the importance of this cultural practice in her life, a truth that the system's categories did not comprehend.

At the same time that Mrs. G.'s statement affirmed the church, it condemned the welfare system. By rejecting the welfare definition of life necessities, she asserted her need to have a say about the criteria for identifying her needs. Her statement was a demand for meaningful participation in the political conversations in which her needs are contested and defined. In the present welfare system, poor women—the objects of welfare—are structurally excluded from those conversations. When Mrs. G. insisted on her need to say for herself what her "life necessities" might be, she expanded, for a moment, the accepted boundaries of those conversations.

Mrs. G.'s statement also spoke to a third dimension of her "life necessity." When Mrs. G. talked about buying Sunday shoes, she defied the rules of legal rhetoric—the rule of relevancy, the rule against "rambling." Had Mrs. G. spoken the language that was proper for her in the setting, her relevant, logical submissive, hyper-correct responses to their questions might have been comprehended. But, by dutifully speaking the language of an institution from which subordinated groups have historically been excluded and in which Mrs. G. felt herself to have no stake, her voice would have repeated, and legitimated, the very social and cultural patterns and priorities that had kept her down. Had she been a *respectful* participant in the legal ritual, Mrs. G. would have articulated someone else's need, or pleasure, rather than her own.

Mrs. G. did not boycott the hearing altogether. Rather, in her moment of misbehavior, she may have been standing her ground within it. Although she appeared, at first, to be deferring to the system's categories and rules, when she finally spoke, she animated those categories with her own experience. She stretched the category of "life necessity" to express her own values and turned it around to critique welfare's systemic disregard of her own point of view. By talking about Sunday shoes, Mrs. G. claimed, for one fragile moment, what was perhaps her most basic "life necessity." She claimed a position of equality in the speech community—an equal power to take part in the *making* of language, making of shared categories, norms, and institutions—as she spoke through that language about her needs.

DISCUSSION QUESTIONS

1. What is the difference between the conventional notion of procedural justice and the "humanist" vision? How important is "meaningful participation by all citizens in governmental decisions that affect their lives"?

2. What did Mrs. G want? What did the author/lawyer want? What difficulty did each have in communicating her wishes? Understanding the other? What tactics were available to them? What were the advantages and disadvantages of each? How did the choice get made? What were the interpersonal dynamics? Who should make such decisions? Would Gabel and Harris view this as non-professional lawyering? Did the strategy ultimately chosen emphasize rights or power? Why did Mrs. G testify as she did? How did all this strategizing affect the outcome?

3. Did Mrs. G win or lose? Was she the master strategist that White depicts? Was she expressing successful resistance? Why does White see her this way? Is "a position of equality within the speech community" the most basic "life necessity"?

SUGGESTED READING

Progressive lawyering has changed radically from the heady days of civil rights and poverty law, when the goal was ringing declarations by the Supreme Court. Conservative courts, legislatures, and executives, diminished resources, and awareness of the limitations of legal reform have led to a reconceptualization of goals and strategies. Early examples include Stephen Wexler, "Practicing Law for Poor People," 79 *Yale Law Journal* 1049 (1970); Gary Bellow, "Turning Solutions into Problems: The Legal Aid Experience," 4 *NLADA Briefcase* 106 (1977). For comparisons of old- and new-left lawyering, see Arthur Kinoy, *Rights on Trial* (1983); Stuart Scheingold, "Radical Lawyers and Socialist Ideals," 15 *Journal of Law and Society* 122 (1988), "The Contradictions of Radical Law Practice," in Maureen Cain and Christine Harrington, *Lawyers in a Postmodern World* (1994); Victor Rabinowitz, *Unrepentant Leftist: A Lawyer's Memoir* (1996). One of the most influential books is Gerald López, *Rebellious Lawyering: One Chicano's View of Progressive Law Practice* (1992). For other accounts, see Lucie E. White, "Mobilizing on the Margins of Litigation: Making Space for Clients to Speak," 16 *N.Y.U. Review of Law and Social Change* 535 (1987–88), "To Learn and Teach: Lessons from Driefontein on Lawyering and Power," 1989 *Wisconsin Law Review* 699; Austin Sarat, "'…The Law Is All Over': Power, Resistance, and the Legal Consciousness of the Welfare Poor," 2 *Yale Journal of Law and Humanities* 343 (1990); Richard F. Klawiter, "¡La Tierra es Nuestra! The Campesino Struggle in El Salvador and a Vision of Community-Based Lawyering," 42 *Stanford Law Review* 1625 (1990); Louise G. Trubek, "Critical Lawyering: Toward a New Public Interest Practice," 1 *Boston University Public Interest*

Law Journal 49 (1991); Rebecca Arbogast, Roger L. Barnett, Ronald C. Slye, and Leslie Kim Treiger, "Revitalizing Public Interest Lawyering in the 1990s: The Story of Our Effort to Address the Problem of Homelessness," 34 *Howard Law Journal* 91 (1991); Anthony V. Alfieri, "Reconstructing Poverty Law Practice: Learning Lessons of Client Narratives," 100 *Yale Law Journal* 2107 (1991), "Impoverished Practices," 81 *Georgetown Law Journal* 2567 (1993), "Practicing Community," 107 *Harvard Law Review* 1747 (1994); Ruth Buchanan and Louise G. Trubek, "Resistances and Possibilities: A Critical and Practical Look at Public Interest Lawyering," 19 *N.Y.U. Review of Law and Social Change* 687 (1992); Stephen Ellmann, "Client-Centeredness Multiplied: Individual Autonomy and Collective Mobilization in Public Interest Lawyers' Representation of Groups," 78 *Virginia Law Review* 1103 (1992); Patricia Ewick and Susan Silbey, "Conformity, Contestation, and Resistance: An Account of Legal Consciousness," 26 *New England Law Review* 73 (1992); "Theoretics of Practice: The Integration of Progressive Thought and Action," 43(4) *Hastings Law Journal* (April 1992); "Symposium: Poverty Law Scholarship," 48(5)

University of Miami Law Review (1994); Luke W. Cole, "The Struggle of Kettleman City: Lessons for the Movement," 5 *Maryland Journal of Contemporary Legal Issues* 67 (1994); Herbert A. Eastman, "Speaking Truth to Power: The Language of Civil Rights Litigators," 104 *Yale Law Journal* 763 (1995); Marc Feldman, "Political Lessons: Legal Services for the Poor," 83 *Georgetown Law Journal* 1529 (1995) (and the commentaries by Gary Bellow and Jeanne Charn and by Alan W. Houseman); "Symposium: Political Lawyering: Conversations on Progressive Social Change," 31(2) *Harvard Civil Rights–Civil Liberties Law Review* (Summer 1996); Ann Southworth, "Business Planning for the Destitute? Lawyers as Facilitators in Civil Rights and Poverty Practice," 1996 *Wisconsin Law Review* 1122; Paul Harris. *Black Rage Confronts The Law* (New York University Press, 1997); Austin Sarat and Stuart Scheingold (eds.), *Lawyering on the Left: Causes, Politics, and Professional Responsibility* (1997). For a critique of post-modernist theories of progressive lawyering, see Joel F. Handler, "Postmodernism, Protest, and the New Social Movements," 26 *Law & Society Review* 697 (1992).